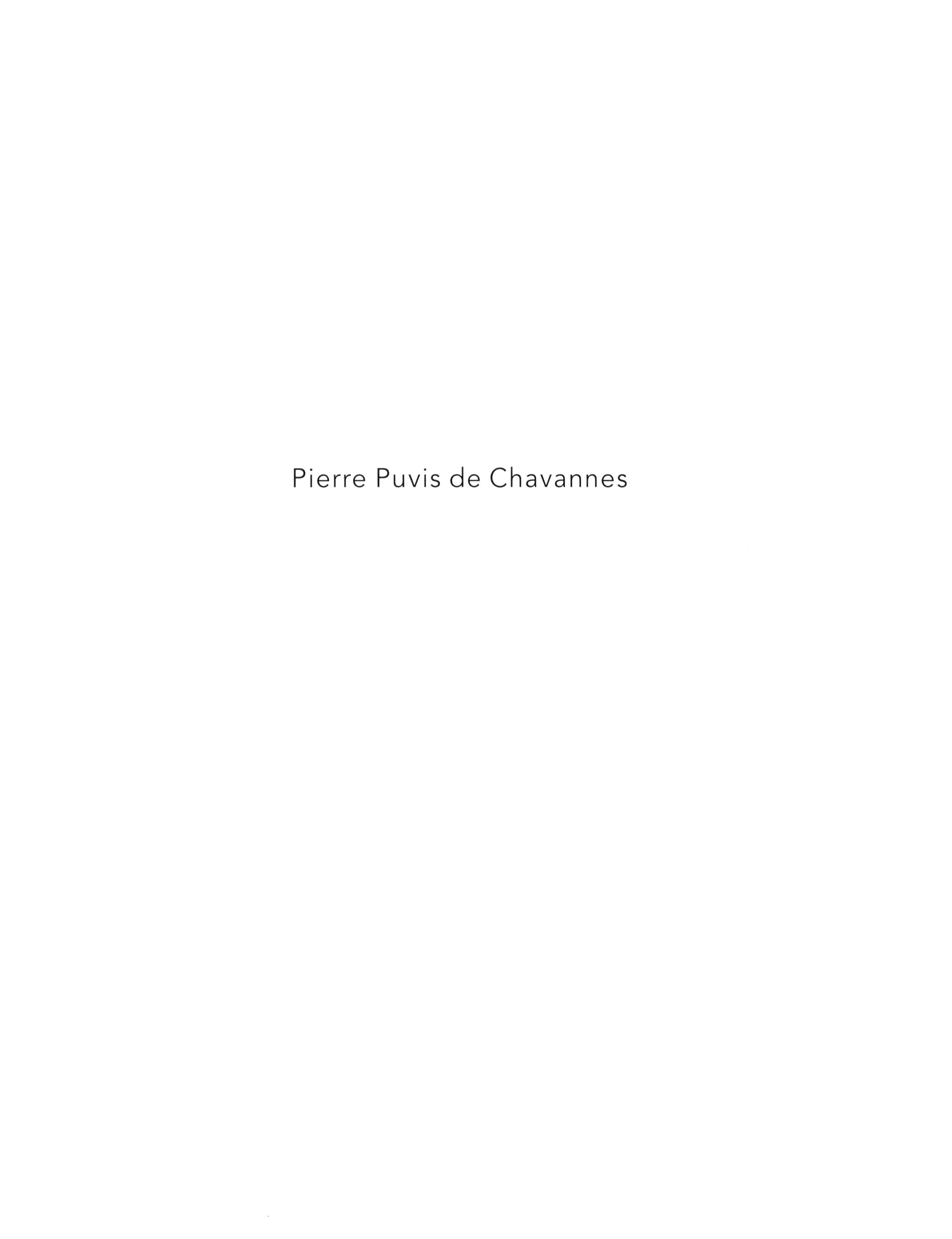

Pierre Puvis de Chavannes

Van Gogh Museum, Amsterdam

Pierre Puvis de Chavannes

Aimée Brown Price

with contributions by

Jon Whiteley

Geneviève Lacambre

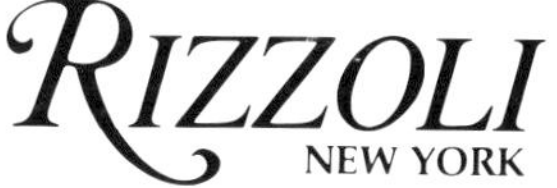
NEW YORK

Contents

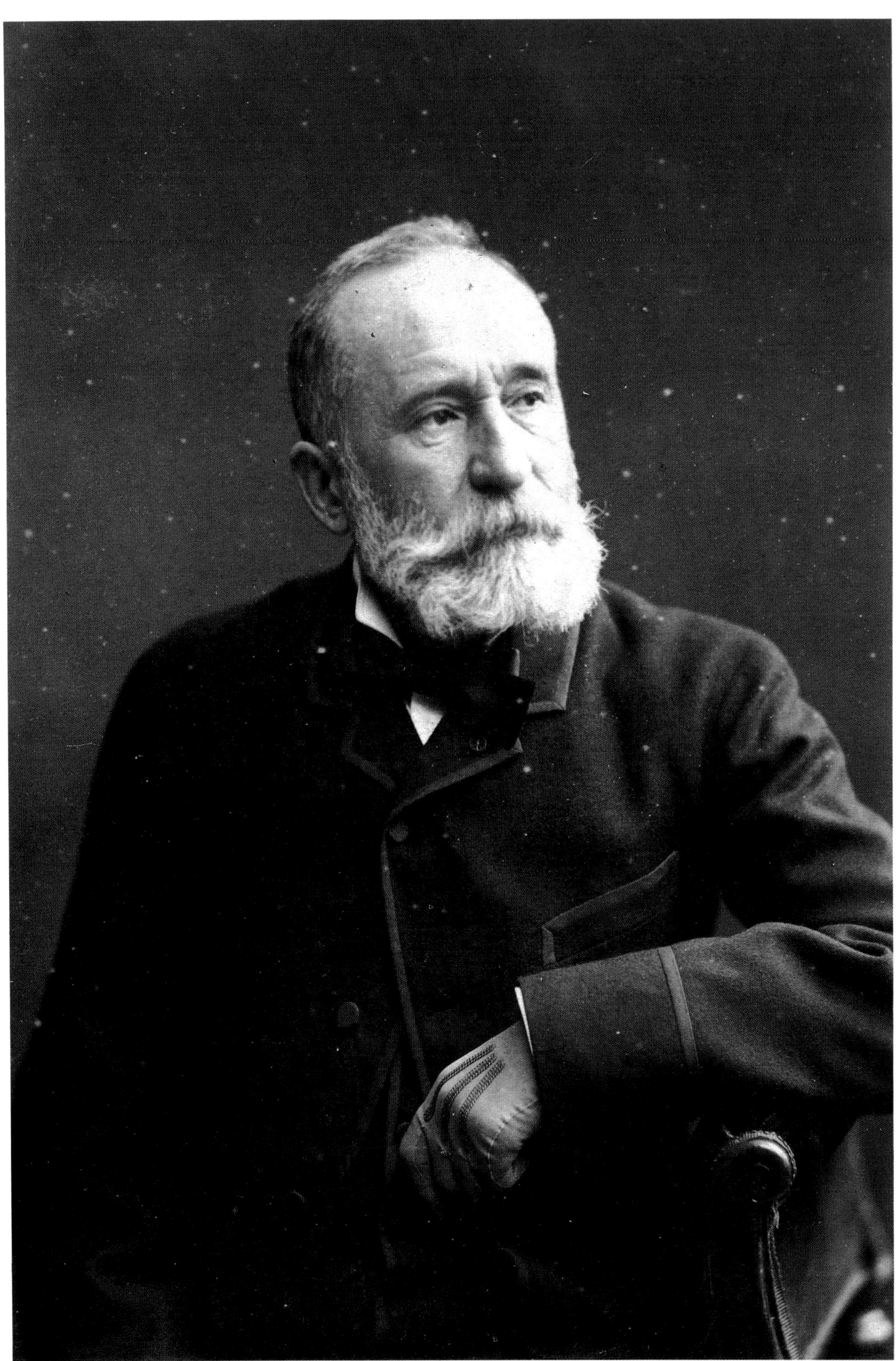

Foreword

A hundred years ago, when he was about seventy, the fame of Pierre Puvis de Chavannes was at its height and his paintings had a great appeal for the generation of Post-Impressionists. His monumental work combined a rigorously pursued aesthetic program with a most individual style. Both these aspects affected avant-garde artists between the 1880s and the turn of the century, among them Seurat, Gauguin, Denis, Rodin and Picasso.

Vincent van Gogh called Puvis a 'prophet' and a 'visionary,' describing his work as 'superb' and 'perfect.' The immense impact of Puvis on Van Gogh is easily traced in his letters, but harder to point out in his work. Rarely did two artists paint in such different ways, and certainly if art history is understood in the narrow sense of a straightforward history of style a connection between the two is difficult to find. Van Gogh felt a particular affinity with Puvis's portraits of contemporaries and considered him a master in this field. Moreover, in his *Inter Artes et Naturam* Puvis had succeeded in giving classic expression to the modern mentality. Van Gogh derived great comfort from it and believed that this ability to console suffering mankind was as much as an artist could hope to attain.

We have to go back to 1905 for the first and last solo exhibition of Puvis's art in the Netherlands, a show of sixteen of his works at the Haagsche Kunstkring in The Hague. In the accompanying folder the critic H.P. Bremmer, clearly rather concerned about the reception Puvis's work would get in the Netherlands, tries to bridge the gap between the Dutch predilection for everyday detail and the 'monumental breadth' of Puvis. The Dutch, being 'first and foremost a nation of still-life painters,' usually prefer the intimate and the *characteristic*, while the French favor the large and *typical*, the image distilled from countless observations. The situation has barely changed since Bremmer's days. Outside France only experts are familiar with the name Puvis de Chavannes. It is the task of museums to draw attention to neglected artists. For many years now the Van Gogh Museum has aimed to provide a richer, more diverse view of nineteenth-century painting in both its collection and exhibition policies. With this retrospective of Puvis de Chavannes the museum is proud to present one of the most significant artistic personalities of this fascinating period.

Puvis' main work - his murals - is of course missing from this exhibition and some important easel paintings could not travel to Amsterdam because of their fragility. However, important works are now on view that were not present at the Puvis exhibition in Paris and Ottawa in 1976-1977, such as *Summer* from the Cleveland Museum of Art and *The Pastoral Life of Saint Genevieve* from the Norton Simon Art Foundation in Pasadena. Thanks to generous loans from museums and private individuals from Algiers to Birmingham, from Canada and the United States to Japan, we were able to assemble a representative collection. We are particularly grateful for the trust placed in us by members of the Puvis de Chavannes family, who are still responsible for a large part of his artistic legacy. They agreed to the loan of a substantial number of works and allowed us access to unique source material.

The compilation and scholarly preparation of the exhibition and its catalogue were in the expert hands of Aimée Brown Price. Her commitment to the project has been enormous and we are profoundly indebted to her. In 1976 she was closely involved in the pioneering Puvis exhibition in Paris and Ottawa, and since then she has worked on a catalogue raisonné of the artist's oeuvre with great dedication. As an authority on Puvis's art she traced many works for us that had neither been published nor exhibited. Considerable attention is paid to Puvis's idiosyncratic draftsmanship, which is the subject of an illuminating essay in this catalogue by Jon Whiteley, Assistant Keeper in the Department of Western Art of the Ashmolean Museum in Oxford. Geneviève Lacambre, Conservateur en Chef of paintings at the Musée d'Orsay in Paris, describes the contemporary art world and the position Puvis held in the artistic establishment of his day.

Martine Stroo, the co-ordinator of the exhibition and editor of the catalogue, has steered the project through many a difficult period with admirable skill, concentration and perseverance. At an earlier stage research assistants Lucas Bonekamp and Dorien Wijstma made their contribution. The handsome catalogue was designed by Pieter Roozen and published by Waanders Uitgevers of Zwolle. Final responsibility within the Van Gogh Museum lay with Andreas Blühm and Aly Noordermeer, head and co-ordinator respectively of the Exhibitions Department.

During the preparation of this exhibition the Van Gogh Museum was fortunate enough to be able to acquire three paintings by Puvis, including the splendid 'modello' for the *Saint Genevieve as a Child in Prayer* in the Panthéon in Paris. It is deeply gratifying to be able to present these acquisitions in this exclusive context.

A century ago many Dutch 'artists of ideas' and proponents of a new movement in monumental art known as 'Gemeenschapskunst' came under Puvis's spell. In an article in the literary magazine *De Nieuwe Gids* the composer Alphons Diepenbrock ranked Puvis de Chavannes alongside Beethoven and Wagner: in their art they had all succeeded in rendering 'symbolic visions of ... moments of the soul.' In May 1888 Diepenbrock's friend, the painter Antoon Derkinderen, had written: 'If I had to cite an example to explain what I want, I could name only one man from our age: Puvis de Chavannes.' In 1905, however, Hendrik Bremmer realized that for a difficult artist like Puvis one had to open one's mind and should definitely not be in a 'crotchety' mood. One should have 'a certain inclination to surrender oneself and love in order to enter into his mind.' In this *fin de siècle* of the twentieth century we hope that visitors to the exhibition will prove susceptible to the solace in Puvis's art.

Ronald de Leeuw
Director Van Gogh Museum

Lenders to the Exhibition

Algeria
Musée National des Beaux-Arts d'Alger, Algiers

Canada
National Gallery of Art, Ottawa

France
Private collections
G. Meunier
Musée de Picardie, Amiens
Musée de Grenoble
Musée des Beaux-Arts de Lille
Musée des Beaux-Arts de Lyon
Musée Municipal des Ursulines, Mâcon
Guy Ladrière, Paris
Collection Galerie du Cygne, Paris
Musée du Louvre, Département des Arts Graphiques, Paris
Musée d'Orsay, Paris
Musée du Petit Palais, Paris
Musée Picasso, Paris
Musée d'Art Moderne, Saint-Etienne
Musée Paul Dupuy, Toulouse

Germany
Clemens-Sels-Museum, Neuss
Graphische Sammlung Staatsgalerie Stuttgart

Great Britain
The Trustees of the Barber Institute of Fine Arts, University of Birmingham
The Syndics of the Fitzwilliam Museum, Cambridge
The Trustees of the National Gallery, London
The Board of Trustees of the Victoria and Albert Museum, London
The Visitors of the Ashmolean Museum, Oxford

Hungary
Szépmüveszeti Múzeum, Budapest

Japan
Ohara Museum of Art, Kurashiki
The National Museum of Western Art, Tokyo

The Netherlands
Vincent van Gogh Foundation, Amsterdam
Rijksmuseum Kröller-Müller, Otterlo
Museum Boymans-van Beuningen, Rotterdam

Russia
Pushkin State Museum of Fine Art, Moscow

Switzerland
Private collection
Museum Stiftung Oskar Reinhart, Winterthur

The United States of America
Private collections
Mrs. John Hay Whitney
The Brooklyn Museum
The Art Institute of Chicago
The Cleveland Museum of Art
Spencer Museum of Art, The University of Kansas, Lawrence
Yale University Art Gallery, New Haven
The City College of New York
Richard L. Feigen, New York
The Metropolitan Museum of Art, New York
The Museum of Modern Art, New York
Stuart Pivar, New York
Robert Miller Gallery, New York
Norton Simon Art Foundation, Pasadena
Philadelphia Museum of Art
The Carnegie Museum of Art, Pittsburgh
Washington University Museum of Art, Saint Louis
The Toledo Museum of Art
National Gallery of Art, Washington, D.C.
National Museum of American Art, Smithsonian Institution, Washington, D.C.
The Phillips Collection, Washington, D.C.

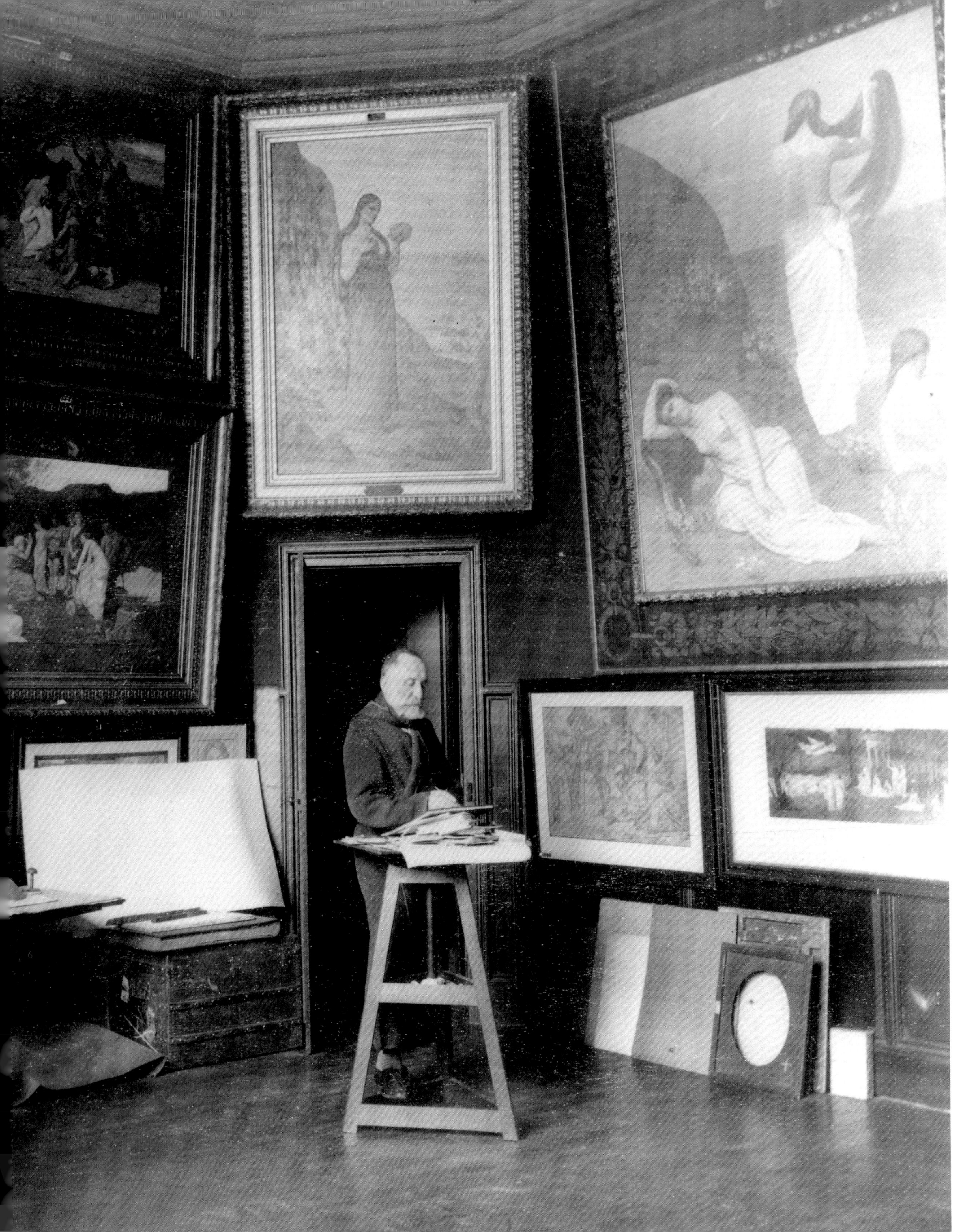

Aimée Brown Price

Pierre Puvis de Chavannes

The Development of a Pictorial Idiom

Although Puvis de Chavannes is best known for producing Arcadian paintings of an epic grandeur, his work does not lend itself to easy categorization. He was an artist of disparate enthusiasms and endeavors, and over a career that spanned five decades – from 1848 to 1898 – his work underwent many transformations. Besides his public paintings, vast mural programs for institutional buildings in many French cities, he executed a considerable number of independent works. He experimented with modernizing allegorical figures, painted warm, personal portraits of friends, and penned wicked parodies even of his own serious work. He produced religious and classicizing statements, still lifes and evocative small watercolor landscapes.

Puvis de Chavannes's mature easel paintings are among his most compelling and original contributions. In contrast to his reassuring official Arcadias, they include melancholic images of great subtlety, reserve and expressive force. As private expressions of isolation and displacement they are an important legacy to modernism and twentieth-century art. The imagery of these more personal works and their radical simplifications are as much a product of the special aesthetic Puvis de Chavannes developed for his murals as are the monumental wall paintings themselves. For most of his career, Puvis was driven by his ambition to create great mural paintings. That is what set him on a search for appropriate styles and to selecting the classicizing imagery with which he is most often identified. That is also what led him to formulate an aesthetic proper to murals. These aspects of his work, the classicizing imagery and the mural aesthetic – that themselves changed over time – were central in the development of his peculiar, idiosyncratic manner that changed the pictorial idiom of his time.

The First Decade of Activity: From Easel Painting to Murals

Puvis's formal training was sporadic. In the late 1840s he spent six months with Henri Scheffer, receiving, it appears, mostly advice and pointers; two weeks with Delacroix (who, ill, then closed his atelier); and three months (perhaps more) with Thomas Couture. He also took a course in anatomy and perspective at the Ecole des Beaux-Arts.[1] He had, however, travelled twice to Italy, staying the second time for over a year; and there he had looked, copied and painted. Upon his return to France, he worked for several years by himself, did some copying at the Louvre, and then for three years worked with several friends, including Gustave Ricard and Alexandre Bida and occasionally the engraver Victor Pollet. Together, they drew after the model and corrected each other at what Puvis, perhaps sardonically, called their 'Academy.'

In the 1850s, with Realism in its ascendancy, Puvis's figurative paintings were, by his own later account, of a 'zealous Romanticism.'[2] He may have so characterized them to explain why after an initial entry in 1850 at the Salon, with a Delacroix-inspired *Dead Christ* (Mokhtar Museum, Guezira, Cairo), his work was not again accepted for exhibition there until 1859. Aside from a score of portraits of family, family retainers and friends, it was these figurative works that absorbed him. For subjects Puvis was attracted to lesser known heroic anecdotes and pathetic dramas. Stories from Roman history, the Middle Ages and the French Revolution were à la mode, and he rendered embellished histories from ancient (cat. 10) to more recent times (see cat. 2), depicting darkly dramatic episodes and harrowing narratives of uncertain outcome (see cat. 19). Puvis rendered his own glosses of well-known compositions, using a Titian *Venus*, for example, as the basis for a sentimental scene from French Protestant history.[3] He studied Venetian artists as fabulists and tried imitating the splendid assurance of their technique. His palette of transparent glazes with shifting tones shows he also looked closely at Delacroix's canvases, as *Negro Boy* (cat. 1) attests. In addition Puvis executed a number of religious works, including drawings based on the *Ecce Homo* theme (cat. 20-22), and a canvas for the church at Champagnat not far from his family's property in Saône-et-Loire (fig. 1).

Amidst all this, in 1854-55, Puvis decided to venture a mural cycle, the most estimable endeavor for a painter of large ambitions. Delacroix,

Couture and Théodore Chassériau, all of whom Puvis admired (having briefly studied with the first two), were then each completing major mural cycles. Delacroix, Ingres and Henri Lehmann were at work on the Paris Hôtel de Ville; Chassériau and Auguste Gendron had completed wall paintings for the Cour des Comptes; and Couture was working on murals for the Church of Saint-Eustache.[4] No public commission was open to the untried artist, and for walls Puvis turned to the newly constructed family château, Le Brouchy, an imposing, medievalizing structure (see cat. 4). In his panels for its dining room (see fig. 2), he for the first time broached the clear definitions and colors, the strong compositional constructions, the discrete forms and sustained narrative vision demanded by mural decorations. Seeking models, he looked at artists from Benozzo Gozzoli to Charles Gleyre and from Raphael to Veronese. In 1859, with an enlarged version of one of his murals, *The Return from the Hunt* (Musée des Beaux-Arts, Marseilles),[5] in a vaguely classicizing and Italianate manner, he once more gained entry to the Salon. That the painting was favorably noted by Théophile Gautier,[6] encouraged Puvis towards creating monumental wall paintings.

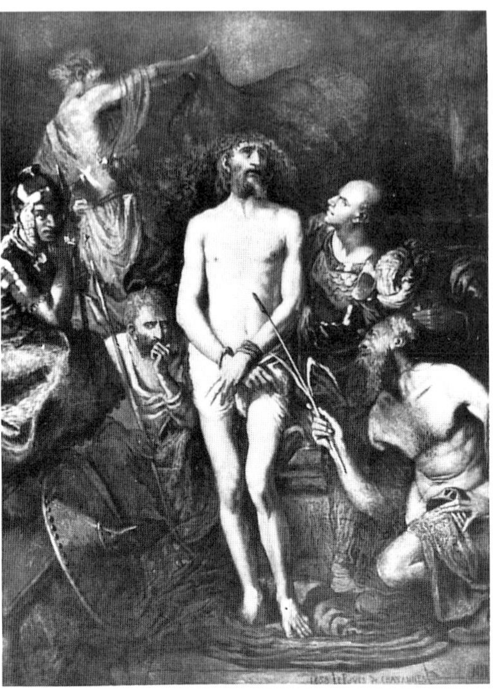

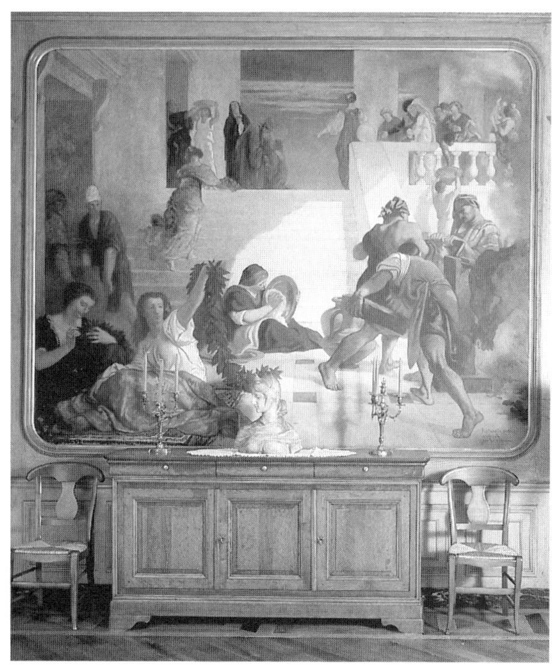

The 1860s: The First Mural Commissions

The prestige accorded mural painting for public buildings in the 1850s constituted a dramatic turnabout from what its status had been early in the century. From the time of Louis XV to that of Jacques-Louis David, mural decorations, because they subordinated themselves to exterior conditions, were thought to lack the dignity of monumental painting, and David proscribed them because they subsumed themselves to architecture. He further dismissed mural decorations as being for sybarites.[7] The hiatus in mural painting in the generation of David and his followers was not on grounds of status alone: during and after the French Revolution, palaces and châteaux were deserted and churches closed. In domestic settings, the popularity of wallpaper from about 1804 to 1855 also decreased demand for wall painting.[8] But during the Restoration (1815-30), murals for churches and civic buildings were reinstituted by government commissions, and during the July Monarchy (1830-48) over forty large-scale complexes were initiated.[9] The restoration of the mural decorations at the Palace of Fontainebleau during the Second Empire enhanced their prominence and made artists aware of such projects while familiarizing them with their special mannerist modes. In the 1840s mural paintings were championed by several critics, Gustave Planche and Théophile Gautier chief among them; and they came to be considered superior to easel paintings in the decoration of buildings, with the muralist viewed as a seeker of the serious and durable in subject matter.[10] By 1870 Henri Regnault could write that 'decoration is the true aim of painting, it hasn't been invented for anything else.'[11]

fig. 1
Christ Before the Praetorial Court, 1858
Oil on canvas, 205 x 160 cm
Parish church, Champagnat

fig. 2
The Return of the Prodigal Son, 1855
Oil on canvas, 252 x 322 cm
Dining room, Château Le Brouchy

In 1861 Puvis presented two monumental wall paintings at the Salon on the epic themes of War and Peace. Executed without a destination, but in a new style formulated for the project, and surrounded with ornamental borders to suggest they were proper decorations, *Bellum* and *Concordia* (see cat. 26-27) were accorded a medal (second class), and the critical notice that led, as Puvis had hoped it would, to his first official mural commissions. Indeed, for most of the 1860s Puvis would be occupied with mural projects: an extensive series of works for new museums at Amiens (to be a veritable compendium of his paintings) and Marseilles, as well as an ensemble of mural decorations for the Paris hôtel of a private patron, the artist and writer Mme Claude Vignon (see cat. 42-45). During the next three decades, he would execute mural programs for other of the new museums that were mushrooming in prospering French provincial cities during the Second Empire and early Third Republic, those at Lyons and Rouen, as well as programs for the city halls at Poitiers and Paris. He would execute two major campaigns at the Panthéon in Paris (the first when it was still the Church of Saint Genevieve), and a panoramic mural for the great amphitheatre of the new Sorbonne. Internationally renowned by the 1890s and the best known mural painter of his generation, he created a cycle of murals for the Boston Public Library, his only wall paintings outside of France.

In 1861 as he first turned to producing monumental public paintings, Puvis de Chavannes sharply modified his imagery and style and embarked on a carefully fashioned, ennobling classicizing idiom appropriate to such projects. The expressive power of various styles had been discussed since the 1840s,[12] with specific styles long considered fitting for particular contexts, official or domestic, religious or profane.[13] A classicizing style was *the* certifiably appropriate mode for official and grand painting.[14] Classical references provided authority, cachet and cultural continuity. Muralists of various aesthetic camps – from Ingres to Delacroix, Lehmann and Chassériau – demonstrate this pervasive orthodoxy. Though *Bellum* was not untheatrical and *Concordia* depended on Renaissance imagery, a bit of Poussin and permutations of classicism from the eighteenth and nineteenth centuries, both were essentially classicizing. The critic Arthur Stevens was shortly to note that Puvis was 'seeking style over everything and walking on the path to great painting, to decorative art.'[15]

Classicism in the Context of the 1860s

Classicizing impulses had surfaced so often and Hellenism was so widespread in nineteenth-century France that each manifestation, though laden with new meaning, was less significant in itself.[16] The first stirrings of the thoroughly French classicism with which Puvis would be involved in the 1860s occurred before 1850 among poets and writers. It was marked by a fervent yearning towards a vaguely defined ancient Hellas. A truism of French education was that Greece was the cradle of French culture, and a nostalgia for Hellenic antiquity was in essence a nostalgia for one's own innocent past. Among the Utopian visions that would haunt painters and men of letters in the later nineteenth century (from 'Oriental' to 'primitive' societies in the distant, exotic Marquesas), that of a Hellenizing Golden Age was the most conservative and pervasive. Classicism functioned as a source of cultural identity, a commonality of received ideas and the reassurance of a would-be hegemony – at least among the members of the educated upper middle class, products, like Puvis, of a lycéen's education in the classics. The framework itself of culture (by that he meant French culture) – science, art, literature, philosophy, government, ethics, diplomacy – complete in all its parts, came from Greece, Ernest Renan intoned in 'The Prayer on the Acropolis' ('La Prière sur l'Acropole').[17] Théophile Gautier, so important to Puvis at the beginning of his career, a fellow poet declared was 'born a Hellene; his homeland ... that of the temples, of white statues, of forests in which the grass had been trod by the steps of the gods; and on the other hand, he was, in spirit, essentially French....'[18] Or as that same Parnassian poet Théodore de Banville succinctly put the sentiment shared by a number of his compatriots, 'I was crazy, as I am still, for anything that touched mother Greece....'[19]

The nostalgia for a Hellenizing Golden Age that would be so much a part of Puvis's mature classicizing imagery was not of recent vintage, but a phenomenon of classical antiquity.[20] The distancing and vague melancholia that would distinguish many of his images was characteristic of Virgil's *Eclogues* themselves; the Arcadia in which Virgil's *Bucolics* is set is far off. Puvis knew his Virgil (and his Homer and Cicero),[21] and reputedly, even as a septuagenarian, was able to recite more of Virgil's verses than someone who had just received his bachelor's degree.[22] The contemporary Parnassian poets also sang the pastness of that longed for Golden Age, with Leconte de Lisle noting its remoteness, the passage of years since then, the 'There' of Baudelaire's 'Là, tout n'est qu'ordre et beauté,/ luxe, calme, et volupté.' That refrain would be as much the theme of Puvis's mature *Pleasant Land* (see cat. 86), as it would be that of Matisse's *Luxe, calme et volupté* a half century later (see cat. 150). This longing for innocence and harmony might be diffuse, encompassing past and future, pagan and Judaeo-Christian concepts, as Victor de Laprade's verses would indicate,[23]

> 'Il est une vallée où l'harmonie habite;...
> Quel que soit le doux nom dont chaque âge la nomme....'[24]

In the 1860s Puvis's epic images were partly generated from classical literature: from *Bellum*, with its resounding *Aeneid*-like Virgilian passages (see cat. 27), to *Sleep*, engendered by specific lines (see cat. 47).[25]

Concordia and *Ave Picardia Nutrix* suggest the easy prosperity of Virgil's Golden Age (see cat. 26). Classical accessories and Latin titles (that one critic thought pretentious) further imbued the works with a sense of the antique.[26]

Puvis also found prototypes for his classicizing work in antique art, insisting it was based directly on nature – understandable, perhaps, in the context of contemporary contrivances. As he put it, 'the antique is nature herself. Go! you can copy the torso of Illisus without fear of taking on a mannerism....'[27] Thus, his easel painting *Autumn* (see cat. 35) features a seated Demeter of Cnidos-like figure; an Amazon of Crésilas becomes *Vigilance* (cat. 45); and later 'bathers' and women at their toilette, draped 'à l'antique' and characterized by impersonal nudity and iconic inactivity, are also based on ancient Venuses (see cat. 76, 96). Landscapes provide a legitimizing environment conferring a bucolic believability, Virgil's *locus amoenus* or place of delight, that was missing from their ancient sculptural prototypes.

Two strains of classicizing images emerge in Puvis's works of the 1860s. A pretty manner, usually for smaller, independent works, typified by *Fishing* (1866, whereabouts unknown) and *The Vintage* (Wallraf-Richartz Museum, Cologne), evokes Golden Age innocence and child-like play; while a more austere group, exemplified by *Vigilance* and *Meditation* (see fig. 30), parallels the stylistic achievements of the contemporaneous Parnassian literary movement with its doctrine of the pre-eminence of form as an impassive, unyielding, Platonic ideal.[28] According to the Parnassians, known before 1866 as 'Formistes' and 'Stylistes,'[29] the Greeks had taught the priority of pure form and simplicity. As Gautier, an adherent of Parnassianism, put it, in a phrase that years later would be echoed by Puvis when he stated that the best ordered conception was the simplest, clearest, most decorative and beautiful:[30] 'Une belle forme est une belle idée.'[31] To read Gautier's criticism in the 1860s is to know that form and line were spoken of abstractly. And to read how Proudhon disparaged this 'idolatrous cult of form,'[32] is to know how important their movement was. Given the Second Empire tendency to ornate surrounds and fancy detail, the serene images and equilibrated phrases that the Parnassians espoused seem the more chaste; nor is it coincidence that Puvis's austere classicizing images should appear in public art at this time of aristocratic opulence and worldliness.[33]

In State-authorized wall painting, the classicizing ideal that Puvis embodied in his Arcadian paintings needed little adjustment to meld with French history and culture. In conflating French and antique culture, and presenting Hellenism as common to both, Puvis set forth a not uncommon idea. His Amiens and Marseilles murals, for example, *Ave Picardia Nutrix* (ill. pp. 102-103) and *Massilia, Greek Colony* (see cat. 50), are at once Greco-Latin and Gallic amalgams. Of the many versions of pastoral, literary and pictorial,[34] that Puvis could turn to as sources for further elaboration of his ideas, Poussin's permutations were particularly cherished by him. Puvis capitalized on the familiarity of the classical mode as an expression of an ideal world and would, later, develop his imagery to indicate that world's displacement.

In the 1860s Puvis also began to develop allegorical themes, whether as individual personifications or whole compositions, for murals and easel paintings alike, ever seeking to be a participant within the great iconographic traditions of Western Art, while making those traditions more versatile and apt for a contemporary context. This was to remain an important issue in his art, one that Thomas Couture had wrestled with as well. Although Couture had advised students to read Homer and Virgil, he also advocated imagery that would not be a digression from the actual world, at least those are his instructions in his *Méthode et entretiens d'atelier*[35]: 'forget lyres and golden harps; since you are a peasant, be a peasant openly, and especially stop putting on your Sunday best.... Why ... these passionless bacchantes? Is it to satisfy the libidinous whims of certain amateurs? .... You are a fake poet, you are a fake classic, you....'[36] Puvis would forgo lyres only intermittently over the years. But he would seek to make his classicizing images germane; in the decades ahead, circumstances were to provide that opportunity.

It was not only classicism, however, that he would embrace. He would exploit the recognition and attendant associations of a fascinating array of pictorial sources to enhance the expressive thrust of his work. These were to include Byzantine and Northern Renaissance as well as Pre-Raphaelite images. His enthusiasms were many: in one breath he would voice his admiration for the decorative character of Simon Vouet's nudes, for Poussin, and for Giotto's colors. Such catholic taste was by no means unique to Puvis: Couture was identified with eclecticism; and that other issue of his studio, Manet, for not disassociated reasons, was called a pasticheur of styles.[37] Before the end of the 1860s, Puvis would return to religious subjects (see cat. 57,62), developing forceful new presentations which he enriched by allusions to religious images from earlier traditions in much the way that he had introduced imagery from earlier classicizing painting into his first classicizing murals. And yet he managed, with his style increasingly bred to decoration, to make these images entirely his own.

The Mural Aesthetic

Critics immediately perceived Puvis de Chavannes's wall paintings and their aesthetic as something new. When *Rest* and *Work*, which would be installed at Amiens, were exhibited at the Salon of 1863, Paul Mantz castigated the abstract nature of the groupings and the 'abridged system of execution and of arbitrary coloration that removes all reality from his figures....'[38] And when that advocate of Realism, Jules Castagnary (who two decades later would be a proponent of Puvis's *The Poor Fisherman*), reviewed Puvis's *Autumn* at the Salon of 1864 – a large easel painting with the characteristics of Puvis's new style – he charged the artist with looking for form for its own sake,[39] and he was quite right.

The differences between Puvis's murals and what one expected of paintings – 'tableaux' – were repeatedly pointed out, whether to justify or condemn them. As his first monumental paintings were executed without a specific destination, Thoré-Bürger maintained that they were called murals simply to justify their 'pâleur.'[40] The style that Puvis developed for his wall paintings can only be understood in the context of what in the mid-nineteenth century was advocated as a proper mural aesthetic. By the middle of the nineteenth century, a fundamental distinction was made between mural and easel painting based on what was perceived as their different purposes.[41] Murals, to decorate a wall, owed their allegiance to it and were to subordinate themselves to their architectural surrounds, not detracting (or distracting) from them or from the planarity of the walls themselves, the integrity of which was to remain inviolate. Paintings, however, were to imitate nature.[42] The 'tableau' and the 'décoration' were to have differing rules, conventions and appearance. Baudelaire was only one of many voices that declared 'décoration' a wholly different endeavor from painting and commented that artists had 'unlearned' how it should be done.[43] Prosper Mérimée (of *Carmen* fame), Inspecteur Général des Monuments Historiques, advised suppressing perspective and other illusionistic effects and evening the intensity of mural surfaces so no single tone would dominate; appealing to a certain luxurious sensuousness, he recommended approximating the colors of a cashmere shawl.[44] The prolific critic Théophile Gautier, who prided himself on being the first to discover Puvis,[45] and whose importance to Puvis must not be underestimated, had declared the sober tones of building walls would teach painters tranquillity of color[46] and recommended that these colors be opaque and whitened, so objects would seem hard and solid[47] – the best tones tender, blond and light, between those of colored relief and faded tapestry.[48] Gautier advocated, 'A balanced composition, rhythmic poses, a sequence of symmetries, qualities that comprise what one might call the architectonic of painting, must ... be sought before all else. To be wed to the monument ... decorative paintings [must] ... respect its disposition and not contravene its lines; ... vigorous tone digs holes that startle the eye.... Clear, matte areas defined by a nicely fixed contour, modeled with moderate relief ... are eminently suitable. Farewell, chiaroscuro, brush play, impasto, lapidary tones, glazes ... sparkling highlights, all those artifices of the palette to which amateurs are so drawn! The wall rejects these niceties: it wants purity of design, grandeur of style and sober harmony of color.'[49] In fact, it was as if Gautier had been just waiting for Puvis to come along, for as he characterized Puvis's mural style as represented in Puvis's first efforts at monumental painting, *Concordia* and *Bellum*, it exemplified precisely those qualities he had repeatedly called for in the 1850s as proper to 'décorations.' Gautier asserted that Puvis was a painter not of 'tableaux,' but of decoration, that what he needed was not an easel, but scaffolding.[50] What was preached as proper was tantamount to an archaizing aesthetic – flattened, lightened, brightened, simplified and non-illusionistic compositions. How widespread these requirements were is documented in Charles Blanc's 1867 *Grammaire des arts du dessin*, a handbook of current dictates, which abrogated perspective in mural painting.[51] But these theories notwithstanding, in practice murals often looked like easel paintings Viollet-le-Duc complained in his *Dictionnaire raisonné*.[52]

Beginning with his first commissions for specific installations, Puvis labored to engineer his compositions with all their elements to fit their sites and the prevailing architecture. As early as 1864 Puvis recognized that he was doing something new and that it did not come easily. It was cold-blooded audacity on his part, he noted, that allowed him to arrest everything 'like geometry.'[53] It was no compliment when Castagnary wrote that Puvis 'doesn't draw or paint; he composes, that's his specialty.'[54] In 1868 Puvis characterized the *veni, vidi, vici* of his method of achieving sobriety and simplicity, 'I've condensed, assembled, packed.'[55]

To maintain the two-dimensionality demanded by wall painting, Puvis nearly eliminated chiaroscuro and produced figurations in which flat shapes and colors are salient. However ample his figures by way of silhouette, without modeling they lost specific gravity, a sense of weight and volume. He was increasingly to heighten and whiten his colors of near tonal equals that, in combination with an overall surface texture, equilibrated pictorial elements in importance and insubstantiality, forming a unit of homogeneous interlocking parts. Puvis also began to use an opaque medium with a matte finish that would reduce light-livened reflections and preserve the legibility of the planar surface. Although fresco was traditionally preferred for murals, as Delacroix had noted in 1849,[56] and Hippolyte Flandrin recommended discreet colorations in fresco as suitable for churches,[57] that medium was ill-advised in the damp French climate.[58] To approximate the inert matte surface of fresco, the next best thing was 'peinture à la cire,' an oil medium with a wax additive, not unlike encaustic, which was what Puvis, like Flandrin, the Ingristes, Chassériau and Delacroix before him, used.[59] In what may have been initiated as imitation of fresco on plaster, Puvis dragged his viscous oil and wax medium drily over the entire pictorial field, overriding the tactile identity of objects represented, and that surface would become rougher, the brush strokes broader and more summary over the years.

Beginning in the mid-1860s, Puvis's mural colors were keyed in chords to those of the surrounding architecture as Gautier said mural colors should be. Puvis wanted it understood that these choices were not based on personal predilection: 'One would have to be quite slow not to understand that the day I have to deal with dark woodwork, strong gold tones, or stained wood floors, I would readily change my color range, without, for that, changing my style....'[60] Yet, Puvis voiced a particular admiration for Giotto's colors, and they were surely to affect his own: 'I found Giotto's palette ideal, so fresh, in which whites, light blues, tender pinks, greens and yellows are wed in such sweet harmonies ... framed by a stone border, I ought to be inspired by this palette.'[61] By the 1890s, readying his Boston Public Library murals, he would acquire a sample of the grey-veined yellow marble used for the walls of the building and took scrupulous care to imitate it.[62] His 'mother tones,' kept meticulously (in crucibles immersed in a water basin), were used throughout a mural's execution.

Contributing mightily to a perception of the decorative character of Puvis's paintings, what made them a suitable embellishment for a wall and completed them, as Gautier noted, were their borders.[63] The prominent borders led to a comparison with tapestries,[64] and that, in turn, helped justify their flat, matte tones and uniform relief and what seemed odd colors 'treated in the manner of fresco painting or of cartoons made as designs for tapestry.'[65] Puvis staunchly defended his borders as absolutely integral to certain of his paintings. He was to introduce borders and ornamented frames over the years in paintings that he wanted thought of as 'decorations': such works as *The Balloon* (fig. 32) and *The Carrier Pigeon* (cat. 65), and the definitive version of *Young Women by the Sea* (see ill. p.10, the frame since lost). Their prominence, even in preparatory drawings and painted studies such as *Labor* of 1862 (cat. 31) and *Saint Genevieve as a Child in Prayer* (cat. 70), indicate how indispensable they were to the conceptual totality of the work, helping to produce the sense of a self-referential, closed unit. Moreover, they confer color, pictorial weight and interest on its outer perimeters. Borders provided a margin of contextual control and psychic and aesthetic insulation. Like the frames of Jacques Derrida's felicitous phrase, they are the 'hors-d'oeuvre' (literally outside the work) to the 'chef-d'oeuvre.'[66] Fully frontal as they are, they also relate the interior imagery to the planar walls of the outlying architecture, leading the way both into and out of the imagery. Without the aesthetic strictures demanded of the contained image, they could be fanciful and ornamental. That pictorial aesthetic was eventually to migrate from the borders to the center of Puvis's paintings.

Because they are perceived as marginal and essentially charming conceits – stylish, arbitrary but somehow gratuitous – the borders engendered an acceptance of a painting as decoration and abetted the development of a sense of the abstract. The bracketing of images with borders – begun by Puvis in 1861 with his first monumental works (see cat. 26-29), and continued into the 1870s in what we call the independent paintings (see cat. 65,76) – plays an important part in a changing definition of the properly pictorial. Their presence signals a painting and creates that expectation for the viewer. The way Puvis's borders functioned to give a sense of an ordered whole was not lost on Georges Seurat, Maurice Denis and Edouard Vuillard, each of whom was to use borders importantly in his own work.[67]

The special aesthetic of Puvis de Chavannes's mural paintings is most apparent in the reduced versions he came to make after them. Puvis first turned to executing such 'réductions,' as he called them, to represent his monumental wall paintings, *Concordia* and *Bellum* and *Rest* and *Work* (that had already been installed at Amiens), at the highly touted Universal Exhibition of 1867 (see cat. 26-29). He thus hoped to further the public recognition he had received when the murals themselves had been exhibited at the Salons of 1861 and 1863. He was to continue this practice, routinely making reductions after his murals, to strengthen his chance for acclaim in face of the inevitable dispersal and inaccessibility of his work.[68]

As the reductions were exhibited virtually as easel paintings, removed from their architectural context, certain elements might be puzzling or seem arbitrary (see cat. 74 and 101). Aside from *Concordia* and *Bellum*, Puvis's murals were executed for specific sites. The rationale for each program, their often ingenious structure, careful cadences, forms and colors were provided by the particular context and the immediate architectural surrounds to which Puvis was increasingly sensitive. No longer explicable in a reduction is the peculiarity of an ivory sky, chosen for a mural in which the stone walls were that color. Divested of their setting, their flatness, the opacity of their lightened colors, their special compositions and the borders themselves seem all the more idiosyncratic. As Camille Pissarro complained as late as 1895 of a reduced version of one of Puvis's murals that was then on exhibition, 'there's an anomaly there, it isn't made to be seen like a picture, no, a thousand times no, on a wall of freestone it's admirable ... but it is not painting....'[69] These reductions made a new generation of painters understand the particularity of the innovative decorative aesthetic at the heart of Puvis's paintings and how that might be exploited.

The 1870s: New Contexts and Imagery

The destruction and deprivations of the Franco-Prussian War of 1870-71 and the horrors attendant on the Paris Commune had their repercussions in Puvis's work. It now took a new turn and assumed an unaccustomed edge. He recorded the painful ironies of the siege and the military presence at Versailles (see cat. 68), referred to how ill-prepared France had been, and sought to invent bracing images in the wake of defeat. His

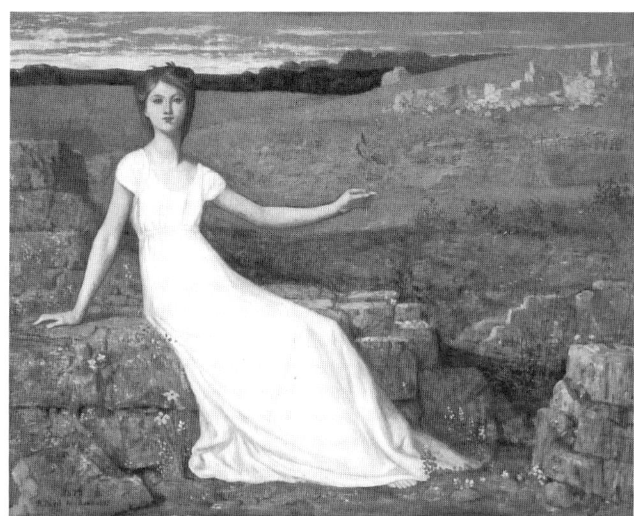

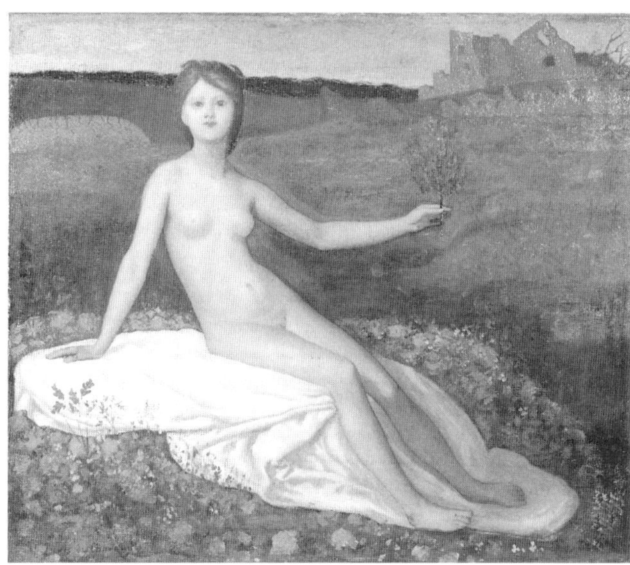

fig. 3
Hope, 1872
Oil on canvas, 102.5 x 129.5 cm
Walters Art Gallery, Baltimore

fig. 4
Hope (second version), ca. 1872
Oil on canvas, 70.7 x 82 cm
Musée d'Orsay, Paris

efforts to develop allegorical figures with particular meaning to his time, begun in 1868,[70] found focus as he tried to devise apt and popular images to resonate with the heroic and less than heroic history of this cataclysmic period. *Symbol of the Red Cross* (Musée du Petit Palais, Paris), *The Balloon* and *The Carrier Pigeon* (fig. 32, cat. 65), *The Sleeping Sentinel* (cat. 63), *Hope* (figs. 3, 4) and *Death and the Maidens* (fig. 33) – all embodied, at varying symbolic levels, recent events. Of his two versions of *Hope*, one was clad in a white dress and might still be associated with religious imagery; but his small, nude *Hope* was a new, nationalistic image honoring renewal for a country in defeat. Modesty and gentle sobriety seemed appropriate during this period of national recovery and soul-searching. In *Hope* Puvis developed a new type of figure whose chaste purity, vulnerability and slight stiffness suggest early Renaissance models – Sassetta, Ambrogio Lorenzetti, Fra Angelico. Puvis would continue to be interested in creating innovative allegorcal personifications, devising in the next two decades such works as *Pity*, in 1887 (cat. 110), and *Charity*, in 1894 (cat. 140); the latter was to be developed as a 'Parisian Virtue.'

After the debacle of 1870-71, classicism was asserted with new vigor as a politico-national ideology. A classicizing past was part of the French identity and pointedly distinguished French-Mediterranean civilization from Prussian Northern Kultur. In the name of nationalism, Numa-Denis Fustel de Coulanges preached a political need for promoting classicizing work and not apologizing for a non-Germanic past. Puvis's classicizing imagery was, through these circumstances, bound up more than ever with patriotic sentiment, a sentiment that continued to be enunciated until the end of the century and beyond: 'Really we French are Gallo-Greeks and Gallo-Latins, and the murky singers of the North who are presented to us as models are nothing but enemies of our ceaselessly threatened race.'[71] Patriotism, Fustel de Coulanges claimed (nimbly rationalizing France's all too recent loss of territory), was not a question of geographic locus: 'True patriotism isn't love of soil, it is love of the past, it is respect for the generations that have preceded us.'[72] The French past was tied to Greco-Roman roots and Fustel de Coulanges urged French artists to celebrate this past with pride and represent 'the Gallo-Roman race at work, busy weaving, building towns, erecting temples, studying law, experiencing at once the labors and the pleasures of peace....'[73] Puvis had idealized the 'Gallo-Roman race' at Amiens and Marseilles. By a society bruised by war and political upheaval, an Arcadian ideal, life at its pastoral best, the idea of fresh beginnings was sought with renewed urgency.

In 1873 Puvis presented his grandly Arcadian, mural size (305 x 507 cm) *Summer* (fig. 5) at the Salon. An adamantly peaceful chronicle of a noble agrarian people harvesting the land's bounty and enjoying respite from their tasks, it is above all restorative. It asserted well-being just when a happy economic situation was not certain.[74] Measured against the deprivations of 1871, this voluptuous paean to the amber fields of France reaffirms possibility. It is a beautiful, conservative return to classicizing imagery and contrasts to such austere wartime images as *The Carrier Pigeon* and *The Balloon*.

In 1874 Puvis received his first commission for a project in Paris, which was also his first program with a religious theme. It was for what was then the Church of Saint Genevieve, the patron of Paris (now the Panthéon, see cat. 70-75). These murals called for yet another idiom, proper for a religious subject. Using an archaizing aesthetic based on early Italian models, Puvis at once simplified his images, gave his work an air of historical authenticity by couching it in an older style more contemporary to the events depicted, and associated his work with the then current idea of the ingenuousness or moral purity of those periods.[75] Recollecting paintings of an age of belief was what Baudelaire had suggested twenty years earlier for religious art; the operative aesthetic was akin to Baudelaire's 'naiveté,' an antidote to affectation and self-conscious-seeming styling. Whether classicizing or Christian, pastoral signified innocence and order. Puvis's inventions are consonant with a return to a simple Christianity, to a faith undissipated by doctrinaire factionalism, a faith such as accompanied the religious revival and anticlericalism at the beginning of the Third Republic. Though the principal sections of the *Saint Genevieve* murals are vaguely Giottesque, the friezes, as was true throughout the Panthéon, were Byzantine in style. For church decoration, similar processionals of hieratic figures against an ornamental background were frequently employed. Byzantinism, familiar in several manifestations, was so widespread that Gautier had congratulated Chassériau for not being swept away by it.[76]

Whether classicizing, archaizing, or neo-Byzantine in style, an affiliation with a past aesthetic tradition lessened immediacy and the naturalism considered unbecoming in monumental and especially religious art. Allusions to a past style also enriched the image at hand. That is, style and a decorative aesthetic kept the subject as anything but a pictorial fiction in abeyance and enhanced the meaning of the religious and classicizing pastoral.

In the 1870s and early 1880s, Puvis perfected a classicizing imagery in paintings such as *The Fisherman's Family* (1875, destroyed; version of 1887, fig. 24), *Young Women by the Sea* (1879, cat. 76, fig. 6), and *Pleasant Land* (1882, see cat. 86), and he would bring this imagery to his official Arcadias of the 1880s and 1890s, the kinds of paintings for which he would best be known. Puvis also came to rely on classicizing imagery in unexpected ways. In paintings such as *Young Women by the Sea* classicism as a sublime orthodoxy could become a vehicle, even a cover for quiet subversion and the pictorial radicalism of the special decorative

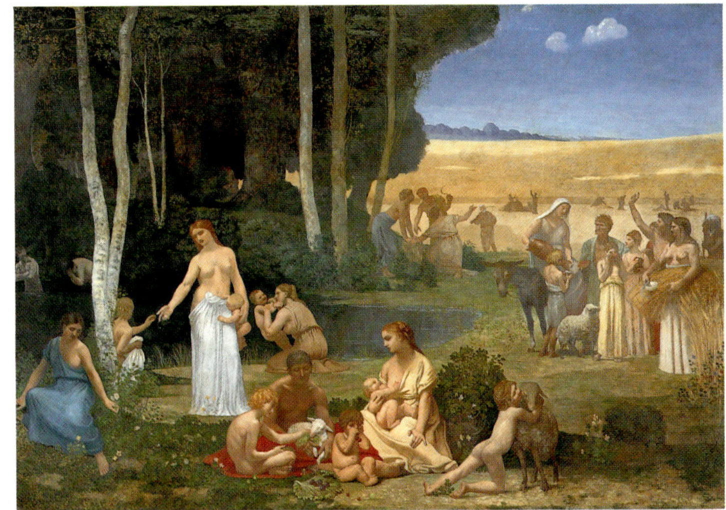

fig. 5
Summer, 1873
Oil on canvas, 305 x 507 cm
Musée d'Orsay, Paris

fig. 6
Young Women by the Sea (large version), 1879
Oil on canvas, 205 x 154 cm
Musée d'Orsay, Paris

fig. 7
The Prodigal Son, ca. 1879
Oil on canvas, 130 x 95.5 cm
Foundation E.G. Bührle Collection, Zurich

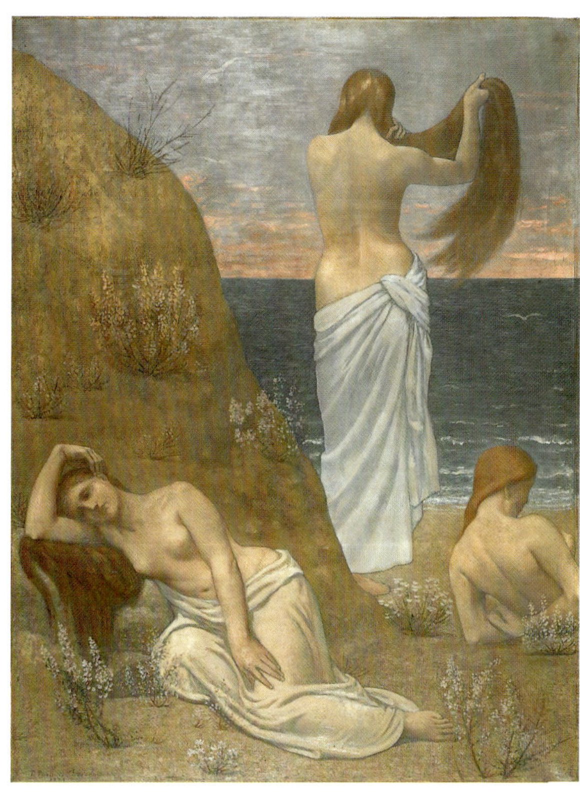

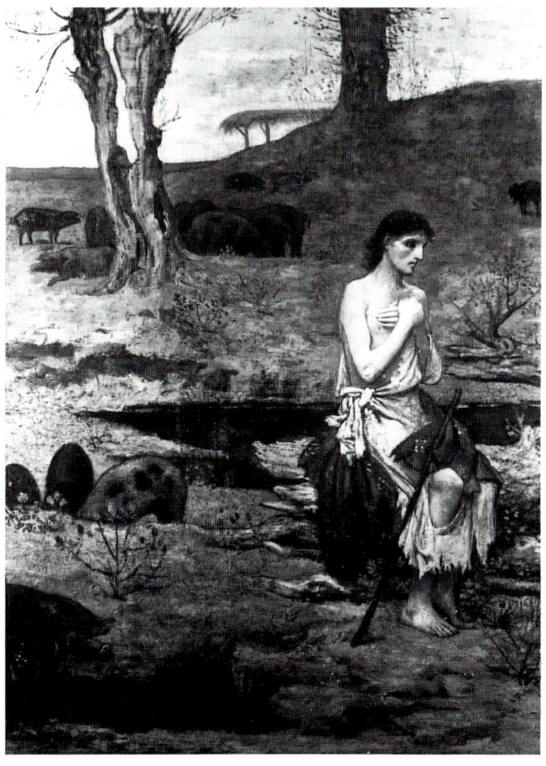

aesthetic with which all his work was becoming imbued. Given Puvis's sensitivity to calibrated placements, a decorous pace and geometries of groupings, a skill he had already honed and that he would continue to develop in his public paintings of the 1880s and 1890s, the structure of *Young Women by the Sea*, and, indeed, other of his independent mature paintings, is that much more audacious.

Puvis's independent paintings of 1879-81, *Young Women by the Sea*, *The Prodigal Son* (fig. 7), and *The Poor Fisherman* (fig. 23), are among his most inventive compositions. His mature aesthetic is represented in *Young Women by the Sea*, the biblical parable of *The Prodigal Son*, and the ascetic would-be genre imagery of *The Poor Fisherman*.[77] Each is a boldly simple and radical composition, their pictorial elements plain, flattened and unexpected. Individual figures are separated and do not interact, even turning from one another to direct an unseeing gaze beyond the physical perimeter of the painting; or they are literally marginalized and even truncated. These works are bound together by a mood of restrained poignancy and attitudes of introspection that range from subdued self-absorption to revery. What distinguishes these paintings, cutting across traditional categories, is an essential melancholy, a sensibility of aloneness and metaphysical isolation which is furthered by the structure itself of the several compositions. Whether faint as in *Young Women by the Sea*, its classicism reassuring that not much could be amiss, or framed as religio-existentialist in the parable of *The Prodigal Son*, or most powerfully and elusively in *The Poor Fisherman*, as emotionally sober and restrained as it may be,[78] it is a growing undercurrent in the tide of traditional subject matter in Puvis's mature personal paintings. The particularity of *The Prodigal Son*, alone in the wilderness, may be measured against *The Return of the Prodigal Son*, one of Puvis's earliest narrative subjects (see fig. 2, cat. 4), in which that erstwhile son returns amidst celebration to the family fold. The expressive motif of moral solitude, melancholy and forbearance that these canvases project – at such variance with the official Arcadias of the public paintings – has not so subtly been termed 'misérabilisme.'[79]

The 1880s and 1890s: The Mature Murals and a New Pictorial Idiom

In the 1880s and 1890s Puvis received commission after commission. In his public pastorals, he brought the grandeur of Utopian idylls – if somewhat stiffly – to France. *The Poor Fisherman* and his other independent paintings notwithstanding, in his public paintings the classicizing modality continued to be preeminent, succinctly transmitting current concerns and normative values. Puvis's contributions at Amiens, Lyons, the Sorbonne and Rouen are sensitive to place, architecture and their respective building program, whether they be museums or a university.

The structure, rhythms, style, materials and colors of these new buildings and the placement within the setting of images as well as the viewer's projected experience of them, came into play in his inventions. *Ludus pro Patria* (ill. pp. 192-193), which completed the Amiens cycle in 1882, depicts an ordered, functioning society, with steadfast communal and familial units. It was patriotic, underscoring communal well-being and a not so veiled call to preparedness at arms. Puvis's commission for the city of his birth, Lyons, brought what has been deemed the quintessential Puvis: an Arcadian grove, *The Sacred Wood* (see cat. 101). *The Sorbonne* (ill. pp. 200-201) would be still another sacred grove, and for Rouen that grove was made gently contemporaneous (*Inter Artes et Naturam*, see ill. pp. 214-215). These images kept actuality at a safe distance while they asserted a cultural history that was the underpinning to the formulation of a certain nationalism[80] and regionalism. At a time of urbanization, industrialization, empire and flux and that much less homogeneity and continuity, these images would serve an integrative function.

Because his paintings subordinated themselves to their buildings, Puvis's services had frequently been secured by architects (Arthur Diet for the museum at Amiens, and Henri Espérandieu for the Palais Longchamp, Marseilles), and now that continued to be the case as Henri Nénot selected him for a major commission for the new Sorbonne (see cat. 112-125). Puvis was also a leading choice in about 1883 to decorate the monumental Louvre staircase – because his work would not detract from the sculpture, landing or galleries of Italian and French masterpieces.[81]

For the most part, his murals were designed for Beaux-Arts institutional architecture, an architecture of regular rhythms and carefully paced sequences, an architecture that might have neo-Baroque styling or ornamentation but lacked the crescendoes of, say, the Italian Baroque. While these buildings might be architecturally decorated,[82] many were sober at heart, of a clarity, symmetry and underlying planarity and constraint that was basically classicizing, with a sense of calm – 'du calme' – long appreciated by the French and not to be underestimated as an ideological desideratum.[83] Their paratactic rhythms are consonant with and a reigning aesthetic in Puvis de Chavannes's developed mural aesthetic.

In painting as in architecture, stylistic pluralism made self-consciously chosen styles, each of which had its own expressive qualities, a matter of calculation.[84] Puvis's use of styles by the mid-1870s and 1880s is arguably comparable to what Henri Labrouste made of stylistic appropriation in his Saint Genevieve Library.[85] The dry regularity, the sense of zones, the tact itself of limited garniture (comparable to Puvis's ornamental borders), the cadences, and what Neil Levine has called a 'mass-positive-space positiveness' is curiously like what Puvis would come to develop, with depicted space eventually counting for as much as depicted mass and, more importantly, mass as little.

Puvis's carefully calibrated placements, his engineering of pictorial components into place were to be hallmarks of his mature aesthetic and pronounced in the murals from the 1880s. In what might be known today as an 'overall' composition, he moved pictorial elements to all parts of the pictorial surface and achieved legible patterns. Puvis would come to advise students also to install their 'theater,' their 'scene,' as he called it, firmly, so it wouldn't dance.[86]

Some critics claimed that Puvis's implacable organizing system was the Golden Section, the classical canon of proportion that claimed validity on mystical, mathematical and scientific grounds, though by the nineteenth century its use might be a mark of cultivation rather than spiritual commitment.[87] Because *Pleasant Land* so influenced Georges Seurat, whose use of the Golden Section has also been asserted,[88] Puvis's canvas has been carefully scrutinized for its use.[89] But Puvis seems to have applied ad hoc regulating principles to his work determined by the site, the prevailing structures, a desire to avoid undue visual incident in any area and to distribute pictorial interest evenly.[90] What is important is that Puvis's geometries demanded explanation. By whatever system, the unyielding placements of his figures led to a sense of the eternally unperturbed and imperturbable. The unruffled evenness of his rhythms was not amenable to depicting dramatic subjects, and his reluctance to take on such subjects – he rejected several such commissions – indicates his awareness of the self-imposed limitations of his style.

Puvis created static presentational areas parallel, tangential to, but separate from the spectator's space and completely at odds with the experiential spaces of artists like Degas and later Cézanne who implied an onlooker's peering presence with close-up views and a penetrating, even invasive visual examination of objects. Puvis's viewer is invited to look upon a staged scene but kept at a safe and discreet distance.

In the interest of compositional cohesion Puvis not only varied pictorial elements – color, shape – but reduced them to the simplest plastic terms. As he put his own credo of austerity, an astonishing less is more aesthetic, 'To simplify, that is to release the thought; the simplest conception proves to be the most beautiful. Painting isn't an imitation of reality, but a parallelism of nature.... Art achieves what nature drafts, pronounces the word that she stammers. How can one arrive at helping nature in its effort to speak? By abbreviation and simplification. Adhere to expressing the important, forget the rest; that is the secret of composition, that is the secret of design, that is even the secret of eloquence and intellect.'[91]

In the 1880s, Puvis would further develop, refine and exploit classicizing imagery. His images would become the more evocative and palatable for lacking specificity. They would be put at a remove from and emptied of mythology. In *Fantasy* (1866, cat. 43), for example, there is still a reference to a winged Pegasus. In *Young Women by the Sea* (1879) and

Pleasant Land (1882) it is the half-draped figures that suggest Hellas, and muted colors and arrested poses that put it at a distance. There is validity to one critic's comment, meant as an accusation, that Puvis was not interested in the spirit of antiquity but only its abstracted husk.[92]

The symbiotic harmony in which figures and their environment are depicted in such pastorals of Puvis's mature idiom as *Pleasant Land* – with their very real interdependent rhythms – corresponds in the most profound sense to that in Virgil's poetry,[93] in which figures and the natural world, a shepherd and a beech tree, are also described in the same terms, as lithe, for example, and are indivisible and functionally equivalent. Just so in *Antique Vision* of 1884 (see cat. 105) or *Virgil, Bucolic Poetry* of 1896 (see cat. 144), figure and vegetation obtain the same shape; a bush and a stony formation may be explained not on botanical or geological grounds but as rhyming constructs.

While landscape settings made pastorals of the classicizing images while localizing them, genre passages domesticated them. Puvis admired Rubens for introducing the 'naturel' in classicizing imagery and included his own homely passages: familial enclaves, children tousling, mothers chiding their young (see cat. 86, 107).[94] By including the quotidian, Puvis made his Arcadian world immediate; and he imbued everyday tasks with importance by using classicizing images to express the nobility of daily occupations. Baudelaire had ridiculed transpositions of the trivialities of modern life into antique circumstances at the 1859 Salon: 'Accordingly, we shall see the ancient brat play ball in an ancient way and at the antique hoop, with antique dolls and antique playthings....'[95] These kinds of genre works presented with antique accoutrements at the 1860 exhibition were plentiful enough to constitute a so-called 'école ancienne,' which came to have a derogatory sense.[96] With his ancients at a fish fry and a kore fingering fabric (destined for a new peplos?) in *Massilia, Greek Colony* (see cat. 50), Puvis came perilously close to banality, but the contained stateliness of his figures generally averted the anecdotal coyness that plagued such canvases by others. By the 1880s, in *Maternity* (cat. 108), and other ostensible genre scenes, a summary abstraction, a gravity, a lack of movement remove the figures from the everyday to allegorical or symbolic status. A number of small canvases of the 1880s of single figures derived from the murals indicate the ready acceptability of a classicizing gloss. With only remnants of a tenuous allegorical function, they are 'idylls' or 'little pictures' in a Virgilian sense. News of pastoral's demise was, indeed, premature.[97]

By the later 1880s, Puvis was represented by the Durand-Ruel Gallery and sophisticated about the commercial potentiality of his work. He wrote his sister-in-law on 4 December 1887, at the close of his retrospective at the Durand-Ruel Gallery, 'an agreeable thing, Platonism has made room for reality.'[98] Whether it was to consecrate his reputation by producing new versions of earlier works or to provide salable works in conjunction with his exhibition, by 1887 he had produced a number of reduced reprises of earlier works and pastels. In some instances he returned to far earlier schemes, paintings dating from over two decades before, to make variants of such paintings as *Autumn* (late variant, Museo de Bellas Artes, Caracas). These reprises provide an opportunity to examine the evolution of Puvis's style. Puvis was aware that the increasing roughness of his technique, evident in oils and pastels alike, might be too coarse for some viewers. Indeed, the astute Félix Fénéon noted about 1883: 'It is in good taste to scoff at Puvis de Chavannes, whose work horrifies painters whose enterprises are display pieces.'[99] In this context, Puvis evaluated a version of his Sorbonne mural (Metropolitan Museum of Art, New York) in 1889: 'I dabbled around a bit to get back on track, replacing with heads, more or less, the small blots that I had had in my large Sorbonne sketch. Thus it took on a less offensive appearance for the bourgeois, – for I must tell you, in honor of the improvement, that its appearance at Durand-Ruel's would have already tempted someone if it had seemed less crude.'[100]

In 1889, having completed his panoramic mural for the Sorbonne – and in direct opposition to his 1879 statement in which he had renounced mural painting (see p. 45) – Puvis declared that he would devote himself to murals, preferring their large spaces to those of easel paintings. The expanses of the late murals allow for flat, uninterrupted color and numerous figures. And now Puvis brought his Arcadian aesthetic to contemporary life, as in *Inter Artes et Naturam*, his 1890 mural for the Rouen Museum. The combination of distant antiquities and crude modernity, as he put it, made Van Gogh think of a rebirth (see cat. 130). It was such a renaissance that Puvis's classicizing images and decorative aesthetic were midwife to after the devastation of the events of 1870-71, and in opposition to the confusing realities of a complicated fin-de-siècle world. The pace at which Puvis was commissioned to execute murals did not lessen. In 1891 he installed his work at Rouen, was working on two cycles for the Paris Hôtel de Ville, and planned tapestry models for Gobelins. That year he refused a project to design tapestry cartoons of *Jeanne d'Arc at Domrémy* and *Jeanne d'Arc at Vaucouleurs*, explaining his care to avoid themes freighted with historical meanings that were inimicable to his own aesthetic priorities.[101] Until 1896 he was occupied with an extensive ensemble for the Boston Public Library (see cat. 143-144 and ill. pp. 54-55). His second campaign for the Paris Panthéon, planned from 1893, was still unfinished at his death in 1898.

Puvis's last great images are simple and clear. What he arrived at is embodied by his late *Magdalene* (cat. 145). With a stunning ecumenical thrust, he used a seated figure derived from a classicizing, pagan tradition to signify a Christian subject pried from all the traditional trappings. The monumentally impassive figure is a statement of moral and existential solitude much as the most individual of Puvis's mature easel canvases are – *The Poor Fisherman, The Prodigal Son, Young Women by the Sea*. The Magdalene has only a title to help establish her identity and a brooding iconic presence to embody the importance – or it may be insignificance – of her existence. Nude and generalized, she could be a bather at the shore.

The originality of Puvis de Chavannes's imagery has a great deal to do with the peculiar circumstances of his developing an officially sanctioned public art as well as an independent idiom. For the former he developed a classicizing imagery of reassurance and a decorative aesthetic of great beauty. His more personal imagery expressed an appreciation of the simple and domestic and a profound sense of solitude and longing. While his inventions were largely carried out within a framework of the most traditional sort and within the constructs of political and religious institutions, he achieved a stunning new vision and imagery.

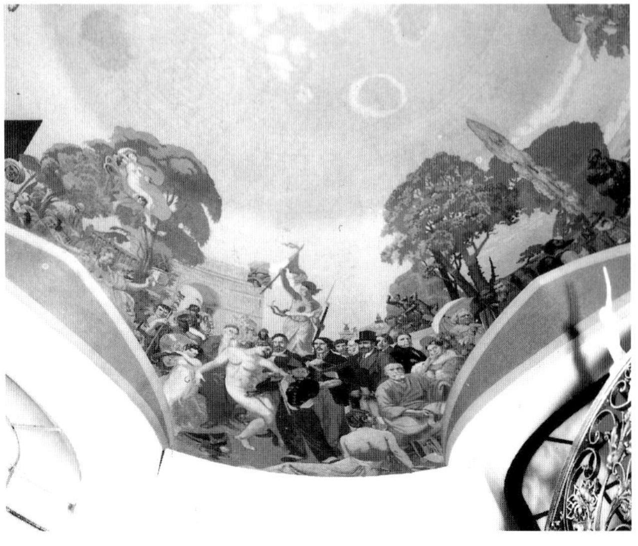

Coda: Puvis de Chavannes's Legacy

Puvis de Chavannes's importance to the development of modern painting has long been acknowledged, if not always understood.[102] His work does not fit the categories that have until recently been so important in encapsulating the art of the time. Not part of a 'movement,' without a satisfactory label, he has fallen through art historical interstices; in limbo, he has been left out in the art historical cold.

During his lifetime Puvis de Chavannes's work came to be often exhibited at the Salons, in the 1890s at the Société Nationale des Beaux-Arts of which he was president, at international exhibitions and at the Durand-Ruel Galllery. It was appraised, disputed and hugely admired for a host of often conflicting reasons. Because his mature idiom was so original, because he produced so much that was basically new and different from the work of others, it was a liberating influence. Puvis was a conduit of ideas that others distilled, and for a long time when his work was approached at all, it was through a backwards leading trail, by wondering how painters from Picasso to Matisse and Seurat to Gauguin came to paint the way they did. Denis, one of the most perspicacious observers of Puvis's painting, contrasted Puvis's firm colors and silhouettes to Delacroix's 'individuals sacrificed by an artificial shadow.'[103] Denis's whitened colors and interlocking shapes show that he took what he saw to heart. The unaccented composition of *The Poor Fisherman* with its sharply defined geometrical shapes was a particularly important influence on his theories as well as his painting. In his 1925 mural tribute to great nineteenth-century artists, part of his *History of French Art* in the cupola of the Musée du Petit Palais in Paris (fig. 8), Denis placed Puvis in the very front, with Ingres just behind him (and a rendering of one of his own figures from his *Inter Artes et Naturam* just before him).[104] Aristide Maillol (a painter in the early part of his career) spoke for Denis and the Hungarian Nabi artist Rippl-Ronai, who all extolled Puvis while showing

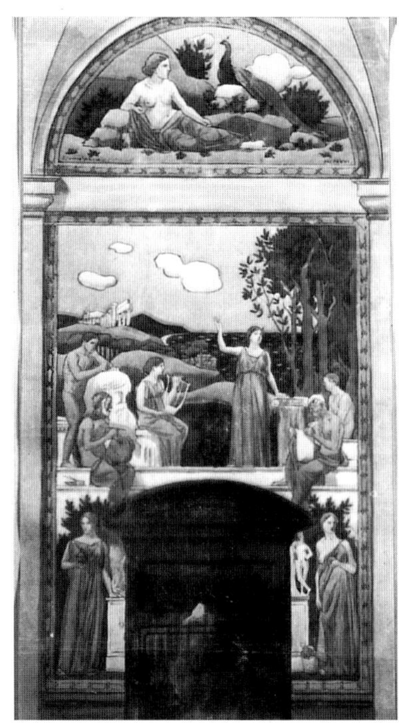

fig. 8
Maurice Denis (1870-1943)
History of French Art, 1925 (detail)
Cupola of the Musée du Petit Palais, Paris

fig. 9
Joaquín Torres García (1875-1949)
Sketch for the Third Fresco in the Palacio de la Diputación de Barcelona, ca. 1912
Watercolor on paper, 1330 x 530 mm
Museo Torres García, Montevideo

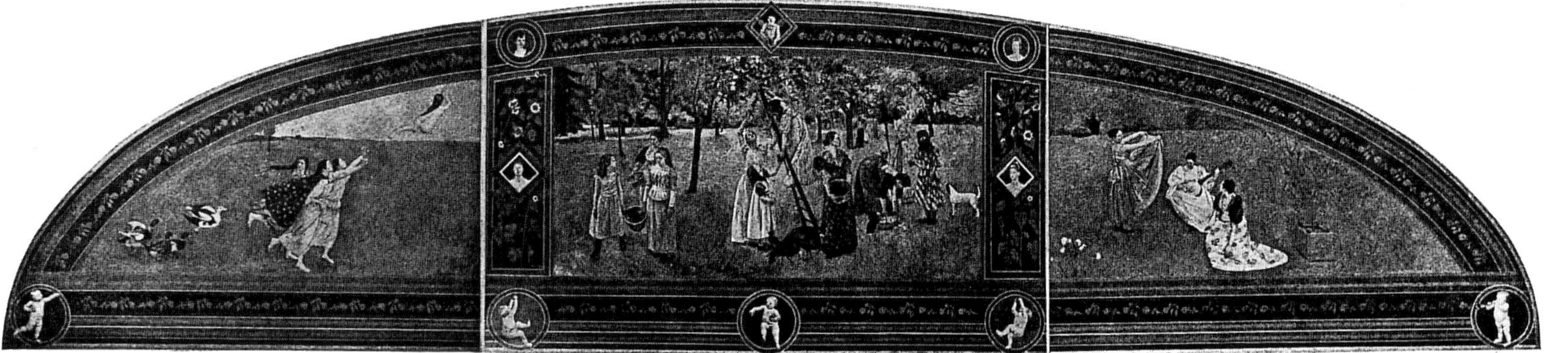

fig. 10
Mary Cassatt (1844-1926)
Modern Woman, decoration of the Woman's Building at the World's Columbian Exposition, Chicago, 1893 (destroyed)

their enthusiasm for his work in their own: 'Puvis! To him we owed the greatest feeling for art in our youth: his fine composition, his beautiful drawing filled us with an impression of poetry....'[105]

There were those who were attracted to the classicizing aspects of his work, among them Alphonse Osbert, Henri Martin and Alexandre Séon, who have been dubbed 'Les Nostalgiques.' Nor can this list exclude a group of pale imitators of his pale work: these include Henri Daras and sometimes Ferdinand Humbert among many others.

Seurat and Picasso noted the essential solitude and isolation of his figures. Seurat's admiration for Puvis is evident in some of his greatest monumental paintings: *A Bathing Place, Asnières*[106] (National Gallery, London) with its similarities to *Pleasant Land* of 1882, and *A Sunday Afternoon on the Island of the Grande Jatte* (Art Institute of Chicago), with its calm, implacable rhythms, which caused Félix Fénéon to call Seurat 'un Puvis modernisant' (see also p. 51). Picasso's bereft Blue Period figures can only be explained through Puvis's paintings. They have everything to do with Puvis's austere *The Poor Fisherman* and *Charity* (see cat. 140), and the late *Saint Genevieve* murals that Picasso, come to Paris at the turn of the century, so assiduously copied at the Panthéon (see cat. 70). From the Neo-Impressionists to Van Gogh, Edouard Vuillard and Henri Matisse (see cat. 150), to Maurice Prendergast (see cat. 151) and Arthur B. Davies in America and to others who understood some of the more profound aspects of Puvis's work, it was a liberating force, an example for their own work and theories. Whether they gained courage from his ineluctable constructs or emulated his borders or intensified the blue color casts of his murals, they all profited from the example of this artist's artist.

There is a whole legacy of public decorations dependent on Puvis's work that stretches far indeed: in France, from Alexandre Séon and Henri Martin to Ferdinand Humbert among many others. In the United States Mary Cassatt's 1893 murals in the Woman's Building at the World's Columbian Exposition in Chicago (destroyed, fig. 10) derived from Puvis's *Inter Artes et Naturam* in a fairly direct way. Indeed , his wall paintings were emulated in many murals in American federal buildings, the collaboration of artists issue of the City Beautiful Movement and admirers such as Edwin Blashfield and John La Farge. In Barcelona, Picasso was not the only artist to take note of Puvis's work in his own. Joaquín Torres-García, whose early work bears a pervasive indebtedness to Puvis's classicism and whose later constructs carry on the order of that aesthetic in the most profound sense, was awarded a mural commission in 1912 at Barcelona and looked to Puvis also, taking his Marseilles murals as an exemplum (fig. 9).

Puvis's decorative aesthetic, developed first for his monumental, mural paintings was a rallying cry for Gauguin and the Nabi circle. Paul Sérusier declared, 'Ne me parlez pas de tableaux, il n'existe que des décorations.'[107] In 1891 Albert Aurier, spokesperson for the group, praised decorative painting for qualities that were not possible within the confines of easel painting as it was then generally understood.

By the end of the nineteenth century, not a little because of Puvis de Chavannes, painters were calling for the kind of decorative aesthetic that Puvis had been instrumental in inventing, and they wanted walls to paint. Willibrord Verkade, for a time associated with the Nabis, described the cry heard from one atelier to the next: 'No more easel paintings! Down with useless furniture! Painting should not abandon a principle of freedom which isolates it from the other arts. A painter's task begins at the point where the architect thinks he has finished. Walls, walls to decorate! Down with perspective! The wall should remain a surface, it should not be broken by the representation of endless horizons. There are no paintings, there are only decorations.'[108]

Notes

1 Vachon (1895), p. 4; Vachon [1900], p. 5; Bréghot du Lut, *Revue du Lyonnais* (1899), 269; Pierre Puvis de Chavannes (28 January 1899), 205. Vachon remains the best general source on Puvis's biography. Puvis's training and its implications are discussed at greater length in the author's forthcoming monograph.

2 'un romantisme à tous crins.' Thiébault-Sisson (16 January 1895).

3 See Brown Price (1992), 50, 55-57.

4 Mid-century projects also included Hippolyte Flandrin's and Camille Corot's work for churches; Paul Delaroche's hemicycle for the Ecole des Beaux-Arts; and Paul Chenavard's huge, ill-fated Panthéon program. Paul Balze's *Progress and New Discoveries in the Sciences, Agriculture and Industry* for the Palais du Sénat (Salon of 1857) was one of many projects generally unknown today.

5 The original at Le Brouchy was 249 x 222.3 cm; the 1859 canvas, 395 x 295 cm.

6 Théophile Gautier, 'Exposition de 1859,' *Le Moniteur Universel* (23 June 1859), 721-722.

7 J. L. Jules David, *Le Peintre Louis David* (Paris, 1880), I, p. 149, an expression of the seriousness of purpose David saw as the intention of painting which should make a powerful contribution to public instruction; Léon Rosenthal, *Louis David* (Paris, 1904), pp. 5-8.

8 Henri Clouzot, 'Au temps où les murs parlaient,' *Renaissance de l'Art français* (1920), 369-375.

9 AN $F^{21}485$ to $F^{21}487$; Malitourne (1848).

10 See Planche (1846), 148; Planche (1855), p. 216; and Gautier (15 May 1848), 114; also Louis Vitet, 'Les Peintres de Saint Vincent de Paul et de l'Hôtel de Ville,' *Revue des Deux Mondes*, s7, IV (October-December 1853), 1002-1003; F. A. de Gruyer, 'Des Conditions de la Peinture en France et des peintures murales de M. Hippolyte Flandrin dans la Nef de Saint Germain des Prés,' *Gazette des Beaux-Arts*, XII (1862), 200.

11 'la décoration est le vrai but de la peinture, elle n'a pas été inventée pour autre chose.' Quoted by Castagnary (1892), II, p. 246.

12 By Baudelaire, 'Salon de 1846,' *OC* (1958), pp. 666-667; by Paul Mantz and others, often in the context of Ingres's style; see also Théophile Gautier, *Paris-Salon de 1847* (Paris, 1847), pp. 16-17.

13 See F. Cummings, 'The Selection of "Style" in Neo-Classical Art as Exemplified in Antonio Canova's *Hercules and Lichas*,' *Akten des 21. Internationalen Kongresses für Kunstgeschichte in Bonn, 1964*, (Berlin, 1967), I, pp. 232-237.

14 And it remained so, as a contemporary account of state purchase procedures by a functionary makes clear: see Gustave Larroumet's 22 December 1890 discourse at the Ecole des Beaux-Arts in Larroumet (1895), *L'Art et l'Etat en France*, Appendix, pp. 331-332; and p. 52.

15 'cherchant pardessus tout le style et marchant dans la voie de la grande peinture, de l'art décoratif.' Arthur Stevens, *Le Salon de 1863* (Paris, 1866), p. 132.

16 Though concerned primarily with literature, Peyre (1932) is an essential introduction. On matters taxonomical see Henri Peyre, *Qu'est-ce que le classicisme*, rev. ed. (Paris, 1965); also J. J. L. Whiteley, 'The Origin and the Concept of "Classique" in French Art Criticism,' *The Warburg and Courtauld Journal*, XXXIX (1976), 268-275.

17 'La Prière' was published in 'Souvernirs d'Enfance,' *Revue des Deux Mondes*, s9, XVIII (1 December 1876), 483-487, but probably dates from Renan's 1865 Greek sojourn.

18 'né Hellène; sa patrie était celle des temples, des blanches statues, des forêts dont l'herbe a été foulée par les pas des Dieux; et d'autre part, il était, d'esprit, essentiellement Français....' Théodore de Banville, *Mes Souvenirs* (Paris, 1882), p. 457.

19 'j'étais fou, comme je le suis encore, de tout ce qui touche à la Grèce maternelle....' De Banville (reminiscing about 1846), *op. cit.* (note 18), p. 253.

20 H. C. Baldry, 'Who Invented the Golden Age?' *The Classical Quarterly*, XLVI (1952), 83-92.

21 Séailles (1888), 141.

22 Durand-Tahier (1895), 29.

23 The poem in its entirety makes this point more clearly. Victor de Laprade's themes were compared to Puvis's for their nobility, 'un peu universitaire'; see Martino (1925), p. 73; for the Puvis/Laprade comparison: Chassé (1938), 529; Chassé (1947), p. 43.

24 'There is a valley where harmony dwells;.../ Whatever the sweet name that each age gives it....' Victor de Laprade, 'Invocation,' see also 'Dédicace. A la ville d'Athènes,' in *Oeuvres Poétiques de Victor de Laprade* (Paris, 1878), I, pp. 3, 285-286.

25 See Brown Price (1968), n. p.

26 Maurice du Seigneur, 'L'Art et les artistes au Salon de 1882,' *L'Artiste*, 52e année, I (June 1882), 632; Bürger (1870), II, p. 264.

27 'Car l'antique, c'est la nature même. Allez! vous pouvez copier le torse de *L'Illisus* sans crainte de prendre une manière....' D. (1898).

28 See Martino (1925), pp. 40, 47, 73 and *passim*; Henri Peyre, *Louis Ménard (1822-1901)* (New Haven, 1932), pp. 329-344 and *passim*.

29 Many of the Parnassians remained particular friends of Puvis and, significantly, were at the 1895 banquet in his honor; see Morhardt (1935), 499-512.

30 Larroumet (1895), *Etudes de Littérature et d'Art*, p. 281, quoting Paul Guigou in *Le Temps* (16 January 1895).

31 Théophile Gautier in *L'Artiste* (December 1856), as quoted in Louis Hautecoeur, *Littérature et peinture en France du XVIIe au XXe siècle* (Paris, 1942), p. 93.

32 'culte idolâtre de la forme,' P. J. Proudhon, *Du Principe de l'Art* (Paris, 1865), pp. 78-79.

33 See R. G. Saisselin, 'Neo-Classicism: Images of Public Virtue and Realities of Private Luxury,' *Art History*, 4 (March 1981), 14-36, with a section on Neo-Classic Painting as 'Administration Art.'

34 Herta Wendel, 'Arkadien im Umkreis bukolischer Dichtung in der Antike und in der französischen Literatur,' *Giessener Beiträge zur Romanischen Philologie,* no. 26 (1933), *passim*.

35 In his words, 'art, which is no longer the art of the world that is being constructed, but that of a bygone world which is in a tattered state ... isn't any longer even an hors d'oeuvre today' ('l'art, qui n'est plus l'art du monde qui s'élève, mais celui d'un ancien monde qui, à l'état de guenille ... n'est même plus un hors-d'oeuvre aujourd'hui'), Thomas Couture , *Méthode et entretiens d'atelier*, 2nd. ed. (Paris, 1868), pp. 108-109. The

Méthode was published in 1867; the second edition of the first volume was issued by early 1868; the second volume, *Paysage. Entretiens d'atelier*, was particularly about landscape.

36 'mais quittez les lyres et les harpes d'or; puisque vous êtes paysan, soyez franchement paysan, et cessez surtout de vous endimancher.... Pourquoi ... des bacchantes gelées? Est-ce pour contenter les velléités libidineuses de certains amateurs? .... Vous êtes un faux poète, vous êtes un faux classique....' Couture, *Paysage. Entretiens d'atelier* (Paris, 1868), pp. 218-219.

37 Manet was called a 'pasticheur' by Thoré, Mantz and Gautier in the 1860s; see Jean Clay, 'Onguents, Fards, Pollens,' in 1983, Paris, Musée National d'Art Moderne, *Bonjour, Monsieur Manet*, p. 6.

38 'un système d'exécution abrégée et de coloration arbitraire qui enlève toute réalité de ses figures....' Mantz (1863), 487. This accusation about flatness was also leveled that same year at Manet, for his *Luncheon on the Grass* (Musée d'Orsay, Paris).

39 Castagnary (1892), I, p. 209.

40 In 1861; Bürger (1870), I, pp. 40-41.

41 See also Brown Price in 1976-77 Paris/Ottawa, pp. 21-24.

42 Thiébault-Sisson (1895), pp. 5-6.

43 Baudelaire, 'Le Salon de 1846,' *OC* (1958), p. 625.

44 Mérimée (1851), 272; see also 331-332; on Mérimée see Aquilino (1989), pp.12-28, 34.

45 Bergerat (1911), IV, pp. 333-334; and Bergerat (1898), n.p.; see letters from Puvis to Gautier (Bibliothèque Thiers, Paris).

46 Théophile Gautier, 'Un Plafond de M. Cabanel,' *L'Artiste*, s7, III (1858), 182.

47 Théophile Gautier, 'Variétés. Salon de 1837. Paysages,' *La Presse* (20 March 1837), 2.

48 Gautier (1847), 2.

49 'Le balancement de la composition, le rythme des attitudes, l'intersé-quence des symétries, qualités qui forment ce qu'on pourrait appeler l'architectonique de la peinture, doivent, en ce cas [of murals] être recherchées avant toutes choses. Pour relier au monument ... les peintures décoratives [must] ... respectent l'ordonnance et n'en contrarient pas les lignes; ... d'intempestives vigueurs de ton creusent des trous qui alarment l'oeil.... Une localité mate et claire, circonscrite par un contour bien arrêté; un modelé de relief mediocre ... conviennent principalement. Adieu le clair-obscur, les jeux de brosse, les empâtements, les martelages de ton, les glacis ... les rehauts pétillants, tous ces artifices de palette auxquels les amateurs sont si sensibles! La muraille repousse ces gentillesses: elle veut la pureté du dessin, la grandeur du style et la sobre harmonie de la couleur.' Gautier (1 March 1863).

50 'Il lui faut, non pas le chevalet, mais l'échafaudage....'Gautier (1861), p. 103; this discussion furthers that broached in the author's essay, 'The Decorative Aesthetic in the Work of Pierre Puvis de Chavannes,' in 1976-77 Paris/Ottawa, pp. 21-26; also a major theme of the author's forth-coming book).

51 Blanc (1876), p. 511; but first published in 1867.

52 E. E. Viollet-le-Duc, *Dictionnaire raisonné de l'architecture française du XIe au XVIe siècle* (Paris 1875), VII, p. 57.

53 Letter of 17 September 1864 to his sister-in-law Valentine (private collection).

54 '[Puvis] ... ne dessine ni ne peint; il compose, c'est là sa spécialité.' Quoted by Michel and Laran (1911), p. 48; see also Gustave Kahn, 'Chronique: L'Art français à l'Exposition,' *La Vogue*, IV (August 1889), 137.

55 'J'ai condensé, ramassé, tassé.' Fabré (1913), 83.

56 In a *Journal* entry of 13 April 1849 on Amaury-Duval, Mottez, and Orsel; see Vol. I (Paris, 1950), p. 287.

57 'The light and discreet colors allow the thought formulated in a studied and deeply felt drawing to triumph all the more; the pale tonalities them-selves convey something serious and spiritual.... The good thing about fresco is that it borrows the tranquil strength from the monument with which it becomes one.' ('Les colorations blondes et discrètes laissent mieux triompher la pensée qu'a formulé un dessin voulu et ressenti; ses pâleurs même ont quelque chose de grave et de religieux.... La fresque a cela de bon que, faisant corps avec le monument, elle emprunte la force tranquille.') Charles Blanc, *Grammaire des arts du dessin*, 2nd edition (Paris, 1870), p. 625; also quoted by Bruno Foucart (1987), p. 61.

58 The few French frescoes quickly began to deteriorate. In 1889 Puvis and his protegé Paul Baudoüin were to study fresco technique in Italy, but their trip was cancelled; see cat. 129.

59 In the 1880s, not a little because of Puvis, interest in techniques of monumental painting spurred Henry Cros and Charles Henry's *L'Encaustique et les autres procédés chez les anciens* (Paris, 1884). On the serenity of wax as opposed to oil surfaces see Gustave Planche, 'Peinture murale; Saint Sévérin, Saint Eustache, Saint Philippe du Roule' [indexed as 'Les Peintures murales dans les églises de Paris 1856'], *Revue des Deux Mondes*, s2, VI (1 November 1856), 46, 49.

60 'Il faut être bien peu doué pour ne pas comprendre que le jour où j'aurai affaire à des boiseries sombres, à des ors puissants de ton, à des parquets teints, je changerais ma gamme très facilement, sans pour cela changer mon style....' Letter of 15 May 1895 (private collection).

61 'Je trouvai la palette de Giotto idéale, cette palette si fraîche, où les blancs, les bleus légers, les roses tendres, les verts et les jaunes se marient en harmonies si douces, et je me dis encadrée dans une bordure de pierre, je devrais m'inspirer de cette palette.' Thiébault-Sisson (11 January 1925), n.p.

62 Letter of 15 May 1895 (private collection); and [Anonymous] (1918), letter of 21 April 1888 to a M. Ricquier.

63 Gautier (1861), p. 106.

64 Interestingly, the tapestry borders to which Puvis's borders were com-pared first developed in the post-medieval era when tapestry representa-tions emulated those of paintings along with their frames in order to sug-gest how similar tapestry was to them.

65 'traitées dans le goût des peintures à fresque ou des cartons destinés à servir de modèles aux tapisseries....' Théophile Gautier, 'Salon de 1861,' *Le Moniteur Universel* (25 May 1861), 731. On the difference between paint-ings and tapestries see Pierre Vaisse, 'La Querelle de la Tapisserie au début de la IIIe République,' *Revue de l'Art*, no. 22 (1973), 66-86.

66 This is the more distinctive in the English translation of Jacques Derrida, *The Truth in Painting*, by Geoff Bennington and Ian McLeod

(Chicago and London, 1987), p. 54, but see *La Vérité en Peinture* (Paris, 1978), pp. 63-64, 93 and the discussion in 'Parergon,' pp. 63-93.

67 On Seurat's borders, see Félix Fénéon, 'Exposition des Artistes Indépendants,' *L'Art Moderne* (October 1889), 339.

68 He called his reductions his 'unsavory labor' ('fade besogne'); see Vachon (1895), p. 88; Vachon [1900], p. 134. Puvis would blame the scattering of his murals for his failure to become a member of the Institut, as he wrote the sculptor Alexandre Falguière in 1889: 'If I never thought of standing for election to the Institut, it is largely attributable to the dispersal of my works, which prevents your colleagues [at the Institut] from getting a very exact idea of my career.' ('Si je n'ai jamais pensé à poser ma candidature à l'Institut il faut l'attribuer en grande partie à la dispersion de mes travaux qui enlève à vos confrères la possibilité de se rendre compte assez exacte de ma carrière.') Letter of 31 January 1889 (private collection).

69 'il y a là-dedans une anomalie, cela n'est pas fait pour être vu comme un tableau, non, mille fois non, sur un mur de pierre de taille c'est admirable ... mais ce n'est pas de la peinture....' Letter to Lucien of 21 November 1895 about a version of *Ludus pro Patria* exhibited at the Durand-Ruel Gallery; see Janine Bailly-Herzberg, *Correspondance de Camille Pissarro* (Paris, 1989), vol. 4, p. 119.

70 Brown Price (1977), 27, 29-35.

71 'C'est que vraiment nous autres Français nous sommes des Gallo-Grecs et des Gallo-Latins, et les brumeux chanteurs du Nord qu'on veut nous donner pour des modèles ne sont que des ennemis de notre race sans cesse menacée.' Marc le Grand, *L'Ame antique* (Paris, 1896), p. viii.

72 'Le véritable patriotisme n'est pas l'amour du sol, c'est l'amour du passé, c'est le respect pour les générations qui nous ont précédés.' Numa Denis Fustel de Coulanges, 'De la manière d'écrire l'histoire en France et en Allemagne,' *Revue des Deux Mondes*, s2, CI (1 September 1872), 245.

73 'la race gallo-romaine au travail, occupée à tisser, à bâtir les villes, à élever des temples, à étudier le droit, à mener de front les labeurs et les jouissances de la paix....' Fustel de Coulanges, *op. cit.* (note 72), 242. Meyer Schapiro indicated the importance of Fustel for Puvis: 'Puvis' subjects are a new body of themes, governed by a characteristic conservative idealization of the past as a model for modern civic life, an attitude perhaps akin to the view of the ancient world in the writings of Fustel de Coulanges.' See Schapiro (1954), 164. Fustel de Coulanges's *La Cité Antique* of 1864 was about the ancient city, the importance of the family and its continuity as a constituent principle, and the national past.

74 Mitchell (1987), 190-191, 193-194, tries to tie the work to specific ideology.

75 On this subject see *inter alia* Melinda Curtis, 'The Pursuit of Primal Purity in the Nineteenth Century,' in 1975, College Park, Maryland, University of Maryland, *Search for Innocence: Primitive and Primitivistic Art of the Nineteenth Century*, pp. 27-69; and Madeleine Lamy, 'Le préraphaelisme Français de 1850 à 1860,' *Notes d'Art et d'Archéologie*, no. 1 (January 1926), 1-7.

76 He attributed its introduction to Overbeck and artists of the Munich and Düsseldorf schools; see Valbert Chevillard, *Un Peintre romantique, Théodore Chassériau* (Paris, 1893), p. 71.

77 This painting is the subject of a separate essay in this book, see pp. 45-53.

78 Among other variants of the general theme are *The Shepherd* or *The Storm* (*Pâtre gardant ses moutons*), 1887, pastel on cardboard, 60 x 41 cm, Musée d'Orsay; Paris, 1976-77 Paris/Ottawa, no. 185; and *Bad Weather* (*Le mauvais temps*) , pastel, 26 x 20.5 cm, formerly collection Bénédite.

79 Feydy (1955-1956), 19-20. In his early *Meditation* (or *Solitude*, destroyed) of 1857 Puvis had broached the theme of isolation and grief; Riotor (1901), repr. p. 91, it was described by Barbier (1858), 340-341; see Vachon [1900], p. 19; Brown Price (1972), p. 287; and 1976-77 Paris/Ottawa , no. 22. This is further discussed in conjunction with *The Poor Fisherman*, see p. 49.

80 Henri Peyre, 'What Greece Means to Modern France,' *Yale French Studies*, no. 6 (1967), 55-62.

81 Chennevières (March 1883), 162-163; also Chennevières (1979), I, pp. 23, 53, 61; II, p. 107; IV, pp. 77-78, 106. The project was not undertaken.

82 The extravagant exterior of the Marseilles museum complex is in notable contrast to the severe interior of the fine arts museum.

83 'Let us have mural painting that harmonizes with architecture, which it serves as an ornament, which is calm and without depth....' ('Laissez-nous la peinture murale s'harmonisant avec l'architecture, à qui elle sert d'ornement, calme et sans profondeur....') Alfred Darcel, 'L'Archéologie à l'exposition universelle des Beaux-Arts,' *Annales archéologiques*, XV (May-June 1855), 189.

84 The use of historical styles to transmit meaning has been closely analyzed by such historians of nineteenth-century architecture as Neil Levine; see his *Architectural Reasoning in the Age of Positivism: The Neo-Grec Idea of Henri Labrouste* [Unpublished Doctoral Dissertation], Yale University (New Haven, 1976), p. 37, see also pp. 589-591.

85 I am grateful to Robert Rosenblum, who years ago got me thinking in terms of architecture by asking what architect Puvis was like.

86 'Installez, installez ferme votre théâtre, votre scène, que ce ne danse pas.' Vachon (1895), p. 50; Vachon [1900], p. 99.

87 Interestingly, a book on the subject, *Le Nombre d'Or: Rites et rythmes pythagoriciens dans le developpement de la civilisation occidentale* (Paris, 1931), by Matila C. Ghyka was dedicated to the Princess Cantacuzène, Puvis's companion. Most recently Marlais (1989) includes schema ostensibly demonstrating Puvis's use of the Golden Section in *The Sacred Wood*, 155-158, figs. 4-5; *Hope*, 160-161, figs. 11-12; *Young Women by the Sea*, 161, fig.13; and *Pleasant Land*, fig. 14.

88 Roger Herz-Fischler, 'Examination of Claims Concerning Seurat and the Golden Number,' *Gazette des Beaux-Arts* s6, CI (March 1983), 109-112, discounts its use; for an opposite view see Marlais (1989), 153-168.

89 Charles Bouleau, *Charpentes: La Géométrie secrète des peintres* (Paris, 1963), pp. 208-209; for speculation on other systems such as 'carrés tournants' see Hautecoeur, *op. cit.* (note 31), p. 104.

90 William Camfield has pointed out the difficulty of determining the Golden Section in a given painting; see his 'Juan Gris and the Golden Section,' *Art Bulletin*, XLVII (March 1965), 130-131.

91 'Simplifier, c'est dégager la pensée; la conception la plus simple se trouvera être la plus belle. La peinture n'est pas une imitation de la réalité, mais un parallelisme de la nature.... L'art achève ce que la nature ébauche,

prononce la parole qu'elle balbutie. Comment arrive-t-on a aider la nature dans son effort pour parler? Par l'abréviation et la simplification. Attachez-vous à exprimer l'important, passez le reste; c'est là le secret de la composition, c'est là le secret du dessin, c'est même le secret de l'éloquence et de l'esprit.' See Emile Bernard, *L'Esthétique fondamentale et traditionnelle* (Paris, n.d. [ca. 1910]), p. 120; a similar but shorter statement is quoted in D. (1898), 2.

92 Richard Muther, *The History of Modern Painting*, rev. ed. (New York, 1907), III, pp. 180-181.

93 Michael C. J. Putnam, *Virgil's Pastoral Art; Studies in 'The Eclogues'* (Princeton, 1970), pp. 275, 302; also p. 294.

94 In a 22 June 1881 letter Puvis advised his assistant Paul Baudoüin of his interest in incorporating such details. Vachon [1900], p. 64.

95 'Nous verrons donc des moutards antiques jouer à la balle antique et au cerceau antique, avec d'antiques poupées et d'antiques joujoux....' Charles Baudelaire, 'Salon de 1859,' *OC* (1958), p. 790; compare the similar sentiment expressed in Bürger (1870), I, p. 16.

96 'Exposition de tableaux de l'école ancienne,' reviewed in the *Gazette des Beaux-Arts*, VII (1860), 260; and Henri Delaborde, *Melanges sur l'art contemporain* (Paris, 1865), pp. 176-179; see also Bürger (1870), I, pp. 12-14.

97 See Patterson (1987) p. 266, who cites Raimund Borgmeier, *The Dying Shepherd: Die Tradition der englischen Ekloge von Pope bis Wordsworth* (Tübingen, 1976), quoting the *Oxford English Dictionary*'s *pastoral* with Thomas Hood's 'The Golden Age is not to be regilt: Pastoral is gone out, and Pan extinct.'

98 'chose agréable le Platonisme a fait place à la réalité.' Letter to Valentine (private collection).

99 'Il est bon goût de railler Puvis de Chavannes dont l'oeuvre fait horreur aux peintres entrepreneurs de morceaux de facture.' Quoted by P. Jullian (1972), 108.

100 'J'ai un peu tripoté pour me remettre en train, remplaçant par des têtes, à peu près, les petits pâtés qui en tenaient lieu dans ma grande esquisse de la Sorbonne. Elle a pris ainsi un aspect moins cruel pour les bourgeois, – car il faut vous dire, à l'honneur du progrès, que son apparition chez Durand-Ruel aurait déjà tenté quelqu'un si elle eût paru moins fruste.' Mandach and Wehrlé (1911), 456. The canvas was sold to the Havemeyers.

101 Brown Price in 1976-77 Paris/Ottawa, pp. 24-25.

102 1976-77 Paris/Ottawa did much to remedy knowledge of Puvis's work; and Richard Wattenmaker, writing in 1975 Toronto acutely linked Puvis's work to that of a great number of other artists including Denis, Seurat, Gauguin, Picasso and Prendergast. Torres-García is among the more important of the artistic heirs missing. The Toronto exhibition was somewhat marred, however, by the inclusion of several works wrongly attributed to Puvis.

103 'personnages sacrifieés par une ombre factice.' Denis (1957-59), I, pp. 163-164, entry of 1 December 1900.

104 Compare also his study for his painted tribute to nineteenth-century art, *Romantic and Realist Art* (*L'art romantique et réaliste*) (sic) at the Musée du Prieuré, Saint-Germain-en-Laye (Inv. PMG 976.1.773).

105 'Puvis! C'est à lui que nous avons dû les plus grandes émotions d'art de notre jeunesse: ces compositions d'un joli style, d'un beau dessin, nous emplissaient d'une impression de poésie par leur science du vaste décor et leur harmonie.' Judith Cladel, *Maillol, sa vie, son oeuvre et ses idées* (Paris, 1937), p. 42.

106 Schapiro (1958); Herbert (1959).

107 As quoted by Armand Séguin, 'Paul Gauguin,' *L'Occident* (May 1903), 298.

108 'Plus de tableaux de chevalet! A bas les meubles inutiles! La peinture ne doit pas usurper une liberté qui l'isole des autres arts. Le travail du peintre commence là ou l'architecte considère le sien comme terminé. Des murs, des murs à décorer! A bas la perspective! Le mur doit rester surface, ne doit pas être percé par la représentation d'horizons infinis. Il n'y a pas de tableaux, il n'y a que des décorations.' Dom Willibrord Verkade, *Le Tourment de Dieu*, transl. Marguerite Faure (Paris, 1923), p. 94.

Jon Whiteley

The Role of Drawing in the Work of Puvis de Chavannes

Puvis's skill in drawing was not admired in his lifetime. Those who liked his work turned a blind eye to the way he drew or else were too indifferent to the art of drawing to care whether he drew well or not. Those who disliked his art, however, invariably condemned him for drawing badly. The Goncourt brothers, both connoisseurs of drawing, shared the irritation of an older generation of critics who were not prepared to forgive Puvis's odd drawing style for the sake of his visionary imagination. 'This Puvis,' Edmond wrote in 1887, 'to think that there are so many fine blank places in our public buildings, condemned to be soiled by these miserable *grisailles*, so badly – worse than that – so stupidly drawn! I do not know any painter since the beginning of painting who has been such a flabby draughtsman.'[1]

When Puvis first came to public notice at the Salons of 1859 and 1861, several classicizing critics, pupils of Ingres, poets and friends of the Academy, alarmed at the growing acceptance of Realism in contemporary art, praised him as an idealist, despite his obvious academic shortcomings.[2] Edmond About, who modeled for a figure in Puvis's early *Christ Before the Praetorial Court* (fig. 1),[3] and admired the work of the academicians Baudry and Cabanel, praised Puvis's *Bellum* and *Concordia* (see cat. 26-27) in 1861, while regretting 'above all that the modeling of the figures has not been taken a little further; one even comes across occasional signs of inexperience in the drawing.'[4] His drawing style, however, made him an easy target for a group of critics, Thoré, Castagnary, Chaumelin and others, who detested the academic and idealist painters of the Second Empire.

As fashions changed and as Puvis's role as a pioneer of the avant-garde became clearer, perceptions shifted among the critics of his paintings. Jules Castagnary, at first one of his bitterest critics, threatened to resign from his post as Directeur des Beaux-Arts in 1887 unless the State agreed to purchase *The Poor Fisherman* (fig. 23) despite the flatness and indifference to conventional drawing which Castagnary had once condemned in earlier and more conventional works as evidence of incompetence.[5] Correspondingly, a number of his friends on the academic front turned hostile. About, in a witty but unkind review, published in the *Le XIXe Siècle* in 1883, voiced the exasperation of many critics who had made allowances for Puvis at his debut but were increasingly distressed at his disregard for the elementary rules of academic drawing: 'When Hell needs repaving, like the Champs Elysées, it will not fail to commit the enterprise to M. Puvis de Chavannes. This artist is, *par excellence*, the man of good intentions, I will even say, of great intentions and vast ideas. For more than twenty years, he has promised himself and he has promised us, a masterpiece which he will never execute because he can neither paint nor draw and he proudly drags into every corner of the realm of art an encyclopaedic ignorance. The lack of primary education is, unhappily, without remedy; neither courage nor perseverance, nor even a certain nobility of soul, will produce an epic in twelve cantos from a dreamer who has not gone to primary school and who lacks not only prosody but the commonest spelling.'[6]

For the most part, critics based their comments on Puvis's drawing style on a knowledge of the paintings. Few of them knew his drawings or realized the extent to which the mannerisms which are characteristic of his mature work were painstakingly developed through a system of preparatory studies. Puvis calculated that for every two months spent painting a major composition, he spent between seven months and a year making the related drawings.[7] Preparatory drawing on this scale was neither new nor uncommon in nineteenth-century France, particularly among painters who decorated churches and other public buildings, but, because of its importance in the academic tradition, critics did not usually associate it with artists like Puvis, who did not conform in all respects to the idea of an academic painter. Puvis, however, based his art on preliminary drawing as thoroughly as any member of the Institut. Extensive preparatory studies enabled him to refine his ideas, to give his finished works an appearance of clarity and order and to paint the final composition quickly and without improvising. Although the final painting appeared at a late and brief stage in the process of composition, the idea of the painting was present in the mind of the artist throughout all earlier stages and dictated every aspect of the preparatory drawings.

About twenty paintings by Puvis, dating from 1849 to 1852, are known. These were doubtless based on preparatory drawings but, apart from the occasional sketch of a composition, they do not appear to have survived. There is little which can be associated with the months which Puvis spent in Italy in 1848 when he must have made studies of sites and works of art of the kind which every artist who visited Italy in the period brought back. The many drawings from the model, drawn in Florence during this trip, which he mentioned in a letter to his friend, Louis Bauderon,[8] have also vanished. They may have been included in a stock of early drawings which he later burnt.[9] To judge by the indifferent quality of Puvis's early paintings, the drawings may not have been much better. He had only begun to take an interest in art in 1846 and did not study it seriously until 1848. A group of sketches and caricatures, dated 1844 and inscribed with Puvis's name, which recently appeared on the art market,[10] suggests that Puvis was not being unduly modest when he dismissed his early drawings as schoolboy scribbles.[11] If the date and attribution are correct, they indicate a startling lack of promise in the work of the nineteen-year-old artist.

The sources of Puvis's early paintings, which suggest that he had studied the Venetians in particular, are less elusive than the sources of his earliest surviving drawings. On his own admission, he picked up little technical instruction from Henri Scheffer.[12] He did not remain in Delacroix's studio long enough to acquire the least trace of the latter's drawing style but the influence of Couture, with whom he studied for three months in 1848-49, is more evident. The hard contours and schematic shading which are characteristic of Couture's method, constitute the basis of all Puvis's figure drawing. The influence of Couture is particularly evident in Puvis's many head studies (see fig.11), just as it is evident in his early portraits, more so, perhaps, than in his compositions, where the influences are more varied. Couture's infectious style was derived from the contemporary academic manner but was simpler and quicker than the kind of polished drawing, practised at the Ecole des Beaux-Arts, which he despised.[13] Following his return from Italy, he attended courses in anatomy and perspective at the Ecole, taking them, like a disagreeable medicine, in the belief that they were of benefit.[14] In later life, he advised one of his own pupils 'to make studies for the sake of making studies. During the nine years that I was refused a place in the Salon, I did nothing else.'[15] Apart from one or two early surviving studies this is the only evidence that the young Puvis habitually drew exercises of this kind. The practice explains his surprisingly rapid mastery in the art of figure drawing in the 1850s which remained the basis of all his later art.

To a large extent the ten years after 1849, when Puvis left Couture's studio, were a period of apprenticeship when contact with fellow artists and self-instruction took the place of formal training. At a stage when most students were still confined to the drawing class, Puvis moved

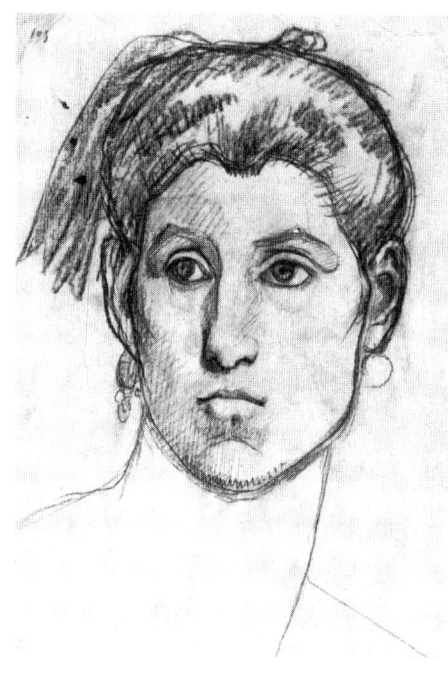

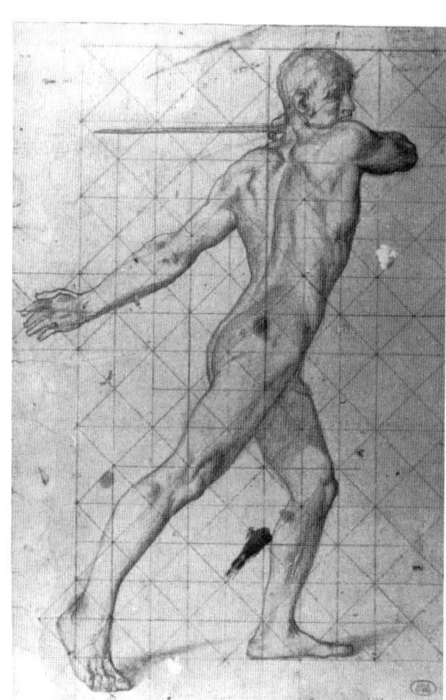

fig. 11
Head of a Woman, ca. 1865
Black pencil on paper, 360 x 255 mm
Musée des Beaux-Arts, Lille (Inv. 2040)

fig. 12
Study for an Executioner, ca. 1869
Red chalk on paper, squared for transfer, 420 x 215 mm
Musée des Beaux-Arts, Lille (Inv. 2005)

quickly into painting. His knowledge of painting was, at first, rudimentary, but he learned by a process of trial and error. As a consequence, several of his early works are flawed by an amateurishness which critics did not easily forget. Much of About's criticism of 1882 would not have been misplaced if he had applied it to the 1850s but it was hardly appropriate to Puvis's later work, which was based on a thorough mastery of figure drawing. Unfortunately for Puvis, the idea that he could not draw became a commonplace. Only with the exhibition of his drawings at the Société Nationale des Beaux-Arts in 1896 and the discovery of hundreds more in his studio after his death in 1898[16] was there a reaction among Puvis's admirers, some of whom began to praise him, with touching exaggeration, as one of the greatest draughtsmen of all time.[17]

The earliest surviving drawings which relate to paintings, were probably all done in the studio in the Place Pigalle which he occupied from 1852 to 1897. For some three years, he shared the studio with the genre painter Alexandre Bida, the portrait painter Gustave Ricard and a successful engraver, Victor Pollet, who had studied at the French Academy in Rome. The life class took place every night after eight and the ritual of correction, usually done by a master in the teaching studios, was here a communal effort.[18] The studies for *Mademoiselle de Sombreuil* (see cat. 2) of c. 1853, the earliest known drawings from this period at the Place Pigalle, were probably drawn shortly after he moved into the new studio. The strong, swelling contours, simplified tonal patches and suppression of detail, as if the artist had observed the model through half closed eyes, recall Couture, but with an expressive awkwardness which is not found in Couture's neat, descriptive studies nor in drawings by Bida and Ricard. The influence of Pollet is harder to assess but it was perhaps no greater than the influence of his friends. Puvis's brutal drawing style in the 1850s probably owed more to his idea of the finished work than it did to the drawing style of other artists. The dramatic character of the early figure drawings, shaded with a broad stroke of chalk, suggests the heavy, rhetorical manner of his contemporary paintings while the strong contrast of light and shade, found in many drawings of the 1850s, recalls his taste in this period for subjects which involved sensational effects of chiaroscuro (see cat. 10, 11).

Puvis's figure studies of the 1850s were often drawn on beige or blue paper, occasionally with highlights in white chalk. Although he sometimes used graphite pencil or pen and ink, he preferred the painterly, tonal effects of chalk for figure drawing. Red chalk, which had passed out of fashion in the 1790s, is not uncommon in his drawings of the 1850s and 1860s. It reappears in the work of a number of other figure painters in the mid-century, sometimes blended with black chalk and white heightening, the classic *trois crayons*, which became more fashionable later in the century following a revival of interest in eighteenth-century drawings. There is, however, nothing rococo in

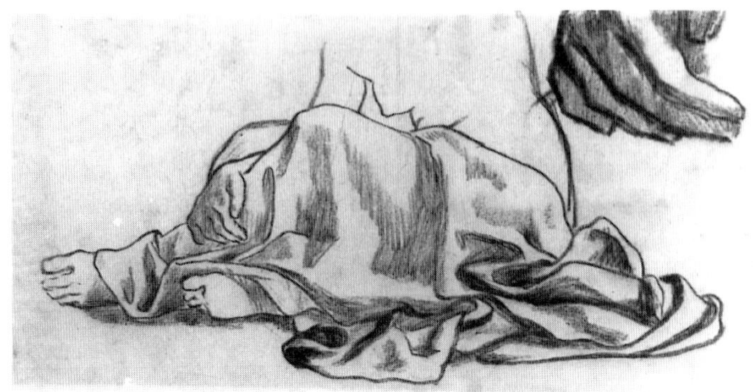

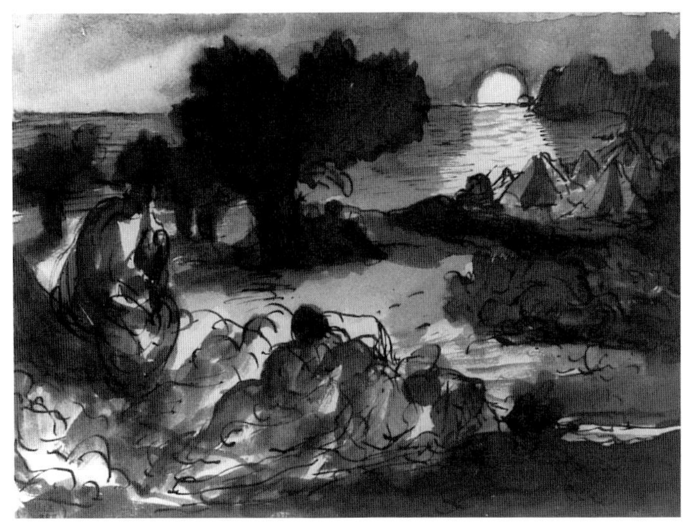

fig. 13
Study for Drapery and Study for Fingers, ca. 1854
Black chalk on tracing paper, 182 x 382 mm
Musée du Petit Palais, Paris (Inv. PPD 285^2; MCB 2)

fig. 14
Study for 'Sleep', ca. 1867
Pen, brown ink and wash on paper, 165 x 225 mm
Musée des Beaux-Arts, Lille (Inv. 2033)

Puvis's use of red chalk, which he valued for its practical effects. Unlike the more friable black chalks, red chalk keeps a good point and has a tonal range and color which are ideally suited to modeling the human figure. Puvis employed it with particular brilliance in several of his studies for *Work* and *Rest* (see cat. 32-34) and it is still found among the studies for *The Beheading of Saint John the Baptist* of 1869 (see fig. 12), although by this date his interest in tonal contrasts was decreasing rapidly. His work as a muralist encouraged him to emphasize the surface of the picture and to modify effects of space and modeling. Consequently, although he continued to use red chalk for drawing fine contours, he largely discarded it for modeling after the mid 1870s in favour of black chalk applied with a lighter and increasingly summary touch.

The most accomplished of Puvis's drawings of the 1850s are associated with the Brouchy murals of 1854-55 (see cat. 4), when he discovered his talent as a mural painter. The nature of the work, undertaken for his brother's dining room, no doubt encouraged him to prepare these compositions with exceptional care. The traditional method of studying the figure in the nude, applying draperies over tracings of the first study and squaring the finished study for transfer to other studies, which he employed for the Brouchy murals, remained the basis of all his later preparatory work (see fig. 13). Some of the Brouchy figure studies are drawn with a bold, open linear stroke, controlled from the wrist, somewhat recalling the drawings of Millet – to whom the Fitzwilliam study for *The Return of the Prodigal Son* (cat. 5) was once attributed[19] – although it is unlikely that Puvis was acquainted with Millet's drawings at this stage as he did not meet the older artist until 1861.[20] Other studies for the murals are outlined with a new precision and densely but neatly shaded in keeping with the clarity of the final compositions.

Because Puvis habitually adapted his drawings to match the character of the work in hand, the neat manner of several of the Brouchy drawings, which ultimately provided the basis of his mature drawing style, was not sustained uniformly through subsequent work. One or two rough, powerful studies for *Christ Before the Praetorial Court* of 1858, in which gestures and expressions are simplified to the point of caricature (see cat. 20), mark a return to the drawing style of the early 1850s. The touches of black chalk are dense and broken, as they are in a number of other studies for paintings in the period 1857-58. The successive decorative paintings which he sent to the Salons of 1859 and 1861, however, encouraged Puvis to resume the more academic style of the figure studies for the Brouchy murals and to perfect it in the preparatory work for the four compositions *War* (*Bellum*), *Peace* (*Concordia*), *Work* and *Rest*, which were acquired in 1863 as decoration for the new museum in Amiens (see cat. 26-29). A number of the studies for the pictures in Amiens demonstrate Puvis's virtuosity in modeling the human figure, although the presence of these figures in the finished compositions occasionally betrays, too clearly, their origin in Puvis's life class. Puvis's later work was never again so ostensibly academic. He now began to eliminate detail, simplify form and diminish tonal contrast in his figure drawings in keeping with his belief that a mural should not dig a hole through the wall[21] but should decorate the surface economically and in harmony with the architecture. His work progressed by a process of reduction. 'My master,' he once remarked, 'has been a horror of certain things.'[22] These things, which filled the mature Puvis with horror, included the dramatic but conventional gestures and strong contrasts of light and shadow which are characteristic of his early figure drawing.

The beautiful studies of 1867 in Lille, associated with *Sleep* (see cat. 47), are already lighter and more delicate than many of the drawings for the Amiens pictures of 1861-63, even though the moonlight scene offered Puvis an opportunity for reviving the strong tone contrasts of his earlier work. The choice of a night scene explains Puvis's uncharacteristic use of pen and wash for a number of the preliminary drawings, including a sketch for the whole composition drawn with a breadth and freedom which recall the more vivid of Claude's nature studies (fig. 14). Puvis often began work on a composition with a preliminary, painted sketch, in oil, watercolor or gouache, in order to establish the broad relationships between tones and colors before he began to work up the details from the model. *Sleep*, which is painted in near monochrome, lent itself to luminous effects of brown wash although Puvis also painted a sketch in oil (cat. 46) which is slightly closer to the final composition than the drawing in wash. Neither is particularly close to the finished work and both must date from the earliest stage of composition.

While the studies for *Sleep* suggest some indecision about the composition in its early stages, the idea for the Panthéon murals, commissioned from the artist in the spring of 1874 (see cat. 70-75), was quickly worked out. The image of the young Saint Genevieve praying in the presence of a woodcutter and his wife, which appears in the right-hand panel of the mural, progressed rapidly from the first patchy watercolor (cat. 71), in which the elements of the praying child, the trees and the onlookers were first established, to the final canvas, exhibited at the Salon of 1876. Several of the studies for the onlookers, although not particularly detailed, are finished with a delicacy and precision which Puvis gradually sacrificed for the sake of unity and harmony in the finished work. The composition developed as Puvis gave greater emphasis to the contrast between the child and the onlookers, exchanging their positions so that the main subject was moved into the middle distance, a device already used by Puvis in a number of paintings of the mid 1850s: *The Return of the Prodigal Son* (fig. 2), *Salome* (cat. 11) and *The Martyrdom of Saint Sebastian* (private collection). To create a mystical contrast between the saint and the onlookers, Puvis exchanged the red dress of the sketch for one in white while emphasizing the realism of the bystanders who observe the child as if she is a vision. The care which Puvis took with the details of this composition is indicated by a number of studies in which he establishes the precise inflexion of the hands of his characters. Refinements of the detail in studies of heads and hands (see fig. 15) are common enough in preparatory drawings by artists from Raphael to Ingres but, as a rule, they concerned Puvis less than the general position of the figure, which he sometimes drew and redrew several times to establish the right pose. Lesser details were, increasingly, left to take care of themselves.

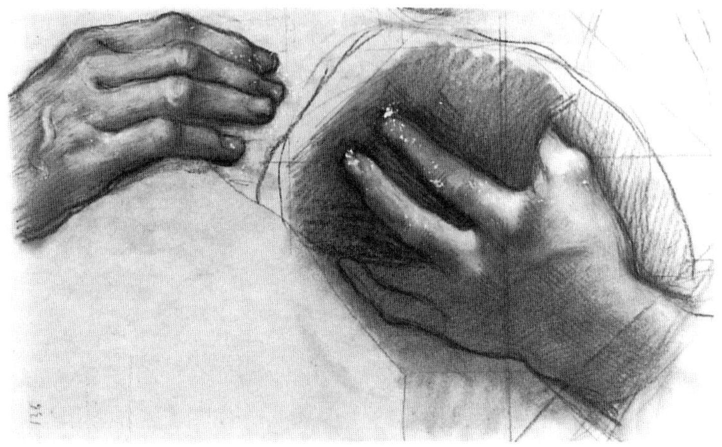

The Byzantine frieze of saints above the main panels in the Panthéon, inspired by Flandrin's frieze in Saint Vincent de Paul, gave Puvis scope to produce several remarkable head studies in a wilfully archaic style, drawn with watercolor and gouache over charcoal, finished with gold paint, and shaded with flat, parallel lines with the tip of the brush (fig. 16). There is also a pair of large, colored drawings in the Musée du Louvre and in the Norton Simon Museum, Pasadena, which appear to be preparatory compositions for the frieze painted in a related style. The abstracted manner of these drawings is unlike any other work connected with the commission. They do not obviously belong within the normal, preparatory process of Puvis's work but may have had a role as supplementary cartoons. They are also, like the frieze itself, untypically archaic in inspiration for, although Puvis has often been classed among the Pre-Raphaelites, he rarely borrowed ideas from artists before Raphael. His manner of drawing derived from contemporary practice and shows no trace of the archaic mannerisms found in the drawings of Overbeck or Burne-Jones.

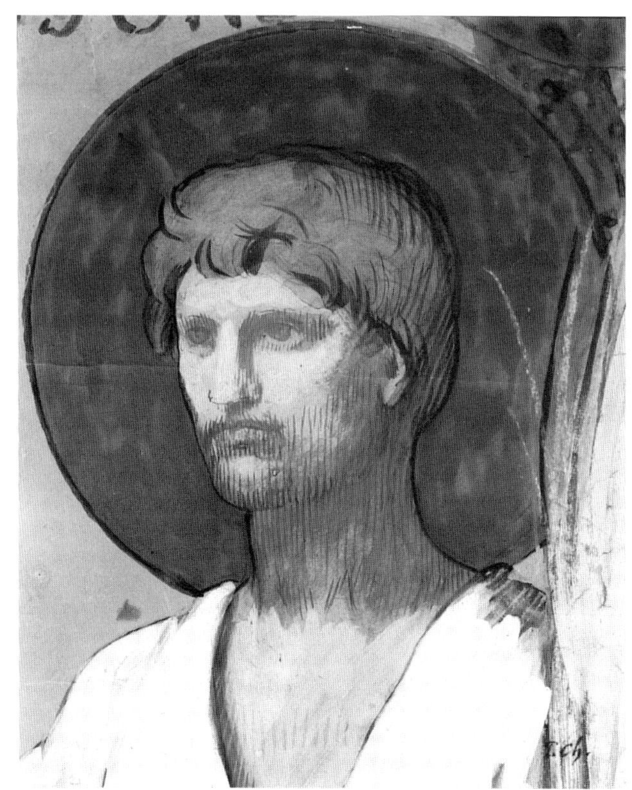

Apart from sketching a handful of rapid notes in watercolor, Puvis rarely painted out of doors, relying on his memory and notes in a pocketbook to retain the essence of a scene. Puvis's account of how the first idea of *Ludus pro Patria* (1882, ill. pp. 192-193) came to him as he watched the landscape of Picardy passing the window of the train to Amiens usefully confirms the importance of this process which may have been at the source of several of his major compositions in which landscape plays a significant role: 'As the shallows of the river, edged with osier, alders and willow, and these low hills which encroach so picturesquely in their varied tones and shapes onto the fields of wheat, rape and beetroot and empty plains and scattered clumps of trees drifted past, I took mental note of the lines and colors; and, back in the studio, I cast a summary sketch onto paper. The vision of that landscape had been so intense, it seemed that a study on the spot would have weakened the sensation and rendered me incapable, on return, of visualizing anything but an impoverished, confused and lifeless image'.[23] Puvis's use of memory to preserve the essentials of an image and discard distracting detail recalls the

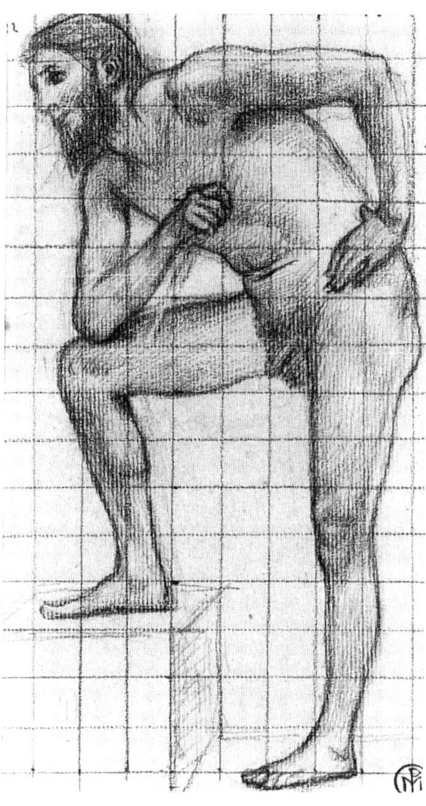

studio practice of Lecoq de Boisbaudron, master of Legros, Fantin-Latour and Degas, and anticipates the methods of the Post-Impressionists. but sets him apart from the Impressionists: 'You do not seem to be painting from nature like Monet, Renoir, Helleu, Gervex and the rest of your friends,' said the Comtesse de Greffulhe to Puvis, when she met him one morning on the beach at Dieppe: 'Madame,' replied the artist, pointing to his head, 'here are my studies, in my memory box.'[24] The landscape of the Rhône and Somme gave Puvis the setting for several of his murals, but it was the Seine and the surrounding countryside which inspired him most. *Inter Artes et Naturam* (ill. pp. 214-215) has a view of the Seine at Rouen in the background. The Grande Jatte provided the landscape for the Panthéon murals and the *Poor Fisherman* was inspired by a view of the Seine estuary at Honfleur.

Puvis's method of studying landscape placed a distance between himself and the model which allowed him to keep what he required and to discard the rest. When he employed preparatory drawing, he developed an analogous method which enabled him to eliminate distracting detail without losing sight of the general idea. The process began with a *croquis*, the first scribbled indication of the idea in the artist's mind, which had been used by painters as a starting point for compositions since the Renaissance. Done, as Vasari put it, 'to test the spirit of the artist's invention,' it provided the artist with an *aide mémoire* which was gradually transformed through months of study from the model into a recognizable composition. The whereabouts of the earliest thumbnail studies for *Ludus pro Patria* is not known but a group of drawings of this type for the Sorbonne, in black chalk and pencil, divided between the Stiftung Oskar Reinhart in Winterthur (see cat. 112-120) and the artist's family, suggests the tentative character of the artist's first thoughts.

Once Puvis had chosen a working variant from his preliminary studies, he began work on the individual figures although, at this stage, the final composition was far from settled. Dozens of figure drawings allowed the artist to develop the composition, experimentally, in the isolation of the studio which he had built at Neuilly in 1867 to accommodate his large canvases. He began the detailed work on *Ludus pro Patria* with a series of strong but summary life drawings in black chalk which provided him with a basis from which he made a first selection, squaring them for transfer, tracing and reversing several as the idea of the composition evolved, and simplifying the figures in the process (see fig. 17). Many of these studies are shaded with long, thin, light, vertical strokes which do no more than indicate, in a summary fashion, the difference between the light side and the shadow. As the drawings evolved through copying and transfer, the contours became sharper and more emphatic and the details more rudimentary. Those selected for a trial run for the final composition were squared up and reassembled in a study of the whole composition drawn, somewhat, in the manner of the large

fig. 15
Study of Hands for 'The Pastoral Life of Saint Genevieve', ca. 1874
Black chalk and white heightening on tracing paper, 248 x 412 mm
Musée du Petit Palais, Paris (Inv. PPD 275^2; MCB 75)

fig. 16
Head of a Saint, ca. 1874
Charcoal, watercolor, gouache and gold paint on paper, 595 x 450 mm
Fogg Art Museum, Cambridge, Mass., Bequest of Grenville L. Winthrop (Inv. 1943.902)

fig. 17
Man in Profile to Right, ca. 1879
Black chalk on paper, squared, 272 x 150 mm
Musée de Picardie, Amiens (Inv. 912bis 2)

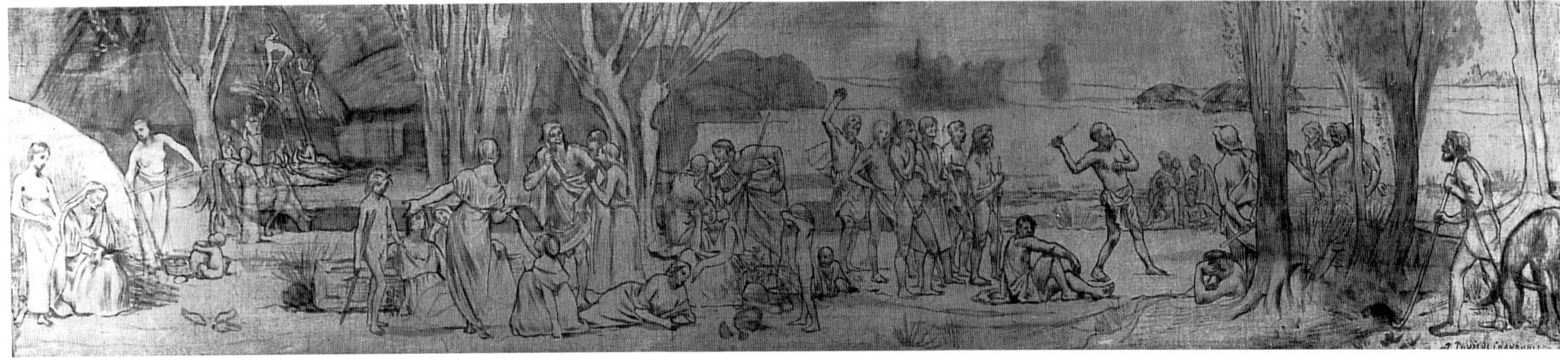

fig. 18
Study for 'Ludus pro Patria', ca. 1879
Pencil, red chalk and oil on canvas, 62 x 251 cm
Musée du Louvre, Paris (Inv. RF 1742)

cartoons, with crayon, red chalk and oil on canvas. Inadequacies could now be corrected by a process of moving the components like pieces in a game about the surface of the work. This is made evident by comparing the final version of *Ludus pro Patria* with the drawing in the Louvre in which Puvis, for the first time, rehearsed his composition with the whole cast (fig. 18). The boy with the crutch in the left foreground of the drawing has been moved further back and nearer the center; the woman reclining on the ground has been put in the boy's place. The man with his hand on his hip talking to a woman at the center has been reversed and transported to the far right of the finished composition; the man seated behind the javelin thrower has likewise been reversed and moved to the left. The child that has dropped a jug and is covering its face at the center has been given a subsidiary role on the left-hand edge. The mural contains many other changes of this nature although very few figures have been sacrificed or added. The only important figure omitted from the final version, the woman holding out her hands to the boy, signifying the maternal, protective aspect of the well-ordered state, was obviously omitted from the final version because of the distracting mannerism of her pose and a desire on Puvis's part to eliminate sentimental asides for the sake of thematic unity. Her place has been taken by the quieter figure of the man leaning against a tree on the right-hand side of the drawing.

The full-scale cartoon, drawn in black chalk on canvas and outlined with the brush in reddish-brown pigment, represents the final stage in the drawing process. These large drawings are not cartoons in the strict sense because they were not traced onto the final canvas and did not represent the composition in its finished form but were perhaps intended to allow Puvis or the Salon public to judge the effect of the composition on a large scale before his thoughts turned to color. Puvis valued his cartoons and often exhibited them in advance of the finished painting. When completing the commission for the Hôtel de Ville at Poitiers, Puvis took the trouble of preparing two full-scale drawings for *Radegonde at the Convent of Sainte-Croix*, sending one to the Salon of 1874 (probably the version now in the Musées Royaux d'Art et d'Histoire in Brussels) while the other (which was possibly not a separate cartoon but the underdrawing on the final canvas) enabled him to continue work on the finished painting. The success of the cartoon for *Ludus pro Patria* (Musées Royaux d'Art et d'Histoire, Brussels) at the Salon of 1880 also had a practical value in persuading the State to commission the painting for 40,000 francs after Puvis had undertaken all the preliminary work at his own expense.

To judge from the cartoons exhibited in Paris and Ottawa in 1976-77, Puvis's cartoons are dry and mechanical by comparison with the smaller drawings[25] but they were cherished by the artist because they represented the idea of the painting or, as he put it, the libretto to the final work.[26] By comparison with the effort which went into the preparatory drawings, painting the final composition was brisk and uncomplicated. Puvis readily employed studio assistants to help him in adding color to his later murals. Like other artists and theorists working in the classical tradition, he valued the idea of a painting more than the execution. His theory that art should represent an ideal of nature from which 'all that is contingent, accidental, all that is momentarily inexpressive' should be rigorously eliminated,[27] places him in the Renaissance tradition of Neo-Platonic artists who, like him, valued the intellectual role of drawing. He had, generally, no sympathy with progressive or modernist ideas and it is not surprising to discover that the increasing simplification of his art, which alarmed his academic colleagues but appealed to artists of the avant-garde, was based upon principles with an impeccable pedigree in the history of European art.

After completing one or two rough, color sketches setting out the broad outline of his composition, Puvis did not return to the palette until the cartoon had been completed. The cartoon provided a basis for a small, painted sketch, the *esquisse*, which became the artist's chief guide in coloring the composition on the final canvas. Rethinking was, if possible, confined to the *esquisse* but, as the composition had already been outlined on the canvas, any alterations introduced at this stage had to be incorporated into the existing drawing. A number of changes of this kind are visible in the murals in the Sorbonne (ill. pp. 200-201), and in the museum at Lyons (see cat. 101) where the original cartoon plainly shows through the overpainting. Tone, which Puvis had largely eliminated in the modeling of his figures, was still important as an element in the surface pattern and although he seems to have introduced tonal notes only when painting the *esquisse*, these must have been in his mind during the earlier stages of composition. Comparison between the preliminary outline drawing of *Ludus pro Patria* and the final composition reveals the importance of these tonal notes which Puvis introduced like a second subject in music, running in a curving sequence from the open door of the hut to the dark foliage and robe of the standing figure on the right. The main line of the composition, as it is established by the figures, runs contrary to this theme, slanting over the heads of the central group and defining a curve which repeats the action of the *picard*, until halted by the target, a pale tree against a dark background of foliage. This brilliant counterpoint of line and tone recalls the sight of the undulating plains of Picardy, seen from the window of a train, which Puvis retained in his memory through months of rigorous experiment and recreated as one of the ruling motifs of his composition.

Each of Puvis's major compositions produced a range of figure drawings which tended to become flatter and simpler as the work progressed but have, also, a common character which distinguishes the drawings for one mural from another. The figure studies for the Sorbonne hemicycle (1886-87), often drawn on blue paper and touched with white, have a statuesque quality (see cat. 121) which is different from the more summary and less supple studies for *Inter Artes et Naturam* at the Rouen museum (1888-90) or from the evanescent studies for the Boston murals (1893-96). Generally speaking, his drawing style became more abbreviated from one mural to another, evolving from the solidly modelled red chalk figures of the early 1860s to the slighter figures of the 1890s which were sometimes reduced to a rapid contour and shaded with a few broad strokes of black chalk. Marie-Christine Boucher has pointed out that figure drawing played a decreasing role in the preparatory work for his last murals in Boston and in the Panthéon, while compositional studies become more numerous.[28] These developments relate to a tendency in Puvis's art to sacrifice the vestiges of realism in favour of a flat, decorative ideal, particularly evident in the Boston murals (see cat. 143-144), in which life drawing had a less essential place than it had in the earlier murals. In Puvis's art, drawing, however important, was always subsidiary to the murals which his drawing served and as the need for figure drawing diminished, his drawings became fewer and more perfunctory.

The great majority of Puvis's drawings consists of preparatory studies. He evidently valued these and presented many of them to friends. A much smaller group, including portraits and copies from his figure studies, were done for their own sake. Caricatures, which he made as a form of private recreation, form another sub-genre of drawings.[29] With the growth of societies for exhibiting and selling prints and drawings in the last four decades of the century, Puvis began to take more interest in producing drawings for their own sake. In 1862, he submitted two etchings to Cadart's Société des Aquafortistes. He involved himself, also, with lithography when that, too, returned to fashion in the 1890s (see cat. 85). These were passing interests but the expanding market for pastels in the 1880s had a more lasting attraction (see cat. 110). He turned to the medium, probably in 1886, composing a number of pastels on motifs borrowed from earlier works or on the theme of women at their toilette, inspired perhaps by Degas. Pastels, however, never became a major concern, probably because, despite the demand among dealers and collectors for this kind of work, he was far too busy with his last mural commissions to devote much time to smaller works. Significantly, all Puvis's prints and most of his pastels were derived from his paintings or from figure studies associated with his paintings and they remained in the margin of the decorative art which he valued above all other.

The role of drawing in Puvis's work was not well understood by his contemporaries. Apart from his pupils, Paul Baudoüin, Alphonse Osbert and Alexandre Séon, who assisted him in painting murals, the younger generation of artists who admired his work, Gauguin, Maillol, Denis, Hodler, Matisse, Picasso and others, tended to imitate the decorative effect of the finished composition, but not the method by which Puvis achieved his result. As Bouguereau and his generation lapsed into critical disgrace in the 1880s, it became very common to praise Puvis at their expense as an artist who had sacrificed academic dexterity for the sake of creating a poetic impression.[30] This view was not misjudged but it tended to divert attention from the importance of drawing in Puvis's art. In the divide which separates the painters/draughtsmen of the nineteenth century from the artists of the avant-garde, Puvis belongs on the side of the Old Masters, with Ingres, Géricault, Bouguereau and Degas, as heir to a tradition of fine drawing which was fatally undermined by the innovators of the 1890s who admired and imitated Puvis but rejected the ancient practices of the drawing class on which his art was founded.

Notes

1 'Ce Puvis, penser qu'il y a tant de belles places blanches dans nos monuments publics qui sont condamnées a être salies par ces tristes grisailles, si mal, pire que cela, si bêtement dessinées! Je ne connais pas, depuis que la peinture existe, un peintre qui ait eu le dessin aussi rondouillard.' Edmond and Jules de Goncourt, *Journal. Mémoires de la Vie Littéraire*, (Monaco, n.d.) vol. XV, p. 13.

2 Goldwater (1946).

3 Vachon [1900], pp. 16-17.

4 'surtout que le modelé des figures ne soit pas poussé un peu plus en avant; on surprendra même ça et la, dans le dessin, certains signes d'inexpérience.' E. About, *Dernière lettre à sa Cousine Madeleine* (Paris, 1863), p. 218.

5 Vachon [1900], p. 161, note 1. On the acquisition of *The Poor Fisherman*, see also pp. 40-41 and 46 of this book.

6 'Lorsque l'enfer voudra se faire paver à neuf, comme les Champs Elysées, il ne manquera pas de confier l'entreprise à M. Puvis de Chavannes. Cet artiste est par excellence l'homme des bonnes intentions, je dirai meme des grandes intentions et des vastes pensées. Depuis plus de vingt ans, il se promet et nous promet un chef-d'oeuvre qu'il n'exécutera jamais, car il ne sait ni peindre ni dessiner, et il promène fièrement dans tous les coins du domaine de l'art une ignorance encyclopédique. Le défaut d'instruction première est malheureusement sans remède; ni le courage, ni la persévérance, ni même une certaine élévation d'esprit ne feront produire un poème épique en douze chants au rêveur qui n'a pas fréquenté l'école primaire et qui manque non seulement de prosodie, mais de la plus vulgaire orthographe.' E. About, 'Le Salon de 1883,' *Le XIXe Siècle* (6 May 1883).

7 Bénédite (January 1900), 19.

8 Guigou (1898), p. 266.

9 Thiébault-Sisson (16 January 1895).

10 I am grateful to Aimée Brown Price for showing me photographs of this collection which was sold at the Hotel Droûot, Paris, 24 April 1991.

11 Thiébault-Sisson (January 1895).

12 Vachon [1900], p. 5.

13 See Boime (1980), p. 448.

14 Alexandre (15 June 1899), 187.

15 'de faire des études pour des études. Pendant les neuf ans que j'ai été refusé au Salon, je n'ai pas fait autre chose.' Vachon [1900], p. 36.

16 In 1898, Puvis's heirs donated large numbers of drawings to French public collections; see Boucher (1979), n.p. Some collections have been catalogued: Boucher (1979) (with an introductory essay which is the essential account for understanding Puvis's drawings); 1984-85 Marseilles (not reliable); see also 1985 Poitiers. Catalogues for the Musées des Beaux-Arts of Amiens and Lyons are being prepared, by Marie-Christine Boucher and Dominique Borel respectively; L. V. Prat has completed a still unpublished catalogue for the Musée du Louvre.

17 E.g. A. Alexandre, *Portraits et Souvenirs* (Paris, 1891), p. 9.

18 Baignières (1881), 418.

19 Louis-Antoine Prat, 'A Drawing by Puvis de Chavannes at the Fitzwilliam Museum in Cambridge,' *Master Drawings*, vol. XVIII (1980), 38-40.

20 He appears to have met Millet for the first time in 1861 at the house of Léon Belly's mother; Mandach and Wehrlé (1910), 675.

21 Thiébault-Sisson (January 1895).

22 'Mon maître ... ça a été l'horreur de certaines choses.' Durand-Tahier (1895), 30.

23 'Au fur et à mesure que défilaient sous mes yeux ces bas-fonds de rivières bordées de saules, de vernes et d'oseraies, ces collines basses, qu'empiècent si pittoresquement, dans la diversité de leurs tons et de leurs dessins, les champs de blé, de colza et de betteraves, de maigres prairies et des petits bois très espacés, je noterais dans mon cerveau les effets de lignes et de couleurs; et, de retour à mon atelier, j'en jetais sur le papier le résumé. La vision du paysage avait été pour moi si intense qu'il me semblait qu'une étude sur place en eut affaibli la sensation et m'eut exposé à n'en retrouver, plus tard, dans ma memoire, qu'une image réduite, confuse et sans vie.' Vachon [1900], p. 146.

24 J.E. Blanche, *Portraits of a Life-Time* (London, 1937), p. 105.

25 See 1976-77 Paris/Ottawa, nos. 107, 109 and 114.

26 Vachon [1900], p. 97

27 Guigou (1898), p. 273.

28 Boucher (1979), n.p.

29 See Brown Price (1991).

30 E.g. Roger-Ballu, *La Peinture au Salon de 1880* (Paris, 1880), p. 3.

Geneviève Lacambre

Puvis de Chavannes and the Artistic Establishment of His Day

Fame often comes to artists only after their death. With Puvis de Chavannes, however, this was hardly the case. According to the obituary Arsène Alexandre published in *Le Figaro*,[1] 'From 1890, victory was assured, and triumph commenced.... The young rushed to him, showering him with admiration and enthusiasm.' The year 1890 also witnessed the first Salon of the Société Nationale des Beaux-Arts; one of the founding members of the Société, Puvis became its president in 1891. His fame reached its apogee in 1895, three years before his death, when *La Plume* devoted an entire issue to the artist and held a banquet in his honor attended by 550 guests.

Puvis had achieved his status of honored master not only by developing a highly personal style, which won acclaim in the 1880s and 1890s, but also because he was attentive to his position in the official French art world.

Though Puvis de Chavannes could take pride in a long list of official achievements, there was one institution he had mixed feelings about all his life: the powerful governing body of the arts known as the Institut de France.[2] Indeed he never took the steps required to be elected as a member. As he wrote in 1887, 'the marvelous Institut neglects no occasion to get at me.... Those people can't tolerate the idea that one can live, work and produce without thinking of them. That becomes an offense and their rage becomes that much greater. They want one to plead, to have the pleasure of refusing one, otherwise they consider one an insurgent, a sort of infidel. Zut!'[3] Nonetheless, on 31 January 1889 he complained to the sculptor Alexandre Falguière that the dispersal of his works stood in the way of his consideration for the Institut; and on 4 June of the same year, he wrote Henry Havard that he did in fact wish to become a member.[4]

Puvis was certainly not unmindful of that barometer of popularity among his peers, namely election to the jury of the Salon. In 1872 he appears for the first time, in seventeenth place, with sixty-nine votes among the supplementary jurors, to whom appeal was made only in case of withdrawal.[5] That year he was not entirely successful as a Salon painter either, as his picture *Death and the Maidens* (fig. 33) was rejected, while *Hope* (fig. 3) was accepted. Puvis would occasionally reappear on the supplementary juror's list, in twentieth place in 1874 and thirty-ninth in 1875. His fortune did not improve notably until the regulations were modified in 1879 and the electoral body was enlarged to include those artists who had already been admitted to the Salon at least three times, besides the members of the Institut and the prizewinners. In the category 'history and figure painting,' 960 voting members for fifteen jurors gave 841 votes to Léon Bonnat and 602 to Puvis, putting him in second place. First place would forever elude him. In 1880, when the government organized its last Salon, he was again second in this category (670 votes), still behind Léon Bonnat (769 votes), with 979 members voting.[6]

Puvis's best years at the official Salon, 1879 and 1880, were undoubtedly the result of the real success won by his first murals for the capital, the *Saint Genevieve* ensemble (see cat. 70-75) which was installed in the Panthéon in 1877 and is known to have attracted 'veritable processions of artists.'[7] Philippe de Chennevières, Directeur des Beaux-Arts[8] until 1879, had given him the opportunity by placing his name on the list of artists charged with the decoration of the imposing structure, but it was Puvis's particular tone, characterized by naïveté, poetry and sincerity, which distinguished him from his colleagues.

The elections to the jury of the Salon organized by the Société des Artistes Français from 1881[9] – with only one jury for painting – were consistently more or less favorable to Puvis. To be sure, he was dissatisfied with the results of the first election, in which he won 681 votes while Bonnat, again in first place, received 1,430, and consequently he withdrew. But until 1889 he was always present, ranging from sixth to nineteenth place.[10]

In 1891, Puvis became president of the Société Nationale des Beaux-Arts, following Ernest Meissonier's resignation on 24 January 1891, several days prior to his death. In December 1889, Meissonier had become the leader of the dissident artists who wished to secede from the Société des Artistes Français.[11] The new Société, of which Puvis was a founding member, was initially located in the town house of Meissonier himself at 131 Boulevard Malesherbes, but subsequently moved to the Palais des Beaux-Arts on the Champ-de-Mars, which was originally constructed for the Exposition Universelle of 1889. We should note in passing that Puvis not only assumed Meissonier's post as president of the Société, but also acquired his late colleague's commission to paint one of the walls of the Panthéon. In 1893-98 this led to the second, equally glorious phase of his decoration of that edifice.

The eight Salons held in the course of Puvis's propitious presidency were to seal his reputation. In 1899, the year after his death, the Salon of the Société Nationale des Beaux-Arts would feature a retrospective of his work. Above the entrance to the exhibition rooms hung a vast composition by Guillaume Dubufe entitled *To Puvis de Chavannes* (fig. 19),[12] showing the late painter seated before his most acclaimed mural, *The Sacred Wood* of 1884 (see cat. 101).

Pierre Vaisse has pointed out that in separating themselves from the Société des Artistes Français, a society that was very serious about representing the entire community of artists – legitimized by its electoral system – the founders of the Société Nationale des Beaux-Arts demonstrated their high estimation of themselves and their refusal to compromise any longer by throwing in their lot with all the rest.[13] The fact of the matter is that, given the system introduced in 1880, a schism was inevitable. In the English fashion, any group of artists was now free to form a society, a freedom of which the Femmes Peintres et Sculpteurs took full advantage as early as 1881, as did the Société des Artistes Indépendants in 1884. Established artists cherished the memory of the selective exhibitions in connection with the Expositions Universelles or that of the Exposition Nationale of 1883. For the latter exhibition, the 'Triennale' – organized, like the old Salons, by the government – the head of the painting division was, as it happened, Meissonier, while the jury of that division, headed by the minister and the Directeur des Beaux-Arts, comprised fourteen members of the Académie des Beaux-Arts and another fourteen nominated by the government, including Puvis de Chavannes.[14]

The catalogue (or *livret*) of the Salon des Artistes Français of 1890, which still listed Meissonier, Puvis and their friends as members, contained (as tradition demanded) the speeches made when the prizes were presented to the artists who had exhibited at the Salon of 1889, a Salon that had been somewhat snubbed by the public. The architect Antoine-Nicolas Bailly, member of the Institut and president of the Artistes Français, noted that at the Exposition Universelle at the Champ-de-Mars in 1889 one could admire the 'arrivés,' the 'triomphants,' whose work had been officially selected from what had been produced in the course of the past ten years, while the Salon gave young novices their chance.[15] The number of items in the Salon catalogues of those years was stagger-

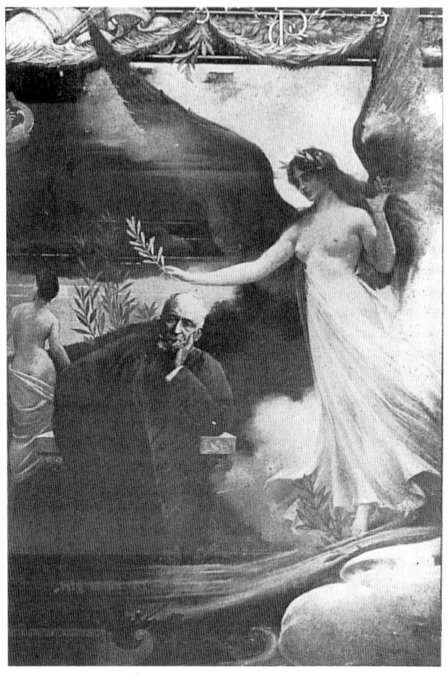

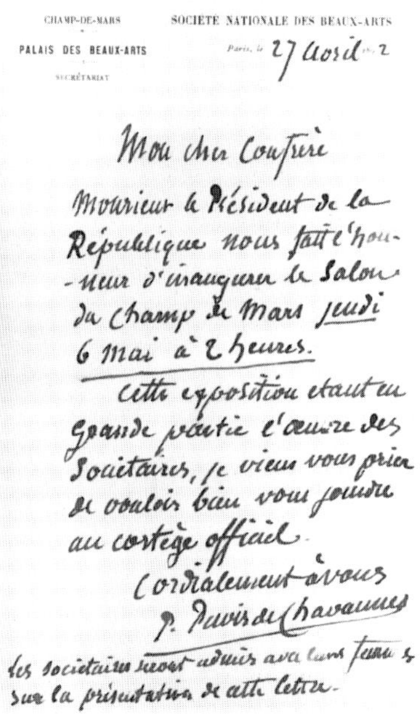

CHAMP-DE-MARS
PALAIS DES BEAUX-ARTS
SECRÉTARIAT

SOCIÉTÉ NATIONALE DES BEAUX-ARTS
Paris, le 27 avril 92

Mon cher Confrère

Monsieur le Président de la République nous fait l'honneur d'inaugurer le Salon du Champ de Mars jeudi 6 mai à 2 heures.

Cette exposition étant en grande partie l'œuvre des Sociétaires, je viens vous prier de vouloir bien vous joindre au cortège officiel.

Cordialement à vous
P. Puvis de Chavannes

Les sociétaires seront admis avec leurs femmes sur la présentation de cette lettre.

fig. 19
Guillaume Dubufe (1853-1909)
To Puvis de Chavannes, 1899 (detail)
Photograph of the painting from the catalogue of the Salon organized by the Société Nationale des Beaux-Arts, 1899

fig. 20
Invitation written by Puvis de Chavannes, 27 April 1892
Documentation department, Musée d'Orsay, Paris
(formerly collection H. Durand-Tahier)

ing, each time exceeding that of 1848 – when the Salon of the nascent Second Republic was held without a jury, and even the artists themselves were dissatisfied with the result. There were 5,523 works in 1888, 5,810 in 1889, 5,301 in 1890, the new rival Salon presumably being the cause of the last year's slight decline.

In the wake of the prestigious events at the Champ-de-Mars to celebrate the centenary of the Revolution, the new Salon had none of the marginal character of the Salon des Artistes Indépendants. One senses that influential individuals assisted at its birth.[16] As for the Salon des Artistes Français, a catalogue and an illustrated catalogue were published and every year Armand Silvestre edited a special volume – likewise illustrated – on the *Nu au Salon (Champ-de-Mars)*, thus continuing what he had published in 1889: *Le Nu au Champ-de-Mars*, with, notably, a commentary on the nude *Hope* of Puvis de Chavannes (fig. 4). There was every reason for Gustave Geffroy to consider the two manifestations as one, held in two different places and opened on two different dates at an interval of fifteen days – 30 April at the Champs Elysées, and 15 May at the Champ-de-Mars – in 1890. And even if Puvis was one of the principal 'émigrés of the Champ-de-Mars,' at the Champs Elysées 'imitations of his manner abound. From large canvases, these imitations have shrunk to easel paintings.'[17] Meanwhile Geffroy remarked that a 'particular tendency is noticeable on the part of the artists encamped among the ruins of the Exposition. There, at the Palais de l'Industrie, history painting, the staging of anecdotal scenes predominates. Here, at the Palais des Beaux-Arts, a preoccupation with the mundane is especially evident.'[18] History painting, as opposed to painting of modern life! The Champ-de-Mars also welcomed the innovators Sisley, Carrière, Rodin and of course Puvis de Chavannes, whose *Inter Artes et Naturam* for the museum of Rouen (ill. pp. 214-215) 'delights the eyes, stirs the soul, through the timeless poetry which emanates from it.'[19]

The regulations of this new Salon differed from those of the Artistes Français, as they did from those of the Indépendants (which had neither a jury nor prizes). While from the beginning it benefited from the Prix du Salon and travel grants awarded by the State, and while the Inspecteurs des Beaux-Arts visited it to decide what the State would purchase, the artists were selected by co-optation, that is they were invited to join by the founding members. As for the associates whose works were admitted, the honor was conferred on them by the membership as a whole. The members were therefore collectively responsible for the tone of the Salon, as evidenced by the invitation composed by Puvis de Chavannes to the inauguration of the 1892 exhibition by the President of the Republic (fig. 20), which read: 'My dear confrère, The President of the Republic will do us the honor of inaugurating the Salon of the Champ-de-Mars.... As this exhibition consists in large part of works by members of the Société, I would like to ask you to join the official procession.' One of the notable differences between the Société Nationale and the Société des Artistes Français is that no prizes were awarded at the former. At the outset the Société des Artistes Français intended to represent every artist, with an elected jury awarding medals to the best.

Save for the legitimate concern they displayed for official recognition, the regulations of the Société Nationale of 1890 closely resembled those of the short-lived Société Nationale des Beaux-Arts, which had been founded for a period of ten years on 15 April 1862, but which in fact did not last beyond 1865. The latter was charged with organizing exhibitions of small paintings on the premises of the dealer Martinet in February each year. The Société Nationale des Beaux-Arts also promoted sales and published reproductions. It thus constituted an attempt by artists to attract private clients without the help of the State, in contrast to the official Salon which was intended to set a qualitative example. The works exhibited were supplied by the two hundred founding members and a roster of regular members who were admitted following acceptance of a work presented to the Comité. Associated with this was a veritable artistic circle, with evening meetings for amateurs who were likewise chosen upon presentation. The president of the Société was the writer Théophile Gautier, and the members of the Comité included Puvis de Chavannes.[20]

The Société Nationale of 1890, which is still in existence, was of a different magnitude but had the same goal as the Société Nationale of 1862. Hippolyte Durand-Tahier, its secretary-general until his death in 1899, took an active interest in selling the works exhibited, and in their price. His Salon was intended to help artists find buyers, the State being concerned with more prestigious events. Moreover the Société Nationale wished to raise the level of its Salon by attracting submissions from celebrated artists abroad. In this connection it is worth noting Puvis's correspondence with Burne-Jones, which evidences his wish to exhibit in Paris the large version of his colleague's *Wheel of Fortune* (now in the Musée d'Orsay), which was never fulfilled.[21]

Durand-Tahier's unpublished archives show to what extent he relieved the president of organizational tasks, freeing him to devote himself to his favorite pastime of scribbling caricatures. When Durand-Tahier reproduced a whole series of them in the special issue of *La Plume* that was devoted to Puvis in 1895, he commented on that aspect of the artist's character: 'This comical verve – which in him is an inbred instinct and an imaginative response – is manifested once again by his surprising talent as a caricaturist. Hundreds of these sketches of an irresistible buffoonery flow from his pen. He had intended to collect them in an album "to attest," he said, "to his regular attendance at the meetings of the Comités to which he belonged." But he feared the malicious tongues "which would not have neglected to say that he had taken the wrong road!"

Charming scruples on the part of the painter of the Sorbonne and the Panthéon!'[22]

Durand-Tahier saved the originals of the caricatures he published. Interestingly enough, two of them were drawn on cards bearing the letterhead of the Société Nationale des Beaux-Arts (fig. 21).

While he may not have published his caricatures until 1895 – in *La Plume* and *Le Rire*[23] – Puvis de Chavannes took pains to ensure that his serious work was shown. He was loyal to the Salons and undaunted by rejection, as for instance during the first decade of the Second Empire – it seems that even the *Dead Christ* he exhibited at the Salon of 1850-51, and then reworked and possibly somewhat enlarged, was refused by the jury of the Exposition Universelle of 1855[24] – or in 1872, the year he was only partially successful at the Salon. When he received a commission, he did not hesitate first to present the full-size cartoon, and then the painting itself before its definitive installation. He ignored neither the Expositions Universelles nor the Exposition Nationale of 1883. Counting his important one-man show at Durand-Ruel's in 1887, works like *Young Women by the Sea* (fig. 6) were exhibited as often as four times during the decade 1880-90, which was a crucial period for Symbolism. Seurat's *Poseuses* (Barnes Foundation, Merion, Penn.), Klinger's *Blue Hour* (Museum der bildenden Künste, Leipzig), Signac's *Women at the Well* (Musée d'Orsay, Paris), Denis's *Orchard of the Wise Virgins* (collection Daniel Malingue) and *Portrait of Mademoiselle Yvonne Lerolle in Three Poses* (Josefowitz Collection) constitute a remarkable legacy. The creators of these works were certainly indebted to their familiarity with this frequently exhibited masterpiece, which also inspired writers and critics.[25] As a further example of his desire for exposure, one could cite his submission of two cartoons for Amiens and the Panthéon to the Exposition Internationale de Blanc et Noir of 1890.[26] One of these, the cartoon of *Ludus pro Patria* (fig. 18), was presented by the artist to the Musée du Luxembourg in 1891, the first of a series of drawings donated during the artist's lifetime. His family presented 201 more after his death, as part of a large donation to French museums[27] which Puvis doubtless discussed with his heirs before he died.

The gesture Puvis made in 1891 toward the Parisian museum devoted to living artists came some years after the State's acquisition of *The Poor Fisherman* (fig. 23) for the Musée du Luxembourg. This had taken place just before the opening of the artist's one-man show at the Galerie Durand-Ruel, which lasted from 20 November until 20 December 1887. Puvis had informed Durand-Ruel that the sale price was 6,000 francs[28]; ten days later, by a decree of 19 November, for the modest sum of 4,000 francs, the minister Eugène Spüller confirmed the choice of his Directeur des Beaux-Arts, Jules Castagnary.[29] The latter had been forced to threaten to resign: clearly Puvis's position was still ambiguous. However, as a

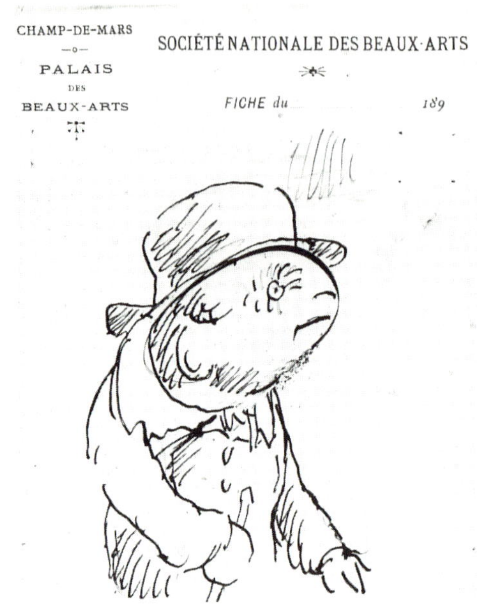

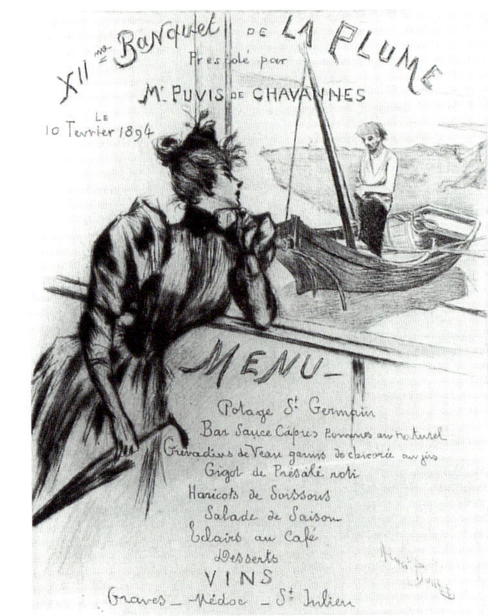

fig. 21
Caricature
Black ink on paper
Documentation department, Musée d'Orsay, Paris
(formerly collection H. Durand-Tahier)

fig. 22
Henri Boutet (1851-1900)
Menu for the Twelfth Banquet of 'La Plume', 1894
Etching, 182 x 140 mm (image)
Documentation department, Musée d'Orsay, Paris
(formerly collection H. Durand-Tahier)

member of the important Conseil Supérieur des Beaux-Arts he was near the center of power.[30] The preface to the catalogue of his show at Durand-Ruel's was written by Roger-Ballu, who held the post of Inspecteur des Beaux-Arts at the time, in addition to other official functions at the Direction des Beaux-Arts such as organizing exhibitions. His text, which is nothing if not enthusiastic, contains some of the finest analysis of Puvis's works by a contemporary. About *The Poor Fisherman* – 'that synthesis of wretchedness' – he wrote: 'What an impressive abstraction of poverty, of desolation, of heart-rending disappointment, in this fisherman, his hands crossed over his chest, facing the empty net. A small, naked child is asleep on the grass; a girl picks flowers. In their insouciance, the two of them rouse our sympathy for the miserable man. And the water of a single tone, which rises and goes far, far away, sad and cold! And the small pink note on the green greys! The eye's enjoyment of the colorations is deeply moving....'[31]

But Puvis had had to wait until the age of 63 before he was admitted to the 'anteroom of the Louvre,' which is what the Musée du Luxembourg amounted to for the most fortunate. It is true that Jean-François Millet and Gustave Courbet managed to penetrate it only posthumously, and that Corot had had to await the fortuitous acquisition of his picture at the Salon of 1850-51 and the shrewd judgment of Philippe de Chennevières before gaining entrance at the age of 57 in 1853.[32] But Henri Gervex (1852-1929) was admitted on the basis of his *Satyr Playing with a Bacchante*, first exhibited in 1874, at 22! And Puvis had close friends who were more fortunate than he: Elie Delaunay (1828-1891), who won the Prix de Rome in 1856 to be sure, had three pictures in the Luxembourg, namely *The Communion of the Apostles* of 1864, *The Plague in Rome* of 1869 and the *Death of Nessus* of 1870; Gustave Moreau (1826-1898) was represented by his *Orpheus*, displayed at the Salon of 1866.

The fact is that the State's acquisitions followed a line that was determined by hierarchy. Puvis de Chavannes's first official mural cycle, installed in the Musée de Picardie at Amiens (see cat. 26-29), only achieved the coherence the artist desired through his gift of *Bellum* to the government, following the purchase of *Concordia* in 1861; in 1865, the State still paid for only half of *Ave Picardia Nutrix* (ill. pp. 102-103). In 1880, finally, that picture's pendant, *Ludus pro Patria* (ill. pp. 192-193), measuring over seventeen metres in length, was commissioned for no less than 40,000 francs. The acquisitions of 'easel paintings ... *large* easel paintings,' as Roger-Ballu said,[33] were intended for Lyons in 1864 (*Autumn* [Musée des Beaux-Arts, Lyons], for 4,000 francs) and for Chartres in 1873 (the immense *Summer* [fig. 5], for 8,000 francs).

We know that Puvis would have preferred to be represented at the Musée du Luxembourg by *Sleep* of 1867 (see cat. 47). He doubtless wished to be regarded as a painter of large formats, since he decorated walls. And Roger-Ballu, in his preface, had not denied that *Sleep* was worthy of the Parisian museum when he lamented the fact that the Luxembourg had not a single picture by Puvis.[34] By no means did the Musée du Luxembourg scorn immense canvases, ever since David or Delacroix, and it still displayed *The Romans of Decadence* by Thomas Couture, *The Divine Tragedy* by Chenavard and *Cain* by Cormon (an artist twenty years Puvis's junior) which, in the *salon d'honneur* of the last official Salon, in 1880, accompanied Puvis's cartoon for *Ludus pro Patria*. Nevertheless, *Sleep* did not enter the Luxembourg: by a decree of 31 December 1887, the work was purchased half by the State and half by the Municipality for the museum of Lille.

But if Paris neglected his large formats, this was hardly the case in Brussels. Evidently for didactic reasons, in the course of 1888 the city wanted to display some of the full-size cartoons Puvis had saved, and to purchase them from him. This explains why the immense, seventeen-meter-long canvas for the *Ludus pro Patria* (now rolled up) is found, along with others for Amiens, Poitiers and the Panthéon, in the Musées Royaux d'Art et d'Histoire in Brussels.[35]

If in the end Puvis had to content himself with having only a work of medium size in the Luxembourg, he need not have had any regrets, as it promptly attained the status of an icon. After all, an amusing, engraved version of *The Poor Fisherman* by Henri Boutet is reproduced on the menu of a dinner organized in 1894 by *La Plume*, at which Puvis presided (fig. 22). The engraving shows an elegant visitor leaning on the balustrade of the museum as she beholds the artist's celebrated work.

Even with the success of *The Poor Fisherman*, Puvis seems to have found his position not as strong as he would have liked – as his student Paul Baudoüin recalled.[36] Baudoüin remembered the master never forgot that for a long time he 'could not enter a room where his works were displayed without hearing offensive comments. "You have to have a strong stomach," he said.'[37] This recollection may explain why he was not willing to compromise his position, which was still tenuous, by taking unnecessary risks. Thus, when Monet organized a subscription to buy Manet's *Olympia* for the State and Berthe Morisot contacted Puvis de Chavannes about it, she reported the following to Monet in a letter of 10 November 1889: 'You cannot imagine how official and complicated he is ... all the same a charming man, but the idea of appearing to oppose the government disturbs him. He would have wanted you to ascertain this government's goodwill beforehand. I told him that this was neither your opinion, nor mine, to which he replied that one should at least have spoken to Proust about it.'[38] Monet had not neglected this official contact with Antonin Proust, but Proust was no more eager to get involved. Gustave Moreau, a close friend of Puvis, was likewise approached,[39] but Monet's request remained unanswered. *Olympia* entered the Musée du Luxembourg, however, where it joined *The Poor Fisherman*.

This episode should certainly not be seen as a sign of indifference toward an artist who had once suffered so much at the hands of the critics while, like Puvis, continuing to exhibit at the Salon, but rather as a sign of profound aesthetic antagonism. According to Hippolyte Durand-Tahier, Puvis was the 'great knight of the Ideal.'[40] Throughout his career he had practised a manner of painting that was described at the time of the Salon of 1872, for example, where he exhibited *Hope*, as 'Pre-Raphaelite.'[41] His manner finally won admiration around 1889-90, as did that of Burne-Jones who, as we have noted, was invited by Puvis to the Société Nationale des Beaux-Arts. Nothing was more antithetical to the style of Manet, who championed a powerful naturalism which, during the same period of 1880-90, had been trivialized and vulgarized by the vast majority of the exhibiting artists, a naturalism that people such as Josephin Péladan, future organizer of the Salons de la Rose+Croix, considered the decadence of art.

The rising generations – Redon, Gauguin, the artists of the School of Pont-Aven, before long the Nabis – attempted, in Puvis's wake, to revitalize art by abandoning the almost photographic rendition of reality to which official naturalism was often reduced. Yet Puvis had diverse admirers and friends. On 16 January 1895 they attended the banquet organized in his honor by *La Plume* at the Hôtel Continental, at which the sculptor Auguste Rodin presided. Facing the hero of the day, Rodin was seated next to Emile Zola, the naturalistic novelist... Among the 550 guests, including writers and artists both French and foreign (Baertsoen, Meunier, Munkacsy, Rusiñol, Thaulow), we should note Signac and Van Rysselberghe, Bourdelle, Bernard and Carrière, but especially Gauguin (between two Polynesian sojourns), Fantin-Latour, Pissarro, Renoir and Monet. For some, this opportunity to pay official tribute to Puvis had come too late: his admirers Seurat and Van Gogh had died some years before.[42]

After receiving the special issue of *La Plume* of 15 January 1895, the following 8 February Puvis sent a (previously unpublished) note to Hippolyte Durand-Tahier, the highly effective secretary-general of the Société Nationale des Beaux-Arts. The note, addressed to the Café Américain with instructions to 'hold until his arrival,' reads as follows: 'My dear friend, I don't know if I'll be able to attend the meeting this evening, or when I'll see you, but in any case before being able to shake your hand and embrace you wholeheartedly, I want to thank you for this essay and for this wonderful publication in which you have managed to assemble – with the exquisite and profound feeling of a friend – everything that could be of interest about me and my work. I am deeply touched and delighted. To you from the heart, 8 February 95, P. Puvis de Chavannes. [the letter continues:] I was anxiously awaiting the appearance of the brochure, when this morning I met my friend Dupré who, having just received it, gave it to me. Do have some copies sent to me. This article is so well written and the whole issue so alive because of everything in it that I want to share it with my village. The idea of having caricatures is very good. I laughed as if I hadn't drawn them myself. Try to come see me on Sunday morning. P.P.Ch.'[43]

Undoubtedly, Puvis's charisma toward the end of his life further enhanced admiration for his oeuvre. His personal style certainly accounts for part of that admiration, but also the care he constantly took to bring his art to the attention of the public in exhibitions of every kind, and, most importantly, his highly admired wall decorations in public buildings.

Notes

1 'A partir de 1890, la victoire est définitivement remportée, et le triomphe commence.... C'est la jeunesse qui se précipite vers lui, qui l'entoure d'admiration et d'enthousiasme.' Cited in *Revue populaire des Beaux-Arts* (5 November 1898), 357.

2 After the Académies were suppressed during the Revolution, the Institut National was created in 1795 and then reformed, first in 1803 and again in 1816. Henceforth the Institut de France comprised an Académie des Beaux-Arts, of which the members were nominated by co-optation and which administered the Prix de Rome, art education and, depending on the era, the jury of the Salon. For more on this subject see, for example, Gérard Monnier, *Des Beaux-Arts aux arts plastiques* (Besançon, 1991).

3 'ce brave Institut ne néglige aucune occasion de dauber sur moi.... Ces gens-là ne supportent pas l'idée qu'on puisse vivre, travailler et produire sans penser à eux. Cela devient une offense, et leur rage s'en aigrit d'autant – ils veulent qu'on les implore pour avoir le plaisir de vous refuser – autrement – ils vous considèrent comme un insurgé, une sorte de Parpaillot. Zut!' Letter of 1 July 1887 (private collection). (I am grateful to Aimée Brown Price for bringing the sources quoted in this note and in the two following to my attention.)

4 Letters belonging to a private collection. For the letter to Falguière, see also p. 26, note 68.

5 Puvis never actually took his place on the jury. As he wrote to the artist Guillaumet on 2 April 1872, 'I am very touched by this token of esteem on the part of my colleagues, but am regretfully unable to oblige, being compelled to leave on urgent business. As a supplementary juror I can allow myself to withdraw without qualms. Nor was there any reason to hesitate; the appointment was made before there was any question of the election in which I was chosen. But this won't cause any harm, for the list strikes me as a good one and offers real guarantees.' ('J'ai été très sensible à cette marque d'estime de mes confrères, mais j'ai le regret de ne pouvoir y répondre étant obligé de m'absenter pour affaires urgentes. Ma situation de juré complémentaire me permet de m'éloigner sans scrupule. Il n'y avait pas d'ailleurs à hésiter; rendez-vous était pris avant qu'il fût question du scrutin d'où je suis sorti. Les choses n'en iront pas plus mal pour cela, car la liste me paraît bien composée et offrir de vraies garanties.') (collection Mme de Mirimonde). A.-P. de Mirimonde, *Catalogue du Musée Baron*

Martin à Gray (1959), p. 134. Later testimonies, such as that of Jules Breton, *Nos peintres du siècle*, Paris, n.d., p. 231, make it clear that the rejection of *Death and the Maidens* – withdrawn by the artist because the jury did not like it and therefore in effect refused it, in a year when the former medalists were not exempted from the scrutiny of the jury – irritated Puvis very much.

6 Each elector had to nominate as many names as there were members of the jury to be elected.

7 'de vraies processions d'artistes,' Chennevières (1885), p. 89. Cf. 1976-77 Paris/Ottawa, p. 134.

8 At the beginning of the Third Republic, the Ministère de l'Instruction Publique comprised a Direction des Beaux-Arts. For more on French institutional history see Monnier, *op. cit.* (note 2) and Genet-Delacroix (1992).

9 The Société des Artistes Français, established on 17 January 1881, was an independent society of artists formed for the purpose of running the Salon, to which the government turned over the exhibition's administration. The Société saw the representation of the artistic community as its mission. As defined by the regulations, the actual workings of the Société differed only superficially from those of the previous official Salon. Nonetheless, the monopoly of the Salon came to an end.

10 Here are, according to the *livrets* of the Salon des Artistes Français, the number of votes obtained by the first-place winner and by Puvis de Chavannes, among a total of 40 jurors of painting (50 in 1882). The number of those voting is not always indicated, but it seems that the first-place winner received two-thirds of the votes on average.

1881: Bonnat, 1430 / Puvis, 681 (last)
1882: Bonnat, 1121 / Puvis, 1241 (8th)
1883: Bouguereau, 990 / Puvis, 847 (12th)
1884: Henner, 1313 / Puvis, 1129 (8th)
1885: Bonnat, 1168 / Puvis, 858 (19th)
1886: Bonnat, 1253 / Puvis, 1101 (7th)
1887: Jules Lefebvre, 1436 / Puvis, 1305 (6th)
1888: Bonnat, 1293 / Puvis, 1096 (15th)
1889: Bonnat, 1372 / Puvis, 1162 (16th)

11. Cf. Constance Cain Hungerford, 'Meissonier and the Founding of the Société Nationale des Beaux-Arts,' *Art Journal*, XLVIII (Spring 1989), 71-77.

12 Partially reproduced in the *Catalogue illustré de la Société Nationale des Beaux-Arts*, ed. L. Baschet, 1899, p. 11. A general view (photograph Roger-Viollet) is reproduced in Brown Price (1977), 28.

13 Vaisse (1979), p. 145.

14 There was likewise Gustave Moreau, an old friend of Puvis de Chavannes, who, in contrast, no longer exhibited at the Salons, preferring to try his luck at the Institut, to which he was elected in 1888.

15 *Société des Artistes Français ... Salon de 1890*, pp. VI-VII.

16 Cf. sale Paris, Hôtel Drouot, *salle* 11, 13 November 1991, lot 74, letter from Puvis de Chavannes of 1892: 'At the moment there is talk of erecting a statue to M. Alphand. I believe we would do well to remember the goodwill and the services he rendered our Société.' ('Au moment où l'on songe à élever une statue à M. Alphand, je crois qu'il est bon de nous souvenir de la bienveillance et des services qu'il a rendus à notre Société.') Jean Alphand was the director-general for the construction of the Exposition Universelle of 1889. It was thanks to him that the Société Nationale obtained the use of the Champ-de-Mars.

17 'les pastiches de sa manière foisonnent. Des grandes toiles, ces pastiches sont descendus aux tableaux de chevalet.' Geffroy (1892), I, p. 141.

18 'tendance particulière peut être signalée chez les artistes campés dans les ruines de l'Exposition. Là-bas, au Palais de l'Industrie, le tableau à explications historiques, la mise en scène d'anecdotes dominent. Ici, au Palais des Beaux-Arts, la préoccupation de la mondanité est surtout évidente.' Geffroy (1892), I, pp. 191-192.

19 'ravit les yeux, invite l'esprit, par l'éternelle poésie qui émane d'elle.' Geffroy (1892), I, p. 217.

20 At the exhibition of 1864, Puvis de Chavannes was represented by a small picture entitled *Jesus Christ Appearing to the Magdalene*, which belonged to Théophile Gautier at the time. It was no. 183bis in the catalogue of February 1864, the only catalogue for a group exhibition that has been preserved (Bibliothèque Nationale, Cabinet des Estampes; Garland reprint). This picture can undoubtedly be identified with that preserved in the Musée des Beaux-Arts, Angers. The 'bis' (indicating that the work was not for sale) can probably be explained by the fact that normally everything was for sale and this work, lent by the president, was not. For more on the dealer Martinet, see Lorne Huston, 'Le Salon et les expositions d'art. Réflexions à partir de l'expérience de Louis Martinet (1861-1865),' *Gazette des Beaux-Arts* (July-August 1990), 45-50.

21 Cf. 1980, Paris, Grand Palais, *Cinq ans d'enrichissement du Patrimoine national 1975-1980*, no. 198 and John Christian, 'Acquisitions – Musée d'Orsay, "La Roue de la Fortune" de Burne-Jones,' *La Revue du Louvre*, no. 3 (1984), 204-211.

22 'Cette verve comique – qui est en lui à la fois comme un instinct de race et une réaction de l'imagination – se manifeste encore par un talent surprenant de caricaturiste. De ces croquis d'une bouffonnerie irrésistible, il en nait par centaines sous sa plume. Il avait songé à les réunir en album "pour témoigner, disait-il, de son assiduité aux séances des Comités dont il faisait partie." Mais, il craignit les méchantes langues "qui n'eussent pas manqué de dire qu'il s'était trompé de voie!" Charmant scrupule du peintre de la Sorbonne et du Panthéon!' Durand-Tahier (1895), 34. The sketch reproduced here (fig. 21) appears on p. 35 (in the lower center) of the 1895 issue of *La Plume*.

23 Cf. 1976-77 Paris/Ottawa, no. 221, and Brown Price (1991).

24 Presently in the Guezira Museum in Cairo, this picture bears the registration number '4891P' on the stretcher. The number does not correspond to the register of the Salon of 1850-51: '1767' (*Enregistrement des ouvrages du Salon de 1850-51*, Archives des Musées Nationaux, Musée du Louvre, Paris). It must therefore have been assigned to the picture at the Exposition Universelle of 1855, the only event where works already exhibited at a Salon could be submitted to the jury. Unfortunately the register does not survive.

25 Cf. De Forges (1970) and: 1975-76 Rotterdam.

26 *Catalogue officiel illustré de l'exposition internationale de blanc et noir, 4e année* (Paris, 1890), no. 392: reduced cartoon 'Ludur [sic] pro patria' with variants; no. 393: reduced cartoon for the Panthéon.

27 Cf. Bénédite (1922), pp. 110-113. See also p. 36, note 16 of this book.

28 Cf. Venturi (1939), vol. 2, p. 95.

29 Cf. Vachon [1900], pp. 161, 162 note 1. On the other hand, the acquisition dossier at the Archives Nationales (F^{21} 2106) shows that the sum retained, 4,000 francs, was only deposited on 14 August 1888, after Puvis had complained on 4 August! See also p.46.

30 Cf. Genet-Delacroix (1992), p. 330. On 15 January 1887 Puvis was chosen to be a member of the Conseil Supérieur des Beaux-Arts – and not for the first time. In 1889 he was called to the new acquisition committee, the 'commission consultative des travaux d'art'; later on, he sat on the Conseil Supérieur des Beaux-Arts by virtue of his presidency of the Société Nationale des Beaux-Arts.

31 'cette synthèse de la misère': 'Quelle impressionnante abstraction de pauvreté, de désolation, de déception navrante, dans cette figure de pêcheur, les mains croisées contre sa poitrine, debout en face au filet vide. Un petit enfant nu dort dans les touffes; une fillette cueille des fleurs: deux insouciances qui augmentent encore la pitié pour le malheureux. Et l'eau d'un seul ton qui monte et s'en va loin, loin, triste et froide! et la petite note rosée sur les gris verts! L'oeil a le plaisir des colorations, et cela vous étreint la poitrine....' Roger-Ballu, Preface to the catalogue *Exposition de tableaux, pastels, dessins par M. Puvis de Chavannes*, 1887, Paris, Galerie Durand-Ruel, pp. 12-13.

32 Cf. 1974, Paris, Grand Palais, *Le musée du Luxembourg en 1874*, no. 55.

33 Roger-Ballu, *op. cit.* (note 31), p. 10.

34 'The Luxembourg doesn't have any of his work yet, neither this picture nor any others, alas.' ('Le Luxembourg ne l'a pas encore, ni celle-ci, ni d'autres, hélas.') Roger-Ballu, *op. cit.* (note 31), p. 14.

35 Cf. 1976-77 Paris/Ottawa, no. 114.

36 Baudoüin (1935), 307-309.

37 'ne pouvait entrer dans telle salle où il avait exposé ses oeuvres sans s'entendre outrager. "Il faut avoir de l'estomac," disait-il.' Baudoüin (1935), 307.

38 'Vous ne vous doutez pas combien il est officiel et compliqué ... au demeurant charmant homme, mais l'idée de paraître en opposition avec l'administration l'agite. Il aurait voulu que vous vous fussiez assuré au préalable de la bonne volonté de cette administration. Je lui ai répondu que ce n'était ni votre opinion, ni la mienne, à quoi il a répliqué qu'il faudrait au moins en parler à Proust.' Quoted in Anne Distel, 'Il y a cent ans, ils ont donné Olympia,' *Quarante-huit/quatorze*, no. 4 (1992), p. 45.

39 Archives of the Musée Gustave Moreau, Paris.

40 'grand chevalier de l'Idéal,' Durand-Tahier (1895), 34.

41 E. Duvergier de Hauranne, 'Le Salon de 1872,' *Revue des deux mondes* (1872), 843-844, who added 'convenient genre for anyone who can neither draw nor paint' ('genre commode pour qui ne sait ni dessiner, ni peindre').

42 For more on the banquet, see Morhardt (1935).

43 'Mon cher ami, je ne sais si je pourrais me rendre ce soir à la réunion, ni quand je vous verrai, mais dans tous les cas avant de pouvoir vous serrer la main et vous embrasser de tout mon coeur, je veux vous remercier de ce texte et de ce recueil merveilleux où vous avez su réunir avec le sentiment exquis et profond d'un ami tout ce qui peut intéresser sur moi et sur mon oeuvre. Je suis absolument touché et ravi – à vous de coeur, 8 février 95 , P. Puvis de Chavannes. [the letter continues:] J'attendais l'apparition de la brochure avec impatience, quand ce matin j'ai rencontré notre ami Dupré qui venait de la recevoir et qui me l'a donnée – faites qu'on m'en envoie – cet article est tellement bien fait et le numéro si vivant par tout ce qu'on y a intercallé que je veux en faire part à mon village. L'idée d'avoir fait figurer des charges est très bonne. J'en ai ri comme si je n'en étais pas l'auteur. Tachez de venir me voir dimanche matin. P.P.Ch.'
Letter formerly in the collection Hippolyte Durand-Tahier .

Aimée Brown Price

The Poor Fisherman

A Painting in Context

'This kind of painting jars in the ensemble of others....'
(Puvis de Chavannes in a letter of April 1881)

In 1879, on the eve of completing his most compelling and important easel paintings, *Young Women by the Sea* (fig. 6, cat. 76), *The Prodigal Son* (fig. 7) and *The Poor Fisherman* (fig. 23), Puvis de Chavannes stated that having proved himself as an official painter much was left to be done in the area of expressiveness. As he put it, 'and then why a large canvas? What subject can I treat in these proportions which isn't a corollary to the large canvases I have already done. Reflection should yield to light as intensity, and the episodic composition to synthetic composition as surface. Works of large dimension make sense only on walls; they take their raison d'être and requirements from them for their execution. Outside of that, one only undertakes them to show what one is capable of; and I wouldn't hesitate if I had something to venture or to prove as a personal tendency; but haven't I done enough of that, Good God! The public and artists would end up by not even noticing it. Instead of that, in the area of expression there are quite a few things to do, and, in that case, surface counts for little!' [1] Developed completely in his own terms, these paintings differ markedly from his murals in subject, structure and level of symbolic communication. Using the special aesthetic bred of his public sphere mural-decorative experience, he broached the radically simplified style with which his mature work would be identified.

There were personal reasons for Puvis's work taking a new and essentially individual turn. In 1878, with his first Paris murals (the *Saint Genevieve* cycle) a resounding success, he seems to have undergone something of a crisis. He was anxious about his prospects, wrote of the conflict of artistic freedom and outside regulations,[2] and noted that 'the artistic horizon as far as it concerns me is quite foggy....' [3] Whether the depressed art market of 1877-78 affected him is not known, but only religious projects were available, which he did not wish to pursue. As he wrote on 7 August 1878: 'in short, I am working, but only for myself, and it isn't without pain that I see time run on, without foreseeing anything great – monuments to decorate are rare, or rather, I am not interested in painting for churches, the only places, however, ready to receive them....'[4] Even public recognition was no salve (at least at this moment), for Puvis cynically noted that the 'centipede one calls the public'[5] appreciated his Salon paintings. While he was at Honfleur, where his *Poor Fisherman* is thought to have been conceived,[6] water leakage destroyed the Panthéon sketches in his atelier and left him further discouraged.[7] That winter, his malaise deepened, augmented by advancing age. As he wrote his family the day before his fifty-fifth birthday, 'we are more and more in an atmosphere absolutely injurious to imaginative conceptions, photography and sewing machines or the like are the true expression of our time – it isn't far from that to a total eclipse of all personal and poetic inspiration....'[8] The sum of this array of incremental concerns was an uneasiness and melancholy coupled with a growing sense that this was the time to make any personal statement that he would.

The last of the independent paintings that Puvis produced during this difficult 1879-81 period is *The Poor Fisherman*, a simple, powerful and elusive painting and one of Puvis de Chavannes's most profoundly original images. Assessed as a special iconographic intricacy, it reveals the power of Puvis's invention and secures his place in the development of modernism.

Puvis developed *The Poor Fisherman* over several years, working and reworking the elements and radically changing its structure, as an extended series of preliminary drawings and other painted studies show (cat. 82-84).[9] Although its essential configuration was established by 1879, as an atypically large painted study (65.5 x 91.3 cm, Pushkin Museum, Moscow) dated (unusually) to that year indicates, the definitive painting was finished only two years later.

Puvis recognized the peculiarity of his curiously enigmatic and compelling masterwork and had anxious second thoughts about exhibiting *The Poor Fisherman* at the Salon of 1881 (the year of its completion). It was clearly different in method and meaning from his habitually reassuring public works. When it was already admirably displayed in readiness for

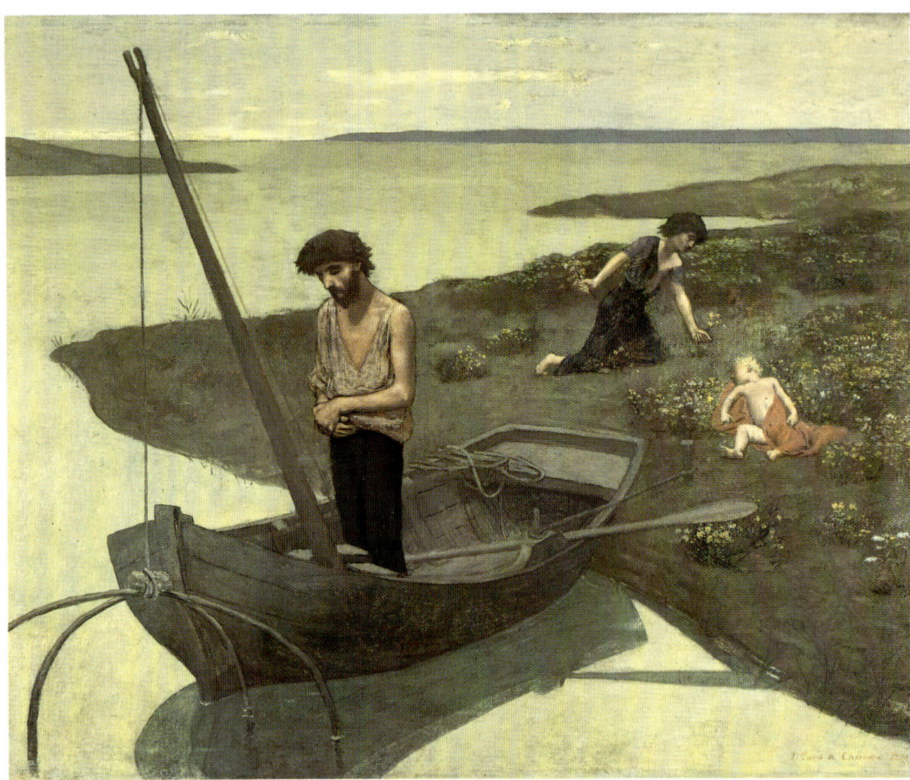

fig. 23
The Poor Fisherman, 1881
Oil on canvas, 155.5 x 192.5 cm
Musée d'Orsay, Paris

the opening, Puvis tried to withdraw it, for he feared a critical thrashing, 'that I don't merit since I would have been the first to condemn myself. Nothing can give an idea of how this kind of painting jars in the ensemble of the others, which doesn't at all modify the feeling it can contain, some boob's first sentiment will certainly be repulsion and there's no need to put it to the test.'[10]

Seven years later, *The Poor Fisherman* was selected to represent Puvis's oeuvre in the French national collection.[11] Puvis was not entirely pleased. On 26 November 1887, shortly after it was bought by the State, he wrote Jules Castagnary, then Directeur des Beaux-Arts, of his reservations. Castagnary, who had been an early champion of Realism, now with more comprehensive views and doubtless a taste for the kind of toiling figure the painting ostensibly portrays, overriding the objections of the notables of the Institut, actively sought its acquisition. In Puvis's own words, 'while far from disavowing the ... [*Poor Fisherman*], which can be curious and interesting in a private gallery, I didn't judge it a museum painting.'[12] Puvis thought that his imposing *Sleep* (see cat. 47), which at 381 x 600 cm, was far larger than *The Poor Fisherman* (155.5 x 192.5 cm), would be more suitable. Moreover, he may have been troubled by the melancholic cast of the fisherman. On 4 December 1887, he informed his sister-in-law, 'As for *The Poor Fisherman*, the affair is in abeyance in the stupidest fashion: the painting was sold to a collector when the Directeur des Beaux-Arts let me know that he wanted it for the Luxembourg. Since the State has priority, the collector [Emile Boivin, who wound up purchasing the large *Young Women by the Sea*, fig. 6, now Musée d'Orsay, Paris] was dismissed; all that was fine but they didn't count (in spite of me) on the Minister [Eugène Spüller], who twice declared that he wanted another painting instead of that one. The Director was nettled by that game and said that he would resign if the painting he chose wasn't taken. – And there I was between the devil and the deep blue sea with one buyer less, for it is probable he will not buy again, the affair having transpired without any consultation with me.'[13] It was presumably in response to this affair, and most likely several years later, that Puvis executed a reduced variant of *The Poor Fisherman* (cat. 81), for his 1881 canvas came to be viewed as unusually important and, having been acquired by the State, was no longer available for purchase.

The Genesis and Meaning of *The Poor Fisherman*

Genre paintings of fisherfolk are abundant in nineteenth-century French painting and fishing and fisherfolk were not infrequent themes in Puvis's paintings. The biblical *Miraculous Draught of Fishes* was among his 1854-55 murals at Le Brouchy representing food and a season as did others in his ensemble. His large (160.5 x 124.5 cm) *The Fisherman* of 1856 (Ohara Museum of Art, Kurashiki, Japan) was essentially an 'académie.'

Fishing as an industry couched in classicizing terms occupied the right-hand portion of his 1865 *Ave Picardia Nutrix* (ill. pp. 102-103, see also cat. 36) and was an incidental passage in an ingratiating, rococo-inspired Golden Age divertissement in his 1866 *Fishing* (whereabouts unknown, formerly Ricketts collection, London). *The Fisherman's Family*, 1875 (see 1887 variant, fig. 24), presents a Hellenizing, idealized image of an archetypal family with a heroic male, female (mother), babe and old man and fishing as a noble, generationally ongoing occupation, the only hint of travail the remains of a battered boat against which the old man rests his head.[14]

In *The Poor Fisherman*, fishing is not ennobled nor presented as a pastime, but it is the patient endeavor of a single person, waiting to see what lot will be his. It depicts a gaunt figure standing in a boat in the foreground of a bleak landscape setting, his head bowed, his hands crossed as he waits for a catch. In the background a woman gathers flowers, a child on the ground nearby.

Puvis said *The Poor Fisherman* was a painting of conscience[15] that he wanted thought of in human, natural terms. Fishing was among the humblest of occupations, and Puvis, sympathetic to the poor, having made the fisherman so prominent in his canvas, remarked at the end of 1881, perhaps referring to his own work, that 'the true poor people, damn it, are invisible.'[16] The thin standing figure and pose of Puvis's fisherman resemble that of the praying peasant in Jean François Millet's *Angelus* (fig. 25), and several preliminary drawings seem to indicate that Millet, whose paintings Puvis admired, was undoubtedly a source.[17] Puvis, like Millet, presents the theme of work, faith, resigned stoicism and passive acceptance of one's lot. Meanwhile, Gambetta pointed to the political ramifications for the dominant classes of that kind of apologia of the ideal peasant, who fatalistically accepts his condition.[18] Indeed, there was real economic hardship among fisherman, with a dearth of fish on the north coast particularly,[19] where, as mentioned, Puvis is said to have conceived the painting.

Detailing the subject of *The Poor Fisherman* to one critic, Puvis concentrated on the background figures on the shore: 'The mother is dead (*sic jubeo*) [so I order] and while the father fishes, the girl entrusted to look after her little brother begins to make bouquets, as that is so natural!'[20] A poor girl and baby had been recurrent images in Puvis's oeuvre, in the early *The Big Sister* (Petit Palais, Geneva), and as outcasts – beggars and 'pariahs' by his own reckoning – at the far right of his *Saint Genevieve* mural of the mid 1870s (ill. p. 150). Elsewhere he explained them this way: 'It isn't a woman, but a young girl at an awkward age. The mother is dead and the little one is there to watch over her brother; she picks flowers with her little monkey hand, feverishly, mechanically. – The child who, in this strange flowerbed didn't do as much would be unnatural. I have a horror of illustrating novels in oils, my only excuse is that I borrowed this vision of misery only from myself.'[21]

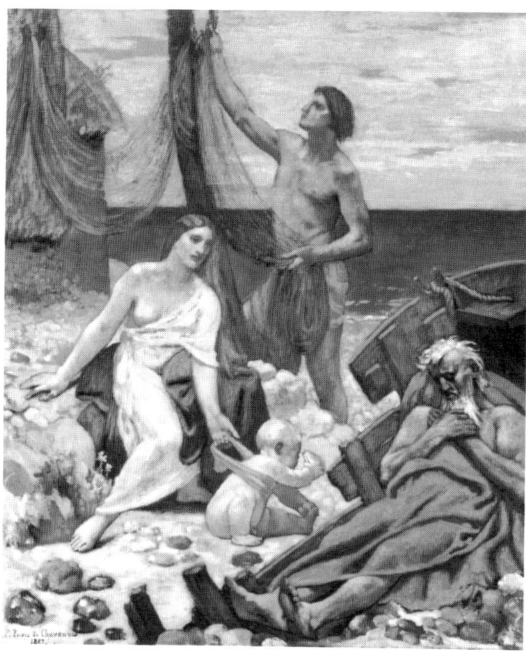

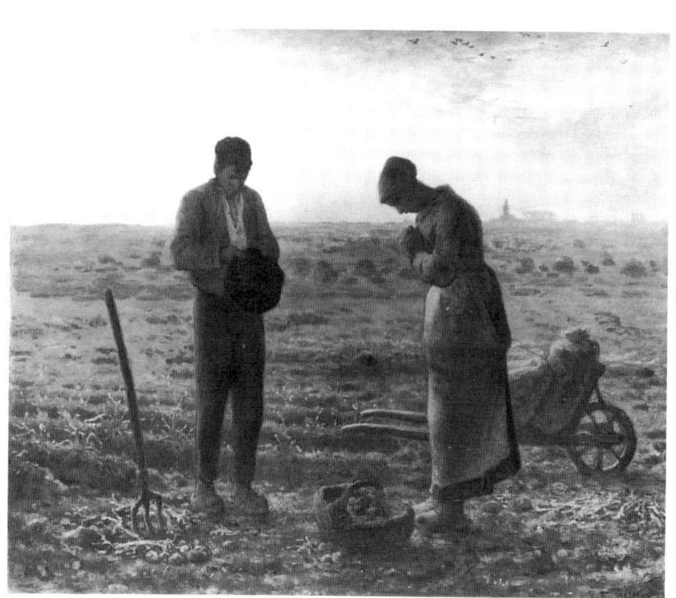

fig. 24
The Fisherman's Family, 1887
Oil on canvas, 82.5 x 71.8 cm
The Art Institute of Chicago,
Mr. and Mrs. Martin A. Ryerson Collection

fig. 25
Jean-François Millet (1814-1875)
The Angelus, 1859
Oil on canvas, 55.5 x 66 cm
Musée d'Orsay, Paris

In antiquity, the piscatorial theme was a traditional companion to pastoral Arcadian motifs of the fecund sweet land and its abundance. Puvis, so well apprised of ancient poetry, doubtless appreciated the ramifications of this pairing for his own work. The fisherman, unlike his Arcadian brother, is customarily not so well off. Typical of a number of ancient poems on this theme is 'The Fishermen' (formerly attributed to Theocritus), which begins: 'There's but one stirrer-up of the boats ... and her name is Poverty. She is the true teacher of labor....'[22] The overlap of pastoral and piscatorial in poetry has itself been remarked: 'Pastoral life may reserve ... a small place for the fisherman, if he does not risk his life on the high seas, but throws his net not too far from shore or sinks his line into a nearby pond or brook. Such a fisherman is twin brother to the shepherd....'[23]

The theme of poverty is important to pastoral, whether pagan or Christian, and its link to a religious meaning has been described thus: 'The ideal of the perfect shepherd or, for that matter, of the complete angler is then based, like the Christian one, on the practice of poverty or, at the least, on its praise. Both Christian theologians and pastoral poets see that condition both as a sign of humility and a token of grace. The former, however, exalt the latter, because it teaches self-contentment. The first alternative connects poverty with self-mortification and self-abasement; the second, with a self-gratification that finds its check in self-control. In brief, Christian poverty is a quest after innocence; pastoral poverty, after happiness as well.'[24]

The Poor Fisherman as a Religious Painting

Fishing is a convention of the Christological literature, first associated with Christ's disciples and Christ's role as a fisher of men. The rich art historical tradition embedded in the construction of *The Poor Fisherman* would signal a religious reading of the work. With his hands crossed modestly before him and his head bowed, the thin, angular, bearded fisherman (so distant from the heroic half-clad fisherman of Puvis's *Fisherman's Family*) approximates a physical type, pose and gesture associated through pictorial tradition with images of Christ. August Strindberg took this to be the case when, in a remarkable letter of 1895 to Gauguin, he voiced admiration for *The Poor Fisherman*, but criticized it as marred by what he saw as an allusion to Christ and a fatalistic acceptance of life's hardships. As he wrote: 'I do not want any part of this pitiful God who accepts blows.'[25] He deplored what he understood as a reference to the crown of thorns and was repelled by the meekness and humble acceptance of one's lot that he saw portrayed (Christian virtues of the kind later condemned by Nietzsche as the transvaluation of values). Contrasting Puvis's God to Gauguin's Vitsuliputsli, 'who eats the hearts of men under the sun,' he concluded that 'No, Gauguin was not created from Chavannes's rib....' As an interesting aside, however, a case can be made that Gauguin's 1889 *Christ in the Garden of Olives* (Norton Gallery and School of Art, West Palm Beach, Florida), widely accepted as a self-portrait of Gauguin as Christ, while following the common posture for the figure, with a squared-off delineation, inclined head and meekly crossed hands, echoes Puvis's *Poor Fisherman*.

The type figure in a passive pose was indeed a well-known topos for Christ. The figure's attitude, the configuration of the setting with a river winding its way to the back and even its grey and silvery tones make the composition strikingly similar to J.B. Corot's *Baptism of Christ* of 1847 (Church of Saint Nicolas du Chardonnet, Paris), which Puvis admired as a 'très belle peinture décorative.'[26] Jean Jacques Henner's *Christ in Prison* (Musée d'Unterlinden, Colmar) of 1860 is also posed in this manner.[27] Most importantly, the figure and pose echo that of Christ in Puvis's own 1858 *Ecce Homo* drawings (see cat. 20-22), which follow a well-known convention that Puvis also used in his *Christ Before the Praetorial Court* (fig. 1). Here, as in his other religious painting, *The Beheading of Saint John the Baptist* (cat. 57) of 1869, Puvis also showed a predilection for a very particularized archaizing figural type for which a distinct taste had begun in Germany. The critic F. de Mercey remarked in 1858 (the very year of the *Ecce Homos*): '[They are] figures with thin and slender forms, with angular and tapering extremities: in the nude parts, the bone structure and skin are curiously studied and the muscle almost erased.... [they have a] pale and cold coloration.'[28]

Although Puvis disavowed mysticism and insisted no philosophy, structured ideas or story be read into images which he said he wanted thought of in human and natural terms, that his poor fisherman would be read as Christ-like is not surprising. Certainly Puvis must have plotted this ambiguity.

In the later nineteenth century there was a shift towards a desacralization of images, and a secularization and migration of symbols within a larger, positivist ideological wave. The ambiguity of *The Poor Fisherman* conforms on several counts to Ernest Renan's revolutionary, humanizing depiction of Christ in *La Vie de Jésus* of 1868. Renan, with roots as a seminarian and anti-clerical prejudices, understood Jesus's early life and, indeed, early Christianity itself, as a charming pastoral;[29] its simplicity, outside of institutionalized religion, worthy of nostalgia.[30] Here faith is a personal matter of the human existential condition, and no reference is made to church, hierarchy or religion. Puvis's movement towards non-specific, even secularized religious iconography continued through to his late, great *Magdalene* (1897, cat. 145).

Melancholy, Modernism and *The Poor Fisherman*

Like *The Prodigal Son* of 1870 (fig. 7), *The Poor Fisherman* is a meditative figure, his hands crossed in a gesture of passivity and constraint. Both compositions underscore the essential isolation of the figure; the former does so in a religious context with a specific moral component generated by the biblical parable, while the fisherman underscores a societal and existential condition. *The Poor Fisherman* is not explained by a single narrative but is rather more elusive. Faith and acceptance are not posed as religious questions within the teachings of the Church, for example, but more vaguely, as a both more universal and personal matter. *The Poor Fisherman* is a special amalgam of vestigial religious referents and secular themes of metaphysical isolation and melancholy that represent the emerging modern mentality.

The melancholy or 'misérabilisme'[31] remarked in *The Poor Fisherman* is consonant with the mood of restrained dejection and disillusionment in Puvis's personal letters of the 1879 to 1881 period. Indeed, a certain melancholia had long been a strain in his independent canvases. A poignant loneliness and sense of moral solitude permeated one of his early paintings, *Meditation* or *Solitude* of 1857,[32] that may be based on a work by Lamartine.[33] Puvis noted his feelings of isolation and apparent depression in 1861, at the time that he had presented his first public paintings of adamant well-being: 'The Musset and Sénancour contagion is not for nothing in my business: I am thus, and so miserable that the sun tires my sight and troubles my soul, especially this autumn sun, which shines madly and doesn't warm....'[34] Melancholia was the 'mal du siècle' that Baudelaire claimed in 1846 was the newest and most remarkable quality in Delacroix's work, what made him a true modern nineteenth-century painter.[35] Indeed, in many quarters isolation and an undefined alienation were viewed as the predicament of contemporary man,[36] with melancholy endemic to modernism.

The roots of Puvis's melancholic imagery might be located in the melancholic indolence that had marked much of Chassériau's work, the 'expressionisme inexpressif' that signaled modernity,[37] its most notable aftermath Picasso's Blue Period imagery. Less grand than pervasive disillusionment seems at stake, an unfocused, bewildered sadness, contained and baleful. These themes with a multitude of permutations would be significant in twentieth-century art.

As emotionally sober and restrained as they are, the expressive motifs of solitude, forbearance and melancholy that underlie *The Poor Fisherman* are at sharp variance with the official Arcadias of Puvis de Chavannes's public paintings. This more personal, private vision, with its inward, reflective imagery of isolation and passivity is a curious foil to the more reassuring public commissions. The latter celebrated societal institutions, family and community. This more personal imagery represents a less expansive outlook. Indeed, by Puvis's account, the family is fragmented, 'sic jubeo,' as he put it. Yet insofar as *The Poor Fisherman* is to be read as a personally expressive statement, that Puvis insisted on the importance of the young woman feverishly gathering flowers in the bleak landscape is important to its interpretation and the meaning of the whole. In view of the public paintings, it is interesting to remark that the concomitant to melancholy, even in antiquity, was a yearning for a Golden Age.

The Decorative Aesthetic in an Independent Painting

The Poor Fisherman is striking for its simplifications, its flat areas of color, its geometry. The unmodulated chalky grey sky and putty sea that, neutral and somber, zigzags back between spits of land, developed from bleak colors of the north coast evident in painted sketches. Its salient features are sharply defined abbreviated forms, rigidly sustained geometric shapes – the arc of the net, the diagonal beam – and stiff figures. The systematic decorative aesthetic that is brought to bear eliminates accent and immunizes the imagery from any sense of verism, making Puvis's explanation in genre terms the more unsatisfactory. That is, *The Poor Fisherman* ostensibly deals with everyday life, but summary styling thwarts a narrative reading and for an audience used to having stories told them this was disturbing. Rather, the generalized mode suggests symbolic meaning. The sense of metaphysical isolation is underscored by a lack of all framing or bracketing devices. Considering Puvis's defense of the borders of his mural decorations, the absence of all such amenities here is the more noteworthy.

The young Maurice Denis very much appreciated these aspects of the construction of *The Poor Fisherman*. It is no coincidence that in the breath directly following his discussion of it, he launched his famous 'Definition of Neo-Traditionism,' the manifesto of a new order of painting: 'Remember that a painting – before being a warhorse, a nude woman, or some anecdote – is essentially a planar surface covered with colors organized in a certain order.'[38]

This thesis issues in the pictorial logic of non-objective and abstract art of the twentieth century. What has not been recognized is that Denis's dictum, even to similarities in expression, echoed what Henri Delaborde had pointed out in 1859, on the eve of Puvis's activity as a mural painter, in defining the special decorative qualities of murals and contrasting them to easel paintings.[39] Not coincidentally, we have come full circle. Delaborde, writing on religious murals, was most probably read by Denis who was intensely interested in religious art. But Denis was to transpose the basic ideas of the mural aesthetic to any pictorial surface – pointedly that of an independent painting – in the same way that Puvis had done so. *The Poor Fisherman* precisely exemplified Puvis's use of a decorative aesthetic, an aesthetic engendered by his experience as a mural painter.

How radical the composition is, with its high horizon, areas of flat color, sharp definition of shapes and asymmetrical placement of water is evident in comparing it to the flattened schema of Japanese prints. But despite similarities to Harunobu's *The Sumida River* (from *The Eight Views of Edo*), with its willowy, flat figures in a similarly shaped boat, there is no evidence Puvis knew this work, and, as drawings demonstrate (see cat. 82-83), he worked his own way to this composition.

Response to *The Poor Fisherman* was immediate and lasting.The painting was out of the ordinary and made people talk. As with any innovative cultural artifact, it was baffling, and some critics proceeded with caution, making and qualifying statements. On the face of it, it was a genre scene and yet it seemed more. The writer Joris Karl Huysmans was both attracted and repulsed.[40] The photographer Nadar (Félix Tournachon) noted that the malicious Grévin said of Puvis's fisherman: 'Yes... he is there, he fishes, he fishes in the water, in the water which isn't water, what do you expect him to catch?'[41]

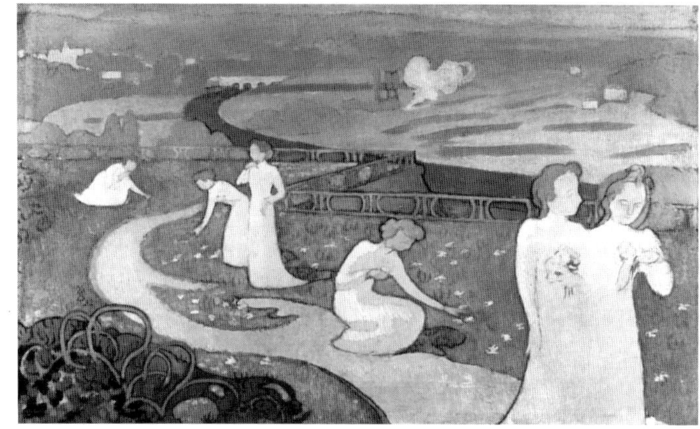

Younger artists acknowledged the seminal nature of this most captivating canvas. *The Poor Fisherman* had its own particular legacy, which included both direct copies, as by the young Aristide Maillol (Musée d'Orsay, Paris),[42] and interpretations.[43] Denis's appreciation of *The Poor Fisherman* is evident in his several versions of *April* of 1892 (see fig. 26).[44] Vastly different in theme, its construction is astonishingly imitative: his topography, winding river and roads are Puvis's waterway; the art nouveau tendrils of vegetation to the lower left corner, a variant of the fisherman's net. Denis's homage came in his emulation of the opaque colors and interlocking shapes that gave rise in the first place to his definition. Denis multiplied the woman picking flowers, with her distinctive, flat and angular pose[45]; she is pale, with a chaste purity and white garb reminiscent of Puvis's young Saint Genevieve. Seurat exaggerated the figure's wooden aspect when he introduced *The Poor Fisherman* into a small (16.5 x 25.5 cm) panel *Landscape with 'The Poor Fisherman'* (also called *Hommage à Pierre P. de Ch*, fig. 27), which he signed 'Puvisse,' a coined superlative for 'Puvis' – the most Puvis. The panel once belonged to the shrewdly perceptive critic Félix Fénéon, who called Seurat a 'Puvis modernisant.'[46] The painting within a painting implies that *The Poor Fisherman* was painted *sur place*. It is itself enigmatic, with only the thin, stiff fisherman retained. Whether this is an ironic comment on its remove from realism or betrays a satirical edge, as has been alleged, is arguable.[47] Loneliness, a motif in a number of Seurat's drawings, must have been an element the young artist recognized as compelling in *The Poor Fisherman*. Perhaps it is only coincidence that his own modest panel, *The Fisherman* (Yale University Art Gallery), is also of a single, slightly bowed fisherman standing in a skiff, isolated and waiting.[48] Gauguin labelled his picture of a fisherman transposed to the South Seas *The Poor Fisherman* (1896-98, Museo de Arte, São Paulo, another version the Hermitage, Saint Petersburg), and in a drawing mimicked the peculiarly posed child.[49]

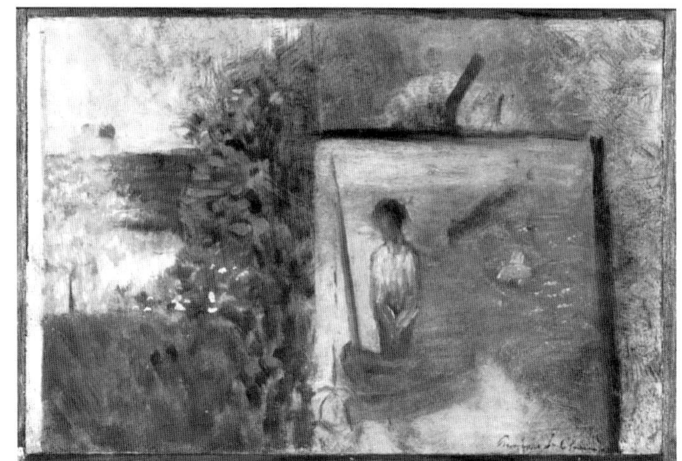

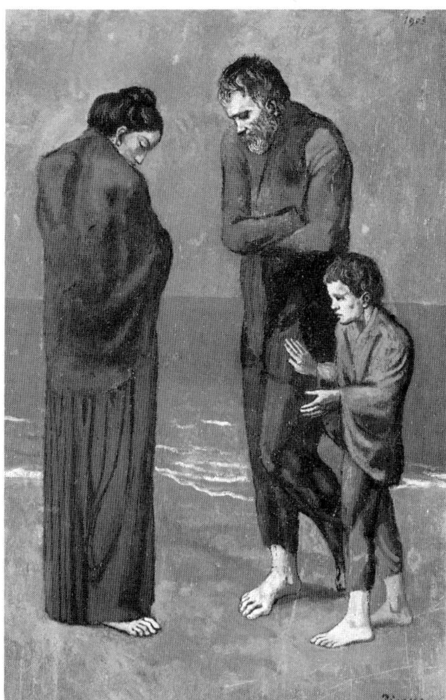

Puvis's *The Poor Fisherman* anticipates Picasso's Blue Period paintings of ca. 1902, particularly his isolated figures and families on a shore, heads bowed, meager, angular, hugging themselves in, such works as *The Fisherman's Goodbye* (whereabouts unknown), and *The Tragedy* (fig. 28).

From Private to Public

By 1915 *The Poor Fisherman* was sufficiently recognizable to function as an icon of helplessness, as in C. Léandre's caricatural image 'A la manière de ... Puvis de Chavannes,' in which the fisherman is a pathetic and laughable foil to a large mermaid who emerges from the sea in a cartoon captioned, 'The British Amphitrite who ridicules the Kaiser, his mines and zeppelins, protects the *poor fisherman*.'[50] Indeed, the canvas inspired a considerable group of satirical caricatures, including figures with gas masks in 'L'Art à la Gare d'Orsay.'[51] By 1925 the painting's familiarity was such that André Marquet could accompany a postal card sketch of *The Poor Fisherman* (Besson Collection) with the words, 'mon nouveau métier d'après Puvis de Chavannes,' meaning that he had gone fishing.

fig. 26
Maurice Denis (1870-1943)
April, 1892
Oil on canvas, 37.5 x 61 cm
Rijksmuseum Kröller-Müller, Otterlo

fig. 27
Georges Seurat (1859-1891)
Landscape with 'The Poor Fisherman' after Puvis de Chavannes, ca. 1881
Oil on wood panel, 16.5 x 25.5 cm
Collection Huguette Berès, Paris

fig. 28
Pablo Picasso (1881-1973)
The Tragedy, 1903
Oil on wood panel, 1.05 x 69 cm
National Gallery of Art, Washington, D.C., Chester Dale Collection

Notes

1 'et ensuite pourquoi une grande toile? Quel sujet puis-je traiter dans ces proportions qui ne soit un corollaire des grandes toiles que j'ai déjà faites. Le reflet doit le céder à la lumière comme intensité, et la composition épisodique à la composition synthétique comme surface. Les travaux de grande dimension n'ont de sens que sur les murs; ils y prennent leur raison d'être et les nécéssités de leur exécution. En dehors de cela, on ne les entreprend que pour montrer ce dont on est capable; et je n'hésiterais pas si j'avais quelque chose à hasarder, ou à prouver comme tendance personnelle; mais en ai-je assez fait, bon Dieu! Le public et les artistes finiraient par ne plus même s'en apercevoir. Au lieu de cela, il y a dans le sens de l'expression bien des choses à faire, et, dans ce cas, la superficie importe peu!' Letter to his student Henri Daras (private collection); compare quotations in Vachon (1895), p. 88; and Vachon [1900], p. 134.

2 In May 1879 he was offered a mural commission for Bordeaux which he rejected, believing that the project was so structured as to abrogate his artistic prerogatives (papers in private collection).

3 'l'horizon artistique en ce qui me concerne est bien brumeux....' Letter of 30 June 1878 to Valentine (private collection).

4 'bref, je travaille, mais uniquement pour moi, et ce n'est pas sans peine que je vois le temps courir, sans rien augurer de beau – les monuments à décorer sont rares, ou pour mieux dire je ne m'interesse pas de peinture dans les églises, les seuls endroits pourtant qui soient prets à les recevoir....' (private collection). It is noteworthy, given this statement, that about this time Puvis must have embarked on the biblical parable of *The Prodigal Son*; religious paintings of a public nature and personal paintings of reli-

gious themes appear to have been differentiated to his mind as surely as his public and private works generally were of two different orders.

5 'mille-pattes qu'on appelle le public,' letter of 19 May 1879 (private collection).

6 Boucher (1979), p. 72, quotes a familial anecdote that Puvis, supposed to meet friends at Saint-Valéry-en-Caux, mistakenly went to Saint-Valéry-sur-Somme and that there, disappointed by his mistake, he conceived *The Poor Fisherman*.

7 Letter of 28 September 1879 (private collection).

8 'nous sommes de plus en plus dans une atmosphère absolument ennemie des conceptions imaginatives la photographie et les machines à coudre, ou autres sont l'expression vraie de notre temps - de là à une éclipse totale de toute aspiration personnelle et poëtique il n'y a pas loin....' Letter of 23 December 1879 (private collection).

9 Among the small oil sketches at its early stages see *Sketch for 'The Poor Fisherman'*, 165 x 237 mm, Musée d'Orsay, Paris (Inv. RF 1983-29); in addition see 1976-77 Paris/Ottawa, nos. 141-142, and also 237, a letter concerning *The Poor Fisherman*.

10 'puisque je ne mérite pas puisque j'aurais été le premier à me condamner. Rien ne peut donner une idée de la manière dont ce gradin de tableau détonne dans l'ensemble des autres – cela ne modifie en rien le sentiment qu'il peut contenir, mais le premier sentiment du badauc serait certainement la répulsion et nous n'avons pas le besoin de le mettre à cette épreuve.' Letter of 27 April 1881 to Valentine (private collection).

11 Arrêté 19 November 1887; he was paid 4,000 francs for it on 14 August 1888. The national collection was then housed at the Luxembourg Palace in Paris; in 1929 the painting was transferred to the Musée du Louvre, Paris; it is now at the Musée d'Orsay, Paris. On the acquisition of *The Poor Fisherman*, see also pp. 40-41.

12 'tout en étant loin de désavouer l'autre tableau [*The Poor Fisherman*] qui peut être curieux et interessant dans une galerie particulière, je ne le jugeais pas être un tableau du musée.' (Letter of 26 November 1887, Musée du Louvre, Cabinet des Dessins); see Vaisse (1980), p. 438 and p. 9; cf. 1976-77 Paris/Ottawa, no. 235.

13 'quand au pauvre pêcheur, l'affaire est en suspense de la manière la plus bête: le tableau était vendu à un amateur, quand le directeur des Beaux-Arts me fait savoir qu'il le veut pour le Luxembourg. L'état ayant priorité, on donne congé à l'amateur – c'est parfait mais on avait compté (malgré moi) sans le ministre qui déclare par 2 fois vouloir d'un autre tableau, à la place de celui-là, qu'il a choisi – me voilà donc entre l'enclume et le marteau, avec mon acheteur en moins car il est probable qu'il ne reviendra pas. L'affaire avait été engagée sans me consulter.' Letter of 4 December 1887 (private collection).

14 See the analysis in Neff (1969), 73-79.

15 Vachon [1900], p. 6.

16 'les vrais pauvres diables sont invisibles.' Letter of 29 December 1881 (private collection).

17 Nineteenth-century critics acknowledged Puvis's general debt to Millet, though the latter was sometimes not thought capable of 'grande peinture'; see Julien Cain and Paul Leprieur, *Millet* (Paris, n.d.), pp. 77-80. Some critics called Puvis a cross between Millet and Corot. When Puvis completed his pastoral *Saint Genevieve* murals in 1877 for the Panthéon he was hailed as the Millet of 'grand art' by J. Rouscanz, Directeur des Beaux-Arts, Brussels; letter of 7 [or 9?] July 1877 (private collection).

18 Jean Claude Chamboredon, 'Peinture des rapports sociaux et l'invention de l'éternel paysan,' *Actes de la recherche et Sciences sociales*, no. 17-18 (November 1977), pp. 6-28 and 22-28.

19 Jules Michelet, *La Mer* (Paris, 1861), pp. 406-407.

20 'La mère est morte (*sic jubeo*) et cependant que le père pêche, la fille commise à la garde de son petit frère se met à faire des bouquets, comme cela est si naturel!' Mauclair (1922), n.p.

21 'Ce n'est pas une femme, mais une fillette à l'âge ingrat. La mère est morte et la petite est là pour veiller sur son frère; elle cueille des fleurs avec sa petite main de singe, fièvreusement, machinalement. – L'enfant qui, dans cet étrange parterre n'en ferait pas autant serait en dehors de la nature. J'ai l'horreur du roman illustré à l'huile, ma seule excuse est de n'avoir emprunté qu'à moi-même cette vision de misère.' Vachon [1900], p. 160. One might speculate as to any possible personal meaning, given the death of Puvis's mother when he was sixteen and the protective familial care rendered by his own older sisters.

22 See J. M. Edmonds, *The Greek Bucolic Poets* (Cambridge, Mass. and London, 1927), pp. 247-252.

23 Poggioli (1975), p. 7.

24 Poggioli (1975), pp. 7-8.

25 'Je ne veux point de ce dieu pitoyable qui accepte les coups.' August Strindberg, 'Préface,' Paris, Hôtel Drouot, 'Vente de tableaux et dessins par Paul Gauguin' (18 February 1895), p. 5. In this famous letter he refused to write an introduction for a sales catalogue of Gauguin's work (because he did not like it). Gauguin in fact used the letter as his preface. Strindberg also gave the painting a banal narrative: the woman was the fisherman's wife who would give him her faithful love when he brought home his prey. For further on the Puvis/Gauguin relationship, see cat. 146 and 148.

26 Guigou (1898), pp. 277-278. Puvis had a photograph of one such image, perhaps this one; it was extremely faded and almost illegible ca. 1972 when this author viewed it in a portfolio of Puvis's belongings (private collection). It is apparently now lost.

27 Though painted in Rome, Puvis might have seen it in Henner's studio, in the same building as his own.

28 'personnages aux formes grêles et élancées, aux extremités anguleuses et effilées; dans les parties nues, l'ostéologie et la peau sont curieusement étudiées et le muscle presque effacé' with a 'coloration pâle et froide.' in 'Les Peintres primitifs,' *L'Artiste*, s7, III (7 February 1858), 86. Also see Suzanne Sulzberger, *La Réhabilitation des primitifs flamands 1802-1867* (Brussels, 1961).

29 Compare Poggioli (1975), pp. 17, 107. These ideas about early Christianity surely colored Puvis's interpretation of the young Genevieve for the Panthéon as well.

30 Maurice Denis also detected Renan's influence, see Denis (1957-59), III, p. 69.

31 See p. 26, note 79.

32 Destroyed (?); stolen from Puvis's studio during the siege of Paris. See Mourey (1895), repr. 173; compare *Drawing for Meditation*, Musée des

Beaux-Arts, Lille (Inv. 2039).

33 Marie-Christine Boucher, 1976-77 Paris/Ottawa, p. 47; the work discussed in the author's forthcoming book.

34 'La contagion Musset et Sénancour n'est pour rien dans mon affaire: je suis ainsi, et si misérable que le soleil me fatigue la vue et me trouble l'âme, surtout ce soleil d'automne, qui brille comme un insensé et ne chauffe pas....' Mandach and Wehrlé (1910), 681-682. Alfred du Musset's *La Confession d'un enfant du siècle* (1836) is about moral solitude; Etienne de Sénancour wrote *Oberman* (1804), about the longings of a 'feeling' man; and in 1819 *Libres méditations d'un solitaire inconnu sur le détachement du monde et sur d'autres objets de la morale religieuse*.

35 Baudelaire, 'Salon de 1846,' *OC* (1958), pp. 628-629. See also Brown Price (1972), p. 319, notes 229-230.

36 An extensive literature ranges through religious and social alienation augmented by such issues as the industrial revolution and the rise of cities. See René Canat, *Une Forme du Mal du Siècle, Du Sentiment de la Solitude morale au XIXe siècle. Chez les Romantiques et les Parnassiens* (Paris, 1904); and on pervasive moral solitude and disillusionment, increased by the 1870-71 defeat, see William Hauptman, *The Persistence of Melancholy in Nineteenth Century Art: The Iconography of a Motif.* University Microfilms, 1975. Feydy (1955-56) notes its beginnings in Hugo's *Préface de Cromwell* which was written in 1827.

37 Feydy (1955-56), 19-20.

38 'Se rappeler qu'un tableau – avant d'être un cheval de bataille, une femme nue ou une quelconque anecdote – est essentiellement une surface plane recouverte de couleurs en un certain ordre assemblées.' Denis's doctrine of Neo-Traditionism first appeared under the pseudonym Pierre Louis as ['Notes d'Art'] 'Définition du neo-traditionnisme' in Denis (1890), 540; reissued in Denis (1913), p. 1; see also Denis (1964), pp. 33-34, 58.

39 'because a painting, having to be in and of itself a totality, an absolute and complete image, the strict likeness of represented objects becomes here a necessary contrivance, one of the principal rules of execution. There [in architectural decoration], however, it is less a question of creating an illusion ... where the planar surface ... does not simulate depth or relief without upsetting the management of the adjacent planar surfaces and even the proportions of the building, it is expedient to treat tone and effect with extreme sobriety, and to leave in a state of summary outlines what would be proper to broach elsewhere without detours and translate without reserve.' ('parce qu'un tableau devant être par lui-même un tout, une image absolue et complète, la stricte vraisemblance des objets réprésentés devient ici un moyen nécessaire, une loi formelle de l'exécution. Là cependant [dans un travail de décoration architecturale] où il s'agit bien moins de faire illusion aux yeux ... où la surface plane réservée au pinceau ne saurait simuler la profondeur ou le relief sans bouleverser l'économie des voisines et les proportions mêmes de l'édifice, il est opportun, il est utile de traiter le ton et l'effet avec un extrême sobriété, et de laisser à l'état d'aperçus des faits qu'il conviendrait d'aborder ailleurs sans détours et de traduire sans réticences.' Delaborde (1859), 882.

40 Huysmans (1883), pp. 178-179; see also Feydy (1955-56), 19-20; and Karageorgevitch (1894), 74.

41 'Oui ... il est là, il pêche, il pêche dans de l'eau, dans de l'eau qui n'est pas de l'eau qu'est-ce que tu veux qu'il prenne?' 'Papiers Nadar,' Bibliothèque Nationale, Paris, n.a.f. 25016, f. 77, noted that Grévin carried malice to everything.

42 Maillol also made a copy after a right-hand segment of Puvis's *Pastoral Life of Saint Genevieve* (private collection, London; it is there attributed to Puvis). See also Wendy Slatkin, *Aristide Maillol in the 1890s* (UMI Research Press, Ann Arbor, Mich., 1982 [1976 thesis]), p. 20. Compare also to the Puvis prototype Maillol's *Prodigal Son* (collection Dominique Denis, Saint-Germain-en-Laye).

43 See 1976-77 Paris/Ottawa, no. 138 for a list.

44 Also see *April* (private collection, Brussels), *Revue de l'art* no. 96 (1992), repr. cover.

45 Compare Denis's similarly posed *Portrait of Mademoiselle Yvonne Lerolle in Three Poses*, 1897(Josefowitz Collection).

46 In Fénéon (1886), reprinted in *Oeuvres* (Paris, 1948), pp. 80-81; see Paul Alexis writing under the pseudonym 'Trublot,' in *Le Cri du Peuple* and quoted in John Rewald, *Georges Seurat* (Paris, 1948), p. 46. Nicolson (1962), 214, points out that Fénéon's statement was misprinted as 'Paris modernisant,' when it first appeared.

47 1991-92, Paris, Grand Palais / New York, Metropolitan Museum of Art, *Seurat*, no. 76, pp. 150, 183-184.

48 Bequest Edith K. Wetmore; according to a 3 March 1937 bill to Miss Wetmore, it was also from the collection of Félix Fénéon.

49 Whereabouts unknown, formerly collection Hugo Perls, exhibited at 1960 Paris, Galerie Charpentier, *Cent oeuvres de Gauguin*, no. 99.

50 'L'Amphitrite britannique, qui se moque du Kaiser, de ses mines et de ses zeppelins, prend le *pauvre pêcheur* sous sa protection.' Silver (1989), p. 104, repr. fig. 74.

51 *Le Canard enchaîné* (17 August 1977), 1 (Courtesy Documentation Department, Musée d'Orsay, Paris).

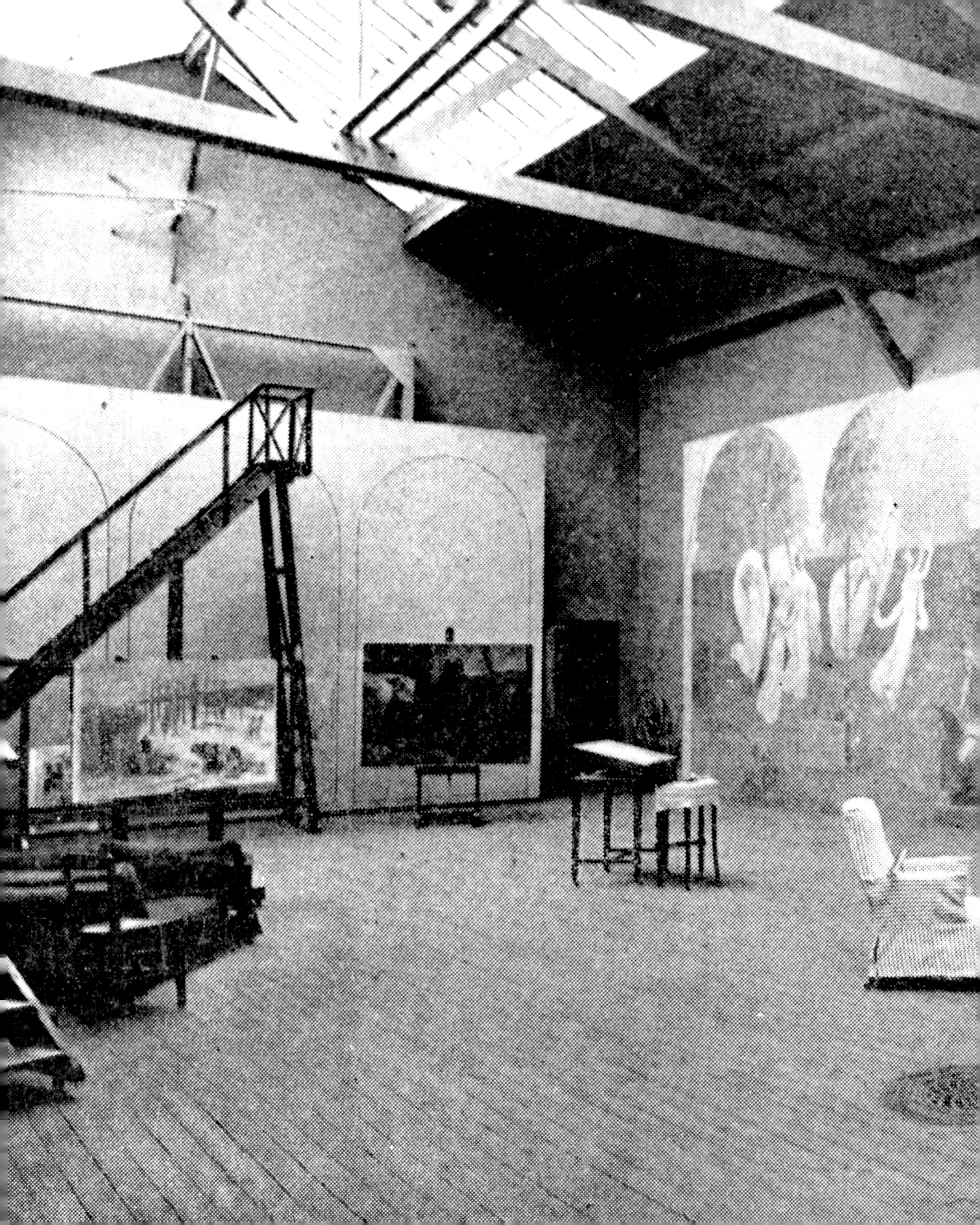

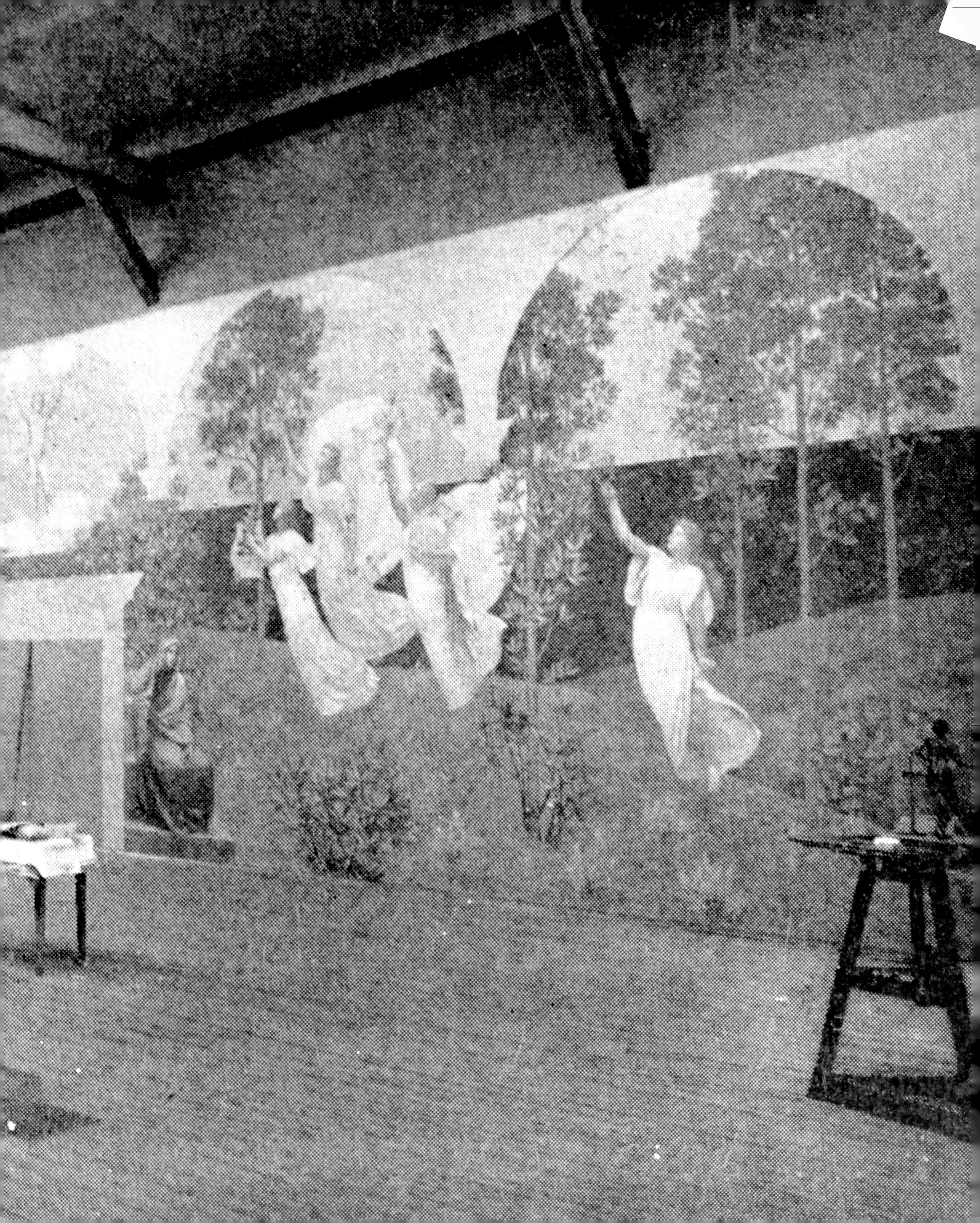

Catalogue

Titles

The artist's own title is given, where possible, or that given to the work when it was first exhibited or sold. Otherwise, the title is that most frequently used in the literature or the author's own descriptive one.

Dates

When a painting is dated, it is so indicated. Approximate dates are preceded by 'ca.' With rare exceptions the drawings were not dated by the artist; they are dated here in conjunction with the paintings to which they relate and on the basis of stylistic criteria.

Signatures and Inscriptions

The following abbreviations are used to locate signatures and inscriptions: u. (upper); l. (lower); l. (left); r. (right); m. (middle).

Atelier Stamp

After Puvis de Chavannes's death, his notary, Maître Delapalme, aided by the painter's assistant Victor Koos, inventoried the works in Puvis's flat and studio. A red wax atelier seal was affixed verso on paintings (as there was no sale, this was not a *cachet de vente*); works on paper received 'côte' (section or, evidently, cabinet locations) and 'pièce' (item) numbers and were initialed by Delapalme with a curly and often misread 'D.' They were stamped 'P.P.C.' The absence of such a stamp does not indicate that a drawing is not authentic, only that it was not among the artist's holdings at his death. Nor is a stamp as such an incontrovertible sign of authenticity, as at least two false stamps exist. Drawings with an authentic stamp are so noted.

Measurements

The measurements of works on paper are given in millimeters and those of other works in centimeters; height precedes width. Most measurements have been verified by the author. 'Sight' measurements are given for those works that could be measured only matted and framed.

Provenance

Provenance is listed in sequence as far as possible.

Selected Exhibitions

Only exhibitions held during the lifetime of the artist and in the year after his death are included, and a very few major exhibitions thereafter: 1937 Lyons; 1972 London/Liverpool; 1975 Toronto; and 1976-77 Paris/Ottawa. The exhibition history of the drawings is difficult to sort out and, for the most part, severely wanting: in catalogues titles are often vague, dimensions and collection omitted, descriptions non-existent. Moreover, records are rarely kept of drawings in private collections and commerce. Therefore, with rare exceptions, only the 1976-77 Paris/Ottawa exhibition is included.

Selected References

The Puvis literature is extensive. Only the most important substantive contributions are here included unless a work is relatively unfamiliar and source material rare, in which case a special attempt at completeness has been made. Specific references to monograph discussions are for the most part not included. The author's doctoral dissertation (Brown Price [1972]) has served as the basis for this catalogue and is not cited under individual entries. Exhibition catalogues that provide discussions of individual works are listed under 'Selected Exhibitions' to avoid repetition. Catalogues of lending institutions are included only if their analyses have added to our discussion.

NB: Complete references, exhibition histories and bibliography are to be included in the author's monograph and catalogue raisonné of the painted works of Puvis de Chavannes, now being prepared for publication.

1

Negro Boy / *Négrillon* 1850

Signed and dated l.l.: P. Puvis Ch 1850
Oil on canvas, 103 x 77.5 cm
Private collection

Provenance Artist's heirs and by descent.
Selected Exhibitions 1976-77 Paris/Ottawa, no. 2.
Selected References Jullian (1938), 240, 243.

In what is essentially an 'académie d'homme,' an exercise in painting a model after life as was prescribed to students following the traditional methods of the fine arts academy, this sensual, young model is spruced up with exotic accoutrements: a red hat, sword and escutcheon or purse that yield an 'Orientalizing,' romantic and sumptuous appearance. No narrative is indicated. The semi-frontal seated pose, the cloth-draped seat and the ruins in the background all presage *Hope* (fig. 4) of some two decades later. The dark-skinned boy is used to exotic and coloristically rich advantage against the turquoise sky and peach-colored clouds, in a manner familiar from Delacroix's canvases. At mid-century in a like manner Alexandre Decamps and Théodore Chassériau used dark-skinned models. Soon Puvis was to abjure the use of shading and highlights, but here he used a palette of transparent glazes of fervid reds, tawny browns and clear turquoises with shifting tones.

Puvis must have taken on the figure to demonstrate his capabilities. These years he executed several relatively large individual figure studies of like composition, with the romanticized figures set in a landscape, a colorful sky in the background. *Diogenes* of 1851, a muscular old man holding up a lamp (two versions, private collections), is such a figure. Exploring various physical types and physiognomies Puvis also executed another painting of a black model, a *Saint Sebastian* (private collection).

2

Study for 'Mademoiselle de Sombreuil Drinking a Glass of Blood to Save Her Father's Life' ca. 1853

Stamp l.r.
Black chalk and pencil on paper, 168 x 128 mm
Private collection

Provenance Artist's studio; artist's heirs and by descent.
Selected References On the painting: Vachon [1900], pp. 61-62; Riotor (April 1896), 266 (listed however as destroyed); Bréghot du Lut (1899), *Le Peintre Puvis de Chavannes: Son oeuvre et sa famille*, p. 11; Bréghot du Lut (1899), *Revue du Lyonnais*, 272; Mauclair (1928), pp. 6-7; Jullian (1938), 240, 243-245, repr. fig. 6.

This is one of at least two drawings[1] for one of the largest (165 x 123 cm) and most complex of Puvis de Chavannes's earliest compositions, *Mademoiselle de Sombreuil Drinking a Glass of Blood to Save Her Father's Life* (*Mademoiselle de Sombreuil buvant un verre de sang pour sauver la vie de son père*) of 1853 (private collection). The more distinct and developed of the two studies (the other hones in on the center section, followed in the painting), it shows a tumultuous street scene contrived to transmit an excited hubbub. Throngs of figures are gathered and gesture dramatically. In the center foreground, a man with his back to us kneels over a prone figure and holds something up to a woman who lunges diagonally forward to reach for it; the pair are encircled by a crowd of other figures, many with their arms raised, one with a musket to his side. Multi-storied buildings are sketched in, a man with a crutch collapses on steps to the left; another figure stands above the crowd brandishing a cloth and holding on to an arched support.

The subject is drawn from a legendary episode of the French Revolution. In September 1792, Marie-Maurille de Sombreuil (1767-1823) defended her father, the imprisoned governor of the Invalides and a Marquis, before a so-called 'jury of the people'; after his acquittal she reputedly was exhorted to drink a concoction mixed with blood, 'à la santé de la Nation.' Contemporaries wrote of her filial devotion without mentioning the blood-laced drink, but by 1800 the story appeared in Ernest Legouvé's *Le Mérite des Femmes*; it was repeated in Victor Hugo's 'La Mort de Mademoiselle de Sombreuil' of 1823 (Ode 9 of *Odes et poésies diverses*);[2] and by Jules Michelet, who reported that Mlle de Sombreuil reputedly swore allegiance to the Revolution and sipped the blood of aristocrats.[3] Alphonse de Lamartine, whom Puvis admired, movingly recounted the episode in his *Histoire des Girondins* (1847), perhaps the source for the painting. As Lamartine wrote: 'Her gesture, her sex, her youth, her disheveled hair, her beauty augmented by the emotion of her soul, her sublime devotion, the ardor of her attentions touched these hired assassins.... As a sign of renunciation of the aristocracy, they demanded she wet her lips with aristocrats' blood that filled a glass. Mademoiselle de Sombreuil grasped the glass with a fearless hand and carried it to her mouth and drank to her father's health. This gesture saved her. They shared in her joy: her assassins' tears mingled with her own.'[4]

Mlle de Sombreuil depicts a woman's valiant act, an ordinary person moved to an extraordinary feat (as Augustin Thierry would

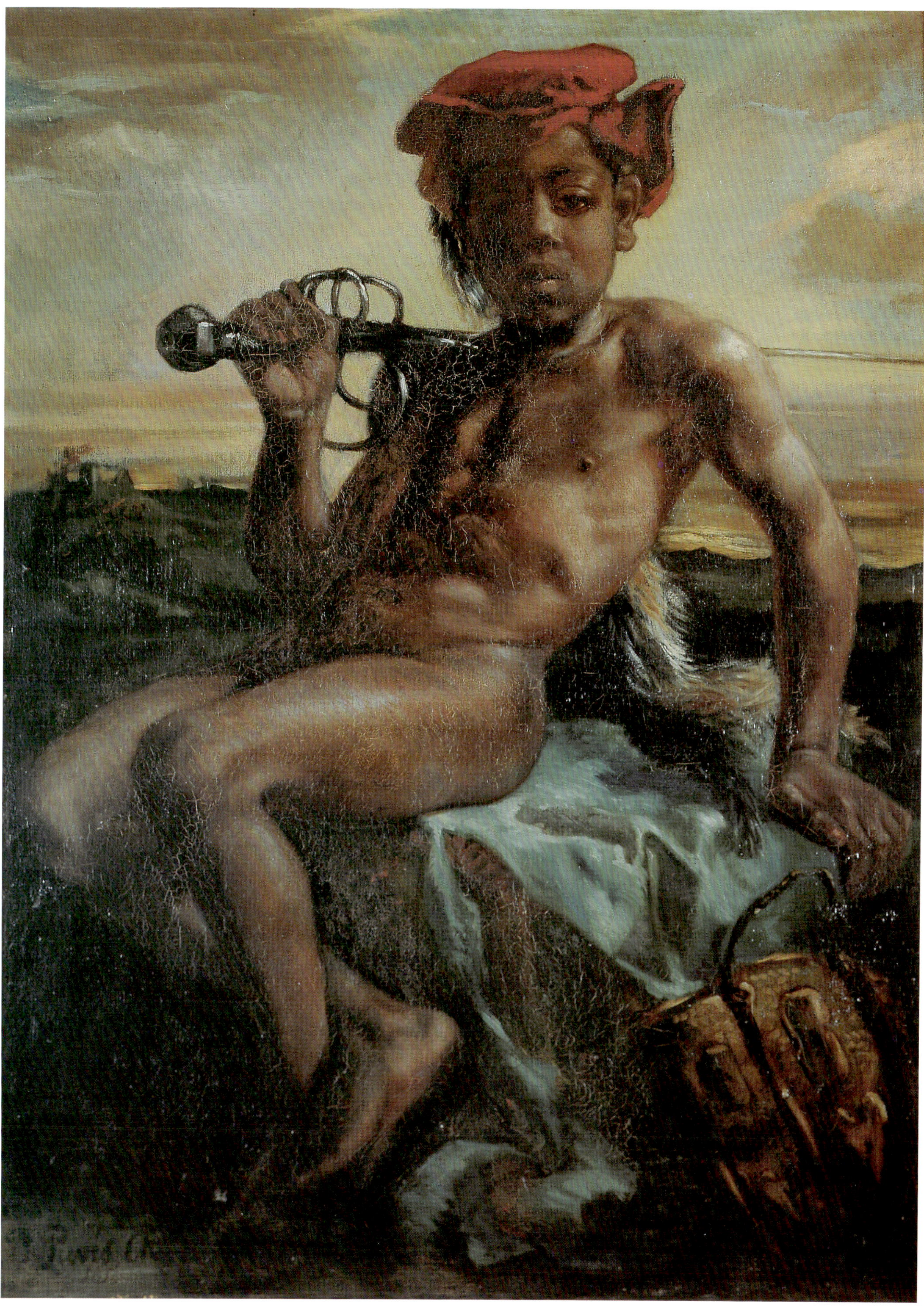

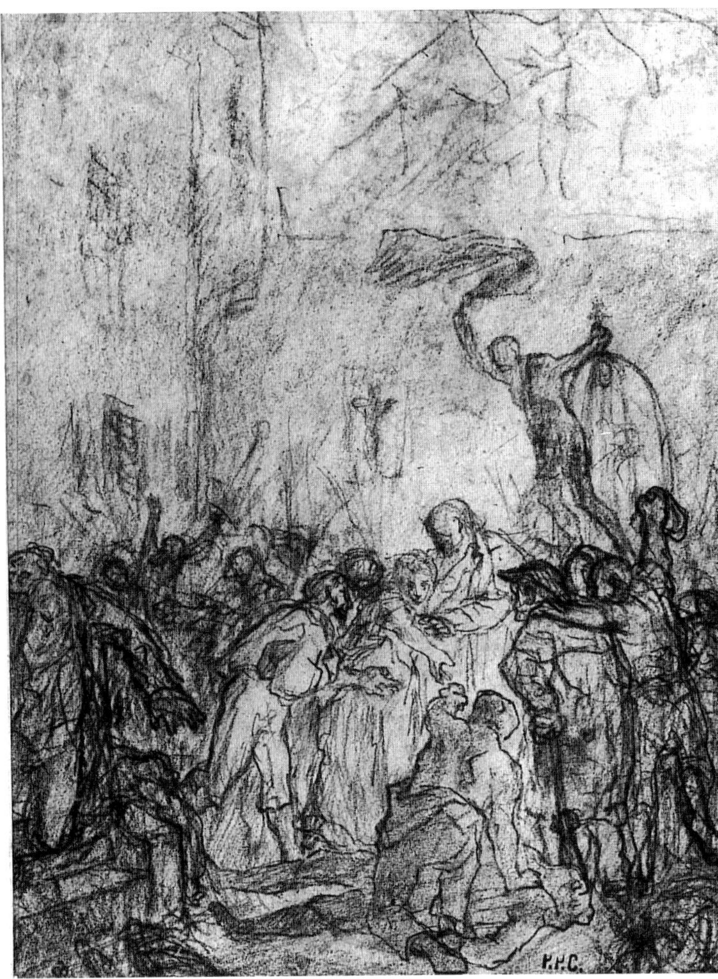

have it in his 1820 *Lettres sur l'histoire de la France*), an action of high drama that the Romantics and Royalists could warm to, that of the heroism of the nobility in the face of insurrection. It was perhaps for that reason that the young artist with his aristocratic leanings[5] was attracted to the theme, as well as for its relative obscurity: these years he sought to depict dramatic and moralizing themes from French history that were not often represented.[6] Here traditional values of loyalty, family, order and devotion are displayed amidst revolutionary upheaval.

In the drawing, the young woman reaches for the famous glass, while supporting her father. Such highly charged commotion is unusual in Puvis's oeuvre, and one critic claimed he rebuffed the painting ('tableau que Puvis a mis au rebut').[7] Many of the figures, smaller, detailed groupings and incidental action of this drawing were to be edited out and are no longer evident in the darkly dramatic definitive canvas.[8]

Puvis may have been inspired by his teacher Henri Scheffer's *Arrest of Charlotte Corday* (Salon of 1831).[9] It too is a revolutionary theme with an excited mob to which Puvis's preliminary drawing in particular bears resemblance.

1 See *Dramatic Scene*, Musée des Beaux-Arts, Marseilles (Inv. D151, Aug. 464); 1984-85 Marseilles, repr. no. 76.

2 Hugo dedicated an 'Ode' to Mlle de Sombreuil in *Les Massacres des Prisonniers de l'Abbaye en 1792*; and alluded to her in Odes 3 and 4 (all early poems written when he had Royalist sympathies); see *Odes et Ballades* (Paris, 1845).

3 J. Michelet, *Histoire de la Revolution française* (Paris, 1849), IV, pp. 161-163.

4 'Son geste, son sexe, sa jeunesse, ses cheveux épars, sa beauté accrue par l'émotion de son âme, la sublimité de son dévouement, l'ardeur de ses applications attendrissent ces sicaires.... On veut qu'en signe d'abjuration de l'aristocratie, elle trempe ses lèvres dans un verre rempli du sang, des aristocrates. Mademoiselle de Sombreuil saisit le verre d'une main intrepide, le porte à sa bouche et boit au Salut de son père. Ce geste la sauve. On s'associe à sa joie: les larmes de ses assassins se mêlent aux siennes.'

5 Of significant social standing, the family, like many others, had abandoned the aristocratic particle 'de Chavannes' at the time of the Revolution, but after 24 January 1852 (when titles of nobility were officially reestablished), asserting their lineage, contrived to have it restored, a matter accomplished on 20 May 1859. See Bréghot du Lut (1899), *Le peintre Puvis de Chavannes: Son oeuvre et sa famille*, p. 397, and Augagneur-Prost (1991), 158.

6 See his *Jean Cavalier at the Bed of his Dying Mother* (Musée des Beaux-Arts, Lyons), also a tale of filial piety; see Brown Price (1992).

7 Jullian (1938), 240.

8 The canvas may also have further darkened over the years.

9 Versions in the Musée des Beaux-Arts, Grenoble and the Walker Art Gallery, Liverpool; a preliminary version, Maison Renan-Scheffer (Musée de la vie romantique), Paris.

3

Nude Standing Man Holding a Saber in His Right Hand, Drawing Related to 'Mademoiselle de Sombreuil' ca. 1853

Black chalk on discolored, greenish paper,
218 x 149 mm
Musée du Petit Palais, Paris (Inv. PPD 258^2; MCB 1)

Provenance Bequest of artist's heirs to the city of Paris (1898); deposited in the Musée Galliera (1899); transferred to the Musée du Petit Palais upon its opening (1901).
Selected References Boucher (1979), no. 1.

This vigorous drawing of a broad-chested nude male of somewhat stocky proportions, his extended arm grasping a sword hilt, relates to Puvis's dramatic 1853 canvas, *Mademoiselle de Sombreuil* (see cat. 2), though

3

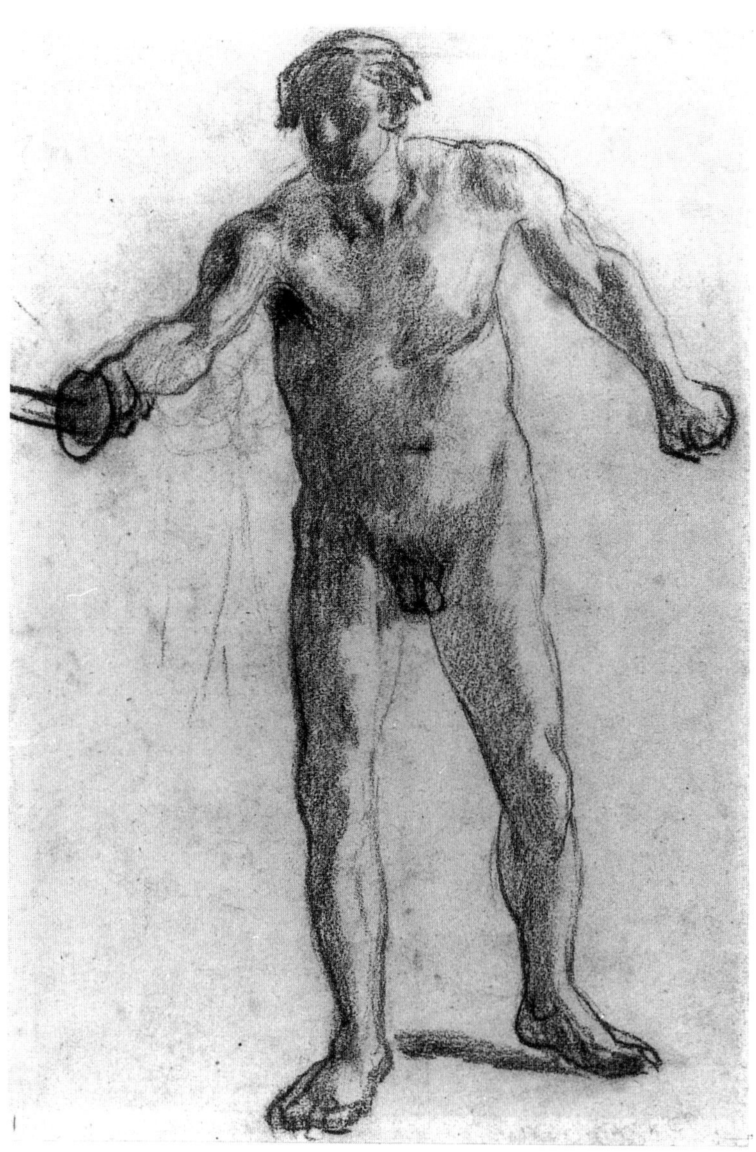

as finally constituted, the composition has no such figure. In a violently expressive, almost caricatural related drawing,[1] a similarly posed figure runs through another figure with his sword; as Marie-Christine Boucher has pointed out, the latter is dressed in eighteenth-century garb, an epoch represented in no other painting by Puvis, and she persuasively concludes that this drawing should be associated with *Mademoiselle de Sombreuil*.[2]

The rugged, if somewhat ungainly pose and forceful, if approximate anatomy also reinforces the idea of an early drawing. The torso is defined in a series of slightly abrupt, curving lines. The topography of face and body are comprised of half-tone areas, the shaping of which obviously fascinated the artist. Thus, the rather square face is almost completely shaded into shapes that only suggest facial features.

1 *Drawing of a Man*, Musée Sainte-Croix de Poitiers (Inv. 899.1.48).

2 See Boucher (1979), no. 1.

4

Study for 'The Return of the Prodigal Son' / *Etude pour 'Le retour de l'enfant prodigue'* 1854

Signed and dated l.l.: P. P. C. 54
Oil on canvas, 52.5 x 67 cm
Private collection

Provenance Artist's heirs and by descent.
Selected Exhibitions 1976-77 Paris/Ottawa, no. 11.
Selected References On the dining room: Segard (March 1914), 5-9, 14, repr. 5; Sâr Josephin Péladan, *L'Art ochlocratique, Salons de 1882 et 1883*, vol. I, *La Décadence esthétique* (Paris, 1888), pp. 25, 48; Vachon (1895), p. 77; Bréghot du Lut (1899), *Revue du Lyonnais*, 266-280; Mandach and Wehrlé (1911), 456; Jullian (1938), 245-248; Chagny (15 September 1959), n.p.; d'Argencourt (1973), pp. 71-82; 1976-77 Paris/Ottawa, pp. 35-41, nos. 10-14.

In 1854-55, Puvis de Chavannes executed his first murals, a series of oil on canvas panels to be inserted into the menuiserie of the handsome dining room walls of the family château.[1] It is for the climactic, large (252 x 352 cm) *Return of the Prodigal Son* (*Le retour de l'enfant prodigue*, fig. 2),[2] that the canvas shown here is a study. Puvis later described the project: 'The dining room of the Château of X..., exactly as large as my Paris atelier, was entirely painted by me in 1854. One can see the Four Seasons there, plus the Return of the Prodigal Son with the necessary calf. It was some nerve on my part, and the family must have had quite some trepidation. Think of it, a completely new beautiful dining room! Evidently, if one were to redo it, it would be better, I believe; but, however, for my debut in decorative art, it's fine. In any case, I found my road to Damascus.'[3] All of the main panels have biblical sources but are designed to be suitable for the dining hall of a country estate. The four other principal panels represent the seasons through biblical scenes in which labors associated with the production of foodstuffs and drink are depicted: *Spring* is fishing, *The Miraculous Draught of Fishes*, symbolic of Christ as the fisher of men; *Summer* is the harvest, *The Gleaners* or *Ruth and Boaz* – Ruth worked in Boaz's fields before she became his wife; the harvesting of grapes and making of wine, *The Vintage*, from the story of Noah represents *Autumn*; and *Winter* is *The Return from the Hunt* or *The Hunt of Esau*. There are four overdoors, *The Sciences*, *The Arts*, *War* and *Peace*.

The Return of the Prodigal Son is interpreted as an opulent genre scene, in which servants make preparations for a feast and carry out the

4

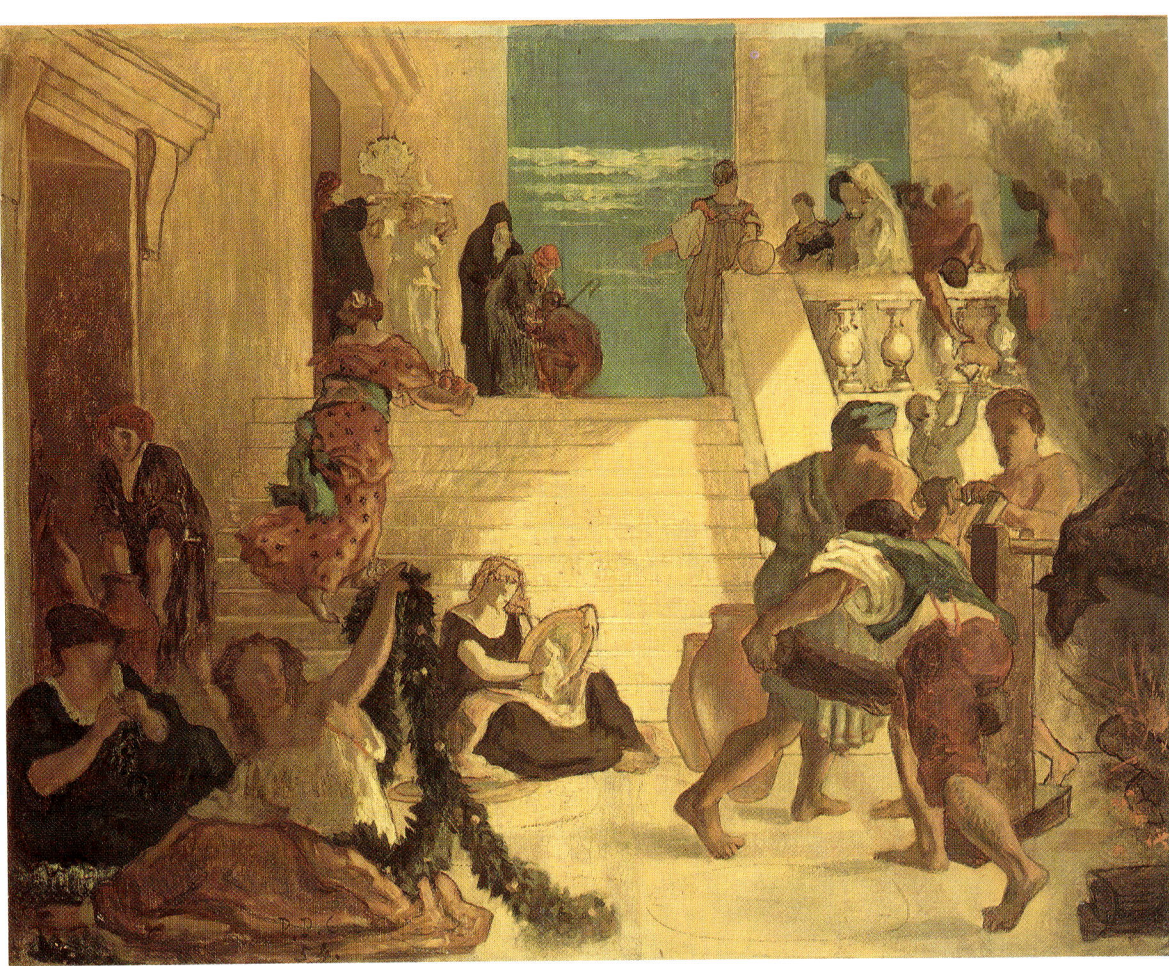

tasks of a wealthy sixteenth-century Venetian household. Amidst the bustle of activity, the son's arrival passes almost unnoticed at the top of the stairs and deflects the customary moralizing lesson of the parable. This way of domesticating pious biblical stories as background vignettes, to be searched out behind ample victuals, was a scheme employed by seventeenth-century Dutch artists. Given the site, a room to be used for festive gatherings, and Puvis's wit (see cat. 6, his caricature of this composition), the theme may well make wry reference to the artist himself as prodigal, having gone to Paris to be educated as a polytechnician-engineer (his father had hoped), but become an artist instead, and now returned to the family fold.

The main elements of the mural are mapped out in this oil study: the architectural setting, the placement of the figures and the play of light creating trapezoidal forms on the steps (the source of actual light is from windows on the right). Puvis relied on others for the authoritative composition, as is not unusual for a beginning artist. The architectural setting of a grand staircase and balustrade, the vivid turquoise sky and ample figures in lavish, brilliant costumes, the rich harmonies of color and general bustle derive from sixteenth-century Venetian painting, specifically Veronese – a like section of whose *Presentation of the Virgin* (Palazzo Ducale, Venice) with precisely these elements Puvis had copied (private collection). Similarities have also been noted to Veronese's *Marriage at Cana* (Musée du Louvre, Paris), Raphael's *Fire in the Borgo* (Vatican Museums) (the woman mounting the stairs) and to Tintoretto.[4] Among contemporaries, Puvis may have found inspiration in one of Courbet's figures in *The Grain Sifters* (Musée des Beaux-Arts, Nantes).[5] The wide stairway, moreover, resembles that in Delacroix's imposing *Execution of Marino Faliero* (Wallace Collection, London) that Puvis could have seen in 1854-55 in Delacroix's studio at Notre Dame de Lorette.

Costumes, details, facial features, a tilt of a head, a cap, a patterned cloth were more sharply defined or somewhat changed in the mural; this is particularly true of the figures to the right who would be garbed in more exotic costumes of patterned fabrics. Already sensitive to the colors of the architecture, as he would continue to be throughout his career as a muralist, Puvis used a robust palette rich in light golden browns, the color of the wood paneling in the dining room. The colors of the sketch, in which tans, reds and turquoise predominate, are not dissimilar from those of Delacroix. In the mural there would also be maroons, pinks and lime. The vivaciousness of this study and the verve of the brushwork were somewhat toned down and hardened in the less intimate wall painting.

5 1 *Summer* and *Winter* are each 250 x 222 cm; *Spring* and *Autumn* are 250 x 205 cm; the overdoors, *The Arts* and *The Sciences* are 45 x 99 cm, and *War* and *Peace* 45 x 151 cm. Slightly earlier, most probably, Puvis collaborated with his friend Bellet du Poisat on exterior frescoes for an annex.

2 The only painting signed and dated; the inscription reads: 'For all the paintings in this room, Pierre Puvis de Chavannes, 1855' ('Pour toutes les peintures de cette salle, Pierre Puvis de Chavannes, 1855').

3 'La salle à manger du château de X..., grande exactement comme mon atelier de Paris, a été peinte entièrement par moi, en 1854. On y voit les Quatre Saisons, plus le retour de l'Enfant Prodigue, avec le veau de rigueur. C'était du toupet de ma part, et la famille a dû avoir une fière peur. Songez donc, une belle salle à manger toute neuve! Evidemment, si c'était à refaire ce serait mieux, je crois; mais cependant, pour mes débuts dans l'art décoratif, c'est supportable. Dans tous les cas, j'ai trouvé mon chemin de Damas.' Mandach and Wehrlé (1911), 456.

4 Jullian (1938), 248.

5 Louise d'Argencourt in 1976-77 Paris/Ottawa, no. 11, points out a congruency of the left-hand side of the composition, which we cannot agree with; however, the central figure is strikingly similar; the dates of the Courbet may be 1853-54 as she asserts, or 1855, too late to explain the coincidence.

5

Study for a Male Figure in 'The Return of the Prodigal Son' ca. 1854

Verso: A lighter sketch of the same figure, apparently a first effort
Black chalk on blue-gray paper, 310 x 239 mm
Fitzwilliam Museum, Cambridge (Inv. PD 86-1961)

Provenance London, Christie's, executor's sale C.H. Dancocks (28 November 1908), lot 16; Louis C.G. Clarke; bequeathed to the museum by the latter (1960).

Selected Exhibitions [Exhibited as Millet at:] 1956, London / Aldeburgh / Cardiff (Arts Council of Great Britain), *Drawings by Jean-François Millet*, no. 2, pl. III; 1969, London, Wildenstein & Co., *Jean-François Millet*, no. 16, repr.; 1976, Paris, Heim Gallery / Lille, Musée des Beaux-Arts / Strasbourg, Musée des Beaux-Arts, *Cent dessins français du Fitzwilliam Museum, Cambridge*, no. 66; 1976-77, New York, Pierpont Morgan Library and International Exhibitions Foundation tour, *European Drawings from the Fitzwilliam*, no. 110.

Selected References Léonce Bénédite, *The Drawings of Jean François Millet* (London and Philadelphia, 1906), pl. 19; *The* [London] *Times* (17 August 1956), n.p.; Wheelock Whitney III, letter of 29 November 1977 to the Fitzwilliam Museum, Cambridge; Louis-Antoine Prat, 'A Drawing by Puvis de Chavannes at the Fitzwilliam Museum in Cambridge,' *Master Drawings*, vol. XVIII (1980), 38-40.

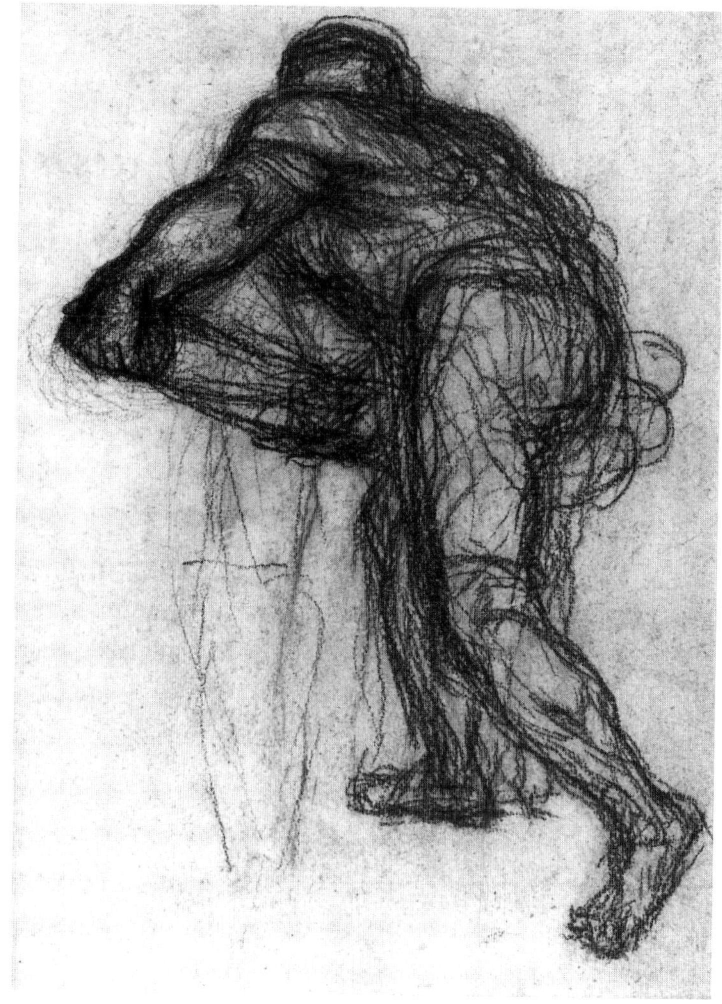

This vigorous, hardy drawing is a study for the foreground figure at the right delivering a log for the fire in *The Return of the Prodigal Son* (fig. 2; see also cat. 4). The pose must have given Puvis some trouble because of its foreshortening and the complexity of the diagonal thrust; the figure, with his back to the viewer, pitches forward and leans into the picture while balancing himself with his extended back leg.[1] Puvis described the action with a multitude of energetic lines, feeling for the form, finding the best lines to describe his figure and emphasizing them.

Doubtless because of its rough style, strong curved strokes and theme of an anonymous laboring figure, bending to concentrate on his work, this drawing was for several decades ascribed to and exhibited as that of Jean-François Millet.[2] Puvis admired the older master and several

6

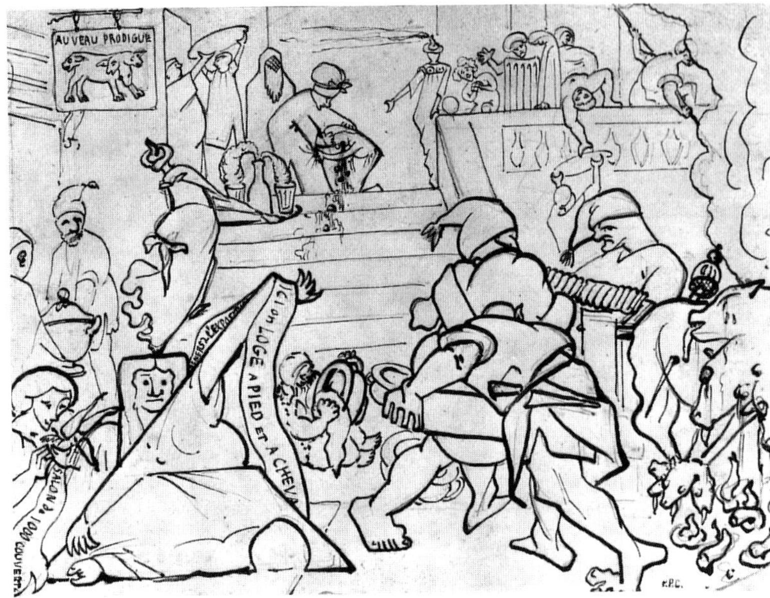

of Puvis's most important works, such as *The Poor Fisherman* (fig. 23), would owe a debt to the Barbizon painter. Indeed, Puvis once visited Millet.[3] At the end of Puvis's career, Emile Bergerat recognized Puvis's affinity to Millet and Corot in a poem, which was included in a special album presented to him at an 1895 banquet in his honor:

> 'Deux aïeux t'ont légué leurs domaines divers,
> Millet, son travailleur aux gravités tragiques,
> Corot, son Arcadie aux crépuscules verts....'[4]

1 The drawing is matted so that the mise-en-page is not visible, but the sheet extends farther at the top and right.

2 Millet executed a figure of similar pose: *A Haymaker Seen from the Back* of 1850-51, Musée du Louvre, Paris (Inv. RF 11350). The reattribution to Puvis was first made by Wheelock Whitney III in 1977 (ref. above).

3 Conrad de Mandach, 'Léon Belly,' *Gazette des Beaux-Arts* (January 1913), 76.

4 'Two forbears have bequeathed to you their diverse domains,/ Millet, his laborer of tragic gravity, Corot,/ his Arcadia of green twilights....' Reproduced in *La Plume* (1895), 55.

6

Caricatural Drawing 'At the Prodigal Calf's' ca. 1854-57

Stamp l.r.; marked l.r.: Benon[1]
Pen, ink and pencil on paper, laid down on cardboard, 214 x 286 mm
Private collection

Provenance Artist's heirs and by descent.
Selected References Letter of 25 April 1937 (private collection); 1976-77 Paris/Ottawa, no. 11; Brown Price (1991), 121-122, repr. fig. 3.

Beginning when he was a schoolboy in the 1840s and continuing throughout his life, Puvis did caricatural drawings.[2] A small number form a distinct stylistic and thematic group: these are stiffly outlined, tight little figurations, drawn with the utmost graphic control.[3] All remarkably parody his own 1850s paintings – those he meant to be among his most important to date – and contain figures and objects that carry through the group. Although 'serious' art was a source of ridicule for caricaturists from mid-century, it is noteworthy that Puvis would use his own paintings as a comic vehicle at a time when his paintings were repeatedly submitted to and rejected by the Salon (1851 to 1859). It is not surprising that most make the Salon the butt of their biting wit and hostility.

In his caricature of *The Return of the Prodigal Son* (fig. 2, see also cat. 4), a sign at the upper left identifies the setting as a tavern or inn, 'Au veau prodigue' ('At the Prodigal Calf's'), and pictures a multi-headed (excessive or prodigal) calf, while a similarly grotesque animal is being roasted to feed the gathering crowd. Much else is excessive in the chaotic scene. Preparations are under way for Salon activities: a banner (replacing the garland held by the woman to the lower left in the painting) announces a Salon of one thousand places. A streamer reads 'Diners à l'Exposition ... Ici on loge à pied et à cheval' ('Exhibition Dinners ... accommodation here for man and horse'), a barb implying the Salon lodges beasts and artists, hardly differentiating between the two. Chamber pots, a favored item in these caricatures, replace the trays a woman polishes in the foreground, and all manner of bizarre persons, one with breasts exposed, another topsy-turvy, are on the terrace that Veronese-like figures inhabit in the painting. The woman mounting the stairs carries a foaming beer bottle, and at its top the prodigal son kneels to vomit. Thus, the opulent Venetian setting has been transformed into a bustling inn of near pandemonium in which prodigality is literally manifest in the many-headed calf.

Puvis's caricatures were essentially private works: he gave some to friends, but kept most. Today these are for the most part still in the collections of collateral descendants. In his lifetime, only a few of his tamest caricatures and grotesques were published,[4] and this was towards the end of his life when his reputation as a painter of public murals had been well established. Puvis was hesitant at least through the 1870s about letting even his easel paintings be known, concerned that they might detract from his murals or jeopardize commissions. Critical opinion did not allow an artist much range, he said, and a painter who paints large must not paint small.[5] He was still less likely to let his caricatures reach the public. In fact, their first publication was greeted with incredulity, and only several years after his death was a whole album published.[6] Most accounts of Puvis's character make the caricatures no less unexpected: he has been considered reserved, withdrawn, a reclusive devotee of work, aloof, official and stuffy. Intimates, however, insisted on his conviviality, saying his aristocratic manner concealed irony and wit. A French commentator ascribed this aspect of his temperament to his regional origins: 'His family was of Burgundian stock, and from this ancestry in which he took great pride he got his taste for ribald discourse and his love for coarse jests. He knew Piron's most obscene couplets by heart and trilled them in a falsetto.'[7]

1 For Puvis's friend Eugène Benon, recipient of several works, see cat. 89; perhaps Puvis meant to give this caricature to Benon.

2 On Puvis as a caricaturist see Brown Price (1991), with bibliography; there was a spate of articles about the caricatures when an album of them was published in 1906 (Adam [1906]); see also 1976-77 Paris/Ottawa, nos. 221-228; Brown Price (1983), 365, and *passim*; R.E. Shikes and S. Heller, *The Art of Satire. Painters as Caricaturists and Cartoonists from Delacroix to Picasso*, no. 19 of *Print Review* (New York, 1984), 20-23. An 'Album de Jeunesse' of 33 caricatural drawings attributed to Puvis, but by several hands were sold Paris, Hôtel Drouot (24 April 1991), no. 98; Puvis allegedly destroyed many of his very earliest drawings; it is not known whether caricatures were among them.

3 On this group see Brown Price (1991), 121-122.

4 See *La Plume* (1895), 31-32, 35-36; reprinted in *Le Rire* (16 February 1895), 3.

5 Ricketts (1908), 12.

6 Some seventy-five caricatures from the collection of Mme. Philippe Gille were published in Adam (1906). See also pp. 39-40 of this book.

7 'Sa famille était de souche bourguignonne, et de cette ascendance, dont il tirait fierté il tenait le goût des propos saletés et l'amour de la gaudriole. Il savait par coeur les couplets les plus grivois de Piron et les fredonnait d'une voix parfaitement fausse.' Thiébault-Sisson (1925), n. p. Alexis Piron (1689-1773) was the author of numerous satires and witty, licentious songs.

7

Bust of a Woman in Profile / *Buste de femme de profil* ca. 1854-55

Oil on wood panel, 53.2 x 44.6 cm
Private collection

Provenance Artist's heirs and by descent.
Selected Exhibitions 1976-77 Paris/Ottawa, no. 24.
Selected References Jullian (1938), 241.

This generously proportioned head is one of the surest and most sensuous of Puvis's earliest works. The woman's head is turned in a lost profile pose, used often by Puvis in the 1850s, the *décolletage* and shoulders announced with powerful contours and defined by a broadly stroked-in bit of red drapery. The pose relates to that of the far right figure in *The Gleaners* (*Ruth and Boaz*) at Le Brouchy; however, it is not clear if the painting was made before or after the mural.[1] Puvis's teacher Couture also often used the *profil perdu* pose, as did one of the latter's other students, Anselm Feuerbach (see *Nana* of 1861, Wallraf-Richartz Museum, Cologne or *Iphigenia* of 1870, Staatsgalerie, Stuttgart).[2] It most closely approximates a pose in Théodore Chassériau's *Ruth and Boaz* (whereabouts unknown), which Puvis may have tried to emulate. The pose engages the viewer while preventing him or her from seeing the subject's features; the figure looks off in revery or is otherwise distracted, frequently by something that the viewer may not be privileged to see.

Puvis must have been attracted by the jagged contours of the face created when the head was turned in such a backward-looking glance, with the earringed ear at center and a mass of large loose knots of auburn hair to the side (compare cat. 10 and cat. 38). The head is set against a strong turquoise background with a hint of green foliage; the faintly indicated background vegetation suggests a larger narrative or perhaps the work's derivation. What may be the model's hand is suggested by two paint strokes. Gusto and flourish relate the panel to Italian models also, notably Veronese, and to Puvis's 1854-55 cycle at Le Brouchy.

1 Jacques Foucart in 1976-77 Paris/Ottawa, no. 24 compares the head to that of *Julia, Daughter of Augustus* (our cat. 10) and dates it to 1857; we think it compares more closely to the earlier work.

2 Pointed out also by Jacques Foucart, 1976-77 Paris/Ottawa, no. 24.

7

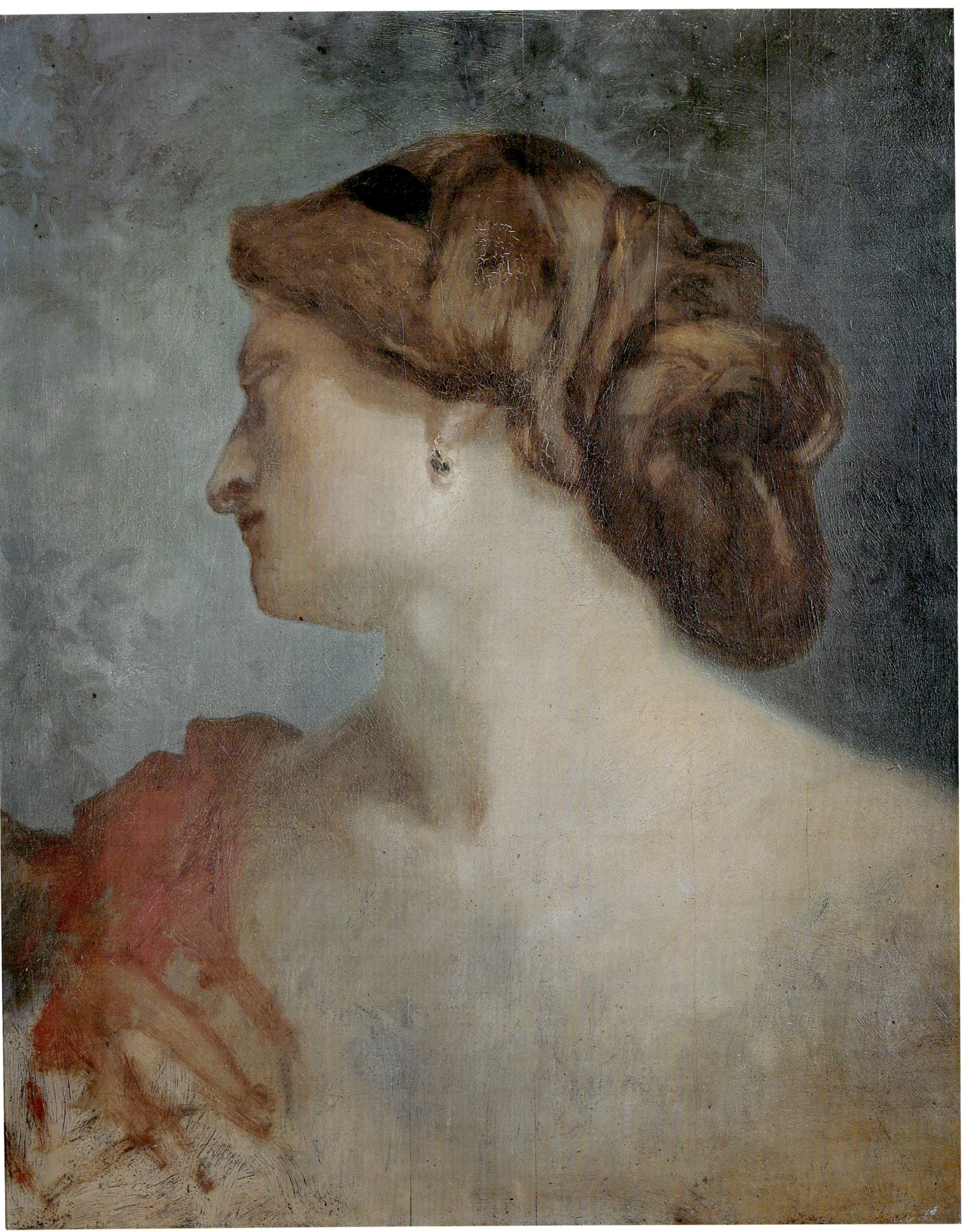

9

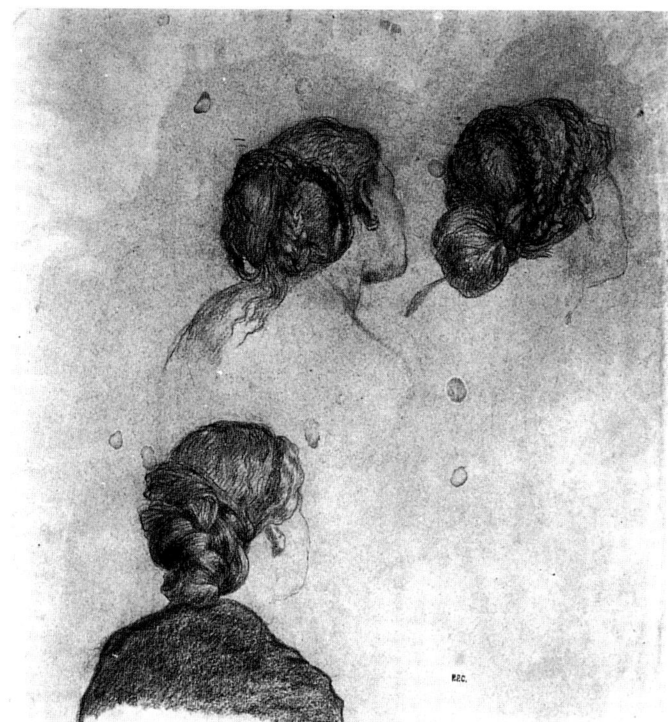

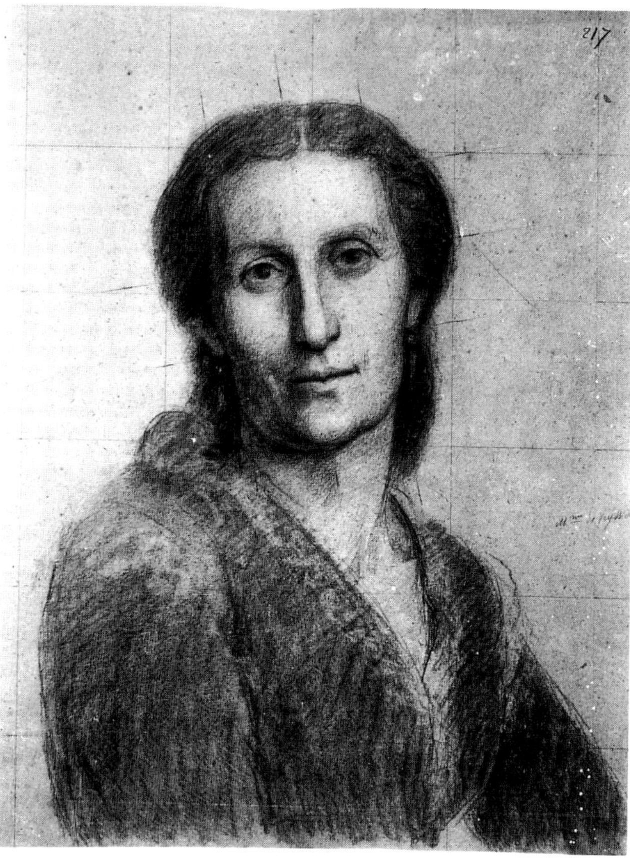

8

Three Studies of a Woman's Head Seen from Behind ca. 1854-57

Stamp l.r.
Black chalk on gray-blue paper, 345 x 320 mm
Museum Boymans-van Beuningen, Rotterdam
(Inv. MB 153)

Provenance Franz Wilhelm Koenigs (1929); given to the Museum Foundation by D.G. van Beuningen (1940).
Selected References H.R. Hoetink, *Franse tekeningen uit de 19e eeuw* (Rotterdam, 1968), no. 215, repr.

Variant coiffures of a chignon and plaited hair are the primary subject of these three renderings of a similarly posed head, apparently of one model. In the variant at the left bottom of the sheet, simple and what may be contemporary clothing suggests a direct study from life. In the other two, the figure is bare-shouldered, bent slightly forward, her head tilted up ever so slightly, a pose that may be preliminary to a narrative painting. In the first study, the woman's hair is gathered in thick bunches and loosely plaited in a bun. At top left, a braid is elaborately pulled around a bun, but loose hair strands are an important, symbolic lapsus, as stray and unruly locks are emblematic of disorder in the otherwise neatly coiffed *Salome* of 1856 (cat. 11), to which this drawing may relate. The elaborate coiffure at the upper right includes a bun with two braids neatly circling the woman's head.

The lost profile pose was, as has been pointed out (see cat. 7), a favored one in Puvis de Chavannes's often dramatic, Romantic paintings of about 1854-57: he used it in *Bust of a Woman in Profile* (cat. 7), the several versions of *Salome* (see cat. 11) and *Julia, Daughter of Augustus* (cat. 10), and executed other drawings of such heads as well.[1] There are other such heads over a range of years: the coiffed head of a nude woman (whom one might expect to be more disheveled) in *Bellum* of 1861 (see cat. 26), and similarly in *Fantasy* of 1866 (cat. 43). This head has also been related to one in the late *Inter Artes et Naturam* (ill. pp. 214-215);[2] the pose is similar and one that Puvis continued to enjoy.

The sheet at the Victoria and Albert Museum also includes a half-length study of a woman with generous features that bears comparison to English Pre-Raphaelite heads. One also thinks of a number of contemporary artists who were also enamored of this pose, Gleyre and Feuerbach among them.

1 For example *Drawing of Woman and Coiffure*, Victoria and Albert Museum, London, Kenneth S. Broad Bequest (Inv. E. 105-1959).
2 Hoetink (ref. above).

9

Head of a Woman (Portrait of Madame de Veyssière) ca. 1851-57

Inscribed with pencil u.r.: 217, and towards m.r. [but seemingly not in Puvis's hand]: Mme de Veyssière
Black and red chalk and charcoal on gray vergé paper, squared, 542 x 430 mm
Museum Boymans-van Beuningen, Rotterdam (Inv. FII 147)

Provenance Franz Wilhelm Koenigs (1929); given to the Museum Foundation by D.G. van Beuningen (1940).
Selected References 1986-87, Baltimore Museum of Art / Los Angeles County Museum of Art / Fort Worth, Kimbell Art Museum, *Nineteenth-Century French Drawings from the Museum Boymans-van Beuningen*, no. 80, repr. p. 127.

This imposing portrait of an older woman is notable for the subject's strong features and an affecting, uncompromising sobriety. The larger, more simplified and abstract of two closely related drawings of the same sitter,[1] this sheet includes a greater portion of her torso. It is likely that Puvis worked here, as he would later, towards simplification and the elimination of distracting elements. That being the case, this drawing would be the second of the two versions, without the decorative scallop detail in the clothing or a head veil indicated by scrawled, crinkly lines, or carefully rendered graying hair. By eliminating stray tendrils of hair Puvis has reinforced its massing, and he has smoothed and evened out the face, making it more symmetrical.

Both drawings would seem to date from the same time; Jacques Foucart dates the more detailed one to about 1860 at the latest, citing its realism and somber vigor of tone.[2] However, because of a tightness of technique, they would both be more convincingly dated to about 1857, if not before. Each sheet is squared twice for transfer, the slightly tilted head at an oblique angle, the upper torso with a vertical grid. The very careful rendering, rare for Puvis, may indicate that these drawings were preliminary to a never executed painted portrait, perhaps a commissioned work. The uncommon calm, simple gravity and pose of the older woman anticipates Puvis's late portrait of the Princess Cantacuzène (1883, cat. 92).[3]

An inscription recto on the Rotterdam sheet and verso on the Rouen version notes a Madame de Veyssière, presumably the sitter, about whom no other information is at present known.[4] Some clue to her identity might be gleaned from the provenance of the Rouen version: from the collection of Paul Auregan (inscribed verso), it seems to have passed to André Joubin, editor of Delacroix's *Journal*. However, their interest may have been that of a connoisseur, not that of a friend or relative.

1 The other: *Portrait of Madame de Veyssière*, ca. 1860, pencil and stump [listed as charcoal], squared for transfer, 425 x 355 mm, Musée des Beaux-Arts, Rouen, Fonds Baderou (Inv. 975.4.3165); see 1976-77 Paris/Ottawa, no. 34.

2 1976-77 Paris/Ottawa, no. 34.

3 Foucart also makes this comparison, see 1976-77 Paris/Ottawa, no. 34.

4 The inscriptions do not seem to be in Puvis's hand.

10

Julia, the Daughter of Augustus, Returning to the Palace in the Morning, Accompanied by a Servant, is Surprised by Soldiers / *Julie, fille d'Auguste, regagnant le matin son palais, accompagnée d'une servante, est surprise par des soldats* ca. 1856-57

Signed l.r.: P. Puvis de Chavannes
Oil on wood panel, 140 x 90 cm
Private collection

Provenance Artist's heirs and by descent.
Selected Exhibitions 1858-59 Lyons, no. 532; 1899 Paris (Durand-Ruel), no. 7; 1937 Lyons, no. 10 [date transposed to 1875].
Selected References Barbier (1858), 338-347; Vachon (1895), p. 63; Vachon [1900], pp. 18, 19, 20; Bénédite (January 1900), 21; Mauclair (1928), p. 7; Jullian (1938), 240, 242-244, fig. 5; Pool (1964), 308.

The notorious Julia of ancient Rome, the corrupt and debauched daughter of the Emperor Augustus, said to have spent her days with prostitutes and her nights with lovers while Rome's armies slept, was described in Macrobius' *Saturnalia*. She was to be banished from Rome by order of the royal house. Puvis described this daughter of Augustus as 'a rake, as you know, who returned home to her spouse Agrippa early in the morning on leaving a party of wild merry-making. Coming upon a band of soldiers, she was afraid of being seen and hid behind a curtain of trees.'[1] Despite her reputation for sexual complicity and nighttime forays, Julia is a relatively subdued if fetching figure as portrayed here in a vaguely Italianate style. Moreover, at first glance her bearing seems

0

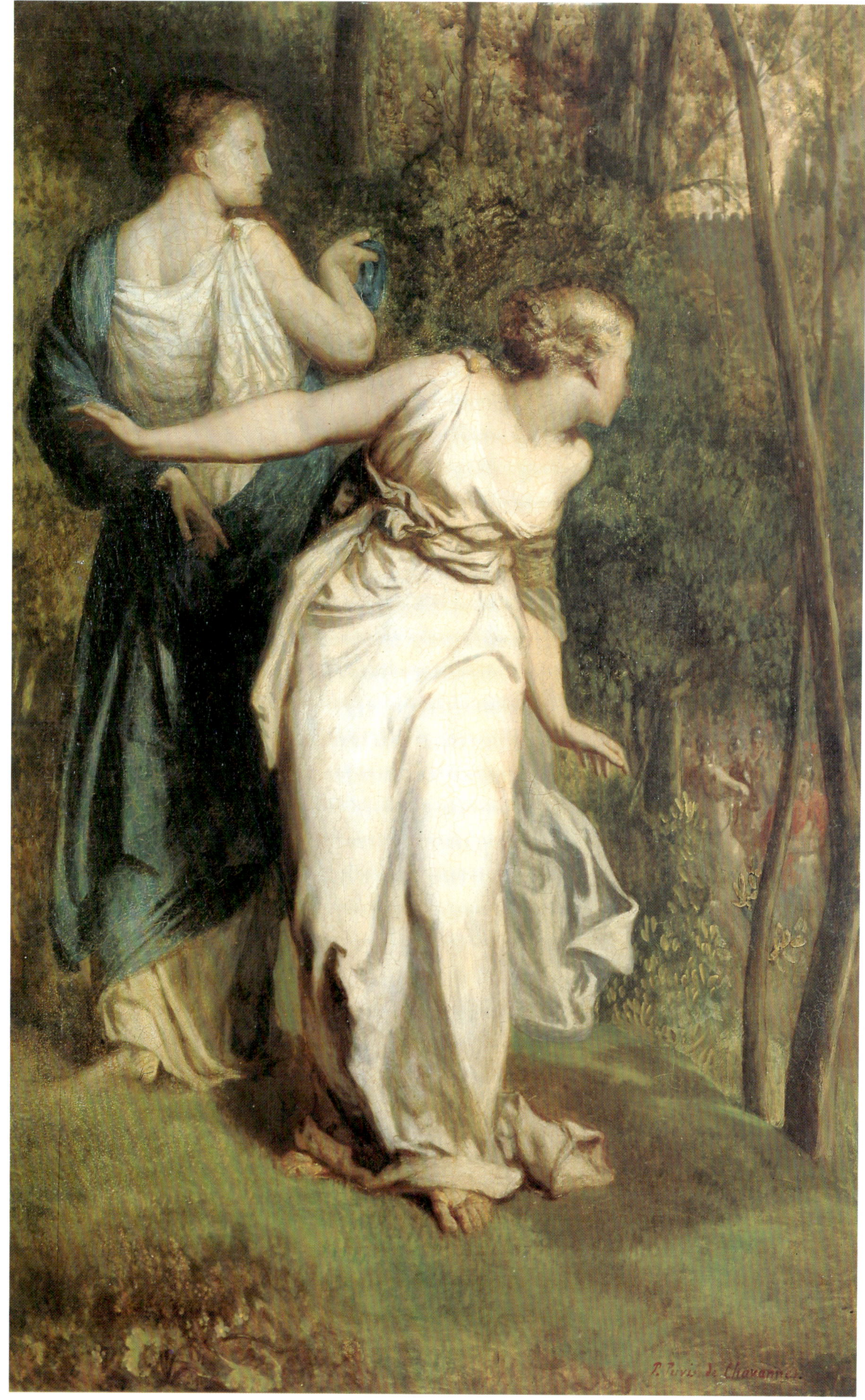

irreproachable enough, for the tones of her dress are so closely allied to those of her flesh that one barely perceives how disheveled she is, her garb fallen revealingly from her shoulder. Indeed, she is here accompanied by a serving woman, as important as a compositional foil as she is as the traditional handmaiden dictated by societal mores, a loyal aide to the principal figure whether or not she is having an escapade.

This kind of tawdry tale had been especially popular during the July Monarchy (1830-48) which 'seems to have been a heyday of translations and retranslations from the Latin classics, especially those that turned about debauchery and decline. New or renewed versions of Suetonius, Petronius, and Juvenal came out in the 1830s, of Ovid, Horace, Catullus, Propertius, and Tibullus between 1840 and 1845. Amateurs of smutty stories had their play cut out, and moralizers their references brought to hand.'[2] Although the vogue for ancient stories of this sort continued,[3] sometimes as moralizing political allegory, this specific theme was certainly not frequent. Pathetic dramas from Roman history, the Middle Ages and the French Revolution were à la mode (compare cat. 2), and in any case, stories of sexual transgressions have never been far from favor.

This painting forms an interesting pair with Puvis's contemporaneous *Salome* (cat. 11): the same size (as are smaller versions of the scenes which correspond),[4] they might even be considered pendants. Drawn from diverse sources, ancient secular and biblical history, each portrays a woman noted for treachery, political ambition and sexual enticement. Each portrays that woman prominently and at full-length, facing into compositions with the *profil perdu* pose Puvis favored these years (see cat. 7).[5] And in both, in Mannerist fashion, small, distant figures are engaged in the narrative action that yields specificity of plot. In these paintings and already at this juncture in his career, Puvis seems to have preferred developing the large, iconic figures to relating stories through figural interaction.

1 'une noceuse, comme vous savez, qui rentre de bon matin, au sortir d'une fête échevelée, chez son époux Agrippa. Rencontrant une bande de soldats, elle craint d'être vue et se cache derrière un rideau d'arbres.' Vachon (1895), p. 63.

2 Eugen Weber, *France. Fin de siècle* (Cambridge, Mass., 1986), p. 16.

3 The imperial courtesan Messalina was of interest in this period and Couture's *Romans of the Decadence* (Musée d'Orsay, Paris) also depicts ancient dissipation.

4 Two or possibly three small versions documented: a *Study for Julia*, signed l.r.: P. de Chavannes 1857 [looks like '1'], oil on panel, 44.3 x 27.3 cm, which may be the same as one mentioned in Saunier (1899) as exhibited at the Galerie Durand-Ruel, and a so-called *Julia surprised*, 47 x 40 cm (whereabouts unknown, formerly collection Félix Bracquemond).

5 Compare also *Study for 'Julia'*, Musée du Louvre, Paris (Inv. RF 2163); and *Profile head for 'Julia'*, Musée du Louvre, Paris (Inv. RF 2164).

11

Salome, the Daughter of Herodias, Ordering the Execution of Saint John the Baptist / *Salomé, la fille d'Hérodiade, donnant le signal du supplice de Saint Jean Baptiste* 1856

Signed l.r.: P. Puvis de Chavannes 1856
Oil on wood panel, 140 x 89.5 cm
Museum Boymans-van Beuningen, Rotterdam; on loan from the Foundation Willem van der Vorm (Inv. VDV 62a)

Provenance M. Peyrusson (1864 or 1879); J. Schmit; Fontainel Dutilleul; 'Amateur de Limoges' (Vachon [1900]); Mme R. Heim [?], Paris; Versailles, Sale (15 March 1959), no. 3411 [as oil on canvas]; Foundation Willem van der Vorm, Rotterdam (1962).
Selected Exhibitions 1858-59 Lyons, no. 531 [?]; Limoges (1864 or 1879), *hors catalogue*.
Selected References Barbier (1858), 338-347; Vachon [1900] pp. 18, 19; Martinie (1925), 13, repr.; Jullian (1938), 240, 244.

One hand on her hip and imperiously holding aloft a platter in readiness for the Baptist's head, Salome dominates this composition. She is turned dramatically from the viewer to face the interior of the composition, the scene of the beheading, in the background below the steps on which she so unswervingly stands. Salome is portrayed as a formidable Roman matron in a stalwart pose, engineer of the Baptist's fate. Above her solid neck only an interesting stray tress in her otherwise neatly plaited hair betrays any duress. Not surprisingly, critics have mistaken this Salome (Hérodiade, as she is called in the New Testament) for her mother Herodias, who advised her to exact the Baptist's head as reward for her dance – in retribution for the prophet's insistence that the mother had illegally and immorally married Herod, her dead husband's brother. Certainly, this Salome is distant from the young girl designated in the Bible. Nor has she anything to do with what was anxiously apprehended in the late nineteenth century as the archetypal, seductive *femme fatale*, who fascinated poets and painters, the alluring temptress of the veils.[1] Puvis's *Salome* is far from such interpretations as Gustave Moreau's exotic vision or Orientalizing versions. Her commanding hand on hip pose and turned position recall that of Christ in Rembrandt's celebrated etching *The Raising of Lazarus*, on which Puvis, who often sought compositional models these years, may have based his own. Puvis was to use the

11

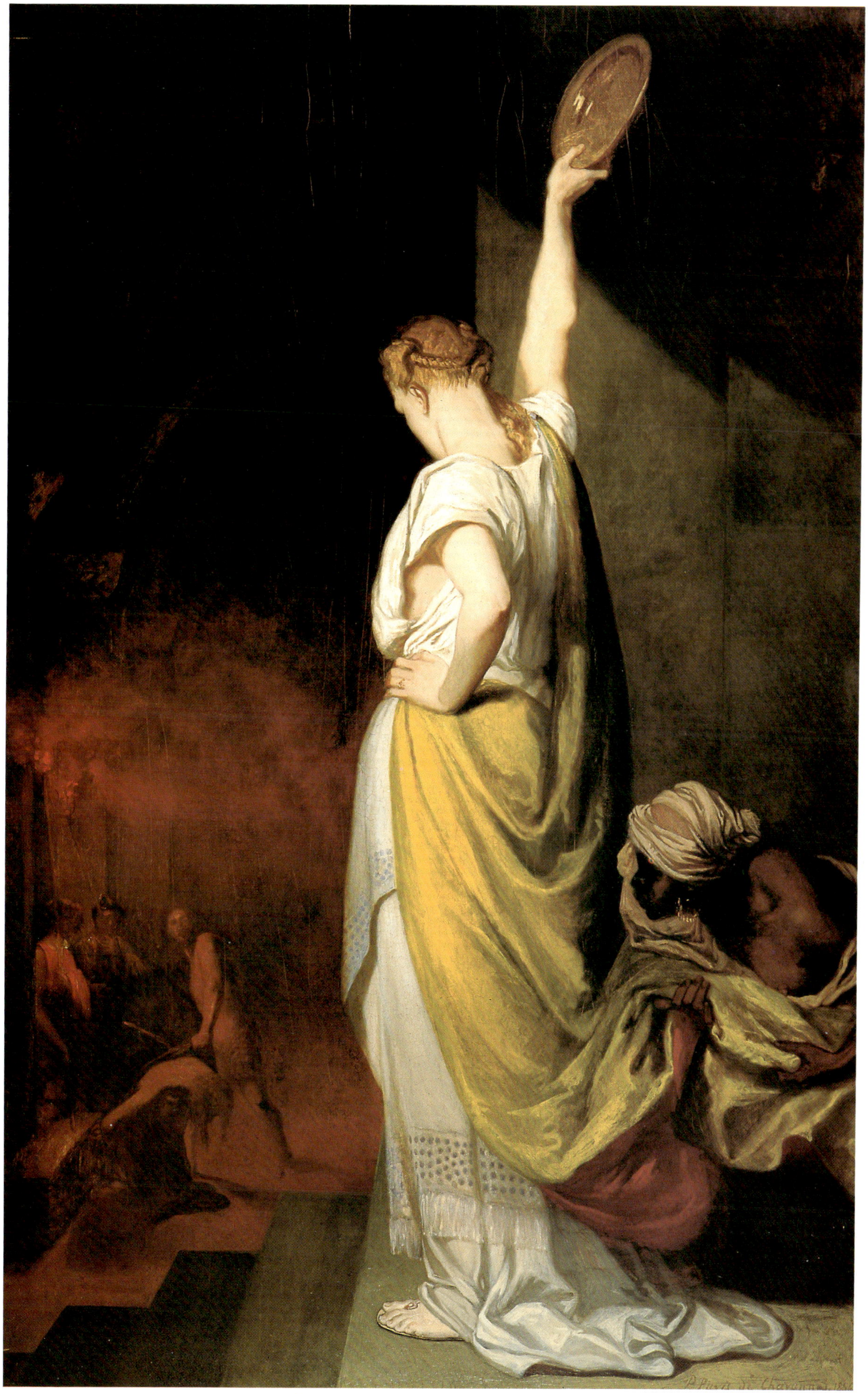

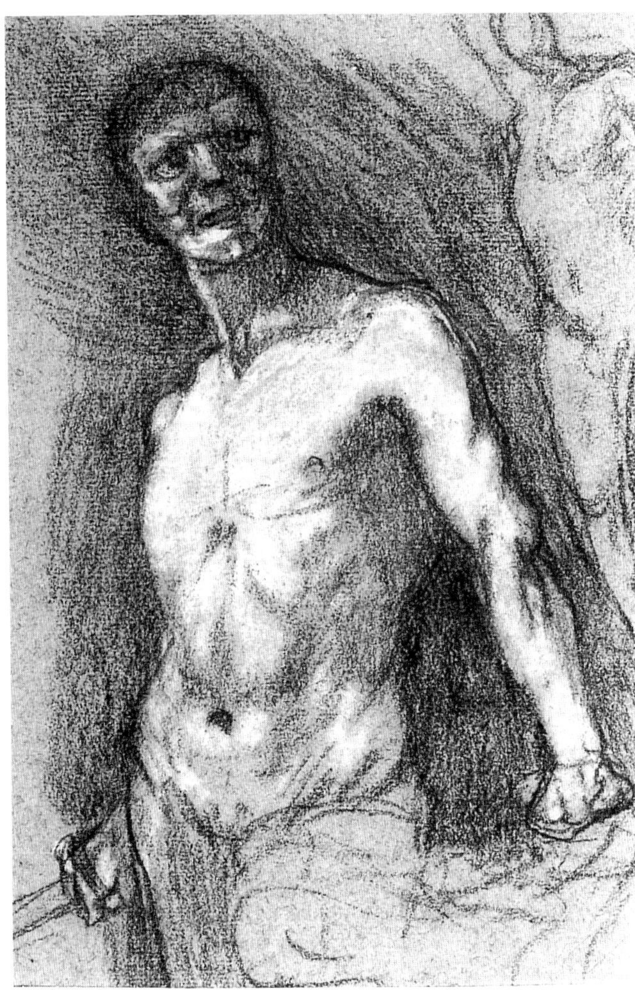

gesture of an upraised arm for a number of allegorical figures (among them *Vigilance* and *The Carrier Pigeon*, cat. 45, 65). Crouched to the right is a pink turbaned Negress,[2] a figure signifying the distant and exotic and familiar from numerous Romantic paintings; her most immediate relative is Chassériau's slave girl in *The Toilette of Esther* (1857, Musée du Louvre, Paris).

The colors of this version of *Salome* are considerably more vibrant and flamboyant than those of a smaller version.[3] At center the draped cloth is a chartreuse yellow with a red lining, opposed to the grayed green drapery and the white turban of the servant in the latter.

Puvis was to take up the cruel story of the beheading again in 1869, moving it to center stage (see cat. 57).

1 See Sylviane Huot, *Le Mythe de Hérodiade chez Mallarmé: genèse et évolution* (Paris, 1977); Mechthilde Hatz, *Frauengestalten des Alten Testaments in der Bildenden Kunst von 1850 bis 1918* (Bamberg, 1972).

2 Compare *Head of a Negress*, stamp l.r., charcoal on green-tinted paper, 300 x 282 mm (sight) (whereabouts unknown, formerly Mlle Berthe de la Conté, Saint Sever, France).

3 *Salome*, oil on panel, 44.3 x 27.3 cm, private collection; see 1976-77 Paris/Ottawa, no. 18.

12 12

Study for the Executioner in 'Salome'

ca. 1856

Black chalk heightened with white on paper, 240 x 165 mm
Musée Paul Dupuy, Toulouse (Inv. 96)

Provenance Bequest of artist's heirs to the city of Toulouse (1898).

This study for the executioner in *Salome* (cat. 11) displays the brutal expressiveness characteristic of a number of Puvis's early drawings. The head and much of the torso of this slightly turned figure are included. The hilt of the drawn sword is visible in his right hand and in his other we know he holds what is not shown here, the Baptist's clothing. At the upper left is a summary study of the whole figure, a slight torsion in his stance (compare cat. 13).

13

Study for the Executioner in 'Salome'

ca. 1856

Inscribed u.r.: 87
Black chalk heightened with white chalk and pencil on gray paper, 315 x 210 mm
Musée de Picardie, Amiens (Inv. 912bis 76)

Provenance Bequest of artist's heirs to the city of Amiens (1898).

Strained tension and ferocity are transmitted by the executioner standing with a sword at the center of this dramatic study for the 1856 *Salome* (cat. 11). He is the most developed of the expressive figures, his strongly lit body alone heightened with white and shaded to create pronounced modeling, accentuating how it twists as he tightens his grasp on his victim and readies his blow. The Baptist kneels to the right; an ancillary figure frames the composition to the left. In the final version, the Baptist would be moved to the left and his pose changed from passivity to bowed helplessness. These forceful figures, which excite the imagination and are central to the narrative but hardly visible in the murky background of the completed canvas, must have been subdued to be searched out (compare a similar device in the composition of *The Return of the Prodigal Son*, fig. 2 and cat. 4), and as not to detract from Salome in the foreground.

13

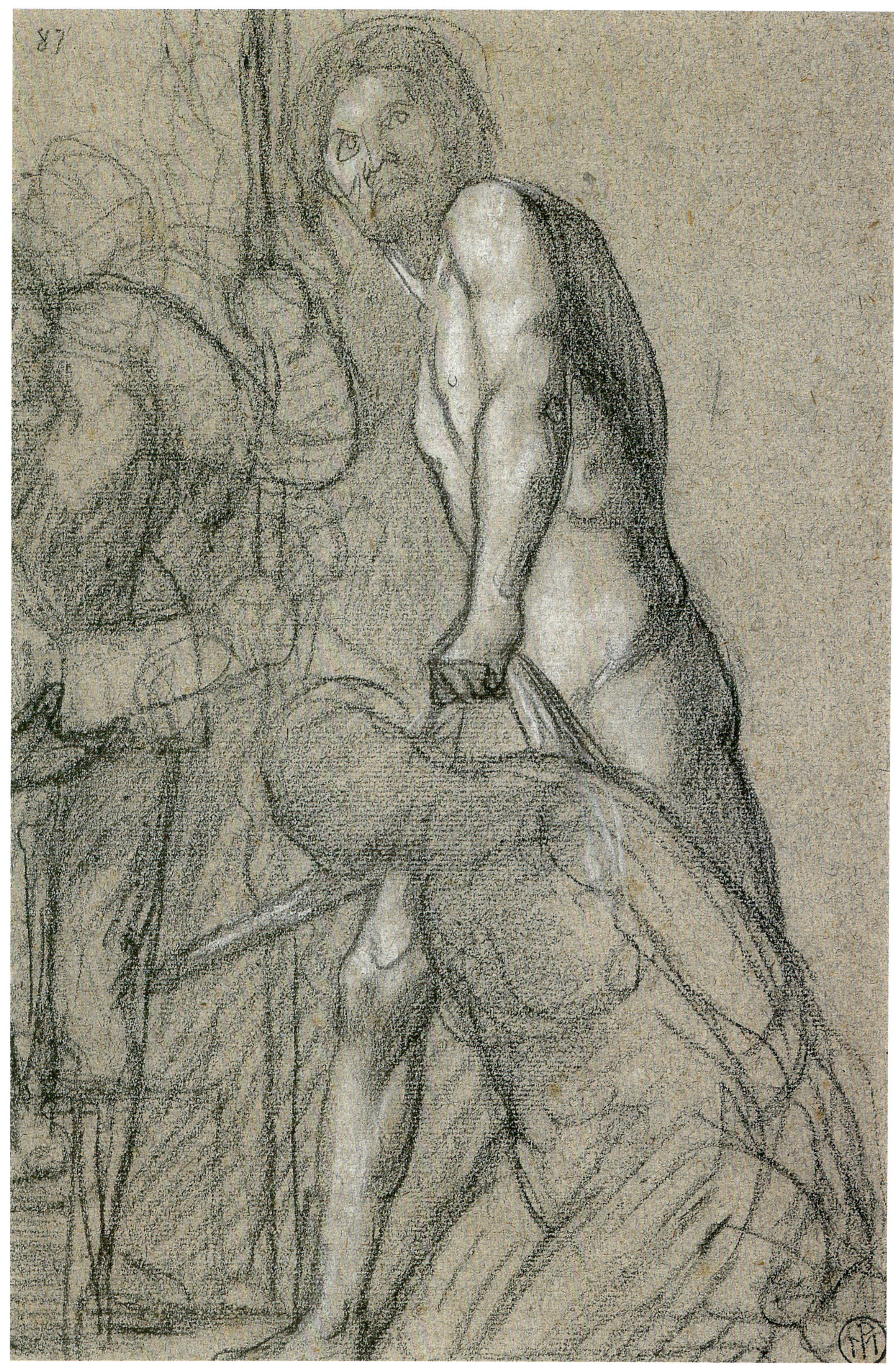

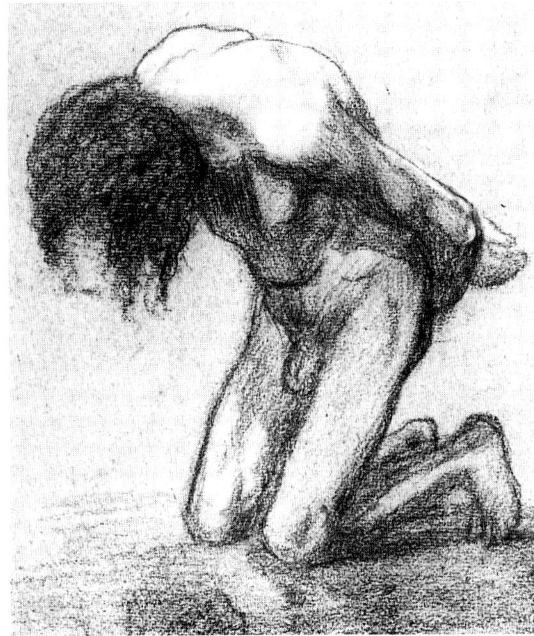

14

Study for Saint John the Baptist in 'Salome' ca. 1856

Black chalk on gray paper, 215 x 185 mm
Musée Paul Dupuy, Toulouse (Inv. 93)

Provenance Bequest of artist's heirs to the city of Toulouse (1898).

The forcefulness and pathos of the crouched, kneeling Baptist, his head bowed, his hair fallen to hide his face and his arms behind his back, awaiting his beheading, is more evident in this study than in the dim, reddened dark recesses of the completed *Salome* of 1856 (cat. 11). In the painting, the figure, reversed, is small and somewhat lost, shunted to the back and side in a composition dominated by the commandeering Salome. The Baptist's utterly helpless pose contrasts to the rigid hieraticism of his posture in the emblematic *Beheading of Saint John the Baptist* variants of over a decade later (see cat. 57, 59-61).

This dramatic study, presumably a life drawing of a studio model, is undertaken much as a preliminary academic study for a painting would have been; first, the model would have been posed nude, as here, and then draped, as in a similar drawing[1] in which drapery has been added and humped up to indicate how it would be pulled in the painting by the executioner.

1 *Study of a Kneeling Man*, ca. 1856, Musée des Beaux-Arts, Lille (Inv. 2066).

15

Self-Portrait / *Puvis de Chavannes, peint par lui-même* 1857

Inscribed verso: A mon bien cher Paul Baudoüin mon portrait peint par moi en 1857 à l'âge de 33 ans P. Puvis de Chavannes
Oil on canvas, 65.5 x 54.5 cm
Musée du Petit Palais, Paris
(Inv. PPP 888; MCB 174)

Provenance Gift of the artist to Paul Baudoüin; Sir Joseph Duveen, London [on consignment?]; bought by the city of Paris from Baudoüin (1931).
Selected Exhibitions 1937 Lyons, no. 1; 1976-77 Paris/Ottawa, no. 23.
Selected References Henri Puvis de Chavannes, personal notes (private collection); Buisson (July 1899), 7, repr. 9; Cortissoz (1925), p. 206; Baudoüin (1935), 297-298, repr. 313; Jullian (1938), 237; H. Puvis de Chavannes (1955), 38; Boucher (1979), no. 174; Brown Price (1991), repr. 128, 131.

Although Puvis referred to himself in drawings and caricatures (cat. 16, 17), he apparently first painted himself only at the age of thirty-three. In this sober, finely modeled portrait he is dark-haired and bearded, his head turned somewhat, the strong highlighting of his temple and nose creating asymmetries and yet, half withdrawn in shadow, he allows us to see him only in part. A goodly portion of his upper torso is included (among early portraits, he used such an extended view only for his 1851 *Portrait of Thomas Alfred Jones* [Musée d'Orsay, Paris], probably his only commissioned portrait). He is suited informally in a dark, unbuttoned coat and appears to be holding a palette (at the lower left what appears to be part of a finger so indicates), a subtle reference to the painter at work. Physiognomy, pictorial structure and mood are more at issue than psychological penetration. Restraint of temperament is matched by that of color: dark warm browns and blacks and a white collar.

Puvis's autoportrait is similar to portraits painted by Edgar Degas, Edouard Manet – another Couture student – and Henri Fantin-Latour from 1857 and into the 1860s, whether of themselves or their comfortable or haut-bourgeois families. They too set forth somber likenesses marked by reticence, quiet seriousness and self-containment. There as here, psychological analysis is tempered by the artists' discretion instigated by the sitters' reserve, sense of privacy and even guardedness.

Puvis's protegé, Paul Baudoüin, to whom the portrait was given, mistakenly stated it was one of only two self-portraits made by Puvis.[1] In

15

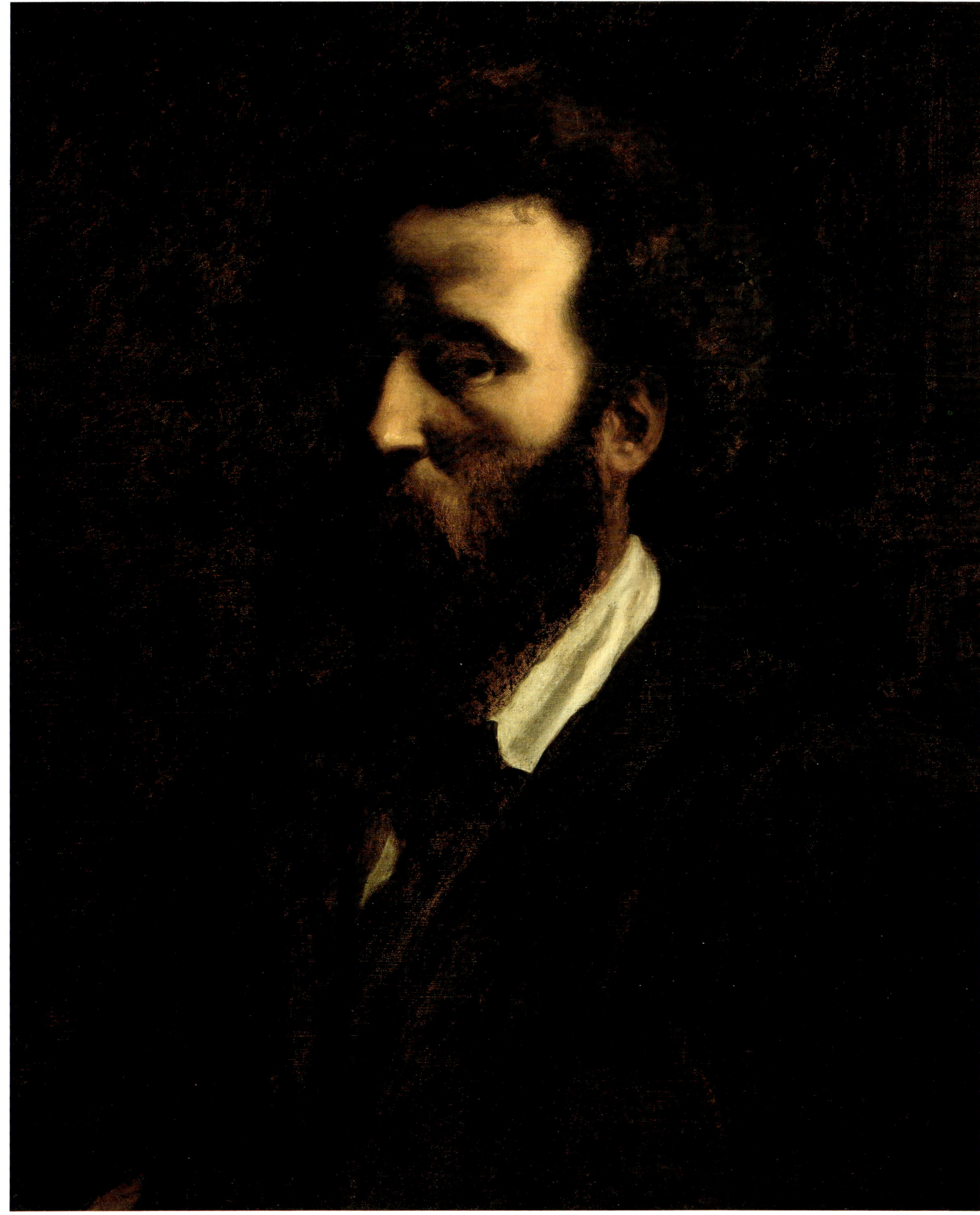

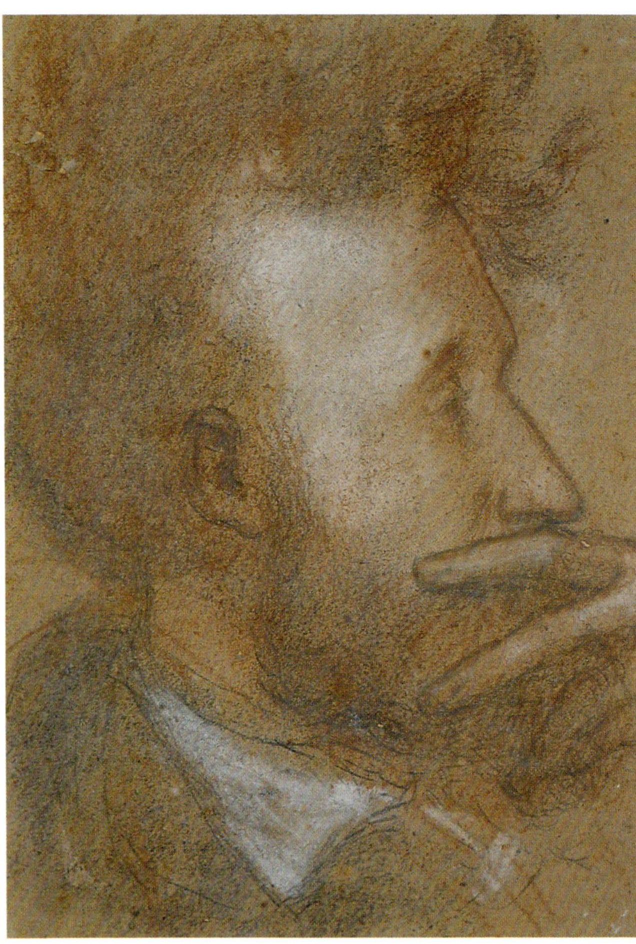

fact, Puvis pictured himself a number of times. In addition to caricatural and expressionistic views that suggest his witty and pensive sides, in later years there are pastels and drawings, an unfinished portrait with a palette (Musée du Louvre, Paris), and an official portrait executed in 1887 for the collection of artists' self-portraits at the Uffizi Gallery in Florence. In the last he depicted himself in profile. In his sixties then, dignified and suited and transmitting the utmost confidence, he shrewdly managed to have an emblem of his achievement at the center of his composition: proudly displayed in his lapel is the small red rosette of the Legion of Honor.

Though he did not often picture himself, Puvis was not averse to posing for others' paintings, drawings, prints and photographs.[2] When Puvis was achieving his first Salon successes in about 1863, both Félix Bracquemond and Gustave Ricard portrayed him,[3] the latter as dapper and serious, an interpretation in which Puvis may have had a say, as he was deeply interested in the impression he made. He worried about his own official self-portrait of 1887[4] and about the sculptured portraits Rodin was to make of him in the 1890s.[5]

1 Baudoüin (1935), 297-298.

2 For a list of portraits by other artists of Puvis de Chavannes, see Boucher (1979), no. 103.

3 Bracquemond portrayed Puvis in two drawings of about 1862-63 (see 1976-77 Paris/Ottawa, no. 238), an engraving of 1862 and an 1863 oil study dedicated in 1899 to Baudoüin (Indianapolis Museum of Art), see Buisson (July 1899), repr. 9. On the Ricard portrait see Louis La Crocq, 'Un Portrait de Puvis de Chavannes par Ricard,' *Bulletin de la Société de l'Histoire de l'Art Français*, I (1929), 167-168; exhibited Limoges, Société des Amis des Arts du Limousin, May 1864, *hors catalogue*, but noted in Albert Guillemot, *Promenades au Salon des Beaux-Arts* (Limoges, 1864), 30, 51-52 (present whereabouts unknown). Guillemot, quoted by La Crocq, described a 'figure fine et bonne dégarnie de cheveux aux tempes, mais à demi couverte d'une épaisse barbe blonde, annonce la force de l'âge mûr' ('a fine and pleasant face, balding at the temples, but half covered with a thick light beard, heralds middle age at its prime'). As Puvis had dark hair, the blond beard in this description gives one pause.

4 See Baudoüin (1935), 301, 303-304.

5 There are cast and carved Rodin sculptures (Musée Rodin, Paris), which are discussed in the author's forthcoming book.

16

Head of a Man in Profile, Hand to Face

ca. 1857 (not in the exhibition)

Sanguine, charcoal, heightened with white chalk
on beige paper, 282 x 190 mm (sight)
Private collection

Provenance Artist's heirs and by descent.

In its informal, expressive immediacy, this drawing is relatively uncommon among Puvis de Chavannes's early works. With its sharp, long nose, small eyes, downward turned brows and bushy hair this profile resembles that of the expressive caricatural head recently identified as an autoportrait (cat. 17) and Puvis de Chavannes's painted self-portrait at age thirty-three (cat. 15), leading to its identification as one of the rare, early self-portraits dating to about 1857. The hand to head pose, with fingers fanning out, transmits an air of thoughtfulness and unpretentiousness as well as of being taken unawares at an introspective and pensive moment. Though a profile pose is not unusual among Puvis's self-portraits, he rarely executed as intimate and unself-conscious a study. As in 1887, in his official portrait for the Uffizi Gallery, he pictures himself in the third person as it were, allowing the viewer to look upon him.

Red chalk, a favorite medium of Puvis's in the 1850s and early 1860s, is used as a warm intermediate tone; charcoal is used for linear definition and white highlights finish the modeling effect.

17

17

Caricatural Self-Portrait ca. 1857

Stamp l.r.
Black chalk on paper, 260 x 190 mm
Collection G. Meunier

Provenance Artist's heirs and by descent.
Selected References Brown Price (1991), 131, repr. fig. 12.

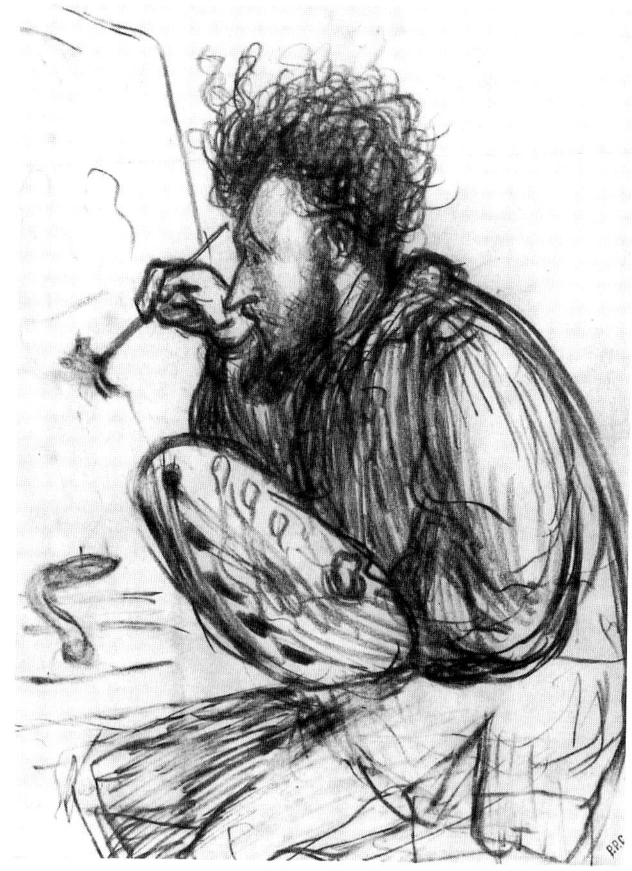

Throughout his life Puvis produced caricatural drawings, which were among the most private and least known of his works. Although in them he referred to himself in a variety of guises,[1] this drawing is a fairly straightforward 'charged portrait.' It must date from about the same time as his staid, introspective portrait of 1857 (cat. 15), in which he appears to be about the same age and which his physiognomy here resembles.

In this spirited, self-mocking portrait of the artist as a young man, exaggeratedly close to his easel, fervently painting away,[2] what is at issue is the artist's absolute concentration on his work. Fraught with the tension of his task, his hair is in disarray as he closely inspects his image. He holds a palette in readiness in one hand while, in the other, a brush with bristles sprouting in all directions informs us that he is forcefully scrubbing away at the panel on which he works. It is a surprising portrait, not only because of its graphic facility, but because we have come to know the artist through his best-known work and his painted images of himself, both of which transmit a sense of composure, reserve and aloof dignity.

The drawing recalls the anxiety that Puvis stated the making of art engenders in the artist. Even several years later, on the eve of presenting his first public murals at the Salon, he betrayed profound misgivings about his training and uncertainties as to his adequacy as an artist. In a letter of 12 March 1861, he asked whether any truly devoted artist 'has in him that marvelous balm known as peace of mind? ... For me peace of mind is cousin to presumptuousness, and if there is an example in the world to show that it doesn't inhabit fine minds, M. Ingres is right there to prove it.'[3]

1 Brown Price (1991), 122-131, 138-139.
2 The curious, snake-like form at his knees appears to be a crank, but its meaning is unclear.
3 'ait en lui ce baume merveilleux qu'on appelle le calme? ... Pour moi, le calme est voisin de l'outrecuidance, et, s'il est, au monde, un exemple à citer pour prouver qu'il n'habite guère les bons cerveaux, M. Ingres est justement là pour prouver.' Mandach and Wehrlé (1910), 677.

18

Portrait of a Woman / *Portrait de femme*
1852 or 1857

Signed and dated to l.r.: P. P. C. 1852 [1857?] CH
Oil on wood panel, 35 x 27 cm
Musée National des Beaux-Arts d'Alger, Algiers (Inv. 1067)

Provenance Félix Bracquemond; Pierre Bracquemond (by 1912); acquired by the museum (1930).
Selected Exhibitions 1899 Paris (Durand-Ruel), no. 4; 1976-77 Paris/Ottawa, no. 6.
Selected References Monod (1912), 323; René Jean, *l'Art français à Saint Petersbourg* (Paris, 1912), pp. 60-61; Jean Alazard, 'Musée des Beaux Arts d'Alger: Exposition des dons et acquisitions,' *Bulletin des Musées de France*, VII (May 1935), 77, repr.; H. Puvis de Chavannes (1955), 39.

Portraits and heads were prominent subjects for Puvis de Chavannes during the first decade of his career. He found sitters among family and friends and among the workers employed at the family estate. About half

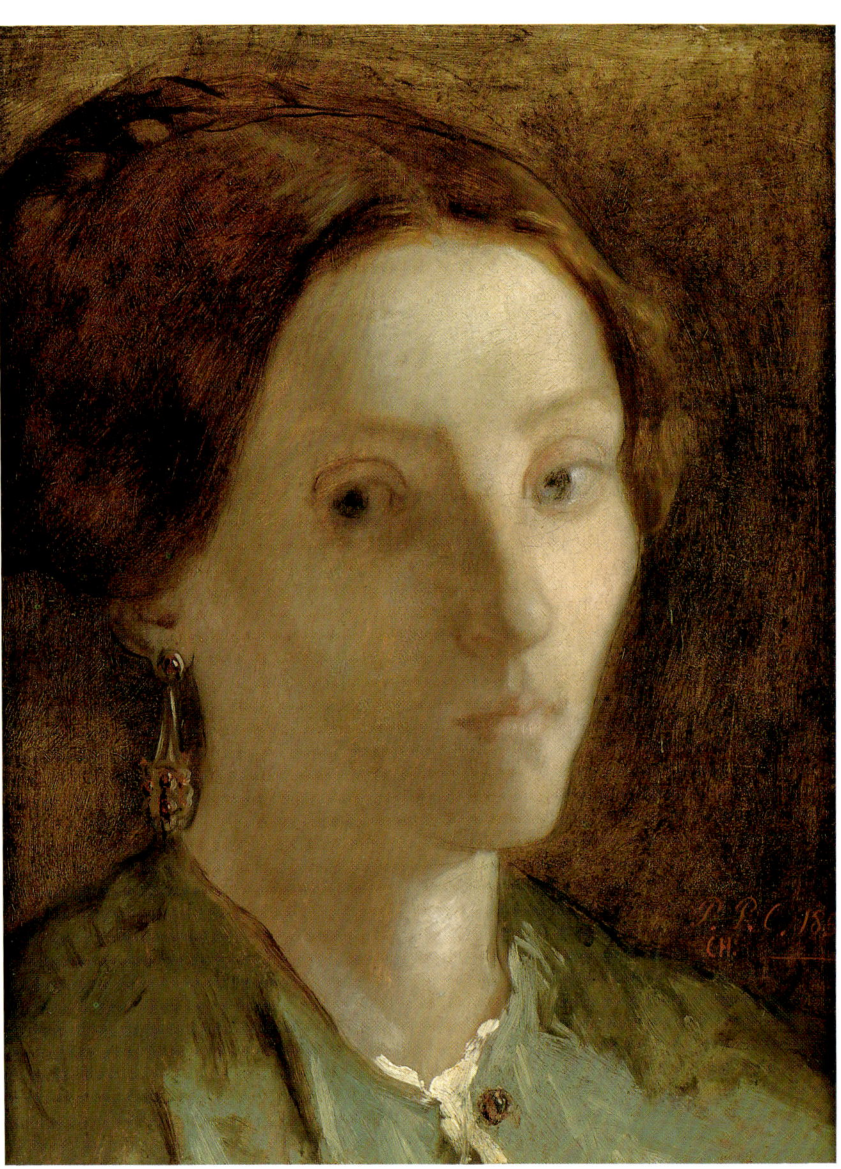

the subjects of some twenty painted portraits of these years, many executed around 1851, can be identified.

Dramatically high cheekbones, widely spaced, round gray eyes, a set small mouth and a pointed chin comprise the distinctive features of this heart-shaped face. Like many of Puvis's early portraits, this one is relatively small and unprepossessing, the head cropped close by the frame. Although marked with an air of intimacy, the sitter's penetrating sideways glance is made somewhat mysterious by the head's being withdrawn into a partial shadow that accentuates its configuration. Warmth and charm are generated through color: the woman's auburn hair blending with the background tones, a bit of white at her throat, the water green dress, a touch of red in the coral earrings.

Although the initialed signature, wooden support, and small dimensions would bolster the 1852 date commonly assigned to the panel, the last numeral of Puvis's dating is not fully legible. The loose, flexible brushwork, strong modeling, secure, painterly notations and play of half light and a comparison with Puvis de Chavannes's portrait of himself, dated 1857 (cat. 15), and that of his nephew Camille of 1858 (private collection) favor the reading of a later date, 1857.

That date would support the hypothesis that the portrait is of the Princess Marie Cantacuzène, who was to become the painter's long-time companion and then his wife. By 1856, Puvis had met her through Théodore Chassériau. Puvis became Chassériau's successor not only as to training and ideas but in this friendship as well.[1] The woman's features and center-parted dark, wavy hair bear resemblance to Chassériau's 1855 (fig. 29) and 1856 drawings of Marie Cantacuzène,[2] and to Puvis's *Portrait of Mme M.C.* (cat. 92), made twenty-six years later.[3]

In the portrait's essential modesty, informality and strength of modeling one may detect traits inculcated by Thomas Couture, with whom Puvis had briefly studied. Couture devoted a section of his *Méthode et entretiens d'Atelier* to portraiture and, for the most part,

19 practiced what he preached: 'Steer clear of giving your portraits theatrical poses; be simple, modest in your poses as in your expressions; we live in the intimacy of the portrait we are looking at.'[4] One critic noted that this panel was 'a curious woman's portrait (about 1860), sharp and delicate like a Ricard.'[5] Gustave Ricard (1823/24-1873), who shared an atelier with Puvis in the early 1850s and considerably influenced his portraiture, was himself influenced by Couture, and was to become a fashionable portraitist.

The first owner of this panel was the painter and printmaker Félix Bracquemond.[6]

1 See Bénédite [1931], I, pp. 490, 494, 496; and Ricketts (1939), pp. 76-77 *inter alia*.

2 Fig. 29 and Bénédite [1931], II, pl. LII (seated portrait of 1856), repr.; the earlier drawing belonged to the Princess and subsequently to Puvis.

3 John Rewald identified the Algiers portrait as of Suzanne Valadon, who modeled for Puvis in the 1880s, rectifying the assertion later; Rewald (1956), repr. p. 28 as *Portrait of Suzanne Valadon*, rectified index, 1962 ed., p. 607.

4 'Gardez-vous bien de donner à vos portraits des poses théatrales; soyez simple, modeste, dans vos poses comme dans vos expressions; nous vivons dans l'intimité du portrait que nous regardons.' Thomas Couture, *Méthode et entretiens d'atelier*, 2nd ed. (Paris, 1868), p. 63; although published after Puvis came into contact with Couture, this book would represent what he taught.

5 'un curieux portrait de femme (vers 1860), aigu et délicat comme un Ricard.' Monod (1912), 323.

6 In 1856 Bracquemond (1833-1914) introduced Japanese prints to his fellow artists in Paris; in 1862 he helped found the Société des Aquafortistes (etchers), in which Puvis participated; in 1863 he proposed doing engravings after Puvis's work; and from 1893 to 1895 he participated in the *L'Estampe originale* project, as did Puvis.

19

Study for 'The Village Firemen' or 'The Fire' ca. 1857

Signed l.l.: P. Puvis de Chavannes
Red chalk and charcoal on paper (horizontal strip added at top, triangular piece at corner l.r.), 630 x 920 mm (sight)
Collection Stuart Pivar, New York

Selected Exhibitions 1894 New York, no. 20.

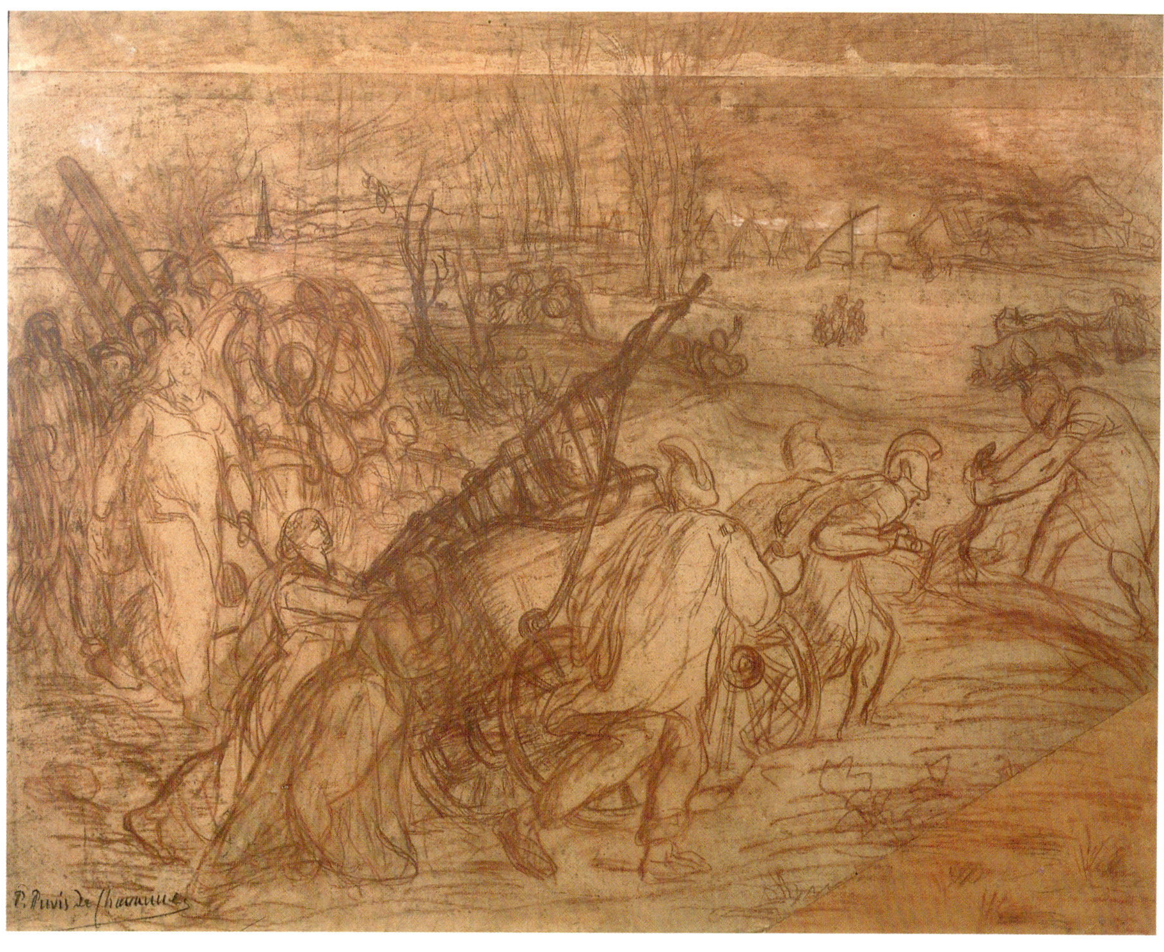

This robust drawing is a study for one of the most complex and largest (179 x 228 cm) of Puvis's canvases of the 1850s, *The Fire* (*L'Incendie*) or *The Village Firemen* (*Les pompiers de village*) (Hermitage, Saint Petersburg). Like Puvis's earlier *Mlle de Sombreuil* (see cat. 2), it is typified by dramatic subject matter which serves as a vehicle for the deployment of a mass of figures in commotion.[1] Smocked and helmeted country firemen and women push and haul firefighting equipment across uneven terrain towards a burning village of thatched cottages and stacked grains or grass. Figures rush in from the left, some with ladders. The rare graphic fervor of this large sanguine, the sense of tumult, drama and catastrophe indicate an early stage in the pictorial process, when composition and format were being formulated. In the painting, all elements of this vigorous drawing were stiffened and toned down.

Rural fires were a major hazard and an important topic of the time.[2] This composition was said to have been inspired by a scene Puvis witnessed from a train passing through the Mâconnais,[3] a region dear to him, in which there were several large fires during 1857, the year of this canvas: 'Fires were sometimes catastrophic. Two such conflagrations occurred in 1857 alone, one destroying 114 dwellings in the little village of Fresne-sur-Apance (Haute-Marne), and the other consuming all 17 houses in the hamlet of Fretterans in Bresse, leaving 100 persons destitute.... people were easily aroused to panic....'[4] Frequent and well-documented, these raging conflagrations were often no accident. Rural fires were deliberately set for political, personal and financial reasons: revenge in disputes between landlords and tenants, political retaliation, blackmail and terrorism. Sometimes set by vagrants, occasionally they were even instigated by companies to coerce the undecided into buying insurance.[5]

Disaster scenes had currency among artists in the 1850s, providing an opportunity to combine realism, then in its ascendancy, and an excited emotionalism, a vestige of Romanticism, proper to the dramatic subject at hand.[6]

The Fire seems to have been created with the composition of Thomas Couture's *The Enrollment of Volunteers of 1792* (the largest version, Musée Départemental de l'Oise, Beauvais) of 1848 in mind, the several versions of which occupied the artist during the months that Puvis was his pupil: the figures dragging fire equipment resemble Couture's men pulling a cannon. *The Fire* is also a country cousin to Gustave Courbet's urban *Firemen Running to a Fire* of 1852 (Musée du Petit Palais, Paris). Evidently, Puvis wanted to make a large-scale painting on an important contemporary theme and Courbet's enormous (388 x 580 cm) canvas would have impressed him. The theme of a community brought together to work constructively in a mutual effort would be a frequent theme of Puvis's murals.

1 Brown Price (1991), 124-128.

2 Eugen Weber, *Peasants into Frenchmen: The Modernization of Rural France 1870-1914* (Stanford, 1976), p. 16.

3 Vachon [1900], p. 120, and repeated by later biographers.

4 Weber, *op. cit.* (note 2), p. 16.

5 John M. Merriman, 'The Norman Fires of 1830: Incendiaries and Fear in Rural France,' *French Historical Studies*, IX, no. 3 (Spring 1976), 451-466, *passim*, especially 451, 462-464.

6 Compare Jean Pierre Antigna's *The Fire*, a fire in an urban apartment (Salon of 1850-51, Musée des Beaux-Arts, Orléans); Ary Scheffer's *Farm Fire* (Salon of 1824, Dordrechts Museum), with which Puvis might have been familiar; and Jules Breton's 1856 *Fire in a Haystack* (exhibited Salon of 1861, Detroit Institute of Arts).

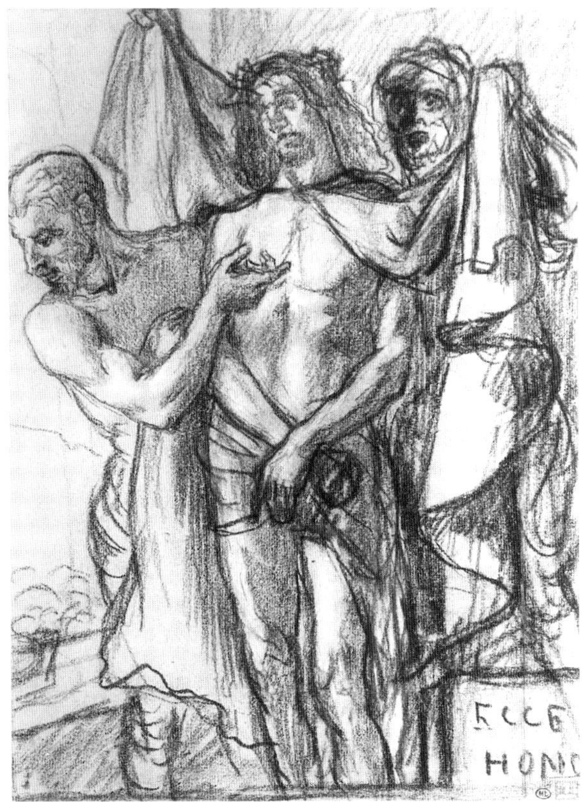

20

Ecce Homo ca. 1858

Inscribed l.r.: Ecce Homo and stamp l.r.
Black chalk heightened with white on gray-pink paper, 293 x 217 mm
Musée du Louvre, Paris (Inv. RF 2159)

Provenance Bequest of artist's heirs to the city of Paris (1899); Musée du Luxembourg; transferred to the Musée du Louvre (1929).

1 This is one of the earliest compositional studies of a splendid series of remarkably strong and expressive drawings[1] undertaken in conjunction with the large (205 x 160 cm) *Christ Before the Praetorial Court* (*Le Christ au prétoire*, fig. 1), executed in 1858 for the church of Champagnat, near the family country estate Le Brouchy.[2] Although the appearance of Christ in the law court (Matthew, 27:29-30; and Mark, 15:9) is the ostensible subject of the latter, the preliminary drawings as well as a lithograph[3] are based on the 'Ecce Homo' (as inscribed to the lower right here) from John (19:5), in which Pilate with the words 'Behold the man!' presents the scourged Christ, who is mocked as King of the Jews in his crown of thorns. He is about to be enrobed and to be given a slender reed in lieu of a scepter.

The essential composition is established here, although revisions were to follow (compare the Petit Palais drawing): the figure that looks down and away from Christ would gaze towards him; the figure at the back would gain a soldier's helmet; the folds of the robe would be simplified. Christ's slightly turned head would be changed to an impassive forward position; his crossed wrists bound and the reed added. In later drawings the focus would move to his upper body, his legs no longer included. Christ would become more austere, his attitude ever one of calm acceptance and passivity. His aloofness and reserve would contrast in the complete composition to the surrounding tumult indicated by the gesticulating soldiers.

Of the ample sources for the composition one must mention Lodovico Cigoli's *Ecce Homo* (ca. 1606, Palazzo Pitti, Florence). But Christ among his tormentors was a frequent theme in the 1840s and 1850s: F.L. Benouville's 1845 Prix de Rome *Christ before the Praetorial Court* (Ecole des Beaux-Arts, Paris); Alexandre Decamps's 1847 painting of the same subject (Musée du Louvre, Paris), particularly the figure to the lower right; and Ary Scheffer's austere *Christ with the Reed* (ca. 1856-57; Dordrechts Museum), are the closest progenitors.

Christ is portrayed as refined, passive and spiritually removed from his harsh tormentors. His submissiveness, the lean figural type and the helpless crossing of his bound hands foreshadow the type and passive stance of Puvis's *Poor Fisherman* of 1881 (fig. 23).

1 Among the many interesting related drawings: *Ecce Homo* or *Composition Study with Three Figures*, inscribed u.l.: 116, black chalk with white highlights on tinted tracing paper, 482 x 378 mm, Musée du Petit Palais, Paris (Inv. PPD 273; MCB 8), 1976-77 Paris/Ottawa, no. 29; *The Descent from the Cross* [sic, an *Ecce Homo*], inscribed: 'A Ch. Durand-Ruel, affectueusement Puvis de Chavannes,' sanguine on white paper, 300 x 230 mm (collection Durand-Ruel, Paris); *Christ and his Tormentors*, medium and dimensions unavailable (private collection); *Figure of Christ for the 'Ecce Homo'*, ca. 1858, black chalk heightened with white on beige-pink paper, 376 x 254 mm, Musée des Beaux-Arts, Lille (Inv. 2023), 1976-77 Paris/Ottawa, no. 30.

2 Exhibited at 1858-59 Lyons, no. 481; called *Ecce Homo* by Vachon (1895), p. 62; and 1936, Lyons, Palais Saint Pierre, *The Mocking of Christ* in *Exposition de l'art réligieux*, no. 77; 1976-77 Paris/Ottawa, no. 28 states Puvis gave it to his brother Edouard for the church.

3 Cabinet des Estampes, Bibliothèque Nationale, Paris (Inv. 1318; 1900).

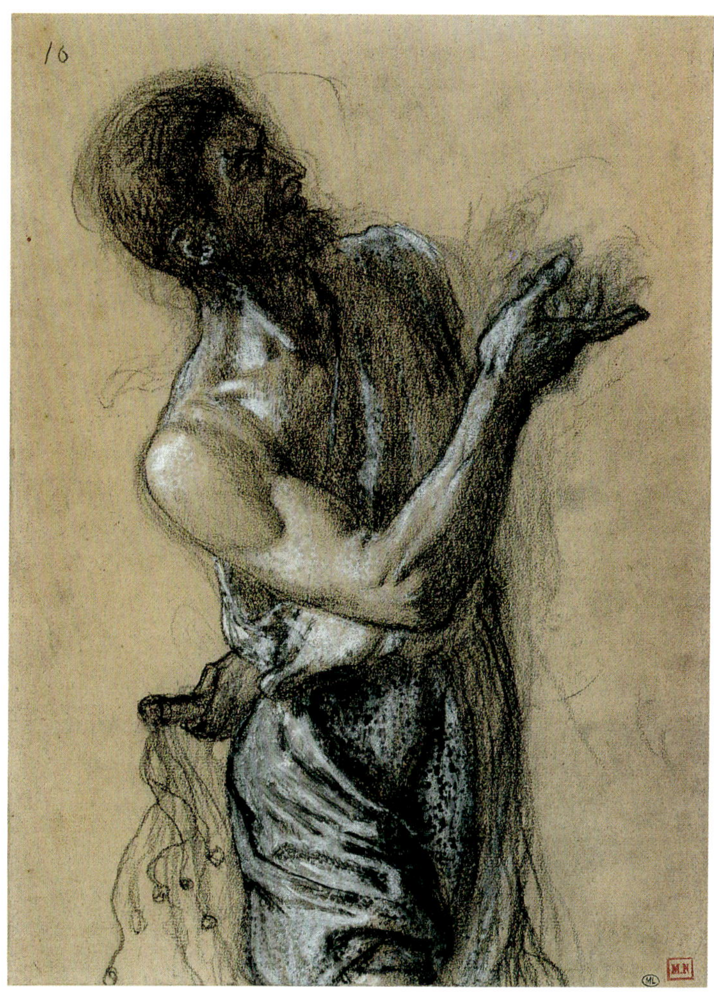

21

Study for the Tormentor in 'Ecce Homo'

ca. 1858

Stamp l.r.; inscribed u.l.: 10 [or 16]
Black chalk heightened with white on beige-pink paper, 308 x 234 mm
Musée du Louvre, Paris (Inv. RF 2160)

Provenance Bequest of artist's heirs to the city of Paris (1899); Musée du Luxembourg; transferred to the Musée du Louvre (1929).

Selected Exhibitions 1976-77 Paris/Ottawa, no. 31.

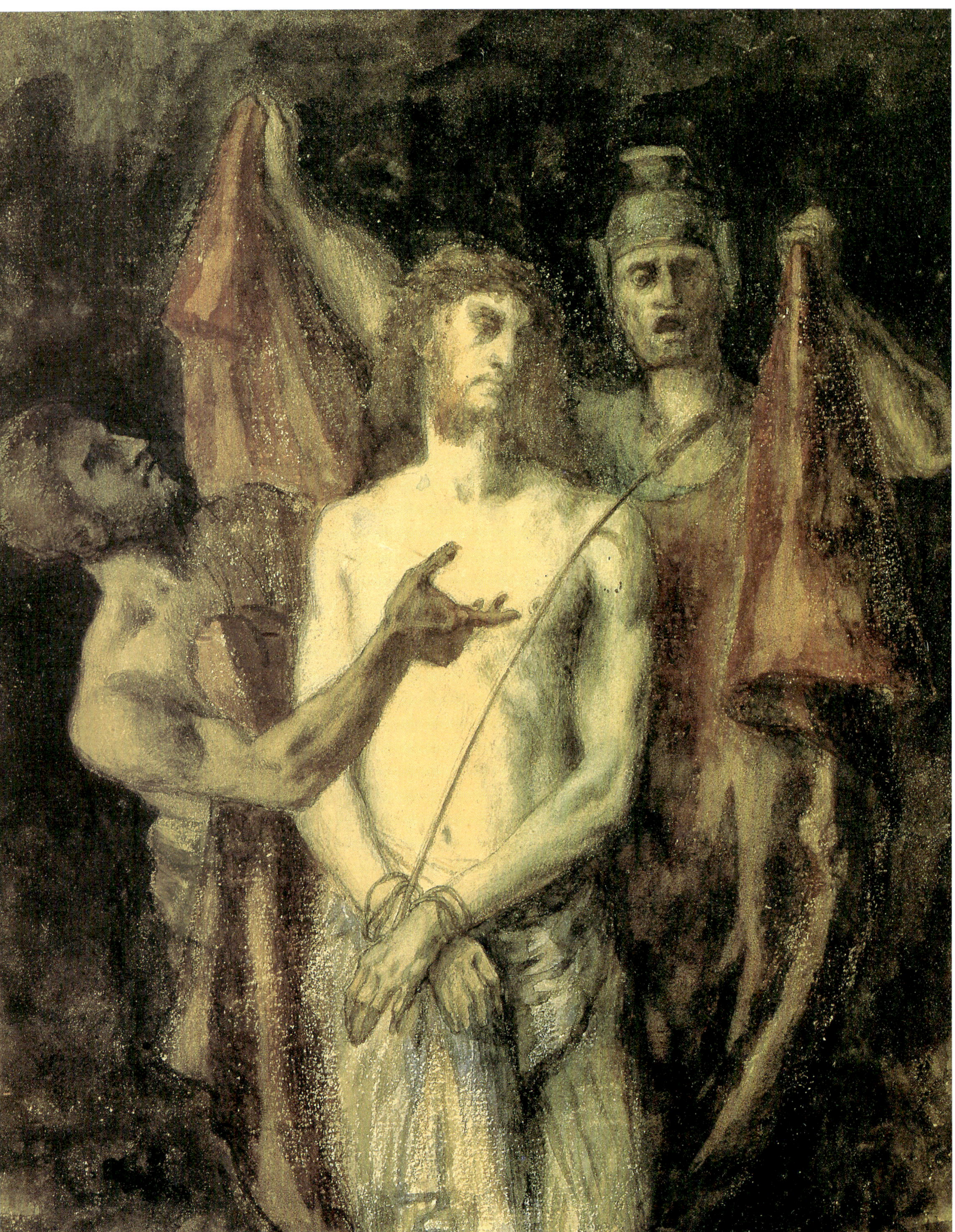

2

This is a variant study of the figure to the left in the *Ecce Homo* drawing compositions of the person who leans around to present Christ, derisively pointing him out with an eloquent, dramatic and cruel gesture. Developed as an individual, the figure here stands in an exotic costume, one shoulder bared (compare the garb of the executioner in the later *The Beheading of Saint John the Baptist* [cat. 57]). In a complicated and mannered pose, notable for its torsion, he conceals a kind of cat-o-nine tails behind his back. Pentimenti indicate minor adjustments made in realizing this brutish figure.

Puvis had been involved in formulating a composition of similarly callous soldiers making light of their vicious duties in his 1857 *Martyrdom of Saint Sebastian* (two versions in private collections).[1]

1 See 1976-77 Paris/Ottawa, no. 19; and also no. 21.

22

Ecce Homo ca. 1858

Inscribed: à ma petite Margot P. Puvis de Chavannes
Watercolor on paper, 234 x 190 mm (sight)
Private collection

Provenance Artist's heirs and by descent.

This refined watercolor of the pale, passive Christ flanked by robust tormentors, the mouth of the figure to the right open in a howl, is another variant of the *Ecce Homo* theme (see cat. 20). With the figure to the left turned towards Christ as in the definitive painting, and the figure behind him in a soldier's helmet, this version would seem to be later than studies at the Musée du Louvre (cat. 20, 21) and the Musée du Petit Palais.[1] Unlike those other versions, however, in which Christ gazes calmly forward, his head is here turned to the right.

The unusually careful and detailed rendering is in part explained by the inscription: this was a gift to 'Margot,' a name we take to be a diminutive appellation for the artist's niece, Marguerite de Vaugelas (born 1839), daughter of his older sister. She may have been particularly close to the artist as well as pious, for a decade later Puvis would again inscribe a religious work to her, a *Magdalene* (cat. 62).

Watercolors are not at all frequent among Puvis de Chavannes's 1850s work. The medium was used here perhaps as suitable for a presentation work on paper, refined, colored and delicate as suited both the subject and its young recipient.

1 See cat. 20, note 1.

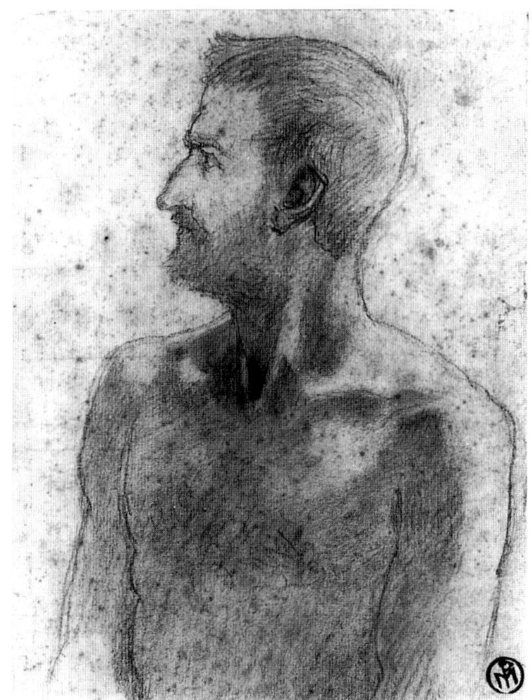

23

Bust of a Man ca. 1850s/1860s

Inscribed l.l.: 72
Sanguine on off-white paper, 225 x 175 mm
Musée de Picardie, Amiens (Inv. 912bis 86)

Provenance Bequest of artist's heirs to the city of Amiens (1898).

This sanguine drawing of the head and upper torso of a man, his head turned in profile, with narrow, squared-off shoulders and an unclothed chest is notable for its simple and direct, unprepossessing actuality and its angularity. It likely dates from the 1850s when sanguine was frequently the artist's medium of choice.

After brief stints at the studios of Henri Scheffer and Eugène Delacroix and a short apprenticeship with Thomas Couture, Puvis eschewed formal art instruction. Instead, in about 1852, he formed an enterprise he called, perhaps sardonically, an 'Academy,' at which he worked with Gustave Ricard, Alexandre Bida and occasionally the engraver Victor Pollet: 'We founded an Academy among ourselves. Every evening, from eight o'clock on we had a life model and we reciprocally corrected each other. Never was teaching better than this mutual instruction.'[1] It may have been this kind of setting in which life drawing was important that provided Puvis with the impetus to execute drawings such as the *Bust of a Man*.

1 'Nous fondâmes une Académie entre nous. Tous les soirs, à partir de huit heures, nous avions le modèle vivant et réciproquement, nous nous corrigions. Jamais enseignement ne fut meilleur que cet enseignement mutuel.' Vachon [1900], p. 14.

24

Group of Figures ca. 1859-61

Inscribed and signed l.r.: dimanche lundi: P P Ch
Sanguine on paper, 140 x 210 mm
Musée de Picardie, Amiens (Inv. 912^{bis}77)

Provenance Bequest of artist's heirs to the city of Amiens (1898).

Quite wonderful figural passages and unusually fluent and engaging poses are to be found in this supple sketch, possibly a study for an unrealized project. An unusually sensuous half-draped figure in the foreground at left swings one arm up and around her person, while another figure lolls deliciously at center. A figure garbed in an antique mode is seated with legs dangling down. Although the drawing does not bear particular resemblance to any other drawing by Puvis known to the author, the figures retain the dramatic gusto of pose one associates with the compositions of the middle to later 1850s. There is a flexibility and knowingness of technique, and a certain loose assurance. The plasticity of the figures and their variable sizes as they are situated within a pocket of space is of some interest to the artist, but would not be so for long. The apparel, such as it is, indicates a pictorial classicism that Puvis arrived at in about 1860. Another element to support this dating is the medium. Puvis particularly favored red chalk during the first fifteen years or so of his activity. 24

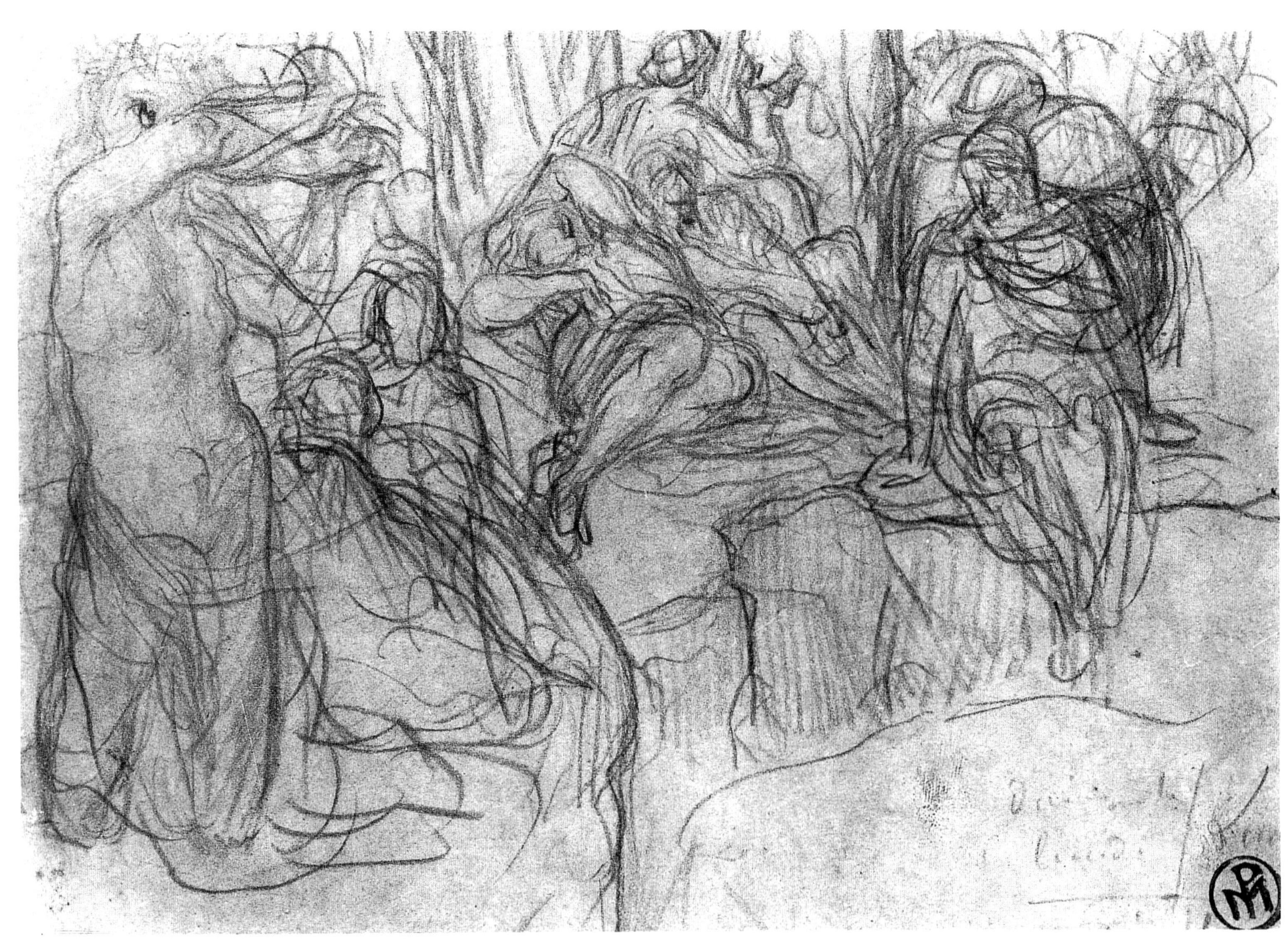

25

Project for a Decoration for the Musée de Picardie, Amiens ca. 1861-62

Stamp: at bottom, five times
Gouache, ink, pencil and red chalk on paper, with overlays, 290 x 1343 mm
The Brooklyn Museum, Charles S. Smith Memorial Fund (Inv. 22.61)

Provenance H. Anglade; Galerie Adam Dupré, Paris; Durand-Ruel, New York (1913); Durand-Ruel, Paris (1913); Durand-Ruel, New York (1922); Brooklyn Museum of Art (1922); Smith Memorial Fund.

Selected References Durand-Ruel Archives, no. 83; photo 7680, no. 10336; Foucart-Borville (1976), p. 66, repr. fig. 16.

Puvis de Chavannes must have executed this striking scheme, a partially colored drawing that translates heroic themes into a decorative vehicle, to show his capabilities and garner his first official project for a specific setting.[1] His first opportunity to produce murals for a public place was for the new Musée Napoléon as it was then called (now the Musée de Picardie) in Amiens, a building that would come to house one of Puvis's most extensive mural cycles, a veritable compendium of his work developed over two decades (1861 through 1882). Ambitious and seeking recognition, Puvis had presented his first monumental paintings, *Concordia* and *Bellum* (see cat. 26-27), at the Salon of 1861, their destination undetermined. Puvis was awarded a second class medal, and the Ministry of Beaux-Arts bought the former on 24 August 1861; Puvis presented its pendant to the State. These acquisitions apparently led the museum's architect, Arthur-Stanislas Diet, to contact the painter.

This design, which includes five framed portals surmounted by oculi and vaulted ceilings, must have been contrived in response to projected plans for the *piano nobile* level at the top of the grand central staircase of the museum, and what Puvis knew or fantasied about the elevations.[2] Five entrances to the collections had been proposed on 19 February 1861, seconded on 21 March 1862 by Charles Dufour, president of the museum commission, and that resolution had been forwarded to the regional prefect.[3] Puvis must have executed this *projet* at the architect's instigation sometime after February 1861 and before late 1862,[4] for by the later date, he was working on *Rest* and *Work* (see cat. 28-29), an indication that the project had been aborted, since several of its motifs, most notably the forgers, were introduced into the new paintings.[5] The proposed mural was to have occupied a long wall and (at either end) two contiguous side walls of the *piano nobile*, a program that differs considerably from the actual cycle which was completed piecemeal and would ultimately include Puvis's 1861 pair of paintings (though in an adjoining grand foyer) that came to the museum officially in 1863.[6] By 1865 Puvis would have finished five large and a number of ancillary canvases for Amiens, three of which – *Rest* and *Work* of 1863 and *Ave Picardia Nutrix* of 1865 (ill. pp. 102-103) – occupy the surrounds of the stairwell where this scheme was to have been.

This carefully rendered drawing is unique in Puvis's oeuvre. The painted turquoise sky functions as a flat unifying agent that diminishes the importance of the narrative figures and testifies to an effort to develop a special aesthetic appropriate to architectural decoration. Two zones are demarcated, each with a separate figurative order and scale: an upper zone with large gamboling putti, a nod to swags and festoons and other decorative conceits – and a manifestation of the Second Empire Rococo revival of the 1860s – and a zone of far smaller classicizing figures engaged in quasi-narrative passages. In the former, the outsize putti, like those Henri Lehmann used in murals for the Paris Hôtel de Ville (destroyed in the Commune), hold attributes ranging from doves to shields; while large, allegorical figures, reminiscent of Théodore Chassériau's figures at the Cour des Comptes (also destroyed), relate to the narratives concerning peace, war, rest and industry. The disjunctive types and scale are not altogether successful. Passages recall sources as varied as Roman reliefs, Renaissance murals and paintings of the Fontainebleau School.

Stanzas on the arts from Horace, Virgil and Dante were proposed as a source, and in an 1866 guide, the Abbé Corblet pointed out emblems borrowed from Ovid, Cicero and Virgil.[7] The project provided pictorial nuggets to be mined at Amiens and elsewhere. Among the iconographic motifs on the six wall segments from left to right are: 1) a triumphal arch (that could represent Roman Gaul), a familial group and figures surrounding a pipe player (much as they do the old man in *Rest* [see cat. 29]); 2) a seated male who recurs as a weaver in drawings for *Ave Picardia Nutrix* (see also cat. 36),[8] 3) an aquatic interlude with bathers, a winged Pegasus, and mounted figures; recreation recalling Chassériau's sketches for a *Summer*,[9] that would also recur in Puvis's late *Summer* for the Paris Hôtel de Ville (see cat. 134), the pond and chilled figures also in his *Summer* of 1873 (fig. 5); 4) figures flanking the central door; Bountifulness or Agriculture at the right relating to the theme of *Ave Picardia Nutrix*, Puvis's 1865 mural; 5) a tiny triumphal arch surmounted by what must be an eagle,[10] a Napoleonic emblem, includes horsemen, trumpets raised as in *Bellum*; 6) the far right segment dominated by a maternity figure, horsemen to the rear and the forgers that would dominate *Work*. The construction of a temple (right), comparable to a Chassériau motif in his *Peace* (Cour des Comptes),[11] was modified for *Massilia, Greek Colony* (see cat. 50) in 1869. Intimations of *Rest* (left) and *Work* (right) are at the far ends of the schema, with scenes parallel to *Concordia* and *Bellum* to the left and right of center.

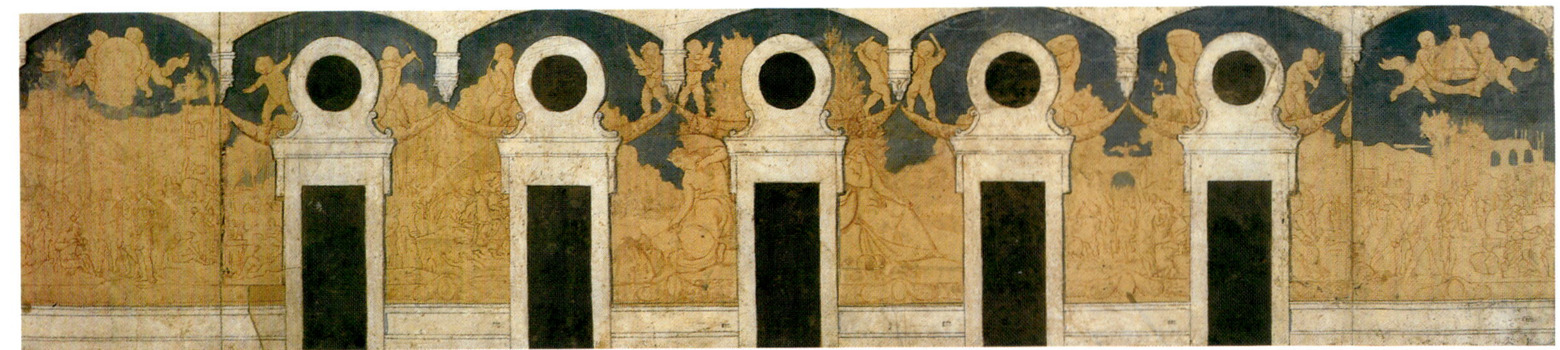

1 Foucart-Borville (1976), p. 66, assumes a drawing done by Puvis for himself; despite the paper overlays (at center and corners) that indicate modified portions, I assume a presentation to the architect or commissioning body.

2 The plans changed considerably in 1861-62 and by 1887 the architecture of the museum would be profoundly modified; see Foucart-Borville (1976), pp. 21-27.

3 CMN correspondance 1862; quoted by d'Argencourt (1973), p. 15.

4 The commission has been analyzed by d'Argencourt (1973); Foucart-Borville (1976), and Boucher (1979); but negotiations or pledges that might have led the artist to formulate this scheme have not been mentioned.

5 Thus a label, verso, with the date 1865 could not be accurate, for by that time Puvis would have completed a number of other works for Amiens.

6 See Viéville (1989), p. 2.

7 Foucart-Borville (1976), p. 61, n. 94. Mythological and literary sources including a so-called 'triumph of the victor' and Diana and Actaeon were ascribed to the drawing when it was exhibited in 1922-23, Brooklyn Museum, *Paintings by Contemporary English and French Painters*, no. 180.

8 Musée de Lille (Inv. 2028-32; I 2687) or Musée de Picardie, Amiens, (Inv. MP-II-12-26A; MP-II-12-2) *inter alia*.

9 Musée du Louvre, Paris (Inv. RF 26055.15 verso).

10 The sculptor Lequesne contributed both large and small eagles to the final decor; see Foucart-Borville (1976), p. 27, note 32.

11 As projected in a drawing, Musée du Louvre (Inv. RF 4518).

The Salon of 1861 with *Concordia*,
which was later installed at the Musée de Picardie, Amiens

Peace, War, Work, Rest: The Reduced Versions of Murals at the Musée de Picardie, Amiens

Puvis de Chavannes had his first success as a painter of monumental wall paintings at the Salon of 1861 with the very works with which he made his public debut as a muralist: *Concordia* and *Bellum*, painted without a destination, were acquired by the State. In 1863, Puvis added *Work* and *Rest* to the first pair. The four were obtained in late 1863 for the Musée Napoléon (later the Musée de Picardie) in Amiens through the efforts of its architect Arthur Diet. In 1864 the ensemble was installed at Amiens and unavailable for further exhibition.[1]

When they were exhibited in 1863, *Rest* and *Work* were not acquired by the State, much to the artist's dismay.[2] On 8 July 1863 he wrote to the Count de Nieuwerkerke, Minister of Beaux-Arts, insisting that the four remain together with a view to having them rendered by the Gobelins workshops; and in a 23 July 1863 letter Puvis further protested to him that they formed an inseparable 'ensemble' with *Concordia* and *Bellum*, which he offered to buy back.[3] *Rest* and *Work* were rolled in an atelier corner until Diet championed them for Amiens.[4] Puvis would ultimately give the second pair to Amiens.

In order to represent his first publicly successful murals at the important Exposition Universelle in 1867 in Paris, Puvis executed reduced versions after this quartet (cat. 26-29). Now the first two received French titles, *La Paix* and *La Guerre* (*Peace* and *War*), considered less pretentious than their original Latin ones and in conformity with the French titles *Le Travail* and *Le Repos* that Puvis had in 1863 given the second pair. French titles served to unify the four, further indicating they were an ensemble, and also helped propel the images from an antique to a

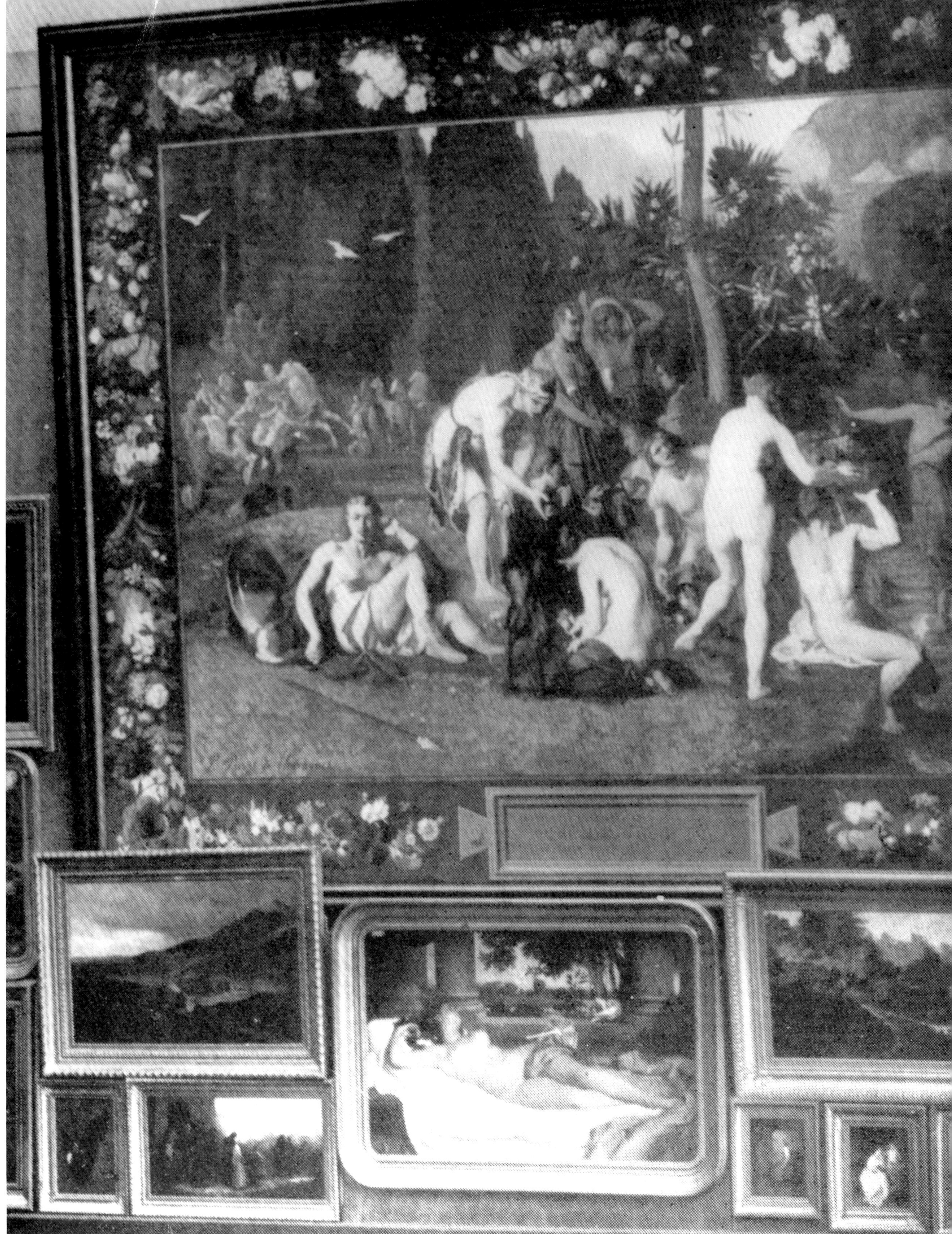

more nationalistic context. In order to enhance his reputation, Puvis would continue the practice of painting what he called 'reductions' after his murals. It was through these reduced versions – virtually as easel paintings – that could be transported, exhibited and sold, that his works would come to be best known. It would be misleading, however, to think of these and, more especially, later versions of other murals as replicas.

Puvis's first four monumental canvases each measure over three and a half meters high by over five meters wide, with an additional meter all around for the borders.[5] The reduced versions measure one by one and a half meters, the size of easel paintings. They are more satisfactory as independent paintings than many of the later reductions, because the murals on which they are based are relatively independent of their setting, designed, as they were, without a specific destination. The four are smoothly executed, their colors somewhat more fully saturated than those of the wall paintings, colors considered more apt for easel paintings, that would have more impact, given the diminished size of the painted areas.

The reductions cannot transmit the importance of the murals granted by size alone, the opulence itself of lavish dimensions and the empathetic reading a viewer makes of life-size figures. Adjustments were made to a smaller format – the brushwork was modified to the size of the objects and with the viewing distance changed, certain characteristics close-up became more noticeable. If the surface had remained the same as the mural surface, it would have been too crude for a small painting and details would have been obliterated; if it had been reduced proportionately, the scumbled effect would have disappeared.

Conspicuous in each of these reduced versions of the murals is a decorated blue border about 14 cm wide. The murals *Concordia* and *Bellum* sported Puvis's first decorated borders, a wide dark band with leafy garlands and entwined attributes and a narrow gold strip. These were important to canvases that Puvis hoped would suggest themselves as being ready for installation as public murals or models for the Gobelins tapestry factories.

The borders of *Concordia* and *Bellum* on which he set such store were eliminated at Amiens, much to Puvis's distress, and the reductions allow us to see them once again. In increasingly heated correspondence in the autumn of 1863, Diet noted that Puvis's first pair of wall paintings needed new borders to be accommodated to their designated places, while Puvis adamantly declared that his borders absolutely belonged with the paintings ('elle est absolument dépendante du tableau') and recommended that the architectural ornament be altered instead.[6] As he put it: 'As actually concerns my border, I will defend it with all my might – with the absolute conviction that its matte texture, its soberness, its neutral quality powerfully serve my painting while giving the stonework a very tasteful pungency.'[7] His arguments were of no avail. He was forced grudgingly to accept the then fashionable decoration of curled and colorful vegetation and ribbons against a Pompeian-red background, which Maurice Denis later characterized (in his *Journal*) as 'meager Pompeian motifs.'[8]

As with these four murals, the artist felt his reduced versions of them belonged together. The four were purchased by the American collector John G. Johnson on 28 November 1888, in exchange for Puvis's *Autumn* and a fee; and Johnson sold *Rest* and *Work* to his friend Peter A.B. Widener, though the artist had insisted to Durand-Ruel that the four be sold together and offered to buy them back himself if that condition was not met.[9]

1 There is an extensive literature on the Amiens murals. Primary sources are: AN F21174; CMN; Archives de la Mairie d'Amiens: Archives modernes: 2 R 7/6; Archives de la Société des Antiquaires de Picardie, Amiens (correspondence, 1864-1865). Monographs on Puvis de Chavannes all include discussions of the Amiens ensemble; there are also special studies. In particular consult: Vachon (1895), pp. 77-94; Vachon [1900], pp. 114-125; Scheid (1907) *passim*; Jean (1925), pp. 17-28; also Brown Price (1972), pp. 307-313, 315-330, 335-336; d'Argencourt (1973), *passim*, with bibliography; Foucart-Borville (1976), *passim*, with bibliography; 1976-77 Paris/Ottawa, pp. 58-64; Viéville (1989), *passim*. Furthermore, there is a large number of related sketches and drawings at Amiens and elsewhere.

2 See Foucart-Borville (1976), p. 32.

3 AN F21174; quoted also in d'Argencourt (1973), pp. 21, 23-24.

4 Foucart-Borville (1976), pp. 29-30.

5 They are 360 x 545 cm, or 460 x 645 cm with borders according to 1976-77 Paris/Ottawa, pp. 62-63; and 340 x 555 cm or 450 x 665 cm with borders, according to Viéville (1989), pp. 10, 12, 14, 16.

6 Letter of 3 September 1863 to Charles Dufour (CMN, 1863); see d'Argencourt (1973), p. 31.

7 'En ce qui concerne directement ma bordure je la défendrai de toutes mes forces – dans l'absolue conviction que sa matité, sa sobriété, sa neutralité servent puissament ma peinture et donnent à la pierre un mordant de haut goût.' Undated letter (private collection).

8 Designed by MM. Chauvin and Gastine; see letter of 7 July 1864, to Dufour. On Puvis's use of borders, see also p. 16.

9 Letter from the curator of the Johnson Collection, to the author.

26

Peace / *La Paix* (reduced version of 1861 mural) 1867

Signed l.l.: P. Puvis de Chavannes
Inscribed at the center of the lower border: LA PAIX
Oil on canvas, 110 x 148.5 cm
Philadelphia Museum of Art, John G. Johnson Collection (Inv. JC 1062)

Provenance Durand-Ruel, Paris (ca. 1872); Hiltbrunner, Paris (1887); Durand-Ruel, New York; John G. Johnson (28 November 1888).
Selected Exhibitions 1867 Paris (Exposition Universelle), no. 526; 1868 Bordeaux, no. 504; 1881 Paris (Musée des Arts Décoratifs), no. 144; 1887 New York, no. 56; 1887 Paris (Durand-Ruel), no. 22; 1892, Philadelphia Museum of Art, *The Johnson Collection*; 1894 New York, no. 16; 1975 Toronto, no. 7; 1976-77 Paris/Ottawa, no. 36.
Selected References Burty (1868), 498, repr. 498; Chaumelin (1873), pp. 109, 219-220; Blanc (1876), *Les artistes de mon temps*, p. 475; [Anonymous] (December 1890), p. 5; W.R. Valentiner, *Catalogue of a Collection of Paintings and Some Art Objects*, vol. III (Philadelphia, 1914), pp. 142-143; Christian Brinton, 'The Johnson Modern Group,' *International Studio*, LXXXVI (October 1922), 11; Venturi (1939), II, pp. 193, 219; Hamilton Bell, 'Temporary Exhibition from the Johnson Collection,' *Pennsylvania Museum Bulletin*, no. 66 (1960), 10.

Puvis's classicizing history paintings *War* and *Peace* represented their sweeping themes as epics redolent of ancient literature and high art, flavored with Renaissance pastoral imagery and goodly portions of Poussin and Fontainebleau. These were shrewd evocations of grand art calculated to impress. In *Concordia* wonderful nude and semi-nude figures are clustered in idyllic interchange, passing the bountiful fruits of the land, before flowering trees. They graciously interact or lie about in a hospitable landscape setting, a protected valley on the banks of a river. Similar themes had been presented to much acclaim by Chassériau, whose generalized rhetoric influenced Puvis in countless formal, stylistic and conceptual ways, and Eugène Delacroix (at the Palais Bourbon).

As was to be Puvis's custom, several figures are drawn from antique and Renaissance prototypes: Mars, a shield by his side, is posed like the Mars (or Dionysus) on the Parthenon's East pediment; the horsemen at the back resemble the Dioscuri; the figure in animal skins, Hercules. Virgilian passages from *The Eclogues* are suggested:

'[But first] as little gifts for you, child, Earth untilled
Will pour the straying ivy rife, and baccaris,
And colocasia mixing with acanthus' smile.
She-goats, unshepherded will bring home udders plumped
With milk....'(IV, 18-21)[1]

The center of the composition, based as it is on the earliest of Puvis's large murals, is the most densely populated area with strongly enunciated, outlined figures. Female figures with marmoreal flesh legible at a distance are the most prominent. The pyramidal group at the center, a nude female flanked by two males, of particular importance to the artist, was also the subject of a separate, small panel painted around 1861 (Hillstead Museum, Farmington, Connecticut). Smaller figures at the sides, in the middle and background shore up the themes through narrative activity. Puvis's mural compositions would radically change over the next decades with pictorial interest spread to all sections of the mural surface, with figurations to be staged and set at unhurried, rhythmic intervals, and a gradual lessening of the figurative interchange that a narrative component demands.

1 Virgil, *The Eclogues*, transl. Guy Lee, rev. ed. (Harmondsworth, 1984), p. 57 (this edition used throughout).

27

War / *La Guerre* (reduced version of 1861 mural) 1867

Signed l.l.: P. Puvis de Chavannes
Inscribed at the center of the lower border: LA GUERRE
Oil on canvas, 110 x 147.5 cm
Philadelphia Museum of Art, John G. Johnson Collection (Inv. JC 1063)

Provenance See cat. 26.
Selected Exhibitions See cat. 26; in addition, note different nos.: 1868 Bordeaux, no. 505; 1887 New York, no. 55; 1887 Paris (Durand-Ruel), no. 21; 1894 New York, no. 17; 1975 Toronto, no. 6; 1976-77 Paris/Ottawa, no. 37.
Selected References See cat. 26.

The source for *War* or *Bellum* seems to be the *Iliad* (Book XXIV, 700-790), which tells of Hector's death during the Trojan War and the lamentations over his body by his parents Priam and Hecuba and his wife Andromache, who are represented here by the old couple and mourning woman. The *Aeneid*'s terse but majestic passages are, however, closer to the spirit of the painting than the Homeric account of the Trojan War. Virgil describes how Creusa, Aeneas's wife, bearing their son Ascanius, was lost in the tumult and darkness (II, 298-318, 705-752), how the Straits of Sigeum lit up from the fires of the burning city, and how shouts arose and trumpets rang. Virgil has Aeneas remember: 'I spread a tawny lion skin across my bent neck, over my broad shoulders, and then take up Anchises; small Iülus [Ascanius] now clutches my right hand; his steps uneven, he is following his father; and my wife moves on behind....'(II, 974-979).[1] The pickaback group on the right suggests Aeneas carrying his father Anchises on his

26

27

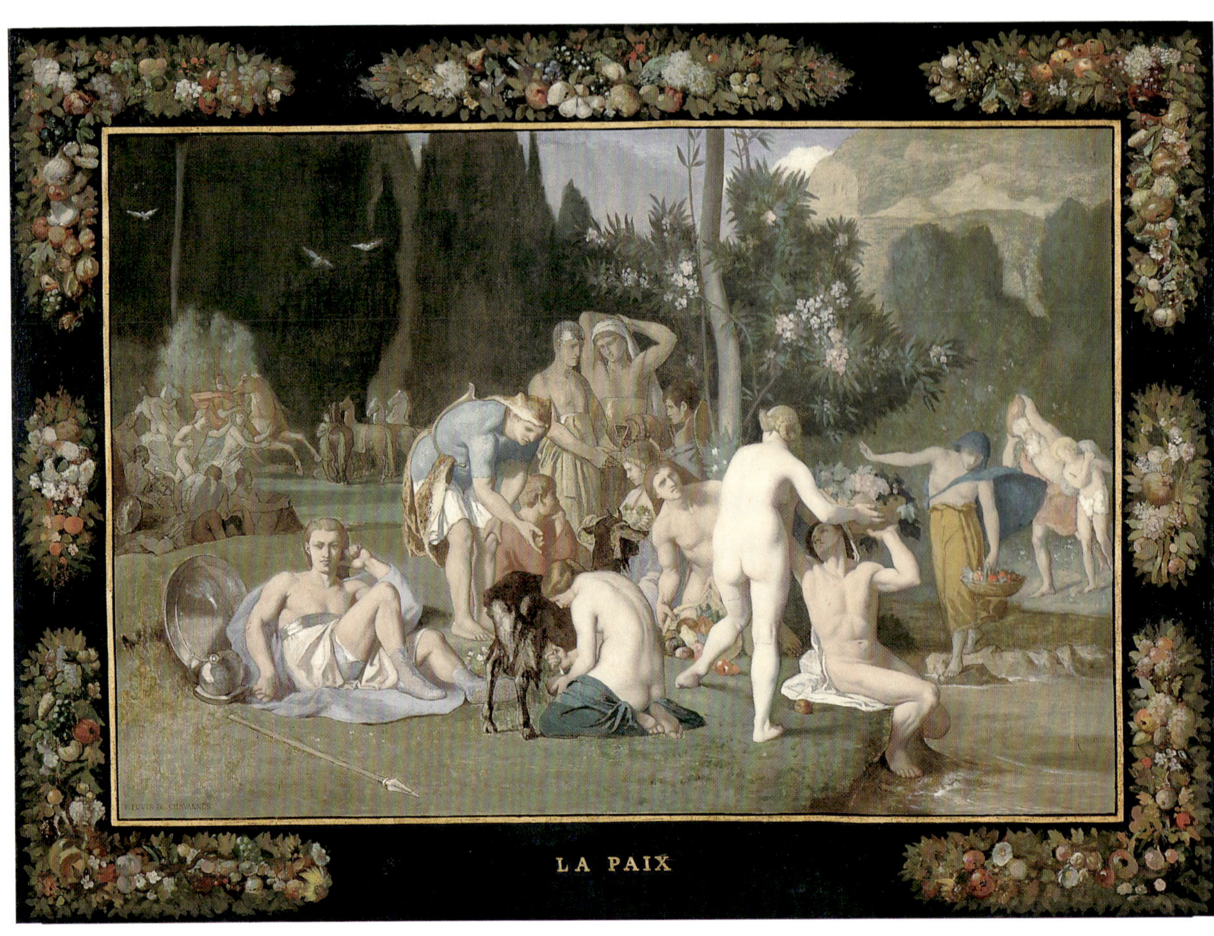

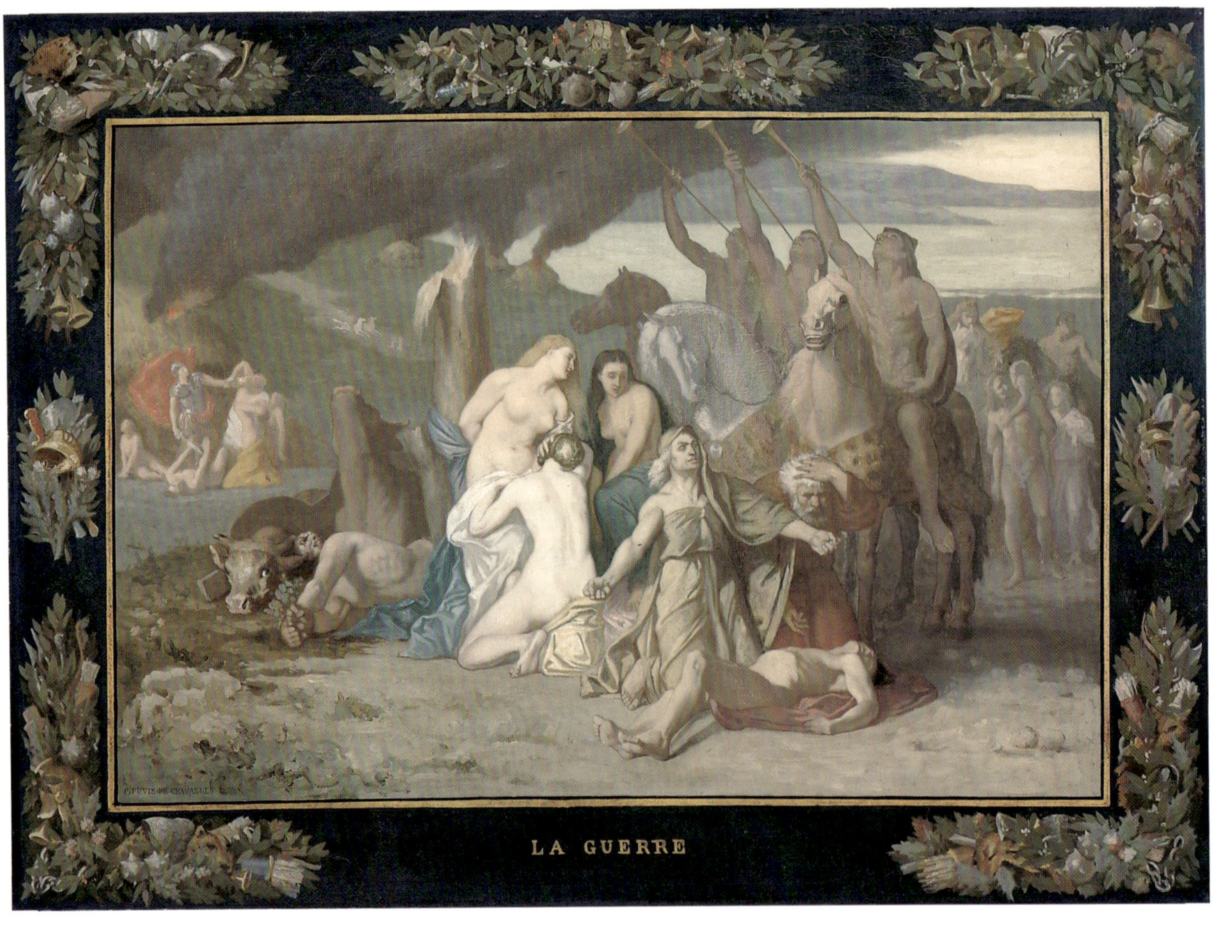

28

29

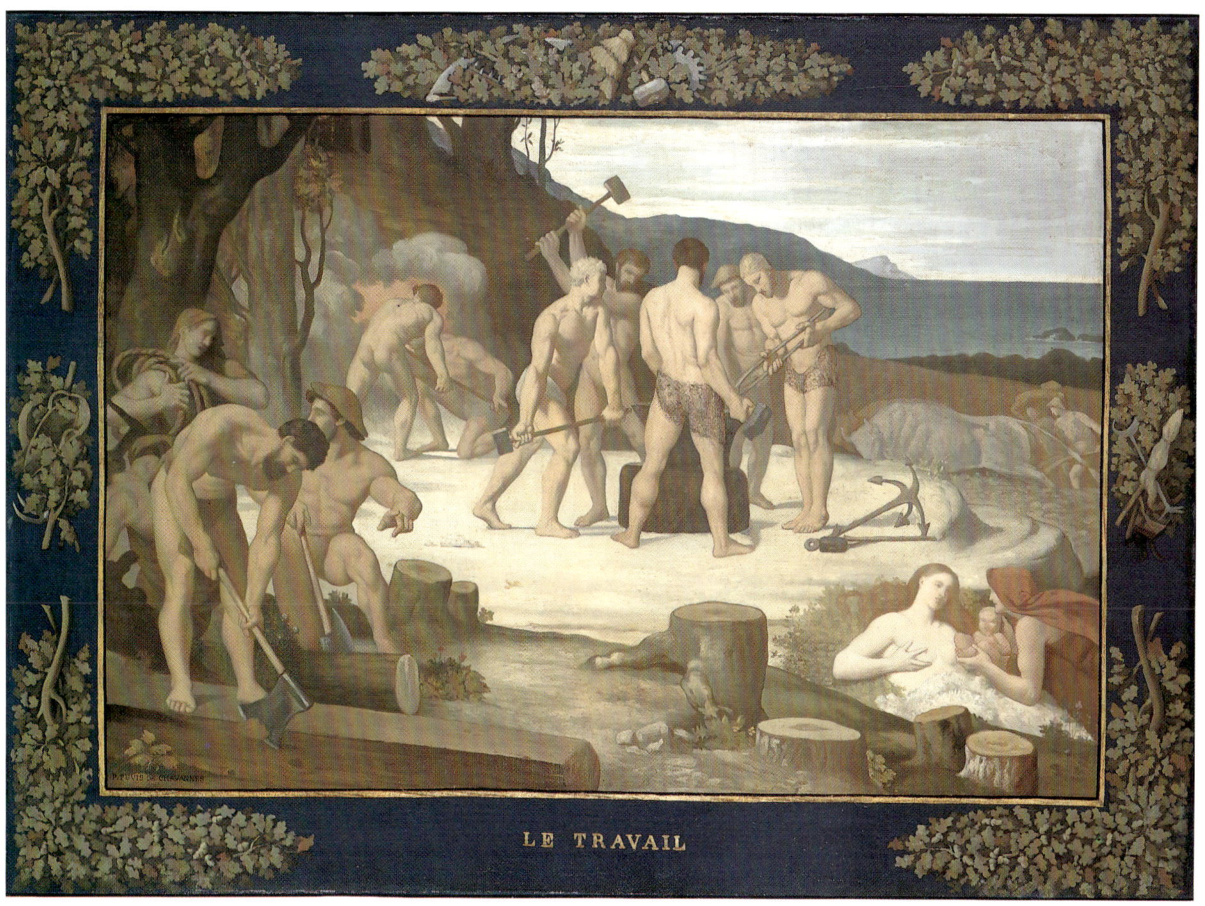

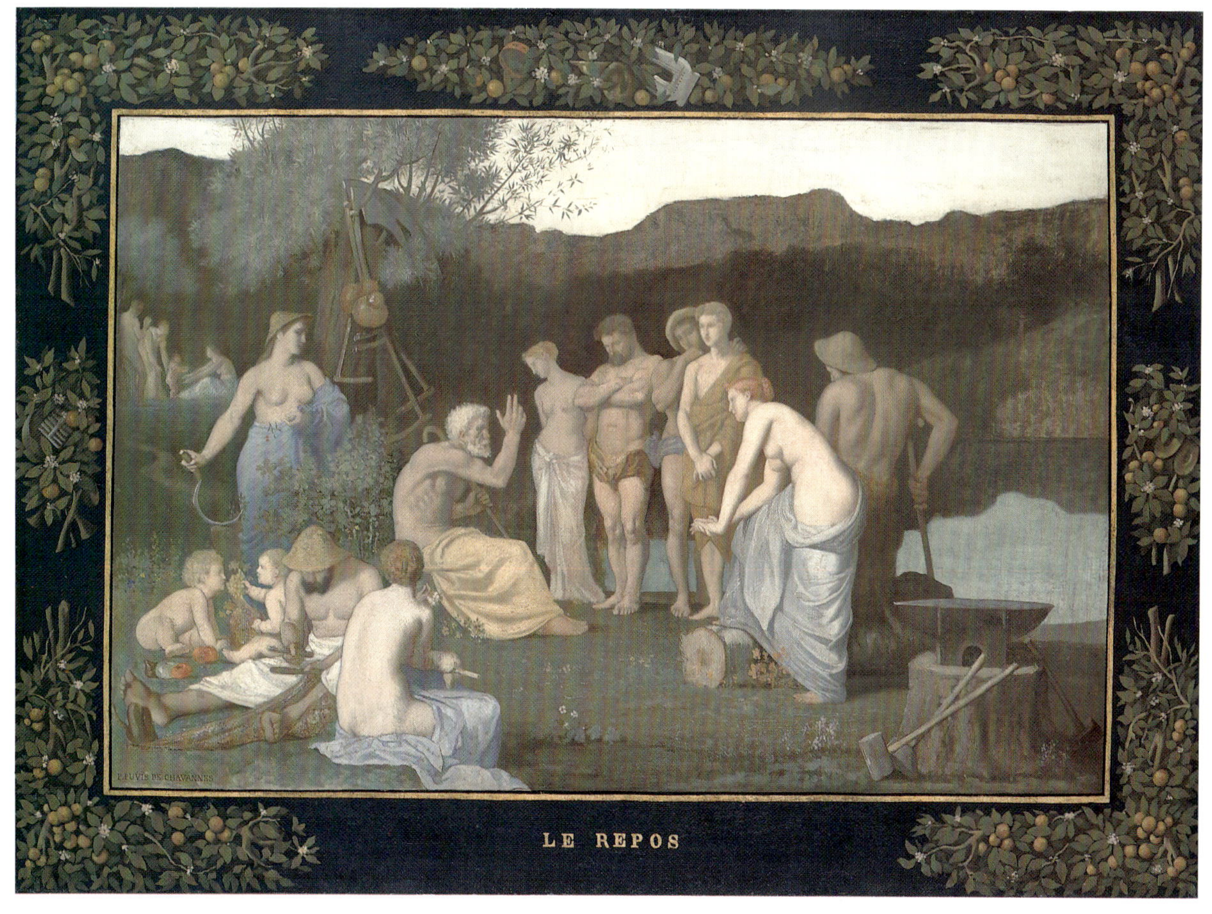

shoulders from the burning Troy, a motif illustrative of filial piety. The three mounted trumpeters who announce war: 'and he calls on battle to issue out .... the brazen trumpets echo hoarse accord' (VII, 810, 812) closely resemble those in Chassériau's *Return from War* (Cour des Comptes, Paris, destroyed), the imagery of which was a model for Puvis in the 1860s. Moreover, Puvis, who knew Virgil well, used lines from the *Aeneid* not far from those above as a source for his 1867 *Sleep* (see cat. 47).

The Trojan War was of singularly special interest to French history: 'It used to be thought that the French were descended from the Franks who themselves came from Troy, and, until the eighteenth century, genealogies going back to Priam were dutifully memorised by schoolboys.'[2]

The immediate iconographic precedent for *Bellum* was Joseph Lies's *Evils of War* (*Les Maux de la Guerre*), exhibited at the Paris Salon of 1859. In turn, Edgar Degas's *Scene of War in the Middle Ages* (Musée d'Orsay, Paris) of 1865[3] seems to owe figural passages to Puvis's canvas. Degas's bending woman resembles the woman tied to the stake and his composition is especially similar to a refined preparatory drawing for *Bellum*[4] with coincident bowing female nudes. Smoke and burning buildings occupy the middle left of both, and pillage and victimization is their theme. Puvis is said to have complimented Degas on the quality of the nudes in his painting when it was exhibited in 1865.[5]

1 Virgil, *Aeneid*, transl. Allen Mandelbaum (Toronto, New York, 1961) (this edition used throughout).
2 Theodore Zeldin, *France 1848-1945. Intellect and Pride*, rev. ed. (Oxford, 1980), p. 10.
3 *Scène de Guerre au Moyen Age*, formerly called *Les Malheurs de la Ville d'Orléans* and *Les Malheurs de Nouvelle Orléans*; see Pool (1964), 306-311, Lies's painting repr. fig. 2. See also 1988-89, Paris, Grand Palais / Ottawa, National Gallery of Canada / New York, Metropolitan Museum of Art, *Degas*, no. 45, pp. 105-107.
4 Musée de Picardie, Amiens (Inv. 912bis 26)
5 John Rewald, *The History of Impressionism*, 4th rev. ed. (New York, 1973), p. 122, without source; repeated in McMullen (1985), p. 126.

28

Work / *Le Travail* (reduced version of 1863 mural) 1867

Signed l.l.: P. Puvis de Chavannes
Inscribed at the center of the lower border:
LE TRAVAIL
Oil on canvas, 108.5 x 148 cm
National Gallery of Art, Washington, D.C.,
Widener Collection (Inv. 1942.9.55)

Provenance See cat. 26; Peter A.B. Widener; gift of J.E. Widener (1942).

Selected Exhibitions See cat. 26; in addition, note different nos.: 1868 Bordeaux, no. 506; New York (1887), no. 57; 1887 Paris (Durand-Ruel), no. 15; [not in 1892 Philadelphia]; [not in 1975 Toronto]; 1976-77 Paris/Ottawa, no. 41.

Selected References See cat. 26; in addition, note different nos.: [W.R. Valentiner], *Paintings in the Collection of Joseph Widener at Lynnewood Hall* (Elkins Park, Pa., 1931), p. 196, repr. p. 197; Barnie F. Winkelman, *John G. Johnson. Lawyer and Art Collector 1841-1917* (Philadelphia, 1942), p. 289.

To complement his first pair of murals for the Museum at Amiens, Puvis executed *Work* and *Rest*. The former shows a pre-industrial Utopian community engaged in what we are given to understand are admirable, satisfying and wholesome enterprises.[1] Each member of Puvis's community, man and woman, willingly and industriously participates in work for the common good, tilling fields, hewing trees, forging tools and anchors for industry and exploration, and nurturing society's progeny. The figures are stationed on a lovely wooded bluff near the seashore, a demarcation of sea and sky establishing a horizontal banding, the kind of topography that was to become one of Puvis de Chavannes's preferred landscapes.

The classicizing, idealized laborers are in no sense challenging as is Millet's *Man with a Hoe*, also exhibited at the 1863 Salon, a haggard peasant, perceived in many quarters as ripe for revolution. In a century of rapid industrialization, new technologies and machinery had replaced skilled workers, and theoretical writings were increasingly devoted to their plight; nonetheless there was migration away from fields and farms to seek work. In the most general sense *Work* glorifies keeping the citizenry down on the farm, and deliberately turns away from these fiercely argued questions. Yet insofar as the imagery resonates with nineteenth-century Picardy, workers might gratefully participate, for in both town and country there was a surplus of labor for *châtelain* or employer.[2]

By choosing to put forgers at the center, Puvis singled out artisans whose way of working had changed far less than that of other trades.[3] Forgers were a frequent pictorial motif at mid-century, as they had been in previous generations. Henri Lehmann's 1852 forgers at the Hôtel de Ville in Paris (destroyed in the Commune) *Men Attend to Their First Work* or *Laboribus urgetur variis*[4] included forgers as well as men felling trees and preparing wood for building homes. Théodore Chassériau's *Order Attends to the Needs of War* or *War* included a section of *Forgers* (Cour des Comptes, Paris, destroyed).[5] A circle of muscular forgers viewed from various angles at progressive stages of performing the same action had proved compositionally inviting, as Tintoretto's *Vulcan's Forge* (Palazzo Ducale, Venice), Velazquez's forgers (*The Forge of Vulcan*, Museo del Prado, Madrid), Goya's (Frick Collection, New York) and Courbet's (Szépmüvészeti Múzeum, Budapest), testify. It is unlikely, however, that Puvis meant more than admiration by his reputed remark, 'If I hadn't been a painter ... I would have wanted to be a blacksmith.'[6] Wreathed around the group of forgers are other laborers: woodsmen, a new mother, a plowman. Tillers and maternity motifs were a commonplace of current civic murals, used for example by Chassériau in his *Peace, Protector of the Arts and Work of the World* (Cour des Comptes). The prominent man with a broadax ignores contemporary debate on deforestation and the government's exploitation of timber reserves. Yet Puvis might have approved the sentiments of the Parnassian poet Victor de Laprade, so often close to his own, in his 'Woodcutter' ('Le Bûcheron') of 1846 in which the woodcutter intones the elegiac: 'Farewell divine trunks.... God wishes it. Cities displace the forest,' though de Laprade continues, 'and often the desert closely follows the city.'[7]

1 See 1977-78, Le Creusot-Montceau-les-Mines, Ecomusée de la Communauté urbane, *La Représentation du travail: Mines, forges, usines*, p. 13.
2 See Robert Forster and Orest Ranum, eds. 'Power and Ideology in the Village Community of Picardy: Past and Present,' in *Rural Society in France: Selections from the Annales Economies, Sociétés, Civilisations* (Baltimore, 1977), p. 113.
3 1977-78, Le Creusot-Montceau-les-Mines, *op.cit.* (note 1), pp. 15-17; on forgers see the discussion of François Bonvin's *The Blacksmith's Shop – Remembrance of the Tréport* of 1857 in Gabriel P. Weisberg, *The Realist Tradition* (Cleveland, 1980), p. 65.
4 See Lehmann drawings at the Musée Carnavalet, Paris.
5 See Chassériau's drawings, Musée du Louvre *Album* (Inv. RF 26067) and Louis-Antoine Prat, *Dessins de Théodore Chassériau*, 2 vols. (Paris, 1988), no. 424. Cf. xcv, no. 1138, p. 226.
6 'Si ne j'étais pas un peintre ... j'aurais voulu être un forgeron.' To Henri Havard; quoted in Vachon (1895), p. 83.
7 'Adieu les troncs divins.... Dieu le veut. Les cités déplacent les forêts, et le désert souvent suit la cité de près.' *Oeuvres poétiques de Victor de Laprade* (Paris, 1878), I, pp. 191-192.

29

Rest / *Le Repos* (reduced version of 1863 mural) 1867

Signed l.l.: P. Puvis de Chavannes
Inscribed at the center of the lower border: LE REPOS
Oil on canvas, 108.5 x 148 cm
National Gallery of Art, Washington, D.C., Widener Collection (Inv. 1942.9.54)

Provenance See cat. 26; Peter A. B. Widener; gift of J.E. Widener (1942).
Selected Exhibitions See cat. 26; in addition, note different nos.: 1868 Bordeaux, no. 507; 1887 New York, no. 58; 1887 Paris, no. 14; [not in 1892 Philadelphia]; [not in 1975 Toronto]; 1976-77 Paris/Ottawa, no. 40.
Selected References See cat. 26, 28; in addition, note different nos.: [W.R. Valentiner (1931), p. 194, repr. p. 195.

A respite from *Work* is *Rest*: the anvil is set aside and tools suspended from a tree. The central theme here is the transmission of cultural values, skills and information – the maintenance of cultural continuity. While the seated old man and his listeners recall Attic stele reliefs and Piero della Francesca's *Death of Adam* (San Francesco, Arezzo), with which Puvis was certainly familiar,[1] figures gathered round an old Homeric character to hear his stories was a recurrent motif in French painting of the epoch: Guillon-Lethière's *Homer Reciting his Verses* (1816) and Paul Jourdy's similar *Homer Reciting his Poems*, which won the 1834 Prix de Rome (Paris, Ecole des Beaux-Arts), are only two examples. Corot's *Homer and the Shepherds* (1845 Salon, Musée de Saint-Lô) similarly groups the bard with three standing, attentive shepherds; and Henri Lehmann's *Menses et sidera signat* (or *Astronomy*, 1852, Hôtel de Ville, Paris, destroyed during the Commune) may have followed the same model. With drapery slipped down to her tilted hip and her arms concealed, the female auditor resembles a Venus de Milo. René Jean has also identified a Homer, Hercules and Apollo (near the daughter of Latona).[2]

Still intent on recognition and acceptability, Puvis looked to authoritative prototypes, whether antique (Hellenistic sculpture), Renaissance or baroque (albeit French classicizing). Classicizing figures with walking sticks, traveling hats and lyres, like those depicted on Greek vases, were anyway frequent subjects of contemporary French academic art. Some disjunctions of scale might be accounted for by Puvis's method of assembling figures from his repertory, and variegated skin tones, particularly the light-skinned females, by Greek convention. Now colors, such as the blue and turquoise of three of the women's draped garments, unify the pictorial surface.

1 Puvis's mature images were to have a striking affinity with that of the fifteenth-century master.
2 Jean (1925), pp. 26-28.

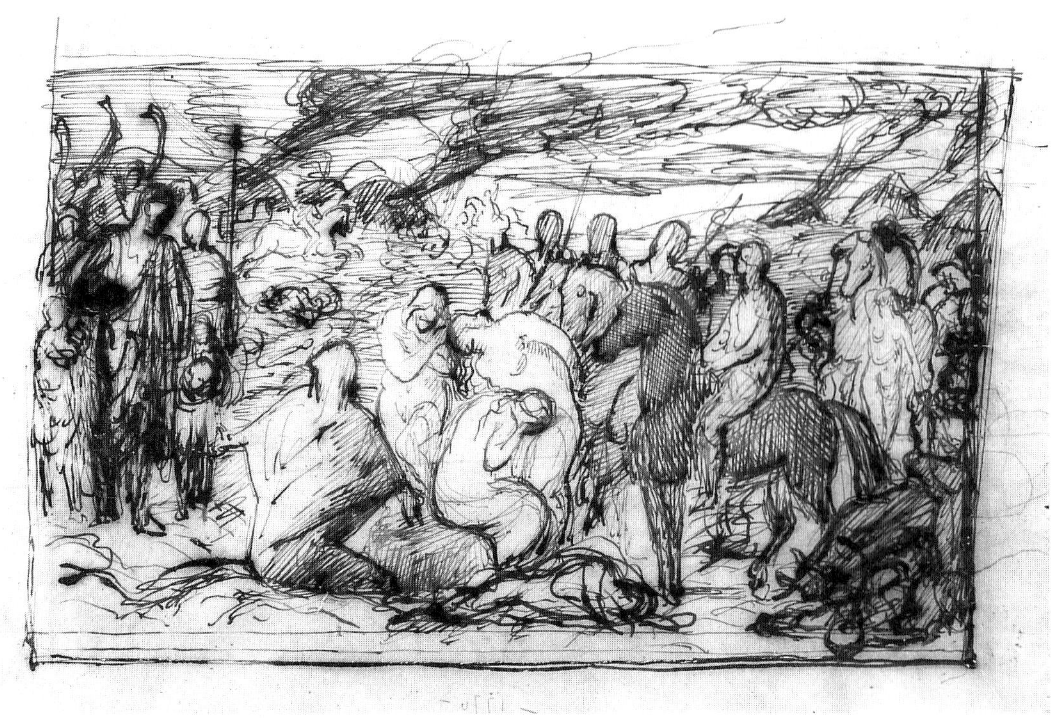

30

Study for 'Bellum' ca. 1861

Pen and red-brown ink on tracing paper, laid down, 150 x 240 mm
Private collection

Provenance H. Puvis de Chavannes, Paris; Mme H. Puvis de Chavannes, Neuilly.
Selected Exhibitions 1976-77 Paris/Ottawa, no. 39.

Puvis frequently planned large murals in drawings of very small dimensions. These required that he formulate essential geometries, vectors and forms important to his decorative schemes without being sidetracked by details. This refined, small study for *Bellum* sharply delineates a multitude of figures. But even amidst the turmoil, with fire and figures streaming in from the left, as in *The Fire* (see cat.19), patterns emerge: the repeated black funnels of smoke, the duplicated trumpeters and horsemen, and the grieving women in a progression of interlaced curves.

In a related, but less complete drawing in pencil and ink,[1] of almost the same dimensions, there are only two females at the center, the pivot around which the scheme would develop: the grieving woman with her head in her hands and the nude figure curved above her.

1 Musée de Picardie, Amiens (Inv. 912bis 26).

31

Labor, Study for 'Work' / *Labor, Etude pour 'Le Travail'* 1862

Signed and inscribed l.r.: au Brouchy – 29 juillet 1862 P. Puvis de Chavannes
Inscribed at the center of the lower border: LABOR
Oil on canvas, 86 x 109 cm
Private collection

Provenance Artist's heirs and by descent.
Selected Exhibitions 1937 Lyons, no. 12, as *Esquisse pour 'Le Travail'* (dimensions as 102 x 120 which must include the frame); 1976-77 Paris/Ottawa, no. 42.

This painted study for *Work* was executed at the family château the summer following Puvis's presentation of his first pair of wall paintings, *Concordia* and *Bellum*, at the Salon of 1861. In a wonderful wooded seaside setting beside a brilliant blue ocean, fine male figures in hide loincloths or nude, the academic paragon of physicality, are stiffly posed at various labors: they hew and prepare wood, forge, and load donkeys. The composition has been generally established, the forgers prominent; in the final, carefully arranged, toned down composition they would be perfectly centered and encircled and bracketed quite symmetrically and prosaically by groups of other working figures. The forgers would also be shifted up and back, the ground plane raised, with these figurations

31

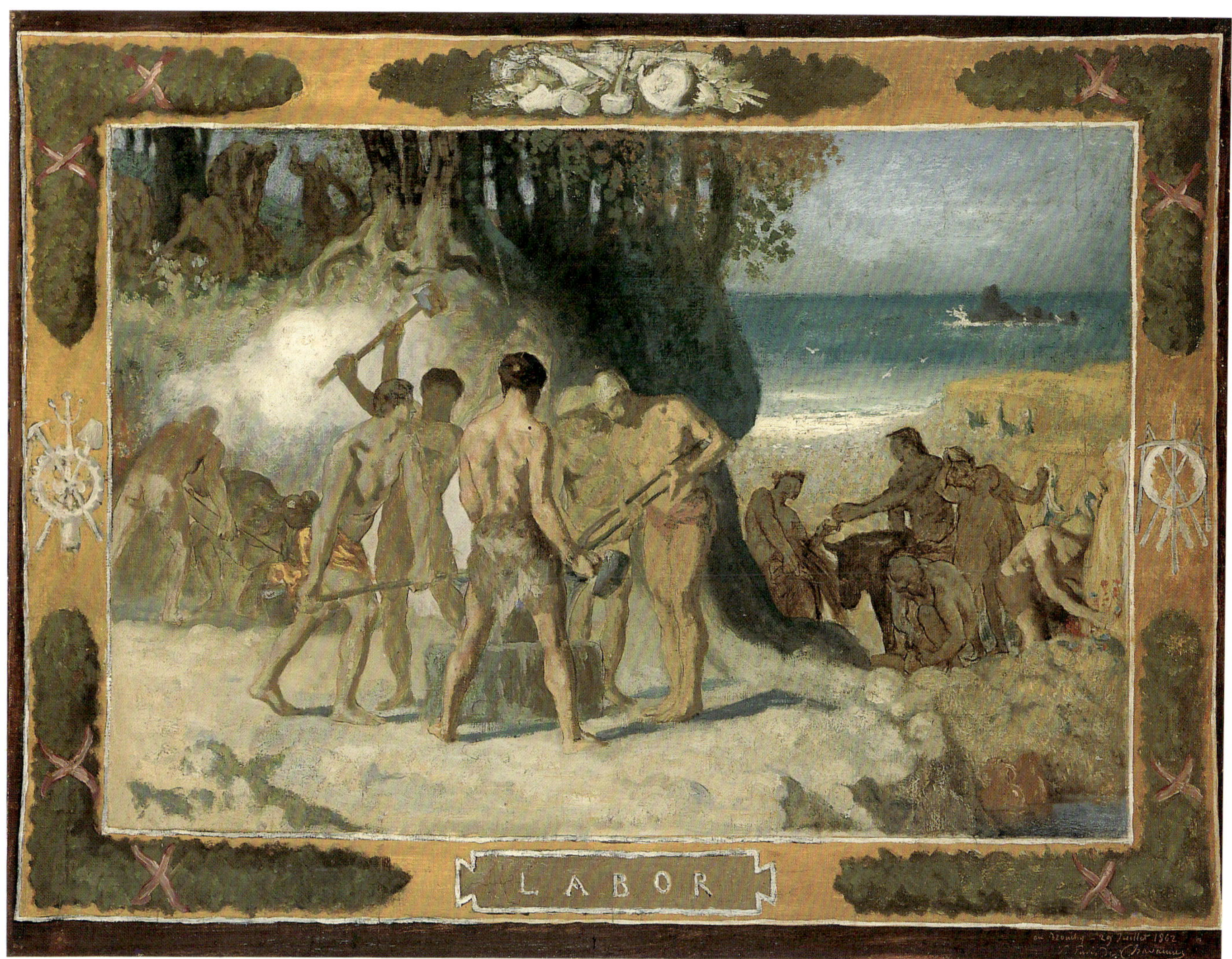

brought more closely to the forward plane (see cat. 28). As would frequently be the case, the artist appropriated some figures from other works, such as the kneeling man from his *Ruth and Boaz* – which he could have examined while he was at Le Brouchy[1] – and eliminated others, which were to reappear in other paintings, as the donkey and rider would in *Summer* of 1873 (fig. 5).

As in Puvis's early pair of murals for Amiens, the Latin title suggests the theme is general and somehow antique; this would be changed in the definitive work to the more nationalistic, less pretentious *Work*. Besides bearing the cartouche with the title, the handsome orange border lends panache to the canvas and – in circumscribing and packaging it – reinforces the idea of the imagery itself as a special phenomenon: this is pictorial decoration, images to adorn an interior architecture, an institutional setting, with all the expectations of presentation and artifice that that specific use was understood to comprise.

1 Louise d'Argencourt has also pointed this out; see 1976-77 Paris/Ottawa, no. 42.

32

Two Male Figures, Study for 'Work'

ca. 1862-63

Inscribed l.r. in red chalk: à Antoine Vollon,
P. Puvis de Chavannes
Red chalk, black chalk, pencil, squared in pencil on paper, 597 x 577 mm; left side of sheet repaired and filled in.
Fitzwilliam Museum, Cambridge (Inv. 2135)

Provenance Antoine Vollon; probably his sale, Paris (22 June 1901); Durand-Ruel, Paris (inscribed support Inv. 6399); E.J. van Wisselingh (17 May 1902); Ricketts (7 August 1901) [according to Durand-Ruel Archives, 1902; Ricketts's edited diaries list 1901]; Charles Ricketts and Charles Shannon; bequeathed to the museum by the latter (1937).
Selected References Ricketts (1939), p. 65.

32

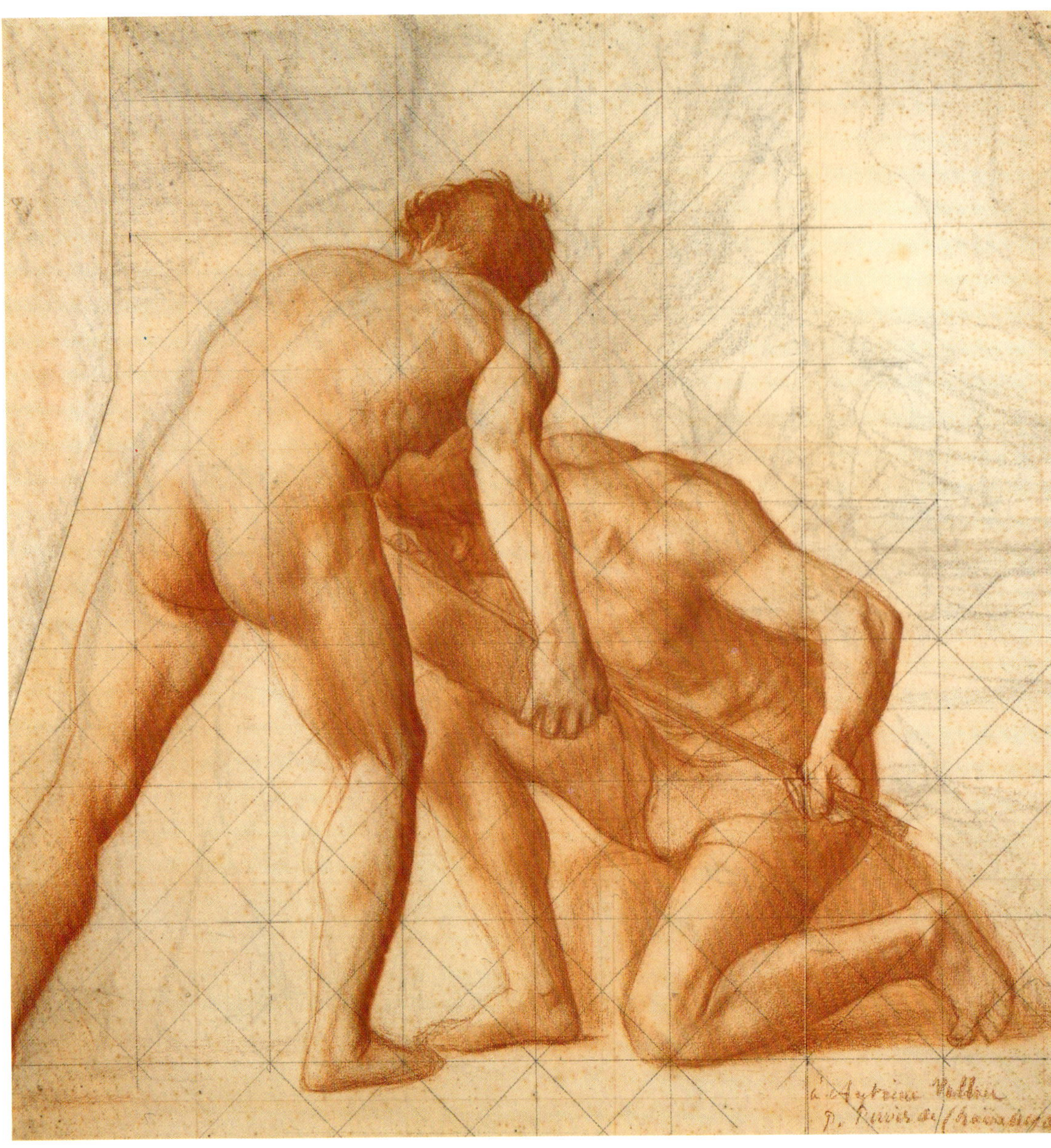

Numerous drawings by Puvis relate to the Amiens murals. These range from small schemes of the entire composition in which a variety of landscape and figurative alternatives with notations as to controlling geometries were tried to large, red chalk studies of two to four figures. The latter were essentially 'académies,' studies of the nude model central to the fine arts training advocated at the Ecole des Beaux-Arts that Puvis never attended. Puvis's figures for the Amiens murals are drawn with deliberate contours and shaded with even tonal gradations that are unlike the kind of drawing that he had engaged in in the previous decade.

The Fitzwilliam sheet is a study of two men for the left background of *Work* and must date from about 1862. In drawing these figures, apparently from life, the artist emphasized the rhythmic forms he saw in his models' bodies. The rendering of the topography of the humped-up back of the figure to the right and the curved outline of the two vigorous figures with the pentimenti show how carefully the artist worked to achieve the right contours and placements. The irregular edges of the support, like those of other of the large sanguine sheets, indicate they are probably fragments of a larger work, and several may have come from the same sheet.

This drawing was for many years the proud possession of the British collectors and aesthetes Charles Shannon and Charles Ricketts, who in 1887 visited Puvis in his atelier and expressed a desire to acquire his work. By then Puvis was known outside of France through his monumental works, his Salon exhibitions and the efforts of the dealer Paul Durand-Ruel. But it was only on 7 August 1901 that Ricketts could write triumphantly of having made a purchase: 'Great red-letter day. One of Puvis de Chavannes's nine[1] stupendous sanguines for the Amiens Museum decorations was bought by me at E.J. Wisselingh's for the huge sum of one hundred thirty-four pounds. I burst into perspiration at the sight of it, so great was my lust of possession. It had just been refused by the British Museum owing to size and cost; the latter, from their point of

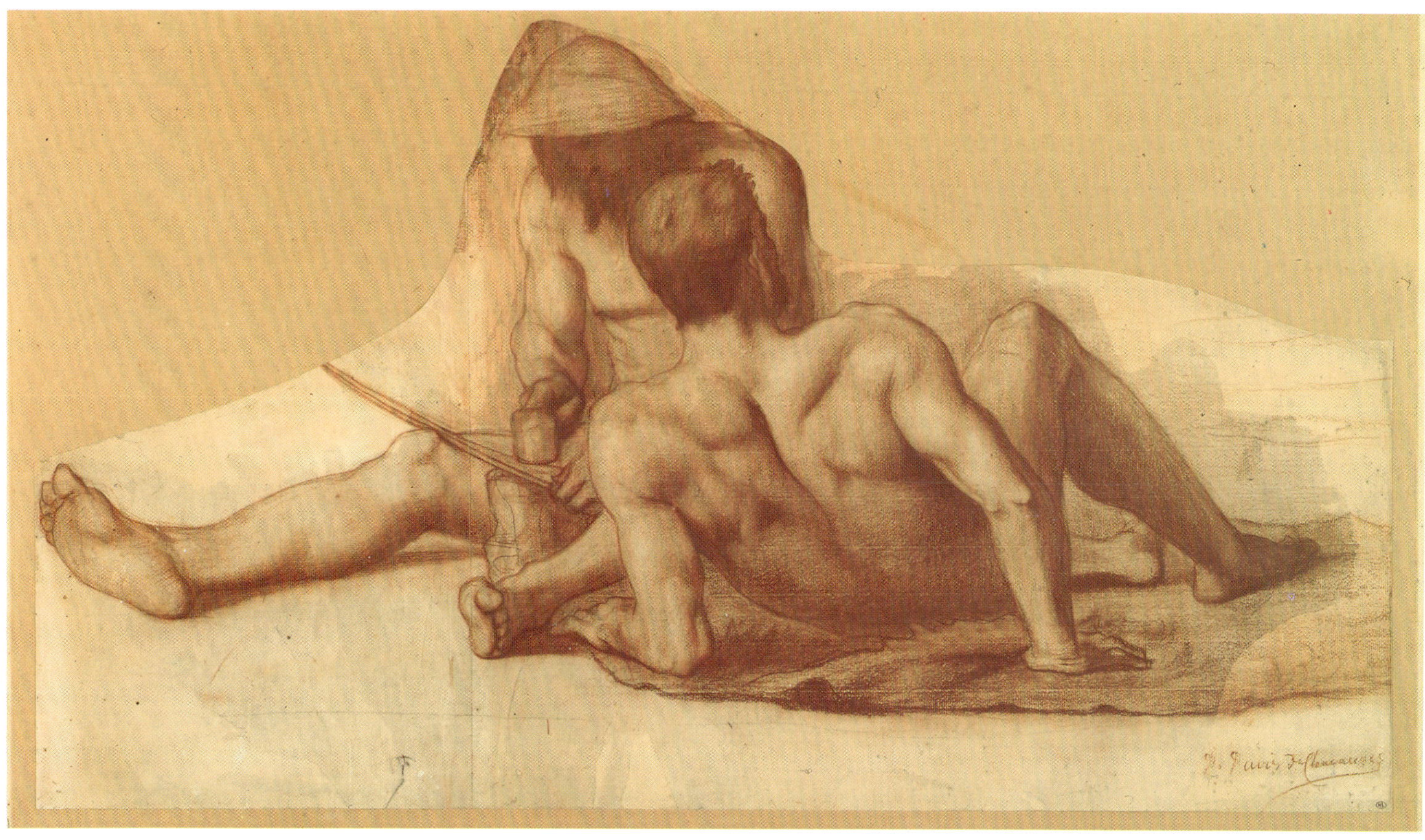

view, is a good excuse, since they did not know how important Puvis is, and how rare is a drawing of this order.'[2] Ricketts described with relish how he first showed his friend the drawing: 'Shannon returned from Lincolnshire. I made him drunk, having placed the Puvis on a table during the grub for him to see when he went into the next room. He blundered in, burbled over his coffee, not turning round towards that side of the room where stood the drawings between two candles. When he turned round, he suddenly became quite sober and serious in an instant, and almost white with astonishment and pleasure.'[3]

1 Large sanguines besides this one include *The Forgers for 'Work'*, Musée Bonnat, Bayonne (Inv. 271/NI), and five others at the Musée du Louvre, Paris (our cat. 33 and 34; Inv. RF 1935, Inv. RF 2008 and Inv. RF 2009). Smaller sanguines of a somewhat different style related to the 1865 *Ave Picardia Nutrix* are at the Ashmolean Museum, Oxford (our cat. 38) and at the British Museum, London (Inv. 1975-3-1-56), which would bring the count to nine.

2 Ricketts (1939), p. 65.

3 On 10 August; Ricketts (1939), p. 66.

33

Study for Two Men Seated on the Ground in 'Rest' ca. 1862-1863

Signed l.r.: P. Puvis de Chavannes
Sanguine and pencil on cream paper, 433 x 768 mm
Musée du Louvre, Paris (Inv. RF 2007)

Provenance Gift of the artist (1895).
Selected Exhibitions 1881 Paris (Musée des Arts Décoratifs), [?]; 1884 Paris (Ecole des Beaux-Arts), no. 920 [?]; 1887 Paris (Durand-Ruel), one of the following: no. 51-52, 54-58; 1887 New York, one of the following: no. 22-24; 1896 Paris (Société Nationale des Beaux-Arts); 1976-77 Paris/Ottawa, no. 45.
Selected References Bénédite (1900), repr. p. 50; Michel and Laran (1911), pp. 33-34, repr.

Seated or sprawled or otherwise low figures occupy the foreground of each of the first four compositions for Amiens. This is a study for two such figures to the lower left in *Rest*: a large man seated on the ground with his legs thrust in front of him, his head bent (and shaded by a hat), and turned slightly, paired with another figure paralleling the first but facing the opposite direction and leaning back on his arm. A seated Ingresque woman was substituted for the man at the right in the painted work, though the general disposition of the two figures was to remain the same. The more sinuous female seems to have been chosen as a counterpoint to the curved outline of the woman leaning forward at the middle right of the painting. The upright position of this new figure enhances the two-dimensional pictorial surface, important to the artist as he increasingly flattened his compositions and visually established a planar surface for his works.

In one of the earliest painted versions of *Rest* (formerly Barbazanges Gallery),[1] only the figure to the left is included; in a somewhat more advanced canvas,[2] the two male figures indicate that these modifications had yet to occur and took place at a late stage of development.

1 Whereabouts unknown; see Werth (1926), repr. pl. 3.

2 Inscribed: P. Puvis de Chavannes à son ami Claude 61 (Collection Joey and Toby Tanenbaum, Toronto).

34

Study for Four Figures in 'Rest' ca. 1862

Signed twice l.r.: P. Puvis de Chavannes
Sanguine, black chalk, pencil and white gouache on cream paper, squared, 740 x 438 mm, left side uneven
Musée du Louvre, Paris (Inv. RF 2006)

Provenance Gift of the artist (1895).
Selected Exhibitions 1881 Paris (Musée des Arts Décoratifs) [?]; 1884 Paris (Ecole des Beaux-Arts), no. 917 or 918; 1976-77 Paris/Ottawa, no. 44.
Selected References Vachon (1895), repr. p. 81; Bénédite (1900), repr. p. 24.

In this masterful drawing Puvis created a distinct characterization of physiognomy and pose for each of four figures while, from a plastic point of view, interrelating them inventively. The woman in profile leaning forward, drapery looped in a lovely curve around her thigh, is placed beside a male figure with his back to us whose muscular limbs rhyme with and continue hers. Two reticent, youthful males stand nearby. As careful as the poses and interweaving of figures are, they would be adjusted in the mural: the woman would become slightly more erect, the figure to her right heftier, his head hatted and placed less persuasively; the two other figures would be somewhat separated, their overlap not so pronounced. These subtleties disclose what the artist was driving at: the lessening of tension in poses, strong characterizations, legible forms and shallow spaces. The motif of the woman leaning forward, her leg up, her back curved, a pose reminiscent of Poussin (*The Arcadian Shepherds, Et in Arcadia Ego*, Musée du Louvre, Paris) and Ingres, was to prove a favorite motif, to be used again in *At the Fountain* (1869, Boston Museum of Fine Arts) and several of its variants (private collection; Musée des Beaux-Arts, Reims). Like many of the other red chalk drawings related to *Rest*, this appears to be a fragment of a larger work.

35

Autumn / *L'Automne* ca. 1863-64

Oil on canvas, 51.5 x 40 cm
National Museum of American Art, Smithsonian Institution, Washington, D.C.; Gift of John Gellatly (Inv. 1929.6.86)

Provenance Probably the same painting used in exchange for the reductions of *Peace, War, Work,* and *Rest* by John G. Johnson, Philadelphia, on 28 November 1888 (see cat. 88); Catholina Lambert Collection, Paterson, New Jersey [perhaps the same, but listed as 101.7 x 81.3 cm]; New York, American Art Association (22 February 1916), to Charles A. Platt; Durand-Ruel, New York (1928); John Gellatly.
Selected Exhibitions 1887 Paris (Durand-Ruel), no. 6 (*Réduction avec variante d'un grand tableau au Musée de Lyon*, probably the version in the Museo de Bellas Artes, Caracas); 1894 New York, no. 11 (possibly this version); 1975 Toronto, no. 2; 1976-77 Paris/Ottawa, no. 55.
Selected References The Durand-Ruel Archives LD 13103 list an *Autumn* with dimensions 53 x 41.5 cm, which may be this work or the study in the Národni Galeri, Prague.

Autumn presents a seated matriarch and two younger women posed in vaguely classicizing dress and undress in a wooded setting amidst seasonal bounty. This unfinished study for his large canvas (280 x 226 cm, Musée des Beaux-Arts, Lyons), which was exhibited at the Salon of

34

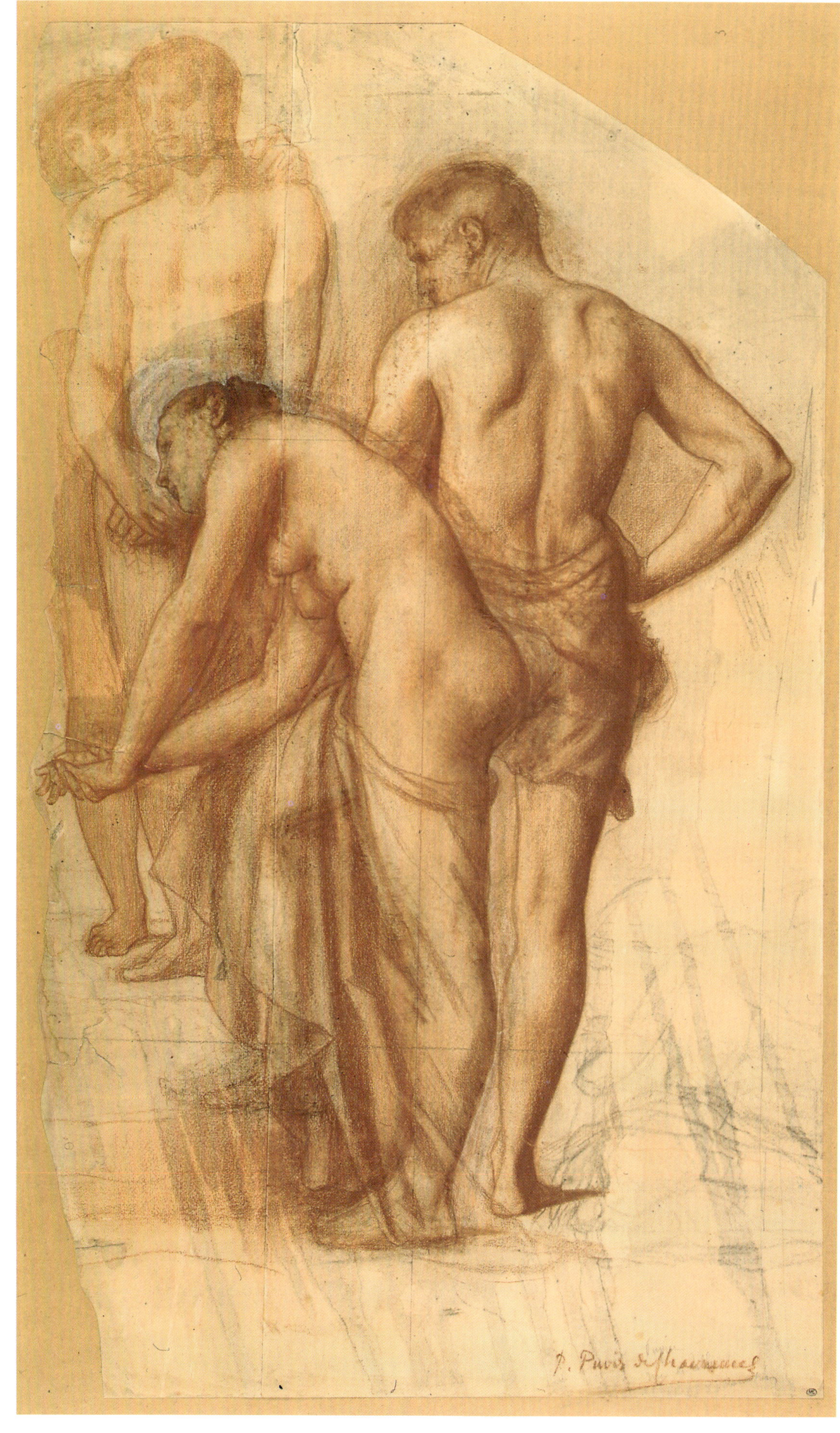

1864, is a rare document of an intermittent stage in the execution of a painting, with the lines defining the curves and arabesques of the three main figures still visible, and the tinting only just begun. The artist primed the canvas with gray pigment and then outlined in umber shapes that had been previously established in drawings and traced onto the canvas. The torso of the figure at right is almost finished, while the central figure remains unpainted, a pink wash indicating the drapery's future, much remarked upon color. Puvis advised his students to follow the same method, an agenda based on having thought through and thoroughly planned a scheme: 'First paint the backgrounds to be quite simple in their effect.... Paint in easily legible tonal values; don't be afraid to go a little beyond your outlines, the drawing will always be seen underneath. You will easily find it, and you will avoid haloes and hardness! .... When you aren't sure whether a thick layer should remain definitively, scrape it off completely to avoid the stickiness which always spoils painting.'[1] His advice seems based on what he learned from Thomas Couture.[2]

Examples from the Fontainebleau Mannerist tradition, Poussin and Ingres must have encouraged Puvis to let anatomical contrivances take precedence over what one knows of anatomy. The acidic artificiality and pallor of the pink and light blue hues have a precedent in the sophisticated palette used in the paintings at Fontainebleau, in which there was renewed interest during the Second Empire when the palace was undergoing restoration in honor of Napoleon III, who had been baptized there. Puvis's work was compared with that of the School of Fontainebleau as Jules Breton afterwards remarked, with Primaticcio's frescoes routinely invoked as were also works by Poussin.[3] The sinuous woman at the right draws on Poussin's distinctive idiom, and one may particularly compare figures in *Apollo and Daphne* (1664, Musée du Louvre, Paris; entered collection 1869); though in one preliminary drawing by Puvis[4] her upper body is in profile, and only subsequently would her back be turned to the viewer as in Poussin's severely *déhanchée* woman.

But Puvis seems to have looked at several sources for his figures. The matron resembles the seated Demeter of Cnidos excavated in 1858 and celebrated as a new acquisition by the British Museum. That antique prototype of a harvest goddess would add a certain historical authenticity to a Demeter (or Ceres) presiding over an autumn harvest. Puvis sought this kind of legitimizing validation for his classicizing paintings of the 1860s. The central figure recalls the Venus de Melos or Capua type, although the drapery concoction is Puvis's own.

When the definitive canvas was shown, critics sought to identify the figures: the three Graces[5] and the three ages of man were proposed; Théophile Gautier saw an allegory of age, a seated woman in the autumn of her life reflecting on youth,[6] and likened its atmosphere to one Theocritus or Virgil might have conceived. He particularly admired the younger figures, appreciated the pink drapery and instructed readers about abstract formal qualities in terms of musical analogies, 'a too lively reality of color would deprive the nudity of its virginal abstraction.... [For the right-hand figure Puvis had drawn] one of those rhythmic poses like a beautiful stanza in which forms balance and equilibrate each other in harmony as sweet to the eye as well-cadenced music is to the ear.'[7]

The general composition, the relationship of figures to each other and the viewer and their placement in a wooded clearing, the foreground still life, even the pose of a bending background figure, bear comparison to those in Manet's *Luncheon on the Grass* (Musée d'Orsay, Paris), exhibited at the Salon des Refusés in 1863. But Puvis's iconography resounds with the traditional: the nudity of his sylvan nymphs aroused no comment; what provoked discussion was how he used style.

The excellence of the definitive *Autumn* was swiftly acknowledged and may have been responsible for Puvis's subsequent Amiens responsibilities. On 26 May 1864, the architect, Arthur Diet, encouraged the President of the Museum Commission to commission Puvis to paint the other seasons, possibly to decorate the Salon de l'Impératrice (the Salon Latour), noting that *Autumn* had been bought by the State and (was it truly only happy coincidence?) was the same height as the Impératrice panels.[8] Although nothing came of that larger project, Puvis's next mural for Amiens, *Ave Picardia Nutrix* (ill. pp. 102-103, see cat. 36), would allude to both the Autumn (at left) and Summer (right) seasons.

1 'Peignez d'abord vos fonds très simplement dans leur effet.... Peignez par grandes valeurs bien écrites; ne craignez pas de faire empiéter un peu sur vos contours, le dessin se verra toujours en dessous. Vous le retrouverez facilement, et vous éviterez les auréoles et les sécheresses! .... Quand vous n'êtes pas sur qu'une forte couche devra rester définitivement, raclez-la tout net pour éviter l'empoissage, qui encanaille toujours la peinture.' Vachon [1900], pp. 112-113, quoted also by others.

2 See Albert B. Boime, *The Academy and French Painting in the Nineteenth Century* (London, 1971), p. 69; and Boime (1980), p. 441.

3 Breton [1899], p. 228.

4 Musée des Beaux-Arts, Lyons (Inv. 305/B607.123).

5 Bürger (1870), II, pp. 24-25.

6 Théophile Gautier, 'Salon de 1864,' *Le Moniteur Universel* (21 May 1864), 720; repeated in Riotor (April 1896), 269.

7 'une réalité trop vive de couleur ôterait à la nudité sa virginale abstraction .... une de ces poses rhythmées comme une belle strophe, où les formes se balancent et s'équilibrient avec une harmonie aussi douce à l'oeil qu'à l'oreille une musique bien cadencée.' Théophile Gautier, 'Les Oeuvres contemporains, "L'Automne" de Puvis de Chavannes,' *L'Artiste* (15 March 1865), 130.

8 Foucart-Borville (1976), p. 54.

illustration on pages 102-103
Ave Picardia Nutrix, 1865. Musée des Beaux-Arts, Amiens

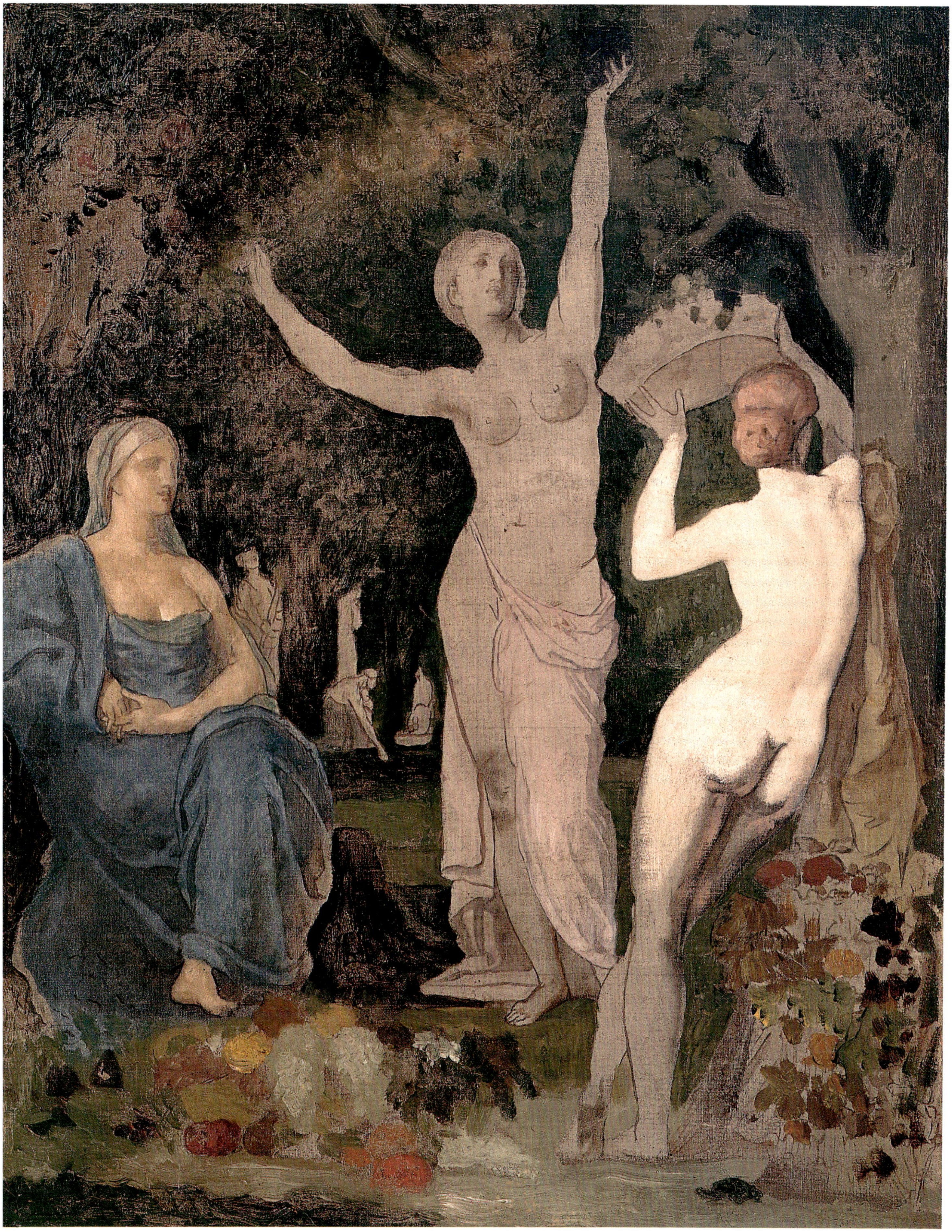

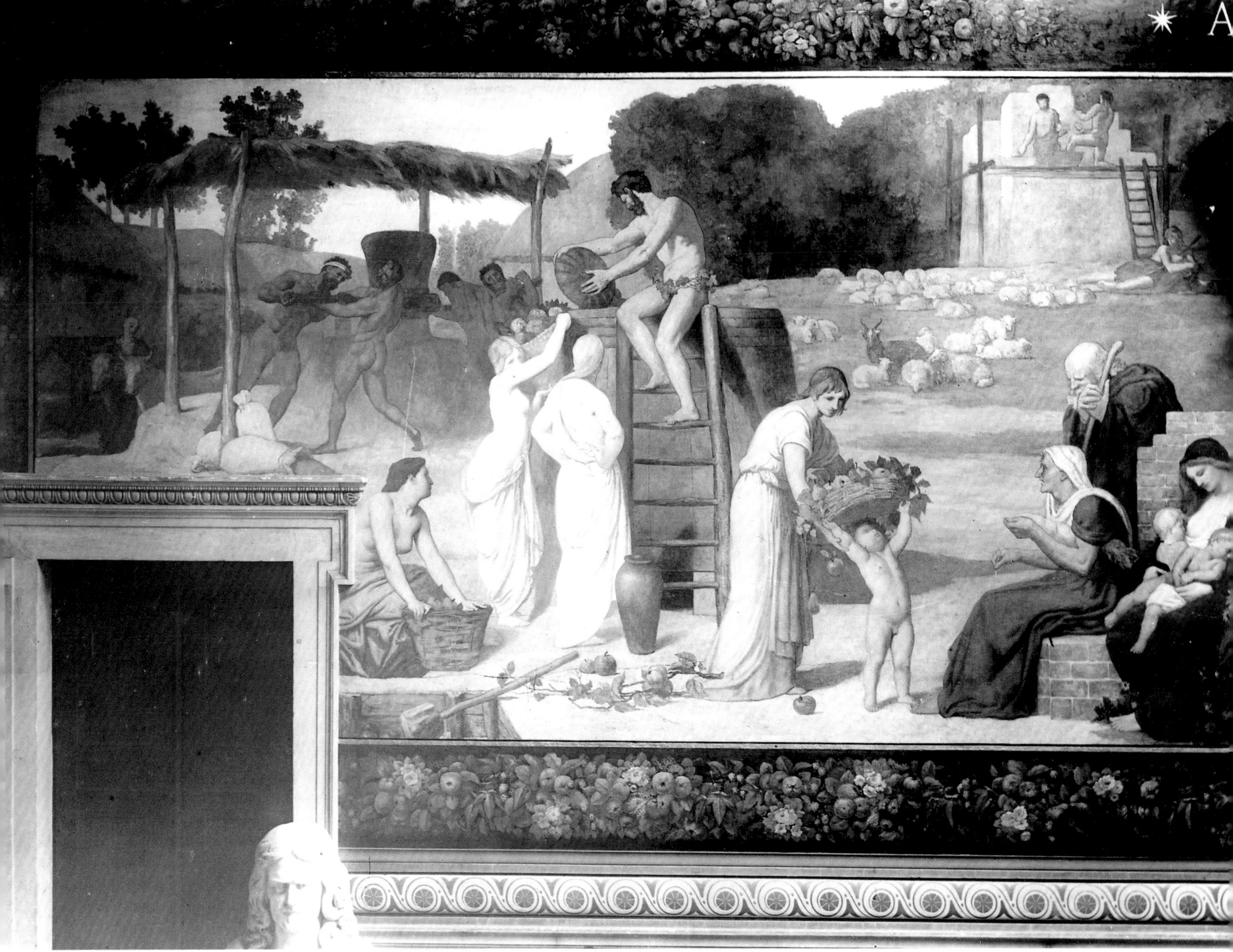

36

Study for 'Ave Picardia Nutrix'

ca. 1864-65

Pencil on tracing paper, 70 x 95 mm
Musée Paul Dupuy, Toulouse (Inv. 83)

Provenance Bequest of artist's heirs to the city of Toulouse (1898).

To embellish a long wall at the top of the great staircase at the Amiens Museum with his largest project (450 x 1750 cm) to that date, Puvis devised a program specific to the Picardy region and its fecundity. *Ave Picardia Nutrix* (*Hail, Picardy the Nourisher*), which he would complete in 1865, was conceived as *The Salute of France to the Dawn of One of its Richest Provinces*.[1] In a letter of 21 October 1864, Puvis described the composition of what would be his 'poem,' which he set 'in a far off time' ('en ces tems reculés').[2] It was divided into two sections, to accommodate three doors to the collection; the theme at left was the grinding of grain and preparation of cider; at the right, fishing and bathing in the Somme, the river that makes the region so fertile.[3]

In preparation for his large compositions, Puvis executed numerous small drawings in which he methodically structured and restructured his compositions and moved figures about, trying many possibilities before fixing on his final arrangement. The outlined configuration and interrelationships of figure and land contours in their simplest state are investigated. This is a study for the section at the right, in which the theme is fishing. As in his other murals for the museum, the activity is portrayed as

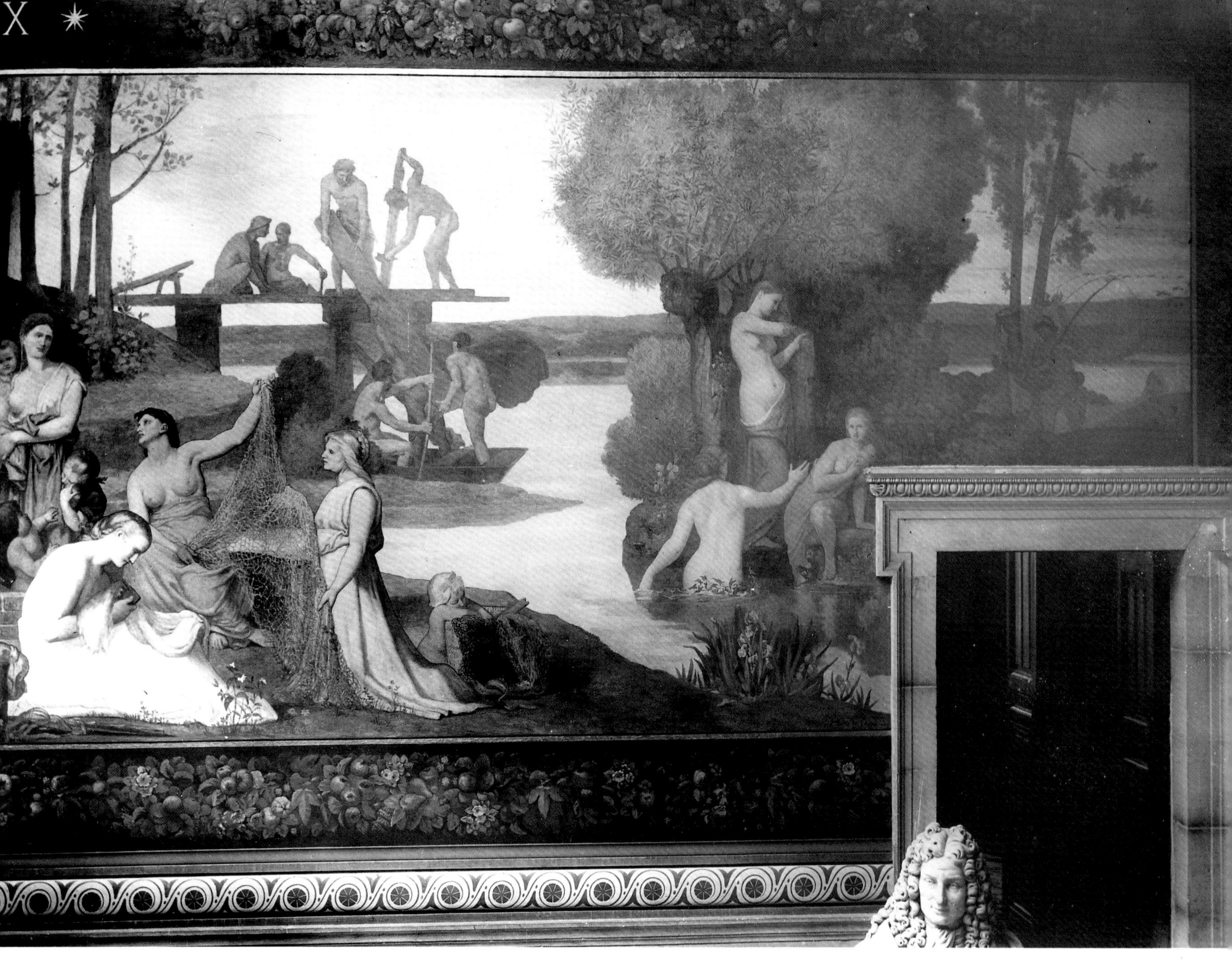

a communal one, with attendant net mending, wading and caring for children. Several of the figural motifs joined Puvis's repertory to be used again over the years. The woman with children at left would appear in the mural and in independent paintings based on it, and serve as the basis for maternity paintings of over two decades later (see cat. 108-109). The man in the foreground would appear as a weaver in a preliminary oil study for *Fishing* (private collection). At the far right, a standing Venus Anadyomene-like figure, wringing her hair, is tried in two positions; she would appear in *The Bathing Place* (private collection) and, modified, in paintings such as *Young Women by the Sea* (fig. 6, cat. 76).

1 *Le Salut de la France à l'aurore de l'une de ses plus riches provinces.* Viéville (1989), pp. 2, 4-5.

2 To Charles Dufour; quoted by Foucart-Borville (1976), n.p.

3 In 1976-77 Paris/Ottawa, p. 62, the photographs have been reversed.

37

Study for a Bather in 'Ave Picardia Nutrix' ca. 1864-65

Red and black chalk on tan paper, 265 x 125 mm
Musée de Picardie, Amiens (Inv. 912bis 20)

Provenance Bequest of artist's heirs to the city of Amiens (1898).

The sensuous nude bather for which this drawing is a study is at the right of a trio of such figures in the right section of *Ave Picardia Nutrix*, devoted to bathers and fishing. The figure is here still being developed from the model. The pose, carefully contrived to align with the sharp vertical of the adjacent doorway, would be further synthesized, the forms and lines strengthened.[1] In several painted variants, (*The River*, ca. 1865, Metropolitan Museum of Art, New York and private collection) and in the mural this figure would be seated on the steep river bank with one leg bent up to brace her body, the other dangling in the water. The slight twist of the upper torso would be nicely accentuated with the figure's right arm reaching up across her body to her left shoulder, creating a rhythmic interplay among the bent and straight limbs. The bathers should be compared to the two other triads of bathers Puvis would develop in *Summer* in 1891 (see cat. 134), the latter also designed for difficult placement proximate to a doorway.

1 Three of the numerous studies in which this figure appears are at the Musée de Picardie, Amiens (Inv. 912bis 9-11).

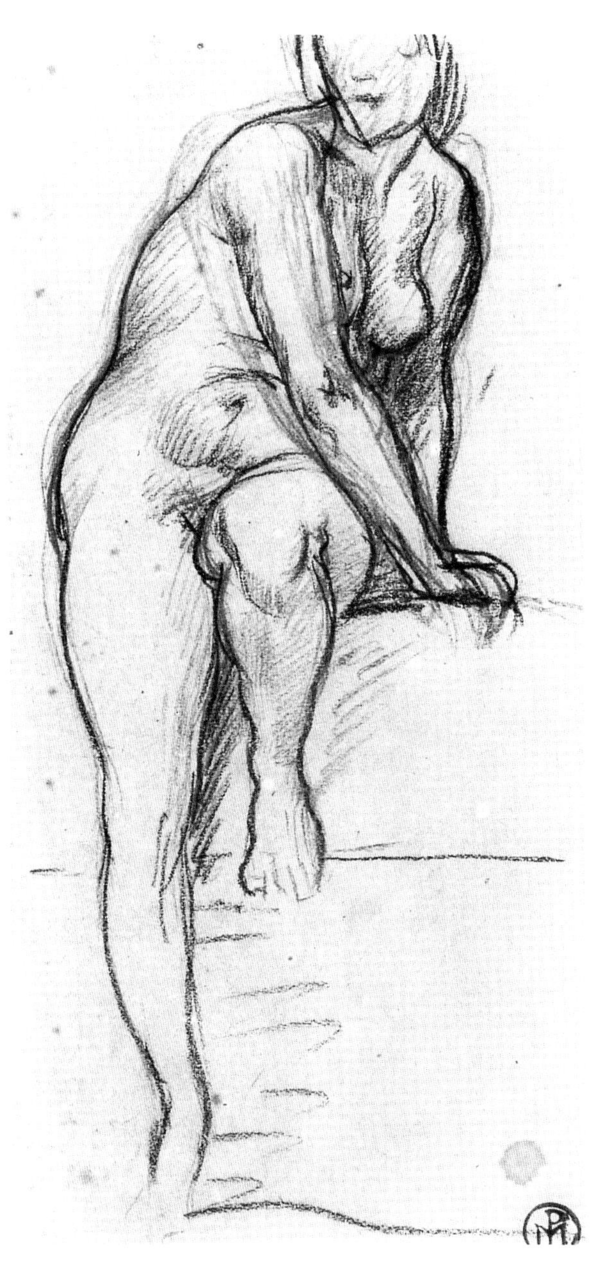

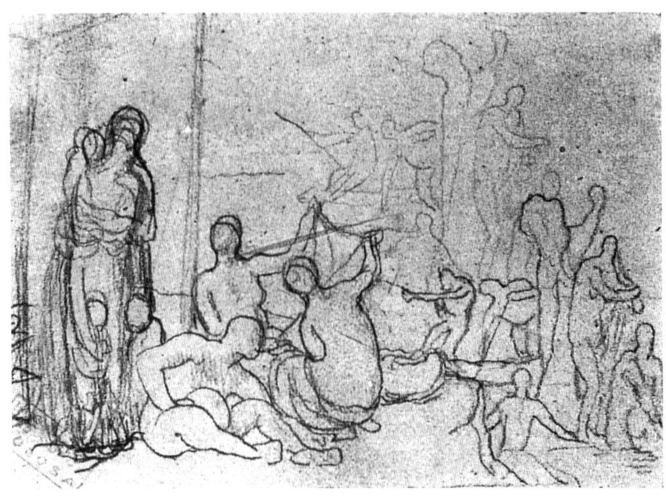

37

38

Study for a Woman in 'Ave Picardia Nutrix' ca. 1865

Signed u.l.: P. Puvis de C
Red chalk, squared, on irregular sheet 432 x 386 mm
Ashmolean Museum, Oxford (Inv. 604.C111)

Provenance Presented to the museum by Sir Michael and Lady Sadler (1925).

This study of a half-draped female figure with a basket is one of the most interesting of the larger red chalk figure studies relating to the Amiens complex.[1] For the left side of *Ave Picardia Nutrix*,[2] the figure is outlined with a new, sharp delicacy that transmits a fullness and sensuousness despite being scarcely shaded in. From about 1865 to 1867, Puvis produced a number of superbly graceful and somewhat mannered figures (see cat. 42). The turned head of this figure, recalling the not unrelated *profil perdu* poses that the artist favored in the mid-1850s (see cat. 7-8, 10-11), is all the more interesting for being oddly exaggerated in construction.[3]

This sheet relates to a red chalk drawing, which is also squared, of a nearby section of the mural: a standing woman in classicizing garment, who leans slightly forward to help a child balance a tray of fruit.[4]

1 A related sheet, *Studies for Ave Picardia Nutrix*, medium and dimensions unknown (formerly Roland Browse and Delbanco and Dr. Leonard Simpson), includes this figure at a more preliminary stage.
2 Compare the independent variant, *Cider*, oil on paper, mounted on canvas, 129.6 x 252.2 cm, Metropolitan Museum of Art, New York.
3 A variant of this figure (reversed) that is less extreme in pose is included in Puvis's *Vintage* (Wallraf-Richartz Museum, Cologne) and his *Wine Press* (Phillips Memorial Art Gallery, Washington, D.C.).
4 British Museum, London (Inv. 1975-3-1-56).

8

39

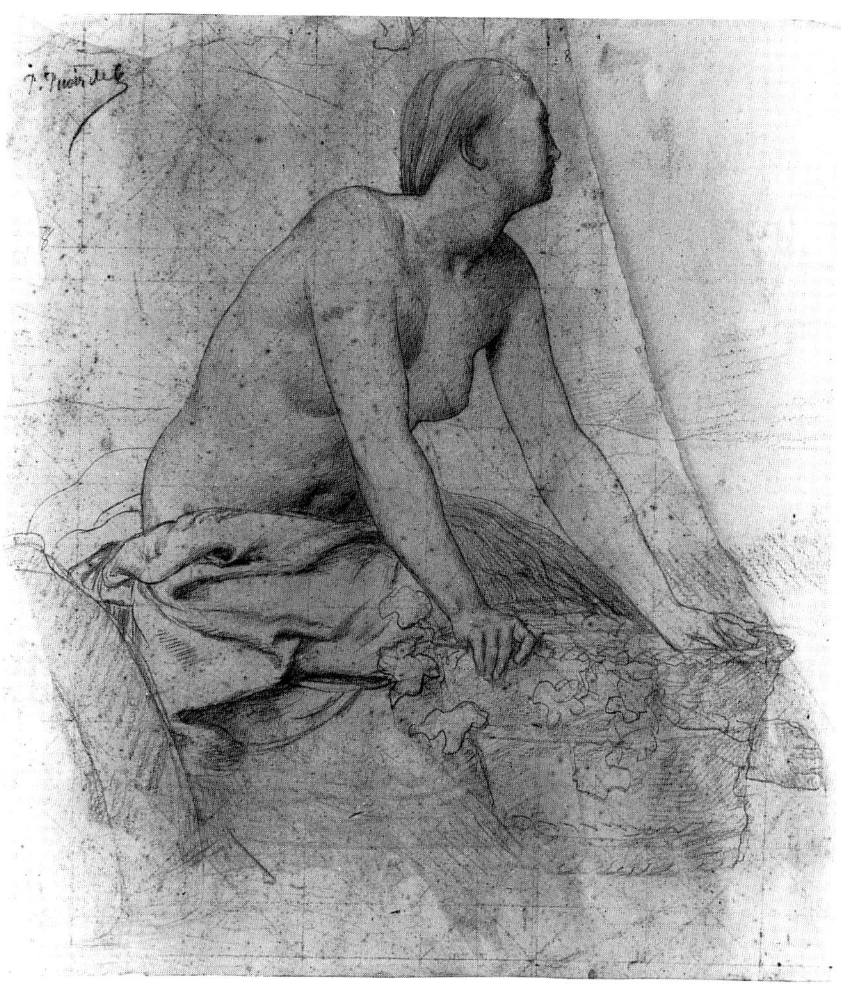

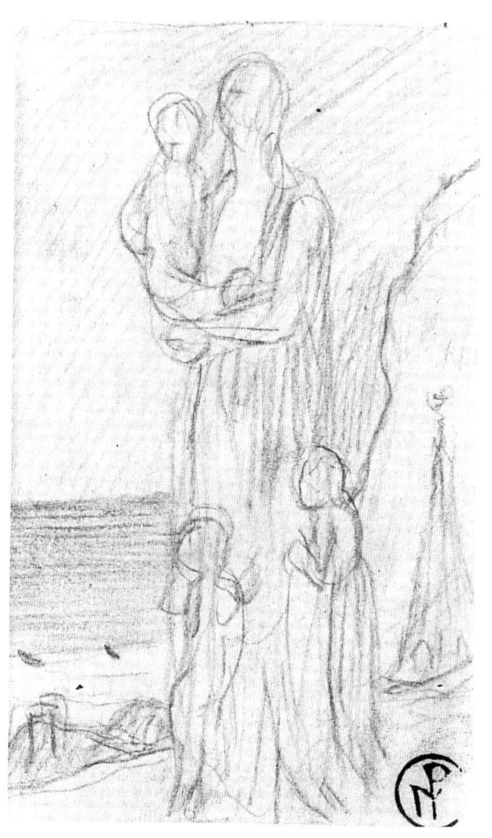

39

Study for 'Ave Picardia Nutrix' and 'La Bresse' ca. 1864-70

Sanguine on off-white paper, 126 x 75 mm
Musée de Picardie, Amiens (Inv. 912bis 15)

Provenance Bequest of artist's heirs to the city of Amiens (1898).

This motif of a mother standing with her three children, first broached in *Ave Picardia Nutrix*, as a compositional drawing (cat. 36) shows, and recurring at several other junctures (see cat. 108 and 109), was a favorite in Puvis's repertory. Here the group appears on a high promontory, a church steeple and the tops of houses just visible beyond, and the ocean in the background. This tiny sketch, fascinating in its summary completeness, is, as the use of sanguine would seem to indicate, probably an early one.

In addition there are related drawings: *'Monique' Head*, pencil on beige cardboard, 173 x 142 mm, Musée du Louvre, Paris (Inv. RF 2169); *Head*, red chalk on off-white cardboard; 227 x 190 mm, Musée du Louvre, Paris (Inv. RF 2170). 40

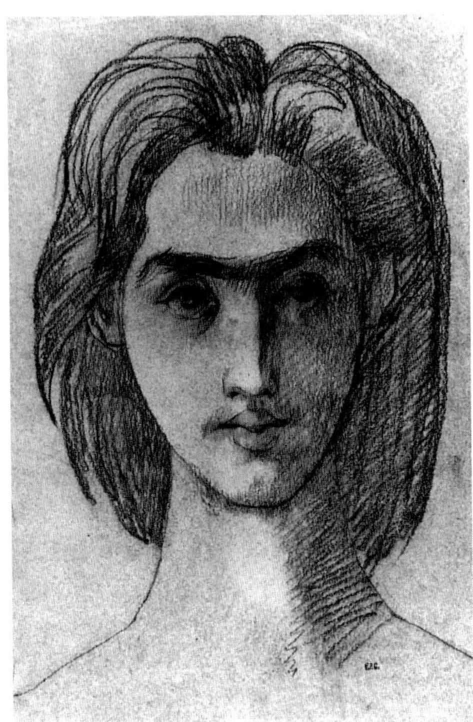

40

Androgynous head ca. 1865

Stamp l.r.
Charcoal on bluish green paper, 360 x 242 mm
Private collection

Provenance Artist's heirs and by descent.

The powerful frontality and symmetry of this oval head with a long nose, small wide lips and heavy brows set on a strong, columnar neck, like several other drawn and painted heads of about 1865,[1] betrays a growing aptitude for manipulating imagery for dramatic, geometrical and pictorial reasons. Puvis was repeatedly to turn to a rigorous frontality – the Baptist in *The Beheading of Saint John the Baptist* (cat. 57), his *Head of a Woman* (cat. 55) or *Hope* (fig. 3, 4) – engendered by the concept of an image as an artificial construct, an icon for a viewer. The most symmetrical of these poses may be likened to hieratic Byzantine stylizations, then used in religious imagery particularly. But these years there was a great taste for frontal heads and portraits – one thinks of Ingres and the Ingristes.

1 *Portrait of a Woman in Pink* or *'Monique'* ca. 1865, 53.5 x 44.5 cm (private collection), 1976-77 Paris/Ottawa, no. 56; *Portrait of Primavera (Ceres)*, 1865, oil on millboard (carton), 50.5 x 39.8 cm (private collection).

41

Lounging Woman ca. 1865

Black chalk on gray paper, 135 x 245 mm
Musée du Petit Palais, Paris
(Inv. PPD 286^{5}; MCB 168)

Provenance Bequest of artist's heirs to the city of Paris (1898); deposited in the Musée Galliera (1899); transferred to the Musée du Petit Palais upon its opening (1901).
Selected References Boucher (1979), no. 168.

Stretched out in some disarray, her head and arm on large cushions, her skirts gathered by the slight twist of her body and her feet emerging with charming unself-consciousness from them, is a young woman identifiable as the Princess Marie Cantacuzène. She is pictured at a seemingly unposed instant of relaxed disrepair, and we are treated to an informality and contemporaneity rare in Puvis's oeuvre, a small record of a private moment born of trusting intimacy. Marie Cantacuzène was Puvis de Chavannes's lady friend and muse, as she had been Chassériau's model and companion (see cat. 18). Both depicted her in a variety of manners: Chassériau as a Madonna, as a woman in a Roman bath, and in more than one sedate portrait (fig. 29);[1] Puvis in expressive drawings and portraits (see cat. 92-95), and as allegorical figures and saints, such as his late *Saint Genevieve Watching over Paris* (Panthéon, Paris). Although she posed often for Puvis, it was seldom with the disarming naturalness seen here. Based on the age of the subject,[2] perhaps in her forties, and the technique, this work must date from about 1865.

We may be used to Manet showing his wife with her legs up on a canapé (*Mme Manet on a Blue Couch*, 1874, pastel, Musée d'Orsay, Paris) or depicting Berthe Morisot plunked down on a sofa (*Repose*, 1870, Museum of Art, Rhode Island School of Design, Providence), but slightly awkward, candid and endearing informality is unexpected from Puvis.

1 She is Mary in two versions of *The Adoration of the Shepherds* (one at the Musée du Petit Palais, Paris) she is twice included as a figure in *The Tepidarium* (Musée d'Orsay, Paris), and one recognizes her features elsewhere also, see Sandoz (1974), nos. 263-264.

2 I am in agreement with Marie-Christine Boucher (1979), no. 168.

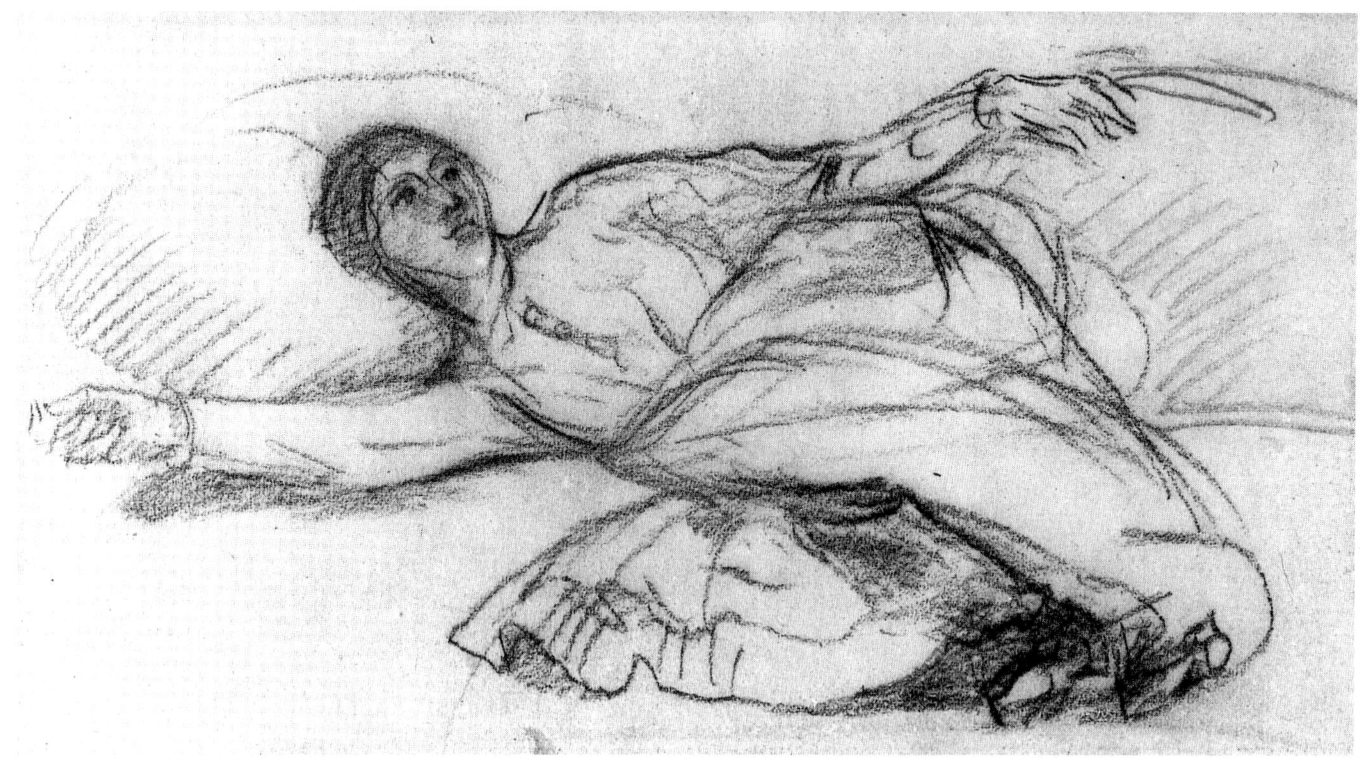

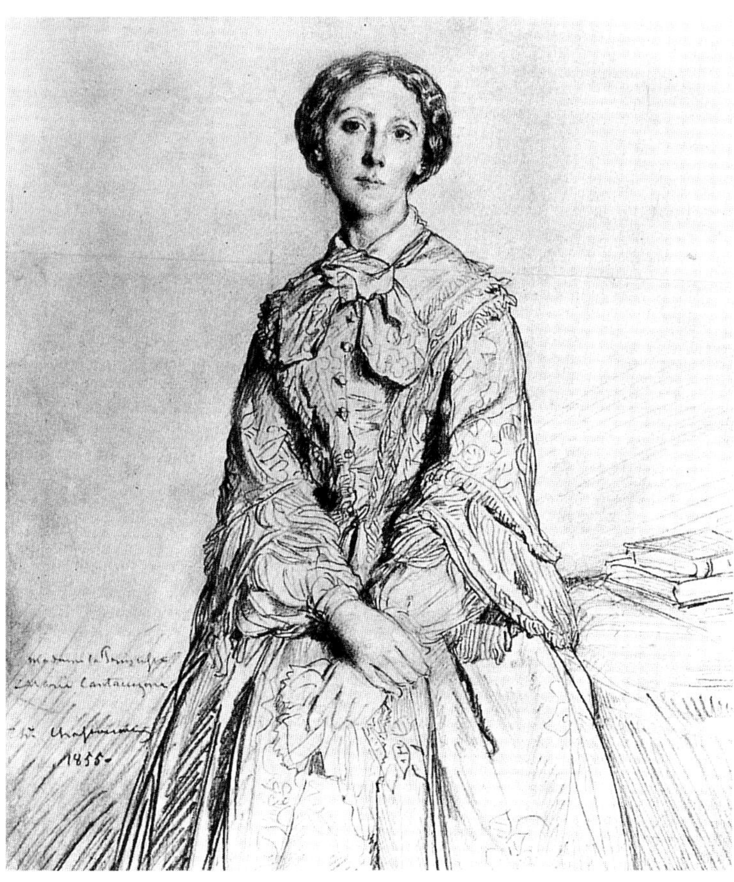

fig. 29
Théodore Chassériau (1819-1856)
Princess Marie Cantacuzène, 1855
Pencil and white heightening on paper, 350 x 270 mm
Private collection

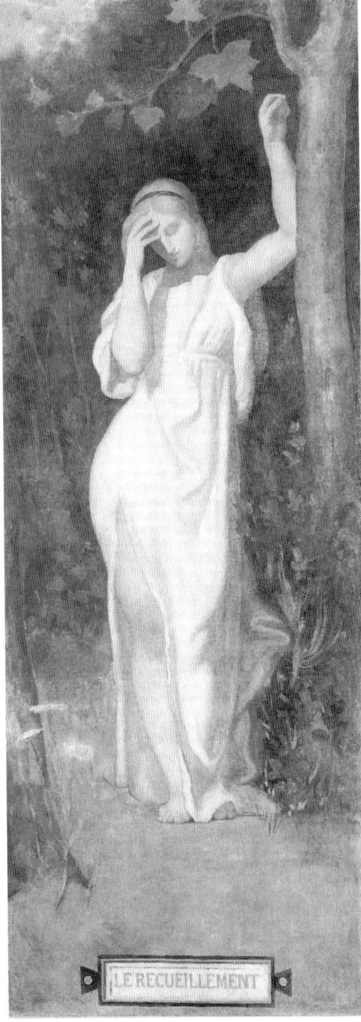

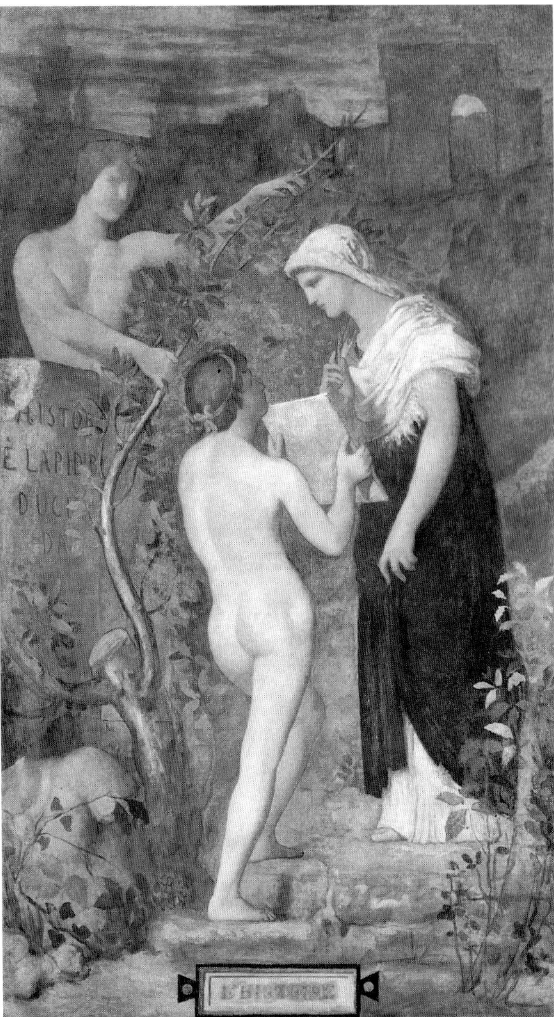

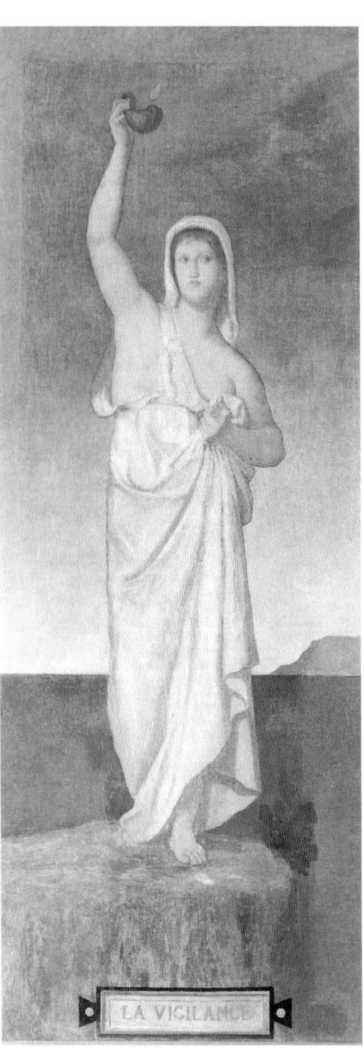

The Decoration for the Hôtel Vignon

As a decorative ensemble for the new home of Claude Vignon, the Balzacian pseudonym (from 1865 to 1885) of the woman sculptor and writer Noémie Constant (1828-1888, née Cadiot), his only commission for a private home,[1] Puvis devised 'quatre figures symboliques': *Fantasy*, *Vigilance*, *Meditation*, *History* (*La Fantaisie*, *La Vigilance*, *Le Recueillement* and *L'Histoire*, fig. 30).[2] This novelist, political essayist and art critic gave Puvis's work the highest marks in her reviews of the 1861 and 1863 Salons for *Le Correspondant*, while pouring scorn on the establishment: 'I don't at all think that Messieurs the members of the Institut are wrong on purpose ... the academicians are mistaken, their judgments seem often incoherent ... Puvis de Chavannes's large murals are the event of the Salon.... One wants to see them as the revival of monumental art.'[3] Puvis must have worked with this accomplished woman on the dimensions and meaning of his ensemble,[4] which was situated in a *salon* on the main floor, near a veranda and a 'Van Dyck' red curtain which Puvis objected to because it clashed with the pale colors of his canvases. *Fantasy* and *History* are somewhat wider than the single figures *Meditation* and *Vigilance*; their disposition is not known, but bilateral balance would demand that the last two bracket one or both of the others.[5]

The first two panels, *Fantasy* and *Vigilance*, were exhibited at the 1866 Salon.[6] Although polychromatic, in comparison to neighboring works they must have seemed sapped of color, which would explain why they were listed in the catalogue as 'peinture en camaïeu; fragment d'une décoration d'un hôtel,' that would have served as notice and mild apologia for those colors, and why Charles Blanc and other critics called them pale 'camaïeus' ('cameo' is not really equivalent and 'monochrome' is misleading).

fig. 30
Decorative paintings for the Hôtel Vignon, 1866
Oil on canvas. Musée d'Orsay, Paris
From left to right:
Meditation (271 x 104 cm)
History (271 x 154 cm)
Vigilance (271 x 104 cm)

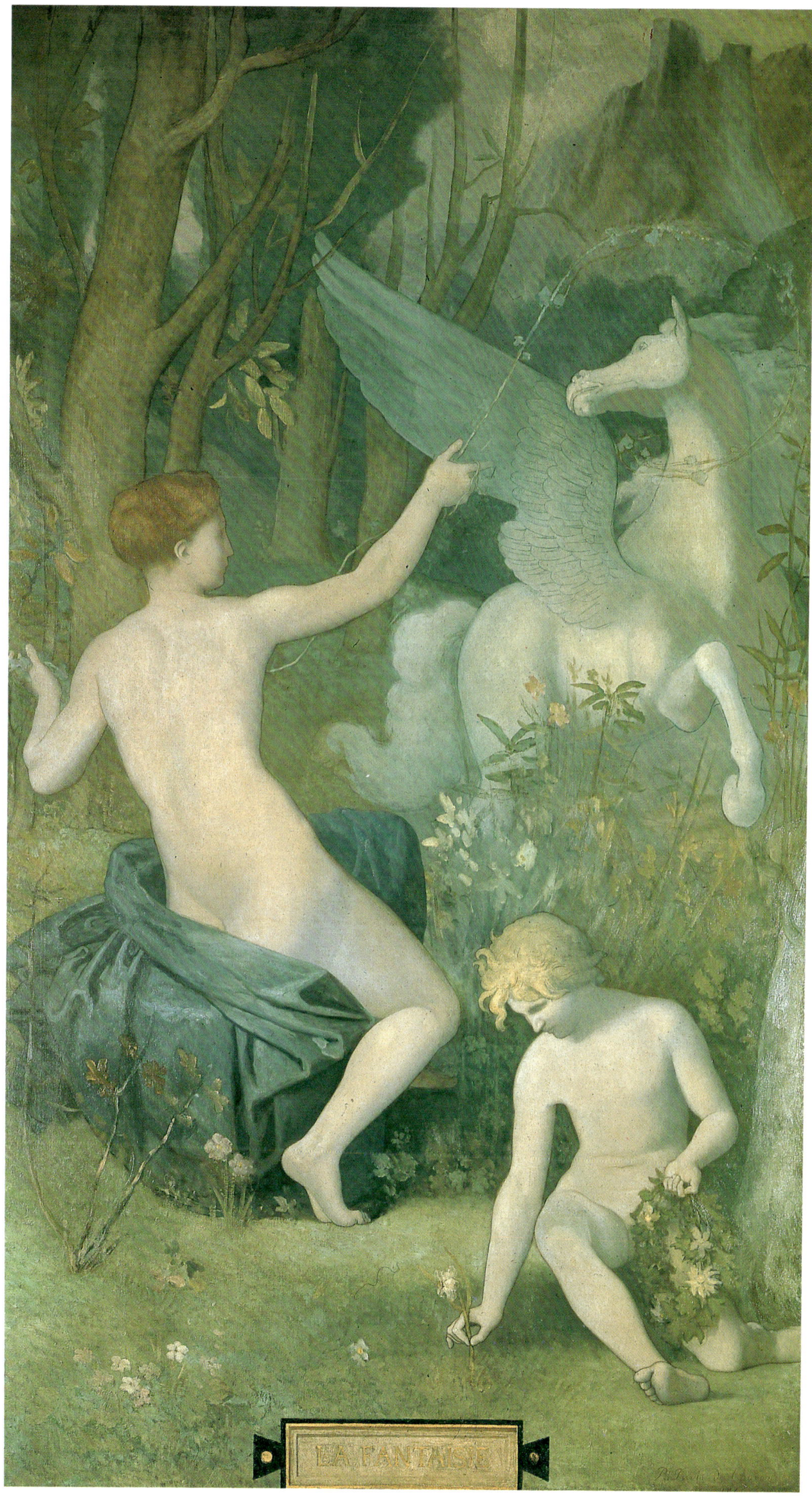
LA FANTAISIE

The Vignon ensemble is the closest Puvis came to the sophisticated stylistic mannerisms of the Fontainebleau School, with its curious mixture of sharp and evanescent forms and its pale, sometimes idiosyncratic colors. One must look particularly to Primaticcio's frescoes in the Ulysses Gallery and the muted hues of the François Ier Gallery (compare cat. 35).

The murals were damaged during the 1870-71 war, but repaired by 1897. In 1872 Madame Vignon married Maurice Rouvier, who kept the canvases after his wife's death and the 1897 sale of their home, which was itself razed in 1912.

1 At 148 rue de la Tour, Paris 16e; her previous house was avidly admired by the Goncourts on 8 October 1861. 1976-77 Paris/Ottawa, no. 59, puts the new house in Passy. A student of Pradier, Claude Vignon exhibited at the 1852 to 1864 Salons using the name of her first husband, the defrocked abbé Alphonse-Louis Constant, who in turn used the pen name Eliphas Lévi and in 1862 had published a book influential in symbolist circles, *Fables et symboles avec leur explication*. Claude Vignon is also the name of a seventeenth-century painter-engraver. On her, see 1981-82, Mont-de-Marsan, Donjon Lacataye, *La Femme artiste, d'Elisabeth Vigée-Lebrun à Rosa Bonheur*, pp. 86, 88.

2 In the older literature *Fantasy* and *Meditation* were called *Dream* and *Poetry*: Vachon (1895), pp. 77-78, ostensibly quoting a letter from Puvis de Chavannes, lists the ensemble as consisting of *La Fantaisie*, *La Vigilance*, *Le Rêve* and *La Poésie*; this is repeated by several later biographers, as Jean (1925), p. 17.

3 'Je ne pense pas du tout que MM. les membres de l'Institut fassent exprès de se tromper ... les académiciens se trompent, que leurs jugements semblent souvent incohérents ... Les grandes murales de M. Puvis de Chavannes sont l'événement du Salon.... On veut y voir une résurrection de l'art monumental.' Claude Vignon, 'Une visite au Salon de 1861,' *Le Correspondant* (1861), 139, also 148-149.

4 I have benefited from Marie-Christine Boucher's astute analyses in Boucher (1978), 98-101, 103.

5 The cycle and the disposition of the panels are discussed in the author's forthcoming book.

6 In the *Salon d'honneur* of the Palais de l'Industrie, according to Geneviève Lacambre in 1984-85 Yamanashi, no. 113. But Edmond About, *Salon de 1866* (Paris, 1867), pp. 88-90 described them in two different rooms.

42

Fantasy / *La Fantaisie* 1866

Signed l.r.: P. Puvis de Chavannes 1866
Inscribed at bottom: LA FANTAISIE
Oil on canvas, 263.7 x 148.6 cm
Ohara Museum of Art, Kurashiki, Okayama, Japan

Provenance Noémie Cadiot [Claude Vignon], Paris; M. Marc Rouvier (second husband of Claude Vignon); Durand-Ruel, Paris (18 May 1903-19 March 1906) and 'rendu'; Galerie Barbazanges, Paris (1919); Torjiro Kojima (October 1922); M. Magosaburo Ohara (1922-1943).

Selected Exhibitions 1866 Paris, no. 1601.

Selected References Durand-Ruel Archives, photo no. 4995, 10476D; A.J. du Pays, 'Salon de 1866,' *L'Illustration*, XLVII (12 May 1866), 299; Charles Blanc, 'Salon de 1866,' *Gazette des Beaux-Arts*, XX (1 June 1866), 512, heliogravure repr. opposite 510, 512; Théophile Gautier, 'Salon de 1866,' *Le Moniteur Universel* (12 June 1866), 737; Edmond About, *Salon de 1866* (Paris, 1867), pp. 88-90; Vachon (1895), pp. 77-78; Boucher (1978), 98-106; 1984-85 Yamanashi, no. 113, repr. p. 148.

Fantasy, one of the compositions devised for the decoration of the home of Mme Claude Vignon, is dominated by a nude Ingresque figure, seated in a landscape, her back to the viewer, a nymph-like figure lassoing a winged horse. In the foreground, near her, an ephebe fashions a wreath, perhaps to crown a poet's head. The winged Pegasus was a not uncommon emblem for fantasy or imagination – an imposing sculptural *Fame Retaining Pegasus* (*Renommée retenant Pégase*), for example, topped Garnier's new building for the Paris Opera and had been sketched out by Eugène Lequesne by 1865. Certainly, the winged horse stood for what was good, classicizing and beautiful in a terse caricature by Puvis (cat. 44).

When *Fantasy* was exhibited at the 1866 Salon, its special blue tonalities were singled out by several critics. The habitually prickly Edmond About found the colors shocking: 'there he is, venturing into perilous paths. He has tackled cameo and carries it to unheard-of dimensions ... he introduces into an obstinately blue painting the discordant yellows of majolica ... one must be fair to the enterprise, M. Puvis de Chavannes puts it under the auspices of Fantasy, a divinity which has been terribly dishonored during the last ten years.... This elegant figure ... with golden hair who throws a creeper around the neck of Pegasus as if it were a lasso is modeled more delicately than all its elder sisters....'[1] As About noted, Puvis valorized the imaginative, a demoded venture in the previous decade (Baudelaire notwithstanding). Théophile Gautier felt compelled to soothe his readers by explaining the strange coloration that seemed to surprise a public unaccustomed to 'camaïeu,' by affirming such painting had been 'so current in the last century.' For him the colors were like those of faience, the blue tones highlighted with yellow touches just like Limoges ware. He wrote of the goddess and Pegasus in 'le pays bleu' ('the blue country'), and acknowledged that *Fantasy* and *Vigilance* contrasted to the 'noisy' ('tapageur') works around them.[2]

43

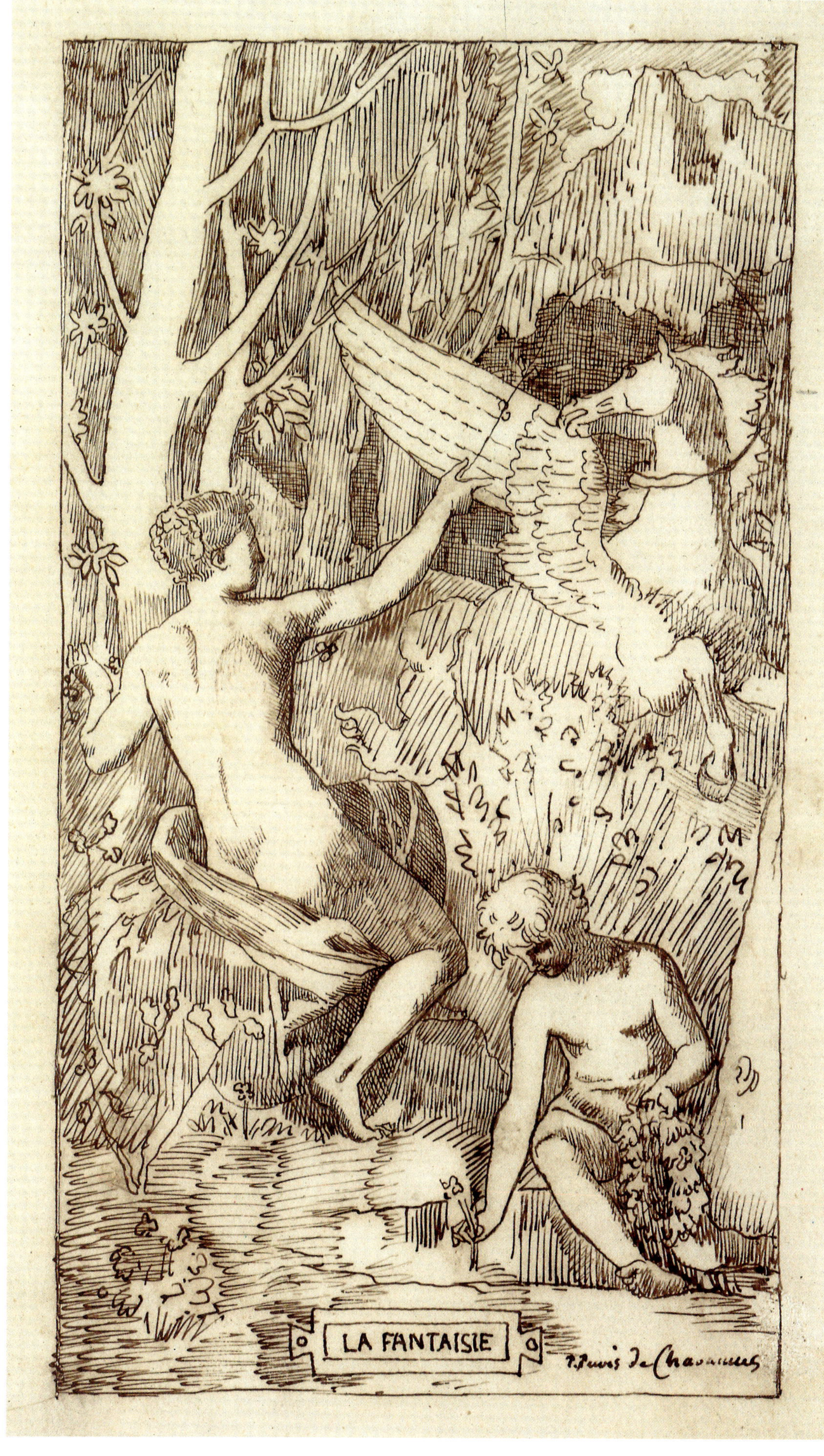

It is not clear why or when *Fantasy* was separated from its companions, but the Japanese collector Ohara (1880-1943) acquired it through Torjiro Kojima in 1922, and it was installed in the Ohara Museum when it opened in 1930.

In contrast to the relative voluptuousness of this *Fantasy*, devised for the Vignon hôtel, there is a smaller version that is considerably different in color and technique, far stiffer, more severe and simplified.[3] Painted with opaque, chalky pastel colors, that version has many of the tonal values reversed and changed – the muse fair-haired – and the composition is flattened. Stylistically it would seem to have been executed long after the Vignon version, probably in the 1880s, when Puvis did a number of small variants of earlier work for exhibition and sale.

1 'le voilà qui s'aventure dans des sentiers périlleux. Il aborde le camaieu, et le porte à des dimensions inouies ... il introduit dans un tableau obstinément bleu les jaunes détonnants de la majolique ... il faut rendre justice à l'entreprise, M. Puvis de Chavannes la met sous les auspices de la Fantaisie, une divinité qui s'est terriblement galvaudée depuis dix ans.... Cette élégante figure ... aux cheveux d'or qui lance une liane autour du cou de Pégase comme pour le prendre au *lazo* est modelée plus délicatement que toutes ses aînées....' About (ref. above), 89.

2 Gautier (ref. above), 737.

3 Called also *Pégase et L'Amour* or *Pegasus und Cupido* (the youth identified as the usual companion to Venus), oil on canvas, 47.5 x 31.5 cm (Emil G. Bührle Collection, Zurich).

43

Fantasy / *La Fantaisie* ca. 1866

Signed l.r.: P. Puvis de Chavannes
Pen and brown ink on paper, 220 x 121 mm
The Museum of Modern Art, New York, lent anonymously (Inv. E. L. 71.623)

Provenance Private collection, New York.

Expressly drafted and surely worked out, this beautiful pen and ink drawing is not a study, but an independent version of *Fantasy* that one must suppose is after the painted canvas. In the large painting interlocking varicolored areas and color cast are important, but line is significant in this far more intimate work. Remarkable for its gamut of sharply etched marks, it is a veritable sampler of energetic lines and squiggles, dashes and curlicues, hooks, loops and cross-hatchings. These signal distinct zones and generate two-dimensional surface patterns and a range of tonalities and textures. Clearly, the artist delighted in modeling limbs and mountains with stitching strokes that change directions as they round corners and in making stiff little flower stems with ink dashes. For all that and the assuredness of the fine, sharp contours and lines, this kind of drawing is rare in the oeuvre.

44

Caricatural Drawing 'Pegasus Vomits Before the Modern Greek'

Stamp l.l.
Black chalk on paper, 200 x 313 mm
Private collection

Provenance Artist's heirs and by descent.
Selected Exhibitions 1976-77 Paris/Ottawa, no. 225.
Selected References Brown Price (1991), 133, repr. 130.

Puvis's caricature *Pegasus Vomits Before the Modern Greek* (*Pégase vomit devant le grec moderne*), includes a winged Pegasus, as in *Fantasy* (cat. 42), a painting that epitomizes his ability to embody a vague antiquity dear to a collective sensibility in the Second Empire. The reason he followed such a pictorial route is forcefully spelled out in the caricature which, though connected ideologically to the painting, is difficult to date. The winged horse, symbolizing the sanctified and marvelous mythic classical tradition, vomits at the sight of the modern Greek, or banal modernity. The implication is that man is no longer heroic (*pace* Baudelaire and the heroism of modern life). Although the Symbolist poet Jean Moréas (born Papadiamantopoulos) was known as 'le grec moderne,' it does not seem likely Puvis, who tried to dissociate himself from the Symbolists – who in turn happily cited him as a progenitor – had him in mind. Nonetheless, the pungent vehicle of caricature tersely enunciated Puvis's aesthetic view.

Puvis's private caricatures are a surprising contrast to his better known public work and, considered with them, an evocative index, sharply enunciating his position, frequently with caustic, editorialized comment, on various issues, aesthetic, topical and personal. Puvis would occasionally do caricatural drawings on the same subject as his painting (see cat. 6). Less than reassuring, they would sometimes vehemently express what was assiduously avoided in the more reserved official work. In using caricature to vent an opinion or present a position, he was not alone, for the use of caricature as manifesto was significant in the nineteenth century, Daumier's 'Battle of the Schools' caricature probably the best known. For Puvis as for other caricaturists of his time, for Cham and Daumier and later Toulouse-Lautrec and

4

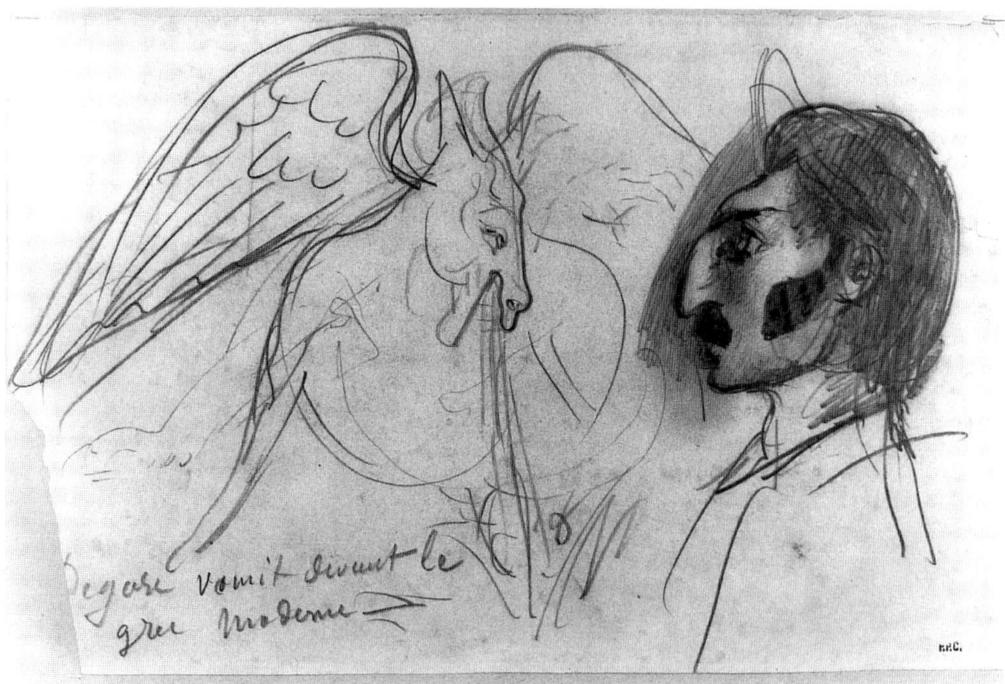

Gauguin, caricature proved an apt and often withering vehicle for the articulation of an aesthetic position – unprepossessing but eloquent. Toulouse-Lautrec's polemical pictorial caricatures were to be used to devastating satirical effect as he brought his case against Puvis's *Sacred Wood* (see fig. 36), ridiculing as out of place just what Puvis celebrated in his *Pégase vomit*.

45

Vigilance / *La Vigilance* 1866

Signed l.r.: P. Puvis de Chavannes 1866
Oil on canvas, 235 x 93 cm
Private collection

Provenance Artist's heirs; Durand-Ruel, Paris (1900-30 August 1902); Chaponay Collection (30 August 1902, returned the same day); Durand-Ruel, Paris (20 January 1903); Paris, Hôtel Drouot (13 December 1941) (same version?); private collection, France.
Selected Exhibitions 1899 Paris (Durand-Ruel), no. 9; 1900 Paris, no. 538 bis, repr. 133; 1937 Lyons, no. 14.
Selected References Boucher (1978), 98-106.

Like Jules Lefebvre's *Truth* of 1870 (Musée d'Orsay, Paris) and Frédéric Bartholdi's *Liberty Enlightening the World* (the 'Statue of Liberty'), *Vigilance* holds a lamp aloft. Although Puvis experimented with what gesture he would use,[1] he decided on this not unusual pose for an allegorical figure, a pose already standard in his repertory (see cat. 11). For his classicizing figure he may have looked to an antique prototype, as was his custom, and his immediate source may have been the sculpture of the Amazon of Crésilas, an engraving of which was illustrated in the *Gazette des Beaux-Arts* on 1 November 1859; true to type, that figure is draped with one breast exposed.[2]

Vigilance was designed for the town house of Claude Vignon, but Puvis apparently made no fewer than five painted versions, the histories of which remain confused.[3] This one is slightly smaller than the Vignon decoration (Musée d'Orsay, Paris), but of a different tonal range and finish; the lower cliff, distant hills and absence of vegetation also distinguish this version. Edmond About's description of amber tones serves to point out what were perceived as unusual color casts in the decorations: 'The blue [of *Fantasy*] gives way to an amber color of a strange smoothness. This tall woman who stands upright on a promontory raising her lit lamp is Vigilance. Dawn appearing behind her comes to relieve her of her long and painful sentry duty. The idea is big and beautiful ... but the morning light slightly veils the delicacies of the model.'[4]

By the later 1860s, this kind of conventionalized figure in antique garb with an arm upraised in what might be viewed as a contrived gesture was not immune from ridicule.[5] With naturalism in its ascendancy, Daumier focused barbed drawings at the artificialities and outmodedness of such classicizing imagery. Two years later, Cham satirized the specific convention of such a classicizing personifying figure by lampooning one that closely resembled *Vigilance*, a sculpture by a M. Bouvier at the 1868 Salon, also posed with a lamp held aloft and draped in classicizing garb. His caption read, 'Une dame éclaire un

4

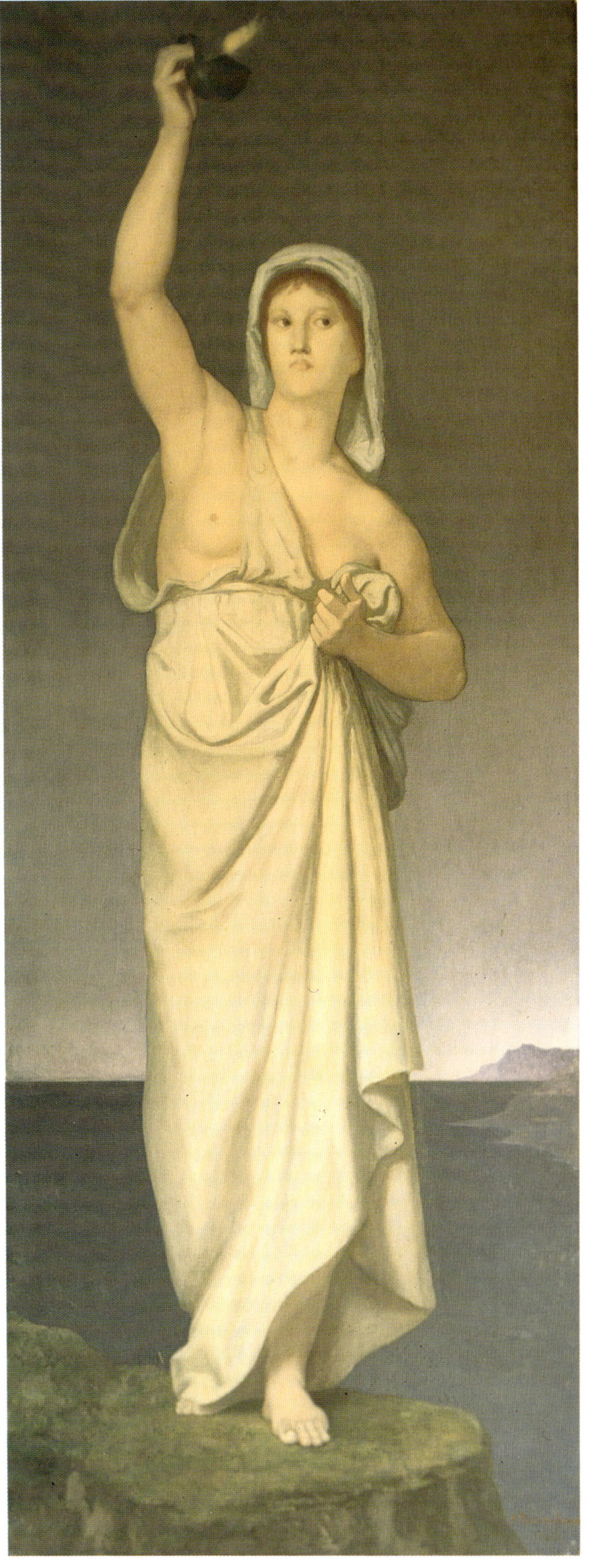

46

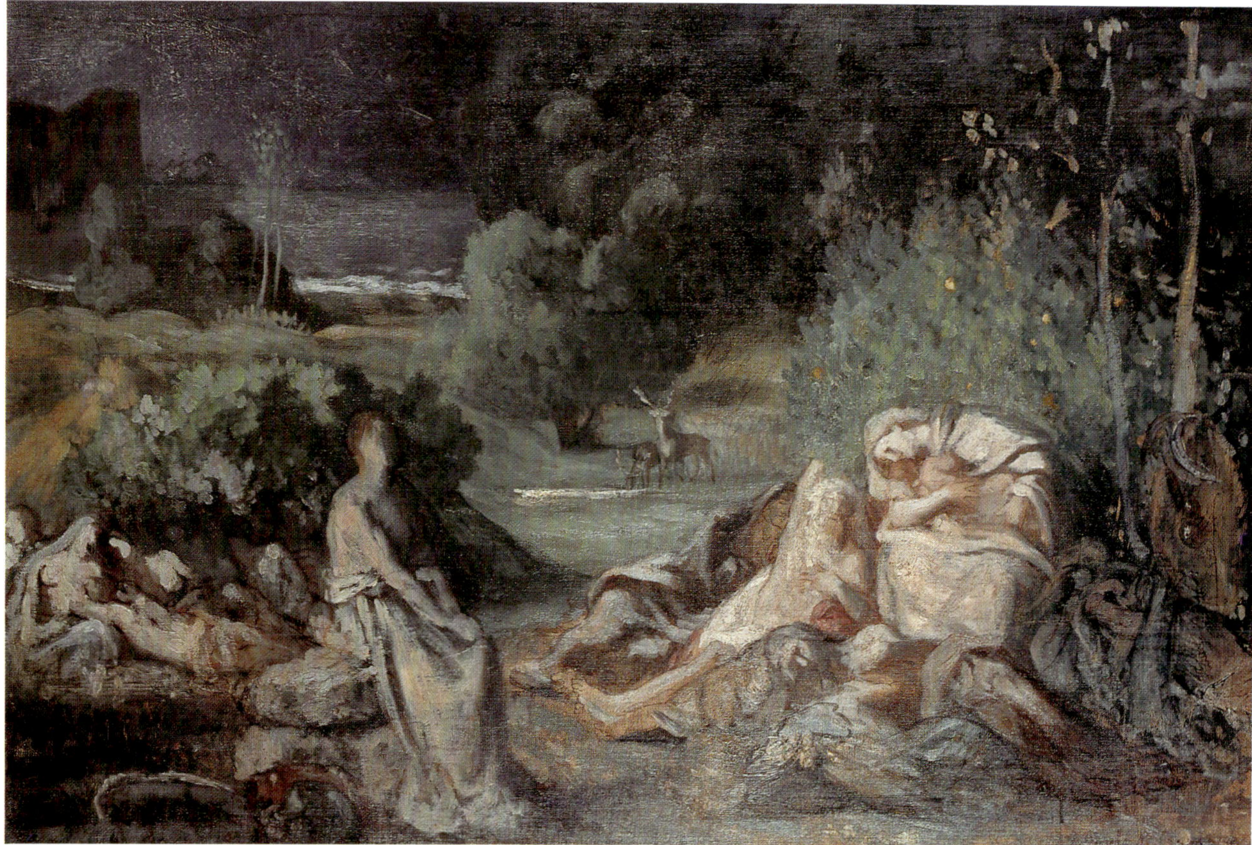

monsieur qui a l'inconvenance de laisser supposer qu'il a perdu ses effets chez elle.' The lamp is held aloft, the caption indicates, so a man who has left something at the lady's place (there has been hanky-panky) might find it.[6]

In the years to come, Puvis would seek to modernize his allegorical personifications (see cat. 65, 139-140).

1 See *Dressed Woman, Leaning to the Left*, black chalk on off-white tracing paper, 310 x 170 mm, Musée de Picardie, Amiens (Inv. 912bis 65).

2 In Greek legend, this race of women warriors were said to remove their right breasts in order that they might better draw their bows.

3 See Boucher (1978), 98, 101, 103. The painted versions include: *Vigilance*, 271.5 x 103.5 cm, Musée d'Orsay, Paris (Inv. MNR 973a), formerly Mme Claude Vignon, Paris; exhibited 1866 Paris, no. 1600 [?], 1976-77 Paris/Ottawa, no. 59; *Truth, Vigilance* or *La Vérité*, dated 1867, 105.7 x 52.5 cm, National Gallery of Scotland, Edinburgh; *Réduction* [*La Vigilance*], 42 x 21 cm, Vente Burty (23 March 1891), no. 24; photographed 1917 by Durand-Ruel, no. 8384. Another reduced version photographed Durand-Ruel, 20 January 1903, no. 4391, without measurements, apparently the same as no. 1176. The problem is made more complex when one reckons with a letter of 27 July (no year) to Puvis from 'Claude Vignon Rouvier' asking for authorization to have *Vigilance* and *Meditation* copied (whether a painting or other reproduction is not noted) by a M. Pollonaire (? almost illegible), a sailor (? 'marin') from Villefranche (Alpes Maritimes) (private collection).

4 'Le bleu fait place à une couleur ambrée d'une suavité étrange. Cette grande femme qui se tient debout sur un promontoire, élevant sa lampe allumée, c'est la Vigilance. L'Aurore qui parait derrière elle vient la relever de sa longue et pénible faction. L'idée est grande et belle ... mais la lumière du matin voile un peu les délicatesses du modèle.' Edmond About, *Salon de 1866* (Paris, 1867), p. 90.

5 See Brown Price (1977), 29.

6 One of an extended series of such drawings lampooning Salon works from 1845 through 1878 by Cham (the pseudonym of Comte Amédée de Noé, 1819-1879); see Brown Price (1991), 122.

46

Study for 'Sleep' ca. 1866-70

Signed l.r.: P. Puvis de Chavannes
Oil on canvas, 55 x 80 cm
Musée des Beaux-Arts, Lille (dépôt de l'Etat, Inv. RF 1943-71)

Provenance J. Francis Auburtin (ca. 1866-1930); Mme Auburtin (1933-1943); Musée du Louvre, Paris (1943); deposited by the Musée du Louvre (1946).
Selected Exhibitions 1870 Limoges, [no. unavailable] (probably this version included, see Burty [ref. below]);

1887 Paris (Durand-Ruel), no. 26 [this version?]; 1972 London/Liverpool, no. 201; 1976-77 Paris/Ottawa, no. 65.
Selected References Durand-Ruel Archives, no. 501, L8284; Philippe Burty, 'L'Exposition de Limoges,' *Gazette des Beaux-Arts*, s2, IV (September 1870), 221-222; E. Foucart-Walter, *Catalogue sommaire illustré des peintures du musée du Louvre et du musée d'Orsay. Ecole Francaise. Annexes et index*, Vol. V (Paris, 1986), p. 321.

This verdant, woodland scene, the ocean far in the background, a lush blue-green place of enchantment, what the French call 'féerique,' provides a sharp contrast in landscape and atmosphere to the arid, sparsely vegetated *Sleep* for which this oil sketch is a study (see cat. 47). Here, stags drink from a pool in a forest clearing, and two female figures[1] are seated prominently in the foreground, watchful, amidst their slumbering companions.

The first owner of this work was Puvis's student Jean-Francis Auburtin (1866-1930), later well-known himself as a painter and responsible for the decorative ensemble of the Paris Conseil d'Etat.[2]

1 Cf. *Study for woman in 'Sleep'*, signed l.r.: P. Puvis de Ch, pencil on blue-gray paper, 285 x 310 mm (private collection).

2 Briend [1991] and Foucart [1991].

47

Sleep / *Le Sommeil* (reduced version)

ca. 1867-70

Signed l.l.: P. Puvis de Chavannes
Oil on canvas, 66.4 x 106 cm
The Metropolitan Museum of Art, New York, Theodore M. Davis Collection, Bequest of Theodore M. Davis, 1915 (Inv. 30.95.253)

Provenance M. Gadala, Paris (until 1896); Durand-Ruel, Paris and New York (1896); Theodore M. Davis (1896); bequeathed to the museum by the latter (1915).
Selected Exhibitions 1870 Limoges, [no. unavailable] (perhaps this version included, see Burty [ref. below]).
Selected References Paris, Fondation Custodia, Institut Néerlandais, Puvis de Chavannes, no. 9281; Philippe Burty, 'L'Exposition de Limoges,' *Gazette des Beaux-Arts*, s2, IV (September 1870), 221-222; Letter of 4 December 1887 (private collection); Théophile Gautier, 'Salon de 1867,' *Le Moniteur Universel* (3 June 1867), 668; Vachon (1895), pp. 80, 185; Michel and Laran (1911), pp. 45-46; Burroughs (1931), 15-16; Baudoüin (1935), 299; Charles Sterling and Margaretha M. Salinger, *French Paintings. A Catalogue of the Collection of the Metropolitan Museum of Art* (New York, 1966-1967), II, pp. 227-228.

Soon after he had finished his imposing *Sleep* (1867, 380 x 600 cm, Musée des Beaux-Arts, Lille), of which the canvas exhibited is a reduced version,[1] Puvis called it his favorite work.[2] Indeed, two decades later, he wanted his unusually large, independent (non-mural) canvas to represent his oeuvre at the Musée du Luxembourg rather than *The Poor Fisherman* that had been chosen.[3]

In a dusky, quiet, moonlit landscape clusters of slumbering figures are barely distinguishable from one another and the outcroppings of rock and vegetation that surround them. In the foreground to the right there is a group composed of a cloaked figure, an old man, a woman with a baby and a young couple, and in the middle distance to the left still other figures, while in the distance, near the shore, a low-lying mass that is very much one with the land might be still other chunky outcroppings or figures. With closely toned colors, browns, ocher, grays and dark red brown, contributing to the partial obscurity, *Sleep* seems to be at least partly about the kinds of half-understood perceptions that somnolence brings about.

A preparatory drawing[4] and the catalogue of the 1867 Salon, at which the definitive canvas was exhibited, both include the inscription 'Tempus erat quo prima quies mortalibus ... aegris incipit,' a fragment from Virgil's *Aeneid* (II, 268) that reads 'It was the hour when for troubled mortals rest – sweetest gift of gods that glides to men – has just begun' and refers to the Trojans's first sleep after they had come to believe that the Greeks had left their land and they were spared from war. Puvis may also have known Leconte de Lisle's almost contemporary verse in his *Poèmes Antiques*,

'C'était l'heure où l'oiseau, sous les vertes feuillées,
Repose, où tout s'endort, les hommes et les Dieux.
Du tranquil Sommeil les ailes déployées
Pâlissaient le ciel radieux.

Sur les algues du bord ... les guerriers épars, rompus de lassitude,
Songaient, sur le sable des mers.'[5]

The pictorial origin of the composition surely lay in Chassériau's drawing of sleeping harvesters in *Harvesters at Rest*, the central section of his *Sleep*[6] which also includes haystacks in the background – such mounds are prominent in an early version of Puvis's scheme (private collection) – and the sleeping apostles in Chassériau's *Christ in the Garden of Olives*, an oil study of which, *Sleep of the Apostles*, belonged

47

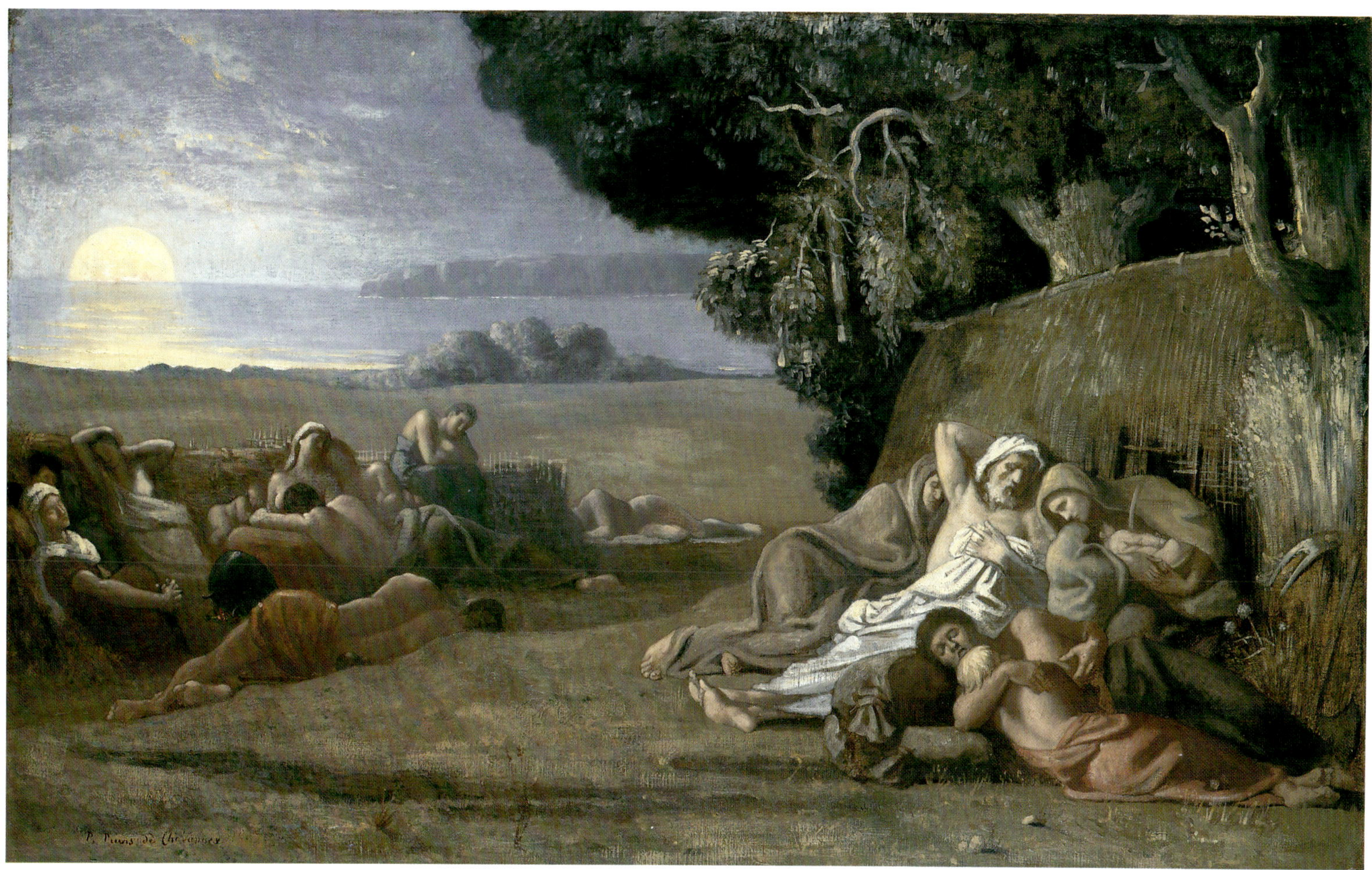

to Marie Cantacuzène and then to Puvis (both Musée du Louvre, Paris). Indeed, Chassériau had intended to make a Virgilian triptych, *Rest* or *Sleep*, the central portion of which, *Sleep*, he imagined much like Puvis's *Sleep*.[7] Dating his remarks 'à minuit 1840,' and noting 'la solitude de la nature la nuit,' he envisioned a frieze of sleep, with nymphs and other figures, and designated the whole be in melancholy half-tones ('à demi ton ... pour que les – seuls sont d'un ton mélancolique'). Chassériau's many drawings of sleeping figures indicate his commitment to the motif.[8]

Recent commentators have argued that Puvis's sketch for *Sleep* illustrates Victor Hugo's 'Booz endormi' (*Légende des Siècles* of 1859), rather than Virgil. He may indeed have found inspiration in its description, for his figures are harvesters rather than warriors: 'Donc Booz dans la nuit dormi parmi les siens; Près des meules qu'on eût prises pour des décombres. Les moissonneurs couchés faisaient des groupes sombres....'[9] Certainly, the poem and Puvis's figures were important to Frédéric Bazille's nocturnal *Ruth and Boaz* (1870, private collection), and Ferdinand Hodler's *Night* of 1890 (Kunstmuseum, Bern) is modeled after a passage of Puvis's work after which Hodler did a preliminary drawing.[10]

Sleep was the theme of a number of French paintings of the 1860s, including Gustave Courbet's sometimes troubled sleepers, as in his provocative *Sleep* of 1866 (Musée du Petit Palais, Paris). The familiarity of the theme notwithstanding, Cham lampooned Puvis's canvas when it was exhibited in 1867 with a parody captioned, 'M. Puvis de Chavannes has perfectly rendered the anguish of a family that can't get any shut-eye for lack of insect repellent.'[11]

This reduced version of *Sleep* postdates the Salon painting, perhaps by a number of years (see below). Some details have been eliminated and the relatively coarse texture of the pigment and scumbling brushstroke have left others less pronounced. The artist increased the coherence of interrelated figures by creating patterns of highlighted body parts and made objects like leaves and wheat more legible by having his assured daubing technique at once describe and comprise them. Figures are larger in proportion to the landscape and highlights and brushstroke technique reduce pictorial space in favor of surface interest.

On 1 April 1870, Puvis elected to send a version of *Sleep*, most likely this one, rather than his four reduced Amiens paintings already shown in Paris and Bordeaux (cat. 26-29) to an exhibition in Limoges. As he put it, 'they [the four] would seem to constitute all my artistic baggage, when on the contrary I haven't since stopped producing works I regard as more or less equal to those. So much for the spiritual[;] as for the temporal, I have no illusions about the luck of lending Limoges four canvases at once, I shall thus vainly deprive myself of them at the most inopportune moment as I then strip my atelier just as the Paris exhibition giving me my bit of publicity could induce an art lover to buy my reductions. I shall thus restrict myself by finishing the painting of sleep that you saw very advanced and send it....'[12]

1 Another version of almost the same dimensions as that exhibited (whereabouts unknown) belonged to Paul Baudoüin. It was 61 x 102 cm, and sold Paris, Hôtel Drouot, Vte. X, 'Vente [Paul] Baudoüin' (24 November 1944), no. 27.

2 See letter from Puvis to the painter Léon Joly Saint François, cited in 1976-77 Paris/Ottawa, no. 231.

3 Letter of 26 November 1887 to the critic Jules Castagnary, then Director of Fine Arts (Musée du Louvre, Cabinet des Dessins); cited also in 1976-77 Paris/Ottawa, no. 235. See also pp. 41 and 46 of this catalogue.

4 Signed l.l.: P. Puvis de Chavannes, pen and brown ink on tracing paper, 249 x 349 mm, Metropolitan Museum of Art, New York (Acces. 10.45.19).

5 'It was the hour when the bird, under the leafy greens,/ rests, when everything, men and Gods slumber./ From tranquil sleep the unfolded wings/ dimmed the radiant sky./ On the seaweed of the shore .../ the scattered warriors, overwhelmed with weariness,/ dreamt, on the sand of the seas.' The poem, 'Hylas,' was first published 1852 (this edition, Paris, 1955, p. 160).

6 Musée du Louvre, Paris (Inv. RF 25.578), see Louis-Antoine Prat, *Dessins de Théodore Chassériau* (Paris, 1988), I, no. 1041.

7 See Musée du Louvre, Inv. RF 25.578, and Inv. 24345, carton 14; cf. Sandoz (1974), p. 28, called there the *Triptych of 'Rest': The Rest of the Harvester, The Rest of the Married Couple, The Rest in Death* (*Triptych du 'repos': Repos du moissonneur, Repos des époux, Repos dans la mort.* Sanchoz's titles are not given in the correct sequence).

8 Musée du Louvre, Paris (Inv. RF 24596-24600).

9 'Thus Boaz at night slept among his own; near the haystacks one might take for ruins. The harvesters sleeping in the open made somber groups....' 1985-86, Paris, Grand Palais, *La Gloire de Victor Hugo*, pp. 605-606.

10 1972-73, Berkeley, University Art Museum / New York, Solomon R. Guggenheim Museum / Cambridge, Mass., Busch-Reisinger Museum, Harvard University, *Ferdinand Hodler*, pp. 72-73.

11 'Puvis de Chavannes a parfaitement rendu les angoisses d'une famille qui ne peut fermer l'oeil faute de poudre insecticide.' Cham, *Cham au Salon de 1867* (Paris, 1867), no. 1252.

12 'elles auraient l'air de constituer tout mon bagage artistique, quand au contraire je n'ai pas cessé de produire depuis des oeuvres que j'estime plus ou moins équivalentes à celles-là. Voilà pour le spirituel[;] quant au temporel je ne me fais pas aucune illusion sur la chance de laisser à Limoges quatre toiles d'un coup, je m'en priverai donc sterilement et au moment le plus inopportune puisque je dégarnirais mon atelier alors que l'exposition de Paris me donnant ma part de publicité pourrait engager un amateur à acheter mes réductions. Je me bornirai donc à achever donc le tableau du sommeil que vous avez vu très avancé et à vous l'envoyer....' Institut Néerlandais (ref. above).

48

Study for Couple in 'Sleep' ca. 1867

Charcoal on paper, 171 X 367 mm
Van Gogh Museum, Amsterdam (Inv. D 1012 M/1991)

Provenance Paris, Hôtel Drouot (23 October 1989), no. 16; Robert Miller Gallery, New York.

Selected references 'Principales acquisitions des Musées en 1991,' *Gazette des Beaux-Arts*, s6, CXIX (March 1992), repr.

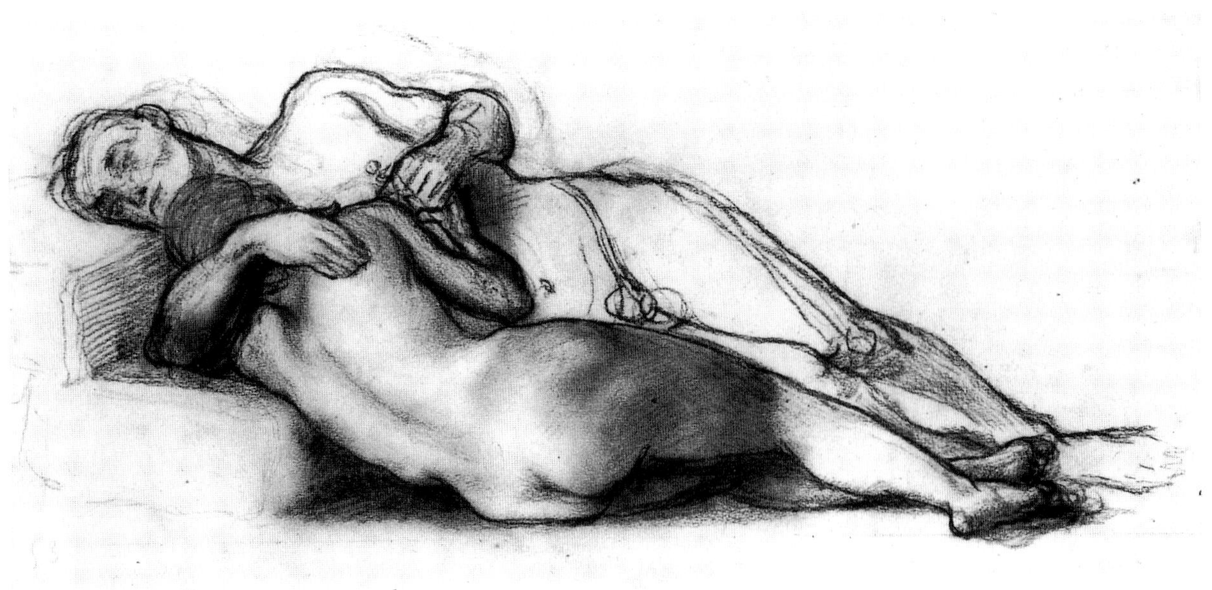

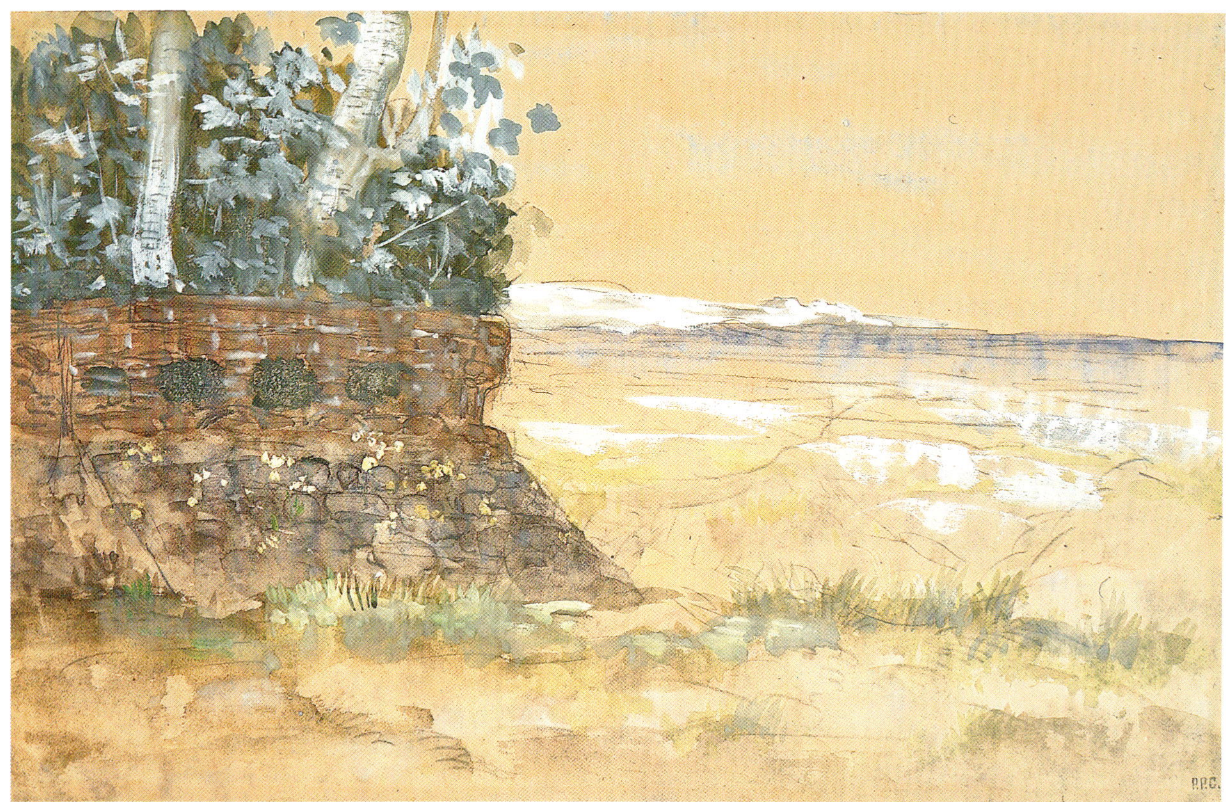

This drawing of a couple lying together in sleep is one of several studies of these two figures[1] for *Sleep* of 1867 (see cat. 47). With the addition of drapery around their lower limbs, they would be among the assemblage of figures lying at rest along a strand. Puvis executed separate drawings of each of these figures: one sheet of the male nude alone against the riser of a platform is a sharply drawn 'académie',[2] that the artist modified to expressive and lyrical purpose in the Amsterdam sheet and subsequent paintings. In another rendition,[3] prepared in conjunction with an early oil variant[4] the female is twisted slightly away from the male, with her knee bent up. The motif of two figures quietly embracing shows a tenderness unusual in Puvis's oeuvre. As has been pointed out by Ronald de Leeuw, 'the difference in the degree to which the figures are elaborated ... the exciting dialogue between a completed and a sketchy form' of 'the female figure seen from the back ... [and the] man depicted with much rougher lines,'[5] contributes to the interest of the sketch.

Another lovely drawing of a more amply proportioned and mature sleeping couple affectionately holding hands and lying in the opposite direction[6] shows that the artist had considered including two such couples, but in the painting he separated these two figures, completely enrobing the female and making her a solitary sleeping figure and the male an older, bearded man deep in sleep, his arm thrust over his head.

1 There are a considerable number of studies and drawings for the composition as a whole and of individual figures. These are widely scattered, although the Musée des Beaux-Arts, Lille, houses the largest group; compare also a drawing of this couple with drapery around them (private collection); 1976-77 Paris/Ottawa, no. 67.

2 Black chalk on gray paper, squared in blue; 220 x 425 mm, Musée des Beaux-Arts, Lille (Inv. 2021).

3 Whereabouts unknown, see *Gazette des Beaux-Arts*, s2, XXXVII (January 1888), repr. 41.

4 *Sleep, variant composition*, ca. 1866-67, oil on canvas, 46 x 47.2 cm (private collection); 1976-77 Paris/Ottawa, no. 64.

5 1991, Amsterdam, Van Gogh Museum, *Aanwinsten/Acquisitions 1986-1991*, p. 35.

6 Signed l.l.: P. P. Ch, black chalk, 190 x 304 mm, Old Jail Art Center, Albany, Texas.

49

Landscape ca. 1867-70

Stamp l.r.
Watercolor, gouache and pencil on paper, 195 x 305 mm
Private collection

Provenance Mr. and Mrs. H. Puvis de Chavannes, Neuilly.

5

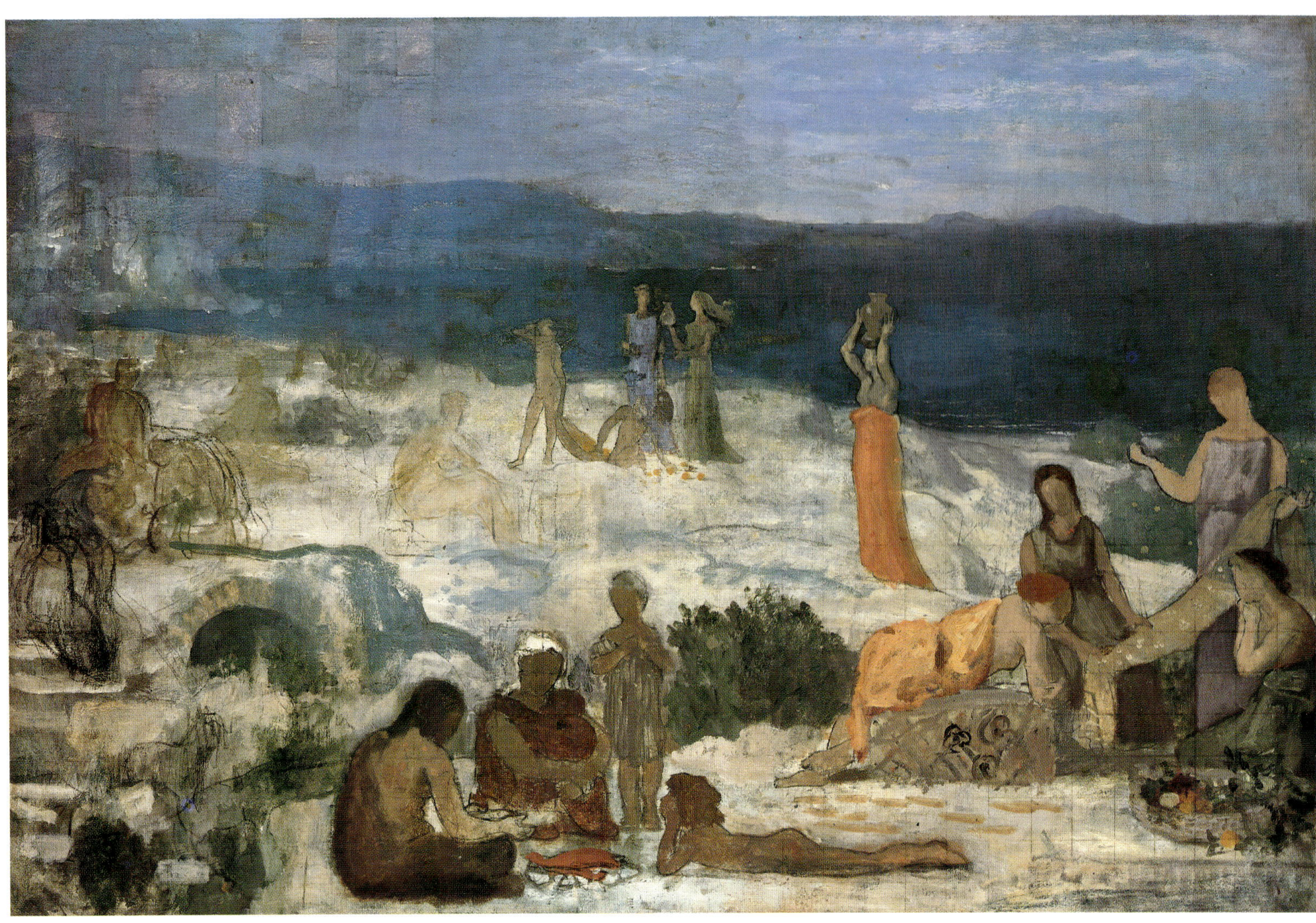

The general configuration of this lovely watercolor landscape, of a wooded bluff near the sea, is in many respects similar to the setting for *Sleep* of 1867 (see cat. 47). The mood also resembles the enchanting atmosphere of one of the preliminary versions of that painting (cat. 46). The whitened tree trunks and white and blue foliage exhibit Puvis's mastery of the brush and watercolor medium. The work is executed with the true calligrapher's light but deft stroke, so that in each leaf the viewer senses a decorative possibility. Indeed, Puvis made much of such foliage from the even bluer and more violet leaves in *History* (1866, see fig. 30) to the golden leaves of *Antique Vision* (1885, see cat. 105) and his Boston Public Library murals (1895-96, see cat. 143-144). The pattern of flat foliate forms plays a part in *The Beheading of Saint John the Baptist* (cat. 57) and *Pleasant Land* (see cat. 86), and these kinds of leaf shapes would be developed and made more familiar later by Gauguin and by Matisse in their work.

50

Massilia, Greek Colony / *Massilia, colonie grecque* ca. 1868-69

Oil, pencil on canvas, squared (visible lower right), 98.1 x 147 cm
The Phillips Collection, Washington, D.C.
(Acc. 1618)

Provenance Durand-Ruel, Paris; Baron Denys Cochin, Paris (1903-1919); Paris, Galerie Georges Petit, Vente Denys Cochin (26 March 1919), no. 19; Bernheim-Jeune, Paris; Gradt; Paris, Galerie Barbazanges; Meyer Goodfriend, New York and Paris; New York, American Art Association, Goodfriend Sale (4-5 January 1923), no. 121; The Kraushaar Gallery, New York; Duncan Phillips (1923); William Rockhill Nelson Gallery of Art, Kansas City, Missouri (housed during World War II).

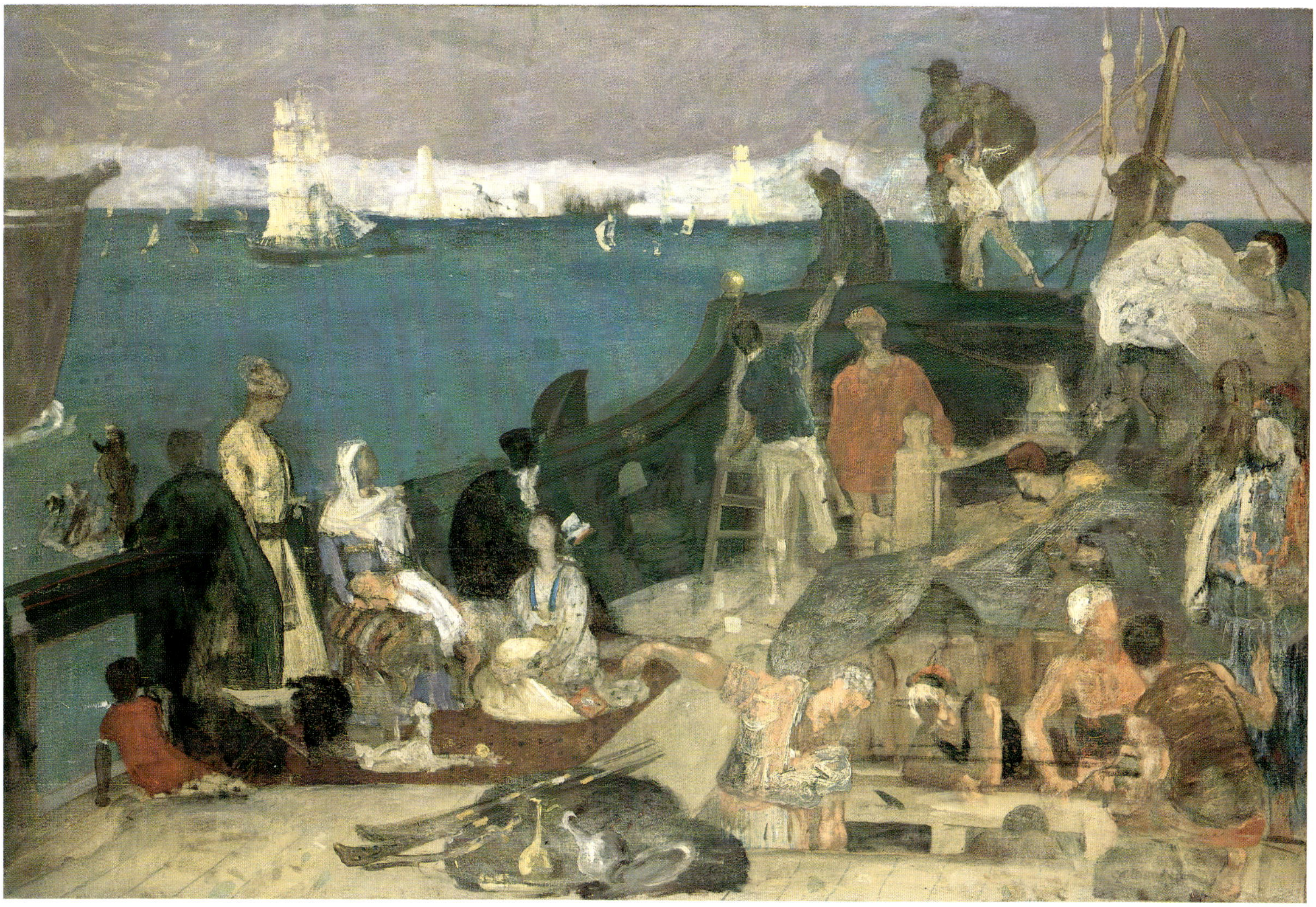

Selected Exhibitions 1894 New York, no. 3; 1899 Paris (Durand-Ruel), no. 18; 1975 Toronto, no. 8; 1976-77 Paris/Ottawa, no. 74.

Selected References On the mural: Chaumelin (1873), pp. 221, 304-306. On this painting: Hutchins (1930), 234-239; 1984-85 Marseilles, no. 3 and pp. 13-50, 51-77; Cafritz/Gowing/Rosand (1988), p. 227.

Art museums that helped frame a city's image proliferated in France in the latter part of the nineteenth century. Second Empire Marseilles was a faster growing city even than Paris. The 1851 population of 198,000 had by 1866 increased to 300,000 and merited such an institution.[1] Surely as a result of the interest in the reduced versions of Puvis de Chavannes's Amiens Museum murals exhibited at the 1867 Exposition Universelle (cat. 26-29), the artist received a contract on 25 July 1867 to execute two murals for the city's new museum, the Palais Longchamp designed by Henri Espérandieu. In 1869 the murals (each 425 x 565 cm, see ill. p. 122) were finished: they were presented at that year's Salon before being transported to the Palais Longchamp, which opened August 1869. Numerous preparatory drawings permit us to trace the project's development.[2]

The contract stipulated that Puvis was to represent antique and modern art in Provence. 'The Construction of the Temple of Diana' (temples of Diana and Apollo were on the acropolis) must have had special appeal to Espérandieu as an architect, who took an active part in the decorative program; 'An Episode from the Life of Puget' was to be about the famous Marseillais sculptor.[3] But the program changed, for reasons unknown to us, and a contract of 18 October 1867 called for murals to represent pagan and Christian Marseilles 'treated in a severe and monumental manner.' By designating Massilia a subject, the commissioning body must have wanted to establish the city's ancient founding, its development as a thriving Greek colony, and its long history and pedigree.[4] Puvis was likely sensitive to the values of the bourgeois sponsors and commercial interests that supported such civic institutions as museums, and those values informed his designs.[5]

His preliminary canvas for *Massilia, Greek Colony* is a wonderfully clear-eyed, remarkably fresh and lovely panorama of the ancient city

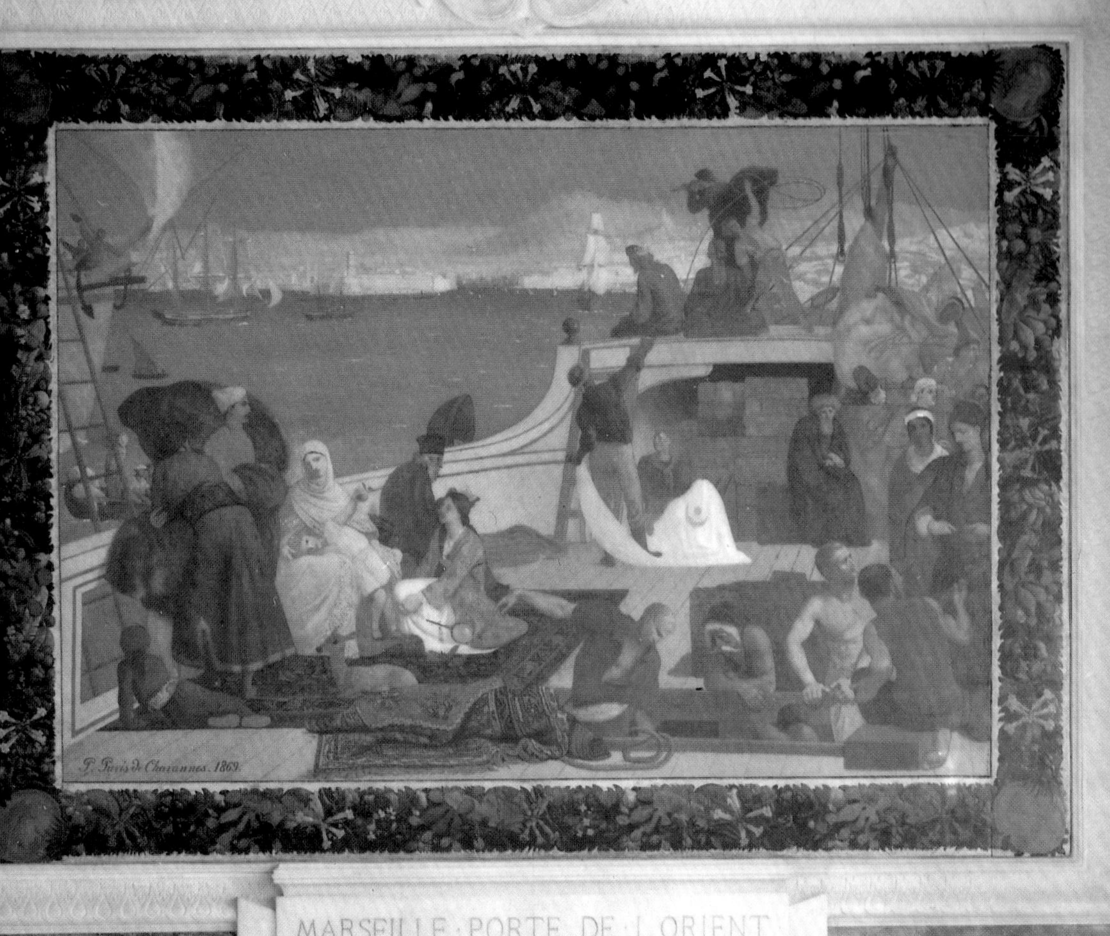
P. Puvis de Chavannes. 1869.
MARSEILLE · PORTE DE L'ORIENT

near the shore. The beginnings of construction, the dressing, for example, of stones, a motif central to the completed mural, are barely hinted at here. The composition is loosely defined and still lacks such devices as the terrace, blocks of stone and tree that would later be used in the mural to separate sections and bracket and interrelate figures. The rapid decrease in the size of the figures is offset by the carpet of clear color – blues, off-whites, salmon pinks and mauve – that pulls images to the forward plane. The daily chores of an imagined 'primitive' population are presented in genre vignettes that are not far removed from modern occupations: cooking a fish, displaying cloth to companions. Chassériau had used the motif of showing cloth in his *Commerce Bringing the People Together – Western Port* (Cour des Comptes, Paris, destroyed in 1871), which Puvis drew on in both his Marseilles murals. Puvis delighted in depicting homely routine pleasures which, he advised a student, he had been intent on including.[6] One particularly effective invention is the boy in the middle distance at center, head facing in one direction, torso turned in the other, a figure used again in the 1871 *Children in an Orchard* (see variant, cat. 127) and one that Degas, himself such a master of pictorial manipulation, appreciated, for he owned a drawing of it.

Pentimenti, such as those above the heads at right, sections in which animals and figures are drawn in, and squared-up portions add interest for the contemporary viewer. Despite patches, crackles and restoration, this study should be counted among Puvis's most celebrated works.

The preparatory oil sketches do not include the final borders, important to the program and specific to the site. As Puvis requested the architect to furnish him with source materials for them on 23 June 1868,[7] he must have already been far advanced in his compositions, and thus these preliminary sketches would seem to date from 1868.

1 Sherman (1989), p. 160.

2 See 1984-85 Marseilles, nos. 5-17, 47, 53; among the most interesting because construction is prominent, *Study for Marseilles, Greek Colony'* ca. 1868, pencil and brown ink on tracing paper, 180 x 255 mm, Musée des Beaux-Arts, Marseilles (Inv. D. 188); also *Composition Study*, pen, black ink and pencil on paper [turned] beige, 121 x 157 mm, Musée du Petit Palais, Paris (Inv. PPD 554[5]; MCB 109), Boucher (1979), no. 109 (there related to the Sorbonne); *Study for 'Marseilles, Greek Colony'* stamp l.r., charcoal and blue on buff paper, 156 x 200 mm, Szépmüvészeti Múzeum, Budapest.

3 A copy of the contract at the Musée des Beaux-Arts, Marseilles; see Geneviève Drocourt, 'Puvis de Chavannes et le décor de l'Escalier d'honneur du Palais Longchamp,' in 1984-85 Marseilles, pp. 13-42.

4 Sherman (1989), pp. 185-187; and Sherman (1987), 49-51, 56, repr. 51.

5 Sherman (1989), pp. 192-193.

6 Letter of 22 June 1881 to Paul Baudoüin, Vachon [1900], p. 64.

7 Etienne Parrocel, *L'Art dans le Midi: célébrités marseillaises: Marseille et ses édifices: Architectes et ingénieurs du XIXe siècle* (Marseilles, 1884), IV, pp. 114-115; also quoted by Drocourt in 1984-85 Marseilles, p. 43.

Marseilles, Gateway to the Orient, 1869
Musée des Beaux-Arts, Marseilles

51

Marseilles, Gateway to the Orient / *Marseille, porte de l'Orient* ca. 1868-69

Oil on canvas, 98.1 x 146.3 cm
The Phillips Collection, Washington, D.C.
(Acc. 1617)

Provenance See cat. 50, in addition, note different nos.: Vente Denys Cochin (26 March 1919), no. 20; Goodfriend Sale (4-5 January 1923), no. 122.

Selected Exhibitions See cat. 50, in addition, note different nos.: 1899 Paris (Durand-Ruel), no. 17; 1975 Toronto, no. 9; 1976-77 Paris/Ottawa, no. 75.

Selected References See cat. 50; Chaumelin (1873), pp. 221-222, 306 (on the mural); Pierre Guiral, '*Marseilles, porte de l'Orient* par Puvis de Chavannes,' *Arts et Livres de Provence*, no. 23 (1954), 78-80 (with bibliography).

The title *Marseille, porte de l'Orient*, displayed in the wide border of the mural, is taken from an 1839 poem by Victor Hugo and suggests a gateway to faraway places: 'Il y a dans les nuits d'Avignon un souffle du ciel de Grèce et d'Italie. On sent à ce courant d'air charmant que la porte de l'Orient est là, tout près, entrebaillée.'[1]

This paean to modern Marseilles pictures a bustling, commercial port and emphasizes the importance of immigration and trade, sources of the city's character and prosperity.[2] Indeed, one message is that this thriving disembarkation point is the welcoming destination for a heterogeneous group of emigrés, as a small commonwealth of strangers in colorful and, for Puvis, unusual costumes are depicted nearing the port of Marseilles on the deck of a ship. The opening in 1869, the year the mural (ill. p. 122) was completed, of the Suez Canal begun by Ferdinand de Lesseps in 1859 – a channel that brought increased trade and shipping to Marseilles – was also legitimized and tacitly celebrated along with commercial interests in Puvis's painting. Yet, as Théodore Chassériau's earlier mural, *Commerce Bringing the People Together - Western Port* showed, an iconography of mercantilism and trade, sparked by a certain *Orientalisme*, was not new. A pre-Suez painting of a similar subject by a M. Barry, *The Entry of the Port of Marseilles*, had been exhibited with its 'diorama' effect at the 1853 Salon.[3]

In refining his ideas, Puvis did his homework, conferred with architect or council and frequently requested detailed information. On 27 October 1867, Puvis wrote he would travel to Marseilles: 'to breathe the air of the region, see the monument, see again the general aspect of Provence and return nicely filled with impressions.'[4] Anecdotes attribute the pictorial conception and vantage point to a Mediterranean boat ride Puvis took – the city is depicted from the sea. But Puvis also requested photographs from the architect: 'You send me real treasures.... As I am insatiable, I still need either a photograph or a sketch of the silhouette of the Château d'If rock and those of the neighboring islands with their distance relationships, while assuming that the viewer be placed in such a manner that the tongue of land on which the imperial residence is, falls perpendicular to the end of the rock of If as in this [accompanying?] figure....'[5]

Puvis's advertisement for Marseilles as a welcoming point for foreigners and goods was optimistic, for its importance as a port was lost to Rotterdam, Hamburg and Antwerp after 1870.[6]

In this freely composed, painterly mural sketch, faintly squared for transfer, with pentimenti, scrapings and visible indecisions, several figures are vaporous and half visible. Although the painter conceived of his borders at least from this stage, as a drawing indicates,[7] they are not included here. As in its companion, fresh color chords contrast to those of the more confined and controlled final work in which the discrete, colored shapes of reds, brown and deep turquoise interlock.

1 'There is in the night of Avignon a breath of the sky of Greece and Italy. One senses in this charming breeze that the door to the Orient is there, quite near, ajar.'

2 Sherman (1987), 47.

3 L. Boyeldieu-d'Auvigny, *Guide aux menus-plaisirs: Salon de 1853* (Paris, 1853), p. 69.

4 'pour prendre l'air du pays, voir le monument, revoir l'aspect général de la provence, et revenir bien réussi d'impressions.' Letter to his sister-in-law Valentine (private collection).

5 'Vous m'envoyez de vrais trésors.... Comme je suis insatiable, il me faudrait encore soit en photographie, soit en croquis, la silhouette du rocher du Château d'If et celles des îles voisines dans leur rapport d'éloignement, en admettant que le spectateur soit placé de manière à ce que la langue de terre où est la résidence impériale tombe à l'aplomb de l'extremité du rocher d'If, comme dans cette figure.' Etienne Parrocel, *L'Art dans le Midi: célébrités marseillaises: Marseille et ses édifices: Architectes et ingénieurs du XIXe siècle* (Marseilles, 1884), IV, pp. 114-115; quoted by Drocourt in 1984-85 Marseilles, p. 43.

6 Theodore Zeldin, *Intellect and Pride*, volume 2 in *France 1848-1945*, rev. ed. (Oxford, 1980), p. 44.

7 Musée des Beaux-Arts, Marseilles (Inv. D. 162).

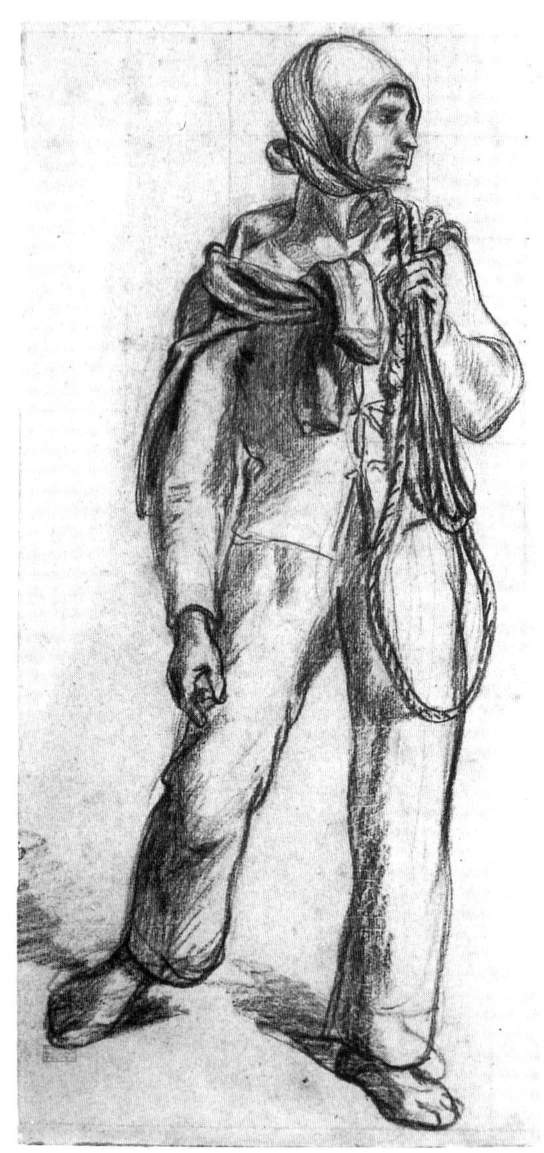

52

Sailor with a Rope ca. 1868-69

Red chalk on gray paper, faintly squared, 483 x 230 mm
Musée Paul Dupuy, Toulouse (Inv. 120)

Provenance Bequest of artist's heirs to the city of Toulouse (1898).

Rare and unusual in its contemporaneity, this relatively large drawing depicts a self-assured worker, his rope a sign of his craft and status. While the figure does not directly relate to any specific figure in the mural *Marseilles, Gateway to the Orient* (ill. p. 122), it may have been made of a Marseilles sailor while Puvis was visiting the city in preparation for his mural program there.

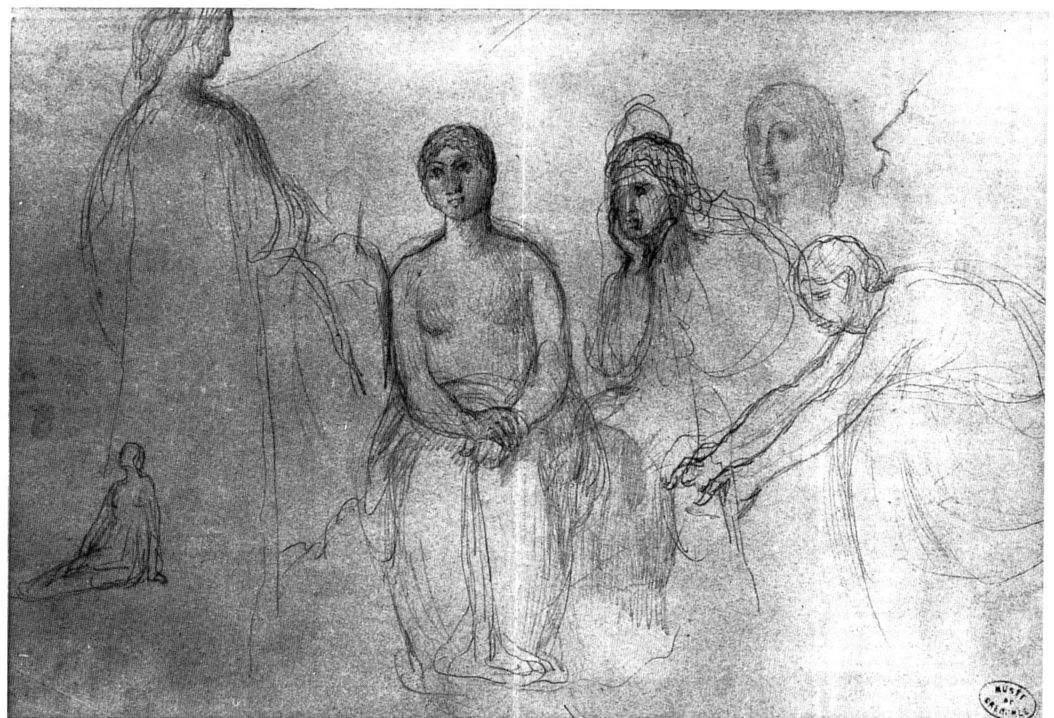

53

Persons Seated and Standing ca. 1867-70

Stamp l.r.
Pencil on beige paper, 187 x 282 mm
Musée de Grenoble (Inv. MG 1220 [5])

Provenance Bequest of artist's heirs to the city of Grenoble (1898); entered museum collection 1899.

The standing and seated figures in this assemblage represent a mix of physical types of a kind not otherwise represented among Puvis's works. The drawing, probably executed after life models in the studio, seems to be an exercise in varying physiognomies.

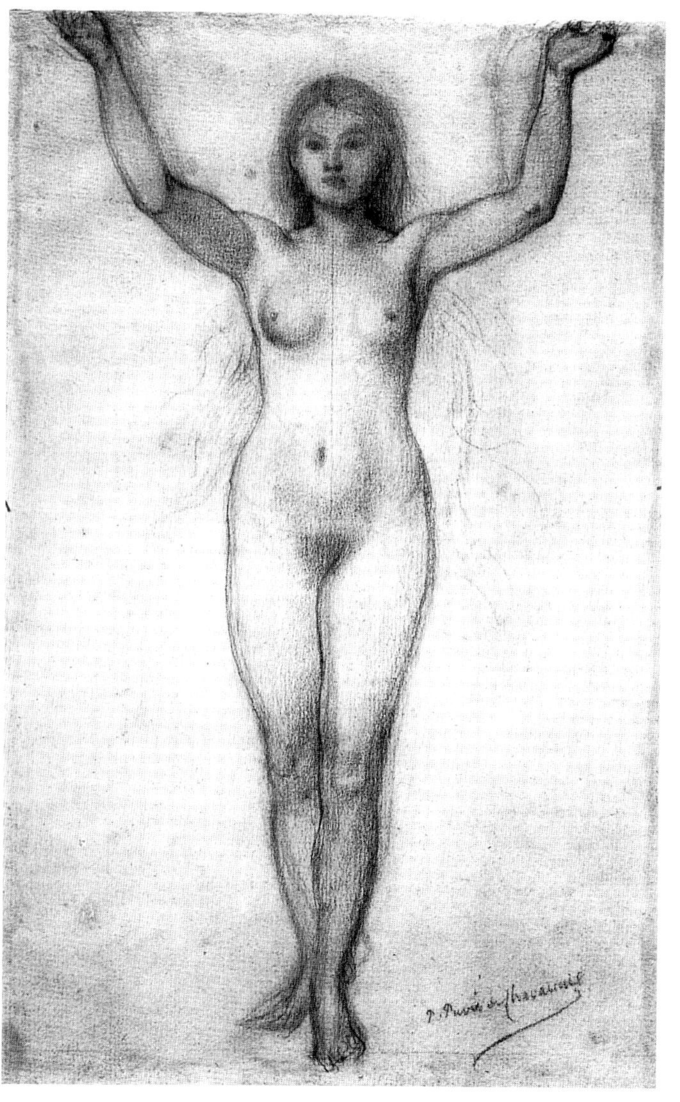

54

Female Standing Nude, Drawing Related to 'Hope' 1869

Signed l.r.: P. Puvis de Chavannes
Pencil on tan paper, 302 x 188 mm
Staatsgalerie Stuttgart (Inv. C59/880)

In several drawings and a photolithograph, the last dated with unusual exactitude 1 August 1869 (cat. 55), Puvis represented the same young woman model facing forward; these works are so closely allied that the date of the lithograph must be considered approximate for the entire group. In one full-length drawing, of a rather demure appeal, the model's arms are extended at her sides. In this one, she is standing on her toes and her arms are held high to either side of her head in a jubilant gesture. One drawing, the contours traced and a vertical plumb line indicating the symmetrical balance Puvis aimed for, puts a single small flower in one hand, a bird's nest with eggs held up in the other (private collection). Puvis varied attributes – the grasping of a sickle might have indicated a Ceres or an initial association with death (J.B. Speed Art Museum, Louisville, Kentucky); the fondling of a bird was another (private collection). The drawings are careful and constrained, a gentle lyricism to the curved forms.

The model is identifiable as Emma Dobigny,[1] who posed for Puvis's *Hope* (fig. 3, 4) and also for Degas and Corot during the years 1869-72.[2] These artists must have been attracted to what appears to be a poised tranquility in her manner, an innocence to her round, soft face, high forehead and wide-spaced eyes. Her adolescent figure touchingly suggests vulnerability and even nostalgic pathos for what would be a lost innocence as it verged on fuller sexual development. As is evident here, she seems to have been supremely unself-conscious about her slim, understated body, and Puvis was keen on developing this pubescent figural type years before he could so aptly put it to emblematic use in his painted personifications of *Hope* of 1872. It was probably about 1869 that Puvis drew her also informally, nude, lying in the seat of an armchair, her legs propped up against the chair wing.[3]

1 Her real name was Marie Emma Thuilleux.

2 She posed for Corot's *Young Greek Woman* of 1868-70 (Shelburne Museum, Vermont) and his *Albanian Woman* of 1872 (Brooklyn Museum) and for Degas's 1869 *Emma Dobigny* (private collection, Zurich, see 1988-89 Paris etc., *Degas*, no. 86 and his 1870 *Sulking* (with Duranty).

3 New York, Sotheby's (26-27 November 1978), no. 814, repr.

55

Head of a Woman 1 August 1869

Signed and dated l.r. in the stone: P. Puvis de Chavannes/ 1er août 1869
Photolithograph, 650 x 410 mm
Collection Galerie du Cygne, Paris

Selected References Published in *L'Estampe Moderne* (April 1896), and in the *Figaro illustré* (February 1899), 2nd série, no. 107.

55

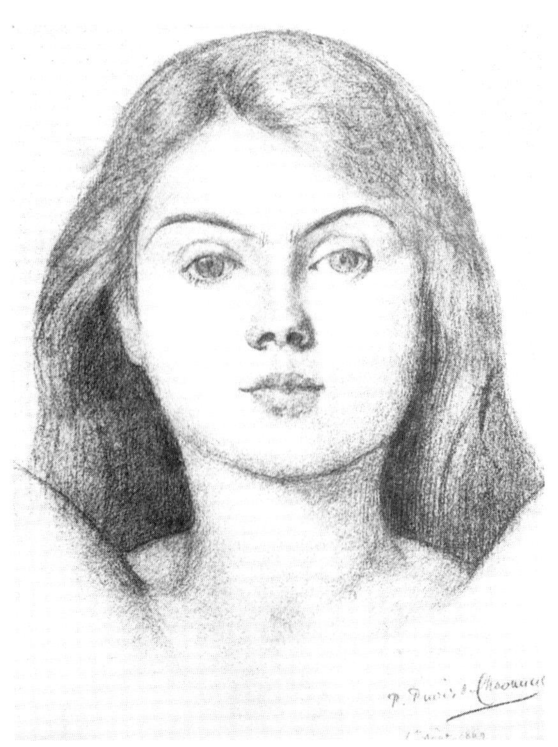

Because of its extremely fine quality, this superbly executed photolithograph has frequently been mistaken for a drawing and is so categorized in several public and private collections.[1] The distinctive, small round face of Emma Dobigny, in a resolutely frontal position with widely spaced, steadfastly gazing eyes, may first be documented in this lithograph dated with unusual precision, 1er août 1869, and in a series of drawings of the nude figure that surely date from the same period (see cat. 54). The head is posed symmetrically. The face, with an expression of poise and innocence, is made particularly distinctive because of the sitter's brows arched in wings over her eyes. The gesture of upraised arms used in at least one related drawing of the full-length figure explains the strong curves at either side of her head in the lithograph; these are the outlines of her raised shoulders.

As Douglas Druick has pointed out in his meticulous analysis of Puvis de Chavannes's printmaking, the artist produced only seven original prints: three etchings, one drypoint and three lithographs.[2] Puvis's early associates, Alexandre Bida and Victor-Florence Pollet, had both been involved with printmaking and may have first interested him in the process. One of his best friends for many years was the artist, printmaker, friend and model to Degas and Manet, Marcellin Desboutin. During the major print revival that began in the 1860s, artists were increasingly encouraged to publish their drawings through the photo-lithographic process in one of many publications, such as *La Vie Moderne* (to which Puvis contributed in 1879 and 1882). Prints made after drawings that were produced from these publications were sometimes sold as drawings to unsuspecting buyers,[3] as has apparently been the case with a print

56 made after Puvis's *The Toilette* (see cat. 100). By the later 1880s and 1890s, however, both critics and artists reacted against these photomechanical processes and there was a return to the original print. It cannot be said, however, of this fine print, which has so often been taken for a drawing, that its production has in any way marred its quality.

1 It is mistakenly listed as a drawing by the Lessing Rosenwald Collection at the National Gallery of Art, Washington, D.C.; also in: New York, American Art Association, John Quinn collection sale (9 November 1927), no. 272, and most recently in 1988-89, Paris etc., *Degas*, p. 148. Although a separate drawing, from which the lithograph was made, has long been assumed (see 1976-77 Paris/Ottawa, p. 113), none has yet been located.

2 Druick (1977), 27, 31, 33-34.

3 Druick (1977), 32.

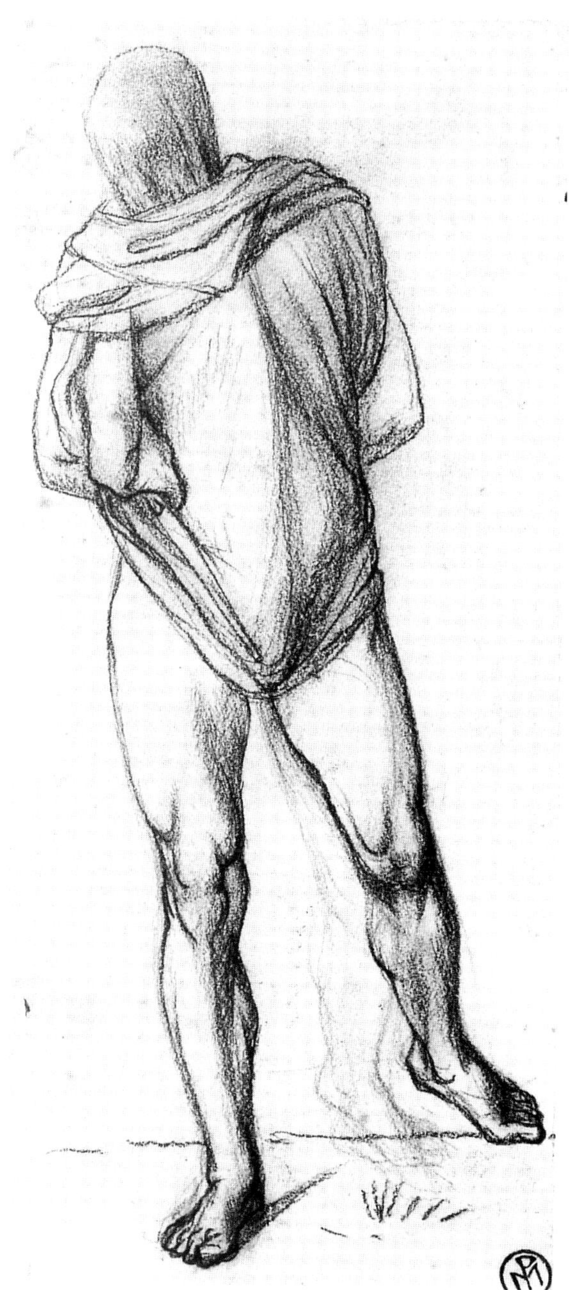

56

Concealed Man ca. 1867-69

Inscribed l.l.: 4
Black chalk on beige paper, 291 x 125 mm
Musée de Picardie, Amiens (Inv. 912bis 102)

Provenance Bequest of artist's heirs to the city of Amiens (1898).

This drawing of a male figure stepping forward, his arms held behind him and his head and torso encased in cloth, is curiously enigmatic. It does not seem to relate to any specific project by Puvis – there is no other drawing of a like figure – and why the figure would be so concealed is not apparent. A specific setting is summarily indicated by the ground line, the briefest mark of shadow behind the heel to the left and the cursory notation for vegetation, and thus a narrative and not just a pictorial exercise is implied. Perhaps the figure is to be associated with some kind of punishment such as the beheading of Saint John the Baptist (see cat. 57). With the head and much of the body of this captive figure so fully wrapped and the sex indicated by the folding of the cloth, it is a disturbing image. Yet pentimenti show a widening of the stride, the right leg poised on the ground line with the figure's muscular legs in an easy, relaxed, even graceful pose. The wrapped figure foreshadows the kind of untoward and troubling imagery that would occupy surrealist artists of the twentieth century.

57

The Beheading of Saint John the Baptist / *La décollation de Saint Jean Baptiste* 1869

Signed and dated l.r.: Puvis de Chavannes 14 xbre [14 December] 1869
Oil on canvas, 124.5 x 166 cm
The Barber Institute of Fine Arts, The University of Birmingham (Inv. 56.5)

Provenance Durand-Ruel, Paris and New York (1878-1911) [but according to Cortissoz, 1925]: Durand-Ruel (1870-1885), then bought back by Puvis]; John Quinn, New York, from Durand-Ruel (October 1911-1927), partly in trade for Manet's *L'Amazone* and $12,000; on loan to the Metropolitan Museum of Art, New York (1915-1927); New York, American Art Association, John Quinn Sale (9-10 February 1927), no. 366; Durand-Ruel (1927);

57

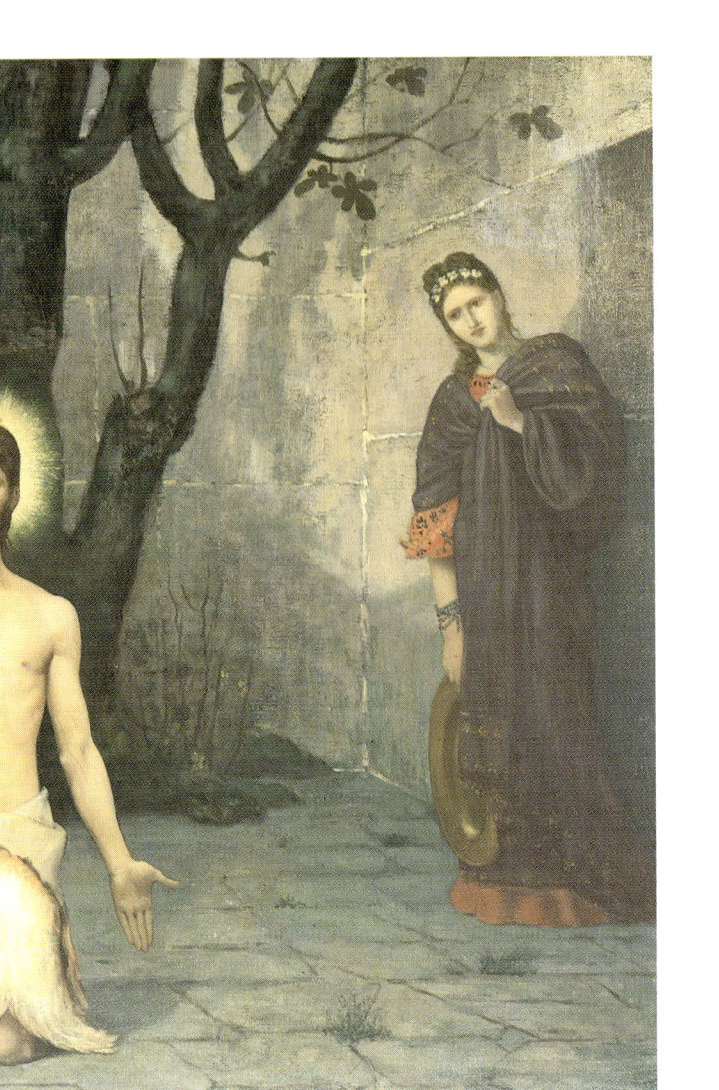

Marlborough Fine Art, London; acquired by the museum (1956).

Selected Exhibitions 1870 Paris; 1887 Paris (Durand-Ruel), no. 16; 1889 Paris (Exposition centennale de l'art français), no. 558; 1894 New York, no. 8 (probably this version); 1895 Boston, no. 2 (this version?); 1896 Geneva, no. 1 (possibly this version); 1898 London (Guildhall), no. 151; 1899 Paris (Durand-Ruel), no. 12 (or 34); 1976-77 Paris/Ottawa, no. 77 (not shown in Paris).

Selected References Cham, *Cham au Salon de 1870* (Paris, 1870), pl. 141; Chaumelin (1873), p. 376; Castagnary (1892), I, p. 420; R. Breuer, 'Ausstellung für Christliche Kunst,' *Deutsche Kunst und Dekoration*, XXIV (1909), 333-334, repr. 313; Michel and Laran (1911), pp. 31-32; [Anonymous], 'The Two "Decapitations" by Puvis de Chavannes,' *Vanity Fair* (May 1915), 34; Cortissoz (1925), pp. 211-212; *The Arts* (April 1926), 90, repr.; Venturi (1939), II, p. 95; B. L. Reid, *The Man from New York, John Quinn and his Friends* (New York, 1968), pp. 94, 105, 145, 200, 660; Mechthilde Hatz, *Frauengestalten des Alten Testaments in der Bildenden Kunst von 1850 bis 1918. Eva, Dalila, Judith, Salome* (Bamberg, 1972), pp. 76-148 (on Salome), 383-384; 1978, Washington D.C., Hirshhorn Museum, *The Noble Buyer*, pp. 23, 179, fig. 8 repr.

John the Baptist kneels in the center of a walled enclosure; an iconic figure, he faces the viewer, his arms outstretched to either side. To the left, an executioner is poised ready to swing his sword; to the right, Salome waits with a platter. This stark, severe interpretation of *The Beheading of Saint John the Baptist*, painted with grayed and muted colors and staged in a highly structured setting, marked (along with *The Magdalene*, cat. 62) Puvis de Chavannes's return to religious imagery after a hiatus of over a decade. The drama depends on spatial and pictorial rhythms rather than on a temporal, sequential or the usual emotionally expressive component. Even the large motion of the executioner is choreographed and locked into place through a system of parallels. In short, Puvis presented this drama ritualistically. In creating this austere and hieratic composition of deadened hues, Puvis may have been influenced by Ernest Renan's recommendation that religious painting be purified of sensuality and materialist concern. Renan had advocated adjusting formal elements to remove or distance the image from the empirical world of specific time and place and withholding color for works with a spiritual component.[1]

Puvis presented his stiff, emblematic version of the subject at the Salon of 1870, and critics generally excoriated it.[2] The figures were called childishly naive, their arrangement impossible for the actions they were performing, the spaces so badly calculated that the Baptist could not possibly have been felled by the executioner.[3] Cham, in his usual merciless caricatural criticism, honed in on what was new and disconcerting, singling out the spatial relationships, with a parody captioned, 'Obliged to cut down the tree before coming to his head, Saint John the Baptist still has a chance.'[4]

The 1869 composition contrasts to Puvis's entirely different configuration of the subject in his *Salome* of 1856 (cat. 11), in which the beheading is shown in terms of narrative action, the Baptist hunched over as he awaits his fate. This later representation of the beheading was worked out in an unusually large number of preliminary sketches, drawings and painted studies that vary considerably from one another and indicate that Puvis struggled with his formulation of the subject. A much larger variant (243 x 316 cm), with a more conventionally dramatic interpretation (National Gallery, London), seems to have been left unfinished. There, the kneeling Baptist, in his hands a slender, glowing cross, averts his head from the sword of the powerfully posed executioner. At right there are three figures: a weeping woman, an impassive, red-robed Herod, and a pensive Salome in a white costume. The crowded figures at right have been edited out of the smaller version.

From at least the 1850s, a severe, hieratic Byzantinism was investigated in religious painting[5] and Puvis's Baptist surely is part of that exploration. The angular figure is also reminiscent of the type used for his *Ecce Homo* ten years earlier (see cat 20-22), which would function with a religious connotation in other works, notably *The Poor Fisherman* (see p. 48). The type also recalls Northern European painting of the early Renaissance which Puvis could have known through an exhibition of Flemish primitives in 1867 in Bruges.[6] Puvis's emotionally remote figures also have a Pre-Raphaelite quality associated with the so-called Lyonnais school of painting (though they had no common doctrine as such), and these years mark Puvis's closest fellowship with this kind of religious painting.

The powerfully posed executioner brandishing his sword is not anticipated in the earliest version of the painting, in which the executioner and the Baptist are pictured at the left, walking into the enclosure.[7] The theatrical stance paraphrases that of a similarly posed figure in Couture's *The Enrollment of the Volunteers of 1792* (1848, Musée Départemental de l'Oise, Beauvais, and other versions).

At the center of all the versions is a large branching tree that has been interpreted as a symbol for the development of Christianity. In the London version it is used as a portentous symbol: the small stump at its base on which the victim would rest his head and the fallen leaves contrast to its majestic branches.

Among the details of the paintings, the artist's special proclivities should not be overlooked: the patterning of the executioner's garment and the decorative circle of large silhouetted leaves at the upper left continuing into the patterned executioner's hat is worthy of Gauguin (see *Te aa Areois*, Museum of Modern Art, New York).

Only rarely did Puvis date his work to the month, and that was during the fall and winter of 1869.[8] This canvas is even more precise, marked 14 Xbre 1869 (14 December 1869), the date of his forty-fifth birthday, possibly, as Louise d'Argencourt suggests, a melancholic equating of his own aging with the irreversibility of the Baptist's fate.[9] As Marie Cantacuzène posed for Salome, any purported identification of the artist with the Baptist would seem to entail a further psychological interpretation. A slightly earlier caricatural drawing dated 11 July 1869 (private collection), in which Puvis showed himself moustached and bearded but swaddled and borne like a baby by a small figure recognizable as Marie Cantacuzène, characterizes her as having utter control of him.[10]

1 Ernest Renan, '"La Tentation du Christ" par Ary Scheffer,' *Journal des Débats* (25 avril 1855), 3.

2 See 1976-77 Paris/Ottawa, no. 77 for several examples.

3 Chaumelin (1873), p. 376.

4 'Obligé d'abattre l'arbre avant d'arriver à la tête, saint Jean Baptiste a encore des chances.' Cham (ref. above).

5 Michael Paul Driskel, 'Icon and Narrative in the Art of Ingres,' *Arts* (December 1981), 100-107; also Bénédite (November 1898), I.

6 See Suzanne Sulzberger, *La Réhabilitation des primitifs Flamands, 1802-1867* (Brussels, 1961), p. 158.

7 These include: *The Beheading of Saint John the Baptist*, ca. 1869, oil on canvas, 118 x 155 cm (private collection); compare *Study for 'The Beheading of Saint John the Baptist'*, ca. 1869, oil on canvas, 32 x 48 cm (private collection).

8 The works so dated include his caricatural self-portrait, see Brown Price (1991), repr. 139; his photolithograph *Head of a Woman* (cat. 55), dated to August 1869; and a version of his *Magdalene* (cat. 62), dated to December 1869.

9 See 1976-77 Paris/Ottawa, no. 77.

10 Brown Price (1991), repr. 139.

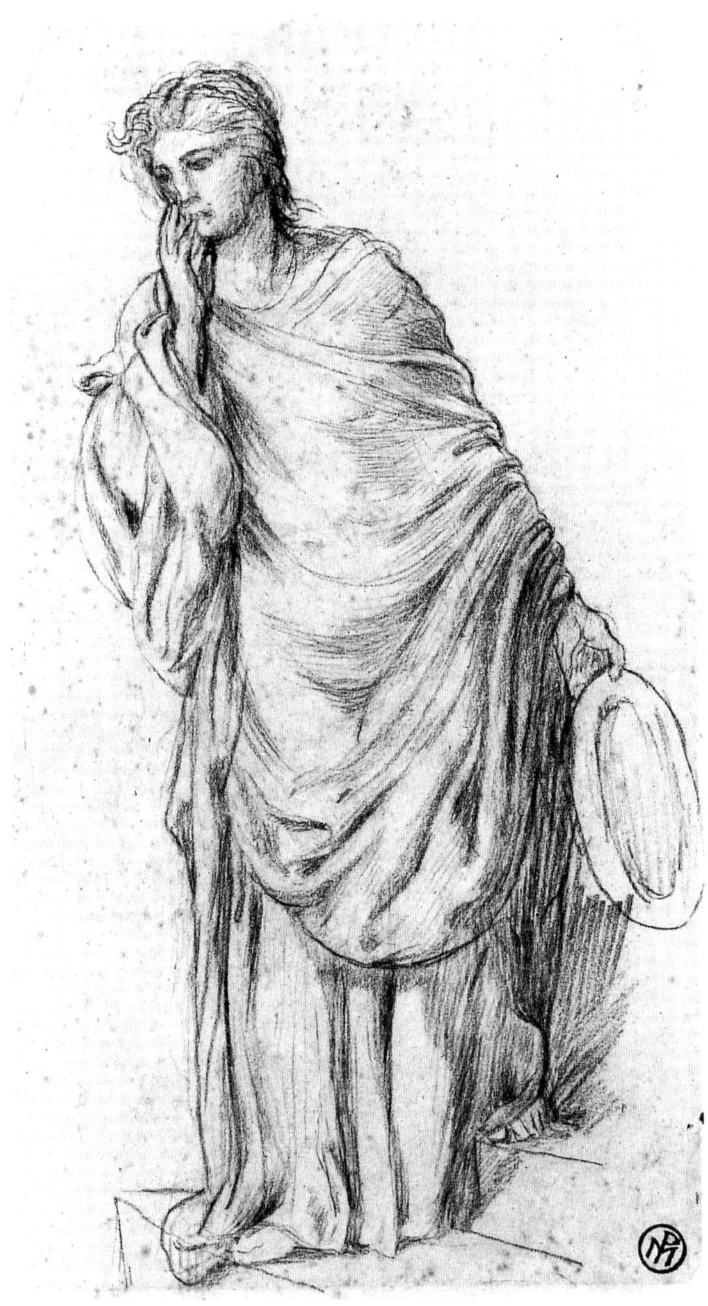

58

Study for Salome in 'The Beheading of Saint John the Baptist' ca. 1869

Black chalk on tracing paper, corners off;
314 x 174 mm
Musée de Picardie, Amiens (Inv. 912bis 56)

Provenance Bequest of artist's heirs to the city of Amiens (1898).

In Puvis's several painted versions of *The Beheading of Saint John the Baptist* (private collections; National Gallery, London; cat. 57), the figure of Salome was altered and her features changed, her attitude towards the scene being played out before her ranging from a certain troubled quality (the version in London) to a stern aloofness (cat. 57). This study of Salome standing half-turned, in a hesitant attitude, her hand to her mouth in a pensive, musing gesture, her foot on a step behind her, as if she has just come or is about to leave, relates to her pose in the large version of *The Beheading* (London). In the series of drawings for the Salome, in which figural type, poses and gestures were tried out and varied, the artist developed a rather lovely, soft and sensuous figure dressed in draped garments, here looped in ample, curved folds.[1] The artist did not often explore subtleties of emotional expression, and the notion of reticence and second thoughts investigated here reverberates with the meaning of the historical narrative.

1 Among them see 1976-77 Paris/Ottawa, nos. 79-80; similar to the last, drawings in the Musée du Petit Palais, Paris (Inv. PPD 284^2; MCB 50) and the Musée de Picardie, Amiens (Inv. 912bis 57).

59

Study for Saint John the Baptist in 'The Beheading of Saint John the Baptist'
ca. 1869

Inscribed u.l.: 173
Sanguine and black chalk on paper, squared,
302 x 192 mm
Musée du Louvre, Paris (Inv. RF 2314)

Provenance Bequest of artist's heirs to the city of Paris (1899); Musée du Luxembourg; transferred to the Musée du Louvre (1929).

This handsome drawing, squared for transfer, is a life study of a kneeling male model facing forward, his arms out to his sides and the palms of his hands open in a pose of helpless acceptance. The pose would be changed in subtle but significant ways in both large painted versions of *The Beheading of Saint John the Baptist* (National Gallery, London; cat. 57), for both would show the Baptist in a rigidly frontal position, though his head is turned in the London variant. The features of this model bear a resemblance to the London version, rather than to the considerably different type in the Birmingham version.

Two related, similar life studies of another model in the same

59

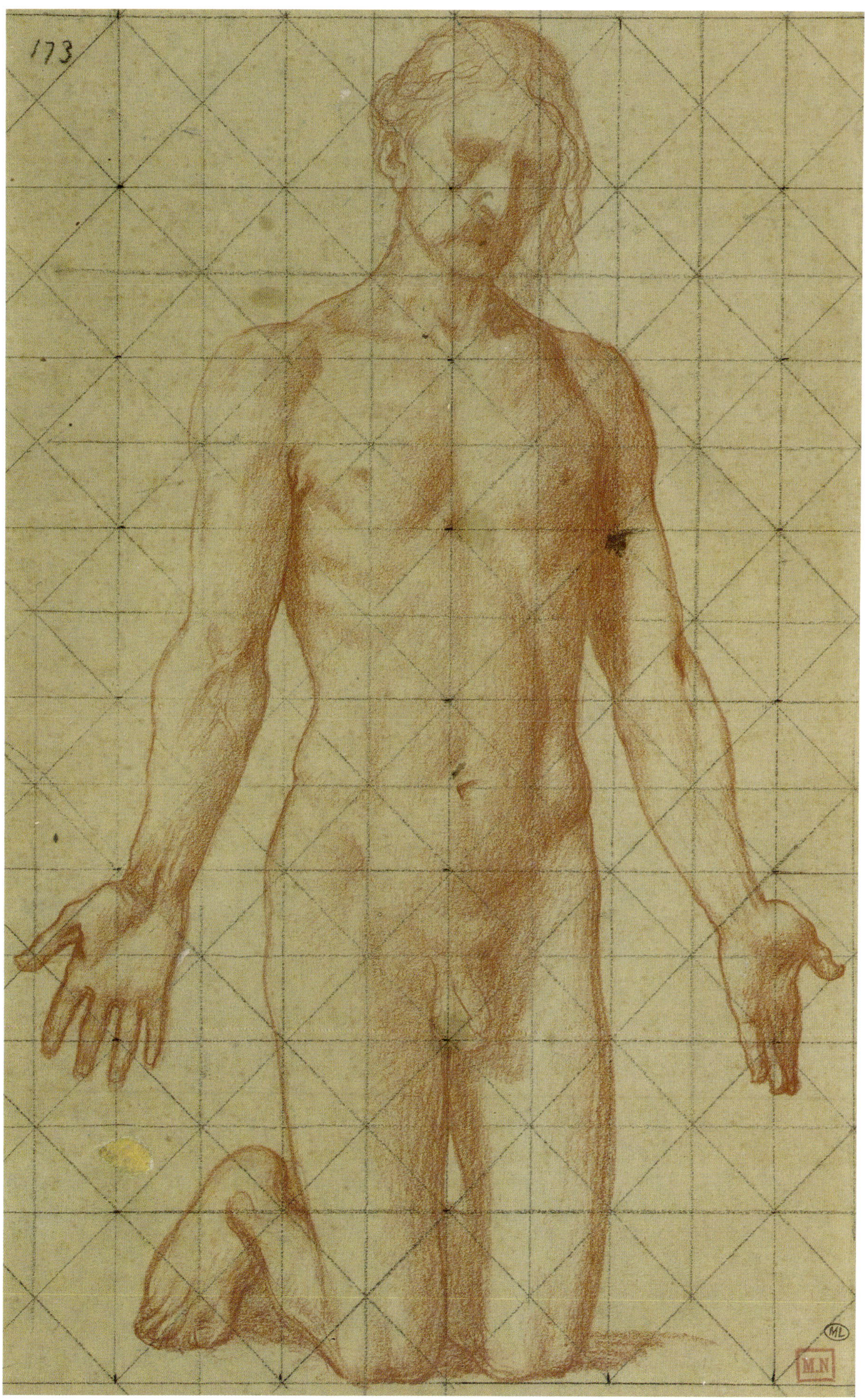

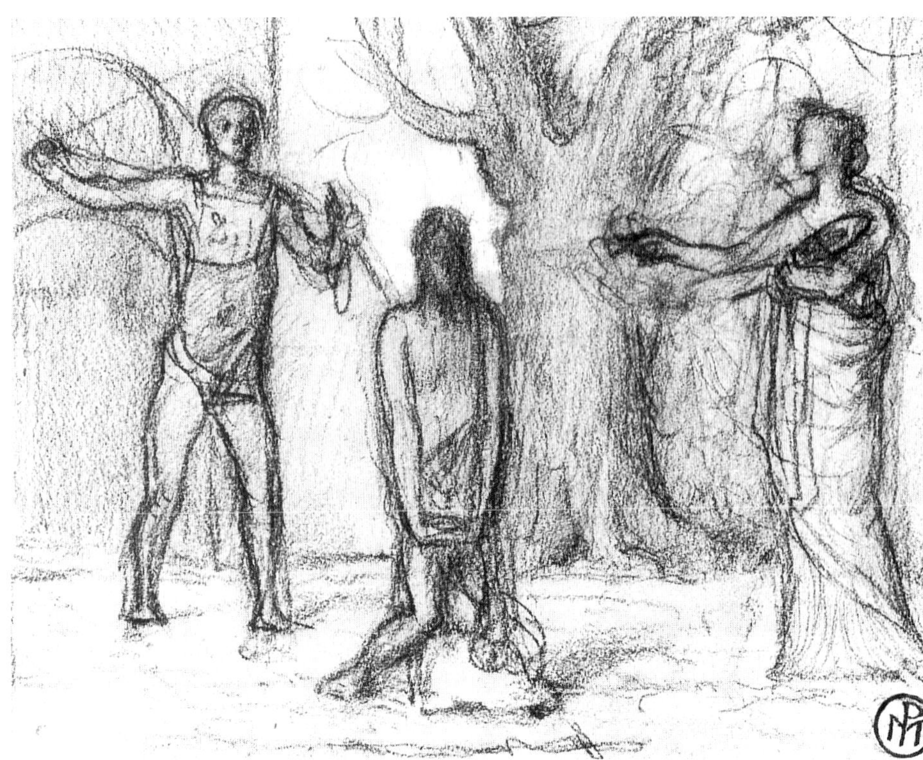

kneeling pose, his head raised,[1] may be linked to an earlier painted head called a *Saint Sebastian*,[2] making the study group still more complex. For behind this painted aureoled head appears a segment of a tree, so important in the composition of *The Beheading of Saint John the Baptist*, as it had been in Puvis's *Martyrdom of Saint Sebastian* of 1857 (private collection). Because of its abrupt edges, the panel appears to be a fragment of a larger work.

1 Musée de Picardie, Amiens (Inv. 912bis 38 and 912bis 37); both drawings heretofore catalogued, perhaps in error, as studies for the Musée d'Angers.

2 *Saint Sebastian* or *Head of a Saint*, signed l.r.: à mon ami Benon, P. Puvis de Chavannes, oil on wood panel, 61.5 x 51 cm, Musée d'Orsay, Paris.

60

Study for 'The Beheading of Saint John the Baptist' ca. 1869

Black chalk highlighted with white on paper,
145 x 190 mm
Musée de Picardie, Amiens, (Inv. 912bis 36)

Provenance Bequest of artist's heirs to the city of Amiens (1898).

Because it approximates the final compositon and yet is lacking the elements that would make the painting so severe a composition, this must be one of the penultimate studies for the Birmingham *Beheading of Saint John the Baptist* (cat. 57). The Baptist is not precisely at center, the tree not directly behind him, and Salome, in a theatrical gesture, points her finger at the Baptist. One of several small drawings that are extremely similar in composition, although unlike a charcoal sketch,[1] this variant is horizontal in format.

1 160 x 120 mm, Musée des Beaux-Arts, Marseilles (Inv. 149).

61

Study for 'The Beheading of Saint John the Baptist' ca. 1869

Pen and brown ink with black chalk and wash of brown ink highlighted with gouache on paper,
151 x 204 mm
Musée du Petit Palais, Paris (Inv. PPD 272^{7}; MCB 52)

Provenance Bequest of artist's heirs to the city of Paris (1898); deposited in the Musée Galliera (1899); transferred to the Musée du Petit Palais upon its opening (1901).
Selected References Boucher (1979), no. 52.

61

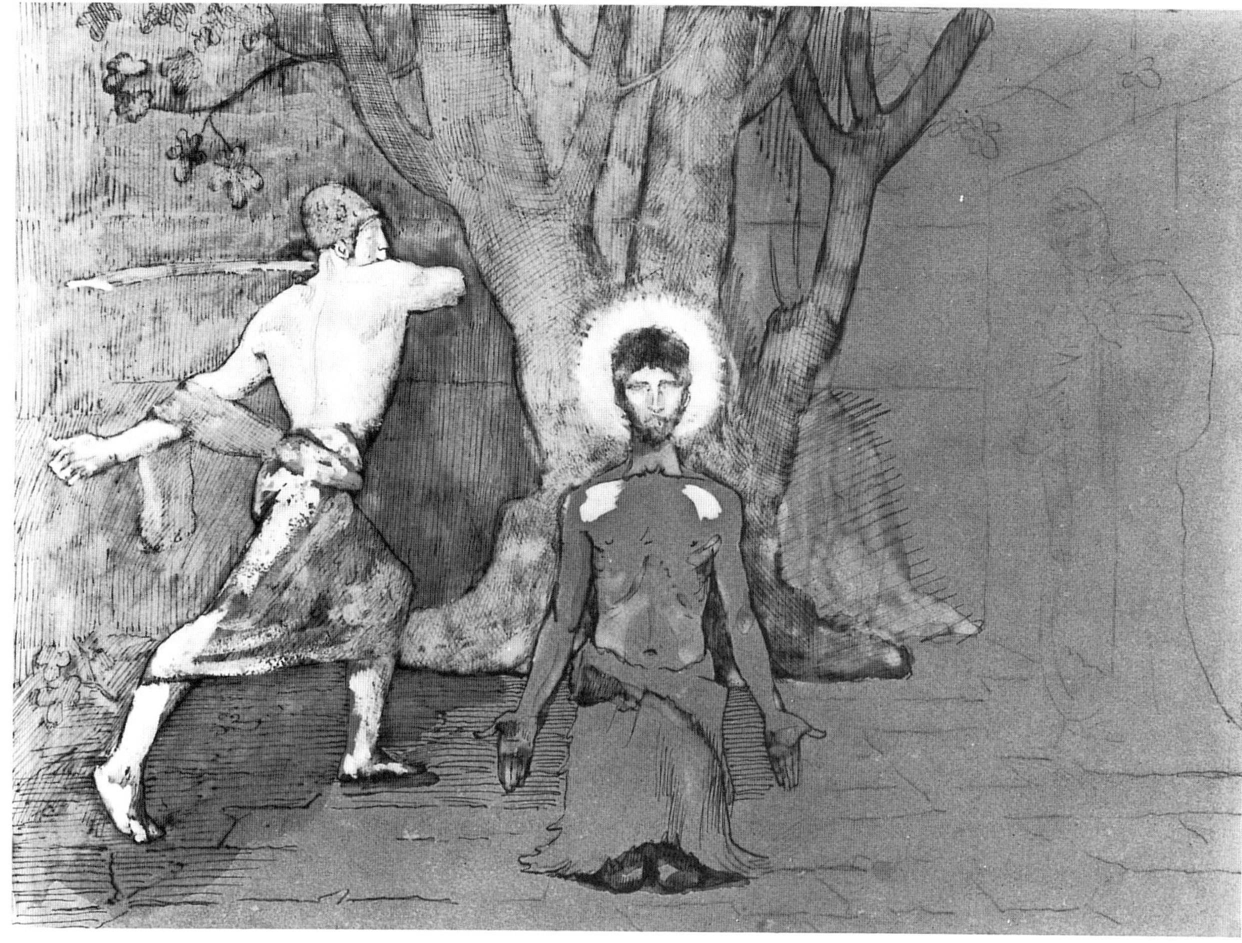

This unusually fine, detailed and deliberately rendered *Beheading of Saint John the Baptist*, a close approximation of the Birmingham painting (cat. 57), may have been prepared with an engraving in mind or as a study of light as suggested by Marie-Christine Boucher.[1] Long parallel pen and ink hatchings indicate the tonality of figures, objects and background. The gouache highlights (on the body of the executioner and the Baptist's head and chest) and the aureole of light radiating from the Baptist's head indicate that it is the several kinds of light and their forms that are of particular interest. In Puvis's religious paintings of the 1850s, light and shadow played an important role in accentuating the drama or mystery of the narrative, and in the 1862 etching of the 1857 *Martyrdom of Saint Sebastian* (private collection),[2] the massing and play of light is important, as is the case here. In the definitive canvas a circle of light falls from above on the left onto the wall above Salome's head and helps situate and isolate the setting, but whether that light would have figured here cannot be determined as that section, to the right in the drawing, is traced but unfinished. In his maturity Puvis eschewed a specific source or play of light in favor of even illumination generated by light, flat areas of color.

1 Boucher (1979), no. 52.

2 See 1976-77 Paris/Ottawa, nos. 19, 21.

62

The Magdalene / *La Madeleine* 1869

Inscribed l.r.: A ma chère nièce Marguerite Pierre Puvis de Chavannes Xbre 1869
Oil on canvas, 53.5 x 37.5 cm
Rijksmuseum Kröller-Müller, Otterlo
(Inv. 1126-43)

Provenance Durand-Ruel, Paris; Emile Bernheim, Paris; Paris, Hôtel Drouot, E.B., Sale [bought in?] (18 November 1933), no. 1948 (dimensions reversed) as *Méditation*, repr.; Paris, Hôtel Drouot (4 March 1935), as *Méditation* [bought in?]; Emile Bernheim, Paris; Huinck en Scherjon, Amsterdam (1943); acquired by the museum (1943).

Selected Exhibitions 1887 Paris (Durand-Ruel), no. 34; 1899 Paris (Durand-Ruel), no. 39 (possibly this version); 1937 Lyons, listed as Bernheim collection, no. 17 (dimensions reversed), repr. pl. VIII; 1972 London/Liverpool, no. 203.

62

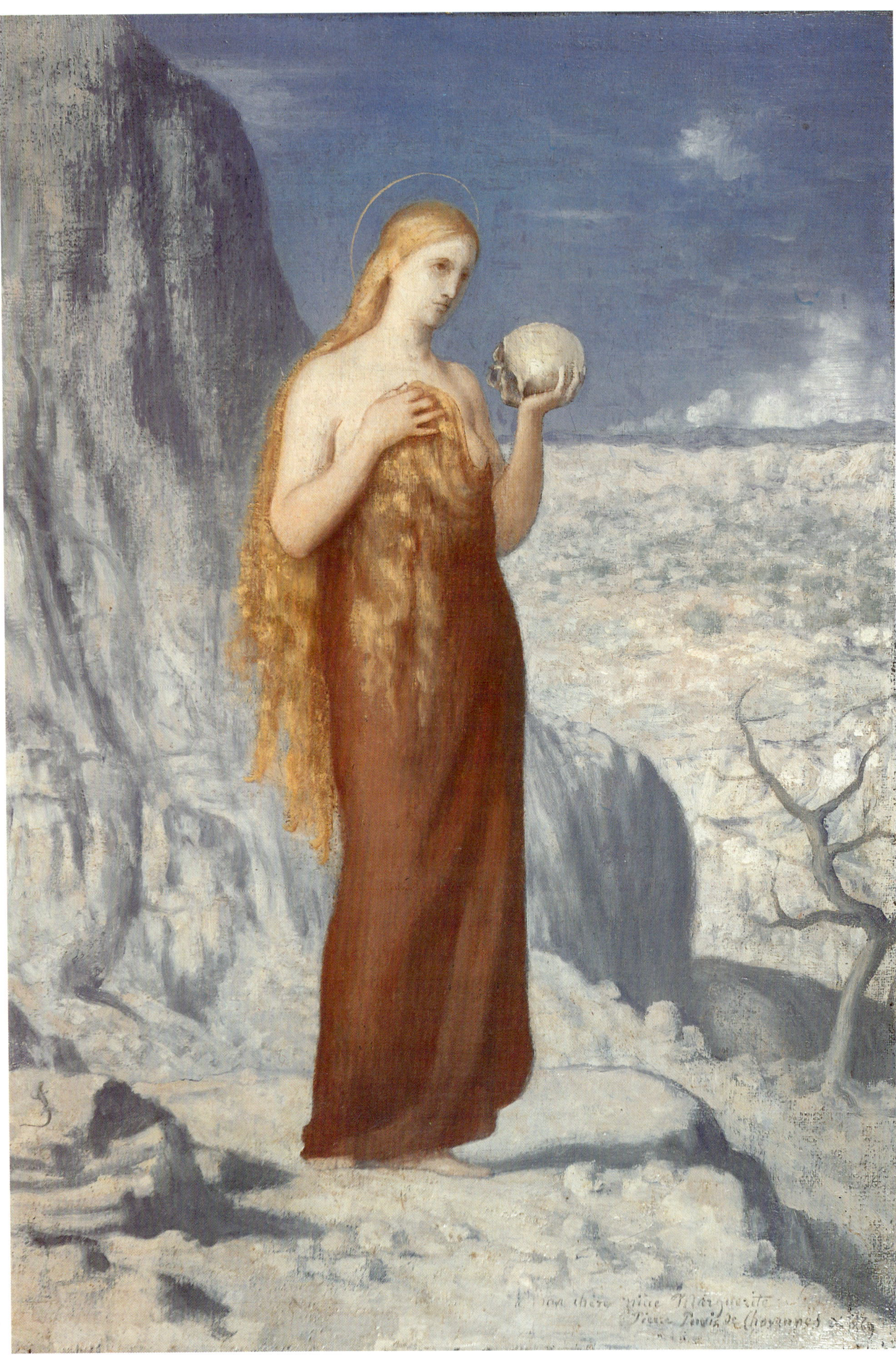

This variant of *The Magdalene* is more intimate in size and less severe than the definitive *Magdalene in the Desert* (156.5 x 105.5 cm, Städelsches Kunstinstitut, Frankfurt, see ill. p. 10) exhibited at the Salon of 1870. One of two small versions,[1] it is dedicated to the artist's niece, Marguerite, and dated to the month, Xbre [December] 1869.[2]

Mary Magdalene stands on a high, barren promontory, a bleached gray-blue desert landscape in the distance. She holds a skull, a traditional attribute of meditation, and her wavy hair is looped under one breast much as in Titian's *Penitent Mary Magdalene* (Palazzo Pitti, Florence). The desolate topography, modeled on the Crau plain near Marseilles,[3] underscores the Magdalene's isolation and invites the viewer to contemplate life, sin and mortality along with her. The coarse, granular texture of muted colors yields a simultaneously abstract and concrete, representational and literal notion of rocks.

This smaller version of *The Magdalene* is more delicate, personal and sympathetic, less aloof and commanding than her statuesque counterpart at Frankfurt with its Italianate-classicizing strain. Even the setting is somewhat less arid, with puffy clouds, a small tree and higher key colors.

The iconography of these canvases is the result of the conflating of several stories. The definitive version of this painting, called *The Magdalene in the Desert* (*La Madeleine au désert*) when it was presented at the 1870 Salon, has also been identified with *The Magdalene at Sainte-Baume*.[4] The biblical Mary Magdalene, an archetypal sinner, recognized her sins and was forgiven. She then anointed Christ with ointment or holy balm (*baume* in French) (Luke, 7:37-38, 45-48). In Burgundy, a cult of the Magdalene added characteristics of Saint Mary the Egyptian to that story; she was frequently portrayed half nude, with long undressed hair, and carrying a skull. In the Burgundian story (which formed the basis for Puvis's *Saint Lazarus and the Holy Marys* [private collection]), the penitent Magdalene retired to the solitude of Sainte-Baume, a holy grotto in Provence where, according to legend, she stayed for thirty years. Indeed, a preparatory drawing in red chalk by Puvis (whereabouts unknown) is inscribed 'in foraminibus petrae/ in caverna maceriae' ('in the cave of stone/ in the grotto of affliction'). 'Baumo,' according to some sources, is a provençal term for cave.

Over two decades later, Puvis would paint another version of the *Magdalene* (cat. 145) abstracted from all the traditional attributes usually associated with the theme.

1 In the other small (40.5 x 25.5 cm) version (private collection), the impassive Magdalene is in a moonlit landscape, an open bible at her feet.

2 Perhaps it was a Christmas gift. In late 1869, Puvis, unusually, dated several works to the month and even the day; see cat. 57, note 8.

3 Puvis could have visited the terrain while preparing his Marseilles murals in 1867-69, see cat. 50-51.

4 1976-77 Paris/Ottawa, no. 81.

63

The Sleeping Sentinel *or* The Seated Warrior ca. 1870-71

Inscribed l.r.: à A. Séon P. Puvis de [scrawl]
Black chalk on paper, 218 x 292 mm
Musée d'Art Moderne, Saint-Etienne

Provenance Artist's gift to Alexandre Séon; gift of Séon to museum (1910).

There is an unusual, fierce expressiveness in this drawing of a nude sentinel slumped in sleep, his spear beside him, another sleeping figure at his side. Among the scrawled background notations, there is a small echo of the sentinel and pyramidal tents. A related drawing, published as *Ludus pro patria, fragment [carton inédit]* (fig. 31),[1] in a special 15-31 January 1895 issue of the periodical *La Plume* (dedicated to Puvis and his work), is an amalgam of both this composition and *Man Throwing a Stone* (cat. 64), with the addition of warriors and tents, and shows the sentinel in the course of being captured. From the reproduction we also learn that the foreground ciphers in our drawing are the beginnings of a shield and helmet.

Since the theme of this and the drawing in *La Plume* is the somnolence of those who should be vigilant and the perilousness of being taken unawares, the Franco-Prussian War might have been their immediate catalyst. This drawing recalls a preparatory drawing for *Sleep* of 1867 in which tents are also prominent, and far back at the shore a curved figure like that of the sentinel can be barely discerned (fig. 14). It too depicts sleeping figures on a seashore and was rooted in passages by Virgil pertaining to the Trojan War (see cat. 47). The earlier drawing would have been an appropriate starting point for this new theme, for the situation that led to the capture of Troy was similar on many counts to the situation in France that many thought brought on the 1870-71 war: a lack of military intelligence, of perspicaciousness and preparedness – indeed, colossal somnolence.[2] The artist Alexandre Séon (1855-1917), a student and protegé to whom Puvis gave the two Saint-Etienne drawings and who donated them to the Musée d'Art et d'Industrie, wrote that these drawings were conceived during the war of '70.[3]

1 The title might indicate the first instance that the artist worked with this theme or a relationship to the (far different) 1882 mural; the whereabouts of the drawing are unknown.

2 See Brown Price (1991), 136-137 for analysis of Puvis's caricatures stemming from the 1870-71 events.

3 His letter of 5 June 1910 to M. Grivolat [at Saint-Etienne]. Archives, Musée d'Art et d'Industrie, Saint-Etienne.

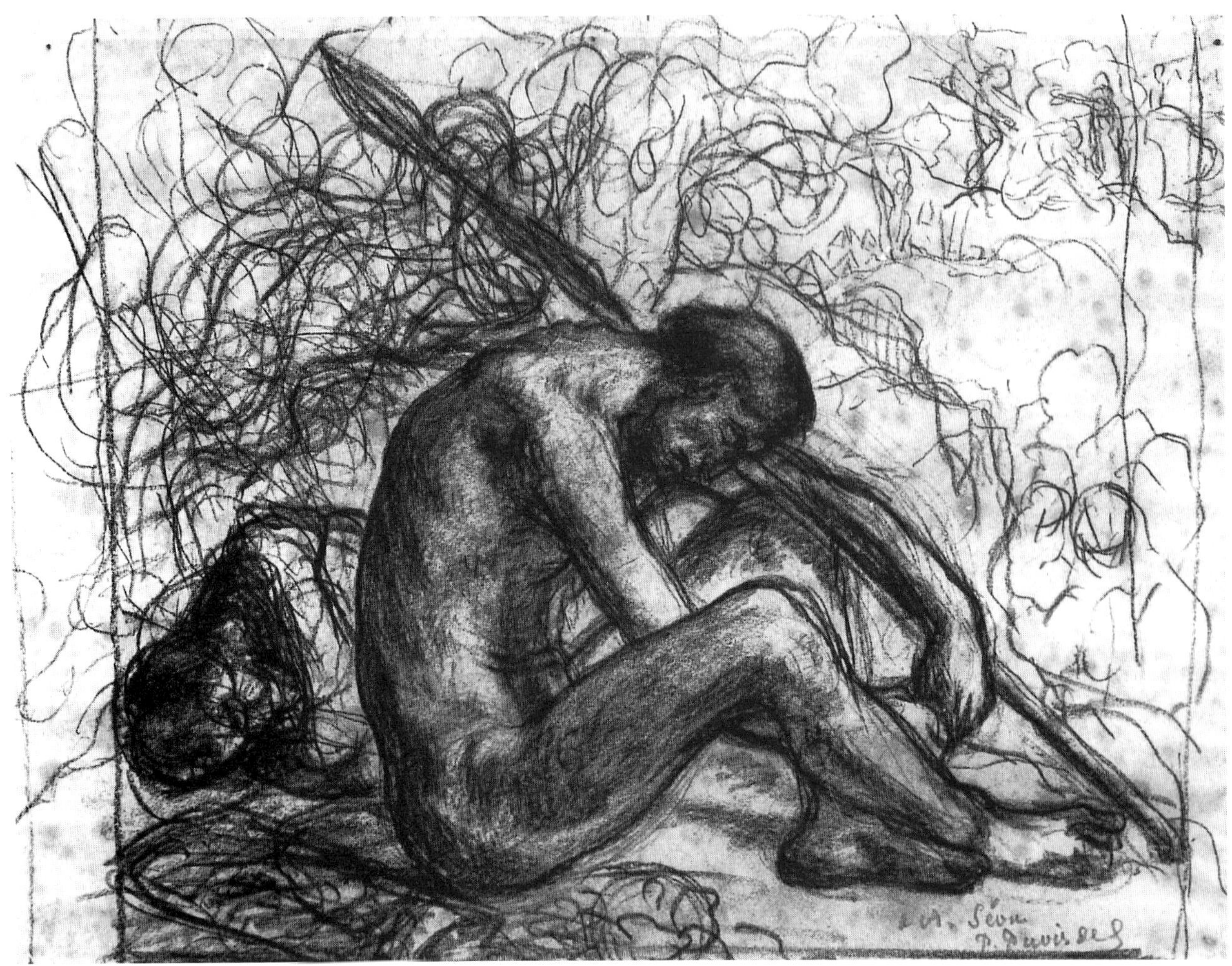

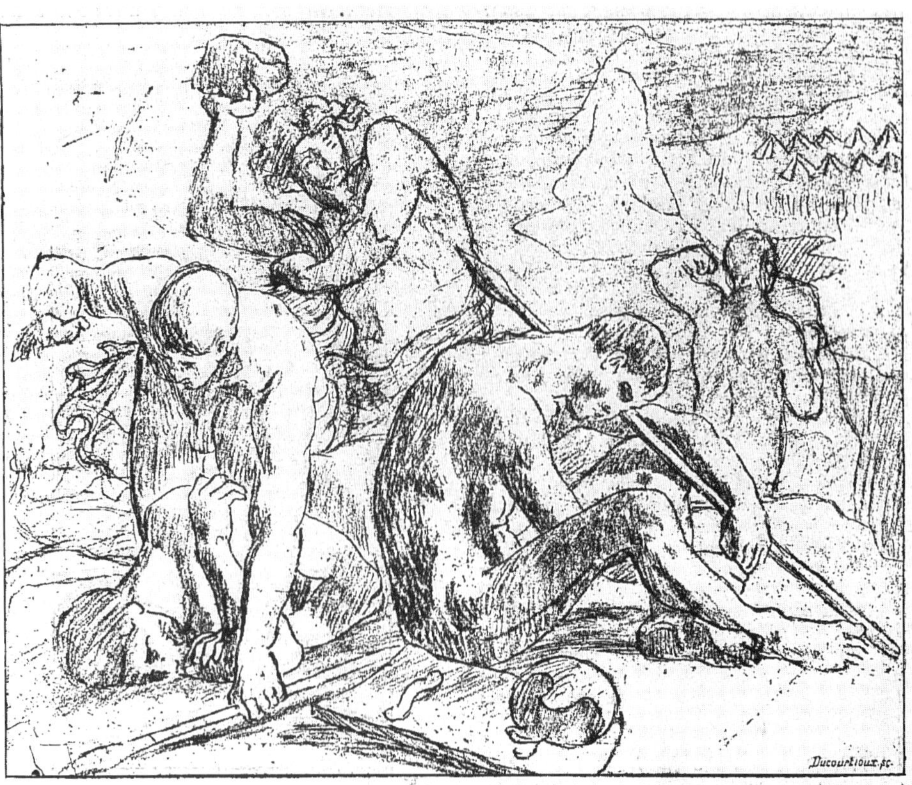

LUDUS PRO PATRIA, fragment (carton inédit) (Musée d'Amiens)

fig. 31
Drawing published in *La Plume*, 15-31 January 1895

64

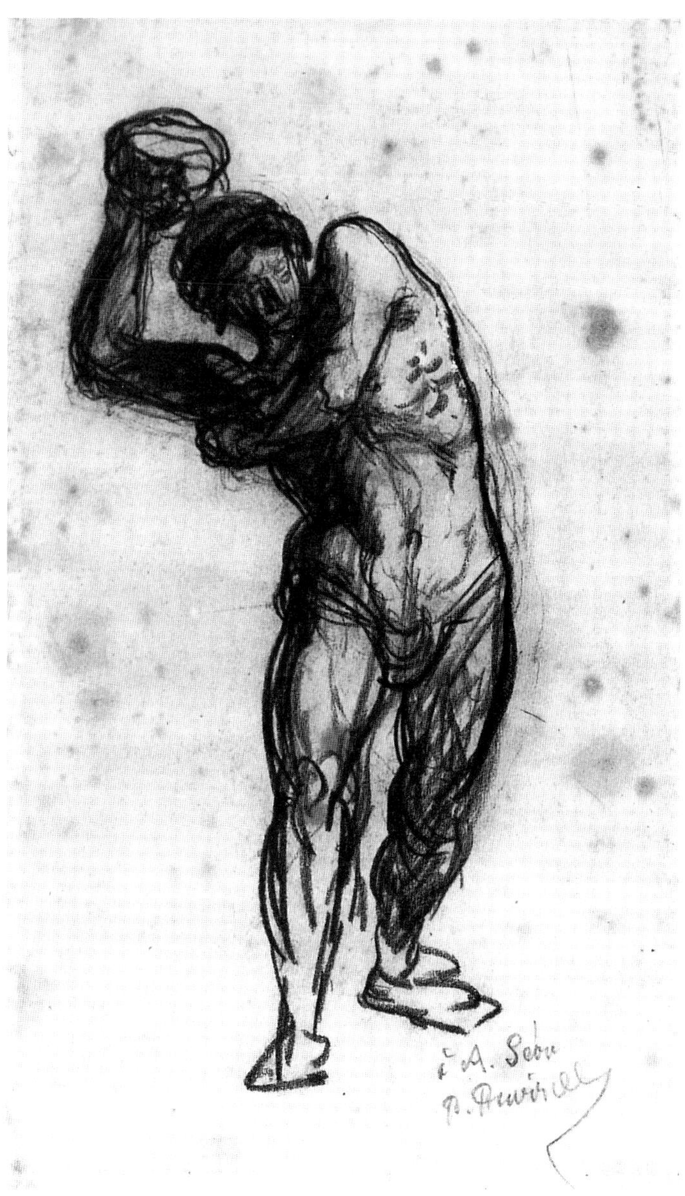

64

Man Throwing a Stone ca. 1870-71

Inscribed l.r.: à A. Séon P. Puvis de [scrawl]
Black chalk on paper, 320 x 185 mm
Musée d'Art Moderne, Saint-Etienne

Provenance Artist's gift to Alexandre Séon; gift of Séon to museum (1910).
Selected Exhibitions 1976-77 Paris/Ottawa, no. 72.

About to hurl a large stone, this tense, muscular figure reappears in a composite drawing published in *La Plume* (fig. 31), in which he is about to attack a sleeping sentinel (see cat. 63). Like the drawing of the sentinel, this work exhibits an uncommon robustness and sense of assurance.

65

The Carrier Pigeon *or* Having Escaped the Enemy Talon the Awaited Message Exalts the Heart of the Proud City / *Le Pigeon Voyageur* or *Echappé à la serre ennemie, le message attendu exalte le coeur de la fière cité* 1871

Signed and dated l.l.: P. Puvis de Chavannes 1871
Oil on canvas, 136.5 x 86.5 cm (163.3 x 112.4 cm with frame)
Musée d'Orsay, Paris, gift of the Acquavella Gallery, New York, 1987 (Inv. RF 1987-22)

Provenance French government; Chicago auction (to benefit a relief fund following the great Chicago fire of 1871); Mr. Lamont, New York; Mrs. James R. Jessup, New York; Metropolitan Museum of Art, New York (1916); Mr. and Mrs. Henry Harkness Flagler, New York; Mrs. Carey, New York (-1953); Mrs. Flagler Matthews, New York; Mr. and Mrs. John Hanke, New York; Acquavella Gallery, New York.
Selected Exhibitions 1975 Toronto, no. 13; 1976-77 Paris/Ottawa, no. 83.
Selected References Letter from Puvis to an unidentified friend, Fondation Custodia, Institut Néerlandais, Paris (86 75K); Letter from Puvis to Paul de Saint-Victor, 28 December 1870; Alfred Darcel, 'Les Musées, les arts et les artistes pendant le siège de Paris,' *Gazette des Beaux-Arts* s2, IV (November 1870), 419 [on litho of *Balloon*]; L. Montigny, 'Notice,' *Le Temps* (30 November 1870), n.p.; Gautier (1871), n.p.; Duranty, 'La caricature et l'imagerie en Europe pendant la guerre de 1870-1871,' *Gazette des Beaux-Arts* (April 1872), 330, 331; Claretie (1874), pp. 190-191; Buisson (1899), 14, 15, 222; Dayot (1901), repr. p. 87; Alexandre (1905), repr. p. 14 [called *Peace 1871*]; Burroughs (1915), pp. 31-33; B. B. [Burroughs] (1916), 12-13; Bradley (1916), 192; Flagler (1923); Brown Price (1977), 29-33; Wilhelm (1949), 12-13; Boucher (1979), pp. 50-52; [Anonymous], 'Les Récentes acquisitions des musées nationaux,' *La Revue du Louvre et des Musées de la France*, no. 5-6 (1987), n.p.; Pierre Cabannes, 'Les petits à côtés imprévus du Musée d'Orsay,' *Le Matin* (26-27 December 1987) 9; 1988, Paris, Grand Palais / Tokyo, National Museum of Western Art, *Le Japonisme*, repr. fig. 18.

Puvis de Chavannes's interest in developing modern personifying figures, apt 'real' allegories for his time, found focus in 1870-71 during the Franco-Prussian War.[1] On 19 July 1870, France declared war on Prussia, and by September the French had been defeated at Sédan. Napoleon III fled France, the Third Republic was declared and the Prussians marched on Paris, surrounded it and cut it off from the outside. The siege continued through the unusually hard winter. To maintain communication between Paris and the rest of France, manned hot-air balloons transported thousands of letters and dispatches to the outside, and carrier pigeons transported microphotographic messages back from the provinces. In October Léon Gambetta escaped in a balloon to organize resistance and sent word back by pigeon of his safety. In January 1871, the capital was bombarded, and by the 28th Paris capitulated and an armistice was signed.

These events inspired Puvis to execute a pair of grandly innovative paintings with figures that were ingeniously contrived to personify a city that could celebrate resistance, but not victory: *The Balloon* (*Le Ballon*) or *The Besieged City of Paris Entrusts to the Air Her Call to France* (*La Ville de Paris investie confie à l'air son appel à la France*) (fig. 32 and study, cat. 66) and this, its pendant, of a woman looming up against the Parisian skyline, and nestling a carrier pigeon while warding off a German eagle. This radically simple figure is a modernized version of *Vigilance* (cat. 45), an allegorical personification made specific to the mournful city. Through adept use of a plain, silhouetted figure, a rather astounding invention with a severity brilliantly furthered by being drained, with its surrounds, of color, *The Carrier Pigeon* and *The Balloon* transmit much about the war and its bleak significance in French history. Of the same dimensions and monochromatic brown and with the same kind of borders, they present the same figure, now recto, now verso, against an urban wartime landscape. Snow, which in its whiteness is used to full pictorial effect, starkly sets off the dark, central figure and is a documentary reminder of the particularly severe winter of 1870-71 in which the Seine itself began to ice over.

Reliance on the use of carrier pigeons to communicate vital messages and help in the rescue of the besieged city fired the creative imagination, particularly when the enemy imported Saxon hawks to intercept the small birds.[2] Paul de Saint-Victor eulogized them as sacred and poetry that contrasted them to the fierce Prussian eagles celebrated 'les pigeons de la République.'[3] Puvis's rendering of the eagle is so similar to that of a Hiroshige print[4] as to indicate familiarity with Japanese imagery, as is also suggested by the depiction of the figure.

Although *The Balloon* is dated 1870 and *The Carrier Pigeon* 1871, Puvis must have conceived of the two together, as preliminary painted studies demonstrate,[5] perhaps executing the definitive canvases at an interval because of difficult wartime conditions. *The Balloon* was planned after the Prussians surrounded the city. By November a lithograph had appeared which, with a purported edition of 50,000, was a huge popular success.[6] By 28 December 1870, Puvis noted he was executing a second painting.[7]

In his definitive paintings, Puvis eliminated the color range of the preliminary oil studies (Musée Carnavalet), and used only dark brown/black and roseate tones which give the appearance of albumen photographic prints of the kind widely used in Europe about twenty years earlier. The images are thus validated as authentic-looking, contemporary documents. Yet, at the same time, by withholding color and yet making the image modern, Puvis brilliantly reinforced a neces-

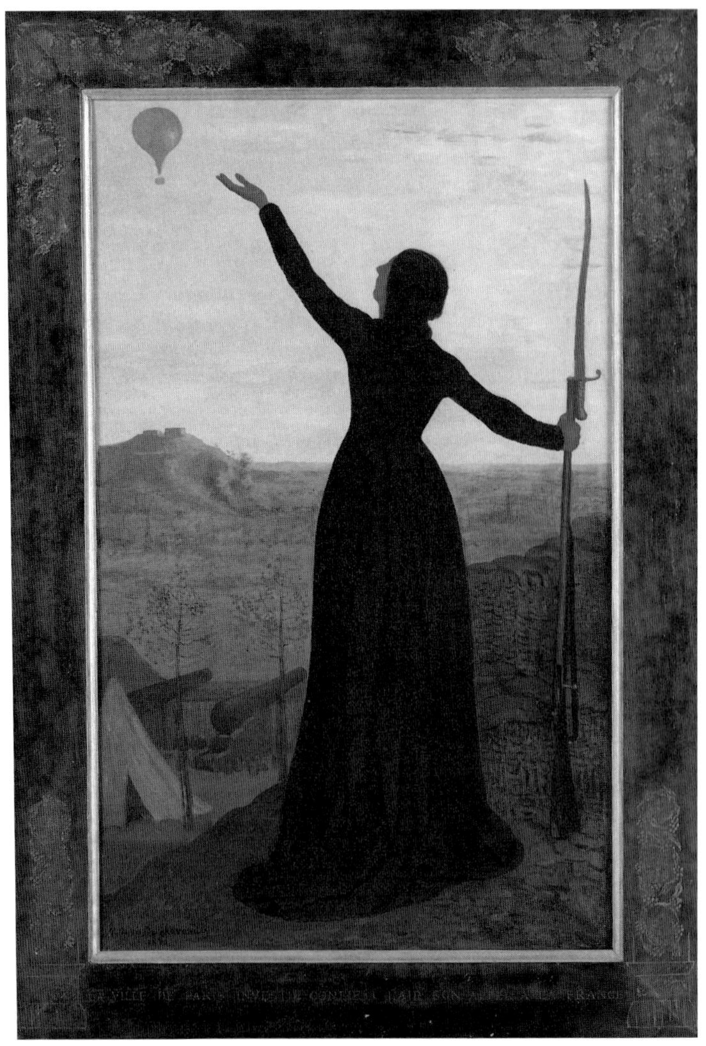

fig. 32
The Balloon, 1870
Oil on canvas, 136.5 x 84 cm
Musée d'Orsay, Paris

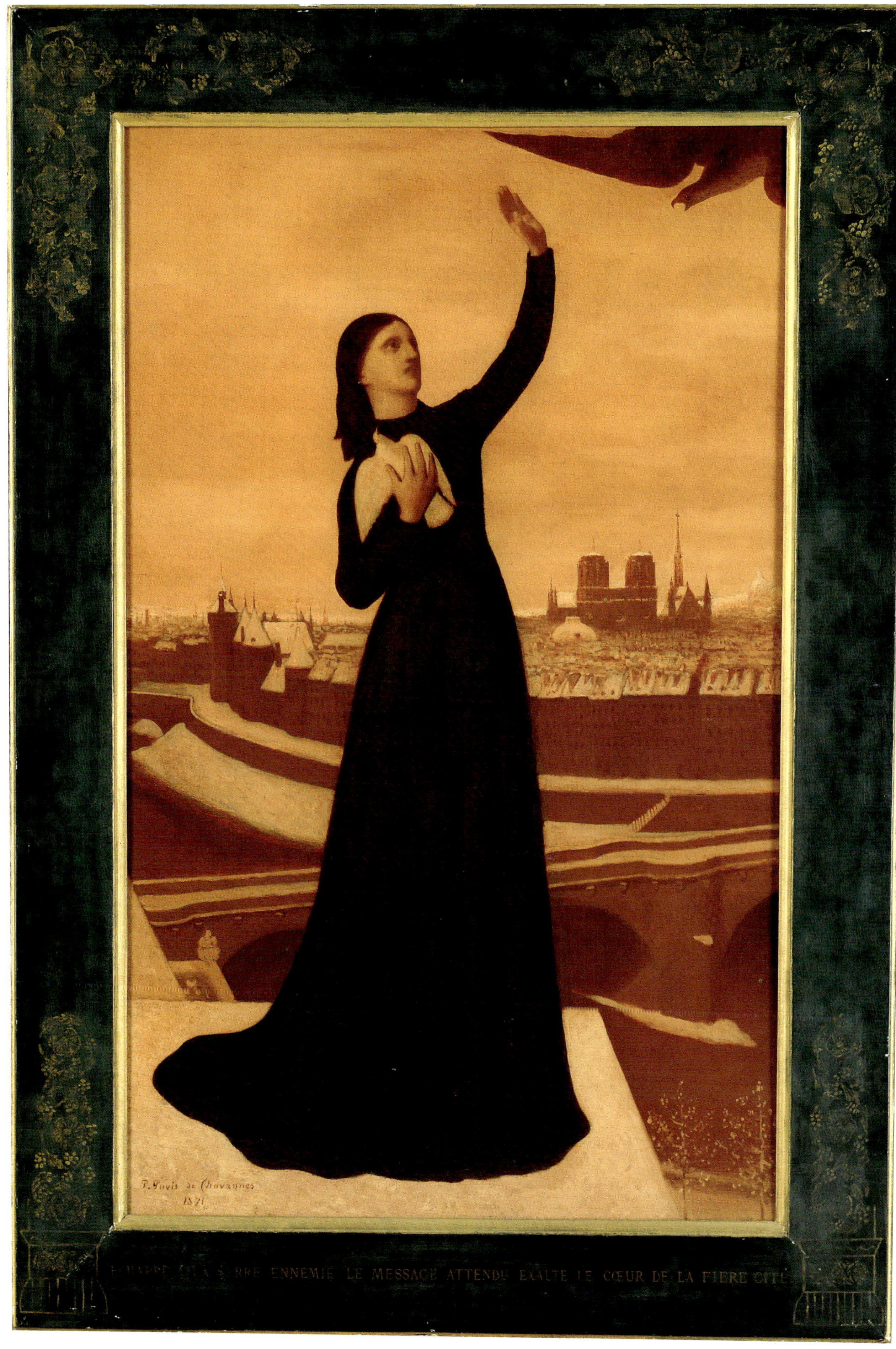
P. Puvis de Chavannes
1871
ENNEMIE LE MESSAGE ATTENDU EXALTE LE CŒUR DE LA FIERE CITÉ

sary gap between allegory and realism; for polychromy would have reinforced realism but at the possible expense of losing a reading of the figure as emblematic.[8]

Though the figure's dress may be black to indicate mourning (or because women of a certain age then affected dark colors), somber dress became the rule during the siege.[9] Nonetheless the figure was singularly austere. As one critic noted, she was not 'one of the talking dolls that Worth dressed not that long ago, but with the features of a noble woman dressed in the costume of our time, which doesn't belong to fashion, isn't of a particular day.'[10] The model for this as for so many other figures by Puvis was Marie Cantacuzène, who is readily recognizable in a preparatory drawing (cat. 67). Indeed, the austere, dark colors presage those Puvis would use for his portrait of her more than a dozen years later (cat. 92). The strongly silhouetted figure influenced Nabis painters, particularly the Hungarian Jozsef Rippl-Ronai's large, monochromatic *Woman in Black* (ca. 1892, collection Arthur Altschul, New York).

The compositions have wide, black painted borders that, planned from an early stage (see the pair at the Musée Carnavalet), are integral to them. Resembling black-edged death announcements or condolence acknowledgements of the time, they tailor the images into strong, even funereal objects.

In gratitude for United States sympathy in 1870 the French government donated *The Carrier Pigeon* and its companion to be sold at a New York bazaar in 1873 or 1874 to benefit a relief fund after the great Chicago fire of 1871. They were stored, seemingly forgotten, and long thought lost, but a privately printed pamphlet described their 1914 recovery from where they had been closeted after their owner had dreamt about them as the Germans advanced once again on France during the First World War.[11]

1 Brown Price (1977).
2 Robert Baldick, *The Siege of Paris* (London, 1964), p. 120. See also Wickham Hoffman, *Camp, Court and Siege* (London, 1877), pp. 185-186.
3 By Eugène Manuel, as noted by Gautier (1871), p. 90; on Puvis see p. 212.
4 1988 Paris/Tokyo (ref. above).
5 See two studies, dated 1870, 41 x 24 cm, oil on paper, laid down on canvas, Josefowitz Collection and *Sketch for 'The Carrier Pigeon'*, 46.2 x 31.4 cm and *Sketch for 'The Balloon'*, 46.3 x 31 cm, oil on cardboard, Musée Carnavalet, Paris; *pace* Geneviève Lacambre in 1990-91 Paris, p. 75, who posited that the second work resulted from the success of the lithographs.
6 1976-77 Paris/Ottawa, no. 82. Buisson (1899), 222, states about 50,000 photographs of the paintings sold within days; he may have meant prints, see Brown Price (1977), 30-32, 39, note 15. *Le Pigeon Voyageur* or *Peace* and *Le Ballon* or *La Ville de Paris investie confie à l'air son appel à la France*, lithographs by Emile Vernier; as no. 23166 in the G. Druet collection (photographs), Cabinet des Estampes, Bibliothèque Nationale, Paris, Vol. II, D 1998.
7 Letter from Puvis to an unidentified friend, Fondation Custodia, Institut Néerlandais, Paris (ref. above).
8 Brown Price (1977), 31.
9 Robert Baldick, *op. cit*, (note 2), p. 104.
10 'une des poupées parlantes qu'habillait Worth naguère encore, mais sous les traits d'une noble femme vêtue de ce costume de nos jours, qui n'appartenant pas à la mode, n'est pas d'un certain jour.'; in *Le Temps* (30 November 1870). This comment is strikingly like what Van Gogh would later say of the dress in Puvis's *Inter Artes et Naturam* (see cat. 130).
11 Flagler (1923).

66

Standing Woman from the Back, Study for 'The Balloon' ca. 1870-71

Inscribed u.l. in black chalk: 179
Black pencil on paper, squared, 314 x 178 mm, upper corners and lower right corner chamfered
Musée du Petit Palais, Paris (Inv. PPD 260[1]; MCB 54)

Provenance Bequest of artist's heirs to the city of Paris (1898); deposited in the Musée Galliera (1899); transferred to the Musée du Petit Palais upon its opening (1901).
Selected References Brown Price (1977), 30-32 and *passim*; Boucher (1979), no. 54.

This study for *The Balloon* or *The Besieged City of Paris Entrusts to the Air Her Call to France* (fig. 32) sets out the essentials of the definitive work, while emphasizing the dominant figure. The woman has her back turned to the viewer and holds a bayonet with a flag swirled around it, a slimly elegant, unadorned weapon in the painting. In the middle distance a row of cannons, manned by a small figure, is aimed out over the landscape, the horizon far higher here than in the painting. The political and military context of the painting would become more precise as the background gained in importance and would come to include a tent and an airborne *montgolfière* towards which the figure gestures. Softening elements such as the flag and details of the figure's hair would be eliminated and the silhouettes pared down and made flatter and crisper as larger shapes would subsume particulars; the dress folds, for example, anyway more difficult to see with the dark tonalities of the dress in the painting, would be hardly distinguishable as an articulated motif.

66

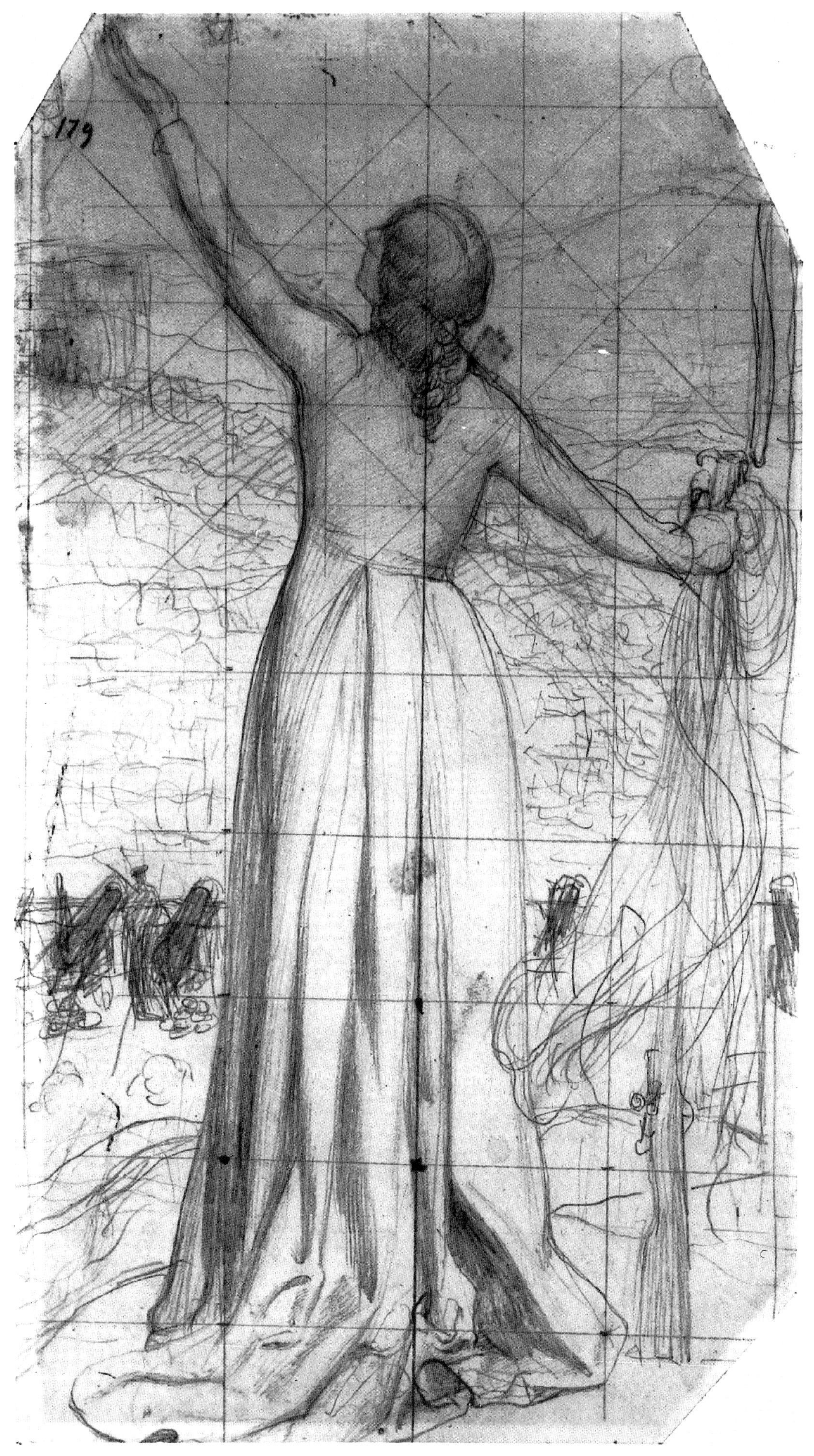

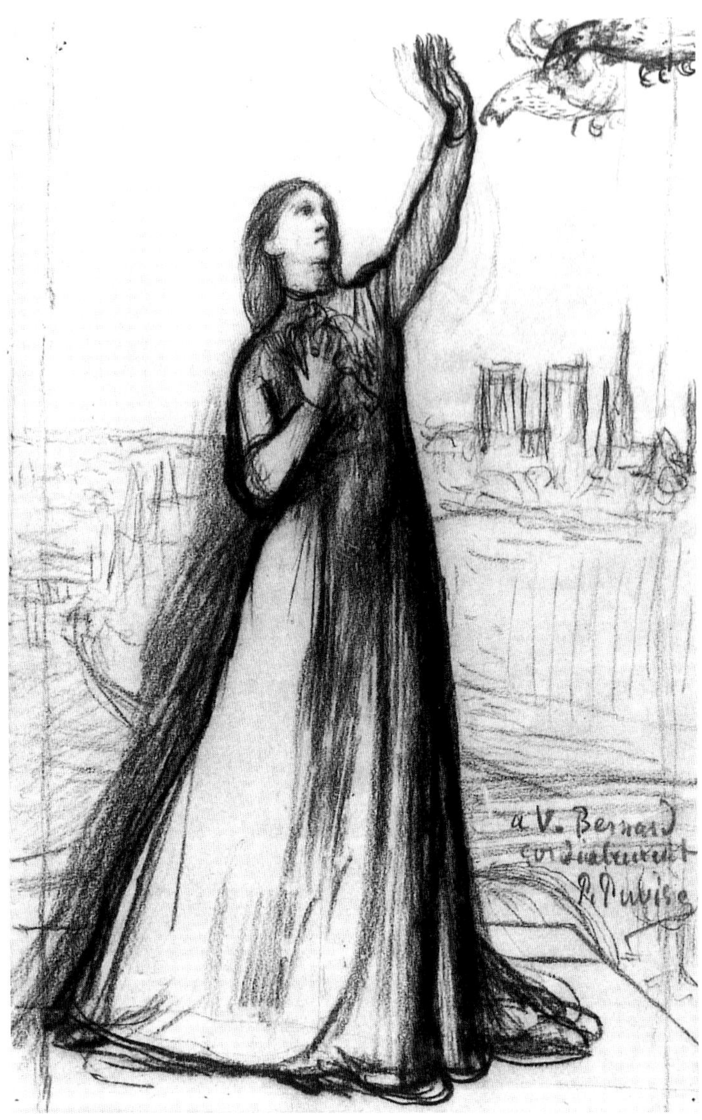

67

Standing Woman from the Front, Study for 'The Carrier Pigeon' ca. 1870-71

Inscribed l.r.: à V. Bernard cordialement P. Puvis C
Charcoal on gray paper, 316 x 212 mm
Musée du Petit Palais, Paris (Inv. D. Dut. 1175; MCB 55)

Provenance V. Bernard; Dutuit (1901); Martin du Nord, Paris (1970).
Selected Exhibitions 1972 London/Liverpool, no. 207, repr. pl. 104; 1976-77 Paris/Ottawa, no. 84.
Selected References Philippe Jullian, *Dreamers of Decadence: Symbolist Painters of the 1890s* (London, 1971), repr. p. 40, fig. 13; P. Jullian (1973), repr. fig. 103; G. Metken, 'Le Retour des Préraphaelites,' *Revue de l'Art* (1974), no. 26, repr. p. 88; Marisa Volpi Orlandesi, 'Camille Corot e l'arte nuova,' *Arte Contemporaneo* (March 1976), no. 16, repr. p. 8; Boucher (1979), no. 55.

This plain, silhouetted figure powerfully looming up against the cityscape is a study for *The Carrier Pigeon* or *Having Escaped the Enemy Talon the Awaited Message Exalts the Heart of the Proud City* (cat. 65). Set against the Seine and the Ile de la Cité, the ancient center of Paris, the city's cherished monuments, the Palais de Justice, Notre-Dame and the Sainte Chapelle are prominent in the background.[1] The process of formulation is legible in the replication of lines defining the figure and the search among them for the proper contour for the finally slimmed down and more angular figure. Pentimenti indicate the ongoing effort: the eagle drawn in near the woman's arm and then farther back in the upper corner; her uplifted left arm adjusted slightly to the right. The sensitive features of Marie Cantacuzène, the model for the figure, are readily recognizable here (compare cat. 18, 92, fig. 29).

68

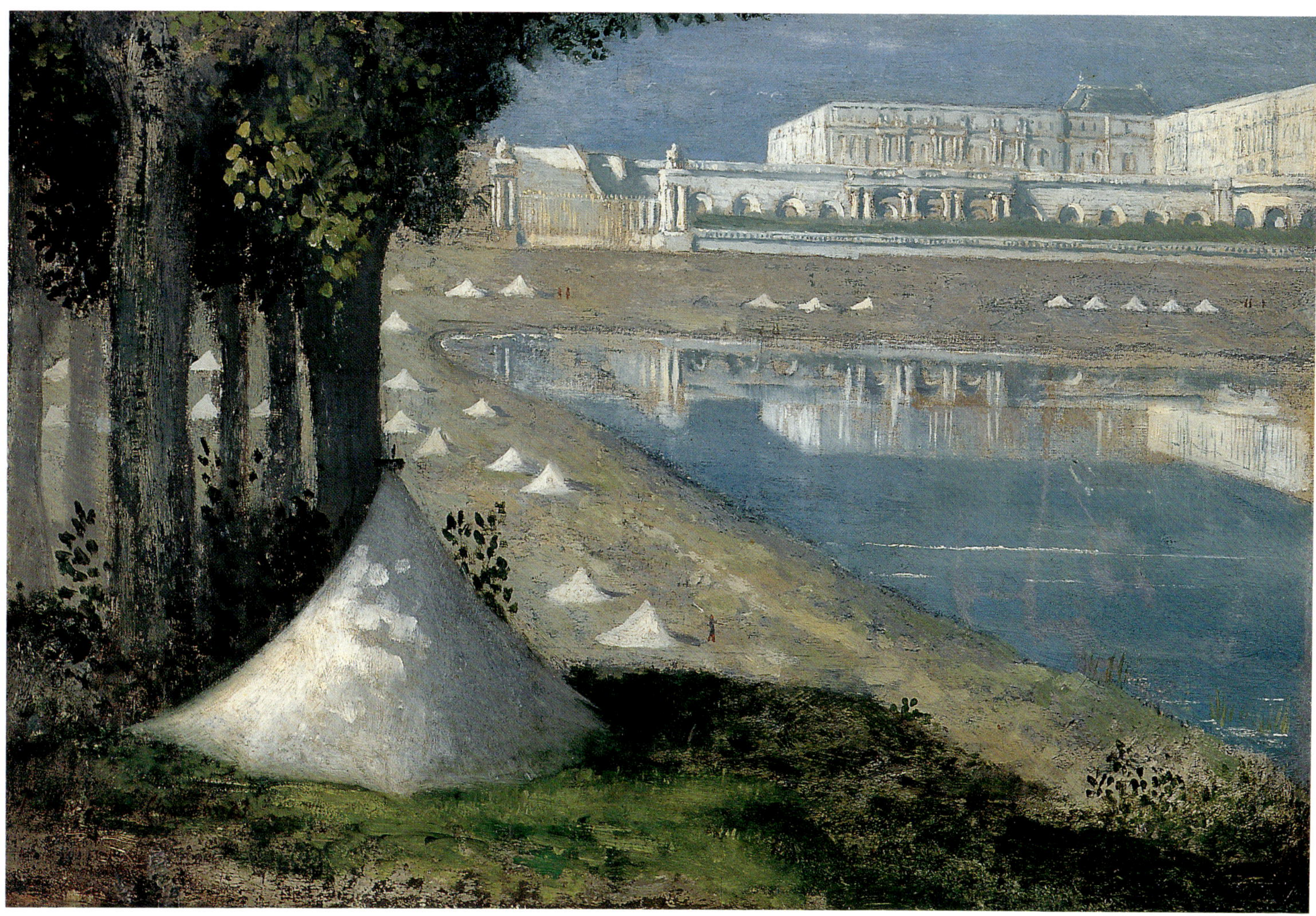

The drawing is dedicated to a V. Bernard, identifiable as Valère Bernard (1860-1936), who, in 1882, as a young artist sought Puvis out and visited him during the following two years, occasionally receiving informal instruction from him.[2] It would have been after that date that the inscription was added. Valère went on to become a Symbolist painter.[3]

1 In Boucher (1979), no. 55, Marie-Christine Boucher sees a boat, but in comparing the painting, what might be perceived as the hull of a boat appears to be the quays, and what might be seen as masts in the drawing, the sketched-in towers on the quai de l'Horloge.

2 See Jean-Roger Soubiran, *Valère Bernard 1860-1936* (n.p. [Marseilles?], 1988), pp. 10-12, 178-180.

3 See Bernard's letters describing his visits and admiration for Puvis in 1981, Marseilles, Musée des Beaux-Arts, *Valère Bernard (1860-1936) Symboliste*, pp. 11-12, 178-80. Marie-Christine Boucher has suggested that V. Bernard could be an assistant to the sculptor Carpeaux (ca. 1818-after 1892), see 1976-77 Paris/Ottawa, no. 84

68

View of the Palace at Versailles and the Orangerie / *Vue sur le château de Versailles et l'Orangerie* April 1871

Signed l.l.: P. Puvis de Chavannes
Oil on canvas, 33.3 x 46.6 cm
Private collection

Provenance Artist's heirs and by descent.
Selected Exhibitions 1976-77 Paris/Ottawa, no. 85.
Selected References Boucher (1979), p. 52.

During the Franco-Prussian War the French government moved to Bordeaux and on 10 March 1871 to Versailles, where the army was organized to recover Paris. The French capitulation on 28 January and new economic regulations were followed by insurrections beginning on 18

March in Paris. Thiers ordered in the National Guard, and so on 21 May began the infamous slaughter of 20,000 people, the 'semaine sanglante.' That spring Puvis found safer quarters at Versailles with his sister and brother-in-law, a member of the Assemblée.[1] In a letter of 30 March 1871 to the artist Berthe Morisot he described his outpost and sentiments: 'I was happy to leave my awful quarter, where informing against one's neighbor is becoming a daily occurrence, and where one may at any moment be forced to join the rabble under penalty of being shot by the first escaped convict who wants the fun of doing it.... If Versailles were not overflowing with refugees, it would be the best place for you.... One is truly bathed in a feeling of grandeur in this admirable and magnificent setting, the sight of which is reassuring, since it recalls a beautiful and noble France, and one can forget for a moment how run down and poisoned she is today.'[2]

Puvis made the army encampments and parading troops in this once royal environment the subject of a series of works.[3] He also filled at least two notebooks with drawings and sketches, some with color notations and remarks penciled in as an *aide-mémoire* for projected works (private collection). The dappled sunlight and oblique view from a dark, cool spot in this landscape recall early Impressionist work.[4] This is one of two landscapes in oils; the other shows soldiers with bayonets mounting the steps of the Versailles palace complex.[5] This one is notable for its penetrating irony: the regal château, reflected in the Swiss Lake, is pictured from afar and diminished, both actually and symbolically, and all but eclipsed by the small military tents pitched among the shady trees that occupy the foreground. That is, the bastion of French government is represented by a mere tent on the magnificent grounds of the emptied stronghold of the Kings of France, the mainstay of French monarchical power and absolutism. Put still another way, the military tent represents the power of government through the force now necessary to maintain it. Puvis must have executed this painting about April, for its composition closely approximates that of a drawing with gouache on paper that has been dated to April[6] and Puvis was at Versailles at that time. Also, it is surely no coincidence that on 1 April Thiers, chief executive of the Chamber of Deputies, had announced that gathering at Versailles was 'one of the best armies France had ever had.'[7]

In Puvis's letters of the period there is a rueful sadness at the passing of an era and a waspishness at the notion that the army was stationed, even if temporarily, on Le Nôtre's parterres, making campgrounds of them. He had a dismal sense of change and a fatalistic view of the dire circumstances of his time.

1 Mandach and Wehrlé (1911), 466-467; Morisot (1950), pp. 51-54.

2 'J'ai quitté avec bonheur mon affreux quartier où la délation s'installe et où l'on peut d'un moment à l'autre être requis de marcher avec la crapule sous peine d'être fusillé par le premier échappé du bagne que cela divertit.... Si Versailles ne regorgeait pas d'émigrants, c'est encore là que vous genez le mieux.... On prend un véritable bain de grand, dans cet admirable et grandiose ensemble dont les vues apaisent en vous parlant d'une belle et noble France. On ne peut oublier un instant combien elle est aujourd'hui fourbue et empoisonnée.' Monique Angoulvent, *Berthe Morisot* (Paris, 1933), pp. 36-37; also in Morisot (1950), pp. 51-54. The English translation by Betty Hubbard (New York, 1957; reissued 1986), p. 64, is considerably softer.

3 These include: *Study for Versailles with an Encampment*, ca. 1871, pencil on paper, 219 x 306 mm (private collection); *Study for Versailles with Cavalry*, ca. 1871, pencil on tracing paper, 178 x 340 mm (private collection); *Parade, Versailles* or *Le Défilé*, ca. 1871, stamp l.r., watercolor, pencil on paper, 155 x 245 mm (private collection); *Landscape with figures*, stamp u.l., watercolor on paper, 115 x 205 mm (private collection); *Study of an Encampment*, stamp l.r., watercolor on paper, 203 x 115 mm (private collection); Paris, Hôtel Drouot (8 February 1949), no. 5.

4 *Pace* Foucart, in 1976-77 Paris/Ottawa, no. 85.

5 Private collection; cf. Brown Price (1977), 31, repr. fig. 4.

6 Musée du Petit Palais, Paris (PPD 256[1]; MCB 56).

7 'une des plus belles armées que la France ait jamais possédées.' Maurice Baumont, *Gloires et Tragédies de la IIIe République* (Paris, 1956), p. 48.

69

Study of a Sleeping Man for 'Death and the Maidens' ca. 1872

Signed l.r.: P. Puvis d
Charcoal heightened with white chalk on tan paper, 149 x 197 mm
Van Gogh Museum, Amsterdam (Inv. D 1013 M/1991)

Provenance Paris, Hôtel Drouot (23 October 1989), no. 32; Robert Miller Gallery, New York.

This half figure of a prone older man apparently sleeping, although close in pose to the figures in *Sleep* (1867, see cat. 47), is a study for the figure of the shrouded, aged grim reaper, lurking, apparently momentarily somnolent, at the lower left of Puvis de Chavannes's *Death and the Maidens* (*Les jeunes filles et la mort*, 1872, fig. 33). In that composition, young women in light costumes are happily dancing and picking flowers, blithely unaware of death nearby. Executed just after the Franco-Prussian War and Commune, it might have to do with the unfolding of these recent events. France, unprepared for a war that might have been avoided, nevertheless undertook this engagement and was tragically defeated. The title, *Death and the Maidens*, recalls Schubert's celebrated song of 1817, *Der Tod und das Mädchen* (*Death and the Maiden*), but the subject is too general to be limited to one source.

9

Submitted to the Salon of 1872, the canvas was rejected after Puvis resigned from the jury. The Parnassian poet Armand Silvestre described the theme: 'the *Sleeping Reaper* ... is an idyll with an absolutely Virgilian composition. Fierce ... is the hand wavering over the laid down scythe. Is it Time who, under the dark mantle from which only his white beard emerges, lies in wait for this charming choir of young girls? Two of them have left the noisy circle and, sweetly intertwined, with their free hand stroke one a fruit, the other a flower. They bathe themselves in the light across the sun-filled plain, but a great fir wood on the slope of the flowered valley preserves the hospitable shadow for their rest.'[1]

Sleeping old men, of which the figure here is a variant, frequently make an appearance in Puvis de Chavannes's work, usually to suggest intergenerational continuity. This figure relates to a similarly posed figure in *Sleep* and to another in *Summer* of 1873 (fig. 5), and again to a similar figure in *The Fisherman's Family* of 1875 (see fig. 24).

1 '[le] *Faucheur endormi* ... est une idylle d'une composition tout à fait virgilienne. Farouche ... est la main flottante sur sa faux couchée, est-ce le Temps qui, sous le manteau sombre dont émerge seule sa barbe blanche, guette ce choeur charmant de jeunes filles? Deux d'entre elles ont quitté la ronde bruyante et, suavement enlacées, caressent de leur main libre, celle-ci un fruit, celle-là une fleur. Elles se baignent dans la lumière à travers la plaine ensoleillée, mais un grand bois de sapin garde à leur repos l'ombre hospitalière, au versant de la vallée fleurie.' Armand Silvestre in his preface to the catalogue *Recueil d'estampes gravées à l'eau-forte* published by Galerie Durand-Ruel (Paris and London, 1873).

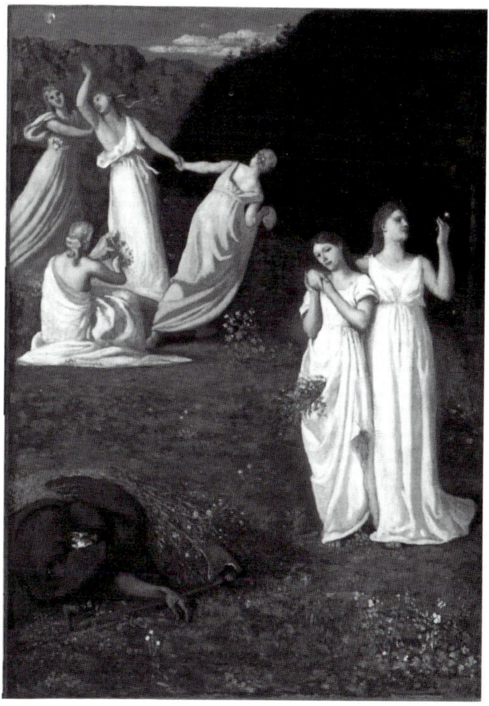

fig. 33
Death and the Maidens, 1872
Oil on canvas, 146 x 105 cm
Sterling and Francine Clark Art Institute, Williamstown, Mass.

illustration on page 146
The Birth of Saint Genevieve and *Saint Genevieve as a Child in Prayer*
Panthéon, Paris, installed in 1877

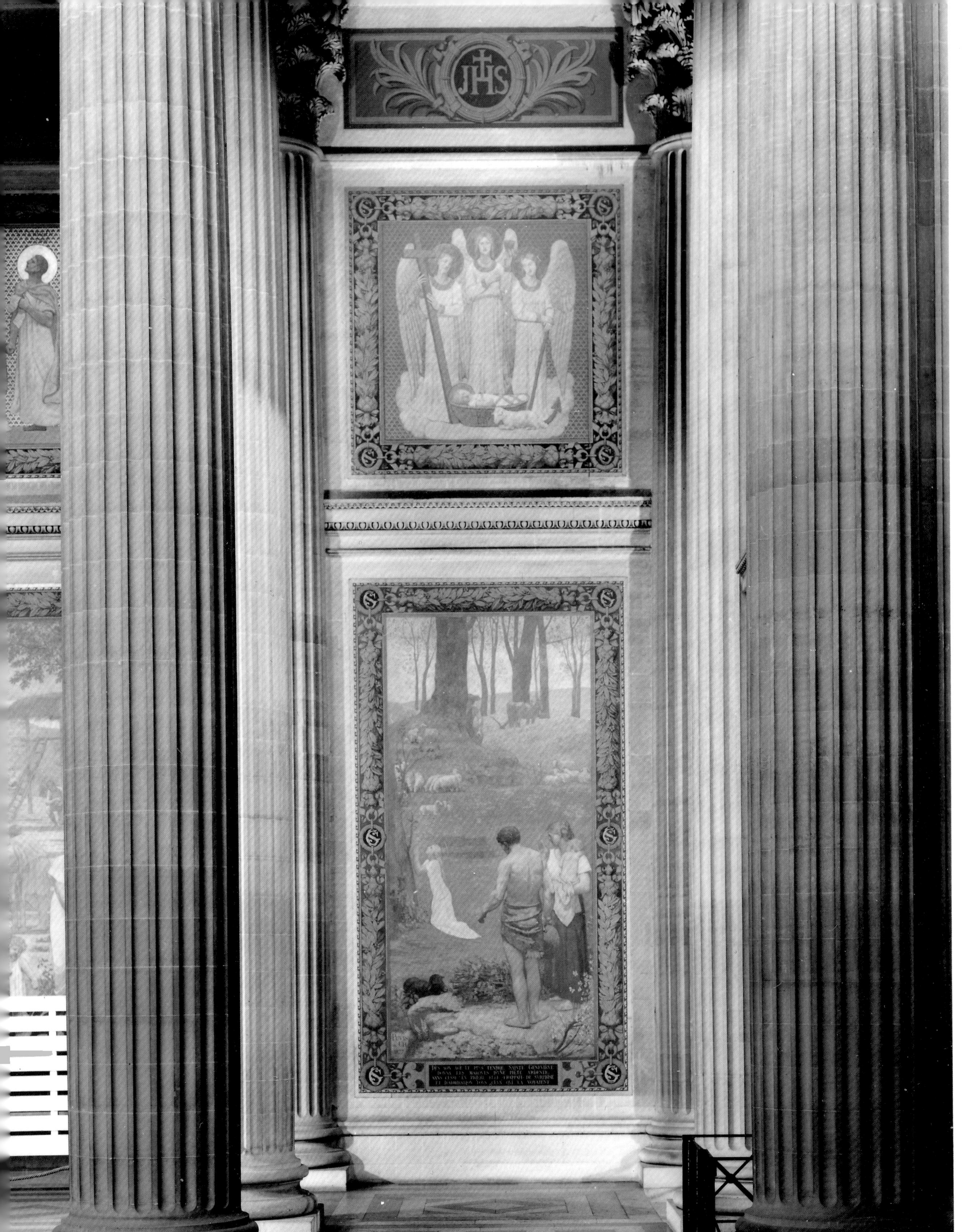
IHS

The Saint Genevieve Ensemble at the Panthéon

Puvis de Chavannes was to execute two great mural cycles for the building known today as the Panthéon. The first program, dating from 1874 to 1877, was his first commission in Paris;[1] he received the commission for his second campaign in 1893 and was completing it at his death in 1898. The earlier contribution was devised for what was then a church dedicated to the founding patron saint of Paris. Designed in the eighteenth century by Jacques Germain Soufflot for a site formerly occupied by an abbey, the Church of Saint Genevieve lost its religious designation after the French Revolution. Reconsecrated after Napoléon III established the Second Empire in 1851, it remained a religious institution until 1885. Under Philippe, the Marquis de Chennevières, Directeur des Beaux-Arts from 1874 to 1878, some forty murals were commissioned for its decoration from artists ranging from Jean-François Millet to Alexandre Cabanel, Léon Bonnat, Jean-Léon Gérôme and Gustave Moreau.[2] Religious figures important in French history were to be depicted – Saint Genevieve, Joan of Arc, Saint Denis – and temporal leaders significant to religious history such as Charlemagne and Saint Louis.

A decree of 14 May 1874 stipulated that the subject of Puvis de Chavannes's mural ensemble be 'l'histoire religioso-nationale de la France' during the first four centuries (A.D.); and an agreement of 15 May designated: 'These paintings should depict 1) in the lower part of the first pair of columns "the education [or upbringing, 'education'] of Saint Geneviève"; 2) in the lower part of the three others, "the pastoral life of the same saint"; 3) in the upper part of the four intercolumniations, above the stone band "a procession of holy persons."'[3] The first mural, interpreted as *Saint Genevieve as a Child in Prayer* (*Sainte Geneviève, enfant, en prière*) (462 x 221 cm, see ill. p. 146), was presented at the Salon of 1876, but dated to the time of its installation, 1877; the second group of three panels, *The Pastoral Life of Saint Genevieve* (*La vie pastorale de Sainte Geneviève*), dated 1877 (left to right: 460 x 277.8, 460 x 343.1, 460.6 x 277.8 cm, see ill. p. 150), was exhibited Paris, Salon of 1877, section 'Monuments publics.' This group is also known as *The Childhood of Saint Genevieve* (*L'Enfance de Sainte Geneviève*). A panel representing *The Birth of Saint Genevieve* (225 x 221 cm, see ill. p. 146), to surmount *Saint Genevieve as a Child in Prayer*, and the so-called 'Frieze' (225 x 280 cm both side panels, and 225 x 347.5 cm center panel, see ill. p. 150), that would surmount *The Pastoral Life of Saint Genevieve*, were exhibited again with 'Monuments publics' at the 1878 Salon.

Saint Genevieve[4] had been revitalized in the French imagination during the disastrous Franco-Prussian War when many prayed for divine intervention. She had delivered the city from the Barbarians centuries before, and the military Governor of Paris himself (under the Government of National Defense), one Louis-Jules Trochu, a man of deep faith, came to believe that she would miraculously reappear to do this once again.[5] Like Joan of Arc, with whom she shared many characteristics, Genevieve had had rustic beginnings: as a young girl she had been driven by a powerful faith that moved her to lead her imperiled country and save it from foreign invasion. It was apt that her life now be recalled.

1.The many references to Puvis's first Saint Genevieve ensemble include: AN F^{21}248, F^{21}4403; contract 15 May 1874 (private collection); correspondence of 15 May 1874; 7 July, 10 August, 11 November 1877; 28 July 1879; 6 June 1888; letter from Raffaelli, 24 May 1877 (private collection); Arthur Baignières, *Journal Officiel* (25 May 1877), n.p.; Charles Yriarte, 'Le Salon de 1876,' *Gazette des Beaux-Arts*, s2, XIII (June 1876), 692-695; Roger-Ballu (1877); Vachon (28 May 1877); Vachon (11 December 1877); Paul Leroi, 'Le Salon de Paris,' *L'Art*, III (1877), 149-150; Chennevières (1885), pp. 72-73, 76-79; 'Le Panthéon' (1889); Sâr Josephin Péladan, *L'Art Idealiste et Mystique. Doctrine de l'ordre et du Salon Annuel des Rose+Croix* (Paris, 1894), pp. 118-120; Mandach and Wehrlé (1910), 688-692; A.D. Sertillanges, *The Legend of Sainte Geneviève* (Paris, [1917]), pp. 10-15; Camille Jullian (1924); 1976-77 Paris/Ottawa, pp. 132-134; Vaisse (1977); Vaisse (1989).

2 Not all these painters ultimately participated, see 1976-77 Paris/Ottawa, pp. 132-134 for a list. See 'Décoration de l'Eglise patronale de Ste. Geneviève; Programme des peintures et sculptures,' AN, F^{21}4403; and Chennevières (1885); Vaisse (1989), pp. 252-258; and Vaisse (1977), 297-299, 302-303, 306-309.

3 AN F^{21}248.

4 For a succinct history of her life and legend see A. H. Delaunay, 'La Chapelle de Sainte Geneviève à St. Germain l'Auxerrois par M. Jean Gigoux,' IV, *L'Artiste* (1843), 321-324.

5 Dennis William Brogan, *The Development of Modern France* (London, 1944), p. 38.

70

Study for 'Saint Genevieve as a Child in Prayer' ca. 1875-76

Inscribed l.l.: au Comte Joseph Primoli
affectueusement P. Puvis de Ch.
Oil on paper, pencil inscription, laid on canvas,
136.3 x 76 cm
Van Gogh Museum, Amsterdam
(Inv. S 438 M/1993)

Provenance Artist's gift to Count Joseph Primoli; Henry Bloome Collection; private collection, Switzerland (1946-84); Robert Miller Gallery, New York (1984-85); private collection, New York (1985-93); New York, Christie's (18 February 1993), no. 12.

This is a study for the first or prefatory composition for Puvis de Chavannes's early complex of murals, which was designated as the 'education' of Genevieve and interpreted by Puvis as *Saint Genevieve as a Child in Prayer* (see ill. p. 146).[1] The future saint kneels in rapt prayer before a crudely made cross tied to a tree. Watched by a peasant couple with a baby and a farmer half hidden by a tree, she is surrounded by the sheep that indicate her pastoral duties. A lengthy cartouche informs the viewer of the narrative while freeing the artist from having to transmit this kind of information pictorially: 'Des son âge le plus tendre/ sainte Geneviève donna les marques d'une/ ardente piété sans cesse en prière/ elle frappait de surprise et d'admi/ ration tous ceux qui l'aperçevaient.'[2]

In his own description Puvis declared that he wanted to indicate several levels of reality, 'I believe, too, to be able – for fear of seeming realistic and in the interests of emotional effect – to give the child in prayer a form and garb smacking more of the angelic than a real being, more of a vision than of reality, the halo that circles her head completes the illusion. – Thus she appeared to this naïvely astonished group.'[3] Puvis, by his own reckoning, resolutely styled his *Saint Genevieve* works so they would not appear naturalistic. To enrich the meaning of their iconography, he chose a primitivizing aesthetic, now respectable enough for religious projects – Gautier had praised Byzantine painting, Giotto and works of a *naive* elegance[4] – which lent a note of innocence and authenticity to the images. The vertical composition and the simply stated slip of a girl in her light dress harken back to the simple, slightly stiff pre-Raphaelite style of a Sassetta or Fra Angelico. Intent on legibility, Puvis developed an opaque finish, and without the chiaroscuro that he abhorred, the surface was read as flat, its rough texture recalling fresco.

The 1870s was a decade of uncertainty and anti-clericalism, a time of cultural and psychological retrenchment that would stress historical continuity in the shock following the 1871 defeat. The setting of the *Saint Genevieve* ensemble is that of an idyllic, pre-lapsarian world of earnest faith, chastity and natural virtues. The image of an innocent young girl in profile at prayer was not totally new, however: Théodore Chassériau had included a like figure in *The Conversion of Mary the Egyptian* (Church of Saint-Merri, ca. 1841-43); there was an analogous figure in F.J. Heim's *Presentation of the Virgin in the Temple* (Church of Saint Sévérin, Paris) of 1849; and in Gabriel Tyr's work. Puvis had established a type of the understated, chaste young girl in his own work with *Hope* (figs. 3,4) of 1872. Puvis's portrait of the devout young peasant girl is related to Millet's depictions two decades earlier of peasants praying in the fields and to Gauguin's later portraits of the faithful in Brittany.

Like many of Puvis's best painted studies, this work permits the viewer the special pleasure of examining the process of execution, of areas left unfinished, and of glimpsing the defining lines of the underlying bistre drawing and the hatchings that are key to the shading. With a proficient, broad technique, the artist patched in color relying on the defining contours of a thinned sepia. The borders he designed would not be executed: in an effort to unify the murals throughout the building, all the actual borders were executed by the 'peintre-décorateur' Victor Galland.

Puvis warmly dedicated what was likely a pre-existing work to the Comte Primoli. The bookish Joseph (or Giuseppe) Napoleon Primoli (1851-1927), was a Napoleonic descendant through his mother, Carlotta Bonaparte Primoli.[5] A great connoisseur and collector, and himself a fascinating photographer,[6] he ultimately bequeathed part of his important collection to the city of Rome to form the basis of the Musée Napoléon.

The images and colors of Puvis's two mural cycles at the Panthéon impressed a number of artists, including the young Aristide Maillol, Picasso and Torres-Garcia. Likely on his third trip to Paris, between 29 October 1902 and January 1903, Picasso copied several sections of these murals and incorporated passages into his own work. The general pastoral idea and foreground figures from *Saint Genevieve as a Child in Prayer* form the basis of his drawing *The Golden Age*, in which the strong male figure to the right is particularly similar to Puvis's peasant.[7]

1 There is also a reduced panel painted after the mural called *The Childhood of Saint Genevieve*, ca. 1879, signed l.l.: P. Puvis Ch, oil and pencil on canvas, 134.2 x 77.1 cm (Fogg Art Museum, Cambridge, Mass.), which corresponds in style and size to the Norton Simon triad (cat. 74).

2 'From the tenderest age Saint Genevieve showed signs of an ardent piety; continually in prayer, she caused surprise and admiration in all those who caught sight of her.'

3 'J'ai cru pouvoir aussi – de peur de la vraisemblance et au profit de l'émotion – donner à l'enfant en prière une forme et un vêtement tenant plus de l'ange que de l'être réel, de la vision que de la realité, l'auréole qui ceint la tête complète l'illusion. – C'est ainsi qu'elle apparaît à ce groupe *naïvement ebahi*.' Chennevières (1885), 88.

4 Théophile Gautier, *Paris-Salon de 1847* (Paris, 1847), p. 60. See also p. 18 of this book.

5 F. Boyer, 'Les Oeuvres d'Artistes français au Musée Napoléonien de Rome,' *La Société de l'histoire de l'art français. Bulletin* (1929), 97-105; Maria Elisa Tittoni, 'Introduction,' *Il Museo Napoleonico* (Roma, 1986), pp. 6-13.

6 He photographed both the poor of Naples and the rituals of the nobility; see Susan Sontag, *On Photography* (New York, 1973), p. 57.

7 Picasso, *The Golden Age*, ink and watercolor on paper, 261 x 400 mm, Museo Picasso, Barcelona (Inv. MPB 110.546), made in Paris, 1902; for drawings most closely based on the second *Saint Genevieve* cycle, note Inv. MPB 110. 468; MPB 110.481; MPB 110.492; MPB 110. 493; and in the Musée Picasso, Paris, MP 461; MP 449.

illustration on page 150
Legendary Saints of France and *The Pastoral Life of Saint Genevieve*
Panthéon, Paris, installed in 1877

70

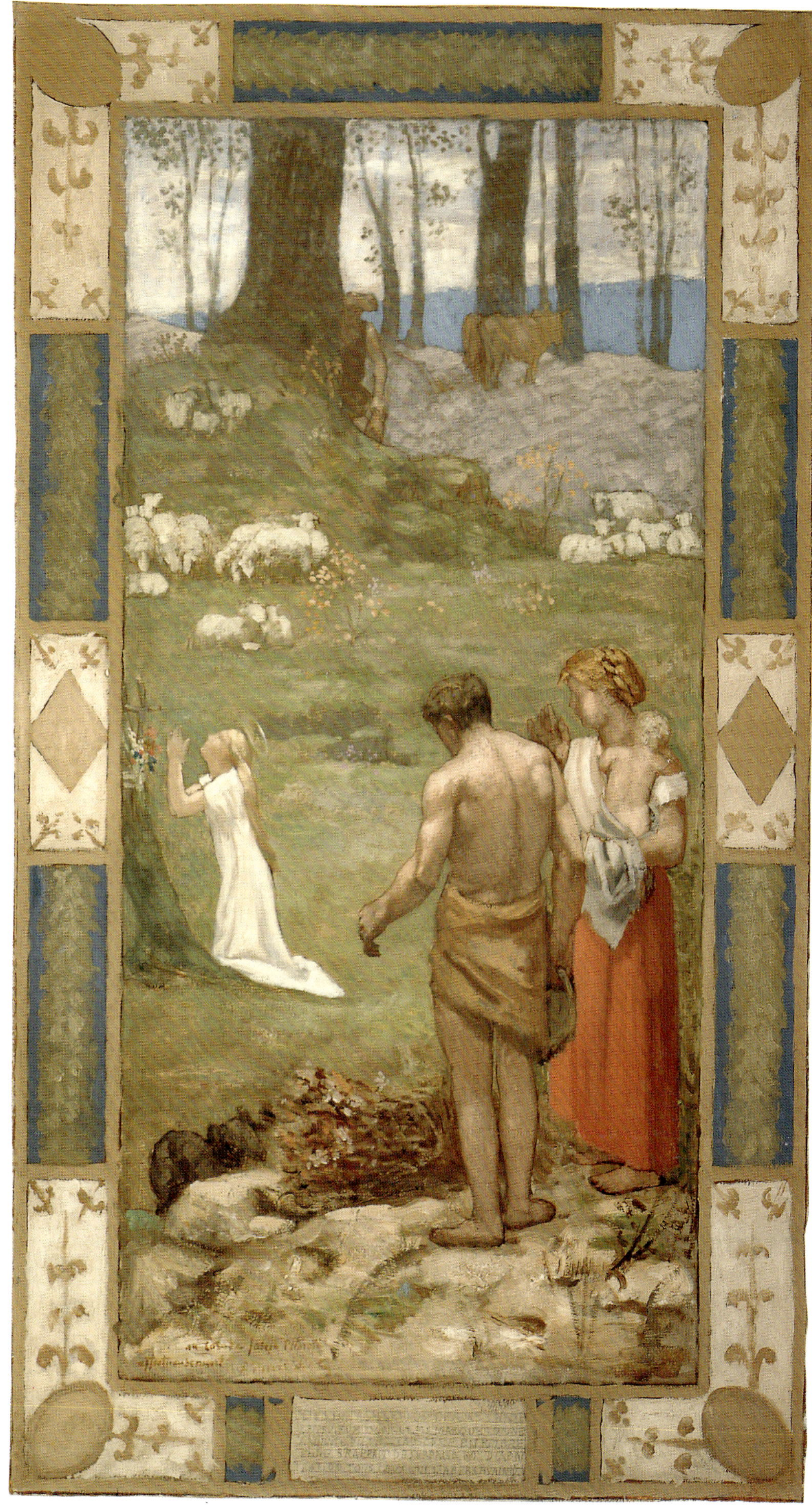

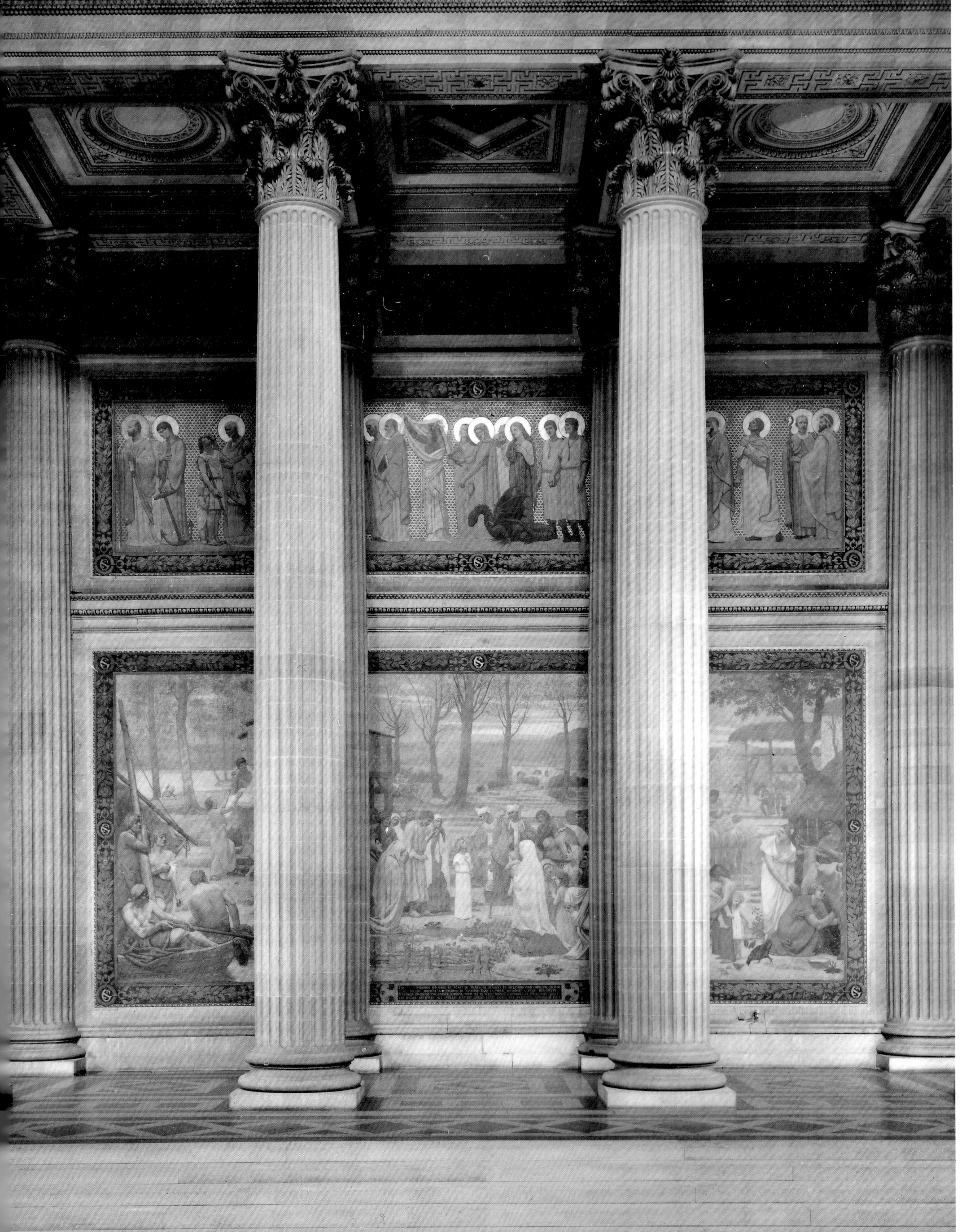

72

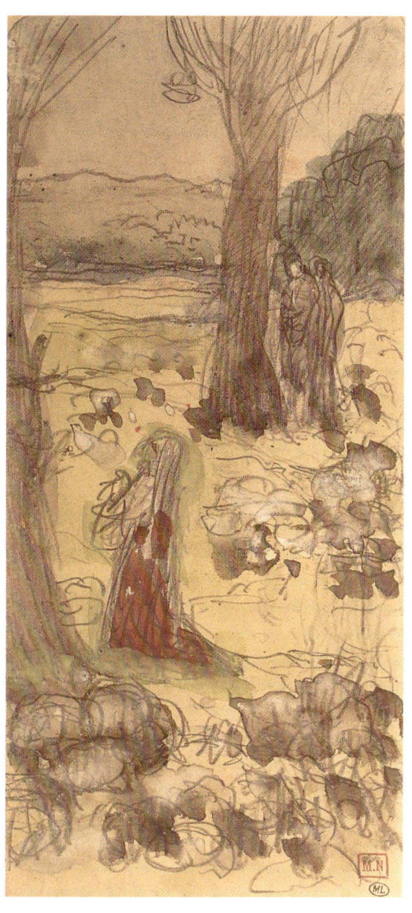

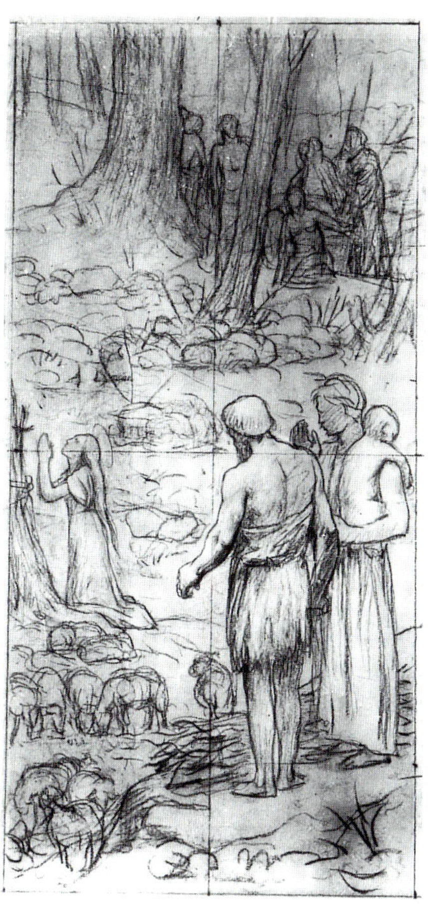

71

Study for 'Saint Genevieve as a Child in Prayer' ca. 1876

Watercolor with white highlights and pencil on beige paper, 253 x 118 mm
Musée du Louvre, Paris (Inv. RF 2199)

Provenance Bequest of artist's heirs to the city of Paris (1899); Musée du Luxembourg; transferred to the Musée du Louvre (1929).
Selected Exhibitions 1972 London/Liverpool, no. 214; 1976-77 Paris/Ottawa, no. 110.
Selected References Bénédite (1900), no. 53.

In the initial stages of preparing a composition, Puvis would often interpolate a small, loose watercolor, such as this one, among his other sketches, testing his pictorial idea with the atmospherics lent by color (though the white of Genevieve's dress would later be an important part of her identification). Here the general idea of Puvis's magisterial Panthéon decoration *Saint Genevieve as a Child in Prayer* (see ill. p. 146) is set down: the unusual sight of a young shepherdess at prayer in a field among her sheep is communicated by the pair of figures who quietly watch at a distance. Repoussoir figures would be added to the foreground to frame the central figure.

72

Study for 'Saint Genevieve as a Child in Prayer' ca. 1874-76

Red and black chalk on paper, divided in quadrants, partially traced with a needle, 570 x 283 mm
Museum Boymans-van Beuningen, Rotterdam (Inv. F II 148)

Provenance Franz Wilhelm Koenigs (1929); given to the Museum Foundation by D.G. van Beuningen (1940).
Selected References H.R. Hoetink, *Franse tekeningen uit de 19e eeuw* (Rotterdam, 1968), no. 220, repr.; 1986-87, Baltimore Museum of Art / Los Angeles County Museum of Art / Fort Worth, Kimbell Art Museum, *Nineteenth-Century French Drawings from the Museum Boymans-van Beuningen*, no. 81, repr.

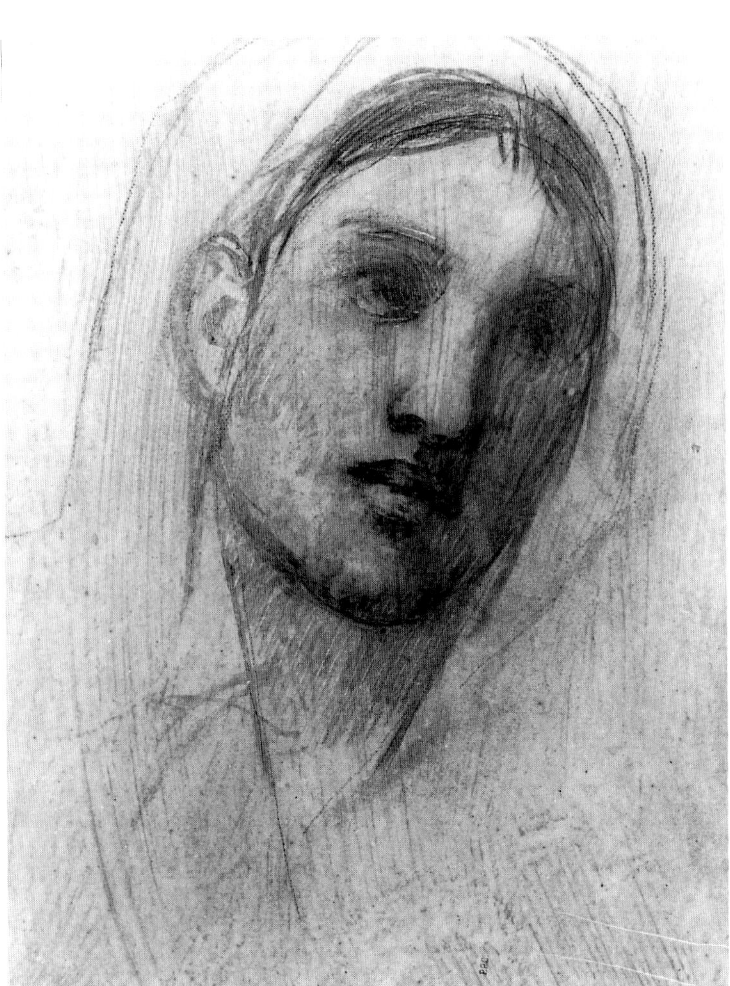

The process of simplification to which Puvis submitted his compositions may be followed in comparing this loose, preliminary sketch to the painted version of *Saint Genevieve as a Child in Prayer* (cat. 70). The onlookers in the background would be reduced to a single figure who would bracket the picture from a high zone and, by facing and corresponding to the viewer, make of him or her a fellow witness to the event. An ox and plow would be added to replace the other figures, maintaining the pictorial weight and visual interest in the upper right and iconographically reinforcing the rusticity of the agrarian setting. The high and narrow panel is divided into quadrants, important in calculating not only bilateral, but vertical balance. Thus, the largest tree trunk, to the upper left, offsets the couple to the lower right; it is made clear that Genevieve's head is just at the center while the heads of the couple are slightly higher. This check on structure indicates a desire to animate the surface in a way comparable to what the Italian 'primitives' achieved, and also indicates how this arrangement parallels that of the later Impressionists and Post-Impressionists, who also strived for a similar overall decorative effect.

73

Head of a Woman ca. 1875-76

Black chalk on tracing paper, 405 x 295 mm (sight)
Private collection

Provenance Artist's heirs and by descent.

In this study, the simple geometrical configuration of a woman's head is emphasized. Its solid ovoid shape is reinforced by the looped curve of the headdress that continues down to form the V of the neck. This hooded head is like those of the powerfully simplified Giottesque figures in the *Saint Genevieve* ensemble, although it does not directly relate to any single one. The facial expression is placid, nothing disturbs the large steady rhythms of the plain, strong facial features. The broad, muted smoothness of the lines seems to indicate that the paper support has a waxed or otherwise treated surface. Once again in Puvis's works we are treated to radical reductions in pictorial thinking usually associated with twentieth-century art.

74

The Pastoral Life of Saint Genevieve / *La vie pastorale de Sainte Geneviève* (reduced version) ca. 1877-79

Signed l.r. of right panel: P. Puvis de Chavannes 1879
Oil on canvas, 134.2 x 81.8 cm; 134.2 x 89.5 cm; 134 x 81 cm
Norton Simon Art Foundation, Pasadena (Inv. M. 1968.49.P)

Provenance Mr. and Mrs. James Byron; Catholina Lambert, Patterson, New Jersey (1894-1916); New York, Plaza Hotel, Catholina Lambert Sale (21-24 February 1916), no. 186; F. von Hellman; I. Johns [same version ?]; Durand-Ruel, Paris (1923-1925); Wert D. Walker; Art Institute of Chicago (until 1955); E. and A. Silberman Galleries, New York (5 December 1963); Huntington Hartford Collection, Gallery of Modern Art, New York (1963-67); Hirschl and Adler Galleries, New York; Norton Simon, Inc.
Selected Exhibitions 1887 Paris (Durand-Ruel), no. 1 [this version ?]; 1887 New York, no. 53; 1889 Paris

(Exposition centennale de l'art français), no. 561 *'Vie de Sainte Geneviève'* [this version ?].

Selected References Delapalme Inventory; [Anonymous], 'Lambert Sale,' *American Art News*, XIV (26 February 1916), 6; [Anonymous], 'Piety of Sainte Geneviève,' *Bulletin of the Metropolitan Museum of Art*, XI (June 1916), 134; *Bulletin of the Art Institute of Chicago*, XVII (11 December 1923), repr. cover, 110; L.C. (1924), 117-120; [Anonymous], 'Chicago Art Institute Gets Mural Studies by Puvis de Chavannes,' *Art News* (15 April 1924), 1; *A Guide to the Paintings in the Permanent Collection*, Art Institute of Chicago (Chicago, 1925), pp. 55-57; *A Guide to the Paintings in the Permanent Collection*, Art Institute of Chicago (Chicago, 1932), pp. 51-53; Venturi (1939), II, p. 95; *Burlington Magazine*, CIII (November 1961), lvii, repr.

While *Saint Genevieve as a Child in Prayer* (ill. p. 146) is about Genevieve's private piety, this triad of canvases after Puvis de Chavannes's mural *The Pastoral Life of Saint Genevieve* produced as its complement (ill. p.150)[1] indicates the moment at which she became part of history. The project director for the Panthéon, Philippe de Chennevières, required that the three mural panels be designed to appear *in situ* as though they were a single composition that passed behind the large stone half-columns that separated them.[2] The surrounds of ancient Paris is the setting, with the Seine, Mount Valérien, and, at a distance from the thatched shelters, stone structures and dwellings and the belfry of Nanterre. But each panel has its own theme and distinctive rhythms.

In the central section, Bishops Saint Germanus and Saint Loup publicly recognize that Genevieve has been marked by God. The panel is symmetrical and static. The bishops and the young white-clad girl are surrounded by a crowd, and there is only a ripple of cursively interlaced gestures to suggest the import of the event, of which we learn not from dramatic action or explicit emotional display, but from an elaborate cartouche: 'L'an 429 Saint Germain d'Auxerre et Saint Loup se rendant/ en Angleterre pour combattre l'hérésie des Pélagiens ar/ rivent aux environs de Nanterre./ Dans la foule accourue à leur rencontre, Saint Germain distingue une enfant marquée pour lui du sceau divin. Il/ l'interroge et prédit à ses parents les hautes destinées/ auxquelles elle est appelée./ Cette enfant fut Sainte Geneviève, patronne de Paris.'[3] Puvis described the narrative to Chennevières: the importance of the look exchanged between Saint Germanus and Genevieve, the controlled emotion of her parents at the left, the 'people of all conditions,' whom he included, the old man who painfully kneels to acknowledge Genevieve, the outcast beggar girl (right) who stands at a distance from the others.[4]

The two wings depict the daily life and activity within the community and yield a further cultural context for the legendary event. At left, in the so-called 'samaritan' panel, an ailing figure (whom Gauguin was to iterate in his *Green Calvary*, 1889, Musées Royaux des Beaux-Arts, Brussels) is carried from a small stone building to a waiting boat to be brought to SS. Loup and Germanus for help. The right panel is devoted to farming and animal husbandry.[5]

To evoke the legend of primitive faith and the time of miracles Puvis used an archaizing style of what was then noted as a 'delicious naiveté.' This brilliant invention may be an extension of what Puvis said he was trying to do: 'I ... wanted, in representing the youth of the heroine, to have everything young – it is spring; the sky is young, it is morning. Finally, its general appearance is tender and sweet like the soul of this child which ought, so to speak, to suffuse and shine through the whole composition.'[6] As noted, Puvis's style, borrowed from an earlier age, suggests the work is almost contemporaneous with the event and thus it lends a note of authenticity to the narrative. The formality of manner, the proportions of the figures, and their costume recall the archaizing simplifications and containment of the sculptural figures of Romanesque portals, notably that of Saint Loup himself on the west door of the Church of Saint Loup de Naud (ca. 1165-70). The plain, cloaked figures, particularly those in the center who are of almost stubby proportions, arrayed as they are in all but isocephalic rows with a stiff but commanding simplicity, and a certain likeness of one to the other, are garbed in mound-like cloaks of marvelously tender colors, and are strikingly reminiscent of Giotto's figures as well. The remarkable colors – cornflower-blue hills, green tree trunks, a turquoise sky – would, through Puvis, help liberate the Post-Impressionists from verism in colors, as his rhythms would be repeated by them (compare Maurice Denis's *Green Trees*, 1893, collection Dominique Denis, to those in *Saint Genevieve as a Child in Prayer*).

There are important differences between the reduced versions after the monumental paintings and the murals themselves. However faithful to the individual mural panels, this reduced version situates them in close proimity to one another, divided only by a narrow molding, causing the scenes to appear disjunctive. Puvis also sought to make allowances for their reduced size, seeking equivalents to the *appearance* of the epic scale and fresco-like surfaces of the monumental work: he instilled a sense of further commodiousness by condensing pictorial elements and aligning them more strictly; the figures are slimmer, the trees pruned and straightened and the composition altogether more crisp. A granular surface and broad technique approximate the appearance of the murals as affected by the viewing distance needed to take in their 'grands traits.'

1 This reduced triptych complements *Saint Genevieve as a Child in Prayer*, Fogg Art Museum, Cambridge, Mass. (see cat. 70, note 1), the dimensions of which correspond to that of each panel of this work. An integrated composition comprising the three panels is *The Meeting of Saint Genevieve and Saint Germanus* ca. 1875-76, oil, pencil on canvas, 52 x 102 cm (private collection), which may be the same as the Delapalme Inventory, no. 55: 'une toile peinte esquisse pour l'ancien Panthéon.' It was perhaps in anticipation of executing these panels that on 9 November 1877 Puvis mentioned consigning a 'Réduction complète des peintures au Panthéon' for sale to Durand-Ruel (Durand-Ruel Archives), which was to be sold for 12,000 francs. A version listed in the Delapalme Inventory as '16) Une esquisse des fresques du Panthéon (à l'état) valeur-mémoire' would seem to refer to three loosely painted pen and ink, oil on paper panels, laid down, 136.5 x 95.2; 136.5 x 113; and 136.5 x 94.3 cm (private collection); except for a different technique and patchy surface it corresponds to the *Saint Genevieve as a Child in Prayer* at the Van Gogh Museum (cat. 70) – both have the same kind of border and each panel is of the same dimensions.

2 Chennevières (1885), pp. 72-73.

3 'In the year 429, Saint Germanus of Auxerre and Saint Loup, on their way to England to fight the Pelagian heresy, arrive in the neighborhood of Nanterre. In the crowd gathered to meet them, Saint Germanus distinguishes a child marked for him with a divine seal. He questions her and to her parents foretells the high destiny to which she has been called. That child was Saint Genevieve, patron saint of Paris.' The versions have slightly different captions: in the mural cartouche, the year is in Roman numerals, and Troyes is designated. Interestingly, the caption and image closely follow a description of what the iconography should entail written by A.H. Delaunay in a scathing critique of Gigoux's interpretation of the subject in Delaunay's 'La Chapelle de Sainte Geneviève à St. Germain l'Auxerrois par M. Jean Gigoux,' IV, *L'Artiste* (1843), 321.

4 Chennevières (1885), pp. 72-73. An important motif in Puvis's work discussed in the author's forthcoming book.

5 Aristide Maillol was to paint a copy of a section at the right, a male and female head with that of a cow in between (private collection, London).

6 'J'ai voulu ... représentant la jeunesse de l'héroïne, que tout fût jeune – c'est le printemps; le ciel est jeune, c'est le matin; enfin, l'aspect général est tendre et doux comme l'âme de cet enfant qui doit, pour ainsi dire, transparaître et baigner toute la composition.' Chennevières (1885), pp. 72-73.

75

74

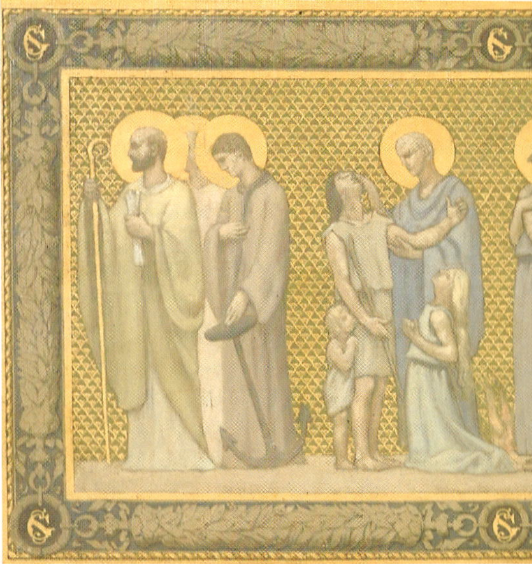

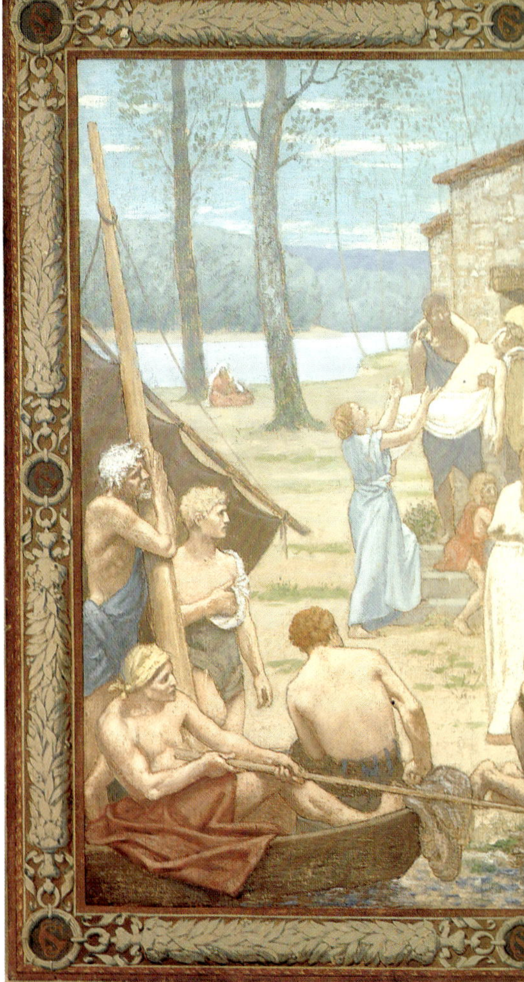

75

Legendary Saints of France / *Saints Légendaires de la France* (reduced version) ca. 1879

Oil on canvas, 77.5 x 83 cm; 77.5 x 89.5 cm; 77.5 x 83 cm
Philadelphia Museum of Art, given by Dr. and Mrs. Richard W. Levy (Inv. 1969-167-001)

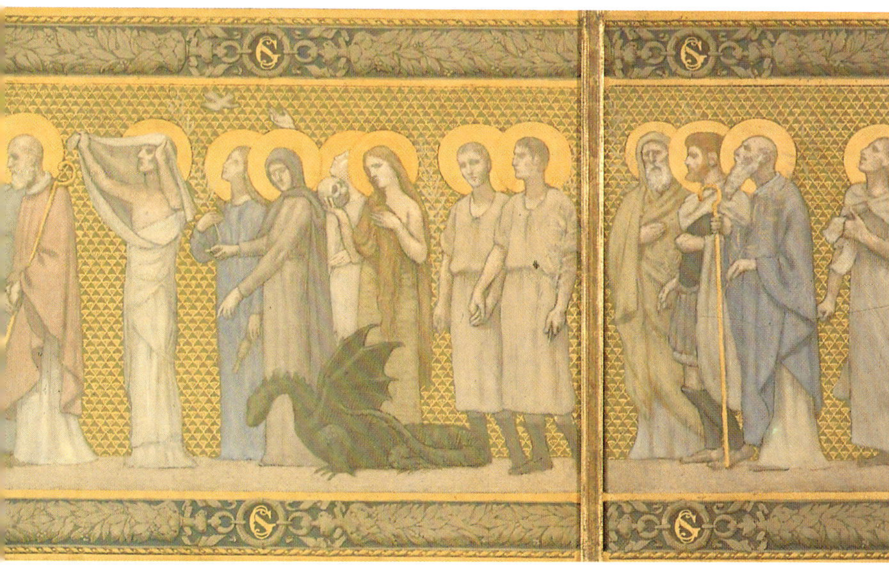

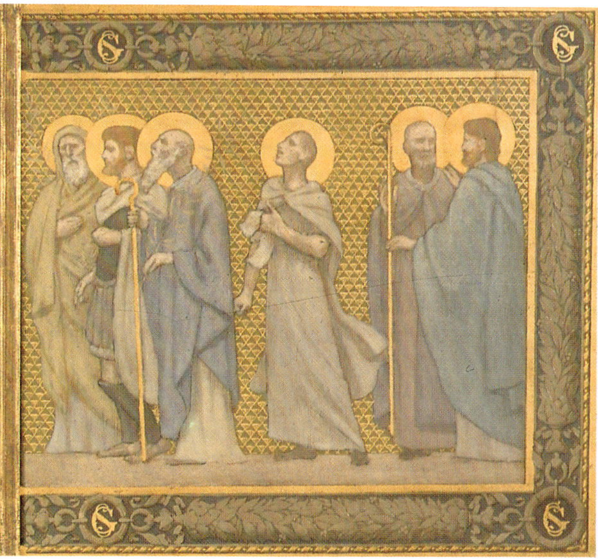

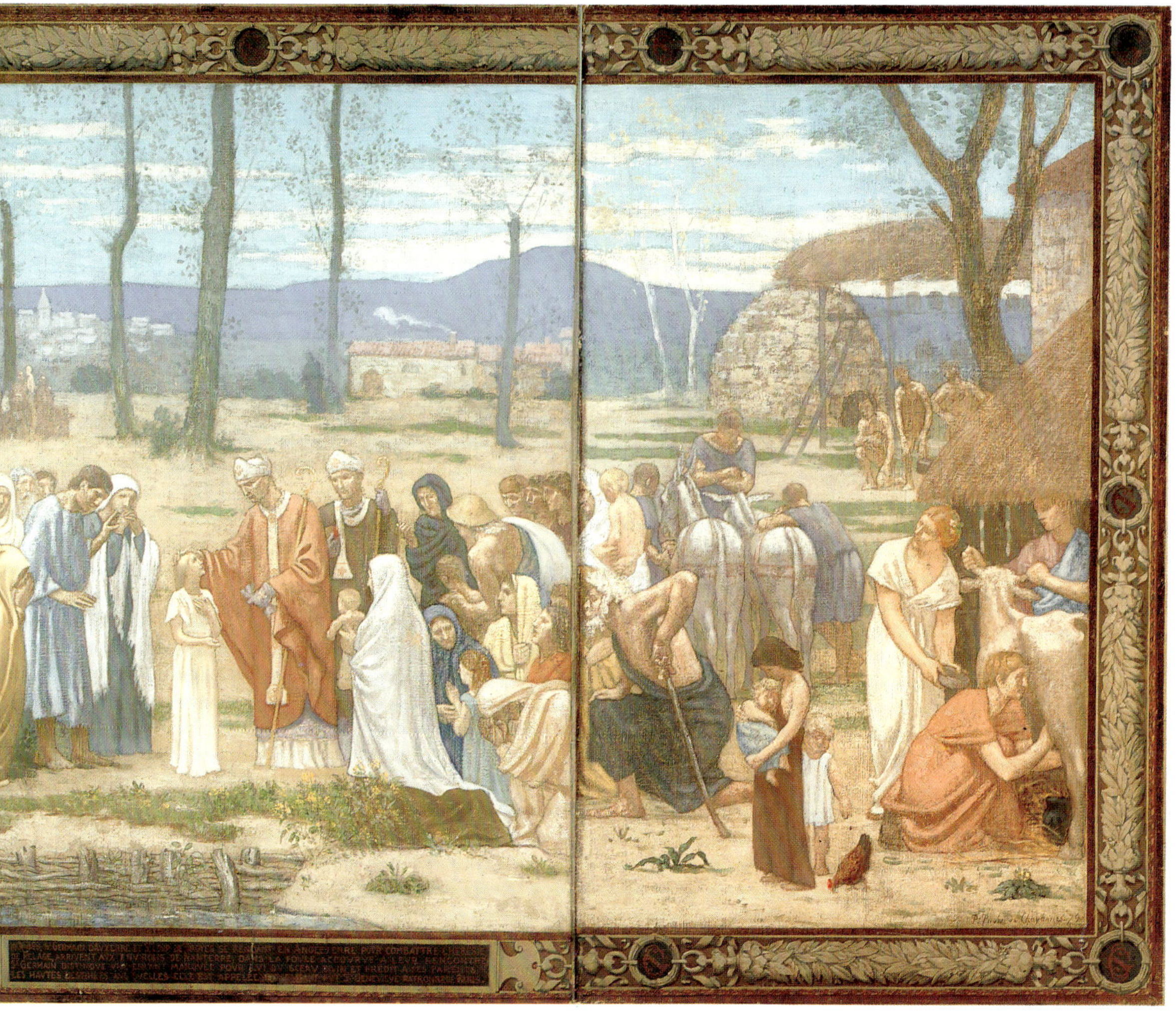

Provenance Catholina Lambert, New York (by 1894); New York, Plaza Hotel, Catholina Lambert Sale (21-24 February 1916), no. 187; Mr and Mrs James Byron (on loan to the Metropolitan Museum of Art (1916-23); F. von Hellman; I. Johns [same version ?]; Durand-Ruel, Paris (1923-25); Wert D. Walker; Art Institute of Chicago (until 1955); on loan to the Brooklyn Museum (1925 for several years); Silberman Gallery, New York (1955); Richard Feigen Gallery, New York (1968); Dr. and Mrs. Richard Levy (1969).

Selected Exhibitions 1887 New York, no. 53 (among 'Reduction of the Paintings at the Panthéon'); 1894 New York (Durand-Ruel), no. 10, possibly the same as 'Decoration of St. Geneviève, 1877 [?] original reduction in several parts.... (2) decoration [or] (3) frieze of the angels in two parts [?]'; 1976-77 Paris/Ottawa, no. 120.

Selected References On the mural: AN F[21]4403, decree of 14 May 1874 [on the Panthéon commission]; Contract of 15 May 1874 (private collection); Vachon (11 December 1877); Vachon [ca. 1877; Amiens], n.p.; *Inventaire des richesses d'art de la France. Monuments civils*, II (Paris, 1889), p. 341; Vachon [1900], pp. 184-185; Bréghot du Lut (1899), *Revue du Lyonnais*, 278-279; 1976-77 Paris/Ottawa, p. 130; Vaisse (1989), pp. 253, 258.

In this reduced version of the so-called 'frieze,' designed to surmount the narrative murals of the pastoral life of the young Genevieve, the procession of figures can be seen at closer range and more clearly than in the large, but high mural *in situ* at the Panthéon (see ill. p. 150). Such friezes, which unified the sundry contributions in the complex, were required of a number of artists who worked on the project. The inclusion of patron saints of provincial French cities, designated by decree of 14 May 1874,[1] and important religious and national historical figures was in keeping with the Panthéon's function as not only a Parisian, but a national monument. Such parades of worthies marching towards an altar or, indeed, forming part of the altar itself, date from antiquity (the Ara Pacis Augustae, for one).

Hippolyte Flandrin had resurrected the gold patterned ground of Byzantine mosaics in his processionals at Saint Vincent de Paul in Paris, Saint Paul in Nîmes, and Saint Germain des Prés – his so-called 'Christian Panathenaics' ('panathénées chrétiennes'), prescribed for parades of theological grandees – and the neo-Byzantine motif became popular among Ingristes and was frequently repeated, particularly in church decoration. The restrained but opulent ground establishes a visually flat barrier, an important exemplum in the development of a decorative aesthetic in later nineteenth-century France.

Watercolor and gouache studies by Puvis include tall, rather undifferentiated saints spaced with an even stateliness.[2] An early study on canvas included their names inscribed above their heads,[3] a reminder, along with the two-dimensional round gold halos, of the origins of such processionals in Byzantine art. In Byzantine painting and mosaics figures are commonly identified by name for the theological purpose of assuring correct identification for worshippers as they address the icons and supplicate them in their prayers.

The saints are differentiated in pose, gesture and attributes. Their individuality and the grand, simple design of the frieze are most clearly and stunningly visible in a series of full-size studies in absolutely flat colors, the most radical to be associated with Puvis's mature aesthetic – light grays, blues, pink, tan, yellow and white, offset by a beige-gold that represents what was to be the final gold 'Byzantine' background.[4]

Despite the care taken to distinguish the figures from one another, the names of the saints, inscribed on the actual panels at the Panthéon, are virtually invisible without special lenses. To add to the confusion of identification, they were slightly different from those designated in the original contract – although Vachon's published list was supposedly based on one from Chennevières that was the same list originally given to the artist. Vachon lists, for example, a Saint Lucanus from Aix, who does not appear in the mural. The saints have been identified as follows:[5] '[left panel:] Saint Paternus, Bishop of Vannes, Saint Clement, Bishop of Metz, Saint Firminus, Bishop of Amiens, Saint Lucian, Bishop of Beauvais; [center panel:] Saint Maximinus, Bishop of Aix,[6] Saint Martial, Bishop of Limoges, Saint Lazarus, Bishop of Marseilles, Saint Solangia of Berry, Saint Martha [of Provence], Saint Columba of Sens, Saint Magdalene [of Provence], Saint Crispin and Saint Crispinus of Soissons; [right panel:] Saint Lucanus of Beauce,[7] Saint Julian of Brioude, Saint Gatianus [of Tours],[8] Saint Fereol of Vienne, Saint Trophimus, Bishop of Arles, Saint Paul, Bishop of Narbonne.'

Puvis portrayed friends and colleagues as various saints: Saint Paternus was modeled after Elie Delaunay (who also contributed murals to the Panthéon), his pastoral hook, one critic said, like a paint brush;[9] Victor Durangel, an artist who worked at Marseilles when Puvis did, is Saint Lucian according to one account, while another names a Saint Victor, perhaps a confusion with his Christian name.[10] Saint Martial was purportedly modeled after Puvis's friend, the engraver Victor Pollet, though other sources again mention a Saint Victor, now of Beauvais, a name saint, but one who is not included. Philippe de Chennevières, the Directeur des Beaux-Arts responsible for the Panthéon commissions, is portrayed as Saint Paul of Narbonne turned to Saint Trophimus of Arles – Puvis himself – and offering him his shepherd's crook. Though why Puvis chose to portray himself as the Arles saint (second from right), or Chennevières, from Normandy, as Paul of Narbonne, is not apparent.

1 Puvis's contract (ref. above) called for 'personnages sacrés.' There were to be twenty saints from the 'first four centuries,' twelve of whom were bishops, 'the first apostles of Paul,' according to 1976-77 Paris/Ottawa, p. 133.

2 *Procession, Study for the frieze of Saint Genevieve*, stamp l.l., watercolor and gouache on beige paper, 320 x 470 mm (private collection), 1976-77 Paris/Ottawa, no. 121. See also *Heads of Saints, Two Studies for a Frieze in the Panthéon*, ca. 1877, black chalk, watercolor, gouache, gold in background, 483 x 431 mm (sight), 595 x 450 mm, Fogg Art Museum, Cambridge, Mass. (Inv. 1943.901-902), see fig. 16; *Heads of Saints*, Fogg Art Museum, Cambridge, Mass. (Inv. 1943.895).

3 *Study for the frieze of Saint Genevieve*, ca. 1877-78, stamp l.r.: ML MN, watercolor and ink on canvas, 285 x 365 mm, Musée du Louvre, Paris (Inv. RF 2211).

4 *Procession of Saints*, gouache on paper laid down on canvas, three panels: 218.5 x 275; 218.5 x 356; 218.5 x 279 cm, Norton Simon Art Foundation, Pasadena, California (Inv. F. 1978.38. 1-3.P).

5 The Marquis de Chennevières, the Abbot Bonnefoy and the Petit Bollandists supplied direction and sources; see discussion 1976-77 Paris/Ottawa, no. 120.

6 This was Saint Lucanus of Beauce according to Vachon (11 December 1877).

7 Saint Saturninus of Toulouse according to Vachon (11 December 1877).

8 Saint Austremonius of Clermont according to Vachon (11 December 1877).

9 Vachon (11 December 1877).

10 Bréghot du Lut (1899), *Revue du Lyonnais*, 278-279; repeated in Michel and Laran (1911), p. 50, or (1912), p. 41.

76

Young Women by the Sea / *Jeunes filles au bord de la mer* (small version) ca. 1879

Signed l.l.: P. Puvis de Chavannes
Oil on canvas, 61 x 47 cm
Musée d'Orsay, Paris, bequest of Comte Isaac de Camondo, 1911 (Inv. RF 2015)

Provenance Robert de Bonnières, Paris (1894); Comte Isaac de Camondo, Paris (1908); Musée du Louvre, Paris (1911; entered collection officially in 1914).

Selected Exhibitions 1899 Paris (Durand-Ruel), no. 23; 1972 London/Liverpool, no. 216; 1976-77 Paris/Ottawa, no. 135.

Selected References De Forges (1970), 241-252; Brown Price in 1976-77 Paris/Ottawa, p. 25.

Nude or semi-nude female figures conventionalized as 'bathers' were an important theme in later nineteenth-century French painting. With this most common of themes and the simplest of settings, Puvis succeeded in creating one of his most extraordinary compositions. While seemingly a classicizing image based on antique ideas, his *Young Women by the Sea* is an idyll of revery and displacement, of sensuousness and emotional remove. The traditional accoutrements of classicism notwithstanding – the central figure draped like a Venus de Milo – this composition is one of Puvis de Chavannes's most original inventions and would inspire an important legacy among other inventive painters (see cat. 148, 152).

From Ingres to Renoir and, of course, far beyond, artists found inspiration for nude bathers in antique prototypes. Here, the central figure standing with her back to the viewer and holding her parted tresses is based on the *Venus Anadyomene* type, a figure holding up her hair as if to wring the sea (from which she was born) from it.[1] Puvis would have certainly been familiar with Théodore Chassériau's rendering of the type in his 1838-40 *Venus Anadyomene* or *Venus Marine* (Musée du Louvre, Paris), well-known as *Aphrogénéia* through popular lithographic reproductions.[2] There were other models nearer at hand for languidly posed bathers: although Puvis's reclining foreground figure is very much his own, it also resembles a figure in Auguste Gendron's *The Voices of the Torrent* (Salon of 1857, Musée des Beaux-Arts 'André Malraux,' Le Havre), a photograph of which Puvis had in his collection.[3]

Puvis presented his majestic 1879 *Young Women by the Sea* (fig. 6), of which this is a reduced variant, at the Salon of that year.[4] Although it was not designed for a particular destination, it had its own painted frame (see ill. p. 10),[5] and was listed as a 'panneau décoratif.'[6] This designation may have been used to justify what might have been perceived as stylistic aberrations in an ordinary painting or 'tableau,' such as the areas of pale, flat matte colors and the intermittent scumbling of the surface. The term might also have been a way of accounting for a lack of narrative. One commentator, Gustave Kahn, would invent a program to explain what seemed otherwise so enigmatic: one of the women was tired of singing, he wrote, and was waiting for a returning boat that never comes.[7] Indeed, the arrangement of the three figures and the composition were as profoundly unusual as was the pictorial presentation.

Although the triad of women evokes a classicizing tradition, this is by no means a conventional work; nor is this rendering of any real actuality, as is William Bouguereau's *The Bathers* of 1884 (Art Institute of Chicago). What may be read as a pyramidal grouping, among the most traditional of compositional conventions, is here shifted to the side, with the figure to the right more than half cut off by the picture edge. The central figure faces away from the viewer and each of the others, placed at an interval, is wilfully turned away from the others to face in a different direction. There is no focus or concerted attention, and no logi-

76

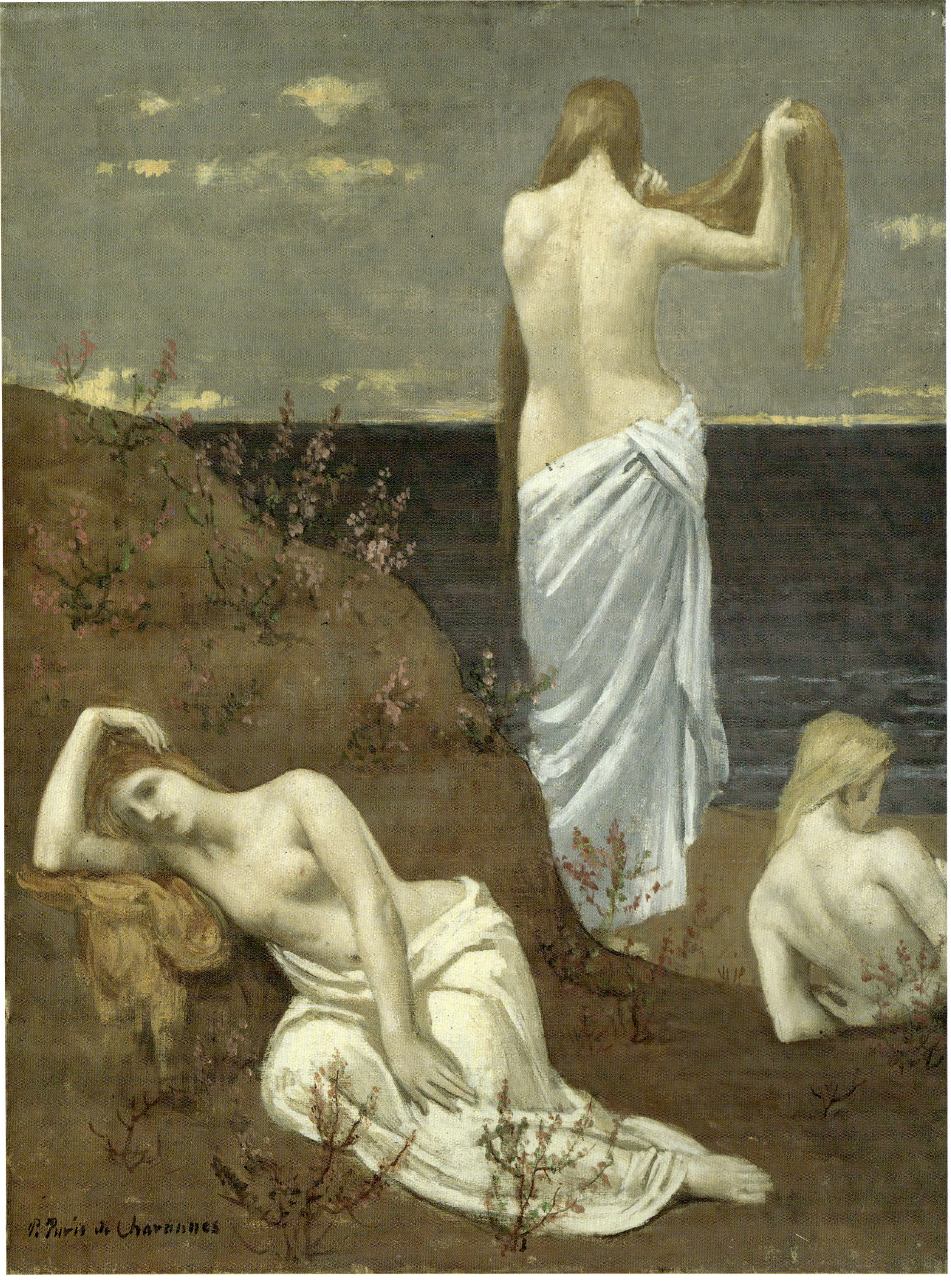

77 cal or explicit transition among them. In the definitive version of *Young Women by the Sea*, a high hill to the left both offsets the central figure and furthers the compositonal asymmetry, limiting the vista and thereby flattening the composition.

This variant of *Young Women by the Sea* appears to be a replica painted after the 1879 version. As if to compensate for its smaller size and what might have been read in a work of these dimensions as slightly wan tonalities, its opaque colors are more intense than those of the large canvas, and, while only slightly subdued, no less audacious – terracotta earth, mauve sky, blond clouds, cyclamen flowers. Forms have been condensed into simpler profiles with slimmer, more angular figures. Technical examination shows that a higher mound was originally to the left, further evidence that this is a replica after the larger work. By reducing its height, the vista was opened out and the central figure monumentalized.

The process of invention by which figures and landscape were formulated and arranged may be followed in numerous drawings. At one stage, all three figures were seated or lying on the ground (see cat. 78). As another drawing makes clear, Puvis came to appreciate the need for a central vertical and toyed with the idea of a tree in the center.[8] Certain postures tried in conjunction with this project were to be used in *Pleasant Land* (see cat. 86). There are numerous studies for the individual figures, some of which are among Puvis's loveliest drawings.[9]

While *Young Women By the Sea* received the encomiums of critics and poets, it also drew barbs for its stiffness and awkwardness – the work of a 'primitive' – and its lack of color.[10] The truncated figure on the right was selected for ridicule by the caricaturist Stop: in his satirical drawing he moved the figure at the left half-way off the canvas too, so that only the lower half of her torso is visible; and he also made fun of the standing woman's long hair that she uses to wave off aggressive gulls.[11]

The composition was to have an important legacy. Variants of the sharply defined figures, each turning her own way, were reiterated in Seurat's *Poseuses* of 1888 (Barnes Foundation, Merion, Penn.), which Paul Signac asserted was as successful as 'the most successful of Puvis and of Renoir, the qualities of which Seurat seems to reunite in this canvas.'[12] Gauguin's women on the strand, particularly *Tahitian Women on a Beach* (cat. 148) are indebted to Puvis's imagery; and Henri Matisse's 1904-05 *Luxe, calme, et volupté* (see cat.150) echoes many elements of this canvas and *Pleasant Land*. The imagery continued to enchant painters, including Picasso, in whose 1918 *Bathers* (cat. 152) there are direct borrowings from Puvis.

1 A Hellenistic bronze of the *Venus Anadyomene* (literally, 'rising from the sea') aroused excitement when it was found in the Saône in the nineteenth century.

2 See P. Jamot, '"La Vénus marine" de Chassériau,' *Revue de l'Art*, XXVIII (July-August 1920), 71-84.

3 Private collection.

4 In addition, there is an unsigned oil on canvas study, 68 x 52 cm, recently auctioned: Bayeux, Hôtel des Ventes (11 November 1993), number not available. Painted with the pale colors of the large version, it includes the high mound with two small trees growing on it.

5 The painted frame is no longer extant.

6 See Brown Price in 1976-77 Paris/Ottawa, pp. 26, also 22-25.

7 Kahn (1888).

8 *Maidens by the Sea*, stamp l.r., black chalk on yellow tracing paper, squared, laid down, 248 x 304 mm, Art Museum, Princeton University, Princeton, New Jersey (Platt Collection) (Inv. 1948-497).

9 For example, *Study for 'Young Women by the Sea'*, black chalk heightened with white chalk on gray paper, squared, 375 x 157 mm, Musée de Picardie, Amiens, (Inv. 912bis 53).

10 See discussions in De Forges (1970), and 1976-77 Paris/Ottawa, pp. 153-154.

11 Stop, *Le Journal amusant* (31 May 1879), n.p.

12 'les plus réussis des Puvis et des Renoir, dont Seurat semble en cette toile réunir les qualités.' Quoted by John Rewald, 'Extraits du journal inédit de Paul Signac, II, 1897-1898,' *Gazette des Beaux-Arts*, s6, XXXIX (April 1952), 272.

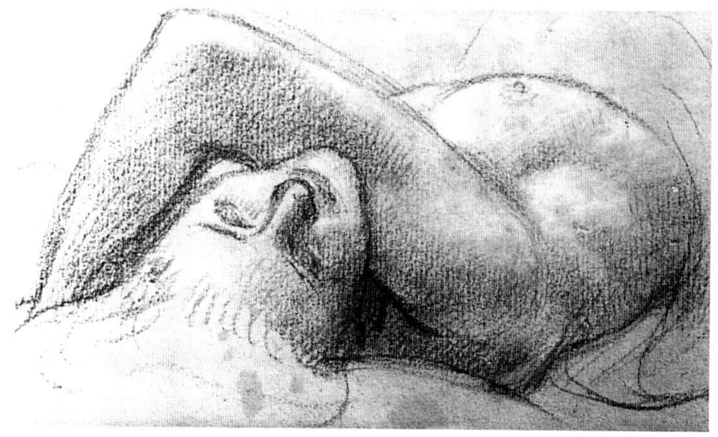

77

Study for 'Young Women by the Sea'

ca. 1879

Black chalk heightened with white chalk on gray blue paper, 117 x 210 mm
Musée des Beaux-Arts, Lyons (Inv. B607.6)

Provenance Bequest of artist's heirs to the city of Lyons (1898).

78

79

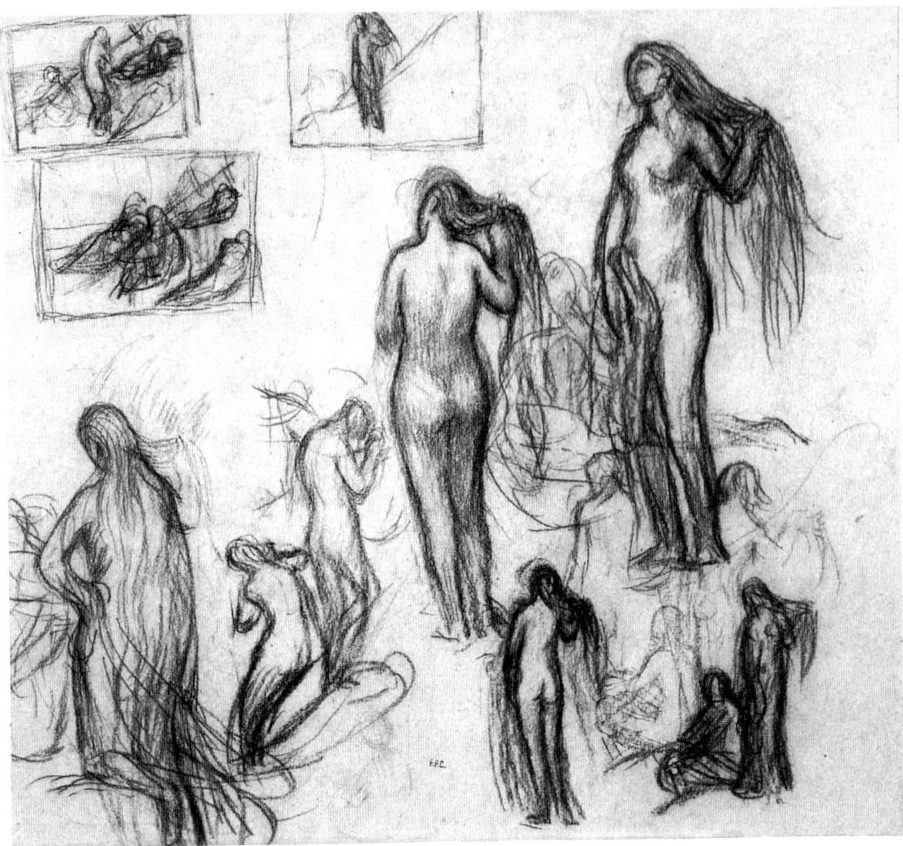

There are a number of variant drawings of this boldly foreshortened, sensuous figure, posed lying on her back with her arm bent to frame her head.[1] In several there are only the slightest of changes. Something of the intellectual and imaginative elasticity with which Puvis conceptualized a work may be gathered from these related drawings, as well as the patient professional process of working and reworking a solution to a pictorial problem, as the artist modified and adjusted his description of head, arms, hands and breast. This pose was not included in the final composition, in which all three figures, as individual as they are and as stiffly posed as they may be, are oriented to the two-dimensional surface and do not pierce that surface as this figure so emphatically does. This pose is included at the right of at least two early cursory sketches for the composition.[2] There, as in the paintings, the figures are placed to face in different directions.

1 Among them: *Drawing related to 'Young Women by the Sea'*, ca. 1879, charcoal and gouache on blue gray paper, 220 x 115 mm, Musée des Beaux-Arts, Lyons (Inv. B 607.69); *Study of a Woman Lying Down*, medium and dimensions not available, Beauvais, Musée départemental de l'Oise; *Study for 'Young Women by the Sea'*, stamp l.l.: black chalk on tracing paper, squared, 348 x 525 mm (private collection).

2 *Study for 'Young Women by the Sea'*, stamp l.l., black charcoal and white chalk, 133 x 172 mm (private collection); *Study for 'Jeunes filles au bord de la mer'*, black chalk on blue paper, 233 x 187 mm, Stiftung Oskar Reinhart, Winterthur (Inv. 2358).

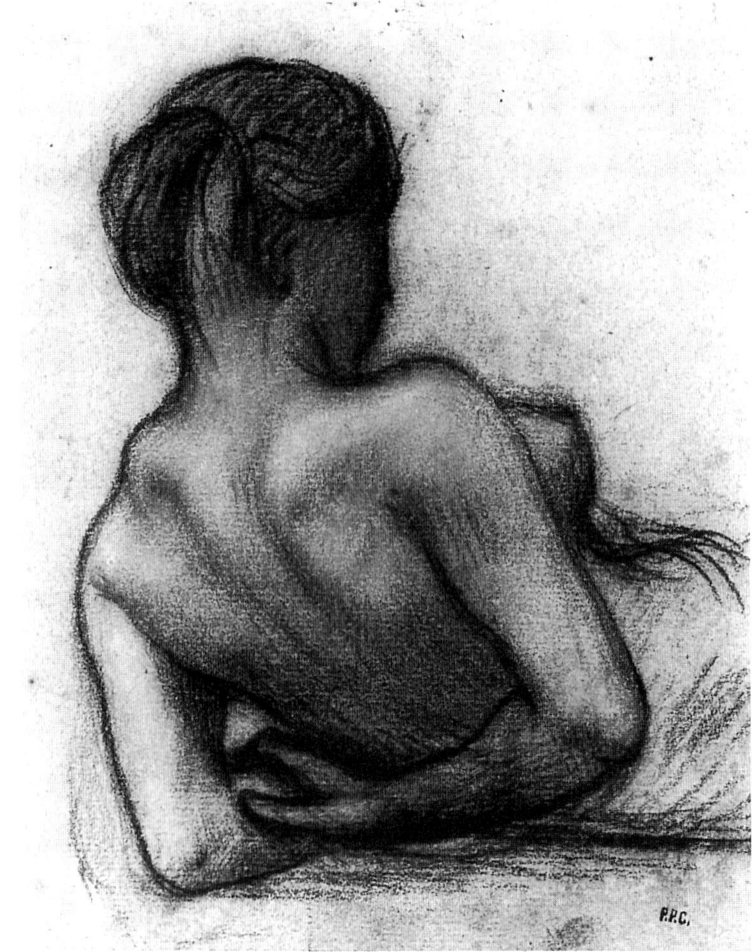

78

Study for 'Young Women by the Sea'
ca. 1879

Stamp towards l. center
Charcoal on blue paper, 345 x 384 mm
Private collection

Provenance M. Brye de Vertamy, Paris.

In this early *croquis* for *Young Women by the Sea* (cat. 76, fig. 6), the artist played with poses and ideas. Sketched from different angles is a standing nude gathering up her hair and slightly wringing it. Finally with her back to the viewer, she approximates the stance of the central figure in *Young Women by the Sea*.

At the top left this sheet is squared off into three compositional studies of one to four figures against a diagonal. One figure, repeated on both sides of these marked areas, seated with her back rounded and her arms around her legs, would be used not in *Young Women by the Sea*, but in *Pleasant Land*, of 1882 (see cat. 86).

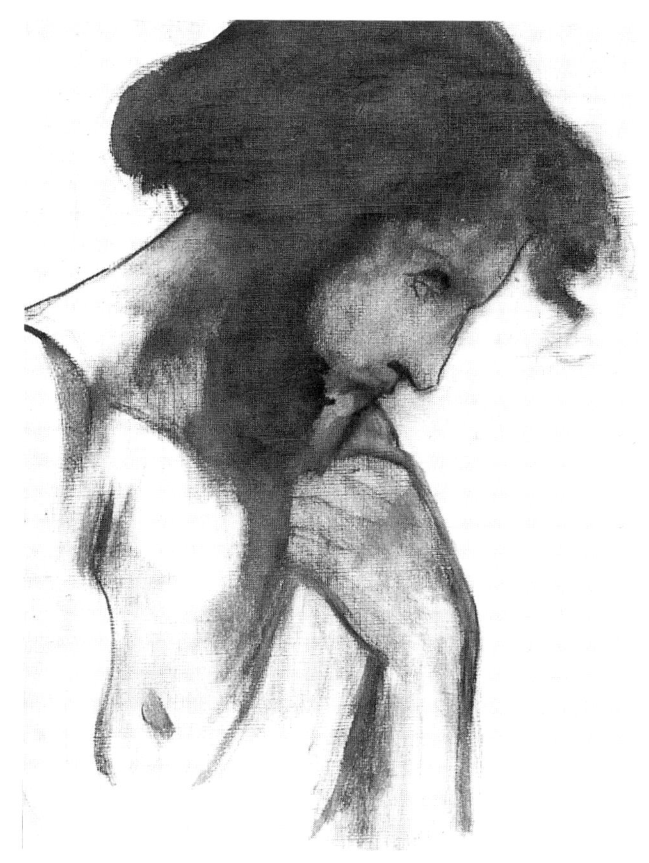

79

Study for 'Young Women by the Sea'
ca. 1879

Stamp l.r.
Black and brown chalk on light greenish paper, 225 x 177 mm
Private collection

Provenance Artist's heirs and by descent.

In the boldly conceived figure to the right of *Young Women by the Sea* (cat. 76, fig.6) for which this is a study, Puvis ventured an unusual and inherently awkward, twisting pose. He made the pose more singular yet by reconfiguring the torso so that the breast of the figure might be included – Ingres might also have done such a thing. Only the head and upper body of the figure, propped up on her elbows, are shown.

The lovely figure is abruptly cut off by the edge of the sheet in a composition similar to what one might expect in the works which Puvis's younger contemporary Degas made about the same time. The strong contours are very much felt out and emphasized, a technique also more generally associated with Degas, at about this same time and later.

80

Study for the Head of 'The Prodigal Son' ca. 1879-83

Oil [sepia?] and washes on canvas, 46 x 41 cm
Private collection

Provenance Artist's heirs and by descent.

Beginning in 1879 Puvis de Chavannes executed several versions of the biblical parable of *The Prodigal Son*. All picture the single figure seated in profile, alone in a bleak landscape, the pigs he tends nearby. The isolated, meditative figure with his hands crossed in front of him is a spiritual brother to *The Poor Fisherman* (fig. 23) of these years. In a version of *The Prodigal Son* in a vertical format that was exhibited at the Salon of 1879 (fig. 7),[1] the ragged figure sits erect on a log. In compositional daring this canvas is similar to *Young Women by the Sea* of the same year (cat. 76, fig. 6), for the figure is literally marginalized, placed to the right of the panel and turned to the right to gaze out beyond its perimeter.

This study of a man's bearded and bowed head and clasped hands, basically a shaded outline drawing on canvas, displays the essential features of the figure in the commanding horizontal variant of *The Prodigal Son* (106 x 147 cm, National Gallery of Art, Washington, D.C.).

There, in a still more barren landscape, the lone, life-size figure is seated on the ground, his head inclined in a posture of dejection. Barer, more austere and bolder still in its simplicity than the Bührle Collection composition (fig. 7), this *Prodigal Son* is more summarily painted with lighter tones and must postdate that one. The development of the composition may be followed in a number of drawings.[2]

1 Another version: *Study for 'The Prodigal Son'* ca. 1879, oil and pencil on canvas, 79.5 x 59.5 cm (private collection).

2 *Nude Male, Seated on the Ground*, Musée du Petit Palais, Paris (Inv. PPD 278[a]; MCB 80); *The Prodigal Son*, pastel, 31 x 40 cm, Whitworth Art Gallery, Manchester; *Study for 'The Prodigal Son'* (private collection), 1976-77 Paris/Ottawa, no. 132.

81

The Poor Fisherman / *Le pauvre pêcheur*

ca. 1887-92

Signed l.r.: P. Puvis de Chavannes
Oil on canvas, 105.8 x 68.6 cm
National Museum of Western Art, Tokyo,
Matsukata Collection (Inv. P 1959 - 175)

Provenance Durand-Ruel, Paris (1892-93); M. Boivin, Paris (1899); M. Beurdeley [? noted by Henri Puvis de Chavannes]; M. Soulange-Bodin; Durand-Ruel, Paris (1920); New York (1921); Mr. Saburo Matsukata; confiscated by the French Government (1944); returned to Japan (1959).

Selected Exhibitions 1899 Paris (Durand-Ruel), no. 16.

Selected References Durand-Ruel Archives (New York), no. 12095; *La Collection Matsukata*, ed. by Asahi Shinbumi (Tokyo, 1955), repr. pl. 7; *Mizue* [special issue] (July 1959); *Catalogue of Paintings, National Museum of Western Art* (Tokyo, 1979), pp. 175-176, no. 227; *Masterpieces, National Museum of Western Art* (Tokyo, 1989), p. 93, no. 87.

The Poor Fisherman (fig. 23) is the painting that was chosen to represent Puvis de Chavannes's work in the French national collections during his lifetime. Curiously enigmatic and compelling, it may be his best known independent work (see pp. 45-53). Preliminary drawings and studies lead to the 1881 version of the composition (see cat. 82-84), presented at the Salon of that year. This variant canvas apparently dates from after that one and was probably painted as a response to the interest aroused by that work.

This later version of *The Poor Fisherman* includes only two figures, the fisherman and the child, now pictured as lying sleeping in the boat and configured not in an angular, flattened fashion, but in a more traditional manner (see cat. 84), emblematic of the differences in signification between the two variants. The composition has been changed from the horizontal of the 1881 version, in which a broad expanse of the bare landscape and estuary are included, with a vista which underscores the emptiness of the setting, to a vertical composition in which the visual field is laterally limited and that barrenness is not quite so strongly enunciated. In the former composition, the isolation of the figures from one another underpins the iconography: two figures, a woman and child, are on the shore and separated from the fisherman, who, in turn, is isolated from them. The separation of the individual figures in that canvas resonates with their solitude in a larger and therefore seemingly starker landscape setting. Now the focus is concentrated on the central figure, who is no longer alone, but accompanied by the child in a work that suggests a more conventional narrative and a narrower range of interpretive readings than the 1881 composition. The presence of the child, for example, deflects the kind of religious reading that the 1881 painting often received (see pp. 48-49). This variant may be somewhat more comfortably associated with a traditional genre painting narrative. Structural changes have accompanied the change in format: the visual field has narrowed at both sides, with the second spit of land brought in so that the water zigzags are more pronounced in shape, while both the top and bottom of the painting have been slightly extended. At the top, more sky is visible, at the bottom, more water, with a larger portion of the boat reflected and the wonderful geometries of which it is comprised somewhat more important. Rather than transmitting a sense of isolation, the vertically augmented spaces subtly suggest an openness and perhaps even a sense of possibility.

In the later 1880s, Puvis executed a number of reprises of earlier paintings. Several of these suggest greater sensitivity to potential buyers. This version of *The Poor Fisherman*, which came to be acquired by the discerning collector Emile Boivin, may have been executed with him in mind or even at his instigation. Boivin was the 'amateur' mentioned in Puvis's letter of 4 December 1887 (see p. 46), who owned several works by Puvis, including *Young Women by the Sea* (fig. 6), and who in fact had already purchased Puvis's *The Poor Fisherman* of 1881 when in late 1887 it was all but requisitioned by the national collection (see pp. 40-41 and 46). This canvas was doubtless meant to console him for his loss.

Interestingly, this variant with its pillar-like format is now in an Asian collection in which that structure might have particular appeal, and in turn is one more reminder of Oriental influences on French nineteenth-century painting.

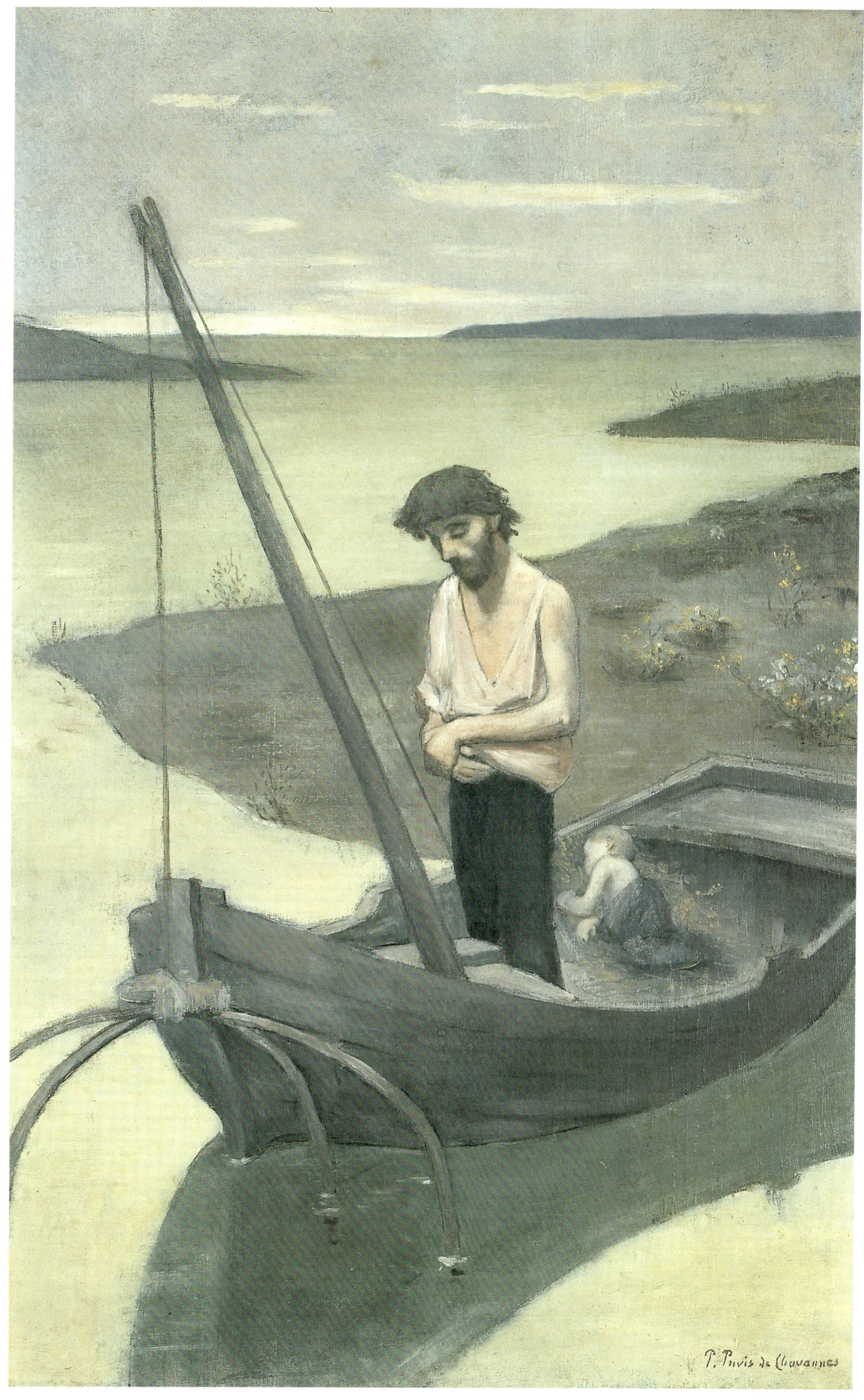
P. Puvis de Chavannes

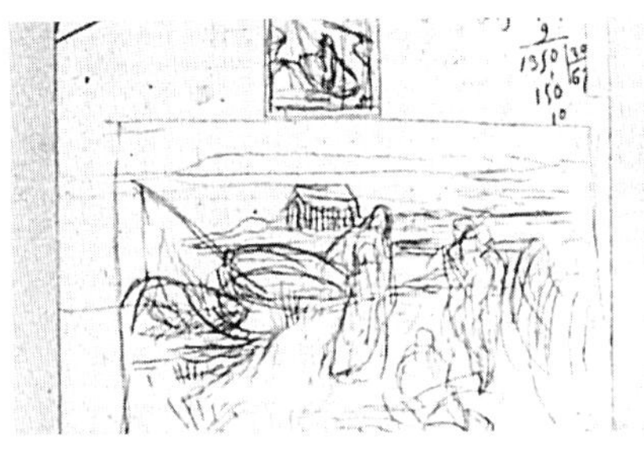
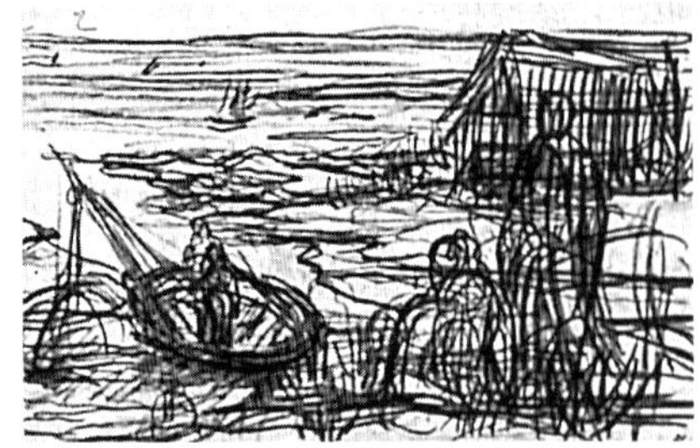
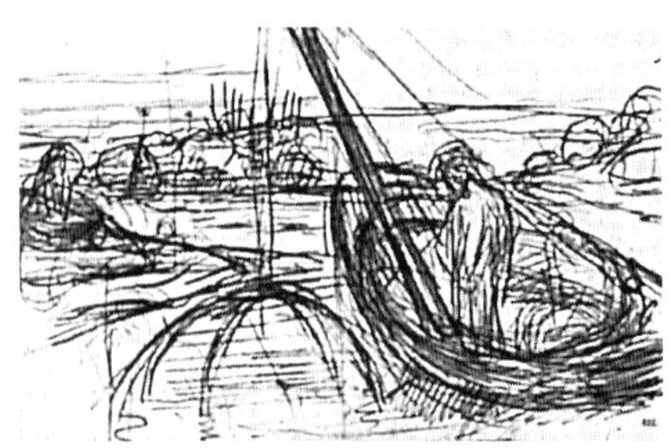
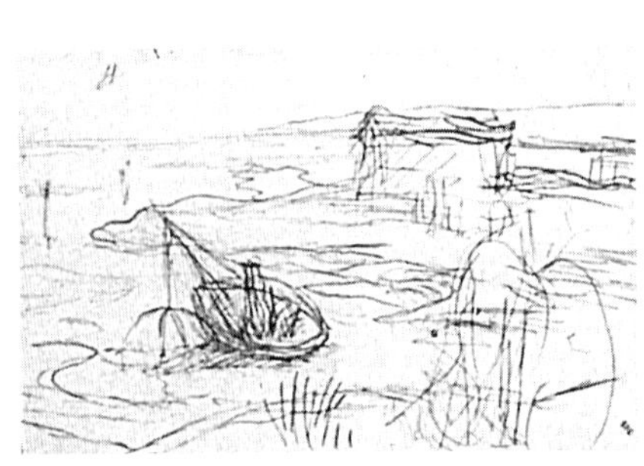
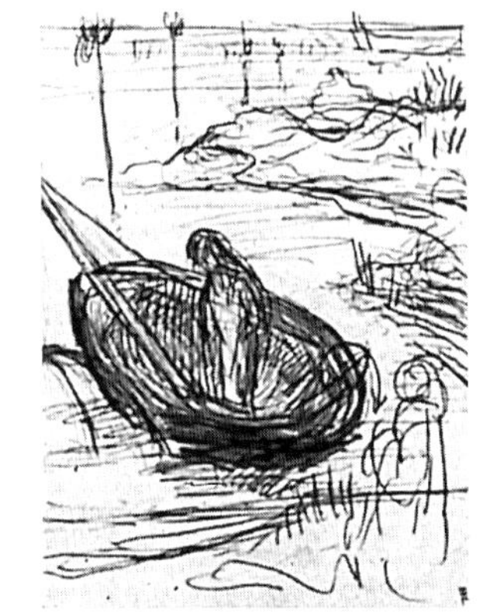
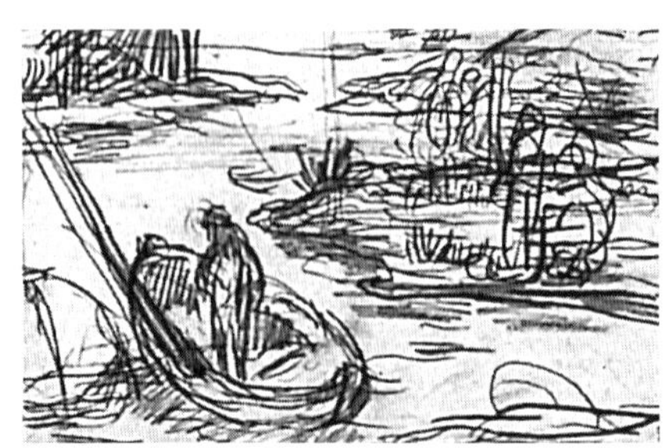

82

Six Studies for 'The Poor Fisherman'

ca. 1879

Each stamp l.r.
Black pencil on paper, l. to r.: top row: 203 x 254 mm; 194 x 305 mm; 194 x 312 mm; bottom row: 198 x 305 mm; 212 x 210 mm; 198 x 305 mm (sight)
Private collection

Provenance Artist's heirs and by descent.
Selected Exhibitions 1896 Paris (Société Nationale des Beaux-Arts), [?]; 1976-77 Paris/Ottawa, no. 143.

The evolution of *The Poor Fisherman* may be followed in these six sketches. The definitive painting (fig. 23) was drastically different from these preliminary drawings and several other early painted sketches (see cat. 83),[1] an extended series that marks an unusual progression in the artist's pictorial thinking. Although in planning monumental painting, Puvis shifted elements and edited considerably, components were never changed with greater consequences for the meaning of the finished work. The isolated fisherman does not seem in question here. Although his position is fixed and that of the boat also (which would be turned in the painting so that he would no longer face towards its side), the landscape configuration, the height of the horizon, the relative importance and size of the figures are explored. The sequence of development most likely reads from the upper left to lower left, then center top to bottom, and finally upper to lower right. In the first four sketches, figures are located in the foreground of the composition, on the near shore; and in the first three of these, there is a shelter in the background. The fisherman gradually gains in importance. An oil study (cat. 83) would seem to have been executed about the same time as the sketch in the center of the upper row, the boat hull substituting for the house.

By 1879 the composition as we know it was established: a painted sketch is so dated.[2] Two years later Puvis presented his finished *The Poor Fisherman* at the Salon.

1 Several small painted *croquis* from early in the formulation of the motif feature the figure of the girl on the near shore: *Preparatory Sketch for 'The Poor Fisherman'*, signed and inscribed l. r: P. Puvis de Chavannes/ Première idée pour le le [sic] pauvre pêcheur, oil and solvent with black pencil on beige paper, 280 x 226 mm, Musée du Louvre, Paris (Inv. RF 15966); and *Sketch for 'The Poor Fisherman'*, oil on wood panel, 16.5 x 23.7 cm (private collection); see 1976-77 Paris/Ottawa, nos. 141-142.

2 *The Poor Fisherman*, signed and dated l.r.: P. Puvis de Ch 79, oil on canvas, 65.5 x 91.3 cm, Pushkin Museum, Moscow.

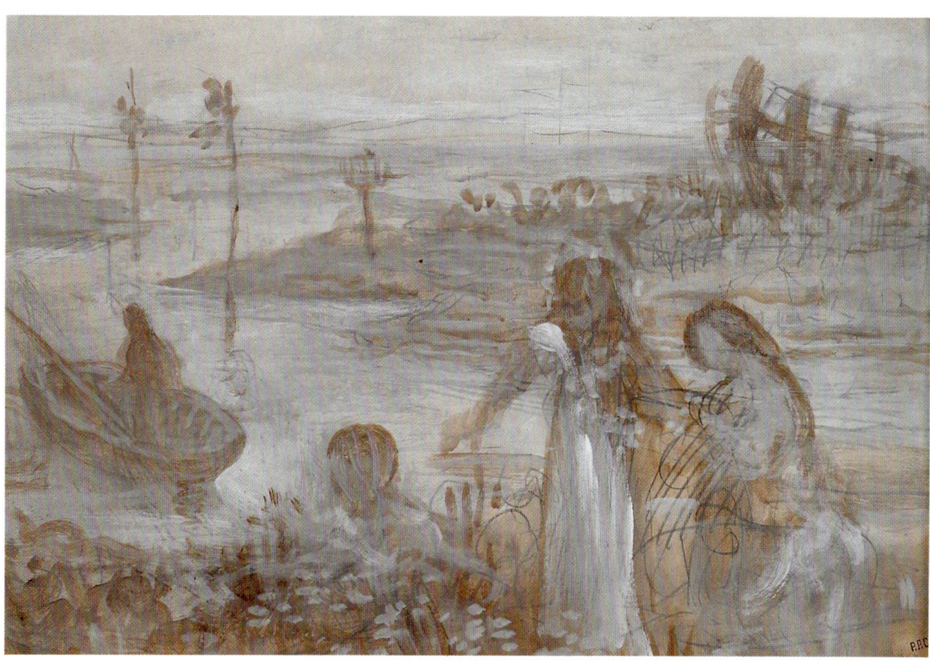

83

Sketch for 'The Poor Fisherman' / *Esquisse pour 'Le pauvre pêcheur'*

ca. 1878-79

Stamp l.r.
Thinned oil [sepia?], gouache and black pencil on paper, 230 x 330 mm
Private collection

Provenance Artist's heirs and by descent.
Selected Exhibitions 1976-77 Paris/Ottawa, no. 140.

The origins of *The Poor Fisherman* (fig. 23) are anchored in this limpid scene of figures on the bank of an estuary. The fisherman is only marginal here, placed to the side and in the middle distance. In a theme all but eclipsed in the completed work, it is women gathering flowers within the sparsest of surroundings who are prominent in the foreground. In this loosely sketched work on paper, two women are depicted quite clearly while two other figures are half visible and barely discernible. A few slim trees punctuate the landscape and the frame of a boat is on the far shore. In an earlier painting of fisherfolk, *The Fisherman's Family* of 1875 (see fig. 24), the battered remains of a boat indicate the precariousness of the life of fishermen. The boat ribs in this work seem to indicate not the decay but the construction of a vessel, perhaps the hopeful sign of a large seaworthy craft. Puvis's sketch of a similar shell of a boat would be reproduced in the special Puvis-issue of *La Plume* published in 1895.

84

Sleeping Child, Study for the Baby in 'The Poor Fisherman' ca. 1879

Charcoal heightened with white, squared; on light brown striated paper, 120 x 116 mm
Musée de Grenoble (Inv. MG 1220 [1])

Provenance Bequest of artist's heirs to the city of Grenoble (1898); entered museum collection 1899.

The sleeping child was not included in any of the earliest drawings and small oil sketches for *The Poor Fisherman*. The first appearance of the child was in the painted study dated 1879, in which he lay on a white cloth in a flowery field in the middle distance, his arm bent and a red ball (a touch of color) in his hand (Pushkin Museum, Moscow). In the definitive work (fig. 23), the child lies outstretched on a reddish cloth in which he is half-wrapped, his arm relaxed and slightly bent.

Puvis's studies indicate a conscientious effort to position the child in such a way as to be read both in three and two dimensions: within a perspectival system that gives the illusion of an object lying back in space and also as a completely legible figuration on the pictorial surface.[1] Although this mission is inherently impossible, its pursuit, as we know from looking at Cézanne, can produce pictures in which a splendid struggle is paramount, which adds vitality and interest to the contested object – not a little because of the awkwardness and pictorial tension inherent in its achievement.

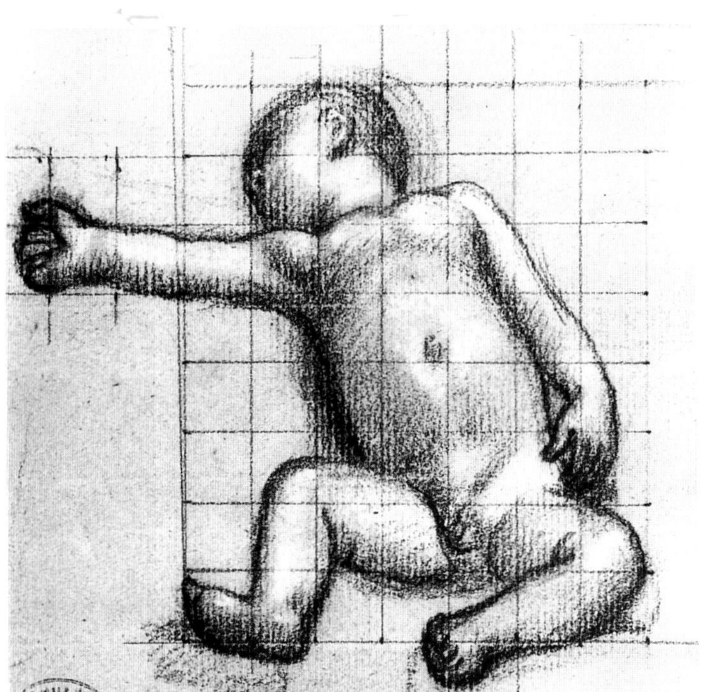

This drawing would have been executed before a closely related study of the nude baby[2] and the differences are instructive: most probably drawn from life, the baby here has been sensitively modeled and heightened with white to indicate the swelling of his belly and a soft plumpness. The child grasps a ball, his right arm bent in the Louvre drawing as in the Pushkin study. In the Louvre drawing forms are consolidated and, more subtly, the head that is turned and dropped back is lightly propped up as it is in the final, painted version.

The radical difference in conception of the Tokyo variant of *The Poor Fisherman* (cat. 81) may be gauged by comparing the two versions of the sleeping child. In the Tokyo canvas, not only does the infant share the boat with the fisherman, thus altering the profound sense of the fisherman's lonely isolation so significant in the definitive painting, but it is posed according to naturalistic convention, turned on its side, its covered lower body, however, without volume. A study for that child makes clear how much more conventional an image it is.[3]

1 *Study for Sleeping Baby in 'The Poor Fisherman'* ca. 1881, stamp b. c., both upper corners cut off, black crayon on off-white paper, 245 x 320 mm (private collection).

2 *Study for Sleeping Nude Child in 'The Poor Fisherman'* 1881, black pencil on tracing paper prepared with yellow ground laid down; squared for transfer, 276 x 228 mm, Musée du Louvre, Paris (Inv. RF 15968); see 1976-77 Paris/Ottawa, no. 147.

3 *Sleeping Child, Left Profile* ca. 1881, black chalk with white highlights on beige paper, 258 x 221 mm, Musée du Petit Palais, Paris (Inv. PPD 291[2]; MCB 83), see Boucher (1979), no. 83.

85

The Poor Fisherman / *Le pauvre pêcheur* 1897

Signed on stone: P. Puvis de Chavannes
Transfer lithograph printed in mauve on paper with watermark MBM, 500 x 650 mm (sheet); 413 x 535 mm (image)
Private collection

Selected References [Ambroise Vollard, ed.] *l'Album des peintres-graveurs* (Paris, 1897); *L'Estampe et l'affiche* (Paris, 1898), II, 19; Delteil (1925), pp. 309-310; Una E. Johnson, *Ambroise Vollard editeur 1867-1939. An Appreciation and Catalogue* (New York, 1944), no. 131, p. 116; cf. rev. ed. Johnson (1977), no. 98; 1976-77 Paris/Ottawa, no. 139; Druick (1977), 30-34.

In 1897, a time of great interest in colored lithography, posters and prints, the entrepreneurial art dealer Ambroise Vollard published his second of two portfolios of lithographs, *L'Album d'estampes originales de la galerie Vollard*.[1] He introduced this series, devoted to original prints after the best known works of well-known artists, with an exhibition at his gallery in December of that year. Puvis participated with this lithograph after *The Poor Fisherman*. Puvis's translation of his painted image into a graphic interpretation is fascinating. The forms are described with a sharp contour line, the geometries and parallelisms of these outlines crisply delineated. The shaded portions are drawn in with parallel hatchings that have little to do with volumetric forms, emphasizing that, if not by 1881 by the later 1890s, illusionistic imagery was of no particular interest to him, though its translation into two dimensions was. Puvis retained the understated quality of his painting by printing his lithograph in only one color. Of the 100 impressions, most were printed in mauve ink, a few in black. The papers vary: many are on white paper, a few on pale blue paper. The combination of mauve ink and light blue paper particularly, as has been pointed out, enhances the melancholy of the imagery and anticipates Picasso's Blue Period.[2]

Puvis had long been interested in printmaking. At the beginning of his career he was to have published etchings with Alfred Cadart.[3] He encouraged several artist printmakers, notably Auguste Lauzet (1855-1898) to make prints after his works.[4] He produced one very fine lithograph in mid-career (cat. 55), and in 1893 he made another relatively freely interpreted transfer lithograph in brown ink after his *Normandy* (cat. 137) for *L'Estampe originale*.[5]

85

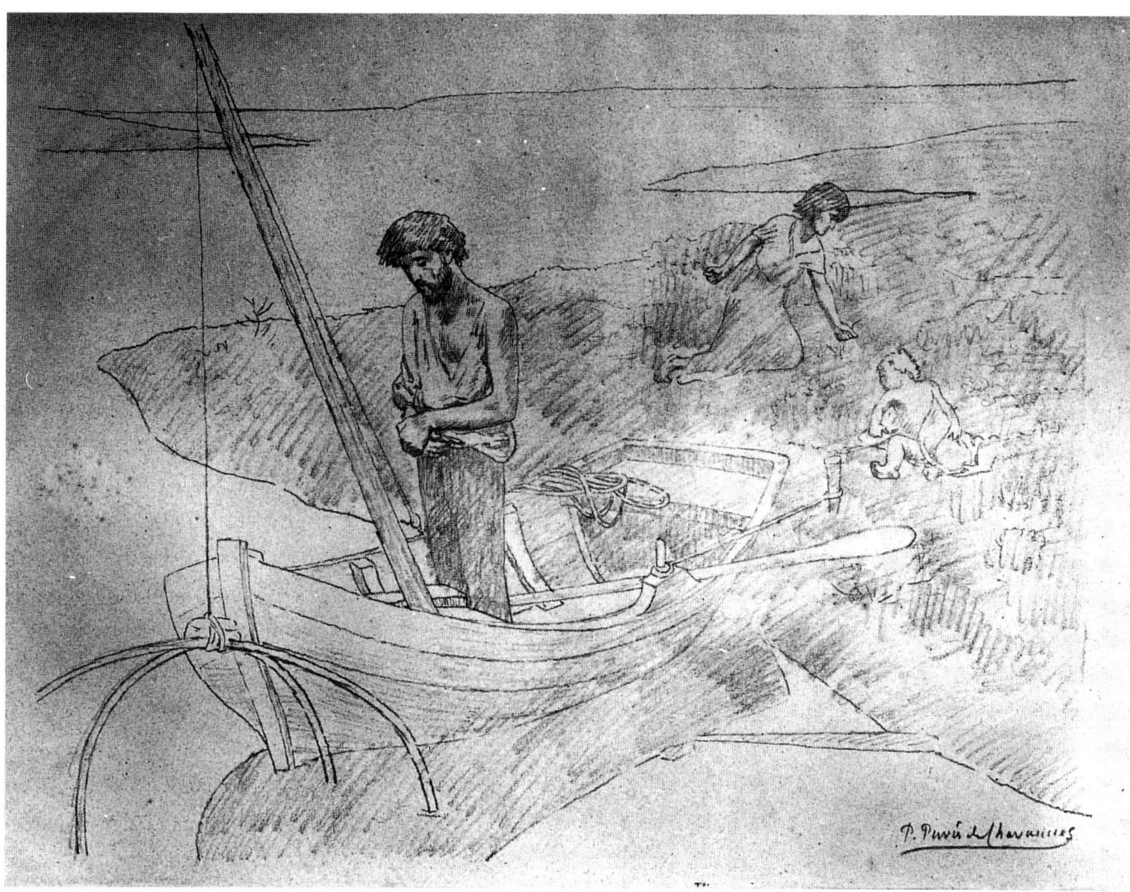

1 *Les peintres graveurs* dated from 1896 (in Johnson [1944, ref. above] *The Poor Fisherman* is listed in that portfolio, though dated 1897; this is corrected in Johnson [1977])..

2 The edition was of 100 impressions. Several impressions were printed in black; these are not to be confused with the 'paniconographie' of 1881 published in the *Catalogue illustré du Salon contenant ... reproductions d'après les originaux des artistes* (Paris, 1881), p. 453, repr. in Druick (1977), fig. 6.

3 In 1862 he was a founding member of the Société des Aquafortistes, which sought to popularize and market prints. See Druick (1977), 27-35.

4 Of which an important collection is at the Victoria and Albert Museum, London.

5 Douglas Druick in 1976-77 Paris/Ottawa, no. 198.On Puvis's prints, see also cat. 55.

86

Pleasant Land / *Doux Pays* (reduced version) ca. 1882

Signed l.l.: P. Puvis de Chavannes
Oil on canvas, 28.8 x 51 cm; with frame: 42 x 62 cm
Yale University Art Gallery, New Haven, Mary Gertrude Abbey Fund (Inv. 1958.64)

Provenance Albert Wolff, Paris (1887); Henri Vever, Paris; Paul Baudoüin, Paris; Paris, Hôtel Drouot, 'Vente Baudoüin' (10 May 1948), no. 34; sold by Kaganovitch, Paris to Dr. Walter Feilchenfeldt, Zurich (1951); acquired by the museum (1958).

Selected Exhibitions 1887 Paris (Durand-Ruel), no. 83; 1975 Toronto, no. 23; 1976-77 Paris/Ottawa, no. 155.

Selected References On the large version: Vachon [1900], p. 203; Michel and Laran (1911), pp 77-78; Schapiro (1958), 22-24, 44-45, 52; Herbert (1959), 22-29; Vincent Ducourau, *Le Musée Bonnat à Bayonne* (Paris, 1988), pp. 104, 114-115. On this painting: Françoise Forster-Hahn, *French and School of Paris Paintings in the Yale University Art Gallery* (New Haven and London, 1968), pp. 22-23 (with additional bibliography); 1976-77 Paris/Ottawa, pp. 172-173; Paul Hayes Tucker, *Monet in the '90s: The Series Paintings* (New Haven and London, 1989), pp. 216-217, fig. 94.

Pleasant Land or perhaps *Sweet Land* – the French 'doux' not completely translated by either – epitomizes the splendid Arcadian vision with which Puvis de Chavannes is especially associated. A Utopia of classicizing figures carefully placed in a landscape, this version is considerably smaller

86

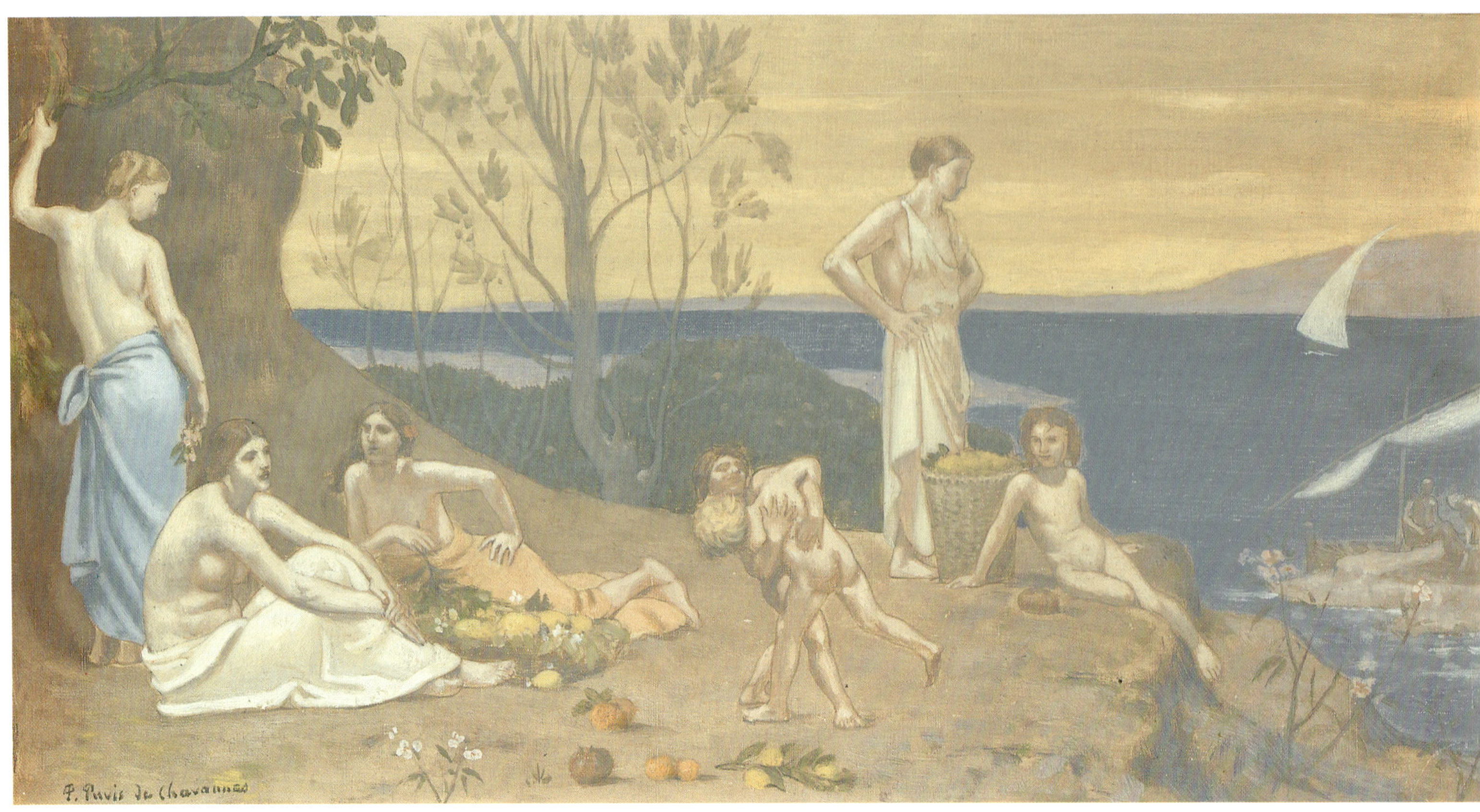

than the canvas which was exhibited at the Salon of 1882[1] and exchanged for his full-length, aristocratic portrait by Léon Bonnat (private collection): it must be a souvenir painted afterwards.[2] Despite a close approximation of the large composition, the sense of the whole has changed from an expansive paradisal universe of grand design and stately rhythms, with unencumbered stretches of flat color and significant visual impact, to a miniaturized world notable for its tiny perfections, a view for the delectation of a single person.

Structure and formal considerations are paramount. They yield the sense of calm and order, logic and perfectibility that is so crucial to Puvis's achievement. Commentators, acknowledging this, have posited various mathematical and geometrical theories as its governing principle, the Golden Section among them.[3] With defined rhythms and linear arabesques controlling the outlined, flattened imagery, and with figure and landscape elements mutually complementary in shape and cadence, a symbiotic balance is established. Puvis transformed the natural into the distinctive and repeated motifs thus formed to create legible patterns. Austere and supremely readable, the shape of a single tree stands poetically – like parsimonious synecdoche – for vegetation, or a sail (a curved repetition of the backs of the figures at left) for navigation. Preparatory drawings (private collections) reveal the artist's preoccupation with defining contours and interrelationships among figures as they parallel each other, echo and continue each other's forms. While rounded and squared off figures are peculiarly awkward individually, together they are right and compelling. The spaces at which these self-contained figures are set reinforces a sense of dreamy indolence and revery, lack of concert and monumental stasis. Conflict is reduced to a tiny duo of wrestling boys poised at the composition's center. This motif, based on that of antique reliefs[4] was, according to family anecdote, posed for by Puvis's uncles Paul and Pierre.[5] The homely image was taken up again in several instances by Gauguin.[6]

As in *Young Women by the Sea*, with which *Pleasant Land* shares thematic and compositional devices, the mood and imagery are enhanced by stylistic distancing. The golden skies, for one, doubtless derive from the gold background of Byzantine art, the kind of ornamental background Puvis had used for his Panthéon friezes (see cat. 75), and they serve as there to remove imagery from a sense of actuality. To increase their special decorative aspect, Puvis took care to bracket both versions of *Pleasant Land*, and the large version of *Young Women by the Sea*,[7] with specially painted ornamental frames.

The large version of *Pleasant Land*, exhibited at the Salon of 1882, made Van Gogh think of Eden, a Lesbos peopled with women.[8] Other young painters took note of *Pleasant Land* in their work, and in our century, *Pleasant Land* has often been approached as a key to the under-

87 standing of the pictorial innovations of a Seurat or a Matisse.[9] Seurat imitated the equilibrated composition to serene aesthetic effect in his 1883-84 *Bathing Place, Asnières* (National Gallery, London), with patterned and controlled figures and landscape – even to similar structures and a similarly placed sailboat. A search for the sources for Matisse's 1904-05 *Luxe, calme et volupté* (see cat. 150), not only as to overall idyllic mood, but to specific figures and topography, also leads to *Pleasant Land*. Whereas Picasso's three *Bathers* (cat. 152) are more clearly related to Puvis's *Young Women by the Sea*, with their now forward, now backward facing poses, they are sharply set off against a band of sea and sky, a few foreground rocks and the single sharp, white, curved form of a sailboat, in a manner that indicates a close look at *Pleasant Land*.

Francis Auburtin's *'Pleasant Land' after Puvis de Chavannes* is one of the most sensitive direct copies.[10] Judging from the number of deliberate imitations and pastiches of various sections, *Pleasant Land* must be one of Puvis's most admired compositions.[11]

1 That version, 230 x 430 cm, decorated a stairway at Bonnat's home on the rue Bassano, was for a time at the entrance to his atelier and is today in the museum that bears his name and his collection in his hometown, the Musée Bonnat in Bayonne.

2 It was for a time in the collection of the critic Albert Wolff, one of Puvis's greatest early supporters but later a detractor who scathingly reviewed *The Poor Fisherman*.

3 Louis Hautecoeur, *Les Beaux-Arts en France, passé et avenir* (Paris, 1948), p. 73, *inter alia*.

4 A similar pair in Degas's *Young Spartans Exercising* (Art Institute of Chicago); see Devin Burnell, 'Degas and his "Young Spartans Exercising",' *Museum Studies*, 4 (1969), 55, and Theodore Reff, 'New Light on Degas' Copies,' *Burlington Magazine*, XCVI (June 1964), 257.

5 An anecdote related by the late Henri Puvis de Chavannes.

6 *Children Wrestling* 1888, Josefowitz Collection; in addition see Gauguin's letter of 24 or 25 July 1888 to Vincent van Gogh, with a sketch for *Children Wrestling*, Van Gogh Museum (Vincent van Gogh Foundation), Amsterdam.

7 Since lost or destroyed; when it was presented at the 1879 Salon the painting was called 'un panneau décoratif,' and the border must have been one component contributing to this special designation. See ill. p. 10.

8 Van Gogh (1958) III, no. 539, p. 43.

9 On the relationship of Seurat to Puvis, see: John Rewald, *Georges Seurat* (Paris, 1948), p. 46; Schapiro (1958), 22-24, 44-45, 52; Herbert (1959), 22-29; 1975 Toronto, pp. 17-19, 101-104. See also p. 51 in this book.

10 Ca. 1892, oil on paper, laid down on canvas, and twice as large as the Yale version: 50.5 x 99 cm (private collection); repr. in Briend [1991], fig. 3, p. 46.

11 See version attributed to Puvis of approximately the same dimensions as the Yale canvas: oil and pencil on canvas, 26 x 48 cm; formerly British Rail Pension Fund; to have been auctioned London, Sotheby's (19 June 1990), no. 62, repr. 119.

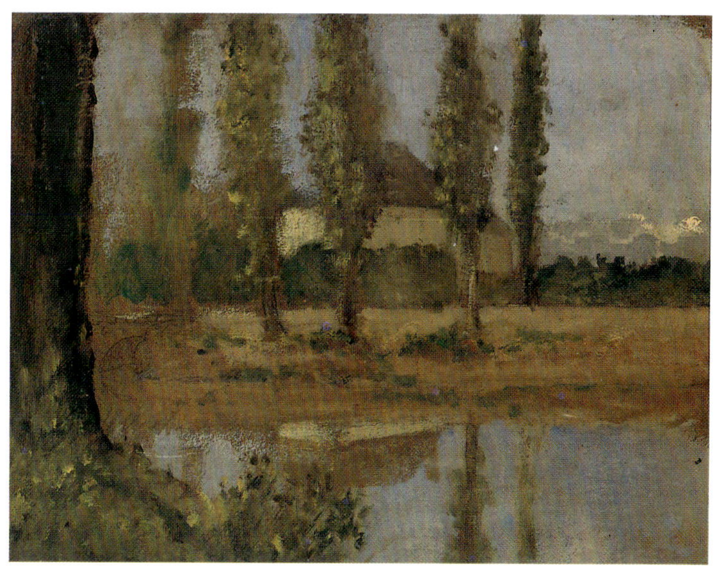

87

Pool of Water and Poplars / *Etang et peupliers* ca. 1875-83

Oil on cardboard, 33.5 x 44 cm

Private collection

Provenance Artist's heirs and by descent.

Selected Exhibitions 1976-77 Paris/Ottawa, no. 89.

Puvis painted few independent landscapes. In his memoir of the artist, his protegé Paul Baudoüin maintained that Puvis executed only three, this one not among them.[1] Yet landscapes play a crucial role in the murals, localizing setting, structuring compositions and, from the late 1860s, furthering a decorative aesthetic. Puvis claimed to have an excellent memory for them, insisting, however, that he had never made a direct study after nature except for a small 'rough draft of a rough draft' ('ébauche d'ébauche').[2] He must have discounted his cahier sketches, occasional drawings and watercolors because he wanted his role understood: it was he who made something durable and constant of nature in a manner we associate with a classical landscape painter, a Corot or a Cézanne. Though the row of trees, light palette and opaque colors of this landscape might remind us of Impressionist canvases, his ways were not theirs. Their ideal rested on a contradiction: 'Nature contains everything, but in a confused way. One must prune away everything momentarily inexpressive....'[3] What he looked for was the permanent character of objects, the body under 'the garment with changing reflections.'[4] 'I have never done a study after nature for my landscapes. I look a good deal, I record, and then it all is a matter of logic. When one knows nature, its habits, the configuration of a poplar, one never forgets its figurative anatomy.'[5]

He was opposed to the landscapes that the Romantics had embraced: grandiose vistas and dramatic topographies, the awe-inspiring and sublime. Certain landscapes were oppressive, he declared: those that did not preserve the feeling of man's power over creation. As for himself, he preferred doing a great deal with little to pursuing beauties not made to man's scale.[6]

The landscape has been associated with that of the Bresse region near Cuiseaux (see cat. 108) and Mervans that Puvis often visited and in which he shared property with his sister and brother-in-law Jordan. Yet the flat ground and band of water, relatively light, opaque colors and a structure that resembles a low-lying, rounded thatched hut are similar to those of the 1882 *Ludus pro Patria* (ill. pp. 192-193), its landscape setting purportedly specific to Picardy. The landscape is oriented in bands parallel to the picture plane, reinforcing a calm planarity, and the trees are set out in regular rhythms, as one might expect from Puvis. When it was previously exhibited, this landscape was dated to 1860-70 because its handling was deemed 'still Realist,'[7] although realism never had an important place in Puvis's vision. A later date would be more appropriate.

Charles Ricketts, among the earliest critics to pay tribute to Puvis's landscapes, tellingly used terms from neoclassical architecture: 'The most original designer of landscape since Rembrandt is Puvis de Chavannes. With him the character of the ground, the drawing of the horizon, have varied more than with any other painter ... with Puvis the distant wand-like trees of Millet have become the colonnades of tree-trunks which we find in the north of France; his trees are recognizable as poplar, willow or sycamore, etc., the leaves [form] ... a strange pattern against the sky, or else sober masses of varying contour supported by varying branch forms; the green trunks have become grey, green or white, and beyond extend horizons ... that have their hour, like the evening hush of the turquoise sky in *Le Repos*, the dry light of morning in *Ludus pro patria*, the weight of noon in *La Vision Antique* or the mauve of a summer night over the stubble fields in *Le Sommeil*.'[8]

1 Baudoüin (1935), 304.
2 Larroumet (1895), *Etudes de Littérature et d'Art*, pp. 287-288.
3 'La Nature contient tout, mais d'une manière confuse. Il faut élaguer en elle tout ce qui est momentanément inexpressif....' Guigou (1898), pp. 272-273.
4 'la robe aux reflets changeants,' D. (1898).
5 'Je n'ai jamais fait ... une etude sur nature pour mes paysages. Je regarde beaucoup, j'enregistre, et puis tout cela est une affaire de logique. Quand on connait la logique d'un être, on sait comment il doit se comporter de toute façon; quand on connait la nature, des habitudes, la conformation d'un peuplier, on n'oublie jamais son anatomie figurée.' Bénédite (1898) *Art et Décoration*, 151; repeated in Bénédite (1922), p. 70.
6 La Farge (1900), 674; a similar statement in Vachon [1900], p. 38.
7 1976-77 Paris/Ottawa, no. 89.
8 Ricketts (1908), 11.

88

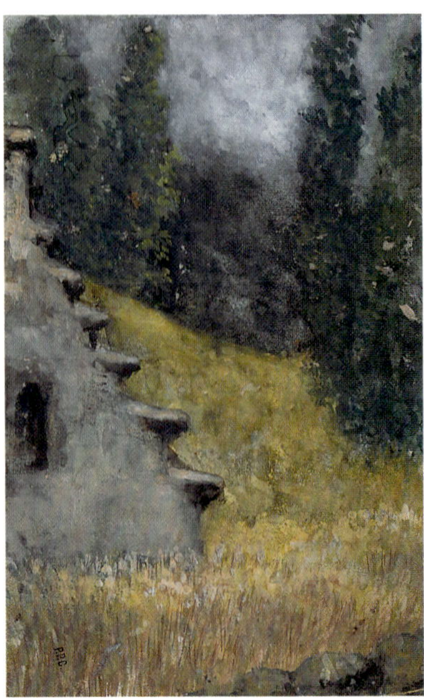

88

The Neighborhood of the Croix d'Arrignat / *Le voisinage de la Croix d'Arrignat* ca. 1875-90

Stamp l.l.
Watercolor and gouache on paper, 225 x 138 mm
Private collection

Provenance Artist's heirs and by descent.

Doubtless, it was this peculiar structure with its distinctively flanged stepped profile roof and high chimney, nestled in the overgrown yellow grasses of a knoll, that attracted Puvis to this site. According to a collateral descendant, this is a sheepfold ('bergerie'), with what must be a shepherd's hut.[1] The ruins of several such rural structures are still at the edge of the woods near the country estate close to Cuiseaux, where Puvis would visit his relatives and where this small landscape must have been executed.

The structure that dominates the sheet is also cropped by the paper edge, in a kind of *mise en page* that is usually associated with works by Degas or the Impressionists. It tacitly implies that the scene is a contingent one, which continues and is casually glimpsed. The grasses and vegetation, the small flecks of surface pigment representing flowers, the beckoning dark green of the trees in the background and the atmospherics of a sky puffy with white furthers an informal immediacy unexpected in Puvis's work.

1 I am grateful to Bertrand Puvis de Chavannes for this information.

89

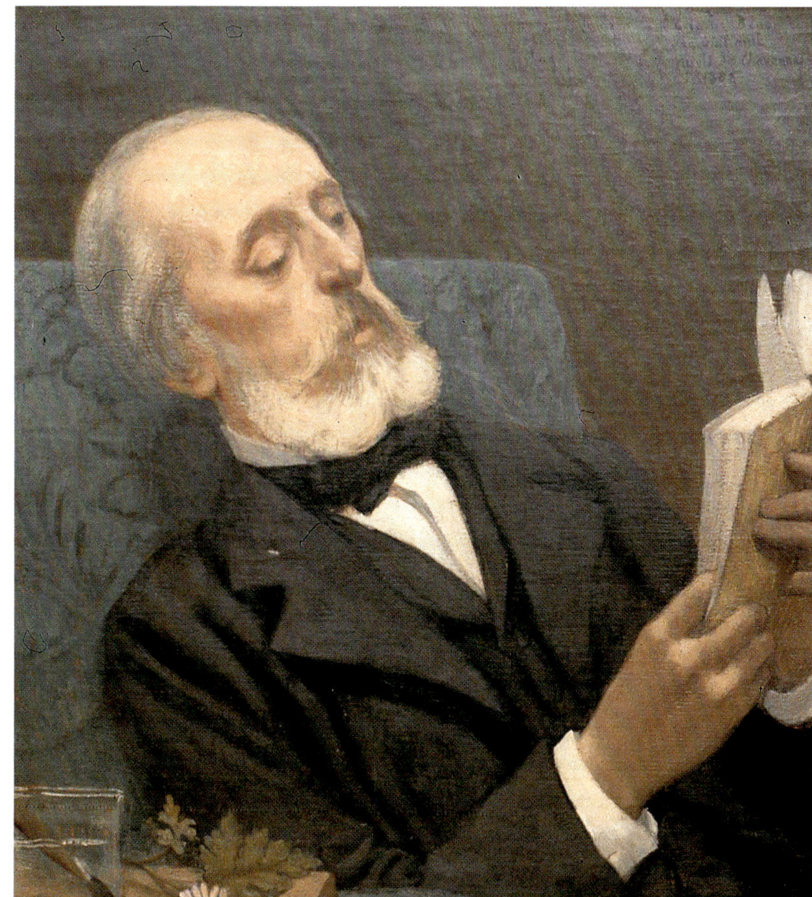

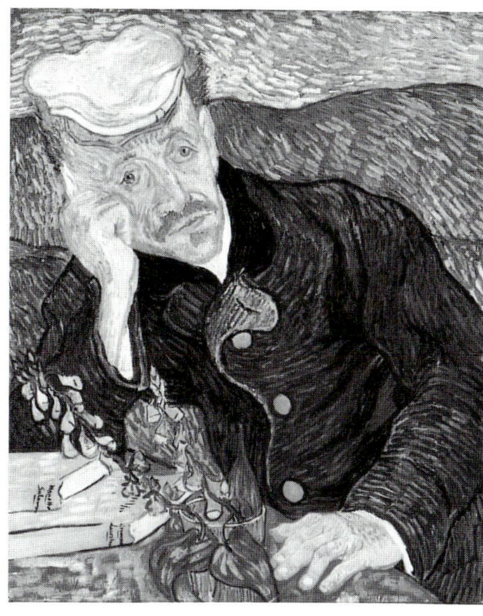

fig. 34
Vincent van Gogh (1853-1890)
Portrait of Dr. Gachet, 1890
Oil on canvas, 67 x 56 cm
Private collection

89

Portrait of Eugène Benon / *Portrait d'Eugène Benon* 1882

Inscribed u.r.: à Eugène Benon son vieil ami P. Puvis de Chavannes 1882
Oil on canvas, 60.5 x 54.5 cm
Private collection

Provenance M. Eugène Benon, Paris, then his son; M. Hermann [?]; Paris, Hôtel Drouot (16 June 1954), no. 48; M. Henri Puvis de Chavannes, Paris; Mme Henri Puvis de Chavannes, Neuilly.

Selected Exhibitions 1887 Paris (Durand-Ruel), no. 20 [?]; 1890 Lyons, no. 639; 1976-77 Paris/Ottawa, no. 159.

Selected References Letters of 6 October 1882 [6 8bre 82] and 11 November 1882 [11 9bre 82] (private collection); Van Gogh (1958), III, p. 238, no. 617; p. 275, no. 637; p. 276, no. 638; p. 470, no. W 22; p. 508, no. B 14 (9); Brown Price (1975), 715, 718-719, repr.

In this affectionate, intimate and astute portrait of a long-time friend, well-being is underscored. Domestic calm yields a private moment in which to read a popular novel – yellow-covered, in the 'format roman.' Benon, who because of advancing age and presbyopia must squint and hold his book away to see, wears a small gold ring on one finger and has modest, thoughtful objects on the table beside him as he sits back in an upholstered armchair. This is not a portrait meant to impress an unknown viewer with the subject's station, and yet a way of life is everywhere detailed.

On 6 October 1882, Puvis wrote of a lull between commissions causing idleness which 'I try to combat by executing two portraits of friends – it's work which is quite new to me and to which I am very much attracted.'[1] By the following month he had finished, for on 11 November 1882 he reported that he had profited from the experience and that Benon's wife and child cried from joy on seeing the results; Puvis was content, 'for it is one of the very rare portraits that I have done, and after work of such a different genre the ordeal was rather severe.'[2]

Little information is available on Benon,[3] though the paintbrush in the glass may indicate that he painted. He apparently died in August 1894, for a letter of the 30th of that month from Puvis to Benon's son

90

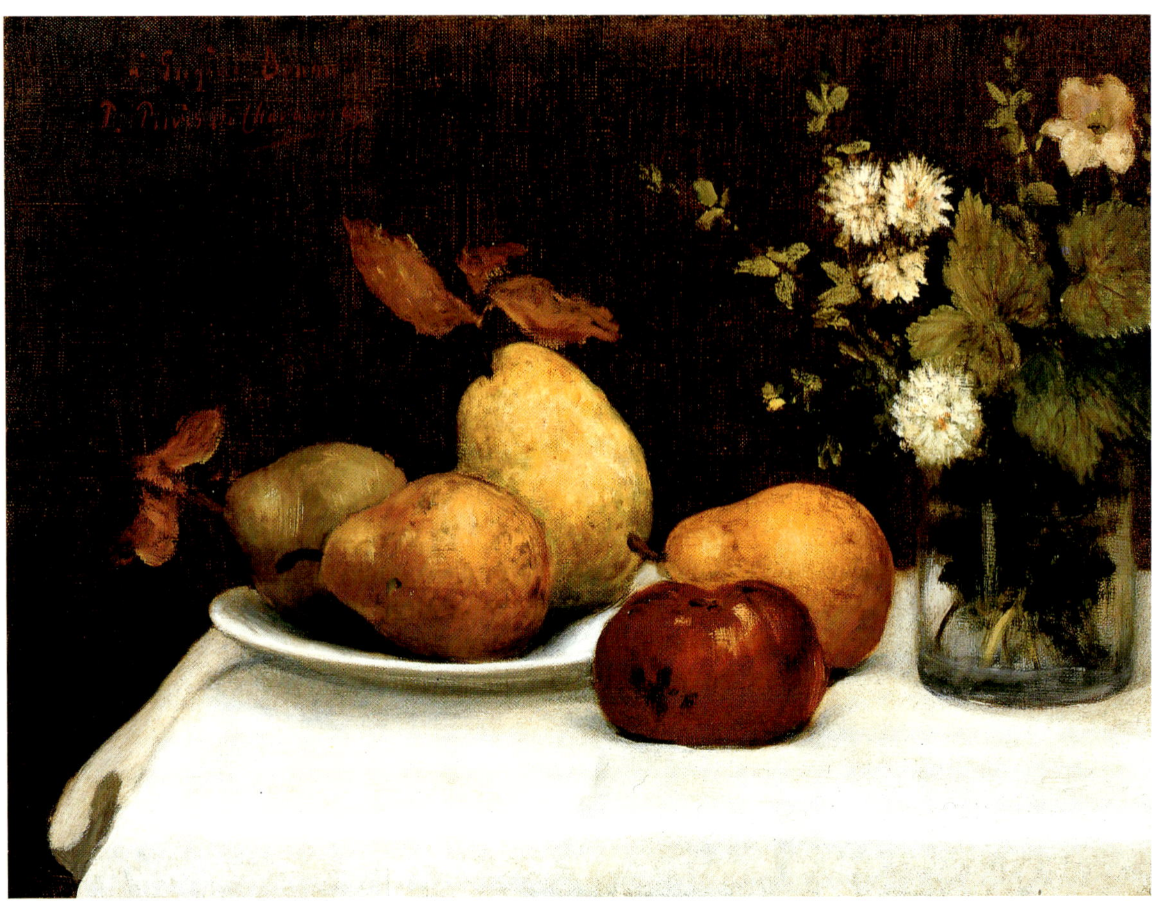

declares that Benon wanted his son to have the portrait and adds, 'Should I disillusion you ... I declare to have known his life only very imperfectly. I can only tell you that in speaking of the Melun House he used to say *My House*.'[4]

Vincent van Gogh, an emphatic proponent of portraiture, who must have seen the portrait at the 1887 Puvis de Chavannes exhibition at the Durand-Ruel Gallery, was among the painting's greatest admirers, writing Emile Bernard in 1888 of 'the serene old man in the clear light of his blue interior, reading a novel with a yellow cover – beside him a glass of water with watercolor brush and a rose in it.'[5] In 1889 he would write it was the ideal portrait.[6] Though the flowers are not roses and are on the table, the fact that Van Gogh took special note of the plain objects of everyday domestic life reflects his own leanings. In the finest form of flattery, he incorporated elements of the Benon portrait, a glass and plant (the foxglove, used for medicinal purposes, in a purple complementary to the yellow book), in one of his two painted portraits of Dr. Paul Gachet (fig. 34), who tried to nurse him back to health in June of the following year.[7] Unlike Benon, peacefully engrossed in reading, Gachet is not diverted from the viewer by the books at his elbow. Whereas Puvis soothed his already peaceful subject with an even, bland technique, Van Gogh created a dynamic painted surface with tense dashes of bright color pastes. Van Gogh appreciated Puvis's wilful simplifications and wrote wistfully of the peacefulness of his portraits to which he contrasted his own modern statement: 'I painted a portrait of Dr. Gachet with an expression of melancholy, which would seem to look like a grimace to many who saw the canvas. And yet it is necessary to paint it like this, for otherwise one could not get an idea of the extent to which, in comparison with the calmness of the old portraits, there is an expression in our modern heads, and passion – like a waiting for things as well as a growth. Sad and yet gentle, but clear and intelligent – this is how one ought to paint many portraits.'[8]

1 'oisiveté ... je la combats en faisant deux portraits d'amis – c'est un travail assez nouveau pour moi et auquel je trouve beaucoup d'attrait.' Letter of 6 October 1882 (private collection).

2 'car c'est un des très rares portraits que j'ai fait et après de travaux d'un genre si différent l'épreuve était assez rude.' (private collection).

3 Correspondence includes an undated congratulatory note from Benon from Interlaken (private collection) and three notes from Puvis, sold Paris, Hôtel Drouot (25 June 1975), no. 138, one of 31 July 1891 bids Benon see a just completed painting by Puvis at Durand-Ruel's about to go to the United States.

4 Private collection.

5 'le vieillard serein, dans son clair intérieur bleu, lisant le roman à couverture jaune – un verre d'eau, dans lequel un pinceau pour l'aquarelle et une rose, à côté de lui.' Van Gogh (1954), IV, p. 221, no. B 14 (9).Transl.: Van

91 Gogh (1958), III, p. 508, no. B 14 (9).

6 Van Gogh (1958), III, p. 238, in a letter to Theo, no. 617.

7 Brown Price (1975), 717-718, repr. 715; see also Judith Sund, *True to Temperament. Van Gogh and French Naturalist Literature* (Cambridge, 1992), p. 242.

8 'J'ai fait le portrait de M. Gachet avec une expression de mélancolie qui souvent à ceux qui regarderaient la toile, pourrait paraitre une grimace. Et pourtant c'est ça qu'il faudrait peindre parcequ'alors on peut se rendre compte combien, en comparaison des portraits calmes anciens, il y a de l'expression dans nos têtes actuelles et de la passion, ét comme de l'attente ét comme un cru. Triste mais doux, mais clair et intelligent, ainsi faudrait-il en faire beaucoup de portraits.' Van Gogh (1954), IV, p. 184, no. W 23. Transl: Van Gogh (1958), III, p. 472, no. W 23.

90

Still Life with Fruit and Flowers / *Nature morte aux fruits et aux fleurs* ca. 1882

Inscribed u.l.: à Eugène Benon P. Puvis de Chavannes
Oil on canvas, 46.2 x 61.2 cm
Van Gogh Museum, Amsterdam (Inv. S 414 M/1990)

Provenance Mme Henri Puvis de Chavannes, Neuilly; Thomas Agnew, London; Sir Alexander Korda, London; London; Paris, Hôtel Drouot (16 June 1954), no. 47; Marlborough Fine Art, Ltd., London; Sotheby's (23 June 1981), no. 51. repr.; London, Sotheby's, 'Nineteenth Century European Paintings and Drawings' (19 June 1990), repr. no. 17.

Selected References Letter of 3 November 1869 (private collection); Brown Price (1975), 717; 1976-77 Paris/Ottawa , repr. p. 10; 1991 Amsterdam, Van Gogh Museum, *Aanwinsten/Acquisitions, 1986-1991*, pp. 32-33, repr.

Although still lifes are frequently included in the figural works (see cat. 35 and fig. 35 *inter alia*) and in ornamental borders, independent still lifes are rare in Puvis's oeuvre.[1] This modest display of fruit is unpretentiously arranged: three pears on a white plate, a pear and apple (or tomato?) casually beside them on a plain white cloth and a handful of small flowers, as if just picked from the garden, unceremoniously placed in an ordinary tumbler. The simplicity and bare domestic setting of this seemingly uncontrived composition compare with certain still lifes by Henri Fantin-Latour. The limited range of brown and tawny hues and the maintenance of stable local color with only slight modifications for shading contrasts with contemporary Impressionist offerings with their tendencies to excite the surface with daubs of paint of myriad hues.

Dedicated to Eugène Benon, whose 1882 portrait (cat. 89) includes similar, unprepossessing objects, it may have been a souvenir for posing and offered in lieu of a still life Puvis mentioned in a letter of 3 November 1869: 'for a long time I promised an overdoor to my friend Benon – these are flowers, on a very narrow canvas that I still see myself rough out in the large dining room of Le Brouchy....'[2] This description suits a horizontal composition of flowers now in the collection of collateral descendants of the artist.

1 Compare *Still Life*, medium unknown, 20 x 27 cm (whereabouts unknown); Paris, Hôtel Drouot, 'Catalogue de tableaux, dessins, aquarelles et autres objets trouvés dans l'atelier de Gustave Ricard' (20 June 1873), no. 64, and *Still Life*, ca. 1883, oil on canvas, 23 x 25.5 cm (private collection); see Paris, Ottawa, (1976-1977), no. 168.

2 'j'ai promis depuis longtemps un dessus de porte à mon ami Benon – ce sont des fleurs, sur une toile très étroite que je me vois encore ébaucher dans la grande salle à manger du Brouchy....' Letter to an unnamed recipient, probably his sister-in-law (private collection).

91

Still Life / *Nature morte* ca. 1882-83

Inscribed l.l.: à Ary Renan/ P. Puvis de Chavannes
Oil on canvas, 55.7 x 46.5 cm
Private collection

Provenance M. Brye de Vertamy, Paris [although he was a collateral descendant, it is not known whether the work came to him by descent or purchase].

This is another of Puvis de Chavannes's infrequent still lifes and the most novel. Placed at regular intervals are glossy green and red apples, a cluster of black grapes, green and tawny pears, and a plum. These fall fruit are here more vivid and sparkling than in the 1864 *Autumn* (see cat. 35), in which they fill baskets and are strewn on the ground.

While some fruit are clustered, most are pictured singly. Read as a whole, the gathering of items stubbornly refuses to be grouped in any customary way. Several are in white dishes, others are put directly on what may be read either as a white cloth or plain white background. The unusual organization is comparable among contemporary works only to Gustave Caillebotte's audacious *Nature Morte* (1880-82, Museum of Fine Arts, Boston), a display of produce in rows as at a greengrocer's.

If this is an exercise in painting individual fruit from different angles, most from the side, with and without shadows, it is no mere amusement. The rendering is unusually finished, and with the figurations at calibrated intervals, a quintessential example of Puvis's pictorial thinking. Is this canvas to be viewed *in toto* as a stunningly inventive and original composition, or as a study of individual fruit set at neat intervals and only coincidentally a distillation of the kinds of regularized rhythms that govern the larger paintings? Our valuation depends on what is taken to be the beginning and end of a motif and the necessity for a cohesive whole. What is complete here are cadences, a subject in this compelling work at least as important as the fruit.

The canvas is dedicated to Puvis's protégé Ary Renan (1857-1900), the son of the prodigious writer and philosopher Ernest Renan.[1] By 1877, if not before, Ary was in Puvis's orbit; the two were to become close, Puvis a surrogate parent and the young man a special charge who in his correspondence addressed Puvis as 'mon bon père.'[2]

1 Cornelius Ary Renan, the grandson of Henri Scheffer (1798-1862), Puvis's teacher, and the great-nephew of Ary Scheffer (1795-1858), was a follower of Gustave Moreau, on whose work he wrote a treatise. Among the other canvases Puvis dedicated to Ary is *Woman in a Landscape* ca. 1882-83, a version of the standing figure in *Pleasant Land* (whereabouts unknown).

2 Letter of 11 September 1877; additional correspondence of Ernest, Cornélie and Ary Renan, particularly in the 1890s (private collection); in addition some 49 letters and notes (information from Dominique Morel, Maison Renan-Scheffer [Musée de la Vie Romantique], Paris). Renan suffered from a physical infirmity.

92

Portrait of Madame M.C. / *Portrait de Madame M.C.* [Marie Cantacuzène] 1883

Signed and twice dated [the second time in gold] u.r.: P. Puvis de Chavannes 1883
Oil on canvas, 78 x 46 cm
Musée des Beaux-Arts, Lyons (Inv. B.606)

Provenance Mme Pierre Puvis de Chavannes, Paris [Mme Cantacuzène]; bequest of Mme Cantacuzène to the museum (1899).
Selected Exhibitions 1883 Paris (Salon), no. 1991; 1887 Paris (Durand-Ruel), no. 18; 1899 Paris (Société Nationale des Beaux-Arts), no. 1187; 1976-77 Paris/Ottawa, no. 169.
Selected References Letters from Puvis de Chavannes of 19 May 1883 and 11 June 1883 (private collections); Lecture notes M. Henri Puvis de Chavannes; Edmond About, 'Le Salon de 1883,' *Le XIXe siècle* (6 May 1883), n.p.; Sâr Josephin Péladan, *L'Art ochlocratique, Salons de 1882 et de 1883*, vol. I, *La Décadence esthétique* (Paris, 1888), pp. 155-156; Galtier (1924), 270-271; Roland Holst (1924), 145-154, repr. [preparatory study] 145; H. Puvis de Chavannes (1937), 115-118, 142; H. Puvis de Chavannes (1938), n. p.; H. Puvis de Chavannes (1955), 40-41; Van Gogh (1958), III, p. 508, no. B 14 (9); p. 238, no. 617; Brown Price (1975), 715, 718-719; Philippe Durey, *Le Musée des Beaux-Arts de Lyon* (Paris, 1988), p. 107.

The Romanian princess Marie Cantacuzène (1817/1822-1898),[1] Puvis's longtime companion, frequently posed for him, as she had for Théodore Chassériau, whose friend she had also been (compare cat. 18, 41). From a family that claimed descent from ancient Greek nobility, the imperial family of Byzantine Constantinople,[2] she had married at sixteen and was widowed. In 1839 she married a distant cousin, Prince Alexander Kantakuzen, from whom she was soon estranged (although she was free to marry again only after his death in 1884),[3] and was subsequently

92

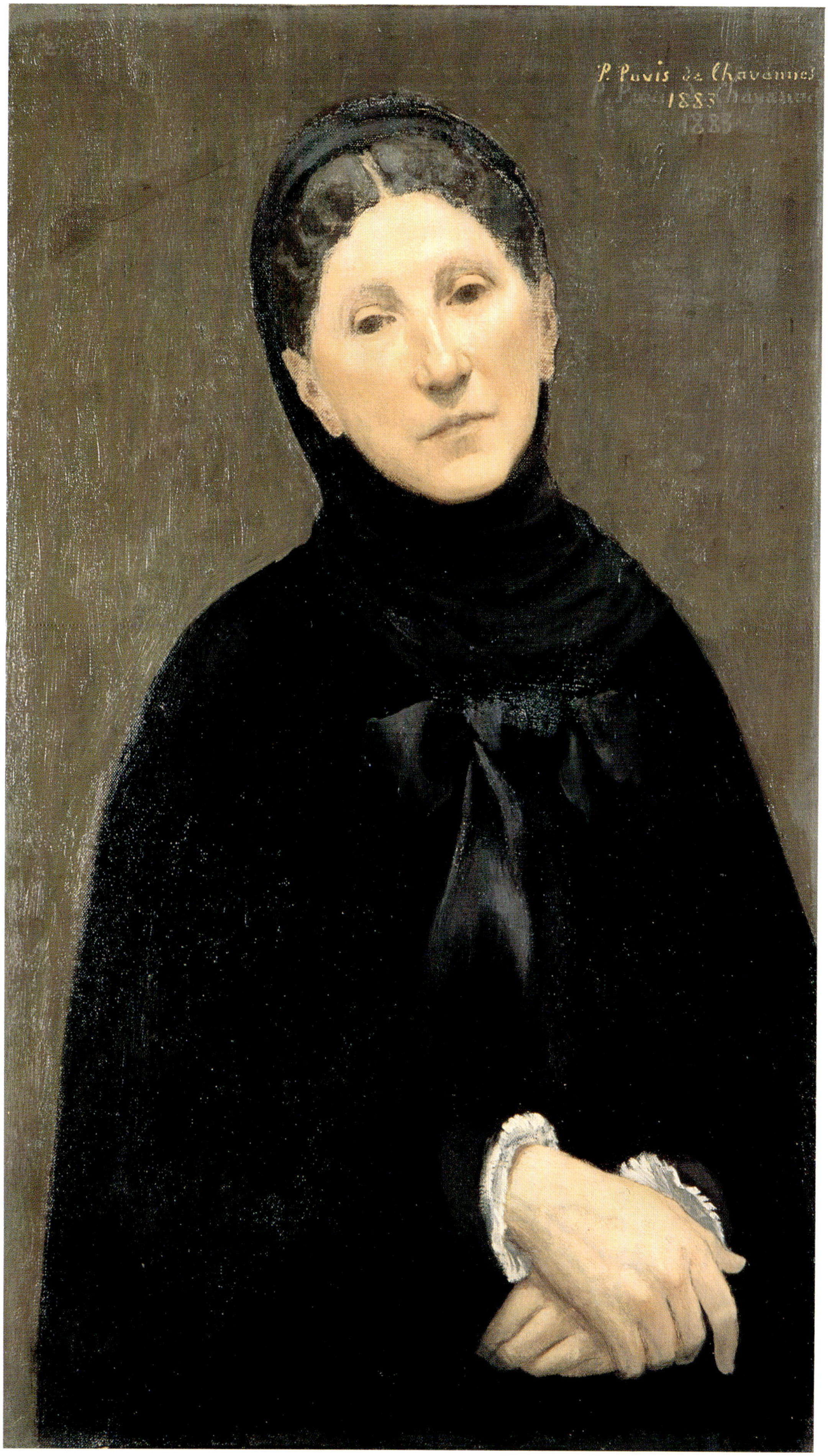

linked to a Romanian revolutionary and a Romanian poet and diplomat. She arrived in Paris about 1850, Gallicized her name, and to her Moldavian relatives became the 'Paris aunt.' Chassériau's 1855 drawing of her (one of two similar works), with hands demurely crossed and pensive expression (fig. 29), came to Puvis's collection through her,[4] and although Puvis's preliminary drawings (cat. 93-95, among others) for this portrait indicate he had thought of showing her seated, reading, he fixed on a pose strikingly similar to the one Chassériau had used. Consciously or not, Puvis took on the Chassériau mantle. In this portrait a certain grandeur is imparted by the elegantly proportioned, slightly elongated canvas that with the frontality of pose recalls Byzantine images and her affirmed ancestral lineage.

Marie Cantacuzène is characterized here simply and affectingly as a woman of a certain age (she was in her sixties), in the dark clothing then worn by older women in France. Although quiet portraits of women in black such as Degas's *Mme Gaujelin* (1867, Isabella Stewart Gardner Museum, Boston) were not uncommon in the preceding decades, a sobriety and steadfast calm are here intensified by the stark austerity of the sharply limited palette: white skin, hands delicately veined in blue, dark brown-black background and severe black dress. This effect was noted when the portrait was exhibited at the Salon of 1883 and more than one critic insisted that widowhood was its subject.[5] So, Sâr Josephin Péladan: 'Puvis .... is so much a thinker, that in making a portrait he ascended to the abstract. *Mme M.C.* is not a widow, she is the widow; he has raised the individual to the type. What more certain mark of his genius! Having come down from his fresco scaffolding, come down to the intimate portrait, he remains the abstractor. That's the essence and spirit of this work ... M. Puvis de Chavannes is incomparably the greatest contemporary painter, even as a portraitist, because he makes a portrait into a type of a state and the abstraction of a sentiment.'[6] Puvis vigorously denied this thesis and explained what must have appeared to be a peculiarly ascetic image by setting forth, on 11 June 1883, the circumstances of its execution: 'I don't want to wait for my return to warn you about the story told regarding my portrait at the Salon. This person is not a widow and if the expression of her face is sad, it is I who am guilty of having involuntarily stressed this side of it. She has a serious, very high-minded, and very kindly character. My only excuse is that I have often seen her with this pensive attitude that has misled you. Reflective people don't think gaily, but in the present instance there is no immediate sorrow. Her dress, which is what she usually wears, however, may also have had something to do with the misconception. This is the truth and the only truth.'[7] In fact the work was attacked to the point that Puvis wrote: 'I am exposed to ... a veritable avalanche of insults, for one can barely call the violent and often crude diatribes with which they try to overwhelm me criticism ... and I ask what is it in this portrait which very frankly bears my imprint that can exasperate to this point.'[8]

Having seen this portrait at the 1887 Puvis de Chavannes exhibition at the Durand-Ruel Gallery, Van Gogh, in an 1888 letter to Emile Bernard, mentioned this 'woman of the world, as the Goncourts have depicted them,'[9] and in 1889 wrote again of 'the *Portrait of a Lady* ... at the same exhibition [1887], a woman already old, but exactly as Michelet felt. There is no such thing as an old woman.'[10] He noted the dignity and containment of the depiction, and like Péladan appreciated Puvis's ability to be at once intimate and transcend the particular even in portraiture.

Marie Cantacuzène's importance to Puvis and the debt he owed her were, he said, incalculable. In his seventies, Puvis reputedly urged Marius Vachon, his most important early biographer, to devote a chapter of his book to her influence on Chassériau's life and his own.[11] A 'jeune femme exquise et supérieure,' she inspired Maurice Barrès's novel *Colette Baudoche*; he wrote that she had perfect taste and was the greatest influence on Puvis, to whom she gave 'des attitudes.'[12]

Although this 1883 portrait is sometimes called *Portrait of Mme Puvis de Chavannes*, Puvis married Marie Cantacuzène only on 21 July 1897, when they were both in their seventies. His collateral descendants have delicately explained that they were 'linked *in extremis*' and that his great-niece had more or less insisted.[13] She died 29 August 1898, and Puvis died two months later, on 24 October.

Mme Puvis de Chavannes bequeathed her portrait to the museum at Lyons, Puvis's birthplace.

1 Sources vary on biographical particulars, including her birth date. References will be given in the author's forthcoming book.

2 Professor Meyer Schapiro suggested in conversation that her genealogy might have been a particular attraction. On the early genealogy see V. Laurent, 'Les Vaticanus Latinus 4789 Histoire et Alliances des Cantacuzènes aux XIVe-XVe Siècles,' *Revue des Etudes Byzantines*, IX (1951), 47-105.

3 Letter from Puvis de Chavannes to an unnamed recipient of 30 March 1884 (private collection).

4 Brown Price, (1975), 715-717; and also *L'Art et les Artistes* (January 1937), repr. 117.

5 Bénédite [1931], II, pp. 483, 498; in 1898, Edouard Aynard wrote an appreciation in which he also described the woman's attire as that of 'grand deuil' and her care-furrowed face as that of sadness; see *Journal des débats* (November 1898), republished in *L'Express* (4 November 1898).

6 'Puvis .... est tellement penseur, qu'en portraiturant il s'élève jusqu'à l'abstrait. *Mme M.C.* n'est pas une veuve, c'est la veuve; il a monté l'individu au type. Quelle marque plus certaine de son génie! Descendu des échafaudages de la fresque, descendu au portrait intime, il reste encore l'abstracteur. Voilà pour l'essence et l'esprit de cet ouvrage ... incomparablement M. Puvis de Chavannes est le plus grand peintre de ce temps, même comme portraitiste, puisqu'il fait d'un portrait le type d'un état et l'abstraction d'un sentiment.' Péladan (ref. above), pp. 155-156.

94

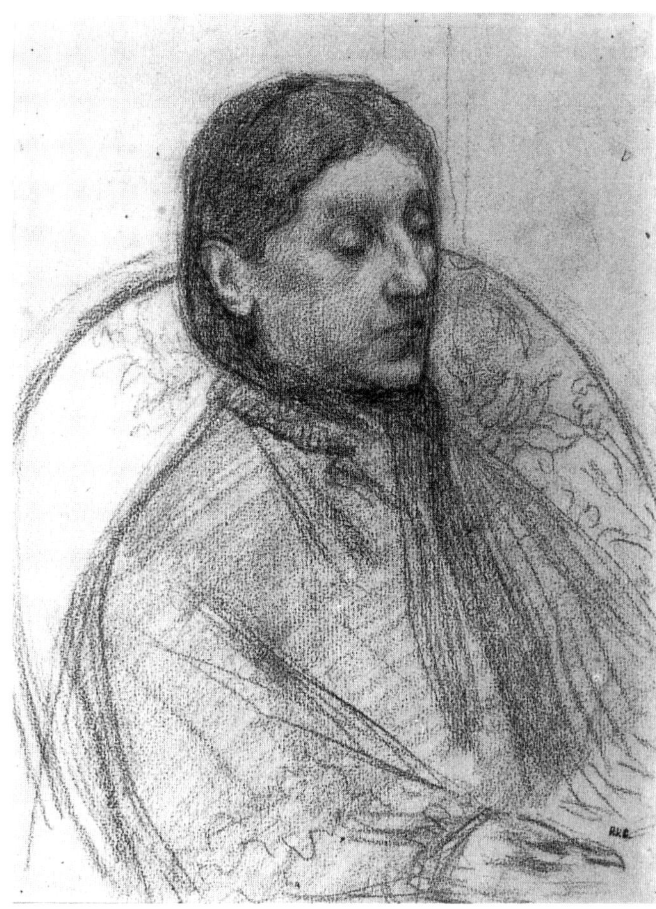

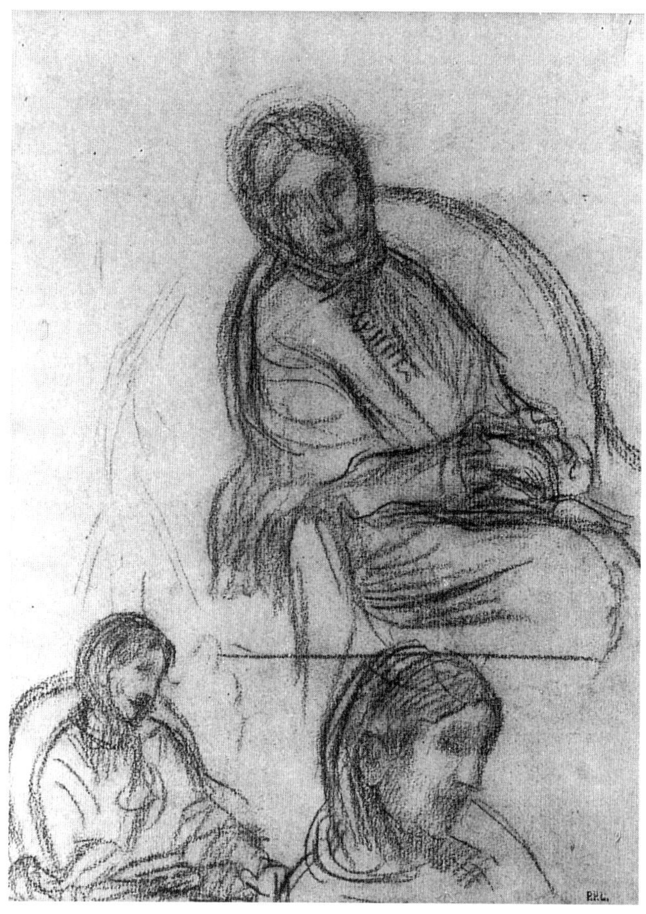

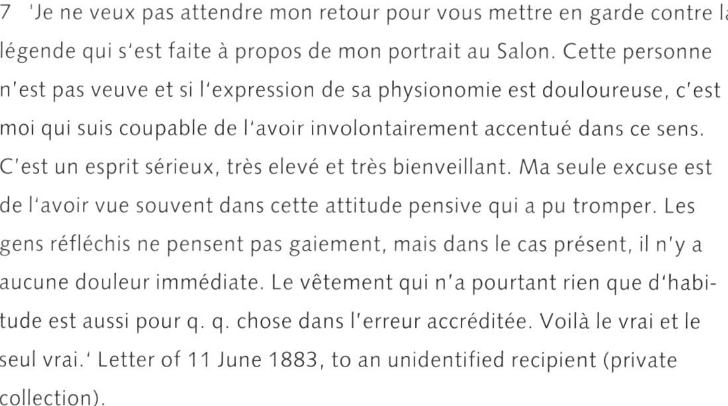

7 'Je ne veux pas attendre mon retour pour vous mettre en garde contre la légende qui s'est faite à propos de mon portrait au Salon. Cette personne n'est pas veuve et si l'expression de sa physionomie est douloureuse, c'est moi qui suis coupable de l'avoir involontairement accentué dans ce sens. C'est un esprit sérieux, très elevé et très bienveillant. Ma seule excuse est de l'avoir vue souvent dans cette attitude pensive qui a pu tromper. Les gens réfléchis ne pensent pas gaiement, mais dans le cas présent, il n'y a aucune douleur immédiate. Le vêtement qui n'a pourtant rien que d'habitude est aussi pour q. q. chose dans l'erreur accréditée. Voilà le vrai et le seul vrai.' Letter of 11 June 1883, to an unidentified recipient (private collection).

8 'je suis la butte à propos du Salon à une véritable avalanche d'injures car on ne peut guère appeler critiques des diatribes violentes et souvent grossières sous lesquelles on cherche à m'accabler .... et je me demande ce qui dans ce portrait et ce tableau qui portent très franchement mon empreinte peut exasperer à ce point.' Letter of 19 May 1883 to his sister-in-law (private collection).

9 'une dame du monde, telle qu'en ont portraituré les deux Goncourt.' Van Gogh (1954), IV, p. 221, no. B 14 (9).

10 'et le portrait de dame qu'il avait à la même exposition, une femme déjà vieille, mais tout-à-fait telle que Michelet le sentait qu'il n'y a pas de vieille femme.' Van Gogh (1953), III, p. 482, no. 617. Transl.: Van Gogh (1958), III, p. 238, no. 617.

11 According to chronicler and administrator Léonce Bénédite, quoted by Sandoz (1974), pp. 67-68.

12 See Maurice Barrès, *Mes Cahiers* (Paris, 1933), IX, pp. 235-236, 434, 625; *Colette Baudoche: Histoire d'une jeune fille de Metz* was included in Barrès's *Les Bastions de l'Est* (Paris, 1905), vol. 2, and published later as a play.

13 In conversation (Marseilles, 1965). The marriage contract, dated 20 July 1897, is in the Delapalme Archives.

93

Study of Madame M.C. ca. 1883

Stamp l.r.
Black conté crayon on light brown paper, 293 x 220 mm
Private collection

Provenance Artist's heirs and by descent.

This thoughtful study of Marie Cantacuzène informally seated in an armchair, turned somewhat to the side, her eyes lowered, perhaps reading, is a nicely realized, personal portrait, a consideration of her head, with a scarf around her hair, and her upper torso.

94

Studies of Madame M.C. Asleep ca. 1883

Stamp l.r.
Black crayon on off-white paper, 292 x 217 mm
Private collection

Provenance Artist's heirs and by descent.

These several sketches of Mme Cantacuzène dozing in a comfortable chair touchingly indicate that the good sitter, so often a model for Puvis over the years, needed an occasional rest. A drawing of her similarly seated (unpublished, private collection), reading a book on her lap, resembles the *Portrait of Eugène Benon* (cat. 89) that Puvis had completed shortly before.

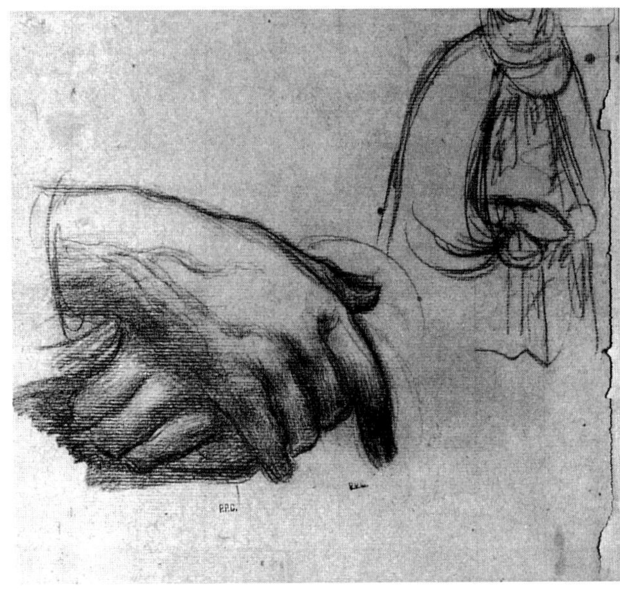

95

Study of the Hands of Madame M. C. and Half-Figure ca. 1883

Stamp twice near lower edge, l. of center
Black crayon on off-white paper, 233 x 255 mm
Private collection

Provenance Artist's heirs and by descent.

Puvis considered several poses and gestures for his 1883 portrait of Madame Cantacuzène (cat. 92). As this still awkward *croquis* illustrates, one possibility was to have her hands folded and holding the sides of her cape together around her. On the same sheet, her hands are more carefully studied, crossed with restraint and equanimity as in the painting, yet also in a way that recalls the gesture of *The Poor Fisherman* of two years earlier (fig. 23) that signaled passive acceptance and humility. Among other preliminary drawings are studies of subtle and quietly elegant details of dress, such as the curved lower edge of the asymmetrical cape and black bow (private collection), niceties that no longer call attention to themselves in the final painted portrait and that in fact indicate how in his paintings the artist would subsume the parts to the whole.

96

The Toilette / *La toilette* ca. 1878-83

Signed l. c.: P. Puvis de Chavann[es]
Oil on millboard, 32.5 x 24 cm
The National Gallery, London, The Lane Bequest (Inv. NG 3267)

Provenance Dezaunais [Dezaunay? a Puvis student?] (July 25, 1902); Durand-Ruel, Paris (25 July 1902-29 May 1906); H. P. Carré (29 May 1906); Sir Hugh Lane (29 May 1906); bequeathed by the latter (1917).
Selected References Durand-Ruel Archives, no. 7118; Fry (1917), 152-153; Lane (1920), 180-183; Gabriel Mourey, 'The Centenary of Puvis de Chavannes,' *The Studio*, LXXXVIII (15 November 1924), 249, repr. opp. 248; Martin Davies, with additions and some revisions by Cecil Gould, *National Gallery Catalogues: French School. Early 19th Century, Impressionists, Post-Impressionists* (London, 1970), no. 3267, p. 195; Boucher (1979), p. 84; 1988-89, Vancouver Art Gallery / Ottawa, National Gallery of Canada / Washington, D.C., National Gallery of Art, *Master Drawings from the National Gallery of Canada*, pp. 213-214.

A woman at her toilette was a theme of great interest to Puvis, as a large cluster of drawings and several paintings by him attest. While a number of them culminated in his 1883 *Young Woman at Her Toilette* (*Femme à sa toilette*, fig. 35), which he presented at the Exposition Nationale des Beaux-Arts (the 'Triennale') that year, his works on this theme are fascinating for their resourcefulness, stylistic diversity and aesthetic range, with manner and mood shifting pronouncedly among them.

The motif of a partly unclothed woman, often with a mirror, preparing her toilette or being groomed, combing her hair or having it dressed, a theme presented in previous centuries within a larger narrative

6

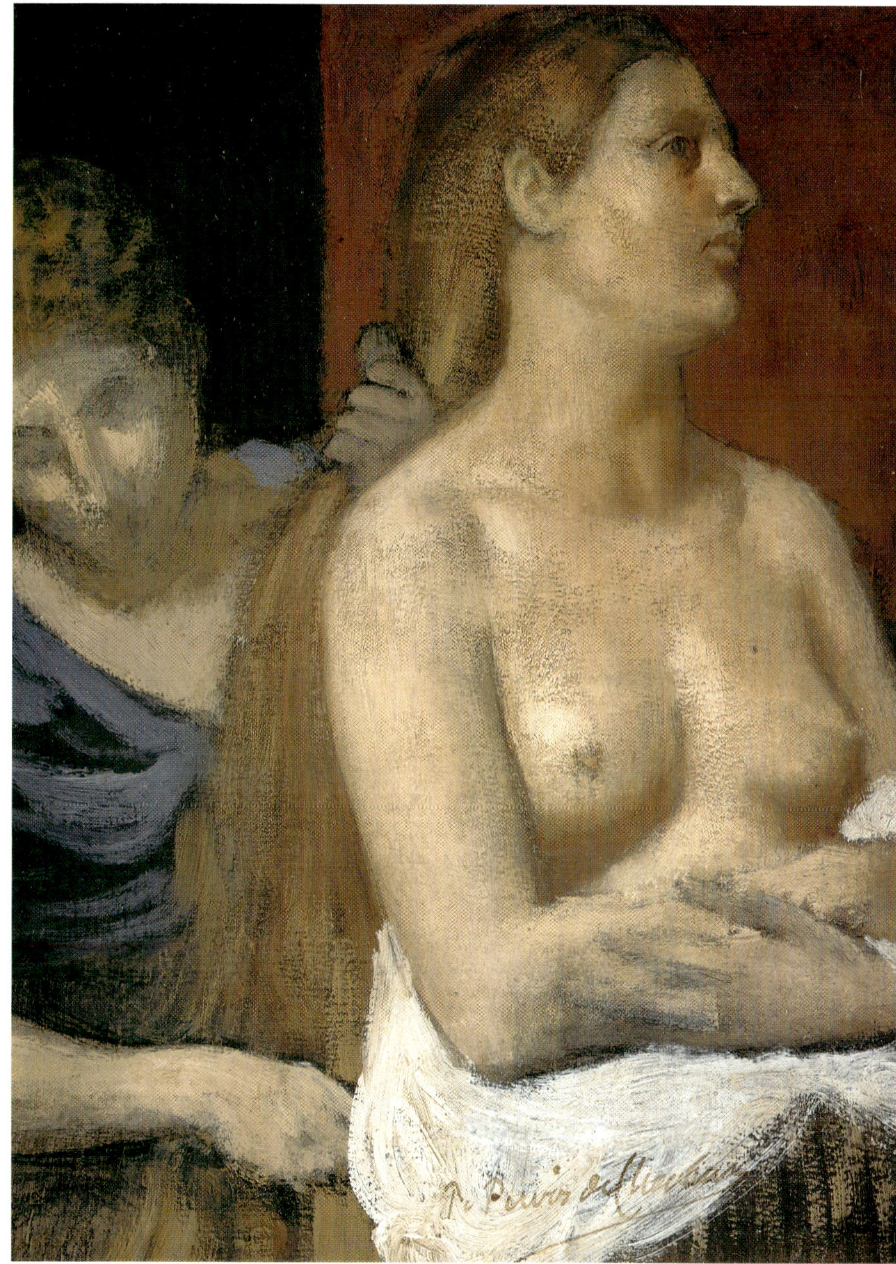

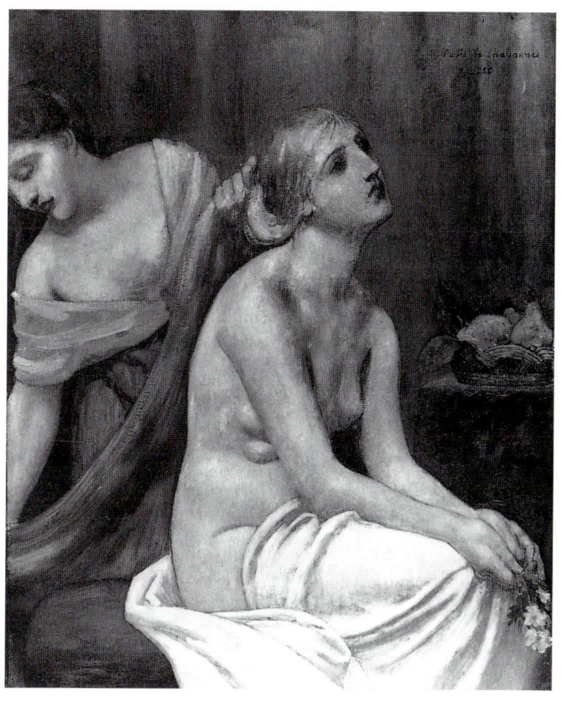

fig. 35
Young Woman at Her Toilette, 1883
Oil on canvas, 75 x 63 cm
Musée d'Orsay, Paris

associated with the mythological goddess of love, Venus, or the biblical Esther, had long been attractive to painters. Titian (*Young Woman at Her Toilette*, Musée du Louvre, Paris) and François Boucher were repeatedly drawn to the theme with its potential for sensuality. But by the 1880s and 1890s, these traditional narratives absented themselves for Puvis as for Degas, for whom the motif was a major one and much commented upon. Though such works by Degas as *Nude Woman Having Her Hair Combed* (1886-88, Metropolitan Museum of Art, New York) echo those by Puvis, the theme is too important and general to indicate anything other than common sources.

This version of the toilette theme is one of the most beautiful and sympathetic of Puvis's independent paintings, a rare foray into domestic intimacy and thoughtful directness. In this small painted work both figures are standing, seen close up and tightly framed. The folded arms of the woman at right frame her body and rest on her garment, which is read as clothing, not drapery. A preliminary, related study is a view of the figures at three-quarter length (cat. 97), showing how Puvis tightened his focus in this panel. In this painted version, the woman is neither plain nor approachably homely, and no longer slumped in posture. The colors are unusually warm, tawny tones with white and mauve, which suggest a directly recorded impression. The naturalism and sensuous volume of this image suggest it must be among the first of the series that led to the 1883 painting, though Puvis had first embarked on this subject some years previously (see below). Although there is a quite similar, sensuous half-nude figure at the far right of Puvis's 1873 *Summer* (fig. 5), the configuration of the two figures here would bring this panel into a closer relationship with the thematic idea of a woman having her hair dressed by an attendant figure, an idea that would seem to work itself out over a span of years that is not that narrow. We would date this painting to the later 1870s.[1]

Amidst the rich group of variants, the question of pictorial progression and dates is a knotty one. The images fall into several groups, indicating the artist took up this theme at several junctures. While a progression among these sundry efforts may be mapped out and their dating calculated, absolute dating is speculative. We would contend that Puvis first formulated his idea for this subject in about 1868 with full-length figures from which he selected his motif (see cat. 97). At some point, we hazard the later 1870s, he executed his idea with a model in naturalistic terms (cat. 98 and this panel). He then went on to ever more classicizing, abbreviated and abstracted interpretations of the motif, in which terse but lyrical linear definitions – particularly in an unfinished, unpublished version[2] – are distinctly Picassesque *avant la lettre*. A decade later, in 1895, he was persuaded to issue a lithograph made after an earlier drawing (cat. 100), which may have inspired him to revisit the theme once more, in 1896, with a mythologized version, *The Toilette of Thetys*.[3]

The attending figure, included in most versions of Puvis's *Toilette*, is shown as secondary. She is frequently truncated by the frame and not as technically finished as the woman having her hair combed. These disparities in rendering of the two figures are all but a convention in Puvis's work on this theme, and increase the sense of a familiar informality, qualities palpable in Degas's works with this subject – in which the servant is also frequently only a fragmentary figure. A subordinate figure is routinely included in treatments of this motif, as in Corot's 1859 *Toilette* (collection Wildenstein, Paris), although it has recently been argued that in Degas's works a certain intimacy among women is more important than the mistress-servant relationship.[4]

1 A date ca. 1870 has been advanced for this panel by Marie-Christine Boucher, and for the subject in Puvis's work, a range of dates beginning in 1861-62 (see 1976-77 Paris/Ottawa, no. 165); Martin Davies dated this panel to about 1877, citing Vachon's 1895 book, which alleges it was exhibited at the Salon that year, but subsequently noting Puvis did not participate that year (ref. above).

2 Oil and pencil on canvas, squared, an arc to the left, 35.1 x 29 cm (private collection); that it is unfinished contributes to the severity of its appearance.

3 Also called *In the Heather (Nymphs)* (*Dans les bruyères [Nymphes]*), oil on canvas, 80.6 x 99.6 cm, Art Institute of Chicago.

4 See Wendy Lesser, *His Other Half: Men Looking at Women Through Art* (Cambridge, Mass., 1991), p. 78.

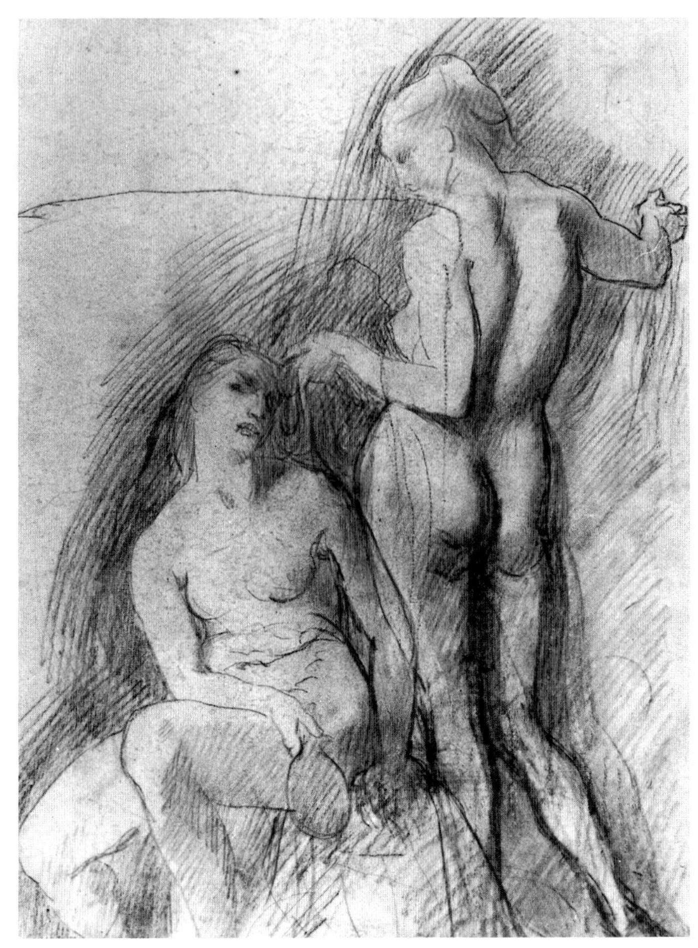

97

Study for 'The Toilette' ca. 1868-80

Stamp l.r.
Pencil and black chalk on yellow paper, white paper bottom center, as if torn and replaced,
320 x 260 mm
Musée du Louvre, Paris (Inv. RF 2162)

Provenance Bequest of artist's heirs to the city of Paris (1899); Musée du Luxembourg; transferred to the Musée du Louvre (1929).

In this drawing of a standing and a seated nude, an early conception for the theme of *The Toilette* is set forth. As the framing rectangle drawn around the seated woman with a mirror indicates, that figure would be the prime focus of later compositions. She would be copied (perhaps by tracing) to produce a closely related drawing with more summary, if hardier outlines; the servant was shifted to her other side, reversed, and only faintly recorded.[1] The servant would subsequently be turned to face the viewer (cat. 99); the spatial interplay between the bodies of the two

98

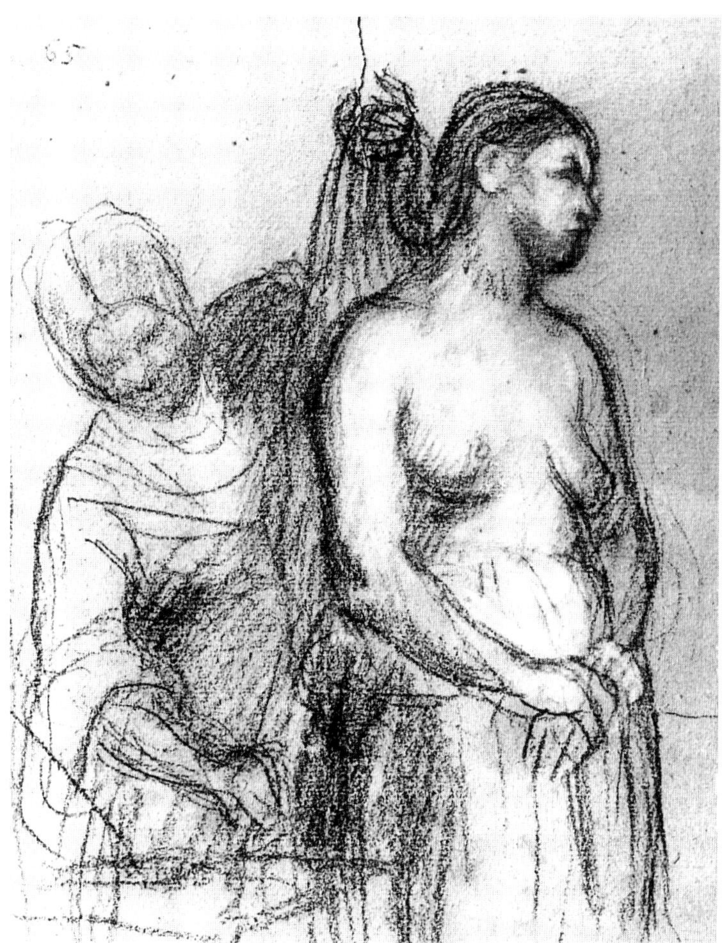

figures would be eliminated as their orientation changed, and the seated figure's pose would be modified so that she would face towards the right,[2] her focus displaced outside the perimeters of the sheet. That last figure would become the source for a series of drawings[3] related to the painted *Young Woman at Her Toilette* of 1883 (fig. 35).

These figures relate generally to the theme of a standing figure holding up her hair that dates from about 1865 and the bathers in *Ave Picardia Nutrix* (see discussion cat. 36). Nonetheless, this current series would seem to date from 1868-69, on the basis of a similarity in the technique and rendering of the figure to such figures as a *Nude Standing Woman* drawn in that period.[4]

1 *Study of a Nude Woman Holding a Mirror*, Musée des Beaux-Arts, Lille (Inv. 2067) and the drawing here presented; according to Mme Boucher, these drawings date from ca. 1861-63 (see 1976-77 Paris/Ottawa, no. 165, with, unfortunately, no discussion of her pictorial reasoning).

2 *Study for 'The Toilette'*, Mills College Art Gallery, Oakland, California (Inv. 1939.15).

3 Our cat. 100, two drawings at the Musée du Petit Palais, Paris (Inv. PPD 269^{3}; MCB 101 and Inv. PPD 285^{3}; MCB 102) and one at the Musée Sainte-Croix, Poitiers (Inv. 892-1-20).

4 Musée du Petit Palais, Paris (Inv. PPD 284^{2}; MCB 50).

98

Study for 'The Toilette' ca. 1879-83

Marked u l.: 65
Black chalk heightened with white on blue paper, 227 x 177 mm
Musée des Beaux-Arts, Lyons (Inv. B607.10)

Provenance Bequest of artist's heirs to the city of Lyons (1898).

The two women in this study are earthier and more naturalistic than the figures in other drawings on the toilette theme and relate to the painted London version (cat. 96). The essential sympathy and lack of idealizing aestheticism in the depiction are rare in Puvis's oeuvre: the woman's sharply observed plain face, stray wisps of hair, slightly sagging breasts and skirt gathered at the waist recall the manner of seventeenth-century Dutch painting by way of mid-century French realism. The social roles of the two figures are not strongly distinguished. The partial undress of the woman being combed is a visual counterpoint to the dress of the attendant. To the left a table or stand is sketched out. The scrawling drawing technique with heightening is a style that Puvis used in the later 1860s and would continue to use into the 1880s.

99

Study for 'The Toilette' ca. 1879-83

Stamp l.r.
Gouache on paper, 256 x 215 mm
Private collection

Provenance Artist's heirs and by descent.
Selected Exhibitions 1937 Lyons, no. 58.

Forthright linear definition and the delicacy of overlaid gouache washes used to suggest diaphanous draped garments characterize this version of *The Toilette*. A very feminine red ribbon in the attendant's hair is piquant for being the only bright spot among restrained, almost monochromatic colors, the browns and whites that define the figures and background. The placement of the attendant at the left and her pose – facing the viewer and slightly bending – and gestures are established as they would remain in several drawings and the painted versions of *The Toilette* (see cat. 100, 96). The seated woman with a mirror turned towards the left, is

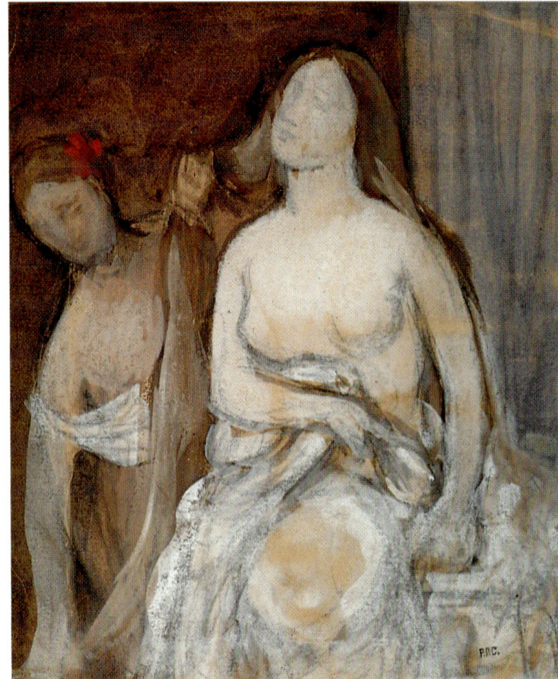

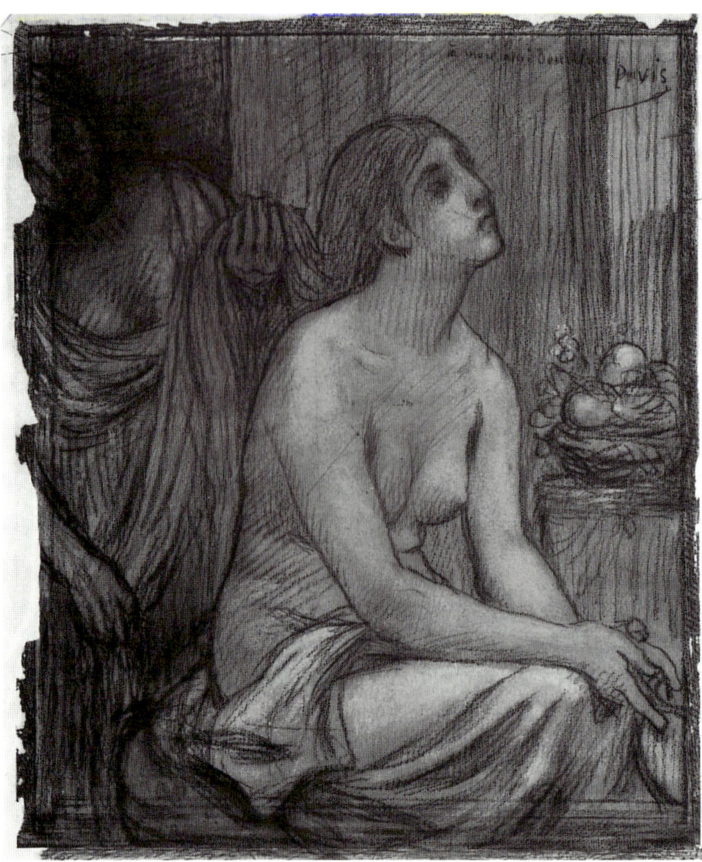

an early variant of the more abstract, classicizing figure who, turned in the other direction, with her gaze lost outside the composition, would culminate in the *Young Woman at Her Toilette* of 1883 (fig. 35).

100

The Toilette / *La toilette* ca. 1882-83

Signed and inscribed u.r.: à mon ami Bouillon/ Puvis
Black chalk with stumping, heightened with white chalk on tracing paper, laid down on textured card, 312 x 261 mm (irregular)
National Gallery of Canada, Ottawa (Inv. NGC 28269)

Provenance Jacques Dubourg, Paris; Paris, Hôtel Drouot (10 December 1981), no. 81 [same? dimensions slightly different]; Margo Pollins Schab, New York; acquired by the museum (1983).
Selected References 1976-77 Paris/Ottawa, no. 166; 1988-89, Vancouver Art Gallery / Ottawa, National Gallery of Canada / Washington, D.C., National Gallery of Art, *Master Drawings from the National Gallery of Canada*, no. 68.

The lovely seated figure, defined by curving contour lines, and the classicizing style of this version of *The Toilette* are striking in this drawing, which, with a related variant,[1] is among those drawings most closely allied to the 1883 *Young Woman at Her Toilette* (fig. 35). While this is the more refined of the two, the other, with its thick contour lines, defines the two figures while flattening them. The heaviness of those lines indicates the artist feeling his way through possibilities to the essential demarcations, a complex of curves the rhythms of which take precedence over empirical observation. At issue in a group of related studies that include only the seated figure, without an attendant, is the figural type: shown as nude and semi-draped, she is a rather young, pubescent girl.[2]

The version presented at the 1883 Salon is of a seated half-draped figure, her head tilted back on a long, Ingresque neck, her preternaturally long hair (designed to offset the placement of her arms) dressed by an attendant. The expression of distracted passivity and revery on her abstracted features, recalling fifth-century B.C. Hellenic heads, serves to dissociate the emotional from the physical self, rendering the figure supremely unself-conscious. In some versions the figure, like a Venus, has a looking glass. In the Musée d'Orsay version, she holds a small bunch of flowers and is supplied with a credible, if rudimentary interior setting, a table and small still life of lemons. The cool, delicate colors and flat, simplified rendering create an abstracted, monumentalized interpretation.

The figure of the attendant in this drawing of *The Toilette* relates in pose to that figure in the painted version exhibited here (cat. 96), though her garment is draped in deeper loops to be more *décolleté*. The seated figure closely approximates the classicizing figure in the 1883 version of the theme.

This drawing served as the basis for a transfer lithograph print of 1895,[3] which was published in the journal *L'Epreuve*. By that time the artist and his images were sufficiently well-known and the idea of spontaneity of drawing sufficiently accepted for this drawing with its smudges and scrawls to be chosen for reproduction.

1 *Drawing related to 'The Toilette'*, ca. 1883, inscribed u.l. c.r: Lundi Dimanche à 10h., stamp l.r., black chalk heightened with white chalk, 310 x 240 mm, Musée du Louvre, Paris (Inv. RF 29111); 1991, Paris, Musée du Louvre, *Repentirs*, no. 7.

2 See the drawings in the Musée du Petit Palais, Paris and the Musée Sainte-Croix, Poitiers mentioned in cat. 97, note 3.

3 *The Toilette* (*La toilette*), 1895, signed u.r. on the stone: Puvis, transfer [?] lithograph, 305 x 250 mm; published in *L'Epreuve* (March 1895), no. 4, planche I; see Delteil (1925), II, p. 310; William Ivins, Jr., *Notes on Prints* (New York, 1930), p. 175, repr. p. 174; 1976-77 Paris/Ottawa, no. 166; Druick (1977), 33 (called photo-lithograph).

101

The Sacred Wood Dear to the Arts and Muses / *Le Bois Sacré cher aux Arts et aux Muses* (reduced version) ca. 1884-89

Signed l.l.: P. Puvis de Chavannes
Oil on canvas, 92.7 x 231 cm
The Art Institute of Chicago, Mr. and Mrs. Potter Palmer Collection (Inv. 22.445)

Provenance Durand-Ruel, Paris (1890); Potter Palmer Collection, Chicago (1890); gift to the museum (1922).
Selected Exhibitions 1975 Toronto, no. 25; 1976-77 Paris/Ottawa, no. 174.
Selected References On the mural: Puvis letters of 4 June 1883; 24 July 1884; 6 August 1884 (private collection); 8 August 1893 (private collection); letter of 1 June 1883 and undated letter (Musée des Beaux-Arts, Lyons; the latter bequest of Mme de Nantois [1934]); Aynard (1884), pp. 6-8, and *passim*; Comte (1884), 288, repr.; Mirbeau (1884), 2; Aynard (1886); Burty (1886), n.p. [3]; Comte (1886); Vachon (1895), pp. 206-211; Vachon [1900], pp. 205, 209-214; Michel and Laran (1911), pp. 85-86, repr. *in situ* pl. xxxv; Lechat (1920); 'T' (1921); Sirieyx de Villers (1924), pp. 128-130; Baudoüin (1935), 300; Charles de Bouleau, *Charpentes: La Géométrie sécrète des peintures* (Paris, 1963), p. 209; 1976-77 Paris/Ottawa, pp. 191-198; Gilles Genty, 'Les Muses aux Bois. La Forêt symboliste, lieu de Révélation,' *Revue d'art internationale*, no. 3 (Autumn 1989-Winter 1990), 119-120. On this painting: Neff (1969), 68-73, 81-82; Richard Brettell, *French Salon Artists, 1800-1900* (Chicago, 1987), pp. 112, 113, 114, 119.

In 1883, at the instigation of its Conseil Administratif headed by Edouard Aynard, Puvis was presented with a commission for murals for the Musée des Beaux-Arts of Lyons. He responded on 1 June that he had received 'the plan for your magnificent staircase, at the sight of its beautiful surfaces all my old decorator's blood bubbled up.'[1] He was to execute one of his most important complexes for the city of his birth and boyhood: *The Sacred Wood* (*Le Bois Sacré*, 1884, 460 x 1040 cm), *Antique Vision* (*La Vision Antique*, 1885, 460 x 578 cm, see cat. 105), *Christian Inspiration* (*L'Inspiration Chrétienne*, ca. 1885-86, 460 x 578 cm, see cat. 106) and, alluding to the two rivers that meet at Lyons, *The Rhône and The Saône* (ca. 1885-86, 460 x 1040 cm).[2]

Calling it a 'fresco' ensemble, Puvis viewed his murals as setting the tone for the building, even sanctifying it: 'The first fresco ... ought to welcome the visitor to the threshold of the Museum, as the baptistry to the threshold of a Church. *The Sacred Wood Dear to the Arts and Muses* generated two others: *Antique Vision* and *Christian Inspiration*, for art is understood between these two terms, of which one evokes the idea of feeling.... If I had painted only [*Christian Inspiration*] ... strictly speaking, one might assert that I had been haunted by medieval Christianity; but, see here, this pagan landscape which so clearly manifests a joy in life on earth, isn't that a sufficient counterbalance to the panel to which it is a pendant?'[3]

Presented here is a reduced version of what the visitor first sees at the top of the museum's great staircase. *The Sacred Wood* is Puvis's paradigmatic Arcadia destined for a public monument: pale muses and figures personifying the arts stationed in a sylvan setting, embodying a cherished, nostalgic idea of Greco-Roman antiquity. A representation of the classical muses is appropriate to a museum; the term 'museum' originated with *museon* or *mouseion*, which Pliny speaks of as the home or realm of the muses. As Puvis described his painting, each poetic detail had a precise meaning: 'In the center of the painting, at the foot of a double Ionian [sic] portico which unites them, appear the three plastic Arts: Architecture seated on the fragment of a column, Sculpture standing at her side, and Painting receiving the tribute of a child who spreads flowers out on her white garment (an allusion to the particular art in which Lyonnais artists have distinguished themselves); near them are dispersed the inspiring Muses: Polyhymnia, with an arm raised, charms and enchants them with her eloquence; Clio, holding her tablets, prepares to write unbiased History; Calliope, seated, unrolling the epic page on which one reads: 'Arma virumque cano,' will extol the glory of the heroes, while two geniuses gather branches of laurel and fashion wreaths. On the left, Thalia, the Muse of Theater, stops attentively, and Terpsichore suspends the rhythm of her steps to listen to the divine harmony of Erato and Euterpe, the two arts of Poetry and Music, who in their long, flowing garments mysteriously traverse the space. In the middle ground, Urania, stretched out on the shore of a lake, contemplates the constellations which are reflected in the waters illuminated by the gold of the setting sun. To the side, under a weeping willow, Melpomene meditates on scenes of Tragedy. The landscape, bathed by the silent light of evening, is bounded by high mountains which close access to this place of delectation and permit only a narrow band of sky to be seen. On the grounds sprinkled with shrubs and flowers stand trees of heroic dimension: laurel, pine, oak.'[4] In Puvis's homage, Music and Poetry actually waft through the air; and the opening lines of Virgil's *Aeneid*, 'I sing of arms and a man,' may be read on Epic Poetry's scroll.

Puvis may have known that Chassériau had also planned a mural with muses and personifications of the Arts,[5] and had made a note on a drawing that all but describes Puvis's enclave of muses: 'introduce a façade, Architecture leaning on one side, Painting executing her drawings at her feet, Sculpture also Poetry and Music would be seated and in this way all the arts would be assembled to be seen.'[6]

Although this reduced version follows the mural composition closely, it is notably different in a number of respects. While presenting the mural in all its particulars, it condenses pictorial elements, showing less fully modeled figures of relatively thinner proportions, thereby making the spaces appear more important. Both background and foreground elements have greater clarity as shapes. As with all the works reduced to a smaller scale, the ratio between the size of the painting and the facture, the paint strokes and scumbling technique, is changed. And of course the visual impact of the works differ. Moreover, the mural *in situ* is visually simpler and more integrated than this reduced version and schemas suggest and photographs usually indicate: the muse of Tragedy (left) and the two narrow-chested, fine and fair-skinned young boys making wreaths (right) are visually and dramatically cut off from the central segment, as they are placed at right angles to the mural on the adjacent walls. This unusual arrangement must have resulted from the artist's wish quite literally to set the Tragic Muse aside ('à l'écart'). Suzanne Valadon told an interlocutor that she modeled not only for the muses, but also the youths.[7]

Puvis may have used his daily walks through the Bois de Boulogne as inspiration for his *Sacred Wood*, for he wrote to Charles Ephrussi on 10 August 1884, when the marouflage was about to take place, that one of two drawings he enclosed was of the 'Boulevard des Malesherbes about three' and, he continued: 'I am sorry not to have been able to add the smell of the park ['bois,' meaning, one might suppose, the Bois de Boulogne] –

101

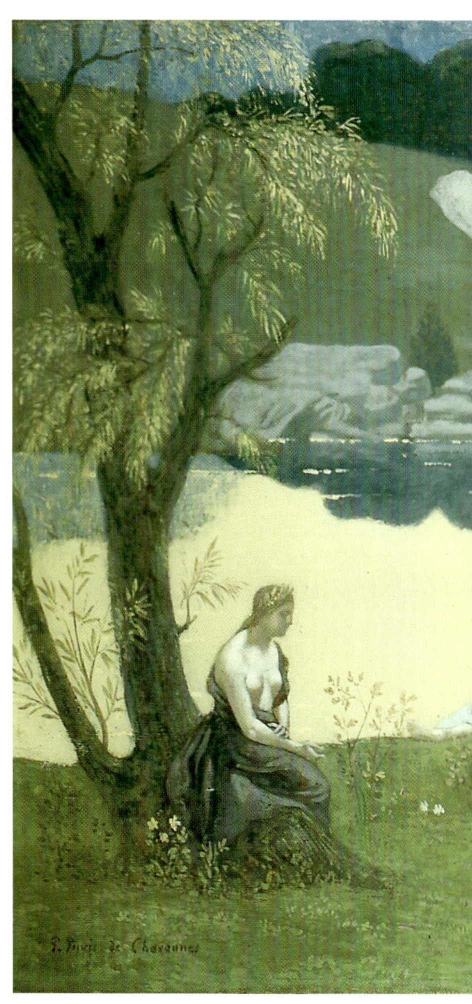

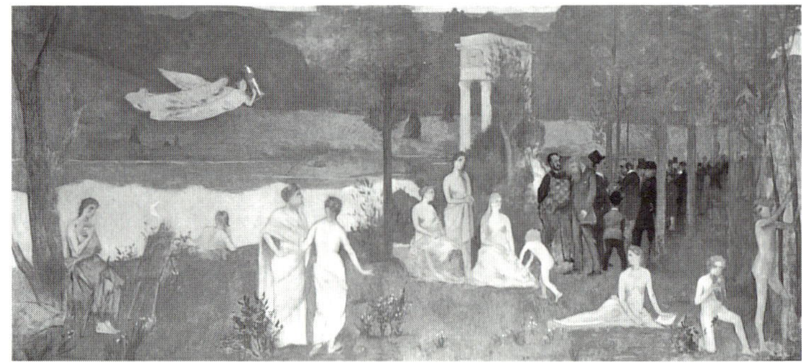

fig. 36
Henri de Toulouse-Lautrec (1864-1901)
Satire of 'The Sacred Wood', 1884
Oil on canvas, 172 x 380 cm
The Henry and Rose Pearlman Foundation, Inc.

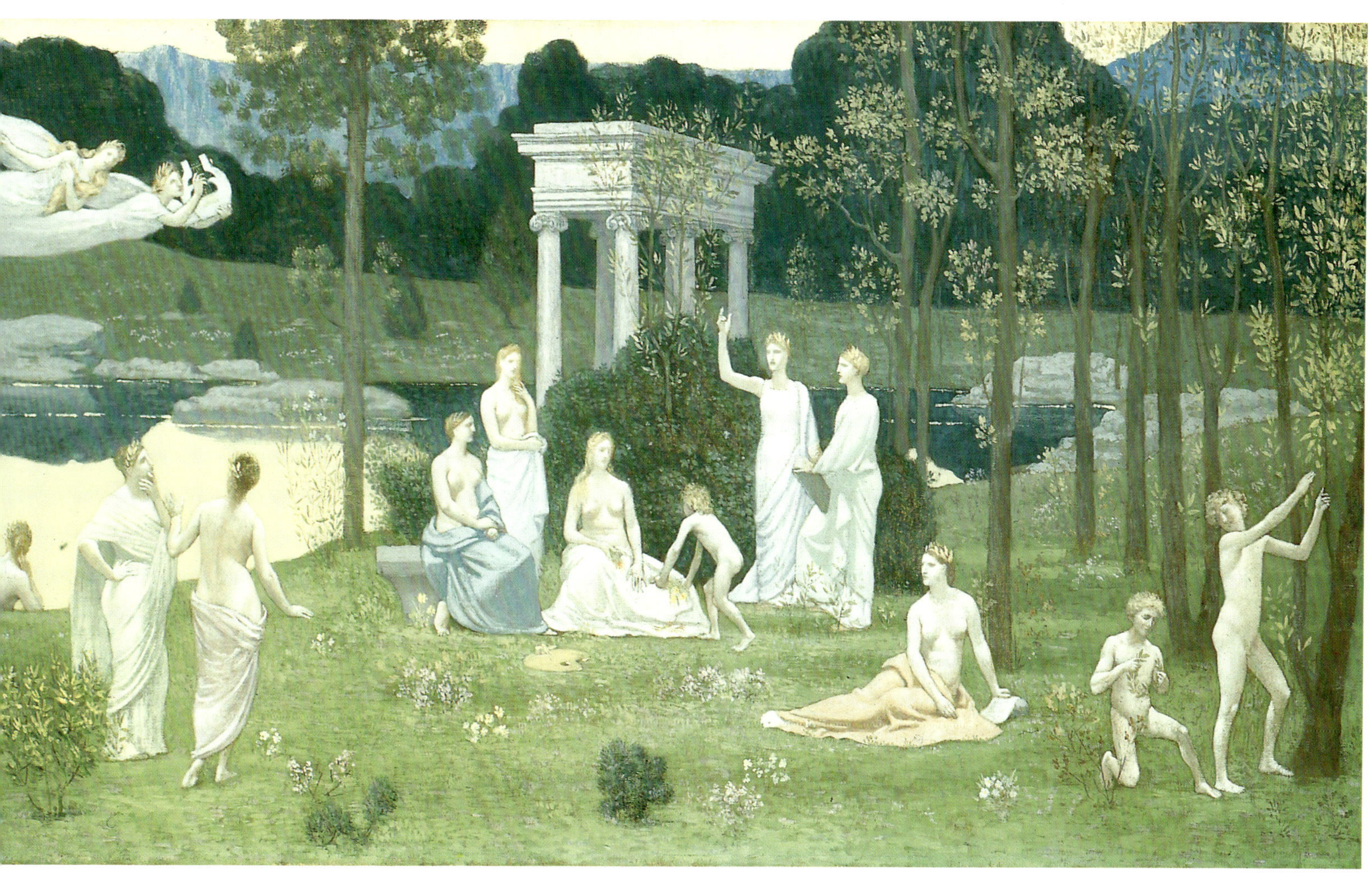

I gave the form of the last to the text of the sacred wood....'[8] Proud of his work, Puvis had stationery printed and tinted in several colors with a variant of his sacred wood in which the muses dance round a herm.[9]

Enthusiastically received at the Salon of 1884, the arrangement ('ordonnance') of the Lyons mural was commended as well as its profound emotion. One critic noted that the charm of what he saw as its almost monochromatic color was lost in reproduction – indeed, an ongoing problem for the proper appreciation of Puvis's murals has always been that their most important qualities – scale, color, and texture – do not reproduce. The critic also noted that Puvis already had his share of followers: 'it is easy to criticize what are generally called M. Puvis de Chavannes's proclivities; it is quite simply the style of a master who too often brings misfortune on the rash souls wishing to imitate him....'[10]

Puvis and his work were something to be reckoned with by the 1880s. In what was essentially a manifesto against Puvis's Arcadia, Toulouse-Lautrec in a large canvas (172 x 380 cm) that satirized *The Sacred Wood* (fig. 36) discounted Parnassus as passé and no longer relevant. He signaled the difference between Parnassus and Paris, with 'real' people – including himself (irreverently turned to urinate) and his friends, Manet and others,[11] trooping through on a would-be guided tour of this exotic site. For Melpomene, the Muse of Tragedy (at the far left), he substituted Puvis's *Prodigal Son* at an easel, painting, underscoring their similarly dejected postures and implying the painter as prodigal. One way or another, artists now had to reckon with Puvis's masterful imagery, and in particular they took account of this painting, whether it was by denying its significance or by quotation. Puvis's art and this painting also became internationally known: in 1884, the Norwegian critic Andreas Aubert, writing in *Christiania Aftenposten*, praised the decorative rhythms and muted colors of *The Sacred Wood*, which he compared to musical harmonies, and Karl Gustav Jensen-Hjell in his 1887 *At the Window* (Nasjonalgalleriet, Oslo), a portrait of a fellow painter (Kalle Lochen) in his studio, prominently included a reproduction of the mural.[12]

1 'J'ai reçu ... le plan de votre magnifique escalier, à la vue de ses belles surfaces tout mon vieux sang de décorateur a bouillonné....', Archive, Musée des Beaux-Arts, Lyons; Puvis apparently made a copy of this letter, 4 June 1883 (private collection), that he kept for himself (compare 1976-77 Paris/Ottawa, no. 234).

2 A gouache maquette clarifies their relationship to the architecture and to each other: 305 x 1720 mm, Musée des Beaux-Arts, Lyons, bequest of

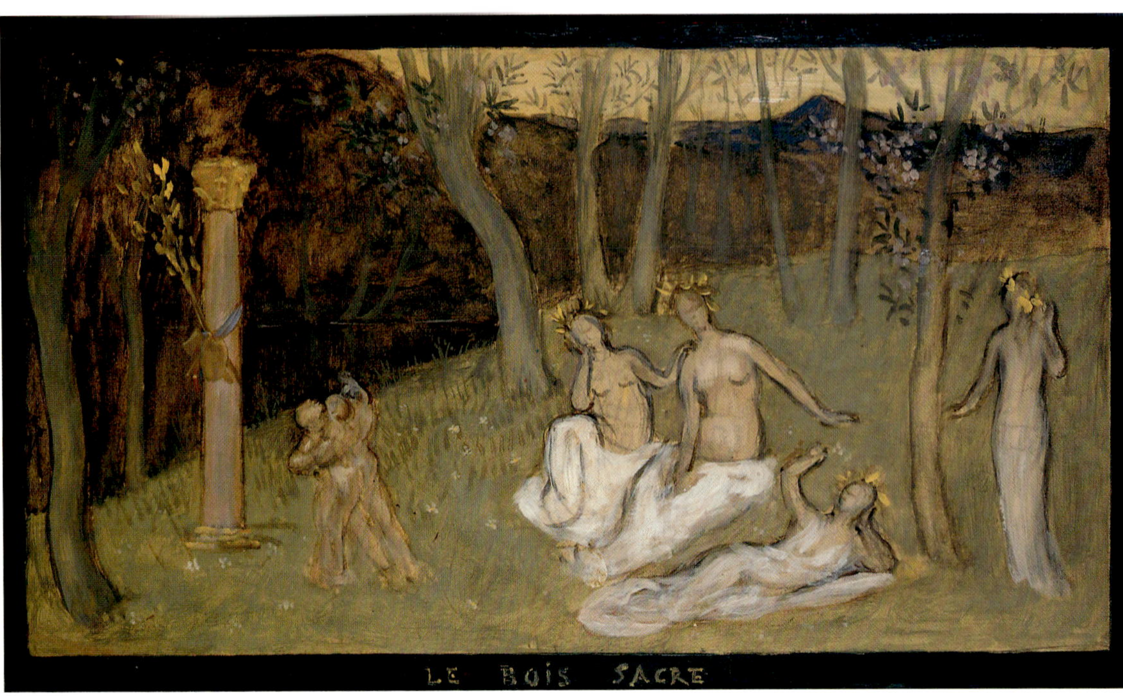

Madeleine Braun (Inv. 1980.12).

3 'La première fresque ... doit accueillir le visiteur au seuil du Musée, comme le baptistère au seuil de l'Eglise. *Le bois sacré cher aux arts et aux muses*, est la génératrice des deux autres: *La Vision Antique* et *l'Inspiration Chrétienne*, car l'art est compris entre ces deux termes, dont l'un évoque l'idée de sentiment.... Si j'avais peint que le sujet de gauche [*l'Inspiration Chrétienne*, actually right if facing *The Sacred Wood*] ... on pourrait, à la rigueur, affirmer que j'ai été hanté par le christianisme du moyen âge; mais, voyons, ce paysage paien qui manifeste si clairement la joie de vivre sur la terre ne faut-il pas un suffisant contrepoids au panneau dont il fait le pendant.' In Sirieyx de Villers (1924), pp. 128-130.

4 Lechat (October 1920), p. 236.

5 Valbert Chevillard, *Un peintre romantique Théodore Chassériau* (Paris, 1893), p. 255.

6 'mettre une façade l'Architecture appuyée sur un des côtés la Peinture peignant ses dessins à ses pieds la Sculpture aussi la Poésie et la Musique seraient assise et de cette façon tous les arts seraient assemblées y permis voir.' Drawing, Musée du Louvre (Inv. RF 25536); quoted more readably in Chevillard, *op. cit.* (note 5), p. 255.

7 'T' (1921).

8 'je regrette de ne pouvoir y joindre l'odeur du parc de bois – j'ai donné la forme dernière au texte du bois sacré....' Letter to an unnamed recipient [Charles Ephrussi] in Switzerland; Bibliothèque Nationale, Paris, Manuscrits (n.a.f. 24839), 496-497.

9 Several variants in private collections.

10 'il est aisé de critiquer ce qu'on est convenu d'appeler les partis pris de M. Puvis de Chavannes; c'est tout bonnement la manière d'un maître qui porte trop souvent malheur aux imprudents désireux de l'imiter....' Comte (1884), 288.

11 Colleagues from his teacher Cormon's studio collaborated on the painting. François Gauzi, *Lautrec et son temps* (Paris, 1954), pp. 116-117, notes the inclusion of Maisonneuve, Terpsichore as La Goulue and Marcelle Lender and Thalia as Sarah Bernhardt in *Phèdre* and even Yvette Guilbert; see Brown Price (1991), for further commentary.

12 See Kirk Varnedoe, *Northern Light. Nordic Art at the Turn of the Century* (New Haven and London, 1988), no. 44, p. 123.

102

The Sacred Wood / *Le Bois Sacré*

ca. 1883-84

Inscribed in the lower border LE BOIS SACRÉ
Oil on paper, laid down on canvas, 38.7 x 65.2 cm
Clemens-Sels Museum, Neuss (Inv. 1962/MA 54)

Provenance Artist's heirs; R. de La Garde, France; Galerie Claude Aubry, Paris (1961); acquired by the museum (1962).
Selected Exhibitions 1976-77 Paris/Ottawa, no. 156.

This small, cursory oil sketch still so different from the final composition for *The Sacred Wood Dear to the Arts and Muses* (see cat. 101) evokes the essential poetry and lyrical mood at its core. It is significant in an oeuvre of methodical procedures in which pencil sketches, numerous studies and drawings habitually preceded painting that at this still early stage color notation is carefully considered and yields a wonderful

103

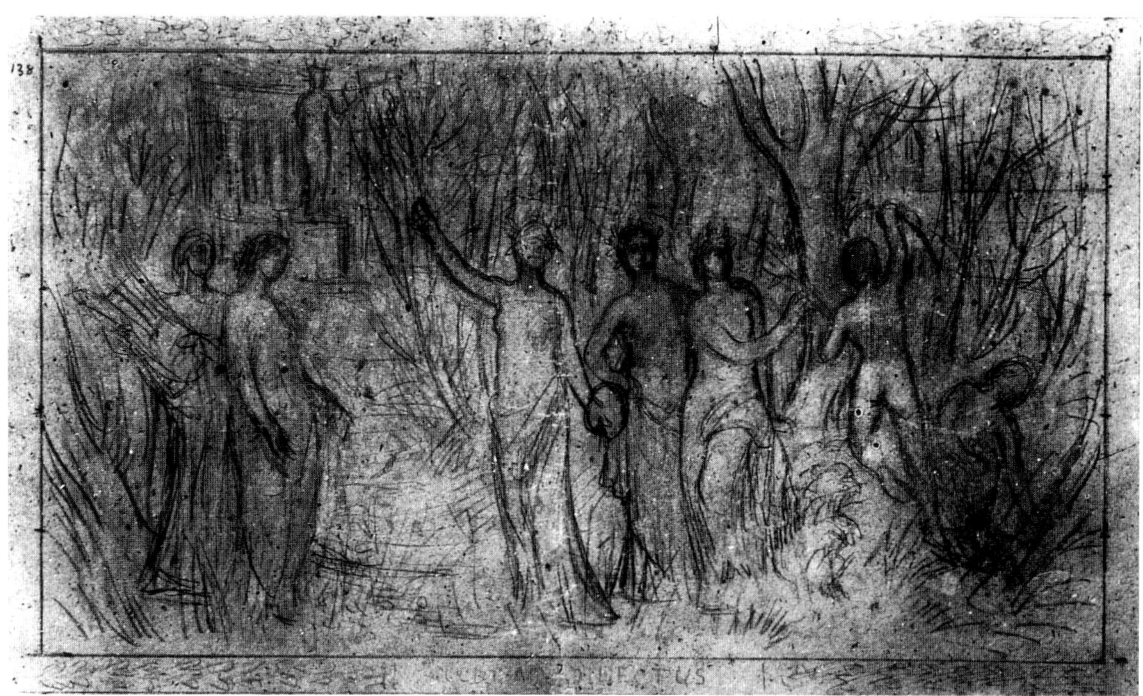

opulence. Because the colors are neither real nor conventional, they play an important part in suffusing the painting with a sense of the marvelous and enchanting. The flowering trees have opaque turquoise green trunks; a light green field is set against a pool of water (left) which is barely distinguishable against a dark ring of hills, and the golden yellow sky is as sumptuous as that of the Byzantine mosaics that it recalls. Furthering the dreamy mood are the single pale pink column and the muses in sparkling white, their heads wreathed with yellow leaves, the whole rimmed with a dark blue painted border in which the title *LE BOIS SACRÉ* is inscribed in yellow.

In several preliminary drawings[1] as here, the rudimentary, circumscribed, essentially cloisonnist little figures – precursors of the highly simplified, flattened and outlined figures that the Nabis painters would develop – document a trail that leads from the wrestling boys, sloping ground, golden skies and single tree of *Pleasant Land* (see cat. 86) to *The Sacred Wood*;[2] and from there, with its sense of playful indolence and qualities of fresh design, to the 1906-07 bucolic idylls of Henri Matisse with their sometimes small, spirited, line-enclosed figures (see cat. 150). In one drawing the figures are basically in the same positions, the single column still to the left (private collection). And in a similar, but slightly larger oil study of a very verdant sacred wood (private collection), an isolated Ionic portico substitutes for the column to indicate classical antiquity.

1 A study in a private collection and *Study for Le Bois Sacré* or *Inter Artes et Naturam* [sic], Národni Galeri, Prague (Inv. K13939).

2 *Pace* Louise d'Argencourt, in 1976-77, Paris/Ottawa, no. 155.

103

'ALLEG AD DILECTUS,' Study for 'The Sacred Wood' ca. 1883-84

Inscribed in lower border: ALLEG AD DILECTUS
Black chalk on dark brown paper, 320 x 552 mm
Musée des Beaux-Arts, Lyons (Inv. B607.24).

Provenance Bequest of artist's heirs to the city of Lyons (1898).

This drawing of companionable muses and boys gathering vegetation – ultimately laurel leaves – in a landscape has elements of several of the classicizing monumental compositions: *Summer* of 1873 (fig. 5; the figure to the far right), most notably *The Sacred Wood* of 1884 (see cat. 101) and what would be *The Sorbonne* of 1886-89 (ill. pp. 200-201). The central figure, an arm raised in a rhetorical gesture used since antiquity in public art, would be Polyhymnia, but now with a palette, she evidently represents Painting. Beside her, the twisting, half-seated woman towards the right, subsequently developed in other drawings, was discarded. To the left a graceful figure plays a lyre, an attribute that in the final composition would be held by one of the flying muses. Puvis frequently included at least a segment of classicizing architecture to help situate his Hellenizing murals. In one early study for *The Sacred Wood* (cat. 102), a single column served; here a small (vestigial) colonnade curves behind a sculpture on a pedestal as would appear to the far right in the Sorbonne mural of *The Sacred Wood* (ill. pp. 200-201). The inscription in the lower border 'alleg[oria] ad dilectus [sic: um]' might be translated, 'allegory for the beloved.'

The dark paper that served to dramatize the scene,[1] was used for several of the earlier drawings for this project[2] but was rarely used elsewhere.

1 Compare also: *Study for 'The Sacred Wood'*, ca. 1883-84, signed and inscribed l.l.: Premiere [sic] pensée du bois sacré/ P. Puvis de Chavannes, charcoal on brown paper, laid down on canvas, 570 x 1175 mm, Walsall Museum and Art Gallery, Manchester.

2 The drawings most closely related to this are one that seems to have just preceded this one, *Study for 'The Sacred Wood'* in the Chrysler Museum, Norfolk, Virginia (Inv. 50.48.71), and a variant of the group to the far right that includes the nude boy from the back at the Musée de Brou, Bourg-en-Bresse (Inv. 898.10).

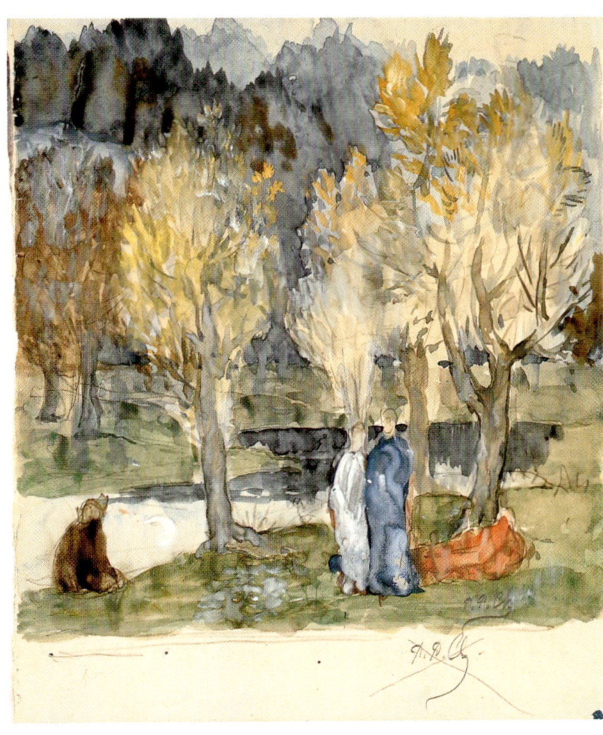

104

Study for 'The Sacred Wood' ca. 1883-84

Signed l.r.: P. P. Ch
Watercolor and pencil on paper, 190 x 190 mm
The Phillips Collection, Washington, D.C. (Acc. 1620)

Provenance Kraushaar Gallery, New York (1922); Duncan Phillips.
Selected Exhibitions 1975 Toronto, no. 24; 1976-77 Paris/Ottawa, no. 175.
Selected References Neff (1969), 68-70, repr.

The light touch and transparent overlays of watercolor in this lovely 104
study for the left central section of *The Sacred Wood* (see cat. 101) transmit the special evanescent beauty of the mythic sheltered enclave. There is a sense of the verdure and fresh ambience of the setting. The foreground figures standing and lying among the trees on the banks of a lake indicate the pastoral character of the work.

105

Antique Vision / *La Vision Antique* (reduced version) ca. 1886-88

Signed l.l.: P. Puvis de Chavannes
Oil on canvas, 105 x 132 cm
The Carnegie Museum of Art, Pittsburgh (Inv. 97.3)

Provenance Durand-Ruel, New York (1895-1897); purchased by the museum from its Annual Exhibition (1897).
Selected Exhibitions 1888 Brussels, no. 384 [this version?]; 1889 Paris (Exposition Universelle), no no.; 1897-98 Pittsburgh, no. 186; 1975 Toronto, no. 28; 1976-77 Paris/Ottawa, no. 176.
Selected References On the mural: Comte (1886), 282; Aynard (1884), pp. 6, 9-10. Vachon [1900], pp. 206-208; 'Antique Vision,' in 'Puvis de Chavannes,' *Masters in Art*, IV (October 1903), 393; Peterson (1961), p. 85. On this painting: Mauclair (1928), p. 163; Peterson (1961), p. 195; Gimpel (1963), p. 106; 'Catalogue of the Permanent Collection,' *Carnegie Magazine*, XXXIX (April 1965), 141, no. 226; *Catalogue of the Painting Collection, Museum of Art, Carnegie Institute* (Pittsburgh, 1973), p. 173; Aaron Sheon, 'Realism to Impressionism,' *Introduction to the Collections of the Museum of Art, Carnegie Institute* (Pittsburgh, 1977), n.p.; Max Kozloff, 'The Anatomy of Disruption,' *Artforum* (December 1980), 66, repr.

The creation of art is one theme of Puvis's Lyons mural complex, and *Antique Vision* evokes art as Form, a Platonic idea, as it pays tribute to a vision of the ancient world. This composition recognizes classical art and Hellenism as the source of an aesthetic and imagery important in Western art. With figures in stilted and angular archaizing poses, Puvis evoked the ancient world as envisioned from the forms of its art. Moreover, surface roughness, pale colors and absence of detail suggest this work itself is ancient in origin.

05

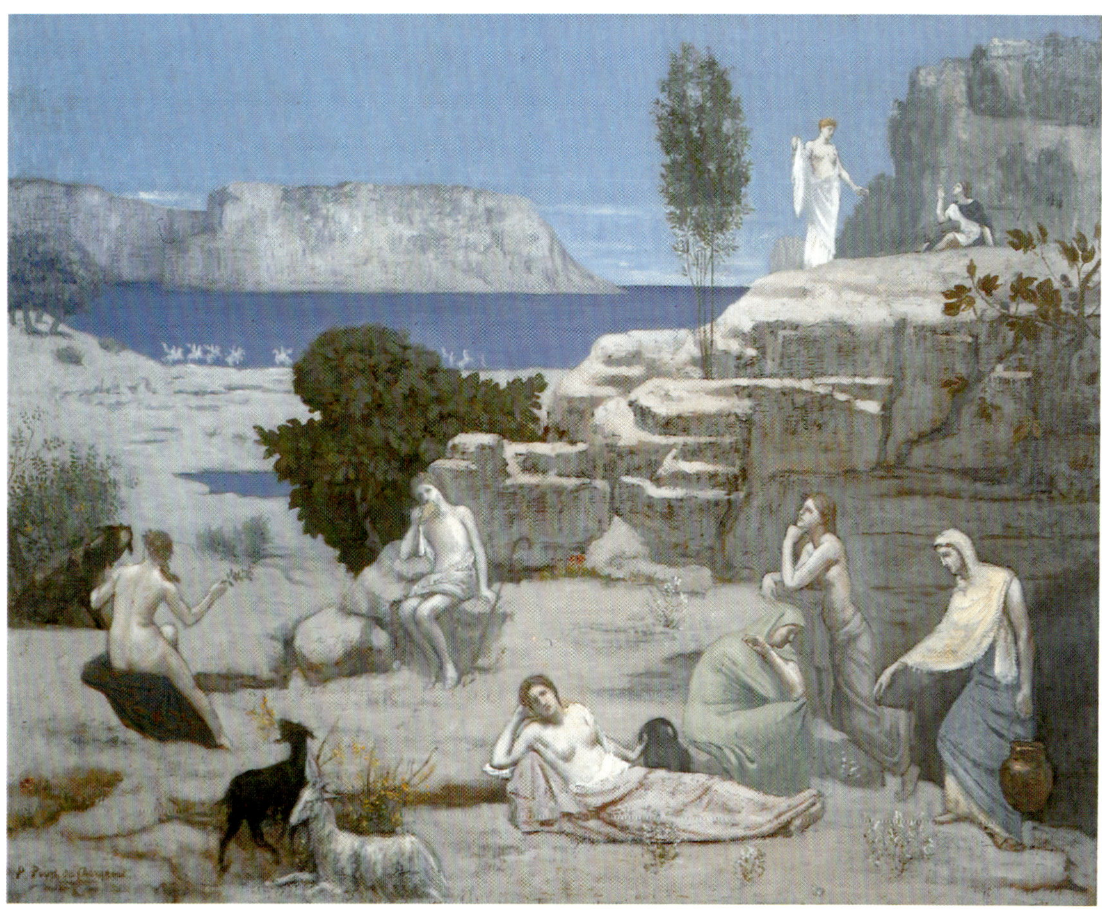

Specific motifs derive from antique sources.[1] Profile figures recall passages of antique reliefs and sculpture: a woman with water jug as on the Parthenon frieze, a recumbent woman like *The Sleeping Ariadne* (Vatican Museums). On the rock to the right, a muse gives a young Phidias a mallet and chisel with which to depict a distant cavalcade of mounted youths such as appears on the Parthenon frieze. *Antique Vision* presents images that were shared by others, as is attested by a dream Théophile Gautier recounted that, in turn, resembles a host of passages in the Parnassian literature of the 1860s: 'I have ... dreams ... of long cavalcades of completely white horses, without harness or bridle, ridden by beautiful nude young people who march past on a band of dark blue color as on the Parthenon friezes, or processions of young women crowned with string fillets with tunics with straight pleats and ivory sistra which seem to turn around an immense vase. – Never fog or steam, never anything uncertain and floating. My sky hasn't any cloud, or, if it does, they are solid clouds trimmed with scissors, made with the fragments of marble fallen from the statue of Jupiter.'[2]

In this as in the other reduced versions[3] of the Lyons murals, colors have been changed, a pot removed, a toga altered. Adjustments are generally towards compactness – the boy's legs moved together, the foliage to the right pruned to a few branches, the branches of the central bush retracted into the main mass – simplicity, abbreviation and flatness.

While the artist allowed himself some freedom in these smaller, portable variants, their colors – here, rose, pinks, tans, a limpid Mediterranean blue and turquoise sky – follow those of the murals, which were carefully keyed to harmonize with the museum walls, just as their shapes were made to resonate with the ambient architecture. The pictorial reasoning is not therefore apparent in canvases not *in situ*; the dusty pink of the landscape and the horizontal stratification of the stone are best explained on formal, not geologic grounds, for they correspond to the framing pilasters and their molding.

1 See Peterson (1961) particularly, pp. 85, 195 and *passim*.

2 'Quelquefois j'ai des autres songes, – ce sont de longues cavalcades de chevaux tout blancs, sans harnais et sans bride, montés par de beaux jeunes gens nus qui défilent sur une bande de couleur bleue foncée comme sur les frises du Parthénon, ou des théories de jeunes filles couronnées de bandelettes avec des tuniques à plis droits et des sistres d'ivoire qui semblent tourner autour d'un vase immense. – Jamais ni brouillard ni vapeur, jamais rien d'incertain et de flottant. Mon ciel n'a pas de nuage, ou, s'il en a, ce sont des nuages solides et taillés au ciseau, faits avec les éclats de marbre tombés de la statue de Jupiter.' *Mademoiselle de Maupin* (first published 1835) (Paris, 1919), p. 211.

3 Another reduced variant includes only the central portion and appears to be a fragment (a recumbent figure is unceremoniously cut off) of *Antique Vision*, oil on canvas, 111.6 x 117 cm (private collection).

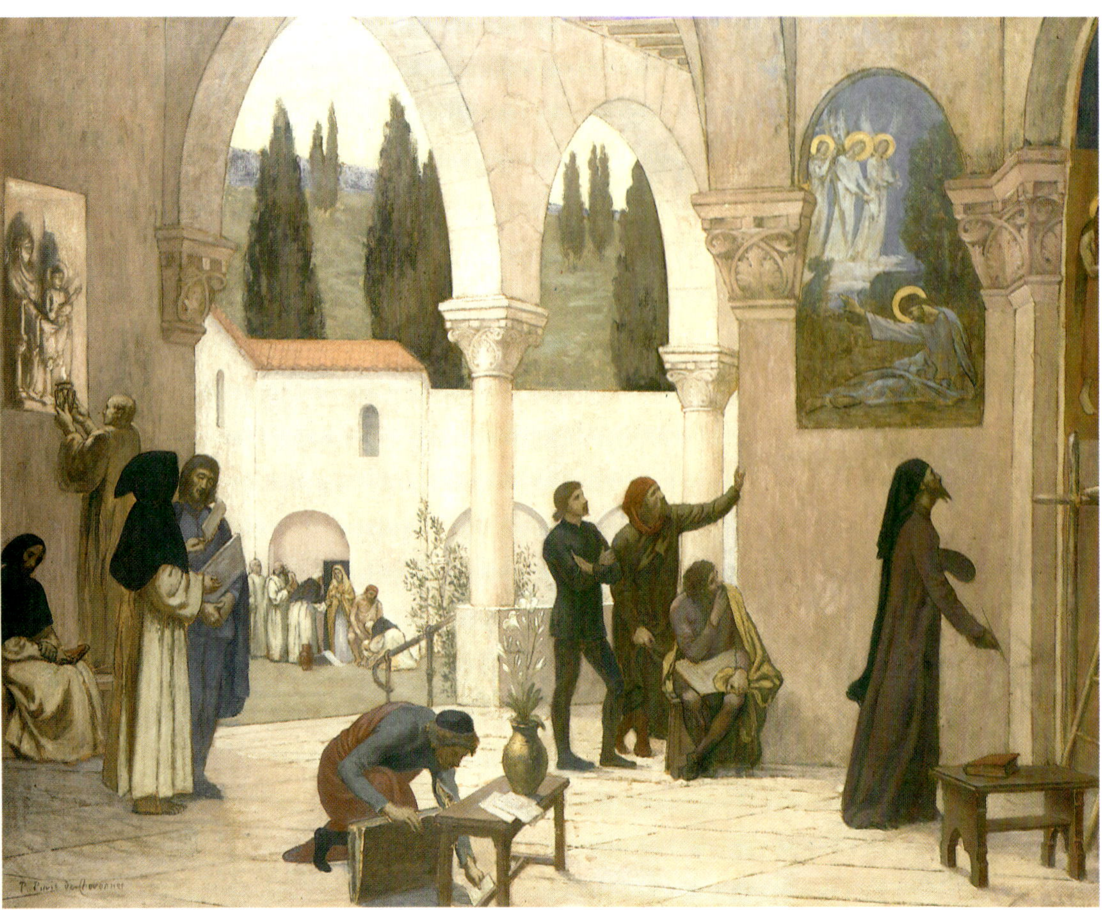

106

Christian Inspiration / *Inspiration Chrétienne* (reduced version) ca. 1887-88

Signed l.l.: P. Puvis de Chavannes
Oil on paper, laid down on canvas, 105 x 132 cm
National Museum of American Art, Smithsonian Institution, Washington, D.C., Gift of John Gellatly (Inv. 1929-6-84)

Provenance Durand-Ruel, New York (1895-1896); R. C. and N. M. Vose, Boston; Mrs. Chauncey J. Blair, New York (1916); Milch Gallery, New York (1928); John Gellatly (1928).
Selected Exhibitions 1888 Brussels, no. 383; 1889 Paris (Exposition Univ.), no no.; 1976-77 Paris/Ottawa, no. 177.
Selected References On the mural: Comte (1886), 282, repr. 308; Aynard (1884), pp. 6, 9-10; Vachon [1900], pp. 208-209; Riotor (1896), pp. 58-59; Michel and Laran (1911), pp. 89-90; Sirieyx de Villers (1924), pp. 128-130; Peterson (1961), pp. 89-90. On this painting: Michel and Laran (1911), p. 90; 'R.C. and N.M. Vose, Boston,' *Art and Archaeology*, XXXV (May-June 1934), 114.

Antique Vision and *Christian Inspiration* represent a bifurcated system of antique form and Christian feeling suitable for Lyons, a city in which religious art thrived. Years before, Théophile Gautier had said that Art was the synthesis of form and feeling,[1] and in 1855, in a frequently repeated phrase, he had exhorted artists to 'baptise Greek art.'[2]

Portraying religion as *functioning* as inspiration for the making of art is a cunning determination particularly apt for a museum setting. Puvis disclaimed any alleged mysticism in his work and discounted a personal connection with the Lyonnais school of religious painters: 'Now, if one really wants to take the trouble to look at my *Christian Inspiration*, will one find the glorification of ecstasy and mortifications? Not at all, here is what I have done: A religious-painter, some Fra Angelico, is busy finishing a mural decoration. Far from being overwhelmed by the infinite, he seems seized with a fever for work, he seems to want to rush to his work to add the last touches: his whole being is in movement. Behind him, as evening approaches, another monk begins to light the lamps, and then, young people arrive, young artists who lean in at the threshhold of the door to learn a lesson from the master by watching him at work. I would very much like to know if there is anything else in all that than evidence of human activity. These men think about God, but first they live, they are involved with their physical and moral strengths. That's my own philosophy and not the contemplative spirit of the Middle Ages.'[3]

Anne Condron Peterson has suggested this scene is not medieval at all, but depicts nineteenth-century Lyonnais painters, the heads modeled after those of Hippolyte Flandrin, Victor Orsel and Paul Chenavard, who are admiring the work of Renaissance artists.[4] Puvis might well have alluded to these artists here without depicting a contemporary scene. He called the man in monkish costume a Fra Angelico figure, which does not disallow the possibility of his being identified with Hippolyte Flandrin, who was called the Fra Angelico of his time, or Viollet-le-Duc, who was responsible for the restoration of many medieval structures. A personal sense may also be imputed to the scene because the painter is a muralist and the work he is finishing resembles Delacroix's *Christ in the Garden of Olives* (Church of Saint Paul-Saint Louis, Paris)[5] as well as Chassériau's version of the same subject (Church of Sainte-Marie, Souillac).

The Camposanto at Pisa, designated in the contract as the setting for *Christian Inspiration*, was the cradle for Christian sentiment in art according to both English Pre-Raphaelites and German Nazarenes, and Benozzo Gozzoli's murals there had inspired Puvis in his murals at Le Brouchy.[6] A maquette of the Lyons Museum stairwell[7] shows the cloister arches were originally meant to respond to and accentuate the tympana above them, but in the final version, a more generalized monastery has been substituted.

More summarily painted than the mural, this reduced version has essentially the same composition, with the addition of a lamp on the right.

1 Louis Hautecoeur, *Littérature et peinture en France* (Paris, 1942), pp. 93-94.
2 Théophile Gautier, *Les Beaux-Arts en 1855* (Paris, 1855), p. 250.
3 'Maintenant, si on veut bien prendre la peine de regarder mon *Inspiration Chrétienne*, est-ce qu'on trouvera la glorification de l'extase et des macérations? Nullement, voici ce que j'ai fait: Un religieux-peintre, quelque Fra Angelico est en train d'achever une décoration murale. Loin d'être abîmé devant l'infini, il semble pris d'une fièvre de travail, il a l'air de vouloir s'élancer sur son ouvrage pour y mettre les touches suprêmes: tout son être est en mouvement. Derrière lui, comme le soir approche, un autre religieux commence à allumer les lampes, et puis, des jeunes gens arrivent, des jeunes artistes qui s'appuient au seuil de la porte pour prendre une leçon du maître en le regardant faire. Je voudrais bien savoir s'il y a autre chose dans tout cela qu'un témoignage en l'honneur de l'activité terrestre. Ces hommes pensent à dieu, mais d'abord ils vivent, ils font leurs forces physiques et morales. C'est cela ma philosophie à moi et non l'esprit contemplatif du moyen âge.' Sirieyx de Villers (1924), pp. 128-130.
4 Peterson (1961), pp. 89-90.
5 Colin Harrison pointed this out; my thanks to him.
6 Brown Price (1972), p. 268.
7 *Maquette for 'Christian Inspiration,'* watercolor, pen and ink, 562 x 595 mm (formerly collection M. Jean Puvis de Chavannes, Paris; present whereabouts unknown), with the mural indicated.

107

Ludus pro Patria *or* The Family / *Ludus pro Patria* or *La Famille* (reduced version, fragment) ca. 1885-87

Signed l.l.: P. Puvis de Chavannes
Oil on canvas, 94 x 125 cm
The Toledo Museum of Art; Purchased with funds from the Libbey Endowment, Gift of Edward Drummond Libbey (Inv. 1951.313)

Provenance Lazare Weiller, Paris (from at least 1887); Paris, Hôtel Drouot, Lazare Weiller Sale (29 November 1901), no. 38 [as *La Famille*]; Bernheim (1904); Prince de Wagram, Paris [at Durand-Ruel, Paris, May-November, 1909; returned to Prince de Wagram] (-1930); Knoedler Gallery, New York; Edward Drummond Libbey.

Selected Exhibitions 1887 Paris (Durand-Ruel), no. 35, *Esquisse* [belonging to Weiller (same?)]; 1899 Paris (Durand-Ruel), no. 14 [called *Réduction du Ludus Pro Patria*, seconde partie (same?)]; 1975 Toronto, no. 20 repr.; 1976-77 Paris/Ottawa, no. 151.

Selected References Werth (1926), pp. 15-25, pl. 15; Ralph Flint, 'Return of the Prodigal Son,' *Art News*, XXIX (1 November 1930), 3, repr. 110. Carlyle Burrows, 'Letter from New York,' *Apollo* (December 1930), 453, repr. 454; Seitz (1951), 20-22; [Anonymous], *Toledo Museum News* (November-December 1951), 1-15 [called *Allegorical Scene*]; Denis (1957), I, p. 152; Foucart (November 1976), 3.

The Family, with the subtext of fecundity, contentment and continuity, a recurring theme in many of Puvis de Chavannes's public paintings, is iterated in this variant of the right section of *Pro Patria Ludus*, Puvis's panoramic (450 x 1750 cm) 1882 mural for the Musée de Picardie, Amiens (see ill. pp. 192-193).[1] After an interval of some seventeen years, France's defeat in war and a change in government, Puvis completed, with this mural, his series of monumental paintings for Amiens that had begun in 1861.

In reassuring, classicizing and Utopian terms, the three sections of this mural celebrate the nation, 'patria,' as a community, while underscoring the continuity of its values and its protection. At left small groups are busy with household tasks, supervising children, conversing within an enclosure of thatched huts. In the center, young men practice war games[2] by throwing *picques* or pikes, the characteristic weapon from which the name of the region, Picardy, is derived.[3] At right, several generations are assembled together, 'le culte du foyer et des ancêtres' that contemporary

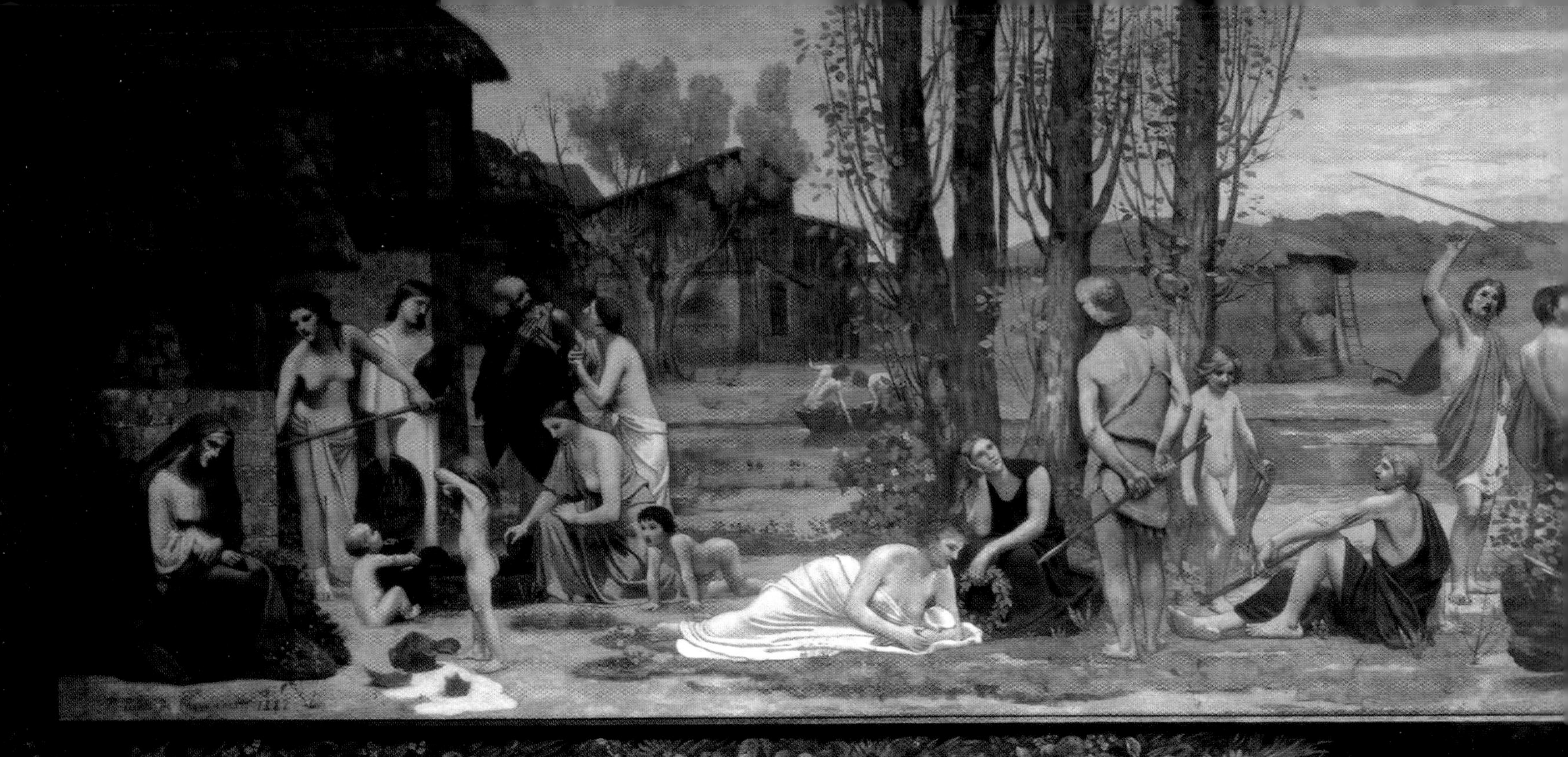

social theorists such as Numa Denis Fustel de Coulanges viewed as the source and center of French culture.[4] Whether as a glowing idealized vision, palliative or diversion, the intergenerational family of this official Arcadia indicated order in a society beset by economic problems, industrial change, emigrations from provincial regions (such as Picardy) and political disruption.

Arranged in frieze-like fashion in a single plane, the classicizing figures are ingeniously interrelated, braided into a concise formation that recalls antique reliefs via Poussin and Ingres. The beautifully mannered pose of the male figure in profile to the right, one leg stepped up to a higher level, his back rounded to a 'C,' a study in angular and curved rhythms, recalls Ingres's Oedipus (*Oedipus and the Sphinx* Musée du Louvre, Paris, reversed) after Poussinesque prototypes. The child facing away from the viewer with his arm about the old man also assumes an Ingresque turned pose, but this is cunningly contrived as a lyrical countercurve balance to the tree to the right.

This canvas is essentially a fragment,[5] albeit a magnificent one, with a larger composition implied: several figures face expectantly towards the left at what would be the center of the mural. The absence of pictorial bracketing yields some abruptness and this canvas contains several puzzling details, such as the pikes in the tree to the right, which have been thrown by figures in the central portion.

The muted blue-green-gray tonalities, dry painting technique and rough, scumbled surface distinguish this variant of *Ludus pro Patria* from the mural, in which there is a fuller range of color chords. The tones, more experimental and adventurous here than in another independent variant section,[6] indicate experience with the pastel medium with which Puvis worked from about 1887 particularly; this canvas may have been executed in conjunction with the 1887 Durand-Ruel retrospective.

The stately women holding children are reminiscent of similar imagery by Chassériau, to whose work on the theme of motherhood Puvis's owes so much.[7] Family and motherhood were not necessarily positive themes or blandly foregone patriotic conclusions. For those with a revolutionary agenda, Family might be a loaded and even inflammatory notion[8]: from this perspective, Puvis's families may be judged as retardataire affronts, social entities that undermined a progressive socio-political program, object lessons in keeping women mothers and preventing their becoming equal members of a labor force. From this viewpoint, public projects had counter-revolutionary iconographic programs that included patriarchal families, and motherhood would then be not so much an iconographical subtheme as a subplot.[9]

Ludus pro Patria, 1882
Musée de Picardie, Amiens

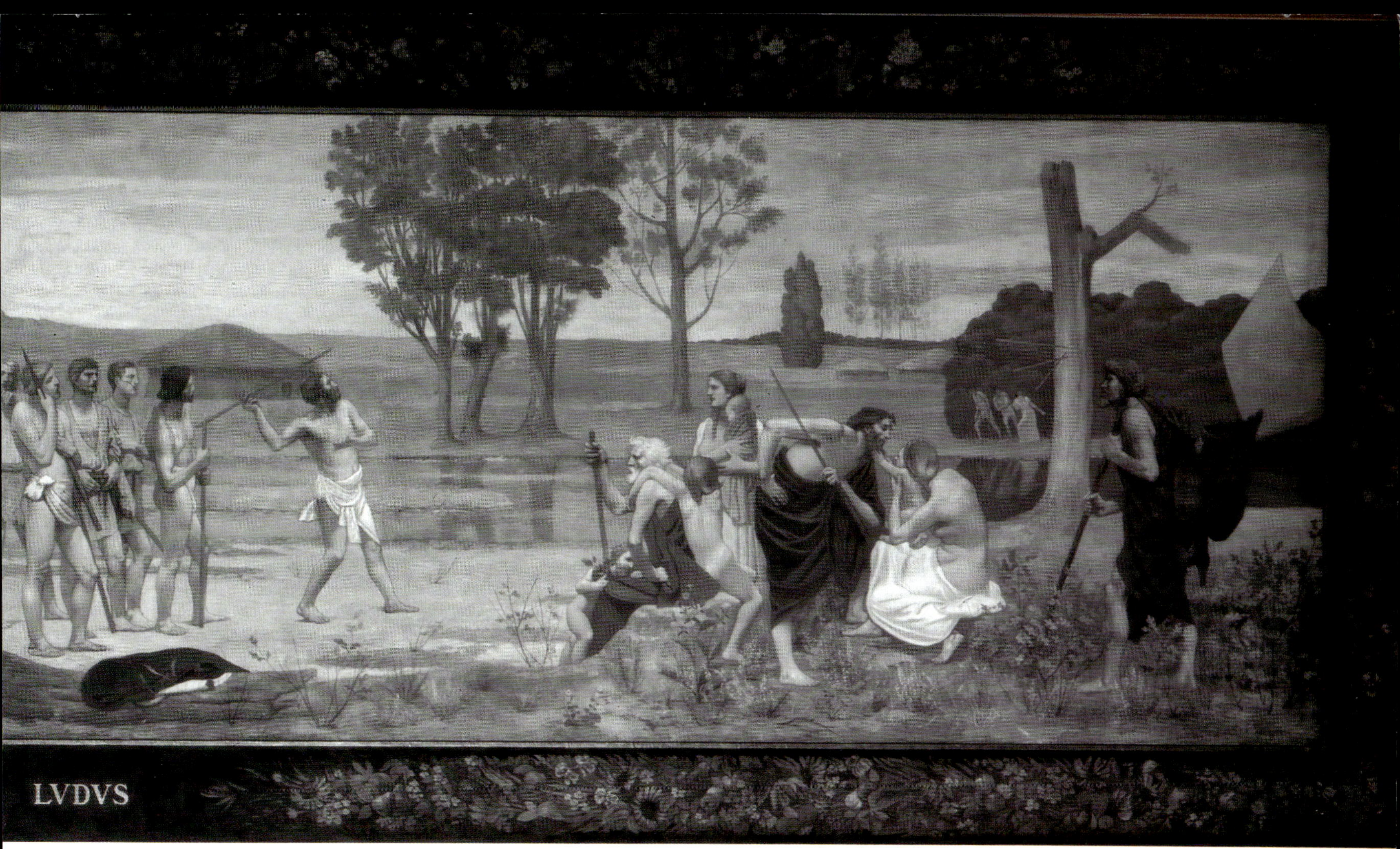

LVDVS

07

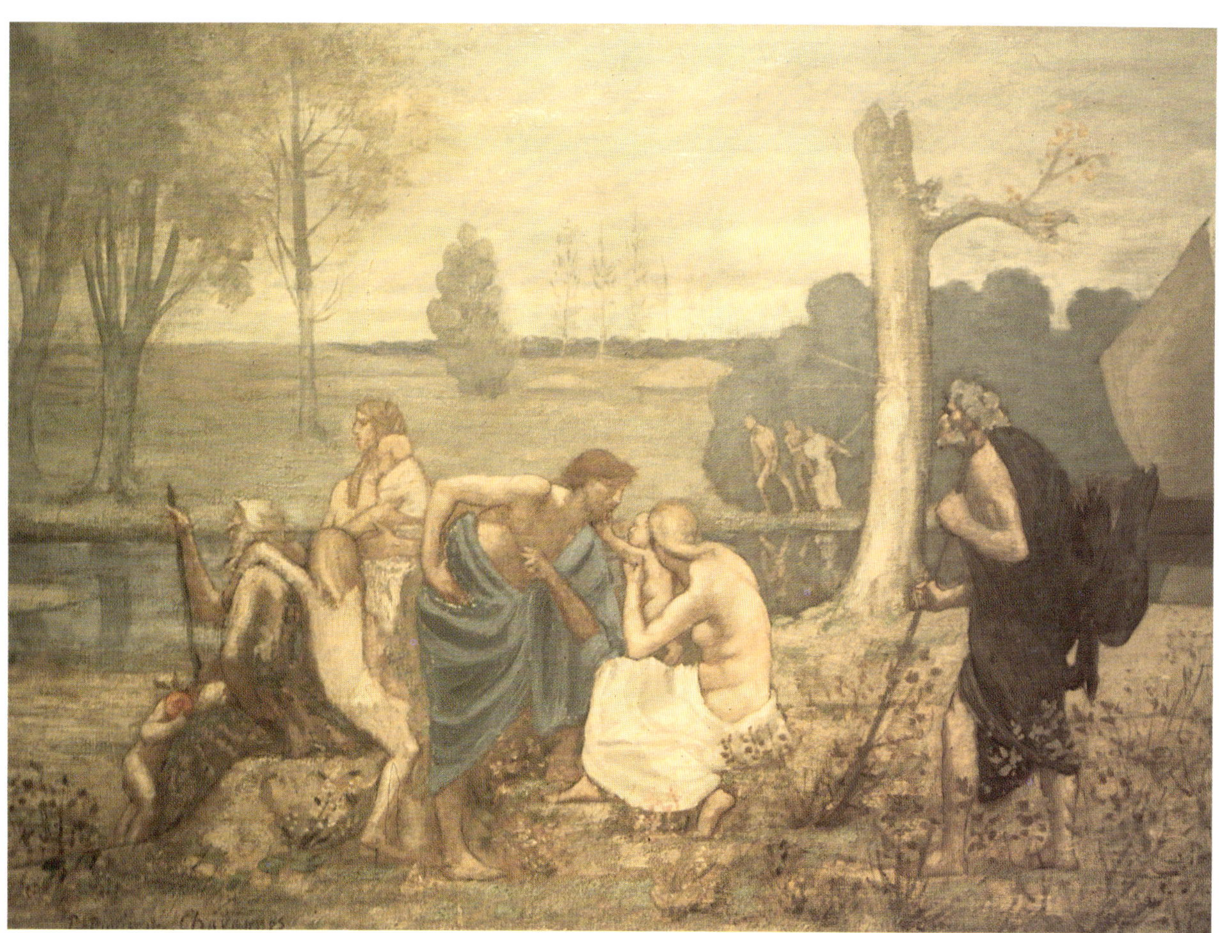

1 Usually named *Ludus pro Patria*, it was presented at the 1882 Salon and installed in 1888; see 1976-77 Paris/Ottawa, pp. 165-167. There is also a reduced version (33.4 x 134.5 cm) at the Metropolitan Museum of Art, New York.

2 Beginning in 1882, still in reaction to the unpreparedness which brought on the 1870-71 war, national societies created 'bataillons scolaires' for military instruction in the schools and just such training; it would seem to be the same sentiments that engendered both the mural and such programs. See *Les cahiers aubois d'Histoire et d'Education*, no. 2 (1978) and Georges Merlier, 'Les Bataillons scolaires en Normandie,' *Cahiers d'Histoire de l'Enseignement*, no. 1 (Rouen, 1973), 99-128.

3 D'Argencourt (1973), pp. 126, 133-139.

4 Fustel de Coulanges established his frame of reference in *La Cité Antique* (Paris, 1864); see particularly pp. 25, 104-110, 416 (of 8th ed., 1880).

5 One day other sections may be located; the Weiller sale included a work of similar dimensions: no. 39, 94 x 280 cm; also mentioned was a canvas called *Sketch for the Primitive Age* (*Esquisse pour l'Age primitif*), 62 x 251 cm; 1976-77 Paris/Ottawa, no. 151, theorizes that one work was cut in two by an American client, implying, perhaps Lambert; this was stated in Thadée Natanson, *Peints à leur tour* (Paris, 1948).

6 See the 1883 variant of the central section, also called *Ludus pro Patria*, 113.5 x 198 cm, Walters Art Gallery, Baltimore; in 1887 Puvis consigned it to Durand-Ruel for sale as 'fragment avec variante très importante du tableau intitulé *Pro Patria Ludus*.'

7 See Sandoz (1974), section 'Les mères,' pp. 47-48.

8 'the *Journal Officiel* of the Commune ... attempting to define what kind of family might develop in a régime of socialism ... began ... with an outright rejection of the word 'famille' in the Academic dictionary; it implied ... a definition of a whole reactionary *society*, a hierarchical group with a father at its head!' Without further citation by Adrian D. Rifkin, 'Ingres and the Academic Dictionary: An Essay on Ideology and Stupefaction in the Social Formation of the "Artist,"' *Art History*, VI (June 1983), 163.

9 Discussion in Mitchell (1987), 191-202; with little differentiation, however, between causality and coincidence.

108

Maternity *or* The Small 'Bresse' / *La Maternité* or *La Petite Bresse* ca. 1887

Oil on canvas, 39 x 24 cm
Private collection

Provenance Artist's heirs and by descent.
Selected Exhibitions 1937 Lyons, no. 52 [as 50 x 30 cm; perhaps the measurements of the frame]; 1976-77 Paris/Ottawa, no. 184.
Selected References Durand-Ruel Archives, no. 179 [same as *La Petite Bresse*, November 1877 (sic?)].

In this superb small canvas on the theme of motherhood, so appealing to Puvis as it had been to Chassériau,[1] the motif of a standing woman with three children was given its independent due. Maternity themes had been included repeatedly in the murals, and this particular passage was first formulated in the context of Puvis's 1865 *Ave Picardia Nutrix* (see cat. 39). Here that group is pictured as a half-draped woman with children clinging closely to her, a hut and sheltering wood nearby. The woman's upper body is nicely framed by the white of her headgear and the cloth around her hips. The faint outlines of a basket (lower left) indicate a careful pruning of elements that might distract from the central theme. There is a larger, strikingly spare variant of *La Bresse*,[2] a personification of the region to which Puvis traced his origins[3] and in which lies the community of Chavannes. Perhaps he wished to pay tribute to his motherland; to do so with a maternity figure would be most apt.

The beautiful grouping of figures, the placement and depiction of the children with their turned heads (particularly at left), show extraordinarily bold liberties taken with compositional structure for the purpose of overall design, inventions that foreshadow twentieth-century ways. Probably to account for its broad technique, dry, opaque pigments and surface texture, *Maternity* was called an unfinished sketch when it was exhibited in 1937 and in 1976-77 as well. Although it may have been painted as a preliminary to the larger *La Bresse*, the setting and figure are considerably different, and it clearly can stand on its own.

1 Bénédite [1931], I, p. 159, repr.; see Sandoz (1974), section 'Les mères,' pp. 47-48.

2 The larger version 61 x 43 cm (whereabouts unknown), see Brown Price (1977), 33-34, repr. 36; also Boucher (1979), repr. p. 54. According to Durand-Ruel Archives, a *La Bresse* was bought from Puvis on 22 March 1872. On 6 November 1890, it is listed as sold to M. Crocker [not in the records of the Crockers of Sacramento, however]; yet a painting of like title is recorded with M. Duret [Théodore Duret, Paris?] (1887), and exhibited 1887 Paris (Durand-Ruel), no. 2. See Durand-Ruel Archives, Paris, no. 1135, 20.331, 459; and Kahn (1888), 145-146.

3 Georges Lecomte, *Ma Traversée* (Paris, 1949), pp. 307-308; and Vachon [1900], p. 140.

109

Study for 'Maternity' or 'La Bresse' ca. 1887

Black chalk on tracing paper, 345 x 147 mm
Musée Paul Dupuy, Toulouse (Inv. 92)

Provenance Bequest of artist's heirs to the city of Toulouse (1898).

08

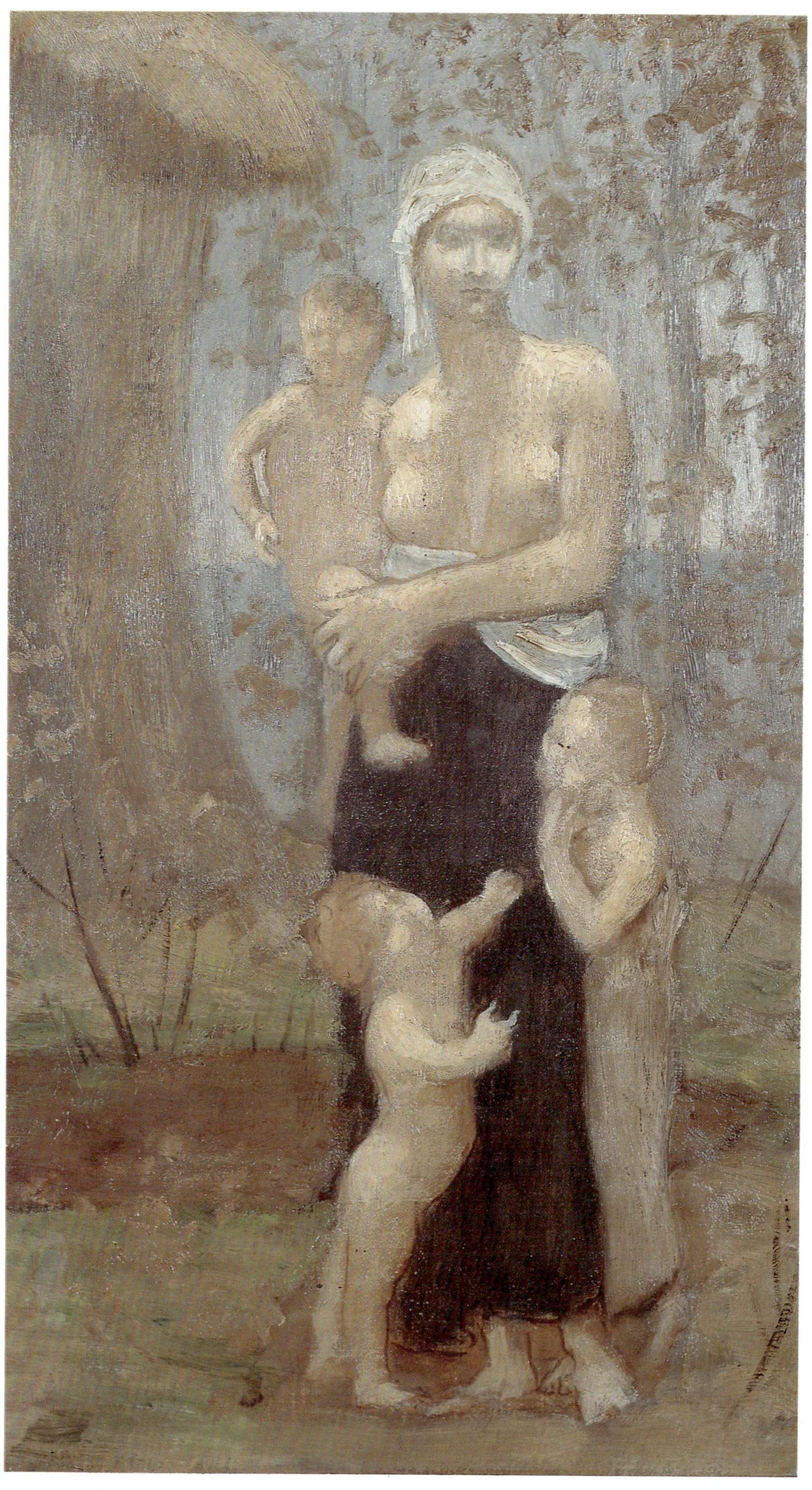

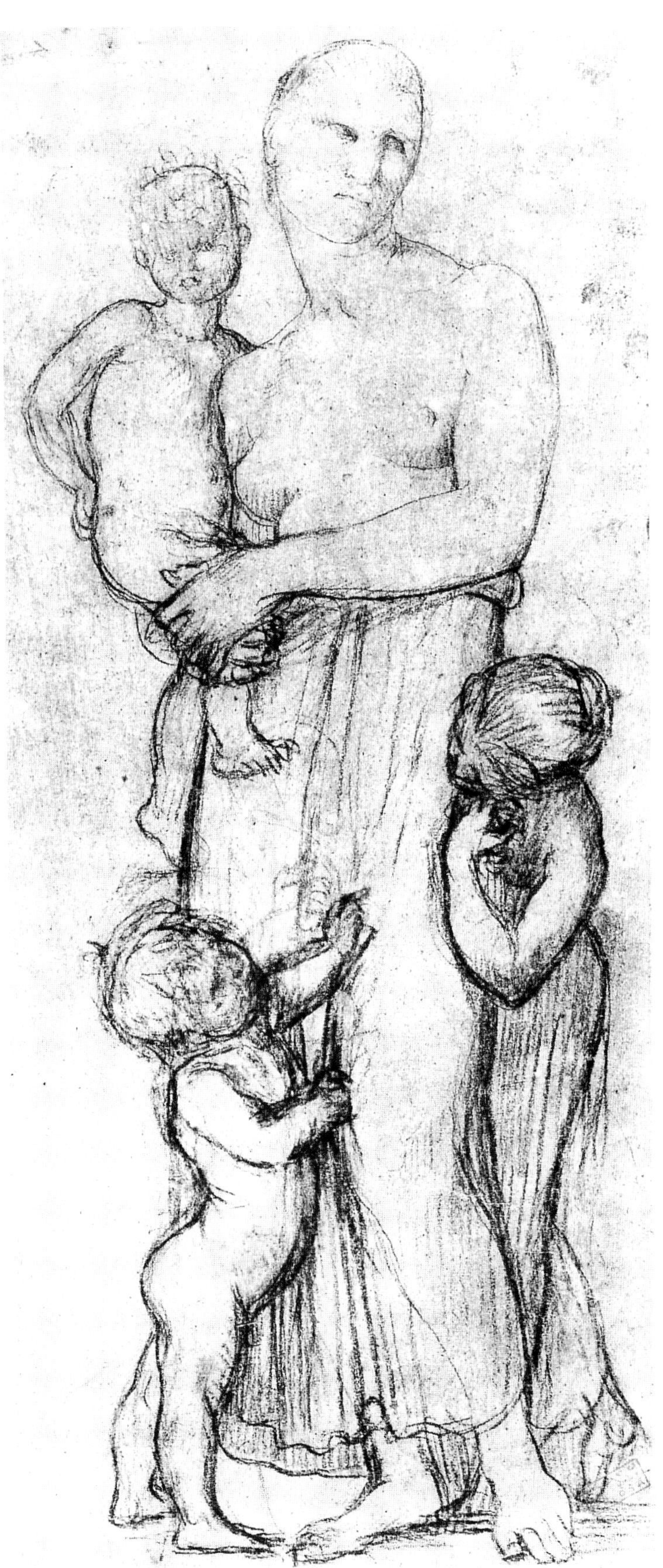

This familiar motif of a mother standing holding a child, her other chil- 10
dren clinging to her for protection and peeping from around her skirts, is here shaved down to its essential curves and countercurves. This drawing is remarkable for its conceptualization of the generously proportioned figure of the woman and the sensualism and pleasure found in the few austere forms themselves, a pleasure we know and are more familiar with in the works of a Picasso. While here the figure is slightly turned and her weight shifted, in the painting she would become more frontal and straightened.

110

Pity / *La Pitié* 1887 (not in the exhibition)

Signed l.l.: P. Puvis de Chavannes 1887
Pastel on canvas, 100.6 x 83 cm
State Pushkin Museum of Fine Art, Moscow
(Inv. 3325)

Provenance Durand-Ruel, Paris; Collection Shchukin, Moscow; Museum of Modern Western Art, Moscow (1918-48).

Selected Exhibitions 1889 Paris (Exposition Universelle, Exposition de la Société des Pastellistes Français), no. 1; 1894 Paris (Durand-Ruel), no no.; 1897 Copenhagen, no. 288; 1899 Paris (Durand-Ruel), no. 50.

Selected References Yriarte (1894), 1; Raoul Sertat, 'Revue artistique,' *La Revue encyclopédique* (15 December 1894), 384, repr. 383; P. Pertzov, *La Collection de peinture française de Stschoukine* (Moscow, 1922), p. 83; *Catalogue of the Museum of Modern Art* (Moscow, 1928), no. 470; L. Réau, *L'Art français dans les musées russes* (Paris, 1929), no. 1055; Brown Price (1977), 34, 40; *La Peinture française au Musée Pouchkine (Moscou)* (Leningrad, 1980), repr. p. 395.

Pity, an unusually large pastel, depicts a disheveled woman, half-sitting, half-lying against a mass of stones, her hand grasped by a compassionate cloaked and hooded figure standing beside her. Puvis had long been interested in inventing new kinds of allegorical figures, and this work, which was solicited as a contribution to a fund-raising raffle,[1] must have been conceived as a suitable vehicle for that occasion.[2] Like Charity, a subject that Puvis would later develop (see cat. 140), Pity is appropriate to the development of the special iconography of mercy and aid. In his *Héroisme de Pitié*, the historian Jules Michelet, whom Puvis greatly admired, wrote approvingly (if condescendingly) of the importance of

110

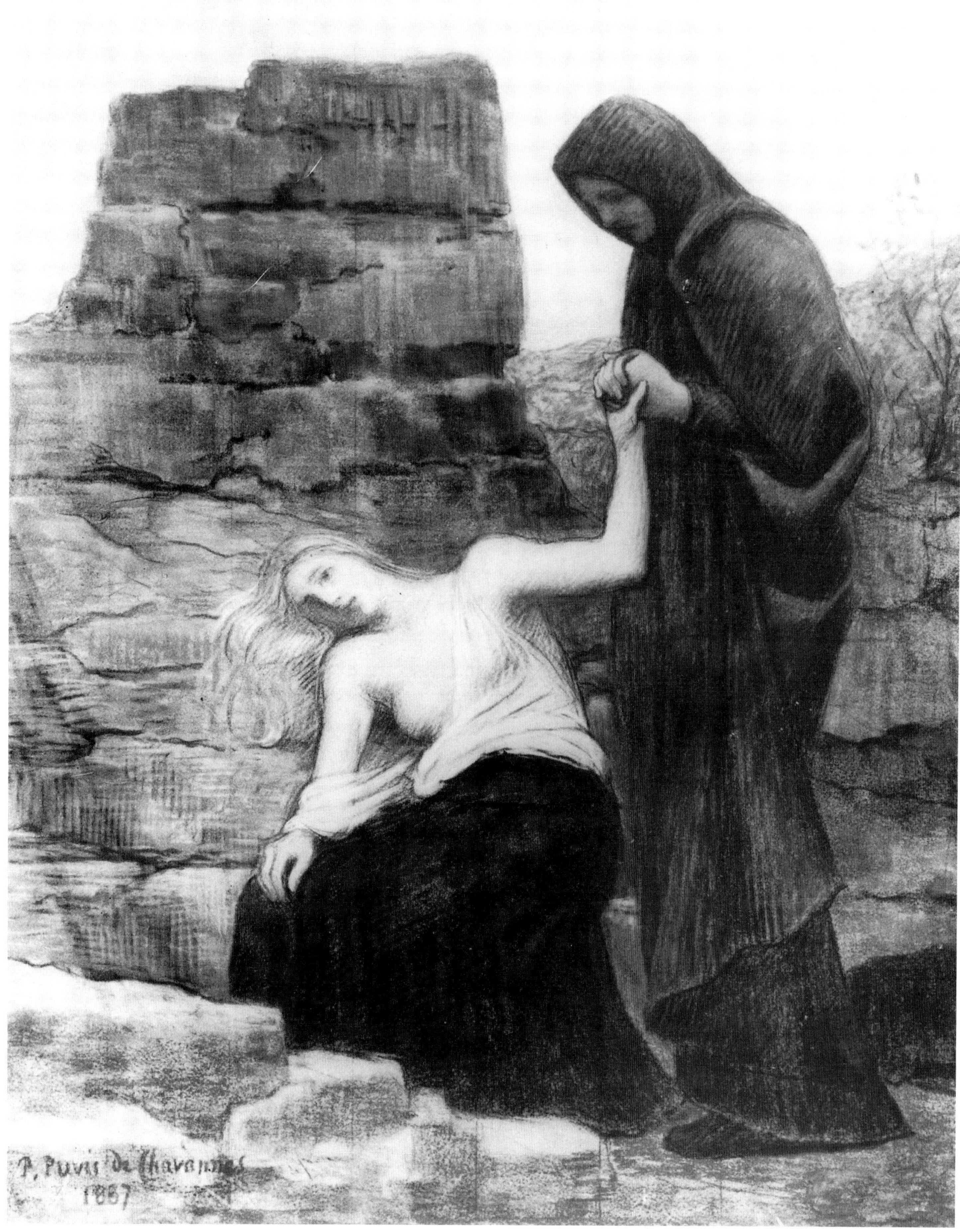

Pity as a heroic female role or as properly embodied by women: 'The first appearance of women in a heroic career ... took place, as one would have expected, through a burst of pity.'[3]

Pity is a secularized transmutation of a *Pietà*, and the composition might be compared to that of Puvis's early painting on that theme with which he had made his Salon debut in 1850, the *Dead Christ* (Mokhtar Museum, Guezira, Cairo). Both the Christ and the subject of *Pity* are posed in a similar manner, while the hooded, succouring and merciful figure, much repeated in paintings of the 1880s and 1890s, is reminiscent of Puvis's early Madonna. There are versions of such figures, posed for by the Princess Cantacuzène, in the 1870-71 *Symbol of the Red Cross* (Musée du Petit Palais, Paris) and continuing through to the 1890s with *Patriotism* (Hôtel de Ville, Paris, and Ohara Museum of Art, Kurashiki, Japan) and *Charity* (see cat. 140). The upper body of the seated young woman resembles that of the figure to the left in the 1879 *Young Women by the Sea* (cat. 76, fig. 6).

Pity is one of Puvis's largest pastels. The medium enjoyed a revival in France in the 1880s, and Puvis came to use it often.[4] Puvis's pastels generally appear from about 1887, and were doubtless encouraged by Durand-Ruel in conjunction with Puvis's retrospective that year. With the exception of this work and one other quite large pastel, *Botany* (Minneapolis Institute of Art), these works were generally small to medium-sized, rapidly executed, often quite lovely and, as colored examples of Puvis's work, readily salable to the growing number of his admirers. While Puvis's pastels are generally light colored and chalky, with few dark or somber hues, colors were adjusted for theme, and *Pity*, with its dark skirted and cloaked figures, is the exception. The texture of the dry, light, opaque medium itself as Puvis usually used it resembled the surfaces of his contemporaneous scumbled, granular oil paintings – and, more importantly, they increasingly resembled pastels. Exposure to Impressionist works and Puvis's own lightened colors of the 1870s must have done much to habituate viewers to the powdery, opaque colors.

1 A letter of 30 April 1887, from Prince Auguste d'Arenberg, President of the Société philanthropique, thanks the artist for his donation to such a raffle (private collection).

2 According to Mme Boucher, without further sources, it was also called *Secours de Nuit* and offered at a charity raffle for L'Oeuvre de l'Hospitalité de nuit; see 1976-77 Paris/Ottawa, no. 202.

3 'La première apparition des femmes dans la carrière de l'héroïsme ... eut lieu, on devait s'y attendre, par un élan de pitié.' in *Les Femmes de la Révolution* (Paris, 1854), n.p.

4 Pastel was used extensively by artists such as Millet, who was partly responsible for its revival, and Degas, who presented numerous pastel nudes at the eighth Impressionist exhibition in 1886. It was promoted by the Société des Pastellistes, founded in the 1880s.

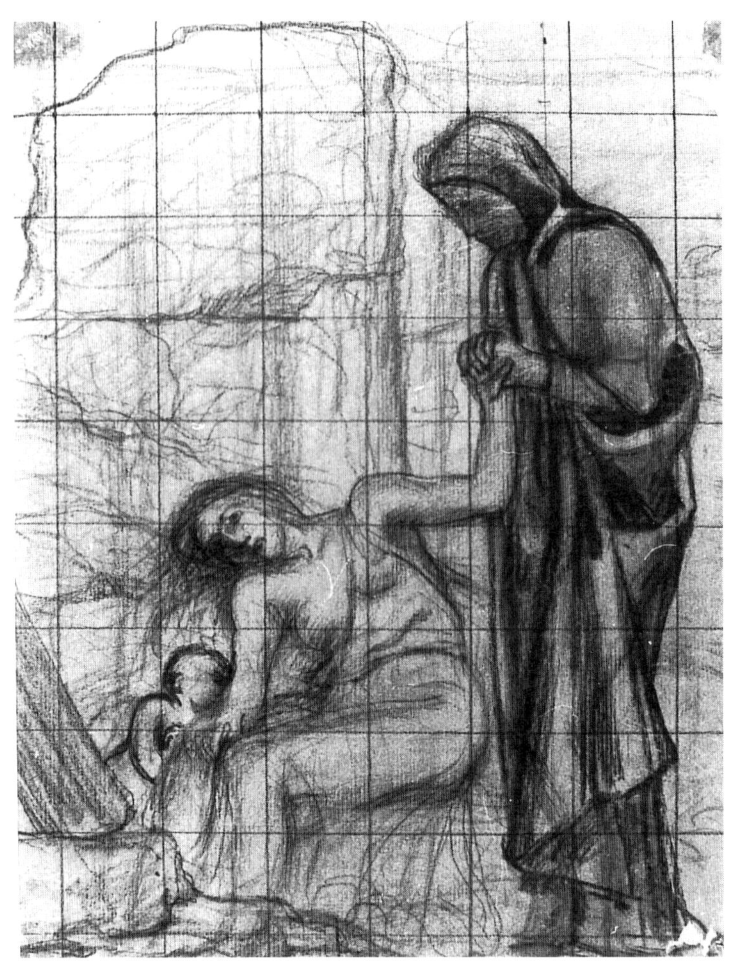

111

Pity 1887-93

Pencil, black chalk and ink on gray paper, squared, 313 x 238 mm

Musée Paul Dupuy, Toulouse (Inv. 104)

Provenance Bequest of artist's heirs to the city of Toulouse (1898).

Beginning with the 1870-71 war and continuing through the 1890s with his series of so-called *'Parisian Virtues'* for the refurbished Hôtel de Ville of Paris (see cat. 139), Puvis created modern allegorical figures, his own 'allégories réelles.'[1] This drawing bridges two of his inventions, his large pastel *Pity* of 1887 (cat. 110) and *Charity* of 1894 (cat. 140; other versions at the Paris Hôtel de Ville and the Gifu Museum, Japan). The child at left in this drawing indicates a link to *Charity*.

1 Brown Price (1977).

The Sorbonne Mural

In 1886, through the offices of Henri Paul Nénot, the architect for the new Sorbonne, Puvis de Chavannes received the commission for a great mural (570 x 2600 cm) for the gently curving wall of what would be the university's principal amphitheater (ill. pp. 200-201).[1] Nénot recognized Puvis's ability to 'obey the laws of architecture' as Philippe de Chennevières had put it, and justified his choice by stating Puvis's paintings would not detract from the architecture – a leading argument, as always, in his favor.[2]

Nénot designed the new building to reflect recent educational reform and provide a structure in which the diverse disciplines of a modern university could have a real rapprochement.[3] The new Sorbonne was to comprise a faculty of letters and 'hautes études,' and a faculty of sciences, with the Ecole des Chartes replacing the former theological faculty. With an ongoing struggle between the secular government and religious institutions for control of education, the administration was especially 'anxious to assert the "spiritualism" of the university's teaching against allegations of materialism.'[4]

On 24 May 1886, having received the official contract and pleased with what he called the possibility of his 'slice of glory,' Puvis privately both gloated and complained, 'if I succeed – to have my name at the Panthéon, the Sorbonne and later the city hall, that's having it in all of Paris. The government patrons know that full well, the rogues, and exploit that position to tighten their purse – the surface that is no less than 170 meters will pay me 35,000 francs....'[5] On 18 June he wrote, 'I am beginning to ruminate on my work for the Sorbonne, but only in my head – I feel as if I were one month pregnant, this work resembles a gestation period. – let's hope that the child will present itself in fine form.'[6]

Although a proposal was made to represent the history of the University of Paris, and Nénot had a Raphael-like *School of Athens* in mind – in part what he got – the Sorbonne was to be another sacred wood: the grove of academe. Puvis's commission called for a single composition set out of doors in which, in a 'very synthetic' manner, he was required to include all the intellectual disciplines of the university, the humanistic disciplines on the one hand, and the theoretical and applied sciences on the other.

Puvis de Chavannes's preliminary drawings (see cat. 112-121) indicate the development of pictorial ideas from a confined landscape of small dimensions to the actual panorama, a hemicycle in which five groups of figures echo the theater space and five cusps of banked rows of balcony seats of the auditorium opposite. The Sorbonne mural is sectioned off via a deceptively simple system that provides both for a basic division into three zones and continuity through overlapping sections.[7] These create symmetrically slackening and, at center, quickening rhythms that match the evenly distributed punctuating accents of the architecture. Mood, color and tone for the mural – ideal, sober, not too vivid, calm – were designated. The figures provide a welcome human modular scale in the three-storey well of space that can seat three thousand – as surely as Le Corbusier's famous 'homme' a century later.

The vice-rector of the University of Paris, Octave Gréard, was the administrator most closely allied with the project. In December 1886, at Puvis's studio in Neuilly, they consulted on the designation and arrangement of the figures: 'It is there that, on a corner of his little work table, in front of an already striking sketch, we together fixed the first features of the description which translated his thought. In the clearing of a sacred wood, seated on a block of marble, the *Sorbonne*; at her sides two geniuses carriers of palms; at their feet, a spring is spouting. At right these Letters: Eloquence standing, Poetry represented by Muses dispersed in diverse poses on the lawn, History and Archaeology investigating the entrails of the past; Philosophy discussing the mystery of life and death. At left [sic; they were to be at the right], the Sciences: Geology, Physiology, Botany, Chemistry symbolized by their attributes, Physics partly opening her veils before a host of young people who offer her, as a first-fruit of their work, a flame of electricity, in the shade of a grove, Geometry meditating on a problem. On this "outline" that I kept, Puvis de Chavannes later put together a developed explanation, proper to use in the interpretation of his work.'[8]

As the central figure for the 'grand amphithéâtre,' characterized as the 'cathédrale du scientisme républicain,' Puvis shrewdly devised the 'Virgin of Science,' a secular Madonna, to communicate the laicization of education while brilliantly resonating with older, religious associations. The personifying figures on either side of her, which serve literally to humanize abstract academic disciplines, are used insofar as possible to embody the discipline within a current context. History, for example, is portrayed as a figure encountering archaeological ruins in accordance with new emphasis on history as the scientific reconstruction of the past through analysis of material remains. Puvis had portrayed History similarly in an 1866 mural complex (see fig 30) and he was to take it up again with the excavation of ancient remains in *Inter Artes et Naturam* (ill. pp. 214-215) and in a mural for the Boston Public Library (see cat. 143). Historical interpretation is depicted separately as Erudition. The then major division between materialism and spiritualism with attendant doubt and pessimism (as emotional components of choice) represents Philosophy.

References to scientific experiment – a phial of bacterial culture, a scalpel – were introduced at the behest of the Minister of Public Instruction, D. Kaempfen, in whom Puvis recognized a powerful ally. Indeed, Puvis accepted his advice along with that of Gréard and no less a personage than Jules Ferry. Puvis even accepted Kaempfen's advice in

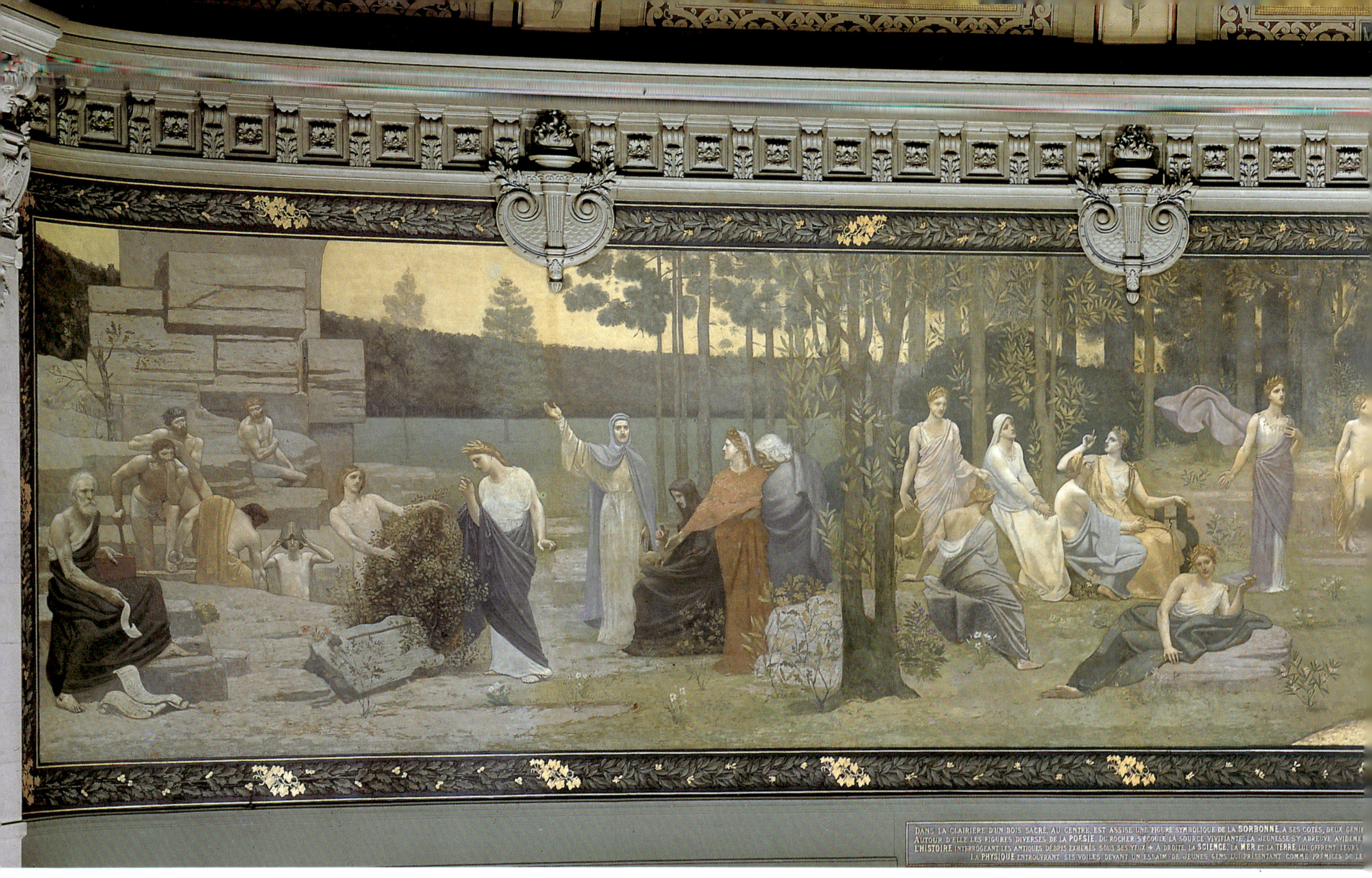

censoring his depiction of Science (to the far right), as he wrote him on 10 March 1887: 'I reflected a good deal on the observations you related to me regarding Science ... all that is very just and when your letter reached me, things were already changed – of course to the extent of the means of which a drawing can dispose [?]; in sum, the study of the phenomena of life is mentioned, but discreetly, for the Sorbonne isn't the medical school – Now one sees on the ground living shell life, sea anemones mingled [?] ... with algae, – a child who dangles them [?] ...holds a scalpel, and examines a lizard that is encamped before him – the other small boy has swapped ... for ... his crystal cube of ... rolls [?] for a phial of cultures – In short ... that can give you an idea of the present state of this cartoon that cannot be governed as one wishes....'[9]

On 5 August 1889, Sadi Carnot, President of France, inaugurated the great amphitheater with pomp and circumstance amidst city, state and university dignitaries and emissaries from foreign universities. Two days later, the mural was officially unveiled, and with artists and notables present, Puvis was named Commander of the Légion d'honneur.

Student revolutionaries in 1968 singled out Puvis's Sorbonne mural for vandalism. With its immutable figures, forever unperturbed and imperturbable, carefully distributed in the best of all Arcadian settings, precisely the sense of authoritative order sought after by the university administration in the 1880s became to the students – who correctly interpreted it – the maddening embodiment of unyielding establishment ideas.

1 Monographs on Puvis all have sections on the Sorbonne mural program. In addition, see: Letters to Valentine, 9 July 1884; 11 [or 17?] May 1886; 24 May 1886; 18 June 1886 (private collection); letter to Kaempfen, 10 March 1887 (private collection); AN F^{21}4867 and F^{21}2106; Aman-Jean (1890); Vachon [1900], pp. 106-108, 225-226; Louis Liard, *L'Enseignement supérieur en France*, 1789-1893, vol. 2 (Paris, 1893); Nénot (1895); Buisson (September 1899), 213-214; Nénot (1903); Smith (1909), 22-23; Mandach and Wehrlé (1911), 454, 456; Michel and Laran (1911), pp. 93-96; Fontainas and Vauxcelles (1922), pp. 296-298; Thiébault-Sisson, 'Puvis de Chavannes d'après des souvenirs personnels, *Feuilleton du temps* (11 January 1925), n.p.; Werth (1926), p. 56; Vaisse (1980), p. 585; Maurice Agulhon, 'Un Décor Républicain,' and Pierre Vaisse, 'Les peintres et le commande officielle,' in Philippe Rivé, *La Sorbonne et sa Reconstruction* (Lyons and Paris, 1987), pp. 151-156 and 165-170 respectively; Paule René-Bazin, *La Sorbonne* (Bellegarde, n.d.).

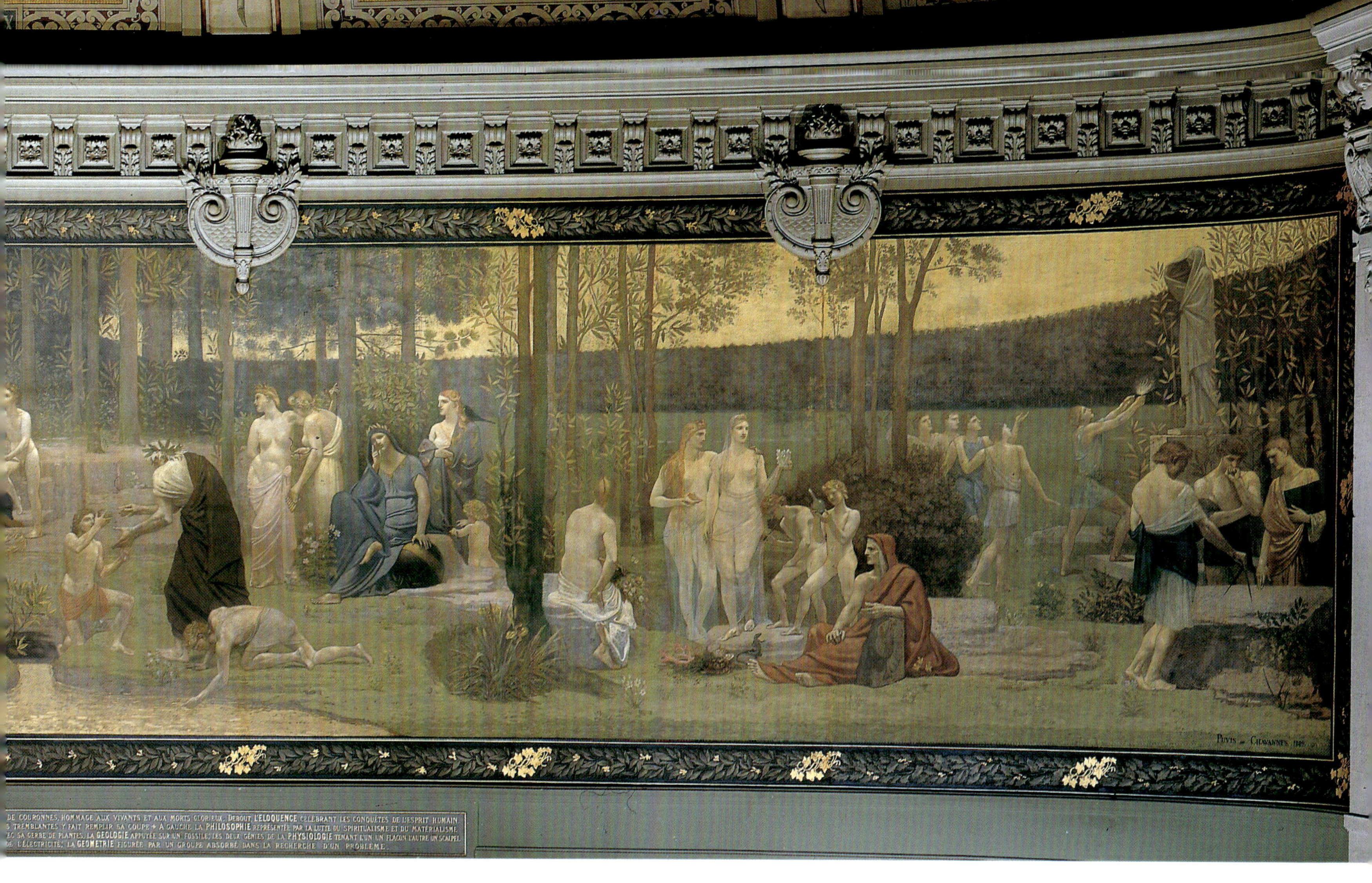

2 AN F21 4867; see Vaisse (1980), p. 585.

3 Nénot (1895).

4 R.D. Anderson, *Education in France 1848-1870* (Oxford, 1975), p. 176.

5 'si je réussis – avore [sic] mon nom au Panthéon, à la Sorbonne et plus tard à l'hôtel de ville c'et l'avoire [sic] dans tout Paris. Les mécenes du gouvernement le savent bien, les malins, et dis en profitant pour serrer leur bourse – cette surface qui n'a pas moins de cent soixante dix mètres superficielles me sera payée trente cinq mille francs....' Letter to his sister-in-law Valentine (private collection).

6 'je commence à ruminer mon travail de la Sorbonne, mais dans la tête seulement – je me fais l'effet d'être enceinte d'un mois, dans ce travail ressemble à une gestation. – espérons que l'enfant se présentera bien.' Letter in a private collection.

7 Charles Bouleau, *Charpentes: La Géométrie secrète des peintres* (Paris, 1963), p. 209.

8 'C'est là que, sur un coin de sa petite table de travail, devant l'ébauche déjà saisissante, nous avons fixé ensemble les premiers linéaments de la description qui traduisait sa pensée. Dans la clairière d'un bois sacré, assise sur un bloc de marbre, la Sorbonne; à ses côtés deux génies porteurs de palmes; à ses pieds, une source jaillissante. A droite ces Lettres: l'Eloquence debout, la Poésie representée par les Muses éparses en diverses attitudes sur le gazon, l'Histoire et l'Archéologie fouillant les entrailles du passé; la Philosophie discutant le mystère de la vie et de la mort. A gauche, les Sciences: la Géologie, la Physiologie, la Botanique, la Chimie symbolisées par leurs attributs, la Physique entr'ouvant ses voiles devant un essaim de jeunes gens qui lui offrent, comme prémice de leurs travaux, une flamme d'electricité, à l'ombre d'un bosquet, la Géometrie méditant sur un problème. De ce "crayon" que j'ai conservé, Puvis de Chavannes a tiré plus tard une légende developpé, propre à servir d'interpretation à son oeuvre.' Nénot (1895), pp. 9-10.

9 'J'ai beaucoup reflechi aux observations que vous m'avez faites à propos de la Science ... tout cela est très juste et quand votre lettre m'est arrivée les choses étaient déjà modifiées – bien entendu dans la mesure des moyens dont peut...[?] disposer un dessin; bref, l'étude des phénomènes de la vie est mentionnée, mais discrètement, car la Sorbonne n'est pas l'école de médecine – On voit maintenant à terre des coquillages vivants, des anémones de mer mêlées [?] ... à des algues, – l'enfant qui le pendre [?] ... tient un scalpel, et examine du lezard qui campe devant lui – l'autre garçonnet a troqué .... du ... son bloc du cristal de roules [?] ... contre un flacon de cultures - ... ce que peut donner l'état présent de ce carton que l'on ne peut pas manier comme on veut – ....' (private collection).

The Sorbonne, 1889
Sorbonne, Paris

112

Composition Study for 'The Sorbonne'

ca. 1886

Stamp l.r.
Black chalk on paper, 93 x 290 mm
Museum Stiftung Oskar Reinhart, Winterthur
(Inv. 2309)

This, the most rudimentary of the composition studies for the Sorbonne exhibited here, and two others (cat. 113 and 114) set forth a formulation considerably different from what ultimately would be pictured in the great amphitheater. The idea was for a 'real' setting, an interior or hall, with a panoramic wall painting of a landscape with an enormous tree-like form branching out and figures under it: a painting in a painting. The decoration sketches are divided into three sections, the large center portion with the painting contrasting to those at the ends with their arch forms.

In June, 1886, Puvis wrote his family he had been thinking of the Sorbonne mural for a month.[1] A Winterthur drawing[2] that is more developed than this one is inscribed '6 août 86,' indicating that the drawing shown here and similar ones must date from earlier that summer. Puvis must have worked on the whole series of compositional drawings in the autumn of 1886, for a cartoon for the central section of the mural was exhibited *hors catalogue* at the 1887 Société des Artistes Français. According to Roger-Ballu it was the apotheosis of the 1887 Salon.[3]

1 Letters of 24 May and 18 June 1886 (private collection).
2 Inv. 2311.
3 Roger-Ballu, 'Salon de 1887,' *L'Illustration* (30 April 1887), 289, 286 repr.

113

Composition Study for 'The Sorbonne'

ca. 1886

Stamp l.r.
Pencil on paper, 106 x 313 mm
Museum Stiftung Oskar Reinhart, Winterthur
(Inv. 2310)

More distinct and developed than the previous study (cat. 112), this one shows a clear interior space, a large schoolroom with a mural on the wall. The arched, curtained entry to the left is surrounded with figures; a table is to the right of center, and at the right a globe and telescope – geography and astronomy – may be seen behind more curtains. High on the wall is a shelf with laboratory equipment – the sciences. A hilly landscape beyond is given as a setting.

114

Composition Study for 'The Sorbonne'

ca. 1886

Stamp l.r.
Pencil on paper, 104 x 403 mm
Museum Stiftung Oskar Reinhart, Winterthur
(Inv. 2308)

This study clarifies a first conception of the mural with its tripartite division articulated through architecture and the indication of arches at each end. The tree form at the center of the interior mural is also further defined.

After having thus formulated a picture within a picture (compare cat. 112-113, 119), the artist may have had a failure of nerve, or it may be the commissioning body was not pleased with his design – though there is no direct evidence as such of this possibility. At any rate, the classroom that he had earlier contemplated disappeared. A sacred grove, like that Puvis had created for his Lyons mural (see cat. 101), was to supplant that idea.

115

Composition Study for 'The Sorbonne'

ca. 1886

Pencil and charcoal on three sheets of paper glued together of irregular heights: left to right: 155, 202 and 155 mm respectively; entire width: 697 mm
Museum Stiftung Oskar Reinhart, Winterthur
(Inv. 2312)

This study is crucial in the development of the actual Sorbonne scheme. The interior envisaged in previous drawings has all but disappeared, with the arcades, through which a landscape setting appears now to be asserting itself, only a faint reminder. A temple-like structure is to the left and a curved stepped structure to the right.

12
13
14
15
16

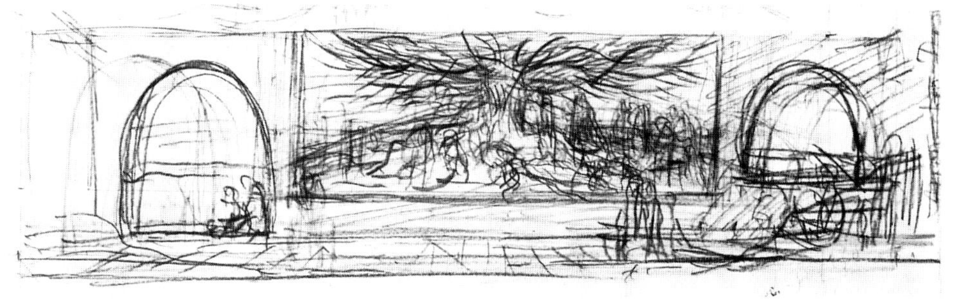

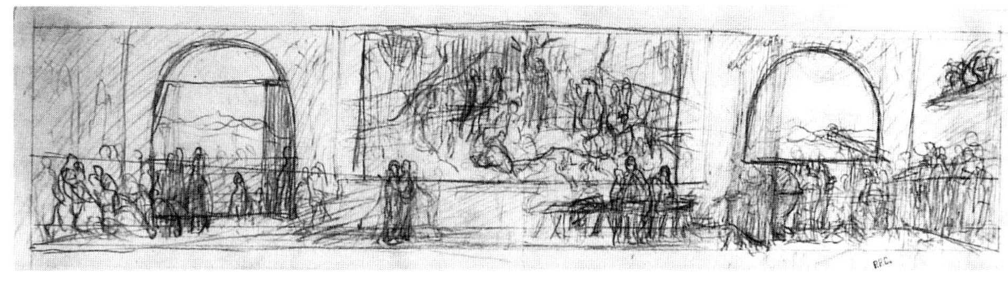

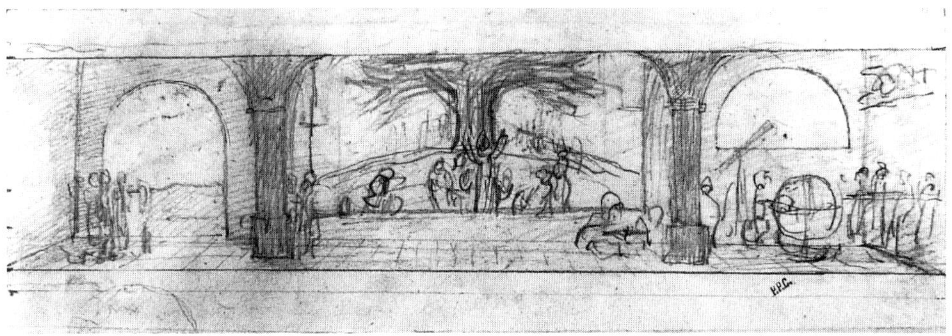

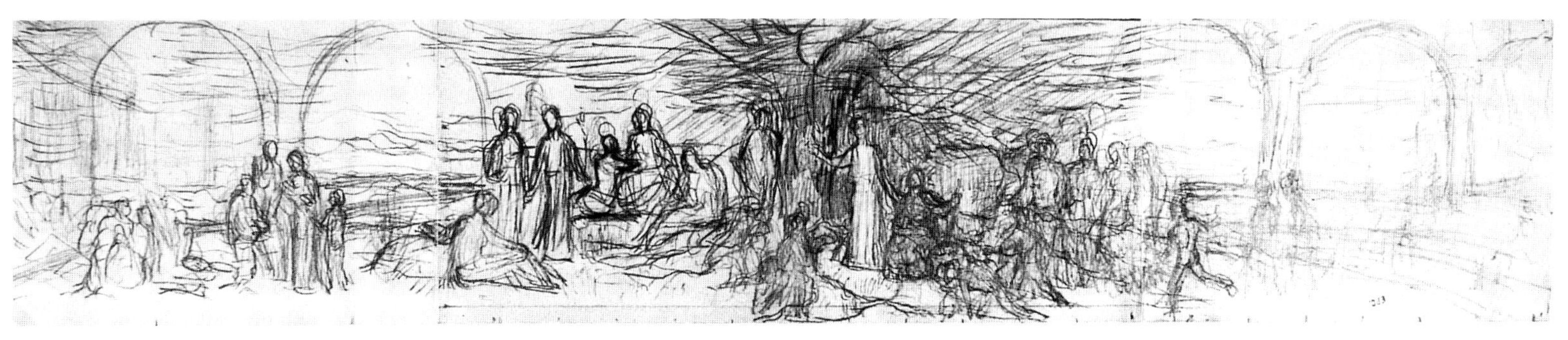

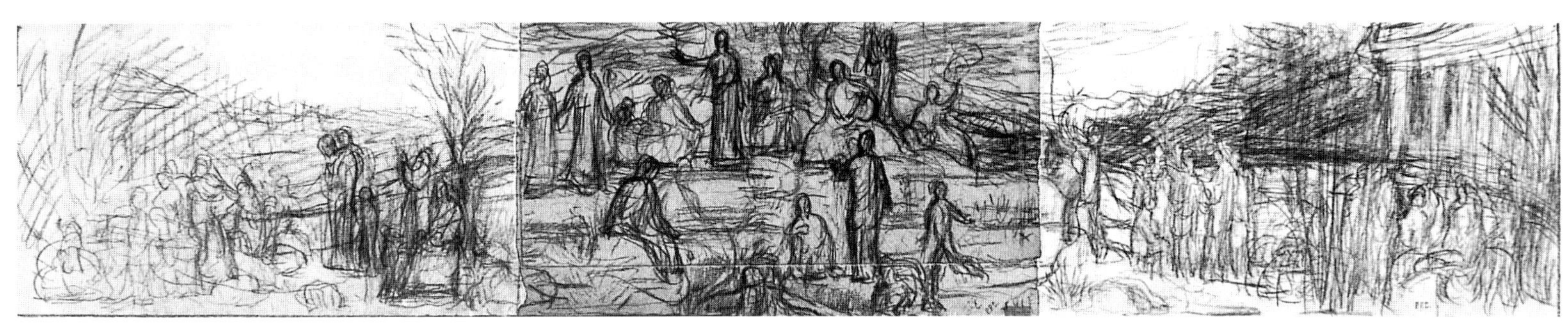

116

Composition Study for 'The Sorbonne'
ca. 1886

Stamp m.r. and twice in center
Black chalk on three sheets of paper joined together, 146 x 761 mm
Museum Stiftung Oskar Reinhart, Winterthur
(Inv. 2320)

Each of the three sections of this drawing has a distinctive setting: to the left and right, classical architecture, a temple and colonnade respectively; and in the center, a mound, stream and majestic tree. Shrubs and roughly indicated trees mark off the divisions, while figures assume many of the stances and rhetorical gestures that they will have in the painting (ill. pp. 200-201).

117

Composition Study for the 'Science' Group in 'The Sorbonne' ca. 1886

Stamp l.r.
Black chalk on paper, 204 x 310 mm
Museum Stiftung Oskar Reinhart, Winterthur
(Inv. 2334)

In this conceptualization for the group at the right devoted to Science, the distinctive posture of the young man measuring with calipers is already established. Other figures surround the sensuous, half-draped woman representing Science or Nature, who would be raised on a pedestal to be presented as a sculptural figure, 'Nature Unveiling Herself,' in the definitive painting (ill. pp. 200-201). Several times during his career Puvis resorted to presenting traditional allegorical figures, considered old-fashioned by the 1870s and 1880s, as sculptural figures as if to justify them.[1] He thereby was able both to use personifying allegorical figures and deliver them into the realm of realism.

1 Brown Price (1976), 29.

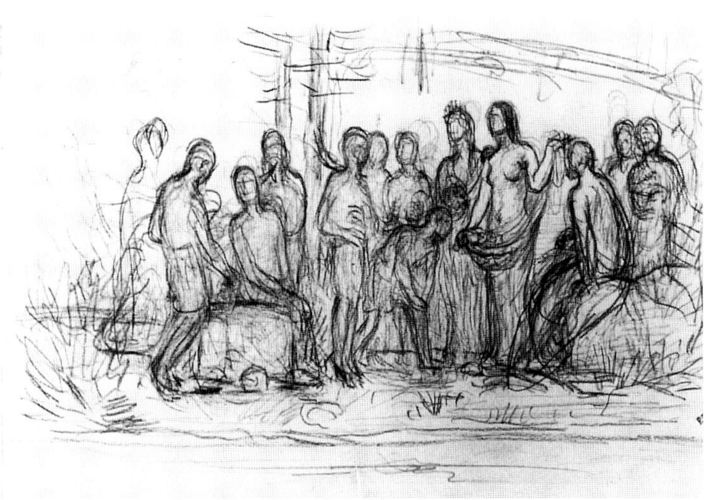

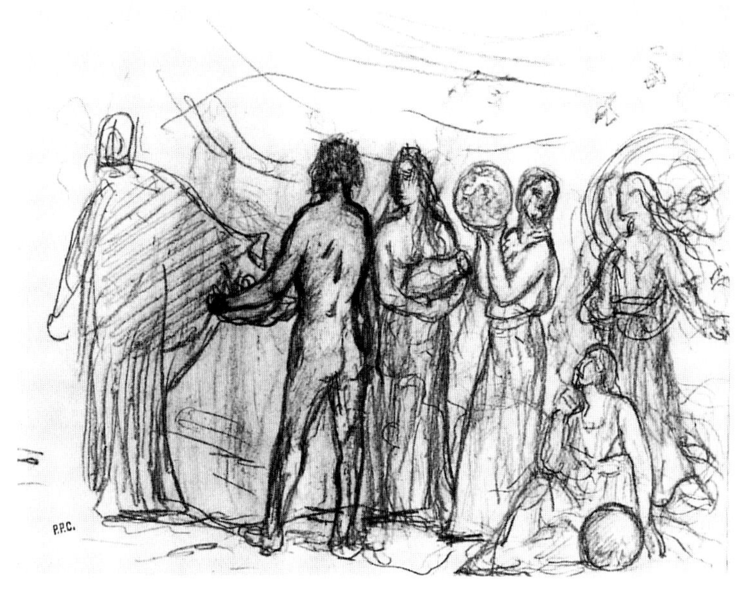

118

Composition Study for the 'Science' Group in 'The Sorbonne' ca. 1886

Stamp l.l.
Pencil on paper, 202 x 247 mm
Museum Stiftung Oskar Reinhart, Winterthur
(Inv. 2337)

These figures with their attributes must have been meant to embody specific disciplines. Except for the figure with a globe, probably Geography, however, which discipline each personifies is not entirely clear. The figure to the right with swirled drapery framing her head shows what compositional liberties the artist would take in his designs and presages a similar design for a muse in the Boston Public Library mural of 1893-96. (see ill. pp. 54-55)

19
20

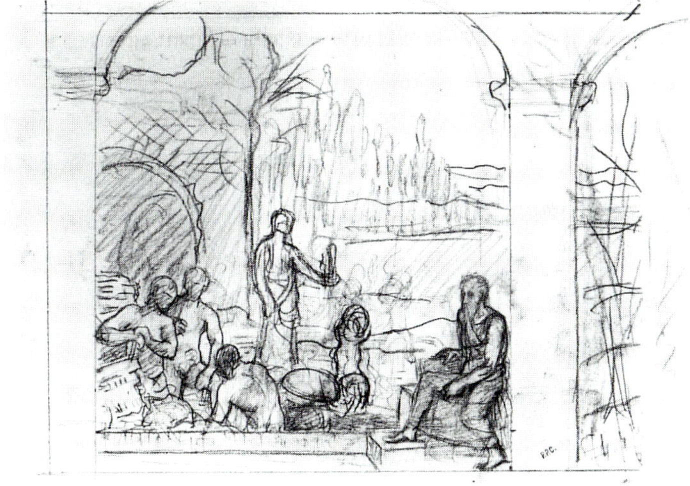

119

Composition Study for the Left Side of 'The Sorbonne' ca. 1886

Stamp to l.r. side
Black chalk on paper, 245 x 329 mm
Museum Stiftung Oskar Reinhart, Winterthur
(Inv. 2341)

This scheme for History (at the far left, see ill. pp. 200-201) would seem to date from the period when the mural would be sectioned by pilasters and arches. Yet this section is far more developed here than in those earlier sketches. On step-like blocks, a bearded old man is seated beside a pier, as if to bridge his own virtual reality and the pictured scene, the painting within the painting that was once envisaged. A similar drawing of a female figure holding books in front of what must have been meant as trompe-l'oeil architecture,[1] also conjoins the viewer's reality with that of the mural.

As in other of Puvis's representations of History, figures are engaged in an archaeological dig. It may have been for this section that Puvis questioned Ernest Renan about a suitable inscription: 'Another important recommendation: – History deciphers an inscription – I don't want Latin or Greek, I want it made of letters unknown to even 99 percent of savants – something like an ancient devilish language [?] – you ought to have that at your place, and you will cabalisticize my old prayer wonderfully....'[2]

1 *Study for the Sorbonne*, crayon, heightened, on beige paper, laid down, 210 x 252 mm, Musée des Beaux-Arts, Lyons (B607.118).
2 'Encore une recommandation importante: – L'Histoire déchiffre une inscription – Je ne la veux ni latine, ni grecque – Je la veux faite de signes inconnus des 99 centièmes même des savants – quelque chose comme une langue antique en diable – vous devez avoir cela chez vous, et vous me cabalistiquerez ma vieille prière à merveille....' Undated letter, before 1892 (the year of Renan's death), Maison Renan-Scheffer (Musée de la Vie Romantique), Paris, feuillet 101.

120

Composition Study for 'The Sorbonne' ca. 1886

Stamp l. border or signed
Watercolor, body color and chalk on paper, 123 x 220 mm
Museum Stiftung Oskar Reinhart, Winterthur
(Inv. 2350)

This study includes several muse-like figures in a wooded area. In front of a gently curving stoa (left) is a figure on a pedestal, doubtless an idea for what would be the sculptural figure at the far right in the mural (ill. pp. 200-201).

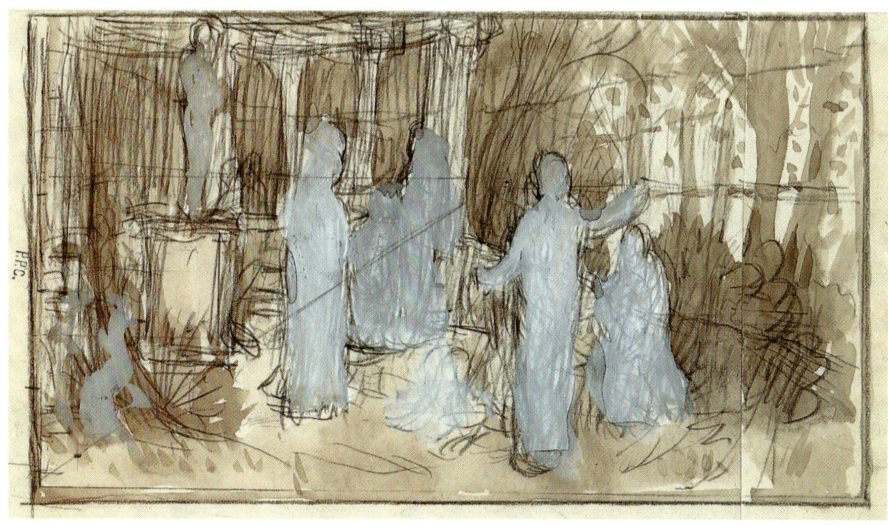

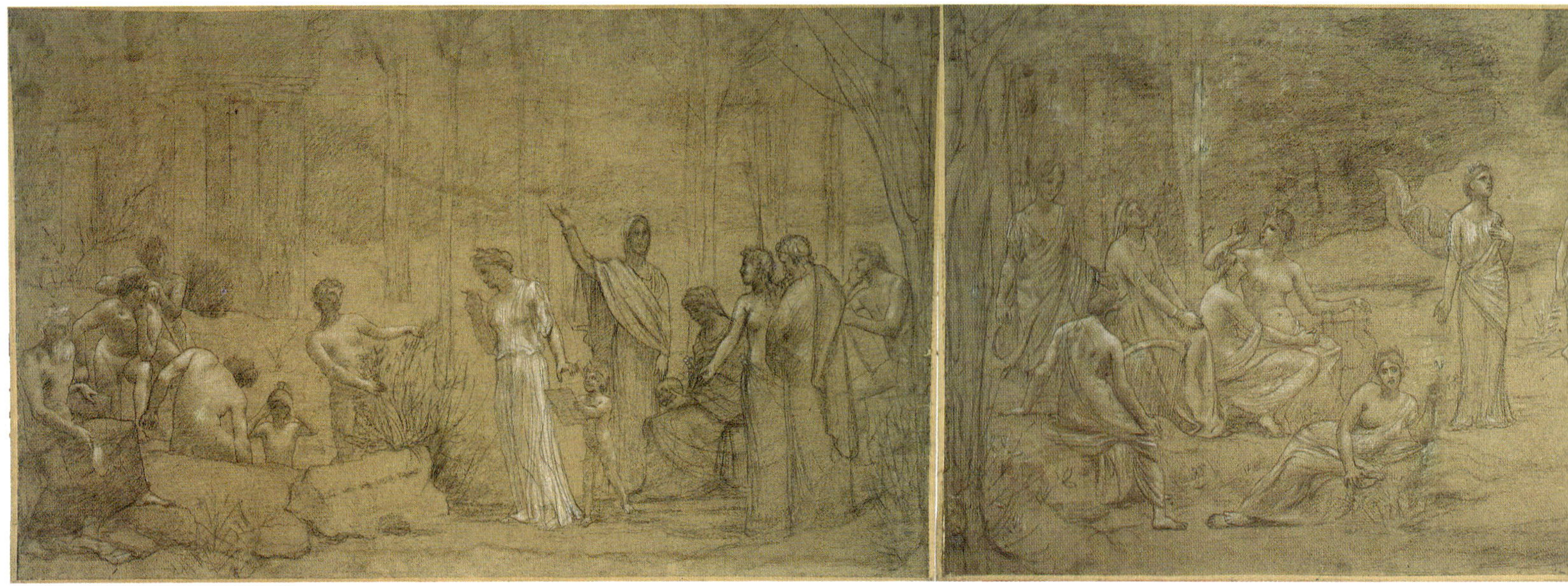

121

Study for 'The Sorbonne' ca. 1887

Charcoal heightened with white on paper, three sheets; left section: 615 x 1030 mm; center section: 605 x 1440 mm; right section: 617 x 1090 mm
Robert Miller Gallery, New York

Provenance Artist's heirs and by descent; private collection.

This triad of drawings is a scheme for the complete Sorbonne mural. The figures particularly are studied, with transparent garb barely veiling anatomical weaknesses. Yet even with its feeble passages, perhaps showing the hand of an assistant, as a whole the study is strong and, as further changes would be made, it is instructive. Ancillary figures were to be eliminated, others to be established. Contrasts were to be heightened and the grove of trees was to be further differentiated and rhythmically patterned.

122

Composition Study for 'The Sorbonne' ca. 1886-87

Stamp l.r.
Black chalk on paper, 240 x 265 mm
Museum Stiftung Oskar Reinhart, Winterthur (Inv. 2313)

These rudimentary sketched figures include the figure that would be further developed separately to become *Euterpe* (cat. 126). A plumb line divides the two sides, and the figure is found in an architectural structure.

Could this study have been meant for a project other than that for the Sorbonne? The arches at the sides of this drawing might indicate a relationship to the Paris Hôtel de Ville commission of 1892 (see cat. 139), the Victor Hugo ceiling being surrounded by not dissimilar shaped spaces.

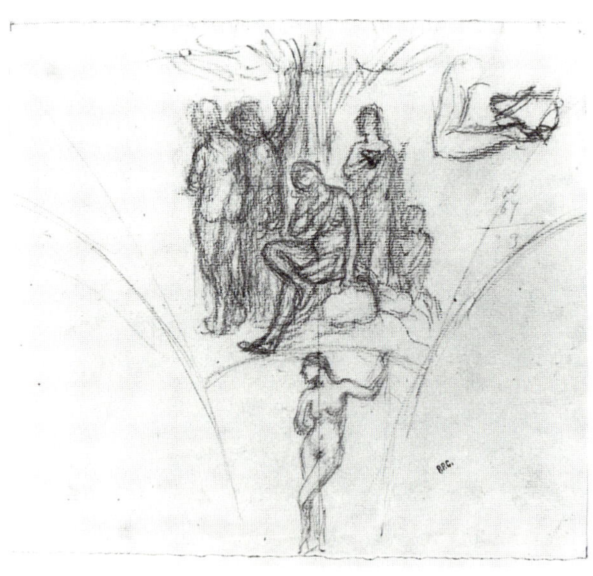

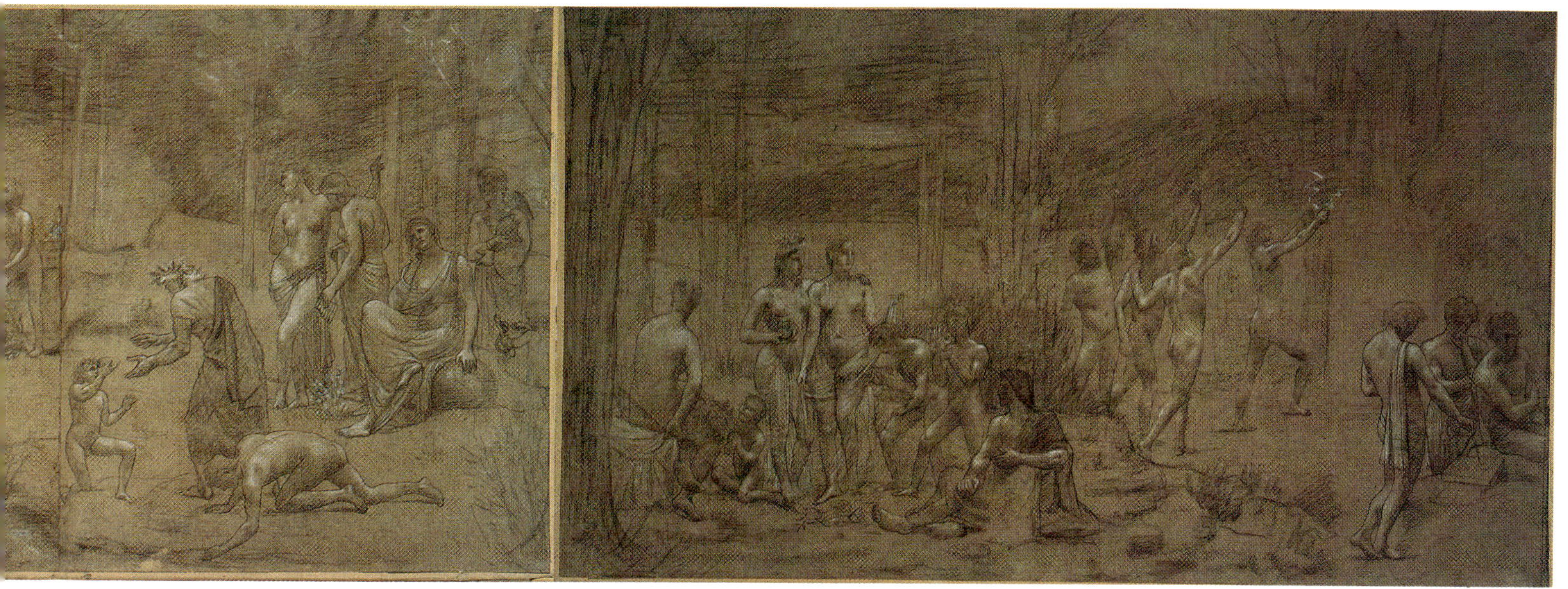

123

Drawing of 'The Sorbonne' ca. 1887-89

Pencil on paper, 750 x 620 mm (slight foxing)
Private collection

Provenance Artist's heirs and by descent.

Translated into three unusually refined, monochromatic, subtly graded pencil drawings (also cat. 124-125), the boldness and subtleties of sections of the classicizing Sorbonne mural compositions (ill. pp. 200-201) are clarified: the audacious, choreographed poses, the mastery of design elements, the formally nuanced but elliptical characterization of the figures, the finesse accorded details.

These records of the various portions of the composition demonstrate that the mural is an aggregate of self-sustaining parts – beautiful verses in a larger poem. While the grouping of figures, seven in each section, is important is establishing periodicity, the phraseology relies largely on the configuration and placement of landscape elements, trees, shrubs and foliage that mark off the beginning and end of groupings.

History and Archeology, at the far left of the mural, are the subject of this sheet. In conformity with then recent efforts to make History as scientific as other branches of learning, the finding of actual artifacts is emphasized. As Octave Gréard described it, 'History and Archeology excavate the entrails of the Past.'[1]

Some parts of the drawing of this section have been completed to every detail while others remain unfinished, with squaring still evident at the lower right, testifying to the methodical care with which rendering took place according to a previously set scheme. The drawings were measured off into squared panels and marked with integers – visible here and along the top of the far right section (see cat. 125) to be faithfully transferred according to calculated rhythmical placements.

1 See p. 199.

124

Drawing of 'The Sorbonne' ca. 1887-89

Pencil on paper, 750 x 620 mm (slight foxing)
Private collection

Provenance Artist's heirs and by descent.

Two of the three superb pencil drawings that Puvis executed of his Sorbonne composition are of contiguous sections that represent the Sciences at the right of the mural: Botany, Physiology, Chemistry and Geology (this sheet), each with an attribute; and at the farthest right, Physics and Geometry (cat. 125). Puvis remarked on his details, pointing out the living shell life on the ground, the sea anemones and algae, the scalpel in one boys's hands and the phial of cultures that another boy holds.[1] A fondness for detail is also clear in the sharply rendered vegetation and the slim tree trunks that are so carefully calibrated.

1 See p. 200.

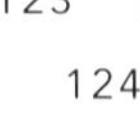

123 124

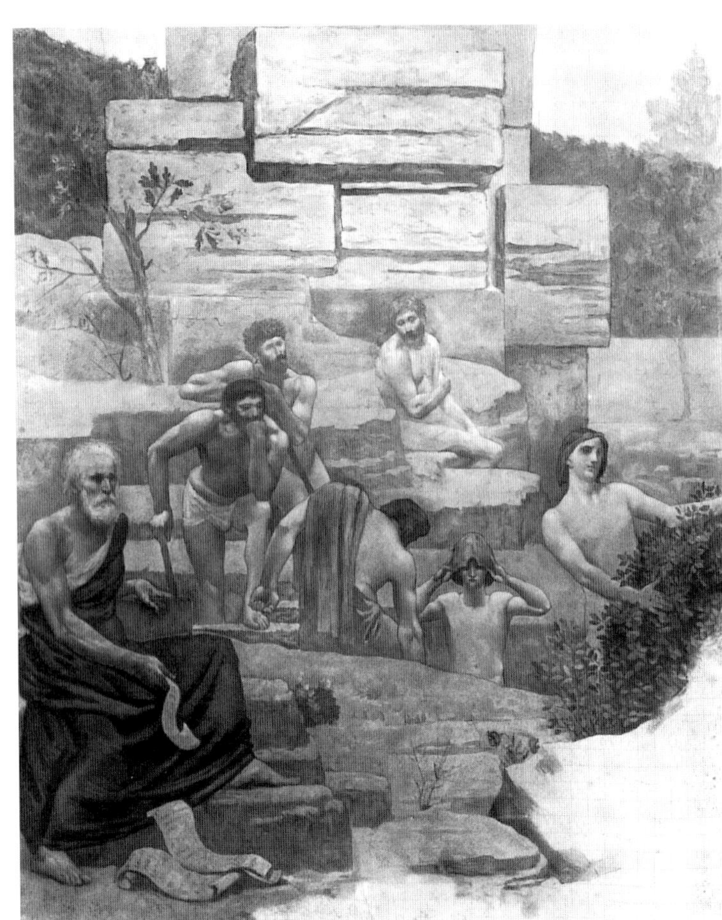

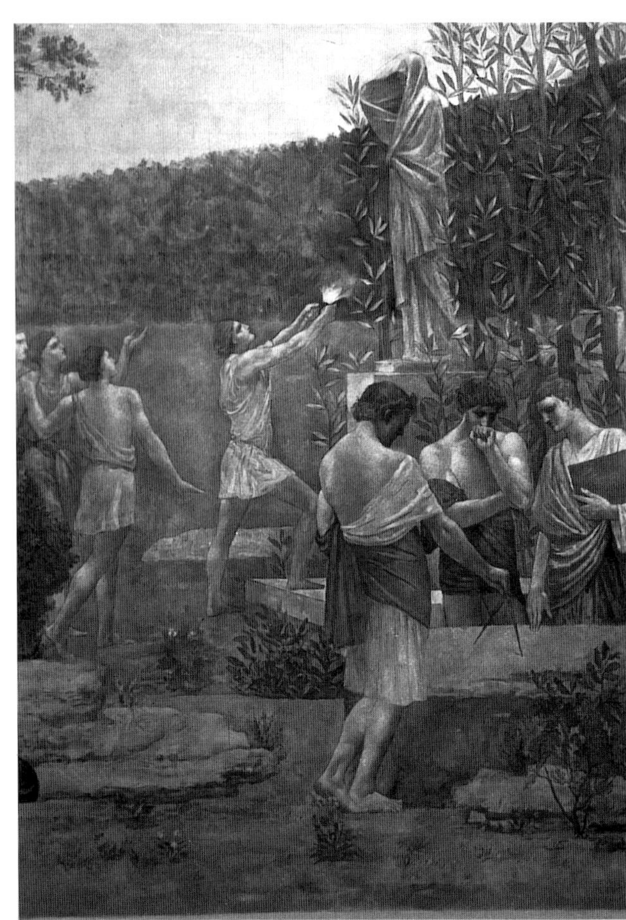

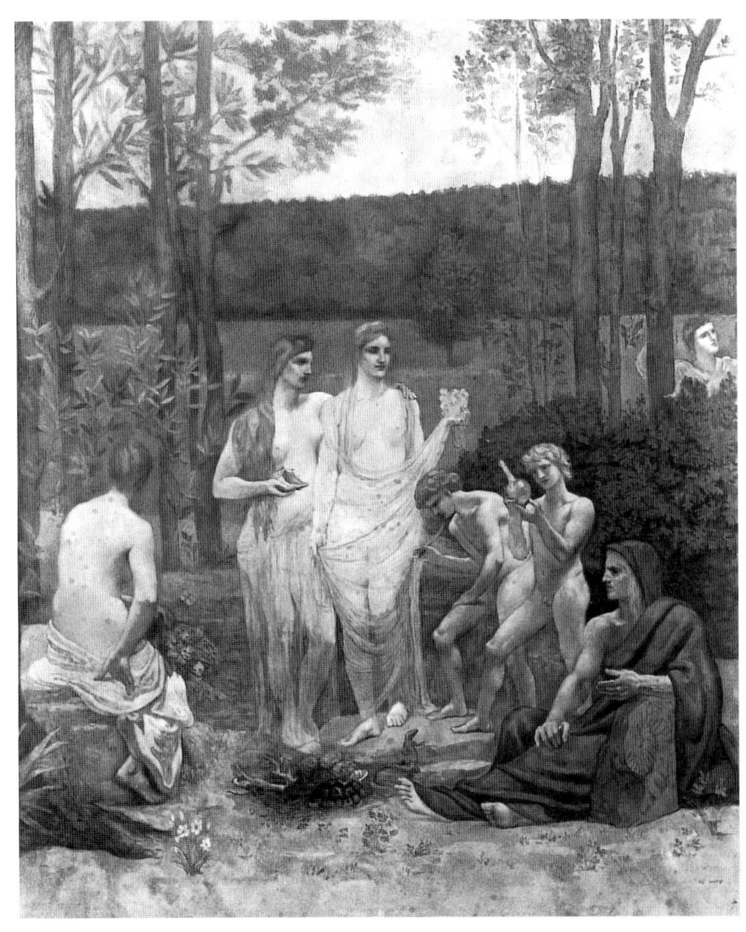

125

Drawing of 'The Sorbonne' ca. 1887-89
(not in the exhibition)

Pencil on paper, 750 x 620 mm (slight foxing)
Private collection

Provenance Artist's heirs and by descent.

Geometry and Physics from the far right of the Sorbonne mural are represented by three figures pondering calculations made with calipers on a flat rock. In the middle distance at the far right Physics, in the person of a sculptured allegorical figure, is represented as revealing her secrets – partly opening her veils before a group of young men, who file before her. With a dramatic gesture they offer her the fruit of their work, a flame of electricity.[1] Or as Puvis explained in a letter: 'Yesterday I painted the statue of Science. She unveils herself a little, very little. That's the way she acted with me, who am as ignorant as a carp.'[2]

1 See p. 199.
2 'Hier j'ai peint la statue de la Science. Elle se dévoile un peu, très peu. C'est ainsi qu'elle a agi avec moi, qui suis ignorant comme une carpe.' Mandach and Wehrlé (1911), 454.

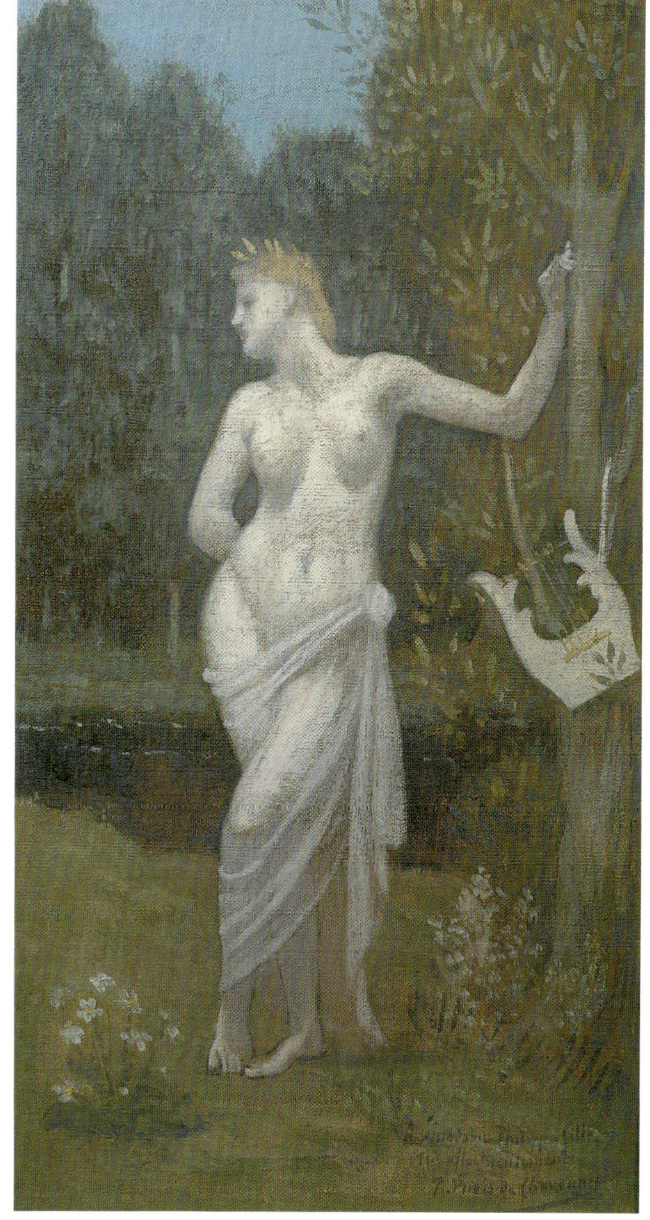

126

Euterpe *or* The Muse of Music / *Euterpe* or *La Muse de la musique* ca. 1889

Inscribed l.r.: A Madame Philippe Gille très affectueusement P. Puvis de Chavannes
Oil on canvas, 43.5 x 24.3 cm
Richard L. Feigen, New York

Provenance Mme Philippe Gille; M. Victor Gille; Durand-Ruel, Paris; Kraushaar Gallery, New York; Knoedler and Co., New York.
Selected Exhibitions 1899 Paris (Durand-Ruel), no. 30 (as *La muse des bois*); 1975 Toronto, no. 27.
Selected References Alexandre (1905), p. 47.

This wonderful, languid, woodland figure is based on a personifying figure in the 1889 mural for the Sorbonne (ill. pp. 200-201, near right side). The dry, roughly textured matte surface and the contrast in color of a milky-skinned figure against a dark background confirm a late date and a reprise of the figure after the mural. Although the subject has traditionally been identified as Euterpe, the Muse of music and inventor of the double flute, the figure could well be the Muse of lyric poetry, Erato, whose attribute is a lyre.[1]

The canvas is dedicated to Mme Philippe Gille (née Alix Massé), the wife of the French dramatist, art critic and writer, whom Puvis had known since she was a young girl.[2] Puvis gave small works as gifts to close friends, and Madame Gille and her sister were the recipients of a number of works, the former receiving caricatures and a pastel *Orpheus* (private collection).

1 Compare *The Muse Erato* (*La Muse Erato*), signed l.r.: P. P. de C., medium unknown, 434 x 320 mm (whereabouts unknown); *Erato*, signed l.r.: verso: 1ere es...17 mars 73, 400 x 320 mm, Paris, Hôtel Drouot [?]

(27 April 1939), no. 174; and *The Small Erato* (*La Petite Erato*), Paris, Hôtel Drouot [?], Vente X (6 March 1940), no. 174.

2 She and her sister Jeanne were daughters of the composer Victor Massé; Jeanne became the wife of the lyricist Léo Delibes, for whom Philippe Gille wrote libretti as he did for Massé. She was given Puvis's *By Moonlight* (*Au clair de la lune*, cat. 142). Gille also wrote the words to Offenbach's *Les Bergers* (1865).

127

Children in an Orchard / *Les enfants au verger* ca. 1885-89

Signed l.l. [pencil]: P. Puvis de Chavannes
Oil and pencil on canvas, 80 x 99 cm
The City College of New York (Inv. 01936)

Provenance Durand-Ruel (1892); sold 10 August 1892 to the Ryerson Collection, Chicago; A 'Mid-Western Educational Institution,' New York, Parke-Bernet Gallery, 'Midwestern Sale,' part II (4 May 1944), repr. no. 48, repr. (but listed as signed l.r. and dated: P. Puvis de Chavannes 1892); Martin Birnbaum; donated by the latter (1960).
Selected Exhibitions 1976-77 Paris/Ottawa, no. 173.
Selected References Durand-Ruel Archives, no. 402; Durand-Ruel photograph L2460; Rood (Autumn 1895); Godet (1912), 47.

Virgil described the spontaneous bounty of the Golden Age in terms of boys picking flowers and strawberries strewn about (*Eclogues*, III, 92). And Chassériau noted that he would like to depict a subject such as pictured here, yet another indication of iconographic filiations between this artist and Puvis de Chavannes: 'two children who fill tubs or baskets make one think of Virgil's *Eclogues* ... put vines in their hair a ray of sunshine on one of them....'[1]

In 1871 Puvis had painted a small (35.5 x 28 cm) version of this subject, *Children in an Orchard* (Detroit Institute of Arts), without the stalwart woman with a sheaf of wheat, a reversed reprise of the sentinel overlooking *Pleasant Land* of 1882 (see cat. 86). That light-hearted divertissement, painted during a time of war and civil unrest, incorporated cunning passages from still earlier work: the child at center with a falling basket a conceit in the rococo spirit from *Ave Picardia Nutrix* of 1865 (ill. p. 102-103, left section), the two boys at left from an oil study of the late 1860s, *Massilia, Greek Colony* (cat. 50). The twisted posturing of the boys is reminiscent of motifs on ancient 'season' sarcophagi, and the variety of supple poses of putti in the carefree design of eighteenth- century decoration. A squared drawing of the boy at left was in Edgar Degas's collection.[2]

This later *Children in an Orchard* combines the sensual, severe and decorative. The exceedingly pale, whitened and neatly defined figures are all but a reverse silhouette against the deep green-gray background. The limited shading and consequent flattening of objects; the roughness of the surface texture and tendency to omit details (leaves and scattered fruit) in favor of a larger statement; the elliptical, curved wreathing of the composition by way of placements, stances, gestures – all contrast to the earlier version and suggest a date at least several years after that of *Pleasant Land*.[3] A date in the later 1880s is also suggested by a related drawing[4] of summary contours and parallel hatchings, a technique associated with later works. The stylistic and coloristic affinities are with works such as *Euterpe* of 1889 (cat. 126).

1 'deux enfants qui remplissent les cuves ou les corbeilles, penser aux Eglogues de Virgile ... leur mettre dans les cheveux les vignes un rayon de soleil sur l'un d'eux....' Inscribed on a drawing, Musée du Louvre, Paris (Inv. RF 25537); quoted slightly differently in Valbert Chevillard, *Un peintre romantique Théodore Chassériau* (Paris, 1893), p. 257.

2 *Study for 'The Orchard'*, signed l.r.: P. P. Ch., medium, dimensions, and whereabouts unknown; Michel (1888), repr. 39.

3 Louise d'Argencourt and Marie Christine Boucher have proposed 1883-85; see 1976-77 Paris/Ottawa, no. 173 and Boucher (1979), no. 99 respectively.

4 *Sketch, variant for 'Autumn'*, black crayon on yellow waxy tracing paper, 230 x 287 mm, Musée du Petit Palais, Paris (Inv. PPD 263[3]; MCB 99).

128

Man Reading / *Le liseur* ca. 1886-95

Signed l.l.: P. Puvis C
Oil and ink on paper, laid on canvas, 55.5 x 46 cm
Van Gogh Museum, Amsterdam
(Inv. S 428 M/1992)

Provenance Artist's heirs and by descent; M. and Mme P. de Vaugelas, Paris; private collection, Paris; Art Research Consultants.
Selected Exhibitions 1896 Lyons, no. 30, repr.; London, Knightsbridge, International Society of Painters, Sculptors, and Gravers, 1898, no. 273, repr.; 1937 Lyons, no. 54.
Selected References A. Bleton, *Lyons, Salon de 1896* (Lyons, 1896), p. 24, repr. p. 30.

27

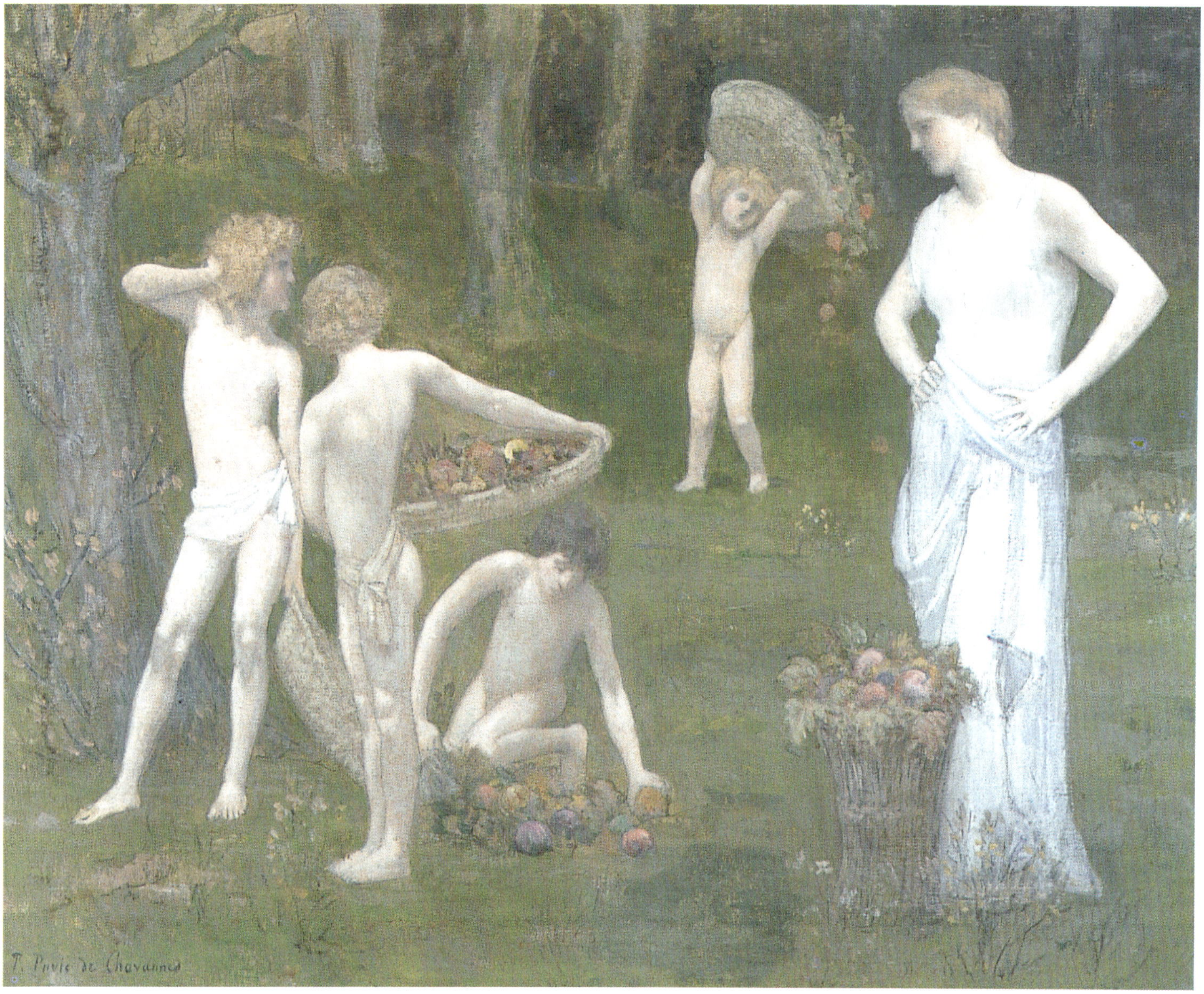

This figure study of a young man in a relaxed pose, at a private moment, contentedly reading in a secluded wooded setting, is made to suggest a certain agelessness: his bleached skin is all but marmoreal; his lower body is wrapped in light gray drapery devised to appear classicizing. What he reads resembles a scroll (in contrast, for example, to the popular novel that Benon reads in Puvis's 1882 portrait, cat. 89). As in Gustave Courbet's *Woman Reading* (1872, National Gallery of Art, Washington, D.C.), a figure at near view is, through the pose of reading, given a reasonable justification for being alone, enjoying a private moment, engaged in his or her own world, in a state akin to revery: these figures are physically present but engaged elsewhere. As in the Courbet, the artificiality of the pose and the would-be natural setting, a peaceful nook of landscape, create a pleasing image to furnish a comfortable interior.

While the date of this composition is not easily ascertained, it is clear that in the 1890s Puvis frequently worked after models, rendering sharp, contemporary features. Several studies of the heads and upper torsos of male figures reading, although not in this precise pose, might have been executed during this period.[1] From about 1887, working in pastels as well as chalk, Puvis also represented half-draped female models posed with, if not reading, books or papers. The contrast of a white-skinned model and dark green surrounds is similar to the tonal contrasts of *Euterpe* and *Children in an Orchard* (cat. 126, 127), and the opacity of the dry pigments and the broad technique also suggest a painting of the 1890s. The theme may be related to that of Aeschylus with his scroll in the mural *Dramatic Poetry* at the Boston Public Library (ca. 1894-96, see p. 230).[2]

1 *Figure in a landscape, head on hand*, pen and pencil on white paper, 180 x 110 mm (private collection); *Man reading in the Landscape*, pencil on paper, 310 x 200 mm (private collection); *Man Reading*, 184 x 237, Musée du Louvre, Paris (Inv. RF 2353); *The Reader*, charcoal on off white paper, laid down, 205 x 186 mm, Musée du Louvre, Paris (Inv. RF 2348);

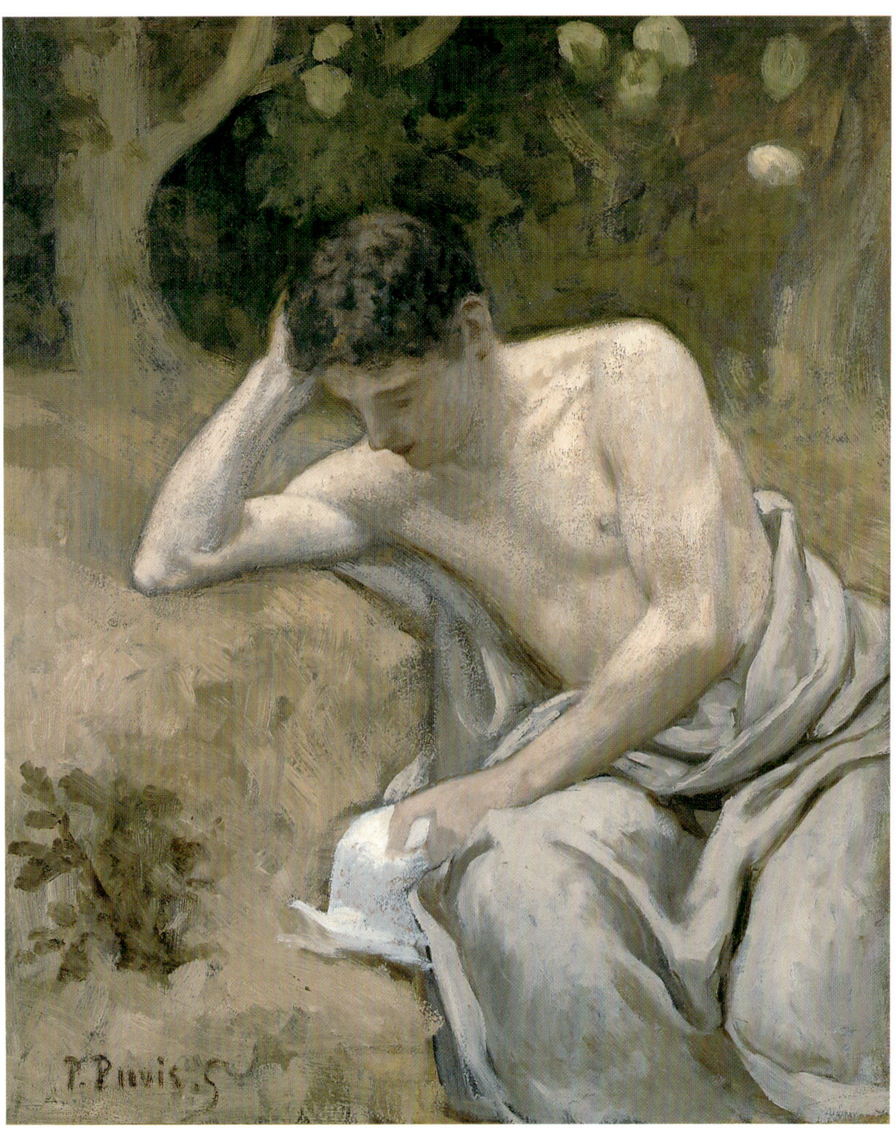

Bust of a Man, black brown chalk with white highlights, squared, 225 x 185 mm, Musée de Picardie, Amiens (Inv. 912bis 99).

2 Cf. *Man Reclining on Steps Reading, 'A Philosopher,' for Boston Library*, ca. 1895; stamp l.r., black chalk on yellowed tracing paper, 182 x 273 mm, Princeton University Art Gallery (Inv. 1948-485).

129

The Benefits of Peace / *Les Bienfaits de la Paix*, Study for 'Inter Artes et Naturam' ca. 1888-89

Signed l.r.: P. Puvis de Ch
Oil on canvas, 64.3 x 170.1 cm
National Gallery of Canada, Ottawa
(Inv. NGC 6331)

Provenance Durand-Ruel, Paris (from 14 August 1894); Paris, Galerie Charpentier, Georges Bernheim Sale (7 June 1935), repr. no. 75; Arthur Tooth and Sons, London (1951-55); acquired by the museum (1955).

Selected Exhibitions 1975 Toronto, no. 29; 1976-77 Paris/Ottawa, no. 190.

Selected References On the mural: Archives du Musée de Rouen, Dossier Puvis de Chavannes; Vachon (1895), pp. 158-165; [Anonymous], 'Peaceful, Exotic, and Decorative; A Current Exhibition of Nineteenth Century Art,' *Illustrated London News*, II (1 December 1951), 904-905; Van Gogh (1958), III, p. 471, no. W22; 1976-77 Paris/Ottawa, pp. 208-209; Helen Raye, unpublished proseminar paper, 11 December 1979, documentation, Metropolitan Museum of Art, New York; Boucher (1979), p. 100; Tapley (1979), pp. 179-182; Sherman (1989), pp. 166-168, 174-176.

'No one knows better than [Puvis] ... how to compose a painting and to place many figures in a large composition....' is what the 17 February 1888 deliberations of the municipality of Rouen stated that would lead to the official commission for murals for the new Musée des Beaux-Arts of Rouen. The authorities had first contacted Puvis about their project in 1883. The Directeur des Beaux-Arts, Castagnary, wanted Puvis and his protegé Paul Baudoüin, who would also be responsible for decorations for the building, to execute their work in fresco and proposed they travel to Italy to study the medium.[1] But Baudoüin fell ill, and Puvis did not want to go without him.[2] Puvis was to execute three works for the museum: *Inter Artes et Naturam* (*Between the Arts and Nature)* (295 x 830 cm), dated 1890 and presented at the new Salon of the Société Nationale des Beaux-Arts that year (ill. pp. 214-215), and the ancillary *Ceramics* and *Pottery* (*La céramique* and *La poterie*, 295 x 165 cm each), both also dated 1890, but exhibited at the Salon of 1891. They were installed on the first and second landings respectively of the great staircase of the museum. Like all Puvis's murals, they were painted on canvas, but because of their textured surface and opaque, matte finish their effect was that of fresco.

The theme of *Inter Artes et Naturam*, for which this is a preliminary study, has to do with the very act of making art and the place of art in society. The transformation of the empirical world into imagery, the cycle of art production from observation and contemplation through manufacture and the rediscovery of works, are all depicted as the most pleasant of enterprises, one that might take place on a grassy promontory (the hill of Bonsecours) overlooking the city, a garden-like spot where mothers and children gather. Here, artists and craftspersons are engaged in what is pictured as essentially the same task: a young woman paints flowers on china, an equally picturesque youth brings a batch of wares to be decorated, art students ruminate and sketch. As befits a city in which ceramics was an important commercial industry central to its mercantile economics, ceramics and their decoration are celebrated and the making and definition of fine and applied art are melded. *Ceramics* and *Pottery* continue the theme of *Inter Artes* by showing various stages in the process of making these wares. As a collection of ceramics was to be featured at the new museum, exhibited along with painting and sculpture and the antiquities found in the region, it was in the museum's interest to have them considered of equal status to painting, sculpture and architecture. This valorization of the decorative arts and crafts concurred with a more general movement in France since the Exposition Universelle of 1878 to bolster French decorative arts and link art and industry.[3] The Musée des Arts Décoratifs opened on 6 January 1879 in the Louvre, Pavillon de Flore. And at the 1891 Salon of the new Société Nationale des Beaux-Arts, held, one may note, at the Palais de l'Industrie, in which Puvis was an *éminence* (and at which he exhibited *Ceramics* and *Pottery*, as noted), the decorative arts were first introduced in a fine arts context.[4] The rapidly changing roles of artist, decorator, craftsperson and art worker were important issues in the late nineteenth century. This was a question not only of respective status in the face of increasing democratization and industrialization, but training, aesthetic expectations and a changing understanding of what constituted art. At the Rouen museum, the fabrication of wares is not portrayed as industrial labor, but as a leisurely, meditative exercise. The enduring importance of art is indicated by the archaeological excavation (middle distance), a reference also to the antiquities displayed in the museum. Uncovered is a relief of a Pegasus, the winged horse Puvis used elsewhere to symbolize *Fantasy* (see cat. 42-43), here perhaps an allusion to the contribution that antiquity made to the collective imagination.

1 Letter of 2-4 May 1888 (private collection). According to d'Argencourt (1976-77 Paris/Ottawa, p. 208), the artist Mazerolle was thought of first (she cites G. Dubosc, 'Le Centenaire de Puvis de Chavannes,' *Journal de Rouen* [14 December 1924]), but previous contact with Puvis had been made.

2 Baudoüin (1935), 301.

3 See Louis Gonse, ed. *Exposition universelle de 1878: Les Beaux-arts et les arts décoratifs*, 2 vols. (Paris, 1879).

4 On this subject see Patricia Mainardi, *The End of the Salon* (Cambridge, 1993), pp. 64-65, 80, 130.

130

Inter Artes et Naturam (reduced version)

ca. 1890-95

Oil on canvas, 40.3 x 113.7 cm

The Metropolitan Museum of Art, New York, gift of Mrs. Harry Payne Bingham (1958) (Inv. 58.15.2)

Provenance Durand-Ruel, Paris and New York (August 1895-99); Oliver H. Payne, New York (1899-1917); Harry Payne Bingham, New York (1917-55); Mrs. Harry Payne Bingham, New York (1955-58).

Selected Exhibitions 1898, Pittsburgh, Carnegie Institute, *Third Annual Exhibition*, no. 210; 1972 London/Liverpool, no. 224; 1975 Toronto, no. 30

Selected References On the mural: see cat. 129.

What is essential to the composition of the panoramic *Inter Artes et Naturam* (ill. pp. 214-215), the complex repetition and elaboration of pictorial elements, is more evident in this reduced version,[1] with its crisp forms and reduced visual field, than in the mural itself. Forms *qua* forms enjoy pride of place. The meticulously organized composition uses the

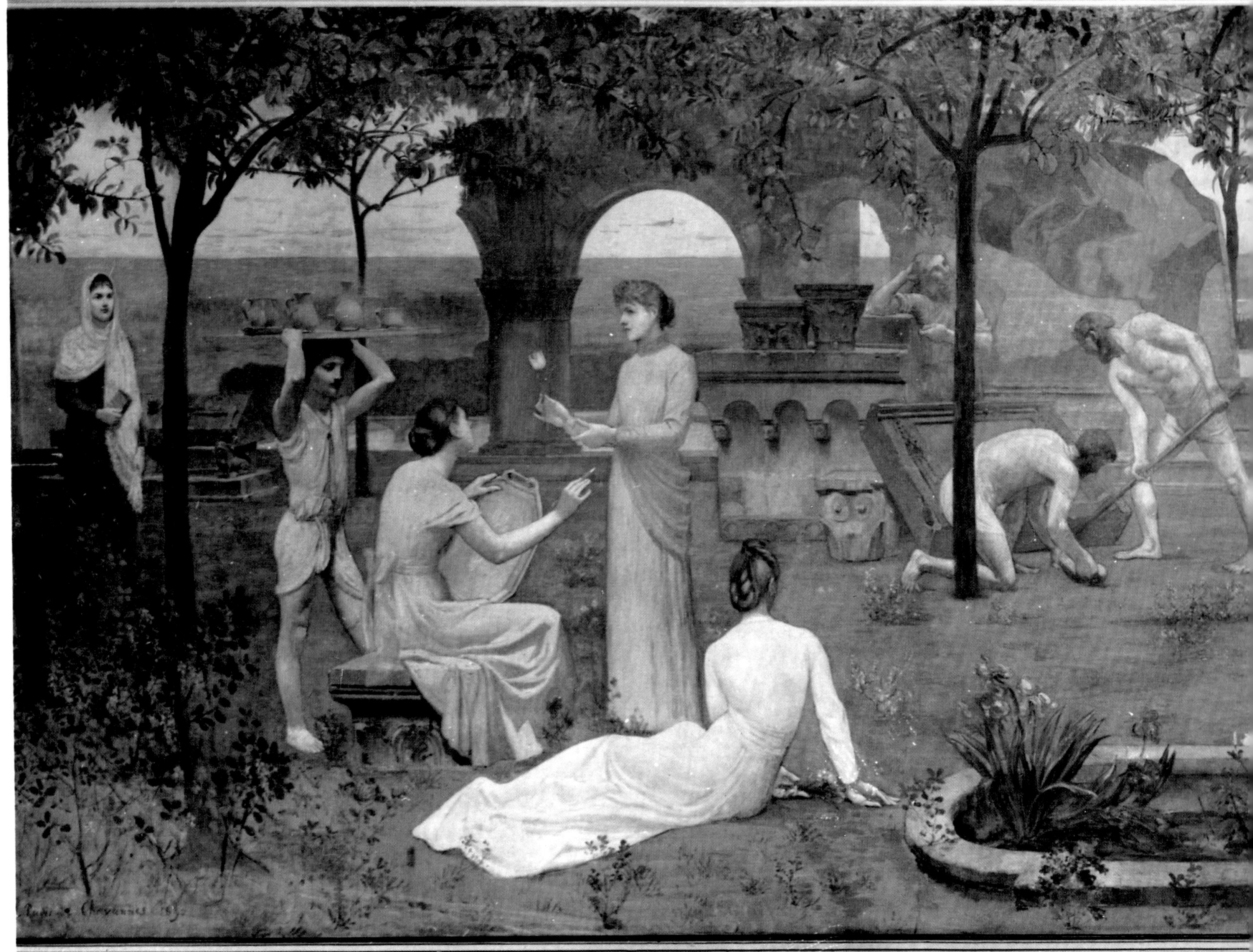

arch as a prevailing motif: an arcade of tree branches forms a canopy across the top; arches frame figures and form a bridge and a triumphal arch and are excavated as ancient ruins. This device furthers the meaning of the title, with nature taking on abstract architectural forms. Moreover, an internal border is approximated by the judicious distribution of pictorial elements to the perimeters of the compositon, an effect reminiscent of the flowered landscape settings and arched tree branches of the Franco-Flemish tapestry tradition.

Though relatively coarsely painted, with squared-off brush strokes, this conceptually complete *Inter Artes et Naturam* contrasts to the unfinished preliminary study (cat. 129), which has been everywhere clarified and sharpened – trees and an arch eliminated, spaces more beautifully shaped. Colors, vertical tree lines and overhead branches anchor the images to the surface, and even middle distance figures, through their conjunction with other pictorial elements, are pulled to the frontal plane. Stiffer and more meager even than those in the mural, the figures here are precisely integrated into the formal structure, and through the painting technique they are integrated into the surface texture.

Though Puvis had quietly essayed modern dress in *Marseilles, Gateway to the Orient* (see cat. 50), *The Balloon* and *The Carrier Pigeon*

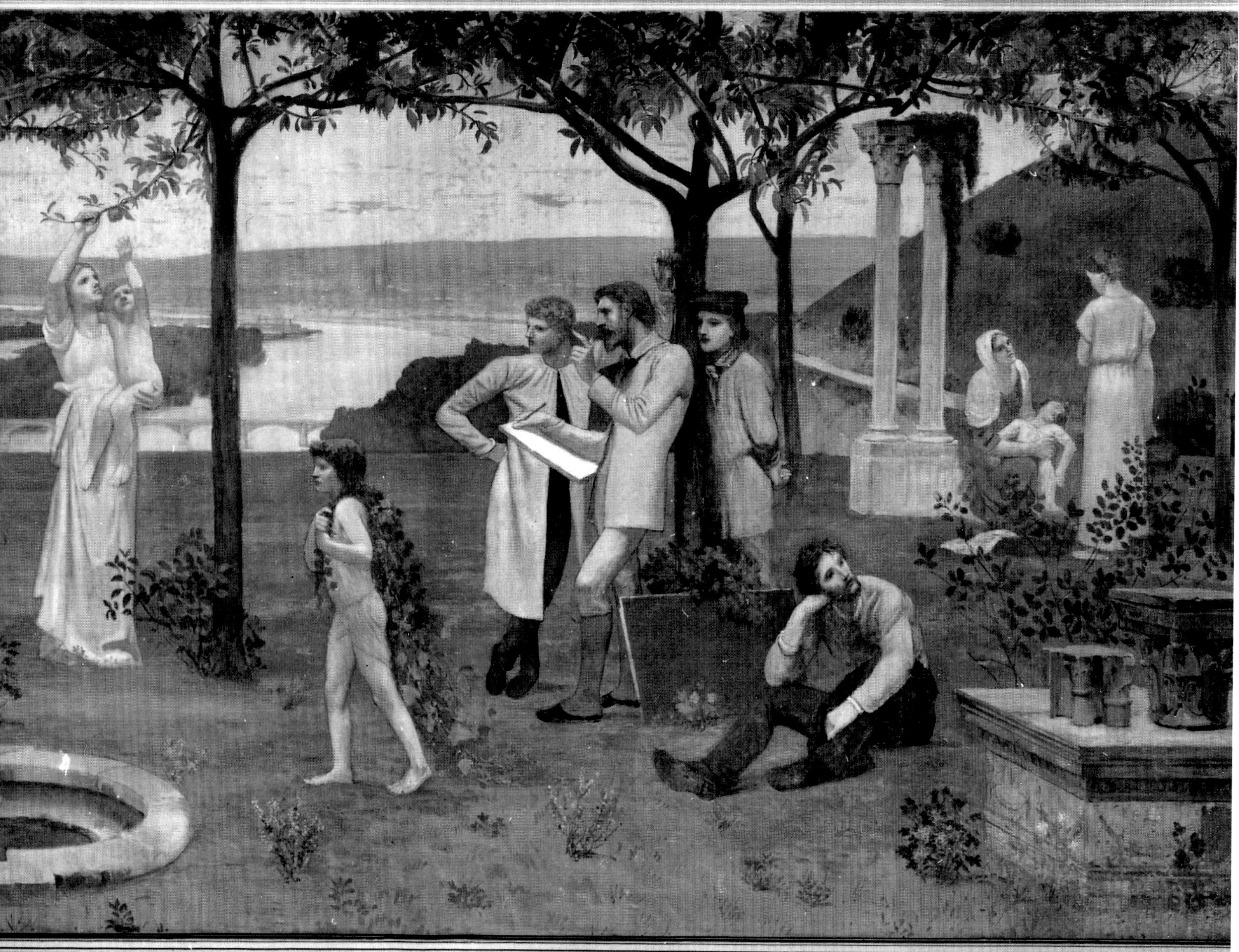

Inter Artes et Naturam, 1890
Musée des Beaux-Arts, Rouen

(fig. 32, cat. 65) and *Symbol of The Red Cross* (Musée du Petit Palais, Paris), the Rouen commission is almost unique among the murals for the introduction of contemporaneity through the figures' clothing. Van Gogh, who drew the mural from memory (cat. 147), wrote his sister in June 1890 that he admired how Puvis combined a sense of distance, antiquity and modernity, finally suggesting a timelessness, 'There is a superb picture by Puvis de Chavannes ... if you look at it a long time you would believe you were witnessing a total [sic: 'fatal'] but benign rebirth in everything you ever believed, in everything you ever desired, a strange and happy meeting of very remote antiquity with raw modernity.'[2] He also noted the colors: 'One figure is a forget-me-not blue, another bright citron yellow, another of a delicate pink color, another white, another violet. Underneath their feet a meadow dotted with little white and yellow flowers. A blue distance with a white town and a river. All humanity, all nature simplified, but as they *might* be if they are not like that.'[3]

The central motif of a woman with a child plucking fruit was taken up by other artists: by Berthe Morisot in her pastel *Picking Oranges* (1889,

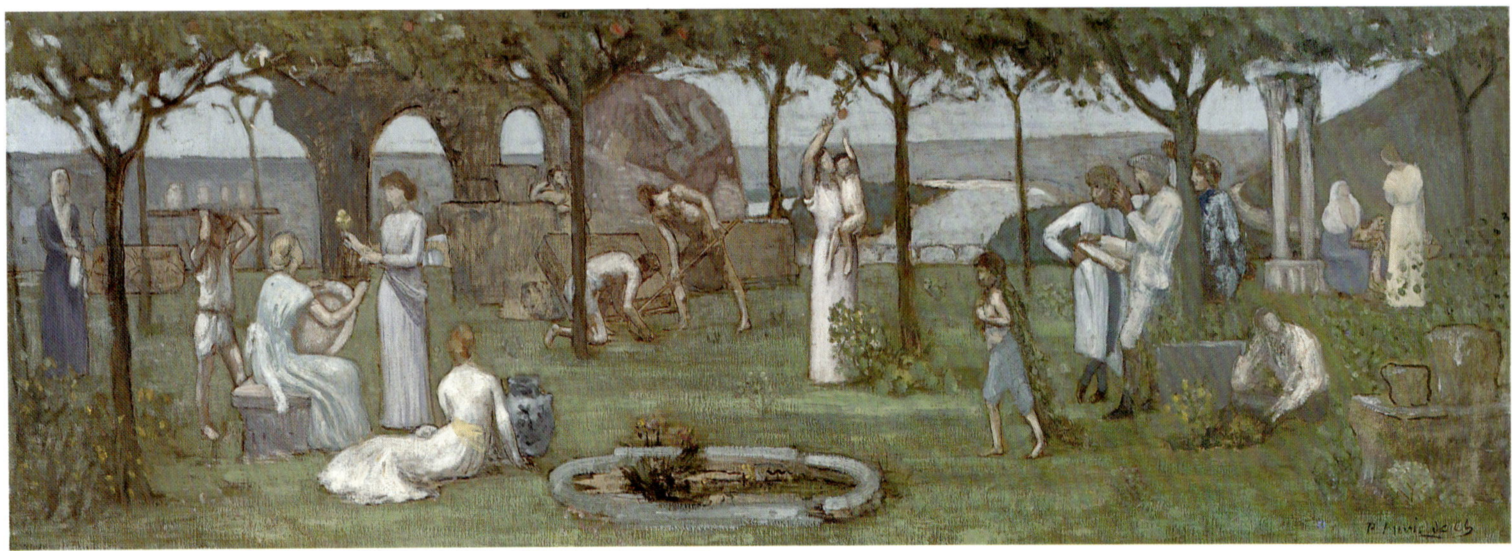

Musée d'Art et d'Histoire de Provence, Grasse)[4] and by Mary Cassatt in her Woman's Building mural for the 1893 World's Columbian Exhibition in Chicago (fig. 10). Cassatt's mural *Modern Woman* (1892-93, destroyed), followed *Inter Artes* closely, particularly the center of her three sections, *Young Girls Pursuing Fame*, *Young Women Plucking the Fruits of Knowledge and Science* and *Arts, Music, Dancing*, in which the story of Eve is inverted with women eagerly seeking these fruits. That Cassatt turned to Puvis's work as a model for her own is perfectly understandable, given his reputation and her relative inexperience with such projects.[5] Paul Gauguin investigated *Inter Artes et Naturam*, as is evident in his central fruit-plucking figure and the measured isolation of each figure in his frieze-like *Where do we come from? What are we? Where are we going?* of 1897 (Museum of Fine Arts, Boston), though he sectioned his work obliquely and filled it with curved tentacles of exotic (art nouveau) vegetation.[6]

1 1976-77 Paris/Ottawa, no. 190, calls this canvas a replica and says it is dated 1889; although it is signed, it is in fact not dated and it is our view that it is a reduced version painted by Puvis in his usual way after having completed the mural.

2 'Il y a de Puvis de Chavannes ... un tableau superbe... en le regardant longtemps, on croirait assister à une renaissance, totale [sic: 'fatale'] mais bienveillante, de toutes choses auxquelles on aurait cru, qu'on aurait désiré, une rencontre étrange et heureuse des antiquités fort lointaines avec la crue modernité.' Van Gogh (1954), IV, pp. 183-184, no. W22.

3 'Une figure sera bleu myosotis, une autre citron claire, une autre rose tendre, une autre blanche, une autre violette. Le terrain une prairie piquée de fleurettes blanches et jaunes. Des lointains bleus avec une ville blanche en un fleuve. Toute l'humanité, toute la nature simplifiée mais comme elle pourrait être si elle ne l'est pas.' Van Gogh (1954), IV, p. 184, no. W22. Transl.: Van Gogh (1958), III, 471, no. W22.

4 A similarity between Puvis's fruit-picking figure and Berthe Morisot's pastel is pointed out in Charles F. Stuckey and William P. Scott with Suzanne G. Lindsay, *Berthe Morisot, Impressionist* (New York, 1987), p. 138.

5 See Nancy Mowll Mathews, *Mary Cassatt* (New York, 1987), pp. 82, 84-85, 152-153; also compare Cassatt's *Cherry Tree* of 1891-92 (private collection), pl. 89, 112 and variants, figs. 89, 109-110, repr.; see also Nancy Hale, *Mary Cassatt*, (New York, 1971), pp. 159-166; and Nancy Mowll Mathews, *Cassatt and Her Circle: Selected Letters*, (New York, 1984), pp. 229, 232-233, 235-238, 335.

6 Jean Alazard put it long ago in 'L'Exotisme dans la peinture française au XIXe siècle,' *Gazette des Beaux-Arts*, s6, VI (October 1931), 250, 253-254: 'Il est banal de le comparer à Puvis de Chavannes, et lui-même aimait à faire cette comparaison.' ('It is banal to compare him to Puvis de Chavannes, and he himself liked to make this comparison.')

131

Portrait of a Bearded Man / *Portrait d'un homme barbu* ca. 1887-90

Oil on canvas, 41 x 32 cm
Private collection

Provenance Artist's heirs and by descent.
Selected Exhibitions 1976-77 Paris/Ottawa, no. 188.

This portrait of a handsome, black-bearded man with generous features and strong cheekbones is posed frontally, a position Puvis favored from about 1865,[1] surely because it warranted symmetry and spatial flattening. Because of its clear sense of simplified form and pattern, contrasting

30
31

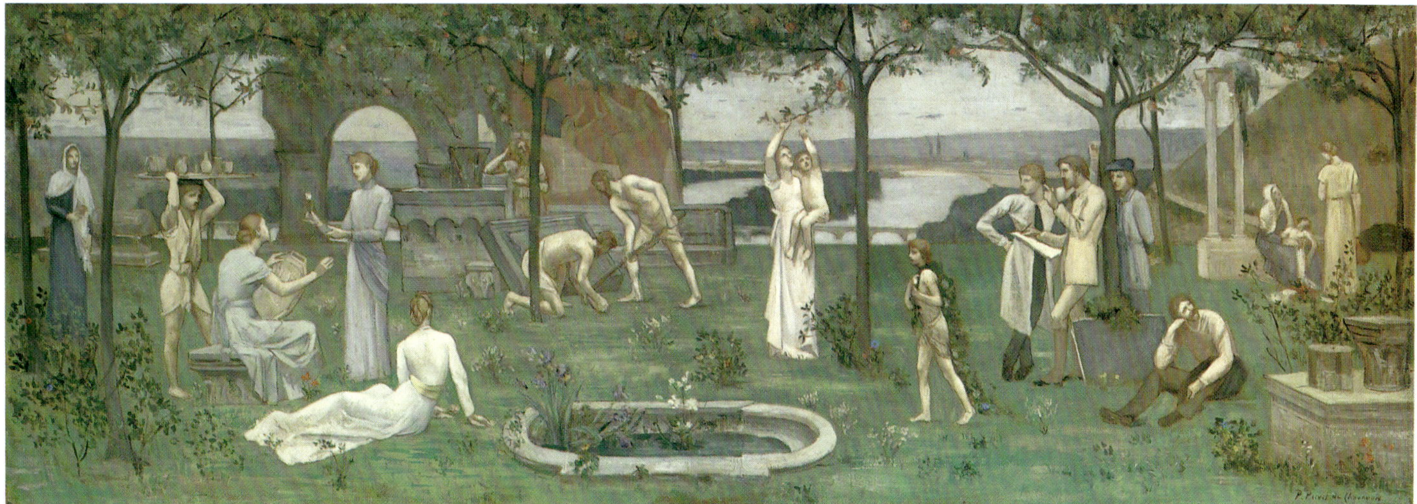

bright colors, and summary style, the portrait would likely have been executed in the later 1880s, postdating the portraits of *Eugène Benon* (cat. 89), *Mme M.C.* (cat. 92) and Puvis's own *Self-portrait* (1887, Uffizi Galleries, Florence), all of which, unlike this limited view, include part of the torso. The patterned fabric seems particularly modern, but Puvis had, from the 1850s, been attracted to patterned clothing,[2] and he had included such ornamented cloth even in the executioner's garb in his *Beheading of Saint John the Baptist* (cat. 57). Indeed, colors, abbreviated form and patterning bring this portrait close in style to that associated with the Nabis.

Who the sitter is might be hazarded. The distinctive square face and hairline, wide-set eyes and full beard, though less robust than we are accustomed to seeing in the many dramatic profile photographs of Auguste Rodin, resemble the sculptor's striking physiognomy. The portrait compares, moreover, to Rodin's own drawn self-portrait after an 1886 full-face Bergerac salt print, and a Paul Boyer photograph dated after June or July 1893.[3] It is not precisely known when Puvis first met Rodin, but the very black hair of the Puvis portrait seems to indicate a somewhat younger man than the then fortyish Rodin, and a certain decorative prettiness (of the kind admired by the Nabis) undermines the force associated with Rodin's features and public persona: there is only a hint of a penetrating glance and none of his characteristically concentrated, knitted brow, both of which are evident in many photographs of him.[4]

Puvis had a very close relationship with the sculptor; their mutual admiration grew because they both felt embattled.[5] Rodin was in charge of the great banquet honoring Puvis in 1895, and it was Puvis to whom he referred on his deathbed. Besides his well-known 1891 bronze bust of the painter, a project for the Panthéon with a *Genius of Eternal Repose* (of 1898), he carved two portraits of Puvis, one of which is a head emerging from a block of marble (Musée Rodin, Paris).

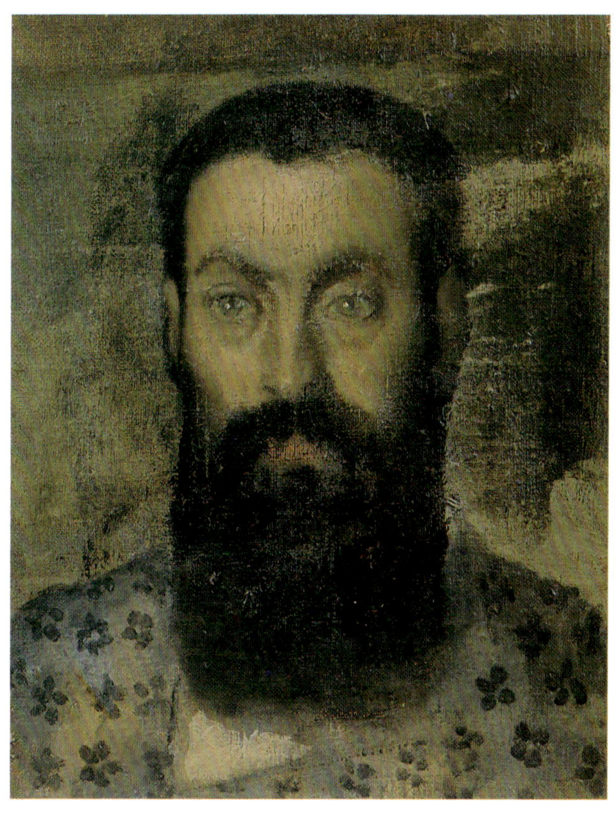

In turn Puvis included Rodin's portrait in his last frieze for the Panthéon, which remained unfinished at his death in 1898, perhaps reasoning that that was how Rodin might be introduced into the hallowed Panthéon, in a contemplative pose with his hand to his head.[6]

1 As *Monique* (private collection), a drawn androgynous head (cat. 40), the head of Saint John the Baptist in *The Beheading of Saint John the Baptist* (cat. 57), the *Portrait of Mme M.C.* (cat. 92), and other works testify.

2 Cf. the apron of *The Big Sister* ca. 1850-54/1862 (Petit Palais, Geneva), the shawl of *The Gondolier* ca. 1848-51 (private collection).

3 Musée Rodin, Paris (Ph 256 and Ph 152); my thanks to Kirk Varnedoe for information about the drawing.

4 In addition, see the following photographs at the Musée Rodin, Paris: Ph 108; Ph 765; Ph 849 by Eugène Druet; Ph 34 by Choumoff.

5 The personal, professional and artistic relationship between Puvis and Rodin is the subject of a section of the author's forthcoming book.

6 See *Cartoon for the Frieze* (unfinished), second campaign cycle of *Saint Genevieve* for the Panthéon (one of four), ca. 1898, oil and sepia on canvas, 230 x 360 cm, Musée d'Orsay, Paris (Inv. RF 20.120).

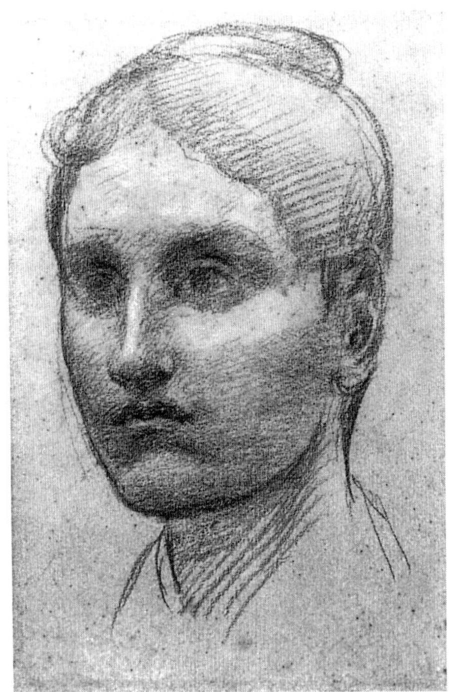

132

Head of a Woman Three Quarters to the Left ca. 1884-95

Black chalk highlighted with white on gray-blue paper turned gray, 198 x 130 mm
Musée du Petit Palais, Paris
(Inv. PPD 268[6]; MCB 166)

Provenance Bequest of artist's heirs to the city of Paris (1898); deposited in the Musée Galliera (1899); transferred to the Musée du Petit Palais upon its opening (1901).
Selected Exhibitions 1896 Paris (Société Nationale des Beaux-Arts), no. 1569.
Selected References Boucher (1979), no. 166.

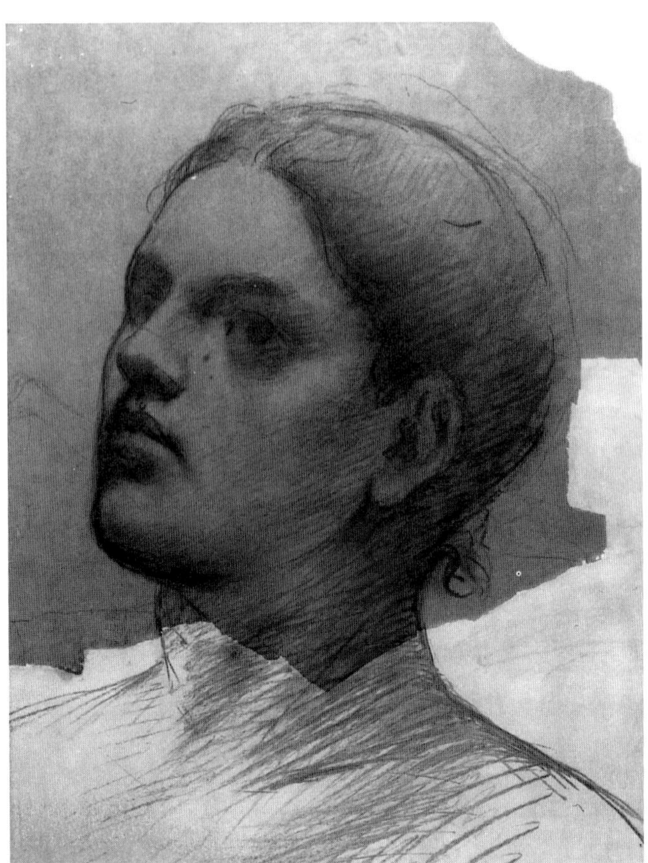

With its even features, calm pose, and spare presentation this head epitomizes the kind of classicizing vision for which Puvis de Chavannes is best known. A refined, delicate but sure technique and clean, strong, geometrical structure make this slightly turned head one of the loveliest of the portrait drawings. While it cannot with certainty be related to any particular project, the head bears some resemblance to that of the more severe 'Mme Lithographie,' a figure depicted on Puvis's 1895 poster for the Galerie Rapp exhibition celebrating the centenary of lithography.[1]

1 Colored lithograph on wove paper, 124 x 84.6 cm (image), 150 x 110 cm (sheet); see 1976-77 Paris/Ottawa, no. 206.

133

Head of a Woman Turned Three-Quarters ca. 1890-96

Stamp l.l.
Pencil and black chalk on torn and uneven tracing paper laid down on white paper, 423 x 330 mm
Musée du Petit Palais, Paris (Inv. D. Dut. 1797)

Provenance Paris, Hôtel Drouot (23 October 1989), no. 15.

The graceful force of this head turned three-quarters to the left is due once more (compare cat. 132) to the search for a configuration that is strong, contained and three-dimensional, at odds with the flatness and symmetry of the frontal heads. In its proportions this head conforms to a classicizing aesthetic rather than showing the particularities that define a specific physiognomy. Yet it is still more specific than the heads in most of the late paintings. We would date it ca. 1890-96.

Large among the drawings of heads, it compares in size to the early *Portrait of Mme de Veyssière* (cat. 9), to which it may be contrasted in pictorial thinking. Assurance drives the contoured lines; strong but minimal shading builds the features, and the artist is no longer working inductively, from the accretion of darting observations and fine notations. The tracing paper sheet, torn at some presumably early date, has been laid down and the drawing of the neck carefully continued onto the paper surrounds, presumably by Puvis's own hand, though with larger, blunter strokes than those of the face.

134

Summer / *L'Eté* 1891

Signed and dated l.l.: P. Puvis de Chavannes 91
Oil on canvas, 149.8 x 232.5 cm
The Cleveland Museum of Art, gift of Mr. and Mrs. J.H. Wade (Inv. CMN 16.1056)

Provenance Paris, Durand-Ruel (1891-92); Mr. and Mrs. Jephtha H. Wade, Cleveland (1892-1916/17); gift of the latter (1917).

Selected Exhibitions 1893, Chicago, *The World's Columbian Exposition*, no. 2964.

Selected References On the Mural and Reduction of the Mural: Correspondence from Puvis to Armand Renaud from 1886-95: letters of 7 and 12 February 1892 (private collection), and 5 November 1892 [?] (Fondation Custodia, Collection F. Lugt, Institut Néerlandais, Paris, 1973, A. 71-72 through 1973.76); Vachon (1895), pp. 127-140, 145, 148-149; Vachon [1900], pp. 231-233; Geffroy (1897), 127-140; 1976-77 Paris/Ottawa, pp. 212-213; Boucher (1979), p. 102; 1986-87 Paris, pp. 379-380. On this painting: Gertrude Underhill, 'Some Recent Acquisitions of the Cleveland Museum of Art,' *Art and Archaeology*, VI (July 1917), 41-49, fig. 3; Van Liere (1980), 112; Robinson (1991), 5-9; Benjamin (1993), 298-300, repr. 299.

Summer is essentially a scene of monumental bathers in a grand landscape that evokes the sultry season, its warmth, a certain torpid laziness, a green and gold day. The painting is dated to the same year as Puvis's mural *Summer* (1891, 590 x 910 cm, cf. fig. 37), which, together with *Winter* (1892, 590 x 910 cm, cf. fig. 38) and four spandrel figures (see cat. 142), comprised one of two mural cycles that Puvis executed for the recently rebuilt Paris Hôtel de Ville (for the other, see cat. 139). The independent variant differs considerably from the mural; comparing the two, makes clear Puvis's mural aesthetic.

Summer was executed for the Zodiac Salon at the city hall, a space which posed almost insuperable problems: it was virtually a foyer for a larger area; it was not well lit; there was a lack of distance between composition and viewer. Or as Puvis put it, it was 'indécorable,' lacked 'recul,' and was 'plongée dans une obscurité decuplée.'[1] Moreover, there was a large door to contend with, and it was on the wall with the door that Puvis elected to put *Summer*. With an inventive, composed setting and a deftly extended landscape providing the opportunity for broad areas of flat color, he solved many of the difficulties.

Integration in scale and harmonious shape of bather to landscape and landscape to portaled wall is at the heart of the success of the monumental wall painting. In the mural, three bathers balance each other at either side of the door, wading, emerging from the water, and lolling on the shore. The scale of the figures integrates the door into an acceptable tripartite division. A semi-circular alignment orders the *dolce far niente* figures and landscape around the door. This gently accommodating arch of figures – the youth emerging from the water at the left and the women lounging at the right – resonates with the arched entrances at either side of the Salon.

Freed from the awkward architectural setting, the composition of the version of *Summer* shown here was condensed, and the bathers proportionately enlarged. The landscape, trees and vegetation were reconfigured, making explicit how much the artist depended on these elements to achieve a decorative unity in his wall paintings. In this more pliable independent composition, the horizon has been lowered and laid back and the background simplified, and the terrain, no longer emphatic in its two-dimensionality, has lost its rakish tilt. Depth is indicated everywhere: water swings back around the central island and not up over it; the boy at left climbs up onto the shore and is not flattened to the forward plane, and the ample women, rather than being set against a lintel-high sward, are placed firmly on the ground with bushes and trees growing up behind them. Because the figures are not subsumed by the setting but rather loom up from it, and because that setting is condensed, they appear larger in this canvas.

The sharply demarcated wide bands of yellow fields and green meadows that unified the two sides of the wall painting are gone, and so

134

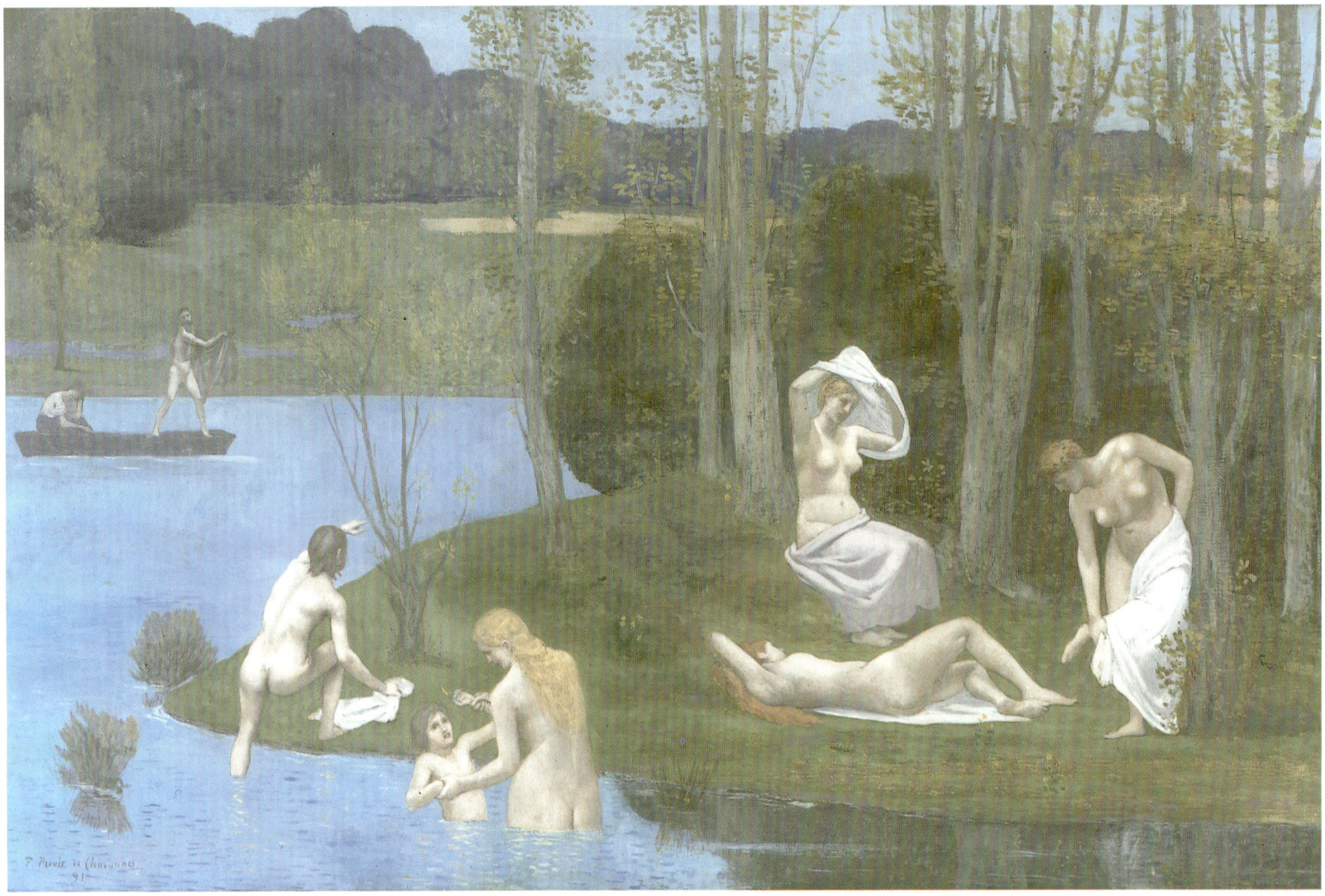

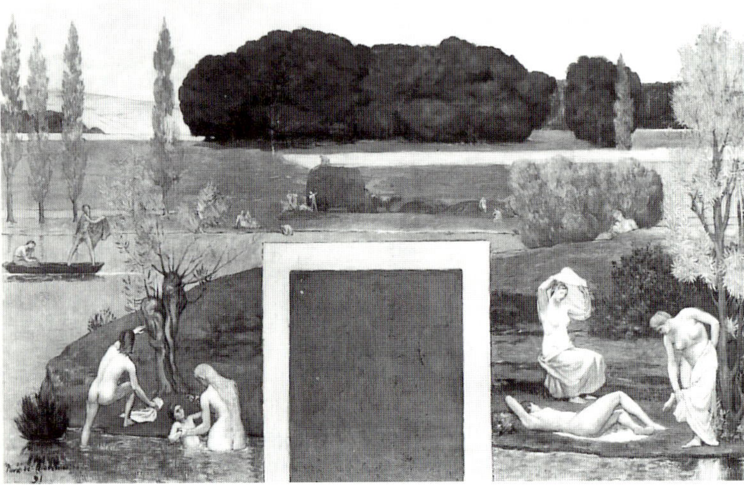

fig. 37
Summer (small version), 1891
Oil on canvas, 54.4 x 86.3 cm
Musée du Petit Palais, Paris

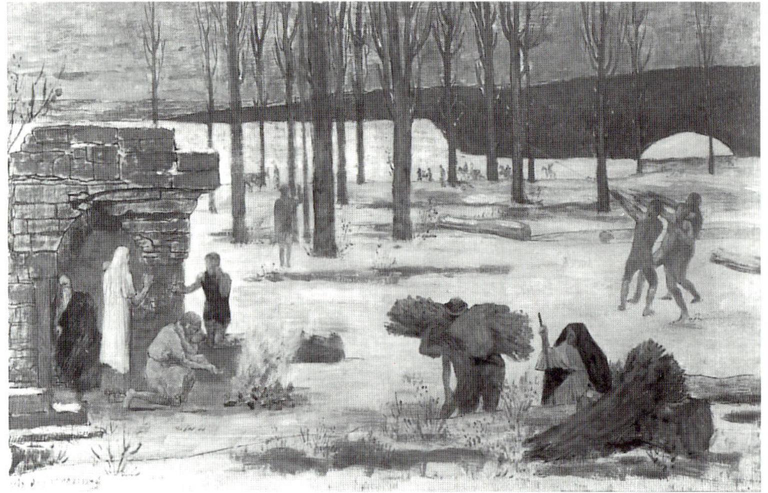

fig. 38
Winter (small version), ca. 1891-92
Oil on canvas, 53.5 x 85.6 cm
Musée du Petit Palais, Paris

35

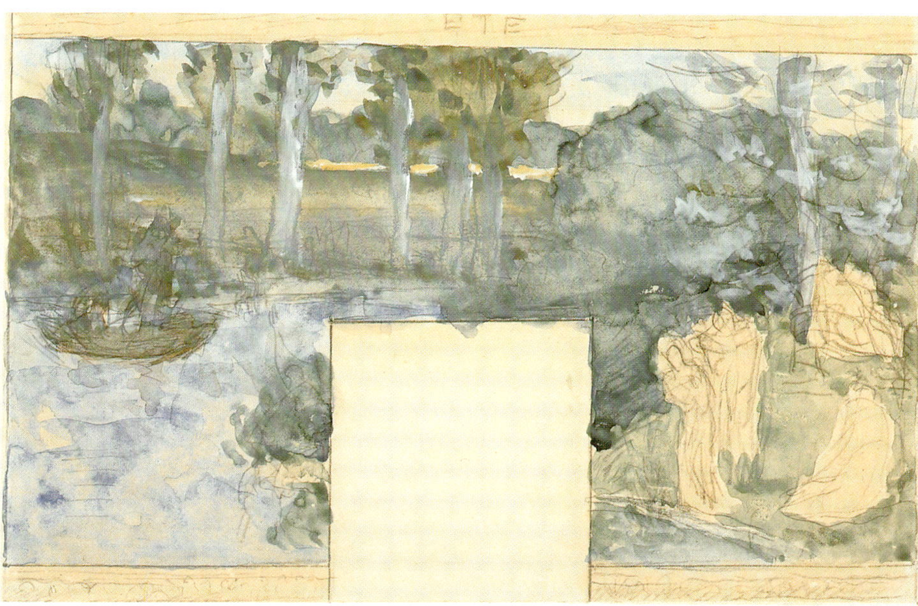

are the trees at each side, put there to frame and strengthen the architecture of the composition. The great mass of trees at the horizon has been changed into a continuous band. Figures and trees are more closely intermingled, the fisherman at left sailing more closely into view. Unlike the wallpainting with its distinct shapes and colors that yield an easy legibility, this *Summer* has a more subdued tonal range and its appearance is made less stark by the proliferation of bare, gray trees with leafy branches.

In *Summer* Puvis reprised earlier motifs, including two bathers from *Summer* of 1873 (fig. 5), bathers that were later drawn on by Picasso for his own compositions (see his 1918 drawing *Bathers*, Fogg Art Museum, Cambridge, Mass.).

Of all the prototypes for figures, the boy emerging from the water and the wading child in Frédéric Bazille's *Summer Scene* (Fogg Art Museum, Cambridge, Mass.) exhibited at the 1870 Salon[2] have aroused the most interest. Puvis had complimented the younger artist[3] and was as apt to have culled his idea from him as from an older source. Another source may have been Chassériau's compelling *Summer* scene, a drawing of figures busily wading through and emerging from the water as here.[4] Sources for the seated woman include Baron Gros's *The Bather* (Musée de Besançon), perhaps via Chapu's relief *Thought* (Salon of 1877, Tomb of Mme la Comtesse d'Agoult, Père-Lachaise, Paris).

1 He would remain disturbed to the extent that, after he finished his murals, he asked that they be returned, for which he would reimburse the commissioning body. Letter of February 1892 (heirs of the artist).

2 Boucher (1979), p. 104, also notes a similarity in the lounging figure and points to Bazille's wrestling figures as prototypes for those of Puvis's in *Pleasant Land* of 1882.

3 On *View of the Village*, 1868 (Musée Fabre, Montpellier).

4 Musée du Louvre, Paris (Inv. RF 56055).

135

Landscape with Figures, Study for 'Summer' ca. 1890-91

Inscribed u. m.: ETE

Watercolor on black pencil on paper, 141 x 225 mm

Musée du Petit Palais, Paris (Inv. PPD 254[4]; MCB 128)

Provenance Bequest of artist's heirs to the city of Paris (1898); deposited in the Musée Galliera (1899); transferred to the Musée du Petit Palais upon its opening (1901).

Selected References Boucher (1979), no. 128.

Puvis developed *Summer*, his 1891 mural for the Paris Hôtel de Ville (see cat. 134) in a series of drawings, pastels, and watercolors. This landscape with its waterways and fertile fields, knolls and trees is set in the Seine region of the Ile de France, as was appropriate for a governmental palace for that zone: it is said to show the Seine from Puteaux, opposite the Bagatelle.[1] At the heart of this watercolor is a sense of the lush and verdant that would contrast to the white and mauve colors of *Winter*, the pendant of the mural (see fig. 38). Although the general massing of the landscape has been found, the wooded bank would give way to a far barer setting, with each element read as a clearer, more distinct colored shape. In the final work, the boat and body of water that dominate the left section of the study will have diminished in importance, and the horizontal elements above the portal would be emboldened and elaborated to bind the two sides together and further embellish the upper reaches of the composition. Figures would be added in the left foreground to further equilibrate the sides, but not before a number of alternative arrangements were tried, including one that reverses the placement of figures at each side of the doorway.[2]

1 Jean (1914), p. 103.

2 *Study for Summer*, ca. 1890-91, pastel, charcoal and gouache on paper, 770 x 1280 mm, Metropolitan Museum of Art, New York (Inv. 1991.464).

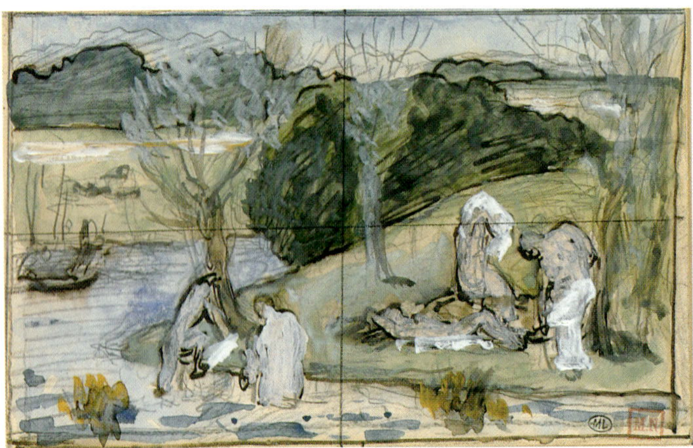

136

Study for 'Summer' ca. 1890-91

Stamp l.r.
Gouache, watercolor, black chalk and ink on paper, 103 x 165 mm
Musée du Louvre, Paris (Inv. RF 2290)

Provenance Bequest of artist's heirs to the city of Paris (1899); Musée du Luxembourg; transferred to the Musée du Louvre (1929)

This watercolor sketch relates to the independent version of *Summer* (cat. 134), in which the doorway, so prominent in the mural for which Puvis devised his composition, has been eliminated. With its secure notations, this watercolor contrasts to the more lyrical and searching study for the mural (cat. 135). The quadrants into which it is divided are helpful in determining the balance of interest and pictorial weight in the sectors. Together, the drawings demonstrate how the artist put landscape elements where he needed them, deploying trees, hills, knolls and water to strategic effect like pawns. Marie-Christine Boucher placed this watercolor before the mural, speculating that Puvis did not first think of situating *Summer* on the wall with the door.[1]

1 Boucher (1979), no. 177.

137

Normandy / *La Normandie* 1893

Signed and dated l.l.: P. Puvis de Chavannes 93
Oil on canvas, 92.4 x 63.5 cm
Private collection

Provenance Durand-Ruel, Paris (1893); Durand-Ruel, New York (1893-94); A.W. Kingman (1895); Durand-Ruel, New York (1896-1901); James Gayley; Mrs. Gano Dunn (1921-), on deposit at Durand-Ruel, New York (11 February 1931); Milliken Collection.
Selected Exhibitions 1894 New York, no. 1[1];1975 Toronto, no. 33; 1976-77 Paris/Ottawa, no. 197.
Selected References Neff (1969), 79, 85; Brown Price (1977), 33-34.

Puvis often went to the Normandy countryside 'to harvest impressions' ('a la recolte des effets').[2] Pride and cultural interest in the various regions of France and their rich diversity grew as a permutation of the rebuilding of French nationalism after the 1870-71 war and a political reaction to increasing centralization. The burgeoning of local historical societies, the promotion of regionalist writing and literature, and the study of the history, dialects, topography and customs of individual provinces were some of its manifestations. The new railroads could speed passengers armed with new guidebooks to what were no longer outlying areas, and painters were among them. And when in the late 1880s and 1890s Puvis executed a series of figural personifications of French geographical regions – *Tamarisk* (*Tamaris*, Metropolitan Museum of Art, New York), emblematic of the Var Valley, *The 'Bresse'* (see cat. 108) and *In the Heather, Nymphs* (Art Institute of Chicago) for Brittany – *Normandy* was included.[3]

In *Normandy*, as in a number of works from about 1870, Puvis endeavored to combine classicizing imagery with germane specificity and to render a symbolic figure of some modernity. As is customary, his figural personification is a woman. She is outfitted in a chemise, skirt and cap, the last as Phrygian – with its implication of Republicanism and nationhood – as it is a servant's or milkmaid's cap. Her quasi-frontal profile pose, with her shoulders set forward, is like that often seen on ancient reliefs. Puvis's drawing of a similarly posed woman in profile[4] resembles the shrouded figures of Attic grave steles (and generally medallions and coins from classical antiquity), which he may have been looking at in preparing his composition. In a lithograph after the painting,[5] the lack of interior modeling and the contoured outlines further emphasize the classicizing aspects of the image.

37

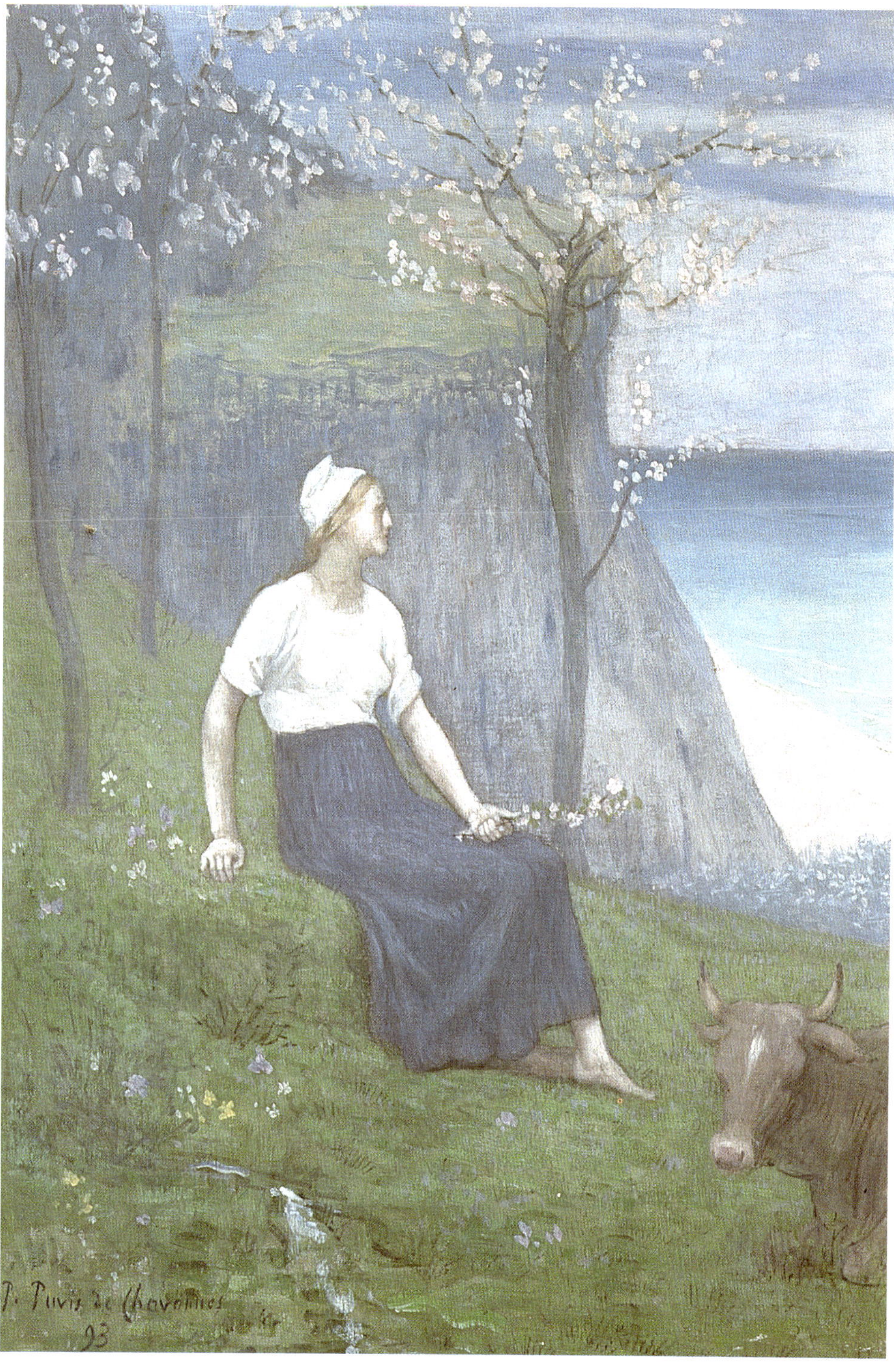

The emblematic figure is seated on a bluff above the sea, likely a limestone cliff for which the north coast is famous, the topography not distant from what enamored Courbet, Seurat and Monet, though its drama is softened by the blossoming trees and mitigated by the subdued, light colors. These matte, opaque chords equilibrate the pictorial surface, which is perceived as a patterned totality. The pink flowers and orchid plants, the light turquoise sea and pale pink shore are muted in tone; notwithstanding that the choices have been made with bold aplomb.

The interposed cow's head shows just how bucolic the pastoral setting is. In Puvis's compositions animals are deployed to add a rustic note and vitalize spaces: Saint Genevieve tends sheep (see cat. 70), the prodigal son, pigs (fig. 7); and goats scamper through *Antique Vision* (see cat. 105) and *Child Gathering Apples* (cat. 138). *Normandy* might be described in terms used to characterize Paul Gauguin's and Emile Bernard's canvases of neighboring Brittany: His [Gauguin's] 'view embraces the region and sets down the synthesis of Brittany: behind the low wall, the white and black cow ... [and] farm servant girl....'[6]

1 Although 1976-77 Paris/Ottawa, no. 197 indicates this work was exhibited in 1894 Vienna, Puvis showed only one painting in that exhibition, no. 129, called *Mädchen* (*Girl*), which possibly could be this painting, though there are no labels verso on the work itself to indicate it travelled there.

2 Raynal (1913), 5.

3 Brown Price (1979), 33-34.

4 Whereabouts unknown; formerly Kraushaar Gallery, New York.

5 *Normandy*, transfer lithograph, signed l.r.; *L'Estampe Originale*, IV (October-December 1893), pl. 36, edition of 100; see 1976-77 Paris/Ottawa, no. 198; and Delteil (1925), II, 310, CDXXXVI.

6 [Paul Gauguin's] 'vue embrasse la région et inscrit la synthèse de la Bretagne: derrière le muretin, la vache noire et blanche ... la servante de la ferme....' Armand Séguin, 'Paul Gauguin,' *L'Occident*, (April 1903), 231.

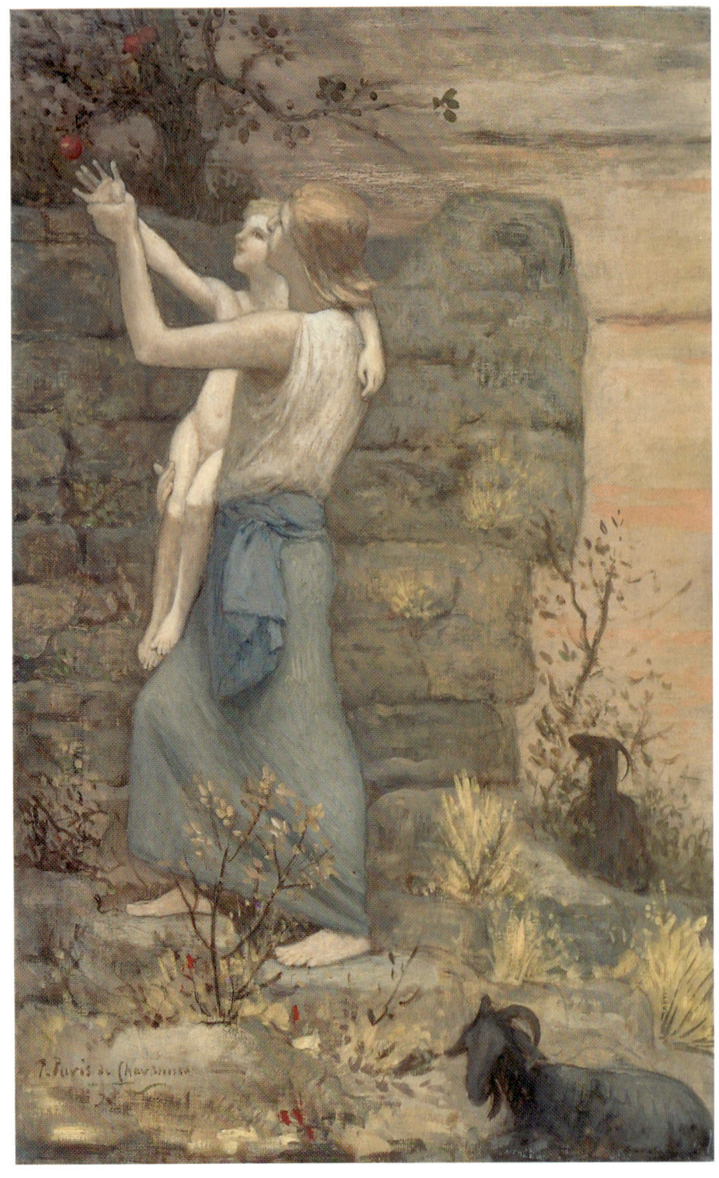

138

Child Picking Apples *or* The Goatherd / *Enfant cueillant des pommes* or *Gardeuse de chèvres* 1893

Signed and dated l.l.: P. Puvis de Chavannes 93
Oil on canvas, 86.5 x 53 cm
Musée Municipal des Ursulines, Mâcon
(Inv. A. 1037))

Provenance Durand-Ruel, Paris (1893) and New York (1894); Mrs. S.D. Warren (1894-95); Durand-Ruel, New York (1895-98); Amelia Küsner (1898); Mrs. Charles Dupont Coudert, New York, on loan to the Metropolitan Museum of Art, New York (1911-27); Wildenstein and Co., New York; London, Sotheby's (7 January 1964), no. 186; Hahn Brothers; private collection, Buenos Aires (1970-74); Michael Hasenclever Gallery, Munich; acquired with the aid of the French government (1975).

Selected Exhibitions 1894 New York, no. 2; 1976-77 Paris/Ottawa, no. 199.

Selected References Alexandre (February 1899), 26, repr.; Michel and Laran (1911), pp. 101-102, repr. pl. XLIII; Burroughs (1915).

Women with children, a frequent motif in Puvis's murals, are also the subject of a number of independent canvases (see cat. 118) derived from them. This woman helping a child pluck fruit from a tree[1] is similar to the central group of *Inter Artes et Naturam* (ill. pp. 214-215), although the two are turned laterally and yield to a slightly stiff, flattened, decorative reading. The elemental stone wall was a favored instrument to foreclose pictorial depth, as in *Pity* of 1887 (cat. 110) and *Charity* of 1893 (cat. 140), although a mound (*Young Women by the Sea*, 1879, fig. 6) or overhang (*In the Heather, Nymphs*, 1896, Art Institute of Chicago) served the purpose as well.

The lyricism of *Child Gathering Apples* is furthered by luminous pastel colors, a tendency to the overly sweet mitigated by the directness of stroke and physically rough surface. Puvis's experience with pastels in the later 1880s affected his painting style.

Goats accessorize the canvas, as in *Antique Vision* (1884, see cat. 105) and *The Shepherd's Song* (also of 1893, Metropolitan Museum of Art, New York), and lend a playful, rustic note to the proceedings, their dark silhouettes a formal interconnection among the pictorial elements.

1 A new Eve, perhaps, domesticated and the mother of the race.

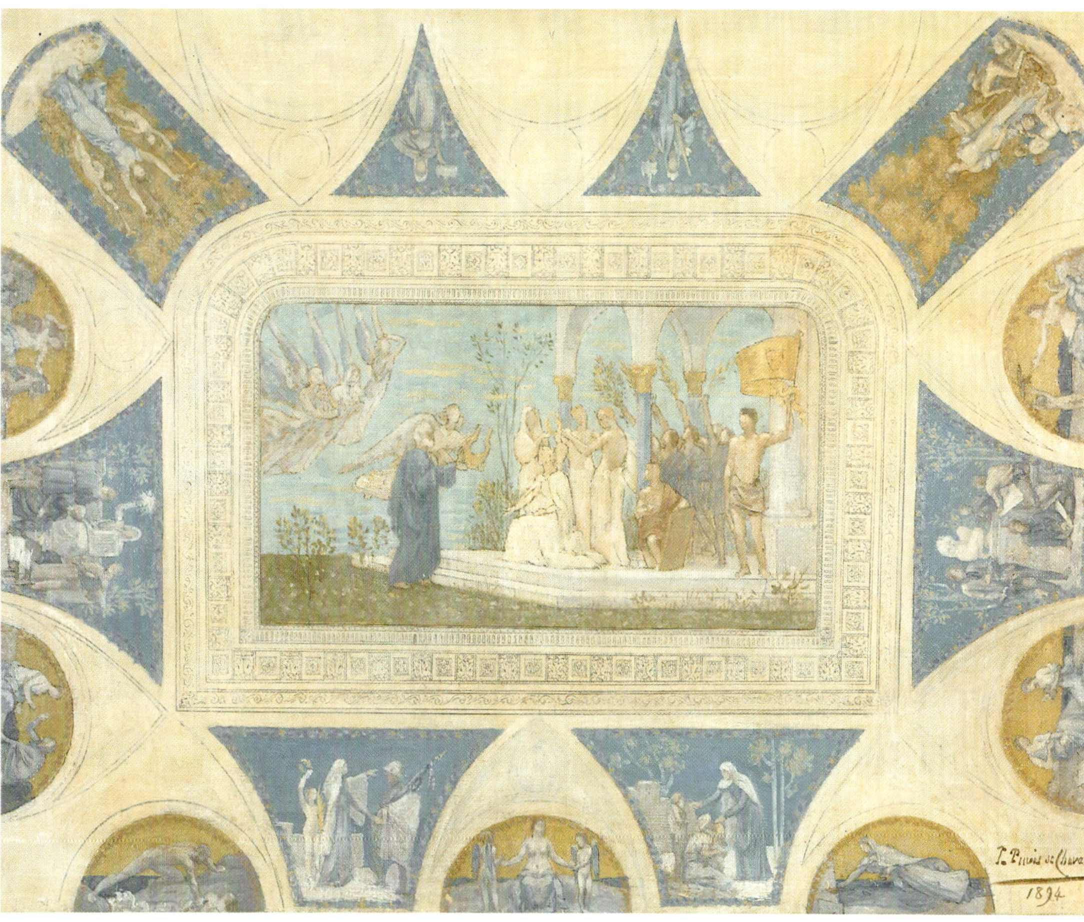

139

Sketch for the Ceiling Ensemble for the Staircase of Honor of the Paris City Hall / *Esquisse d'ensemble pour le plafond de l'escalier d'honneur de l'Hôtel de Ville, Paris* 1894

Signed and dated l.r.: P. Puvis de Chavannes 1894
Oil, pen and ink on canvas, 67.1 x 83.5 cm
Musée du Petit Palais, Paris (Inv. PPP 2361; MCB 180)

Provenance Artist's donation to the city of Paris (1894), deposited with works belonging to the city in Auteuil; Musée Cernuschi (1897); Musée Galliera (1899); transferred to the Musée du Petit Palais upon its opening (1901).
Selected Exhibitions 1895-96 Paris; 1899-1900 Paris, not in catalogue; 1976-77 Paris/Ottawa, no. 200.
Selected References On the Murals: Letter from Puvis to his family, 29 March 1892 (private collection); Vachon (1895), pp. 146-154; Geffroy (1895), IV, pp. 130-137; Vachon [1900], 233-240; Vachon (1905), pp. 192-196; 1976-77 Paris/Ottawa, pp. 220-221; 1986-87 Paris, pp. 63-71, 214-216, 285-287, 379-383. On this painting: Boucher (1979), no. 180, 1986-87 Paris, p. 288, no. 118.

Puvis executed two complexes for the Paris City Hall: murals for the Zodiac Salon (see cat. 134), and a decorative cycle that surmounts the great ceremonial Staircase of Honor.[1] Puvis (like Michelangelo) viewed the prospect of a ceiling decoration as something of a punishment: 'And then ceilings? but, I would prefer collecting dung on the highway!'[2] After having developed a mural aesthetic of flattened forms that would not break the planar aspect of a wall, he was not likely to have chosen trompe l'oeil effects or *di sotto in sù* perspectives, but when the mural was finished, he was roundly criticized for not having done so.

What he devised can best be analyzed in this schema, in which the central ceiling painting and the complex of fifteen dauntingly variegated shaped spaces that comprise its coved surrounds – curved vaults, semi-circular tympana, triangular areas and modified squinches – what Puvis called the small 'morceaux' (bits) that fit the 'morcellement' (parcelling out)[3] of the architecture – are flattened out and the most legible. The ornamented bands that are carefully penned in (perhaps by an assistant), represent the stucco relief frames. This oil sketch is part of a collection of such schemas at the Musée du Petit Palais, the result of a prefectural decree of 29 January 1889 requiring the donation to the municipality of a sketch of each commission for the newly reconstructed city hall.[4] This canvas appears to be a rendering produced to fulfill that requirement and not an early study presented to the commission (as has elsewhere been argued).[5]

The program was set by 12 December 1892: 'Having to represent the Glorification of the City of Paris in a ceiling and fifteen complementary compartments, I have chosen for the principal subject a scene that can be divided thus: the City of Paris, crowned by Letters, Sciences and Arts, receives the homage of the universal bard who celebrated her. Victor Hugo, his hand on his lyre, presents it to the city. The fifteen compartments that serve as a support and corollary to the principal subject are: for the four wide vaults: The Intellectual Home [or Study, at left in this schema], Artistic Ardor [at right], Charity [bottom to right], Patriotism [bottom to left]; for the two vaults: Medieval Paris [sometimes given as Lutetia, its ancient name, holding a model of the Sainte Chapelle], Modern Paris [with a model of Garnier's Opéra; both at top]; for the seven tympana: Wit [lower right], Beauty [called Elegance by Puvis, upper left], Urbanity [lower left], Fantasy [upper right], The Cult of Memory [also translated as Remembrance or Nostalgia, bottom right], Fearlessness [bottom left], Generosity [bottom center]. The two vaults remain to be determined. [These would be *Enthusiasm*, first projected as *Renown*, and *Industry*, at the upper corners].'[6]

Puvis now developed his '*Parisian Virtues*', an updated, urbanized, cosmopolitized version of the ancient theme. Though in 1892 Puvis was still not sure of the colors for his decoration, proposing camaïeux, this canvas maps out what were to be its limited but varied hues – dull gold, turquoise, blues, green, subtly modulated mauves, grays and white – with individual placement within the series determining the disposition of color as it did the composition of each within the whole.

His central image was *Victor Hugo Offering his Lyre to the City of Paris*.[7] Hugo (1802-1885), whose writing Puvis admired, had been involved in politics and lived in exile from 1851 to 1870; his *Les Châtiments* (one of the works to which reference is made in the painting) had attacked Napoleon III, and after his return he had become a Republican senator. Here he is reconciled to the city that figured so prominently in several of his novels and of which he had written an appreciation that had been included in a special 1867 Paris guidebook.

How to combine what was current while transcending the contemporary concerned the ad hoc committee of 32 charged with the program just as it admittedly did Puvis: 'First of all, I was concerned to ward off all elements that would have dated my work. Do you see a Victor Hugo in a jacket? To insure the reality of the person, it sufficed to reproduce the poet's head, that inspired head with the jutting forehead. In a word, it's the eternal human bard I wanted to paint.'[8] Puvis was close to Rodin at this period, and the latter's *Monument to Victor Hugo*, commissioned in 1889 for the Panthéon, may have affected Puvis's theme. The second version of Rodin's project, developed in 1890 but ultimately aborted, apotheosized Hugo with personifying figures bearing laurel and representing the *vox populi*.[9]

1 1976-77 Paris/Ottawa, pp. 220-221 reviews the history of the project, for which Paul Baudry and Elie Delaunay were selected prior to Puvis. Puvis received the commission 22 January 1892, almost a decade after his first bid of 21 January 1882 had failed (letter in a private collection).

2 'Et puis des plafonds? mais j'aimerais mieux ramasser du crottin sur la grand'route!' Vachon (1895), p. 35.

3 1986-87 Paris, p. 286.

4 Boucher (1979), no. 177.

5 1976-77 Paris/Ottawa, no. 135; Boucher (1979), no. 180; and 1986-87 Paris, p. 288. The 1892 date is untenable because by 16 December 1892 Puvis had not yet arrived at the subjects Enthusiasm and Industry and was thinking in terms of camaieux; see A.D.A.C., PV, 16 December 1892; cited in 1986-87 Paris, p. 288.

6 'Ayant à représenter dans un plafond et quinze compartiments complémentaires la glorification de la Ville de Paris, j'ai choisi pour sujet principal une scène qui peut se diviser ainsi: la Ville de Paris, couronnée par les Lettres, les Sciences et les Arts, agrée l'hommage du chantre universel qui l'a célébrée. Victor Hugo, la main sur sa lyre, la présente à la Ville. Les quinze compartiments qui servent d'appui et de corollaire au sujet principal sont: pour les quatre voussures larges: le Foyer intellectuel, l'Ardeur artistique, la Charité, le Patriotisme; pour les deux voussures: Paris Moyen-Age, Paris Moderne; pour les sept tympans: l'Esprit, l'Elegance [Beauté], l'Urbanité, la Fantaisie, le Culte du Souvenir, l'Intrépidité, la Générosité. Restent à déterminer deux voussures.' See A.D.A.C., PV, 12 December 1892; in 1986-87 Paris, p. 286. In a letter of 29 March 1892 (ref. above) Puvis labeled the variously shaped canvases A through D, described the 'glorification intellectuelle' of Paris and the 'immortel' bard and listed the tympana in another order: Esprit, Générosité, Fantaisie [schema C is a shallow tympanum], Elégance, Culte de Souvenir, Vaillance [ultimately Intrepidité or Fearlessness], Urbanité.' *Intellectual Home* and *Artistic Ardor* were reversed.

7 *Hommage de Victor Hugo à la Ville de Paris* was its title at the Salon of 1893; it was renamed *Victor Hugo offrant sa lyre à la Ville de Paris* at the 1894 Salon. In a letter of 29 March 1892 (ref. above) he described the panel: 'La ville de Paris, couronnée par les lettres, les sciences et les arts agrée l'hommage du chantre immortel qui l'a célébrée – Victor Hugo lui présente sa lyre à la suite apparaît un trio de figures volantes – symbolisant l'essence même de son oeuvre – Poésie lyrique, Légende ou roman, drame, ou les châtiments. Sous le portique, le groupe d'éphebes, faisant cortège à la ville brandit des palmes – l'un d'eux s'apprête à écrire sur le livre d'or, un autre tient l'étendard ou brille le titre glorieux créé par Hugo: Paris, Ville Lumière.' (The City of Paris, crowned by Letters, Sciences and the Arts

40 receives the homage of the immortal bard who celebrated her – Victor Hugo offers her his lyre, in his train appears a trio of flying figures – symbolizing the very essence of his work – Lyric Poetry, the Novel *The Legend of the Centuries*, Drama or *The Punishments*. Under the portico, there is a procession of young ephebes, comprising the City's attendants, brandishing palms – one of them prepares to write on the Golden Book, another holds the standard on which one may read Hugo's glorious title: Paris, City of Light.')

8 'J'ai tenu, tout d'abord, à écarter tous les éléments qui auraient daté mon oeuvre. Voyez-vous un Victor Hugo en veston? Il suffisait, pour assurer la réalité du type, de reproduire la tête du poète, cette tête génial, au front débordant. En un mot, c'est le barde humain, éternel, que j'ai voulu peindre.' [Anonymous], *L'Art Français* ([?] 1894), p. 33. My thanks to Susannah Wolfson, for bringing this to my attention.

9 Jane Mayo Roos, 'Rodin's *Monument to Victor Hugo*: Art and Politics in the Third Republic,' *Art Bulletin* (December 1986), 632-656.

140

Charity / *La Charité* 1894

Signed and dated l.r.: 94 P. Puvis de Chavannes
Oil on canvas, 92.4 x 74.3 cm
Washington University Gallery of Art, Saint Louis, University Purchase, Bixby Fund, 1908
(Inv. WU 2105)

Provenance Durand-Ruel, Paris (6 September 1894); Durand-Ruel, New York (1894-1908).

Selected Exhibitions 1894 Paris (Durand-Ruel), no no.; 1894 New York, no. 7; 1895, Saint Louis Exhibition and Music Hall, no. 455; 1896 Pittsburgh, no. 234; 1899 Paris (Durand-Ruel), no. 47; 1975 Toronto, no. 35; 1976-77 Paris/Ottawa, no. 203.

Selected References Durand-Ruel Archives, no. 573 L3120; [Anonymous], 'Exposition de M. Puvis de Chavannes,' *Chronique des Arts* (20 October 1894), 52; Yriarte (1894); Alexandre (February 1899), 26-35, repr.; Smith (1909); Brown Price (1977), 34-37.

One of the modernized, secularized *Parisian Virtues* Puvis developed for the Hôtel de Ville (see cat. 139) was *Charity*. This virtue is depicted as a simply clad, caped figure ministering to a woman huddled with ragged children in the snow. This canvas, an independent variant, is not as bleak and stark as the mural decoration, designed to be viewed from a con-

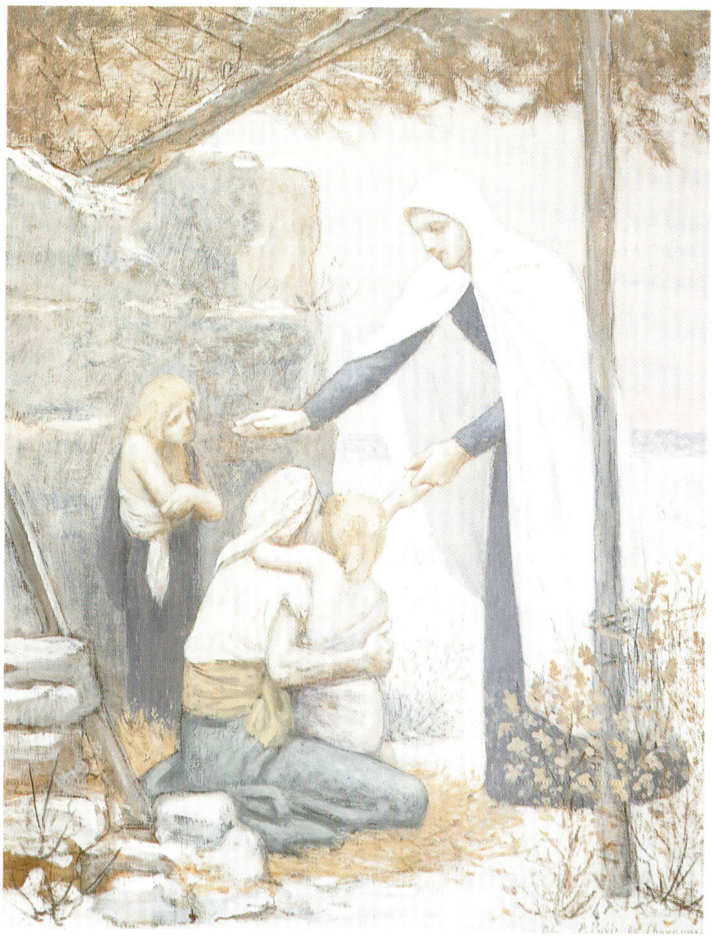

siderable distance, or a monumental preliminary sketch for it.[1] On this more intimate scale, the artist permitted himself the niceties of a tender facial expression for the standing altruistic figure, and slightly more elaboration of the now varicolored garments of the bare-armed, destitute trio. The latter are enframed but scarcely sheltered by a stone outcropping, a tree and a bower of branches. Certain elements are spatially ambiguous: the tree and diagonal support cannot be firmly located, and, as in a Cézanne, may be read as an illusionistic image within the pictorial spaces or within a system of formal geometries on the pictorial surface. The gestures and structure form a system of parallels that lock the composition into place. The use of chalky colors – a white-blanketed, bare landscape, pale pink sky, frosty blue sea and sparse, gold leaves – mutes the objects and lightens the composition both visually and emotionally, yielding an oddly removed, poetic image.

Charity was part of a familiar Christian theological trilogy, with Hope and Faith. But this is not a religious allegorical personification. Giving is promoted as a civic, secular, humanitarian virtue, with the ennobled poor pictured as helpless innocents, though whether the poor were responsible for bringing on their own plight was a controversial issue at the time. Public charity in Paris had traditionally been carried out by the

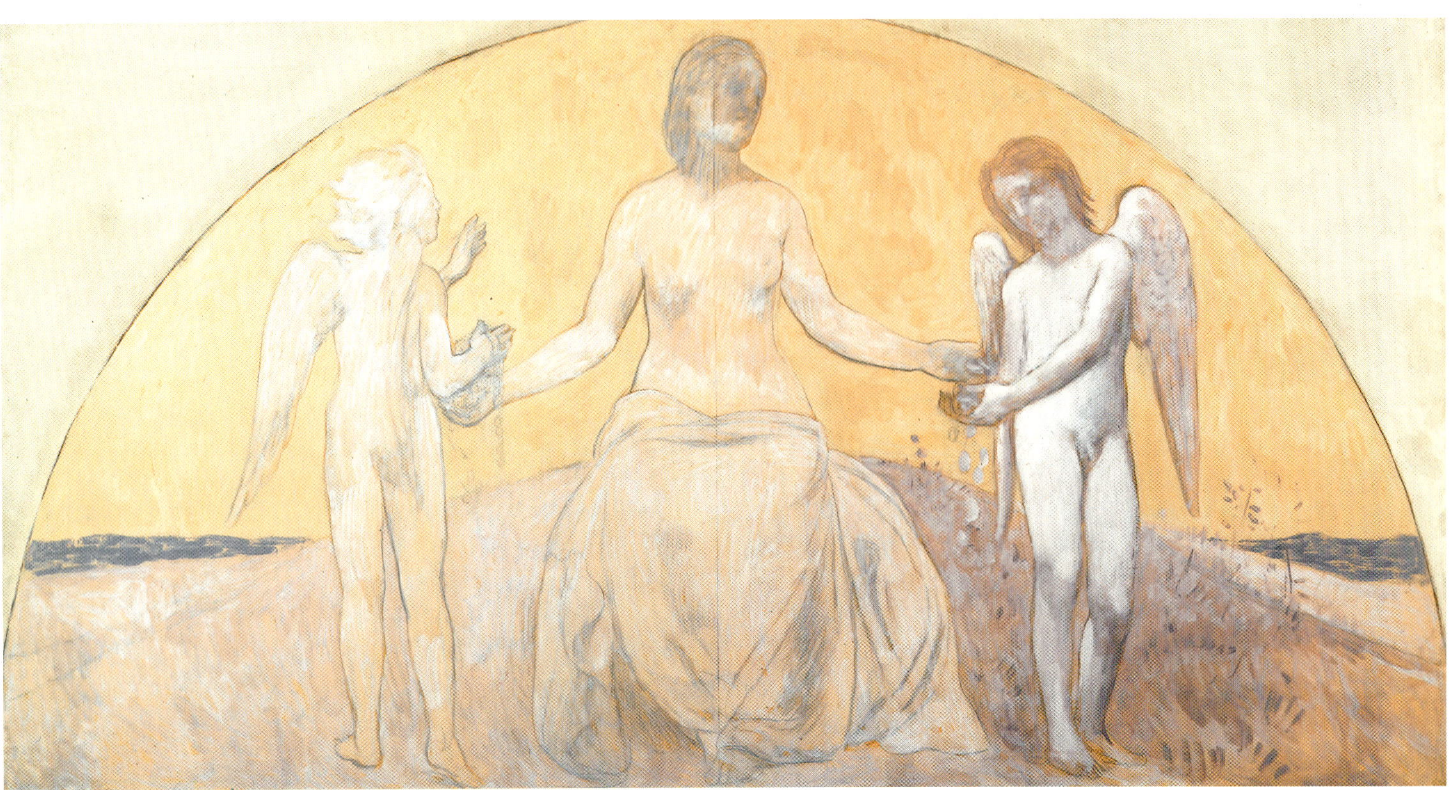

Church, but in the late nineteenth century city government increasingly appropriated this function, and whether administrative authority over aid to the poor should be under the auspices of church or state was the subject of intense debate.[2] Clearly, the government wanted to portray *Charity* as a civic duty; the Public Assistance program was under its jurisdiction. The central figure here, garbed in a plain blue gown, though secular, transmits the sense of a sister of mercy or a lay Madonna. This figure, modeled after the Princess Cantacuzène, has its counterpart in other examples of Puvis's late work – in *Patriotism* at the Hôtel de Ville and the 1898 *Saint Genevieve* at the Panthéon.

The theme and pictorial idea for *Charity* originated with Puvis's large 1887 pastel *Pity* (cat. 110), with a similar setting and ministering figure. Picasso, painting his wretched, meager outcasts in equally restrained colors during his Blue Period, less than a decade later, would owe much to *Charity*'s theme of poverty, its rudimentary seaside setting, its gaunt, angular figures, with their hugged-in poses, and its opaque colors of an overriding tonal cast.

1 *Charity* ca. 1894, oil over pencil on paper laid down on canvas, squared, 241 x 350.5 cm, Gifu Museum, Japan; there is also a preliminary version, *Charity*, oil on canvas, 49.5 x 42 cm, collection Joey and Toby Tanenbaum, Toronto.

2 Pierre de la Gorce, *Histoire du Second Empire*, vol. II (Paris, 1894), p. 180.

141

Generosity / La *Générosité* ca. 1893

Oil and pencil on paper, mounted on canvas, 142 x 284 cm
Victoria and Albert Museum, London
(Inv. E.917-1911).

Provenance National Art Collections Fund (1911).
Selected Exhibitions 1972 London/Liverpool, no. 227.

This is a loosely painted study for *Generosity*,[1] the seated half-nude woman handing coins and jewels to winged putti in Puvis de Chavannes's series of *Parisian Virtues* at the Paris Hôtel de Ville (see cat. 139). The simply conceived and broadly executed outlines, the inventive and daring colors and shapes may be associated with twentieth-century rather than nineteenth-century painting. Many of these qualities may in part be explained by the origin of *Generosity* as an architectural decoration, to be legible at a distance, and its position at the center of a series of shaped canvases (between *Patriotism* and *Charity*), along the coved wall framing the ceiling decoration. The satisfaction taken in symmetry is evident in the double square proportions and the exact placements assured by carefully marked vertical guidelines on which the figures are so precisely placed.

42 The colors are few and daring: a pink hill, a yellow gold background. Like the flat yellow gold background that Puvis used elsewhere (see cat. 86), they may be explained as part of a programmatic commitment engendered by the then fashionable neo-Byzantinism prevalent in architectural decoration since mid-century.

Individual placement within the series determined the color and goes far to explain the composition of each of the panels that had their origins in the Hôtel de Ville series of *Parisian Virtues*. Thus *Generosity*, at the center of one side of the ceiling, is bilaterally symmetrical, while *Patriotism* and *Charity* (compare cat. 140) which bracket it, share many of the same elements: a tall, gowned figure facing towards where *Generosity* would have been, young boys, a third figure, and similar background walls. The rudimentary landscapes often include a blue sea which provides an ongoing horizontal sectioning of the background against which the figures were placed. The symmetry, hieratic poses and colors are muted recollections of the ascetic but opulent Byzantine style.

1 This work corresponds to *Generosity*, not *Charity* as recorded by the Victoria and Albert Museum. *Urbanity*, which represents an old woman giving flowers to a young woman, was once also called *Generosity* (see 1894 Paris [Société Nationale des Beaux-Arts], no. 934), perhaps leading to the confusion over the Victoria and Albert composition.

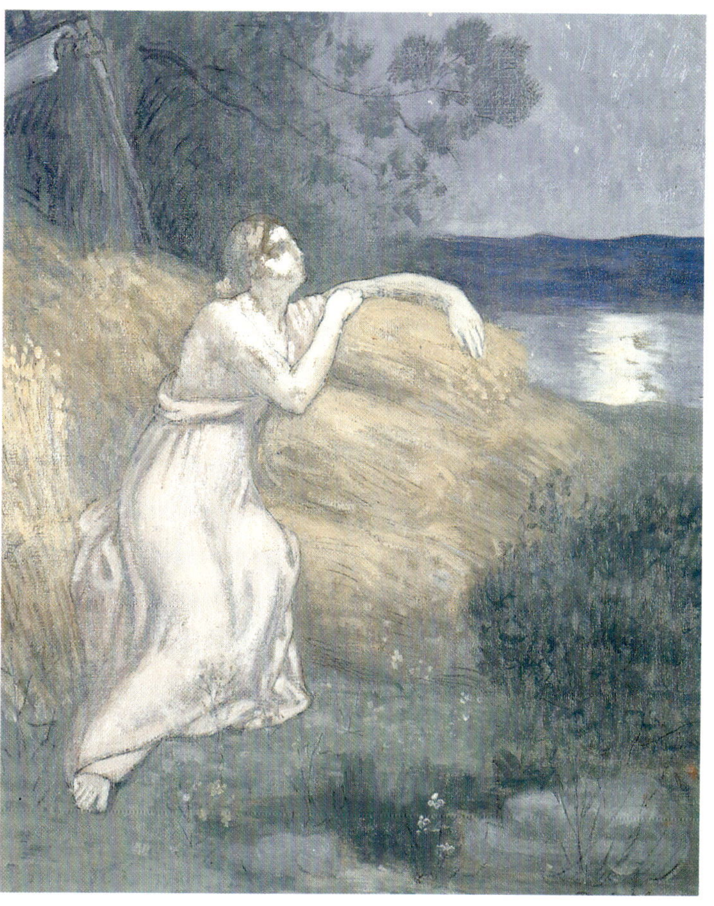

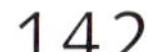

142

By Moonlight / *Au clair de la lune*

ca. 1893-95

Signed l.r.: Puvis de C; and l.l. a trace of a signature, overpainted: P. Puvis de C va nes
Oil on canvas, 46 x 38.1 cm
Spencer Museum of Art, The University of Kansas, Lawrence (Anonymous Gift) (Inv. 56.51)

Provenance Artist to Mme Léo Delibes, Paris; Paris, Hôtel Drouot, Mme Léo Delibes Sale (4-5 July 1919), no. 205; M. Rosenberg; Galerie Georges Petit, Paris; J. Allard et Cie., Paris; M. Knoedler and Co., New York; J.J. Emery, Cincinnati; Cincinnati Art Museum (1924-45); New York, Parke-Bernet Galleries [Museum Sale], 'Property of a Mid-West Educational Institution' (18 October 1945), no. 43; Mr. and Mrs. Harold Kaye, New York; anonymous gift to the museum (1956).

Selected Exhibitions 1975 Toronto, no. 26; 1976-77 Paris/Ottawa, no. 207.

Selected References Robertson (1957), repr. 148.

In this lyrical canvas Puvis has adapted the seated figure of a woman leaning on a sheaf of wheat from his spandrel decoration, a difficult architectural space, at the Zodiac Salon of the Paris Hôtel de Ville (see cat. 134) and placed her in a moonlit landscape, the light reflected off the surface of a pond in the background, the stars glinting in the sky. The title, like the dedication verso, 'A Mme L[eo] Delibes/ au clair de la lune/ par son ami Pierrot,' plays on the old ballad and children's tune. Léo Delibes (1836-1891) composed music for the ballets *Coppélia* and *Sylvia* as well as a song, *Mon ami Pierrot*.[1] Puvis inscribed several small works to Mme Delibes (née Jeanne Massé), whom he had known since she was a young girl.[2] That Puvis referred to himself as Pierrot, a turn on his Christian name, is of course because of the song; but Pierrot was also a common sobriquet for painters, a pantomime character associated with the sometimes melancholic and good-natured minstrel.[3] Puvis's use of this name betrays a charming, slightly self-deprecating familiarity.

1 See Robertson (1957); the song on which it is based dates back at least to the eighteenth century.

2 She and her sister were daughters of the composer Victor Massé; her sister became the wife of the composer Philippe Gille, for whom Delibes wrote libretti as he did for Massé.

3 See Brown Price (1991), 128.

The Murals for the Boston Public Library

Puvis de Chavannes's mural ensemble for the imposing new Boston Public Library, which was installed in 1896, was to be his only mural project outside of France.[1] Beginning in 1891 he was courted by a delegation of Americans to take on the commission for the 'monumental, *very monumental* staircase,'[2] but he was reluctant to undertake a program for a building he was never to see and murals he was not to know *in situ*. But models and information were sent; a fee several times greater than any other Puvis had received before was offered, and the commission was finally secured on 18 May 1893, with a contract sent 7 July 1893. Henry Brooks Adams and the artistic and literary circle surrounding him, including the painter John La Farge and the sculptor Augustus Saint-Gaudens, who considered Puvis the first among muralists, were great supporters of the choice, with Adams himself, somewhat given to hyperbole, later writing of the Boston murals that they were 'the greatest things ever painted.'[3]

The program for Puvis's first library decoration was based on the idea that a library is a conservatory of human knowledge. There were to be eight panels 14 by 7 in 'English feet' ('pieds anglais'), each of which was to represent the 'prime aspects of knowledge'; and a large work, 12 by 50, to be executed first, was to represent in one vast scene the results of knowledge. With shrewd practicality, Puvis based the division of knowledge on Boston's own codification system for classifying books. The visitor ascending the ceremonial staircase would first see *Chemistry* and *Physics*, which flank the windows lighting the open space, and then three paintings on each side wall, *Philosophy*, *Astronomy* and *History* (see cat. 143) on one, and *Virgil (Bucolic Poetry)* (see cat. 144), *Aeschylus (Dramatic Poetry)* and *Homer (Epic Poetry)* on the other (each panel 435 x 220 cm). On the landing at the top of the stairs, be yond a balustrade opposite the windows, on a wall pierced by a door to the collections was the culminating *The Muses Welcome the Spirit of Light* (*Les Muses inspiratrices acclament le génie, messager de lumière* (485 x 1545 cm) (see ill. pp. 54-55). The compositions, motifs and colors of each of the panels are best understood in terms of its placement in relationship to the others and to the point at which a visitor would first see them. Thus *Philosophy*, *Astronomy* and *History* are all visually bracketed by the Ionic colonnade in the first, which resonates at the other end of this series with the large Doric column in *History*. The principal canvas, *The Muses Welcome the Spirit of Light* is filled with airborne muses, a composition astutely devised so as to be seen above a balustrade.

1 Official and informal correspondence and contracts for the Boston Public Library murals are with the Archives of the Trustees and the Archive and Manuscript Collection, Boston Public Library; the New York Historical Society Library, New York, the McKim, Mead and White papers, the Manuscript Archives; and in private collections. See also: Frank H. Chase, *Boston Public Library. A Handbook of the Library Building, Its Mural Decorations and Its Collections* (Boston, 1922), pp. 13-16; Theodore Child, 'Some Modern French Painters,' *Harper's New Monthly Magazine*, LXXX (May 1890), 817-830; Arthur Wesley Dow, *Boston Evening Transcript* (23 January 1892), n.p.; Ernest F. Fenollosa, *Mural Painting in the Boston Public Library* (Boston, 1896); Mandach and Wehrlé (1911), 468; Thiébault-Sisson (10 October 1896), 1008; Vachon [1900], pp. 250-256; M.G. van Rensselaer, 'The New Public Library in Boston,' *The Century Magazine*, L (June 1895), 260; Waern (1987).

2 'escalier monumental, *très monumental*,' letter of 25 September 1891 (private collection); see Ruth Clark, story in *The Boston Transcript* (11 October 1924), n.p.

3 Letter from Paris of 8 September 1896, to Mabel La Farge; see *Henry Adams and his Friends, a Collection of his Unpublished Letters*, introduction by Harold D. Cater (Boston, 1947), p. 385.

143

History / *L'Histoire* ca. 1895-96

Stamped l.r.: P. P. C.
Oil, charcoal, pencil and wash on canvas, squared for transfer, 124.5 x 64 cm
Collection Guy Ladrière, Paris

Provenance Artist's heirs and by descent; Inscribed verso: apporté de la Croix d'Arrignat [the property of collateral descendants] en 1931.

Selected References Official and private correspondence and contracts (private collection); Raymond Bouyer, *L'Art aux Salons de 1896* (Paris, 1896), pp. 74-75.

On several occasions Puvis represented *History* as the discovery of an artifact or ruin or, as in Poussin's *Et in Arcadia ego* (Musée du Louvre, Paris), the uncovering of ancient writing on a stone stele: at the Sorbonne (ill. pp. 200-201) and in *Inter Artes et Naturam* (ill. pp. 214-215). In a panel at the Boston Public Library, for which this canvas is a preparatory study, as in his 1866 *History* (Musée d'Orsay, Paris), Puvis represented Clio, the Muse of history, accompanied by an ephebe, a genius of learning (with book and torch). Here Clio gazes at a sunken Doric column. In conjunction with his earlier interpretation of *History* Puvis had asked: 'What is History? A curious woman, who searches and probes the past in order to reconstruct life by means of documents, of which the most precious are furnished by the ruins of monuments....'[1]

43

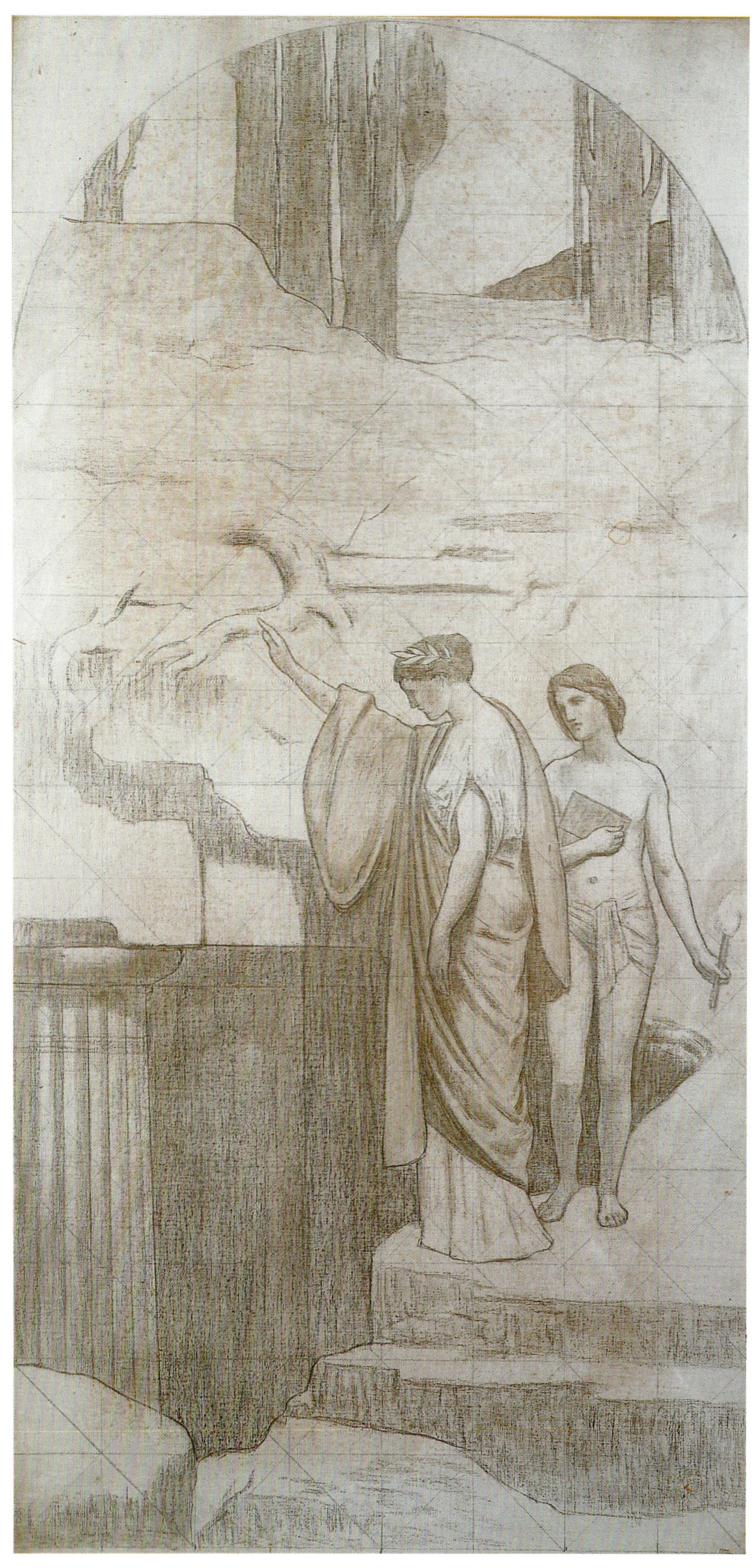

In a move away from the allegorical, perhaps even to the scientific, and most likely also in a rhythmic response to the stoa of columns in *Philosophy*, a mural at the other end of the wall at Boston, the column replaced a hoary old man who evidently represented a bygone time in a preliminary study.[2]

With its sharp outlines and austere geometries this precisely rendered preparatory cartoon for *History* is squared for enlargement and transfer. The unusual aesthetic appeal of plain geometries and pared-down ascetic forms is clearer still in this magisterial design than in the mural, as is the columnar effect of the trees and the strong central band of the landscape set against the darker cavern below and the responding vista above. The refined stepping of the geological outcropping from several angles is also more readily appreciated in this uncolored work. The final mural would include several branches of leaves and flowers, making its effect slightly less severe.

1 'Qu'est l'Histoire? Une curieuse, qui cherche et fouille dans le passé pour en reconstituer la vie au moyen de documents, dont les plus précieux lui sont fournis par les ruines des monuments....' Vachon (1895), p. 140.
2 Oil and charcoal on canvas, 66 x 32.2 cm (rounded at top) (private collection).

144

Virgil, Bucolic Poetry / *Virgile, Poésie des Champs* (reduced version) 1896

Signed and dated l.l.: P. Puvis de Chavannes 96
Oil on canvas, 124 x 63 cm
Private collection

Provenance Durand-Ruel, Paris; New York (1896-97), no. 3998; Charles A. Tweed; Durand-Ruel, New York (1926); R.T. Paine, II, Brookline, Mass.; Mrs. Alan Cunningham, Brookline, Mass.; Ruth Brown.
Selected Exhibitions 1975 Toronto, no. 39.
Selected References Durand-Ruel Archives, no. 835, no. 1669.

Emile Bernard called Puvis a 'French Virgil,'[1] and his work surely had an affinity to that of the ancient poet whom he chose to represent *Bucolic Poetry* in a mural panel at the Boston Public Library. This is a reduced version of that work, part of Puvis's only mural commission outside of France. Puvis's tribute to Virgil includes the ancient poet in the kind of idyllic setting he often described. Virgil was a preferred author to Puvis, as he had been to Chassériau. One of Puvis's earliest paintings included the poet,[2] whose imagery was of lasting import in his work – for specific iconographic passages in the earlier works such as *Concordia* and *Sleep* (see cat. 26, 47) and later, no less potently, for a more pervasive sense of the pastoral. Indeed, a love of Virgil was not unusual for a French artist; his poetry was a staple of a French schoolboy's education in the classics. By the nation's own cultural reckoning, the Virgilian and Augustan age was the antique beginning of civilized French society. It is no wonder that Virgil would represent bucolic or pastoral poetry in a series of panels representing various genres of literature and the academic disciplines at the Boston Public Library.

The beehives prominent in the foreground must refer to the apiarian lore in Book IV of the *Georgics*. They also foretell the end of the Golden Age: during Saturn's reign honey fell from heaven as dew, but when those times ended Jupiter shook the honey from the leaves and thereafter bees laboriously had to make it. Beehives are represented at another library as reminders that poets are the honey of literature and 'instar apis debet varies excerpere libris mellifluo ut manet dulcis ab ore liquor' ('Just as the bees distil honey from flowers so should we draw sweet essence from literature').[3]

The golden tree leaves are also a very Virgilian motif[4]: in the *Aeneid* trees have golden foliage, boughs and pliant twigs, metallic leaves and flowers (Book VI, l. 200 ff.); to enter the earth's hidden places, one first must pluck the golden foliage that marks the entrance to the underworld.

The measured, distinctly colored, interlocking forms of this composition transmit the sense of a serene order in which everything fits together, in which human and landscape forms respond: at left the columnar figure and trees, at right rounded landscape shapes. In the far background we see bucolic episodes: a tiny background figure plows the fields, while another, whose shape is repeated in the nearby tree boughs, declaims to a recumbent figure on the ground.[5]

1 Bernard (1903), 277.
2 A painting that has been called *Pia*, see 1976-77 Paris/Ottawa, revised, English edition, no. 8; see the author's forthcoming catalogue raisonné.
3 André Masson, *The Pictorial Catalogue. Mural Decorations in Libraries* [The Lyell Lectures, Oxford 1972-1973], transl. David Gerard (Oxford, 1981), pp. 10-11 in describing Michel Boeckn's (1688-1742) panels for the library of Saint-Lambrecht in Styria, a Benedictine abbey.
4 As noted by Professor Martin Ostwald (Swarthmore College) and related by the collector; they proliferate in the main mural at the library, *The Inspiring Muses*, and are also included in several of the other ancillary panels; they also extend to the wall beyond the images.
5 As noted by the collector.

144

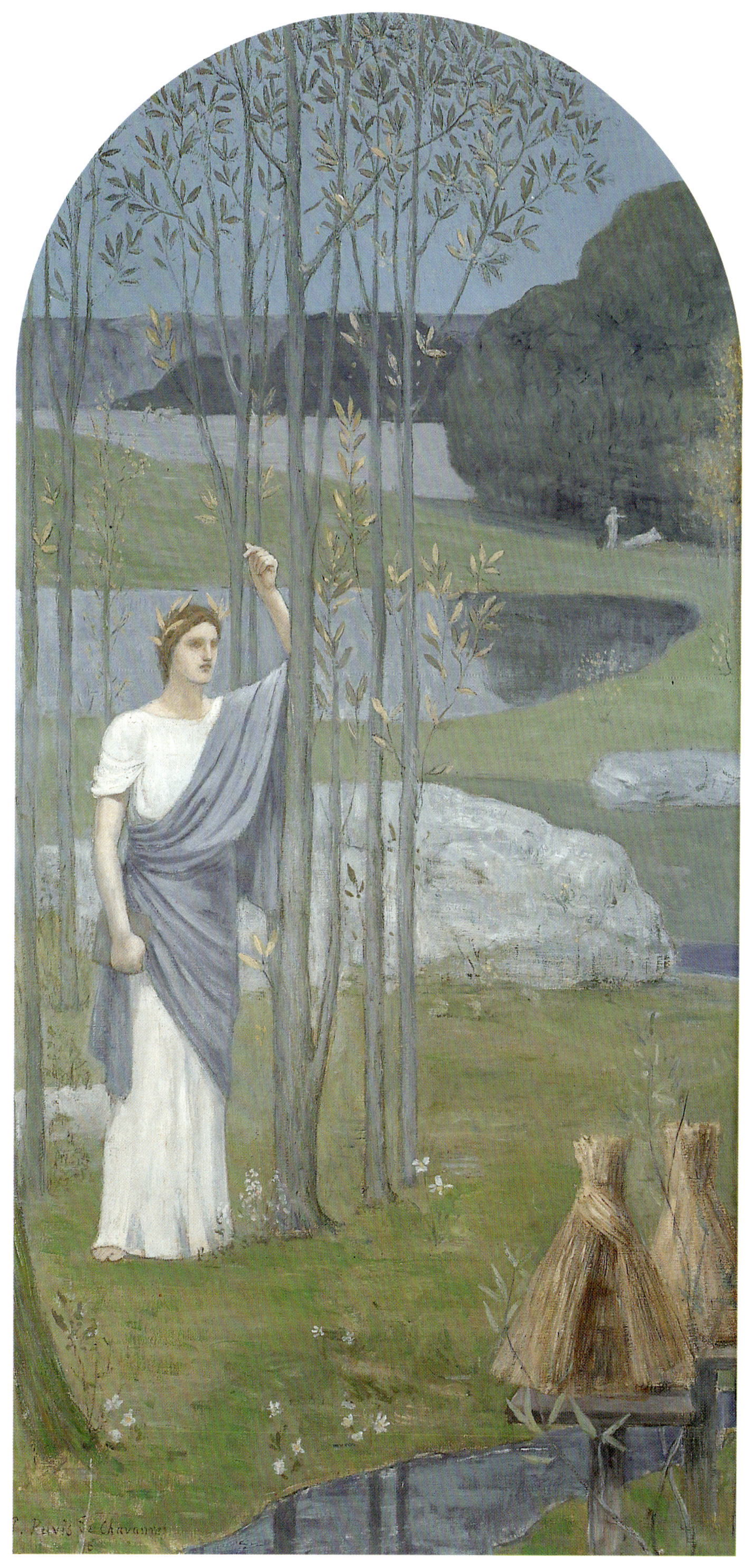

145

The Magdalene / *La Madeleine* 1897

Signed and dated l.r.: P. Puvis de Chavannes 1897
Oil, pencil on canvas, 115.5 x 89.2 cm
Szépmüvészeti Múzeum, Budapest (Inv. 389.B)

Provenance Durand-Ruel, Paris (1897); Baron Adolf Kohner, Budapest; acquired by the museum (1930).
Selected Exhibitions 1897 or 1898 Paris, Durand-Ruel [? according to 1976-77 Paris/Ottawa]; 1898, Vienna, Künstlerhaus, *Jubiläumskunstausstellung*; 1899 Paris (Durand-Ruel), no. 39; 1976-77 Paris/Ottawa, no. 216.
Selected References Alexandre (1898), n.p.; G. Lengyel, *Nyugat*, I (1908), 1, 18; Hugo Haberfeld, 'Die Französischen Bilder der Sammlung Kohner,' *Cicerone* (1 August 1911), 584; Alexis Petrovics, 'Baro Kohner Adolf gyüjtemenye' ['Baron Adolf Kohner's Collection'], *Magyar Muvészet*, VI (1929), repr. opp. 316, 317; *Az Orszagos Magyar Szépmüvészeti Muzeum Evkönyvei* ['The National Hungarian Fine Arts Museum Annual Books'], VI (1929-1930), 139, fig. 11; D. Csanky, *A XIX. és XX. sz. külföldi mesterei* [*Masters of the XIX and XX Centuries*] (Budapest, 1939), p. 78, repr. p. 78. Albert Gyergai, 'French Art in the Museum of Fine Arts,' *Budapest*, III (1947), 454; Istvan Genthon, *From Romanticism to Post-Impressionism, French Paintings in Hungary*, trans. Eva Racz (Budapest, 1964), p. 44.

This monumental Magdalene, except for her gravity, might be a bather seated at the seashore. Classicizing and remote, defined in the simplest terms, she is a powerful presence. She has none of the traditional trappings of the religious narrative, neither skull nor lizard. She does not, as was frequently the case with other nineteenth-century Magdalenes, appear distressed. Nor is she used as a pretext for sensuality, as had happened so often in earlier images, for it was said that the Magdalene so burned with the love of God that she could not bear to be clothed. While far from being sensual and fleshy in the way Renoir's contemporaneous large bathers are, she recalls them. She too is seen to the hips, in a figure and landscape composition that is reduced to a few simple elements. The Magdalene was the last step in Puvis's continued secularization of traditionally religious subjects. The narrative meaning of the figure is more ambivalent as the pictorial decisiveness is ever more assured.

Arsène Alexandre reported meeting the painter on the street in 1897, and Puvis said of the *Magdalene* on which he was then working, surely referring to one of the preliminary drawings: 'You would not guess what I am doing at the moment.... I am executing an academy! ... yes, a life figure, completely stupidly, to see where I am in drawing. You can't imagine how it amuses me simply to copy a bit, like a student, a "segment from life." Oh, how stupidly all those things are taught in the School of Fine Arts. They don't deviate from their iron wire drawing. They see nothing, and their eyes are still hidden.'[1] Apparently, Puvis outlined the figure onto his canvas, painted it in, and then pencilled in further details. Strong outlines intermittently rim the figure. Pencilled marks at brow and jaw and crosshatchings at the right breast and left side are especially evident after recent cleaning. In a composition in which the spaces are not meant to read back convincingly in three dimensions, flowers are used as a spatial organizer, separating foreground and background rocks.

This is a reprise of the subject of the *Magdalene* for Puvis: in 1869 he had painted his sober and introspective, austerely colored, readily identifiable *Magdalene* (Städelsches Kunstinstitut, Frankfurt and cat. 62). But Puvis's solid sculptural image derives at least as much from figures in his secular work, like the woman in *The Fisherman's Family* (fig. 24) and a seated bather in his 1891 *Summer* (see fig. 37), as from his religious imagery.

This kind of massive sculptural figure, with her simple large features and body, described so succinctly and memorably, at once voluptuous and restrained, was a significant forerunner of the similarly posed, classicizing seated women that Picasso painted, particularly about 1921-23. Indeed, in many ways, from the Blue Period works to the poses of figures to these classicizing figures, Picasso's images would be indebted to those of Puvis.

1 'Vous ne vous douteriez pas de ce que je fais en ce moment.... Je fais une académie! ... oui, une figure d'après nature, tout bêtement, pour voir où j'en suis du dessin. Vous n'imagineriez pas comme cela m'amuse de copier tout simplement un morceau, comme un élève, un "morceau d'après nature." Ah! comme on enseigne bêtement toutes ces choses-là à l'Ecole des beaux-arts. Ils ne sortent pas de leur dessin en fil de fer. Ils ne voient rien, et on leur cache encore les yeux.' Alexandre (1898), n.p.

illustration on page 236
Paul Gauguin (1843-1903)
Still Life with Sunflowers and Puvis de Chavannes's 'Hope', 1901 (detail)

45

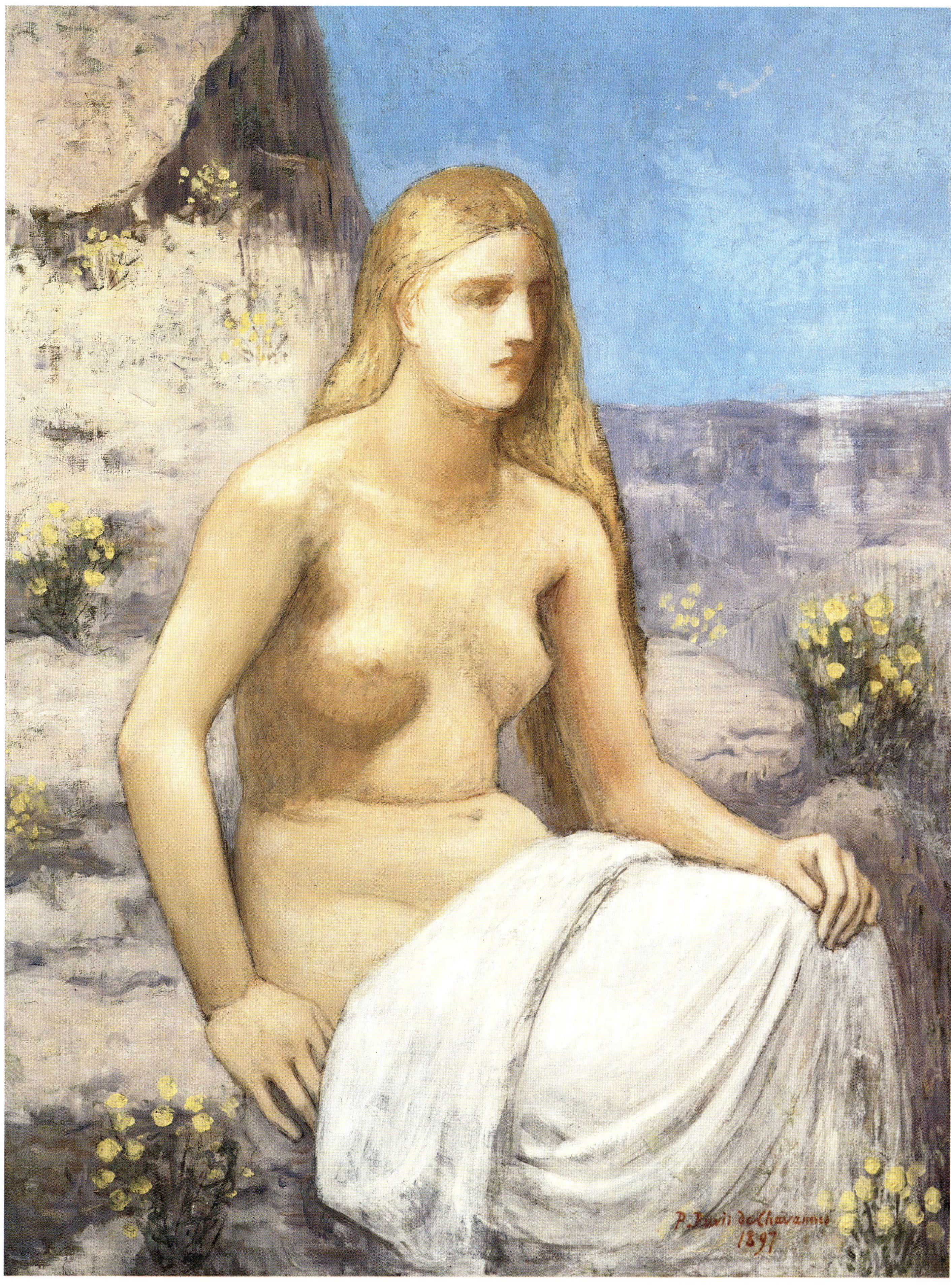

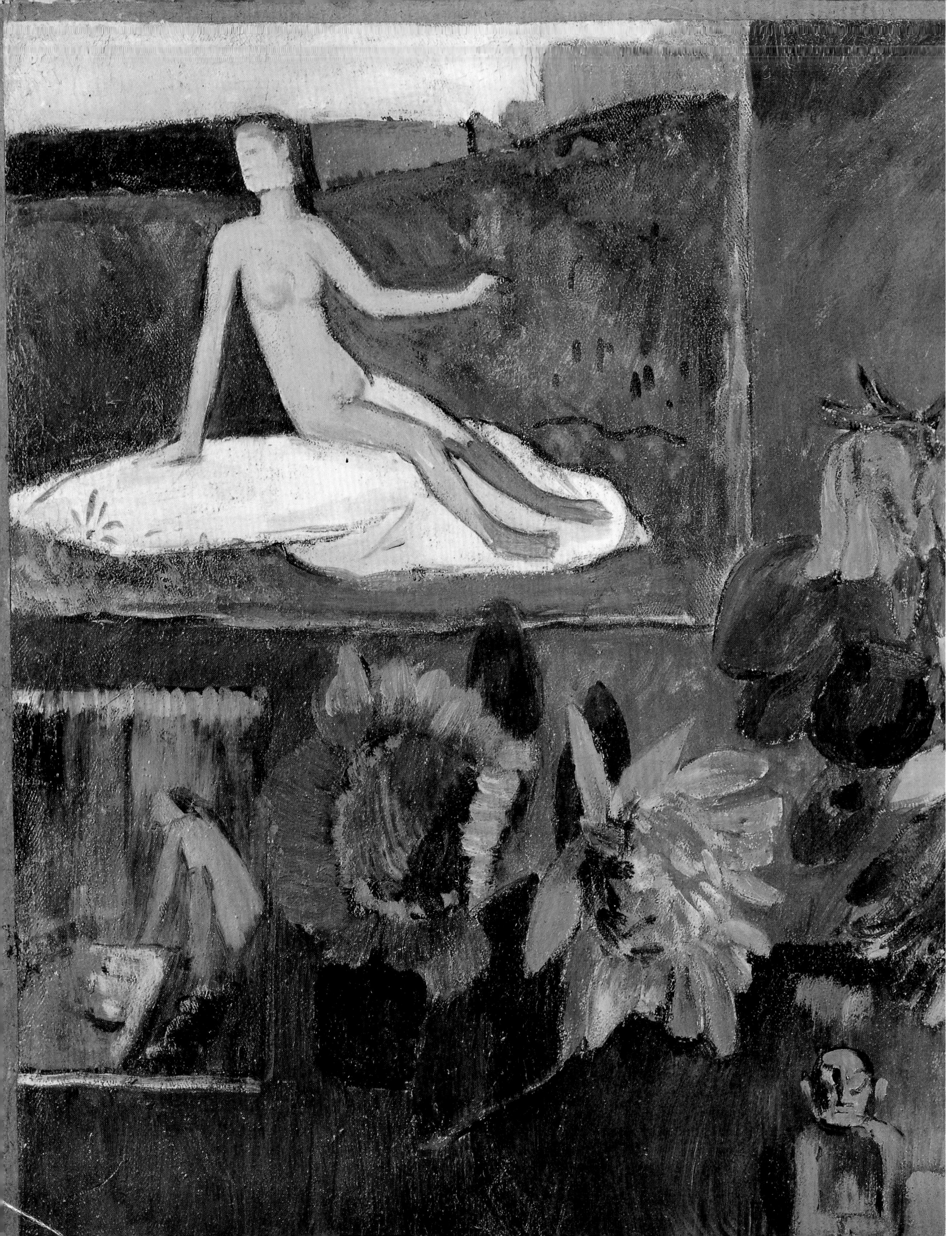

46

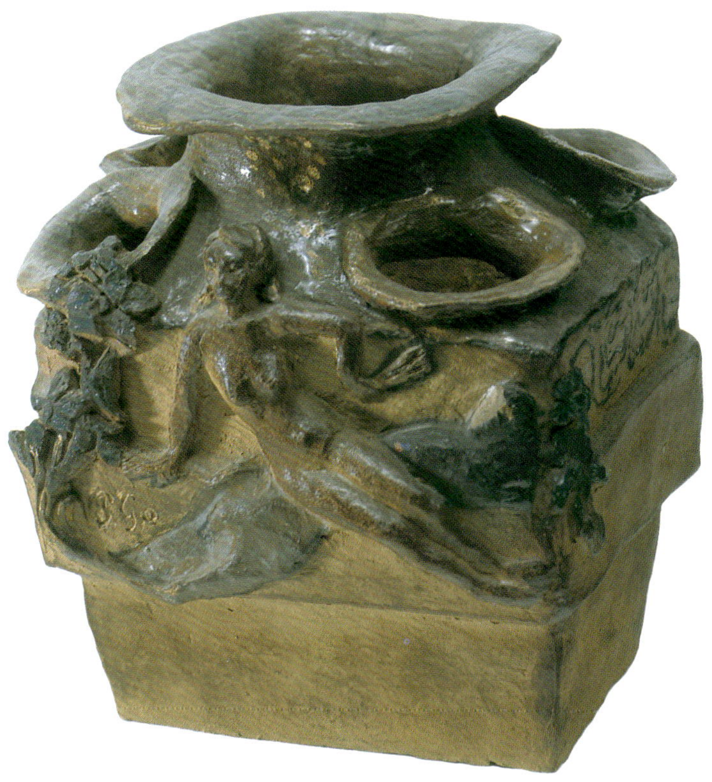

146

Paul Gauguin (1848-1903)

Vase with 'Hope' *or* 'Cleopatra' Vase
ca. 1887

Signed l.l.: P. Go.
Clay, partly glazed, 14 x 129 cm
Van Gogh Museum (Vincent van Gogh Foundation), Amsterdam (Inv. V 37 V/1978)

Provenance The artist to Theo van Gogh, Paris; Johanna van Gogh-Bonger; V.W. van Gogh, Laren.
Selected References M.E. Tralbaut, 'Rond een pot van Gauguin,' *Vrienden van de Nederlandse Ceramiek. Mededelingenblad*, no. 18 (April 1960), 15-19, with English summary, 31; Christopher Gray, *Sculpture and Ceramics of Paul Gauguin* (Baltimore, 1963), pp. 15-16, no. 37, p. 147; Merete Bodelsen, *Gauguin's Ceramics. A Study in the Development of His Art* (London, 1964), pp. 158-159, sketch for repr. figs. 110-111; Evert van Uitert, ed. *The Rijksmuseum Vincent van Gogh* (Amsterdam, 1987), p. 104.

Gauguin began making ceramics in the spring or summer of 1886, after his friend, the artist Félix Bracquemond, introduced him to a ceramist, Ernest Chaplet.[1] Gauguin proceeded with great vigor, executing over fifty-five pieces by January 1887 and at least two more before he left for Martinique in April of 1887.[2] Their forms were often boldly original, influenced by oriental and perhaps Mexican and Peruvian pottery. He made several drawings before working in clay, and the so-called 'Cleopatra' vase is usually dated to 1886 on the basis of a related drawing that is in the 'Brittany' notebook ascribed to that year.[3] It is a basically rectangular vase with one large and four smaller, irregular round orifices; there are incised marks, which form a pattern or perhaps a cryptic notation. The main image is a seated relief figure with her legs to the side. It is based on Puvis's nude *Hope* of 1872 (fig. 4) which Gauguin must have seen before it was first exhibited at the end of 1887 at the Durand-Ruel Gallery.

While Gauguin protested more than once that Puvis's works were of little interest to him, it would be very much in his bravura, contrary character to turn Puvis's chaste *Hope* to perverse purpose. He transformed the innocent pubescent young woman whom Puvis had pictured into a nude woman with large, pendulous breasts, who, rather than delicately holding up an oak twig, has her hand close to her hip and holds what appears to be a fan with which to flirt. Gauguin himself called this the 'Cleopatra' pot.[4] In the nineteenth century, lewd ideas of sexuality were attributed to Cleopatra, *femme fatale* that she was, and these contrast to the purity of Puvis's *Hope*. The other side of the vase includes rooting pigs, interpreted as having an 'erotic' nature.[5] Although Gauguin frequently included farm animals in his works, in this symbolic piece, which cites Puvis on one side, he may have been alluding to the pigs in Puvis's *The Prodigal Son* (fig. 7) on the other.

Gauguin used the image of Puvis's nude *Hope* repeatedly, insisting all the while, with characteristic bravado and *amour-propre*, how backward-looking the older artist was.[6] Given Gauguin's claims to absolute originality, we cannot call these Puvis-inspired works homages so much as appropriations – *Te aa no Areois* (*The Seed of the Areois*, 1892, Museum of Modern Art, New York) was a Tahitian *Hope* (reversed), even to the (patterned) drapery on which the figure sits and the theme of regeneration.[7] Gauguin's fold-out drawing of the figure accompanied Charles Morice's 1894 poem 'A Puvis de Chavannes,' in the *Mercure de France*.[8] Gauguin kept a photograph of Puvis's 1872 image in his hut in the South Seas,[9] and incorporated it as a photograph – with the figure's head slyly turned – in a 1901 still life (Metropolitan Museum of Art, New York, and Joanne Toor Cummings, see ill. p. 236). This last is a disquisition on the levels of pictorial equivalences for ideas – from that of readily recognized personification to more singular or hermetic images for the initiated. Gauguin shunted his representation of the photograph of *Hope* above and to the side, and placed a bouquet of sunflowers prominently in the center of his painting. They were a more abstract, less conventional and thus arbitrary symbolic signifier of gratitude for Gauguin as for his friend Van Gogh. Gauguin insisted that Puvis could not surmount conventional symbolism, but still misidentified (purposively?) *Hope* as *Purity* ('Pureté').[10] 'Puvis explains his ideas, that is very true, but he does not paint them. He is a Greek, whereas I am a savage, a wolf without a collar in the forest. Puvis will entitle a work "Purity," and to explain it will paint a young virgin with a lyre in her hand, a well-known symbol, which everybody can understand. Gauguin, faced with the same title of "Purity," will paint a landscape with limpid streams, no sign of pollution by man, perhaps one human being. Without going into details, Puvis and I are divided by a whole world. Puvis, as a painter, is a wordsmith, not a man of letters, whilst I am not a wordsmith, but perhaps a man of letters.'[11]

What did Gauguin and many others (see cat. 149) see in this stiff little frontal image of a nude girl? It declared an innocence, an appealing unschooled quality that moved a generation disenchanted with academism and the tricks of that trade. In Gauguin's renditions of the seated figure, one sees a veering off into a further sharpened and flattened, 'primitivizing,' Egyptian-like prototype used in a still greater number of his works, such as *Vairaumati tei oa* (*Her Name is Vairaumati*, 1892, Hermitage, Saint Petersburg).

Gauguin appropriated freely from Puvis, and his mature style is explicable only with reference to that of Puvis: the synthetism, the interdependence and scale of figures and landscapes in what are essentially the Tahitian Arcadias of his maturity, the strong symmetries of the panoramas, the rhythmic spacing and paratactic rhythms of his monumental *Where Do We Come from? What Are We? Where Are We Going?* (1897, Museum of Fine Arts, Boston), while he adamantly volunteered, 'ce n'est pas une toile faite comme un Puvis de Chavannes....'[12]

1 Gray (ref. above), p. 5.

2 Bodelsen (ref. above) puts this pot to about 1886 and Gray (ref. above), pp. 16/18 to 1886-87 and two more pots to the spring of 1887.

3 See Gray (ref. above), p. 16; related drawings repr. fig. 9c, p. 15 (reproduced from Gauguin, *Carnet de croquis*, no. 37) and fig. 10c, p. 17 (reproduced from *Album Gauguin*, p. 25, recto and p. 73 respectively, Cabinet des Dessins, Musée du Louvre, Paris); Paul Gauguin's *Carnet de croquis*, texts by Raymond Cogniat and John Rewald (New York, 1962), no. 37. Also see Bodelsen (ref. above), fig. 110; Gauguin had also used pigs in an earlier pitcher of two Breton girls with pigs (Bodelsen, fig. 36).

4 Gray (ref. above), no. 37, p. 147; see unpublished postscriptum of his letter to Schuffenecker published in Claude Roger-Marx, *Europe* (15 February 1939), p. 170, cited by Tralbaut (ref. above).

5 Van Uitert, ed. (ref. above).

6 As in Jean de Rotonchamp, *Paul Gauguin* (Paris, 1906), pp. 128-134.

7 A variant monotype, *Seated Figure* (whereabouts unknown), is attributed to Gauguin by Richard Field in 1973, Philadelphia Museum of Art, *Paul Gauguin: Monotypes*, no. 32, repr.

8 A double page pull-out, *Mercure de France*, XIII, no. 62 (February 1895) (present whereabouts unknown).

9 Reproduced in *Art News Annual*, XXV, part 2 (1955), 144; Gauguin also had reproductions of works by Puvis on his walls at Le Pouldu; see Armand Séguin, 'Paul Gauguin,' *L'Occident* (March-April 1903), 16.

10 Letter to Daniel de Monfried, February 1898, in *Lettres de Gauguin à sa femme et à ses amis* (Paris, 1946), p. 286.

11 'Puvis explique son idée, oui, mais il ne la peint pas. Il est grec tandis que moi je suis un sauvage, un loup dans les bois sans collier. Puvis intitulera un tableau "Pureté" et pour l'expliquer peindra une jeune vierge avec un lys à la main – Symbole connu; donc on le comprend. Gauguin au titre Pureté peindra un paysage aux eaux limpides; aucune souillure de l'homme civilisé, peut-être un personnage. Sans rentrer dans des détails il y a tout un monde entre Puvis et moi. Puvis comme peintre est un lettré et non un homme de lettres tandis que moi je ne suis pas un lettré mais peut-être un homme de lettres.' Letter from Gauguin to Charles Morice, July 1901, in *Lettres de Gauguin a sa femme et a ses amis, op. cit.* (note 10), pp. 301. Transl.: Gauguin, *Letters from Brittany and the South Seas. The Search for Paradise*, selected and introduced by Bernard Denvir (New York, 1992), pp. 136-137.

12 Letter of July 1901 to Charles Morice, quoted in the latter's *Paul Gauguin*, 2nd ed. (Paris, 1920), pp. 248-249; and in *Lettres de Gauguin à sa femme et à ses amis, op. cit.* (note 10), pp. 299-303; also Gray (ref. above), p. 36, who dates the letter September 1888.

147

Vincent van Gogh (1853-1890)

Letter with Sketch of 'Inter Artes et Naturam' June 1890

Pen and ink on paper, 22 x 17 cm
Van Gogh Museum (Vincent van Gogh Foundation), Amsterdam (Inv. B 722 / V1962)

Provenance Willemina van Gogh (-1941); heirs of Willemina van Gogh; V.W. van Gogh, Laren.

Selected References 1973-74, New York, Metropolitan Museum of Art, *Van Gogh as Critic and Self-Critic*, no. 44; 1975 Toronto, no. 49, pp. 111-114.

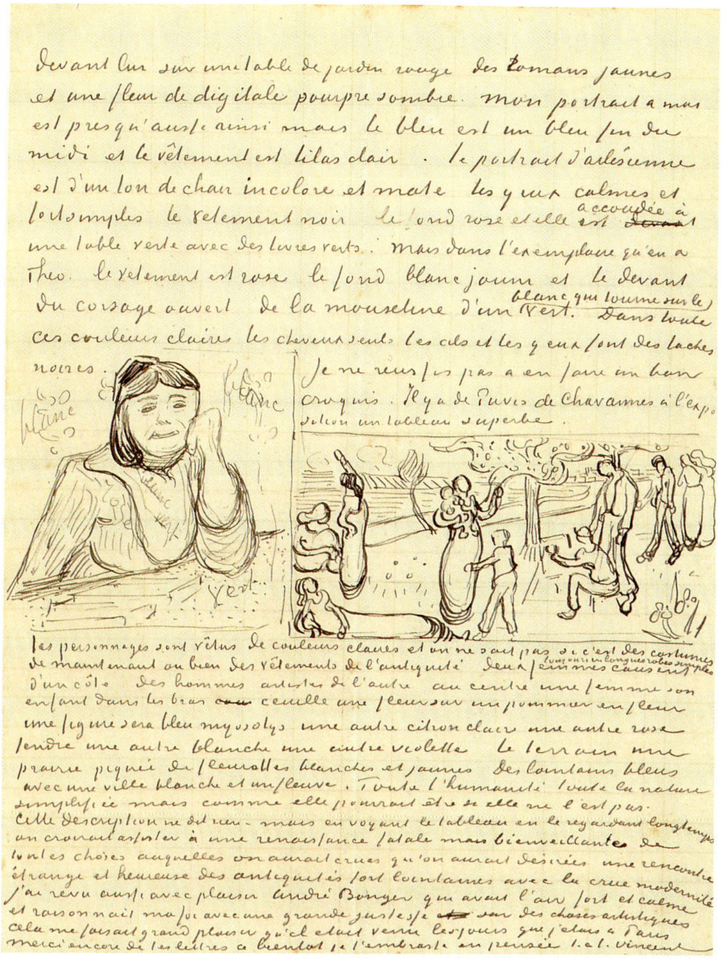

On a number of occasions, Van Gogh wrote in detail and penetratingly about Puvis de Chavannes's paintings, deftly encapsulating the effect of the latter's work and what he cherished in it (see cat. 86, 130). He wrote no less acutely and attentively of Puvis's quiet, measured portraits of Eugène Benon and Marie Cantacuzène (see cat. 89, 92) than of his more spectacular large, public paintings. His admiration for the calm and paradisal order of Puvis's paintings is the more moving because of his own fervent search for order. As he wrote to Emile Bernard from Arles in June 1888 (prefacing a discussion of Puvis's *Portrait of Eugène Benon*): 'We artists, who love order and symmetry, isolate ourselves [from anarchy] and are working to define *only one thing*. Puvis knows this all right, and when he, so just and so wise – forgetting his Elysian fields – was so good as to descend amiably into the intimacy of our time, he painted a fine portrait indeed....'[1] And when he found an actual landscape setting particularly beautiful, he might compare it to one by Puvis, as when he wrote in 1888 to Theo about the South of France, 'when you have seen the cypresses and the oleanders here, and the sun – and the day will come, you may be sure – then you will think even more often of the beautiful "Doux Pays" [*Pleasant Land*] by Puvis de Chavannes, and many other pictures of his.'[2]

Puvis's *Inter Artes et Naturam* (ill. pp. 214-215) was exhibited in 1890 at the newly founded Société Nationale des Beaux-Arts, and Van Gogh transmitted his enthusiasm to J.J. Isaacson, a Dutch critic and painter, as part of an extensive discussion of Puvis's importance. Van Gogh compared Puvis's colors and modern sentiment to those of Delacroix, whose equal he believed Puvis to be – and with whom, in his analyses, he often paired him.[3] As for *Inter Artes et Naturam*, it seemed to allude, 'to an equivalence, a strange and providential meeting of *very* far off antiquities and *crude* modernity.'[4] He claimed that Puvis's canvases had become vaguer and even more prophetic than those of the Romantic painter: 'before [Puvis's paintings] ... one feels an emotion as if one were present at the continuation of all kinds of things, a benevolent renaissance ordained by fate.'[5]

In June 1890 Van Gogh wrote at some length of *Inter Artes et Naturam* to his sister Willemina, again dwelling on the difficulty of placing the scene in time: 'There is a superb picture by Puvis de Chavannes.... The figures of the persons are dressed in bright colors, and one cannot tell whether they are costumes of today or on the other hand clothes of antiquity.'[6] With great subtlety he described the particular nuances of Puvis's palette, marveling at how the colors themselves and the simplified composition contributed to a sense of the ideal: 'One figure is forget-me-not blue, another bright citron yellow, another of a delicate pink color, another white, another violet. Underneath their feet a meadow dotted with little white and yellow flowers. A blue distance with a white town and a river. All humanity, all nature simplified, but as they *might* be if they are not like that.'[7]

What Van Gogh found most compelling was a melding of the antique ideal with the contemporary, the former conferring a sense of timeless perfection on the modern. To conflate the enduring with the current was indeed what Puvis had for some time tried to do. As Van Gogh put it, 'when one sees this picture, when one looks at it for a long time you would believe you were witnessing a total [sic: 'fatal'] but benign rebirth in everything you ever believed, in everything you ever desired – a strange and happy meeting of very remote antiquity with raw modernity.'[8] Declaring, however, 'This description does not tell you anything,' he included a drawing from memory of *Inter Artes* in his letter. Of some interest in his spirited sketch is what he remembered, what he invented and what he omitted. Repeating the panoramic horizontal format of Puvis's *Inter Artes*, Van Gogh clearly demarcated a distinctly horizontal composition and landscape, and he repeated the general disposition of the figures, though he included eleven rather than the eighteen of Puvis's large painting. There was no forgetting the woman with the child picking fruit, and the boy at center, in a friendly fashion, is gathered nearer. The tree and flowered lawn were the kinds of pastoral elements so important to Van Gogh's own painting and not likely to be left out. The river in the background and city on the horizon are also duly noted. All the figures are dressed in far more contemporary fashion than Puvis had allowed them. The contemplative sketcher of Puvis's painting is almost centered and transformed into an animated artist turned to paint the distant landscape. Van Gogh recalled the two women standing together at the far right (whom he had described). And he importantly remembered the woman seated on the ground (here facing the viewer), her long gown trailing off horizontally to the (here, other) side and underscoring the elongated shape of the composition itself. To the far left, a woman seated with her arms around her legs seems to have been imported from Puvis's *Pleasant Land*. Van Gogh did omit all reference to archaeology in the left middle ground, all the arched ruins, and the border of trees at the top.

Having arrived in Auvers on 20 May 1890, Van Gogh described the lovely countryside and quiet which he yet again compared to a Puvis: 'This is in an almost lush country .... there is so much well-being in the air. I see ... in it a quiet like a Puvis de Chavannes, no factories, but lovely, well-kept greenery in abundance.'[9] He now embarked on his own series of distinctive horizontal format compositions, such as *Wheatfields* (Österreichische Galerie, Vienna) and *Wheatfields under a Clouded Sky* (Van Gogh Museum, Amsterdam). As Richard Wattenmaker has pointed out, he went to some trouble in so doing, for only one of these conforms to a standard French size.[10] He also took to heart the pale colors of what 'might be,' such as he had described them in Puvis's work, painting in somewhat whitened colors several of his own idyllic landscapes and figures, such as *Mademoiselle Gachet in Her Garden at Auvers-sur-Oise* (Musée d'Orsay, Paris) and *Women Walking Along in the Fields* (Marion Koogler McNay Art Institute, San Antonio).[11] Puvis de Chavannes's paintings gave Van Gogh not only profound pleasure, but moved him in his own work in important directions.[12]

1 'Nous, artistes, amoureux de l'ordre et de la symétrie, nous nous isolons et travaillons à définir *une seule chose*. Puvis sait bien cela, et lorsque lui, si sage et si juste, a voulu – oubliant ses Champs-Elysées – descendre aimablement jusqu'à l'intimité de notre époque, il a fait un bien beau portrait....' Van Gogh (1954), IV, B 14 (9), p. 221. Transl.: Van Gogh (1958), III, B 14 (9), p. 508.

2 'Mon cher Theo, lorsque tu auras vu les cyprès, les laurier-roses, le soleil d'ici – et ce jour-là viendra, sois tranquille. – Encore plus souvent tu penseras aux beaux Puvis de Chavannes Doux pays et tant d'autres.' Van Gogh (1953), III, no. 539, p. 311. Transl.: Van Gogh (1958), III, no. 539, p. 43.

3 See letter to Theo, Van Gogh (1958), III, no. 615, p. 233.

4 'à une équivalence à une rencontre étrange et providentielle des antiquités fort lointaines et la crue modernité.' Van Gogh (1953), III, no. 614a, p. 477. Transl.: Van Gogh (1958), III, no. 614a, p. 232; compare also pp. 231, 233.

5 'devant ses toiles de ces dernières années on se sent ému comme assistant à une continuation de toutes choses une renaissance fatale mais bienveillante.' Van Gogh (1953), III, no. 614a, p. 477. Transl.: Van Gogh (1958), III, no. 614a, pp. 232.

6 'Il y a de Puvis de Chavannes à l'exposition un tableau superbe. Les personnages sont vêtus de couleurs claires et on ne sait pas si c'est des costumes de maintenant ou bien des vêtements de l'antiquité.' Van Gogh (1954), IV, no. W 22, p. 183. Transl.: Van Gogh (1958), III, no. W 22, p. 471.

7 'Une figure sera bleu myosotis, une autre citron clair, une autre rose tendre, une autre blanche, une autre violettte. Le terrain une prairie piquée de fleurettes blanches et jaunes. Des lointains bleus avec une ville blanche et un fleuve. Toute l'humanité, toute la nature simplifiée mais comme elle pourrait être si elle ne l'est pas. Van Gogh (1954), IV, no. W 22, p. 184. Transl.: Van Gogh (1958), III, no. W 22, p. 471. The colors mentioned are strikingly similar to those that Puvis had years earlier said he admired in Giotto's paintings. (See p. 16 of this book.)

8 'en voyant le tableau, en le regardant longtemps, on croirait assister à une renaissance totale [sic: 'fatale'] mais bienveillante, de toutes choses auxquelles on aurait crues, qu'on aurait désirées, une rencontre étrange et heureuse des antiquités fort lointaines avec la crue modernité.' Van Gogh (1954), IV, no. W 22, p. 184.

9 'Cela dans une campagne presque grasse ... il y a beaucoup de bien- être dans l'air. Un calme à la Puvis de Chavannes j'y vois ou y crois voir, pas d'usines, mais de la belle verdure en abondance et en bon ordre.' Van Gogh (1953), III, no. 637, p. 518. Transl.: Van Gogh (1958), III, no. 637, p. 275.

10 1975 Toronto, pp. 23, 112.

11 1975 Toronto, pp. 111-114.

12 See in addition, among other references to Puvis in Van Gogh (1958), III: Van Gogh's letter of 28 January 1889, no. 574, p. 132, that mentions Puvis's *Hope*; letter no. 539, p. 43 on *Pleasant Land*; and letter no. 587, p. 158 on Puvis's *Young Women by the Sea*.

148

Paul Gauguin (1848-1903)

Tahitian Women on a Beach / *Tahitiennes sur la plage* 1892

Signed l.r.: P. Gauguin
Oil on canvas, 109.9 x 89.5 cm
The Metropolitan Museum of Art, New York, Robert Lehman Collection, 1975 (Inv. 1975.1.179)

Provenance Ambroise Vollard; Alphonse Kann; Barbazanges Galerie, Paris; M. Oliver Esq., London; Bignou, New York; Robert Lehman.

Selected References Marius-Ary Leblond, *Peintres des Races* (Paris, 1909), repr. p. 225; Rewald (1956), repr. p. 508; John Richardson, 'Gauguin at Chicago and New York,' *The Burlington Magazine* (May 1959), 191; Richard S. Field, 'Paul Gauguin. The Paintings of the First Voyage to Tahiti,' [Unpublished] doctoral dissertation (Harvard University, 1963) (New York and London [Garland] 1977), pp. 93-95, 341-342; Georges Wildenstein, *Paul Gauguin* (Paris, 1964), no. 462; De Forges (1970), 252; 1975 Toronto, p. 122.

Gauguin's mature idiom, so very powerfully his own, is explicable only through reference to Puvis de Chavannes's accomplishments. The decorative aesthetic that Puvis developed, his way of condensing, flattening and synthesizing images, was an important example to Gauguin, and to the painters of the 'school' of Pont-Aven and the Nabis with whom he was involved, encouraging them to advance even further – and more bluntly – towards these same goals. Gauguin's tastes were exceedingly adventurous and catholic, and he was on the alert to new imagery as he tried to disengage himself from the mainstream of traditional European art as understood in later nineteenth-century France. In that connection, Puvis's masterful ability to create simple, legible postures of a somewhat stilted hieratic formality had a special appeal to Gauguin – and he often paraphrased them. In the 1880s when Gauguin was in Brittany, he derived images from the Breton calvaries and regional wooden sculpture; and further seeking the unschooled and primitive, in the early 1890s when he went to the South Seas, he looked to the reliefs from Borobudur; still later it might be a sharply defined figure in a Lucas Cranach painting (*Sleeping Nymph*, 1537, Musée des Beaux-Arts, Besançon) on which he might model one of his own figures (*The Noble Woman* [*Te arii vahine*],1896, Hermitage, Saint Petersburg).[1] During his first stay in Tahiti, from 1891 to 1893, Gauguin had with him photographs and reproductions of art, doubtless a comfort to him as well as useful in terms of images to which he might refer.[2] Gauguin's wide-ranging interests flourished, but Puvis's work remained an abiding source, a rich pictorial lode that he continued to mine.

Despite a tropical exoticism, there is not a great distance between Gauguin's South Seas *Place of Delight* (*Te Nave Nave Fenua*, 1892, Ohara Museum of Art, Kurashiki), or *Day of Delight* (*Nave Nave Mahana*, 1896, Musée des Beaux-Arts, Lyons) and Puvis's more conservative, Hellenizing image of an idyllic *Pleasant Land* (see cat. 86), either in theme or underlying iconography or basic aesthetic. Gauguin produced intensely colored figurative paintings of figures working and resting in tropical settings, but the fundamental elements of his work are to be found in Puvis's compositions. The flowered cotton cloths (*pareus*) wrapped around their waists notwithstanding, his *vahinés* (women) are costumed essentially like the white and pastel draped figures in Puvis's Arcadian paintings; their somewhat stiff poses, the manner in which they are separated from one another and deployed in the landscape, and the collapse of space into sharply defined areas of flat color itself had all been enunciated by Puvis. Although it may be only coincidence that Gauguin's *Man with an Axe* (private collection, Basel) of 1891, a figure repeated in *Death (Matamoe*, Pushkin Museum, Moscow) of 1892, is posed like one of Puvis's forgers in *Work* (see cat. 28), in 1892 Gauguin quoted repeatedly from Puvis. One of his favorite images was *Hope* (fig. 4), the contrived, twisted angularity of her pose emphasized in his own taut *The Seed of the Areois* (*Te aa no Areois*, 1892, Museum of Modern Art, New York) and a cluster of variant compositions (see cat. 146).

Puvis's tenderly colored, classicizing *Young Women by the Sea* (fig. 6, cat. 76) are rarefied hothouse plants compared to Gauguin's hardier, tropical *Tahitian Women on a Beach* with its fully saturated colors, but they are the seedlings that engendered them. Gauguin's trio of sharply articulated Tahitian women are set against a background of variegated, intense dark and sharp blues and patches of vivid lime green. Although a favorite motif for Gauguin was women viewed from the back bathing in the sea, a subject he had painted several times in Brittany (*Ondine*, 1889, Cleveland Museum of Art), the standing woman at the center of *Tahitian Women on a Beach* is based rather on Puvis's Venus Anadyomene transposed to the South Seas. Facing away from the viewer, she too raises her arm and gathers up her hair in her hand. Corresponding to the dramatically truncated figure at the right in Puvis's canvas is the figure at left in Gauguin's composition, whose head and shoulders alone are visible as she stands below a ledge that is in the foreground. To the right a crouching woman, seen from behind, because of her low placement, suggests the general configuration of Puvis's composition.[3] The churning water curling around the rock in the background is defined here as elsewhere by Gauguin in a Japanese manner, with linear arabesques and

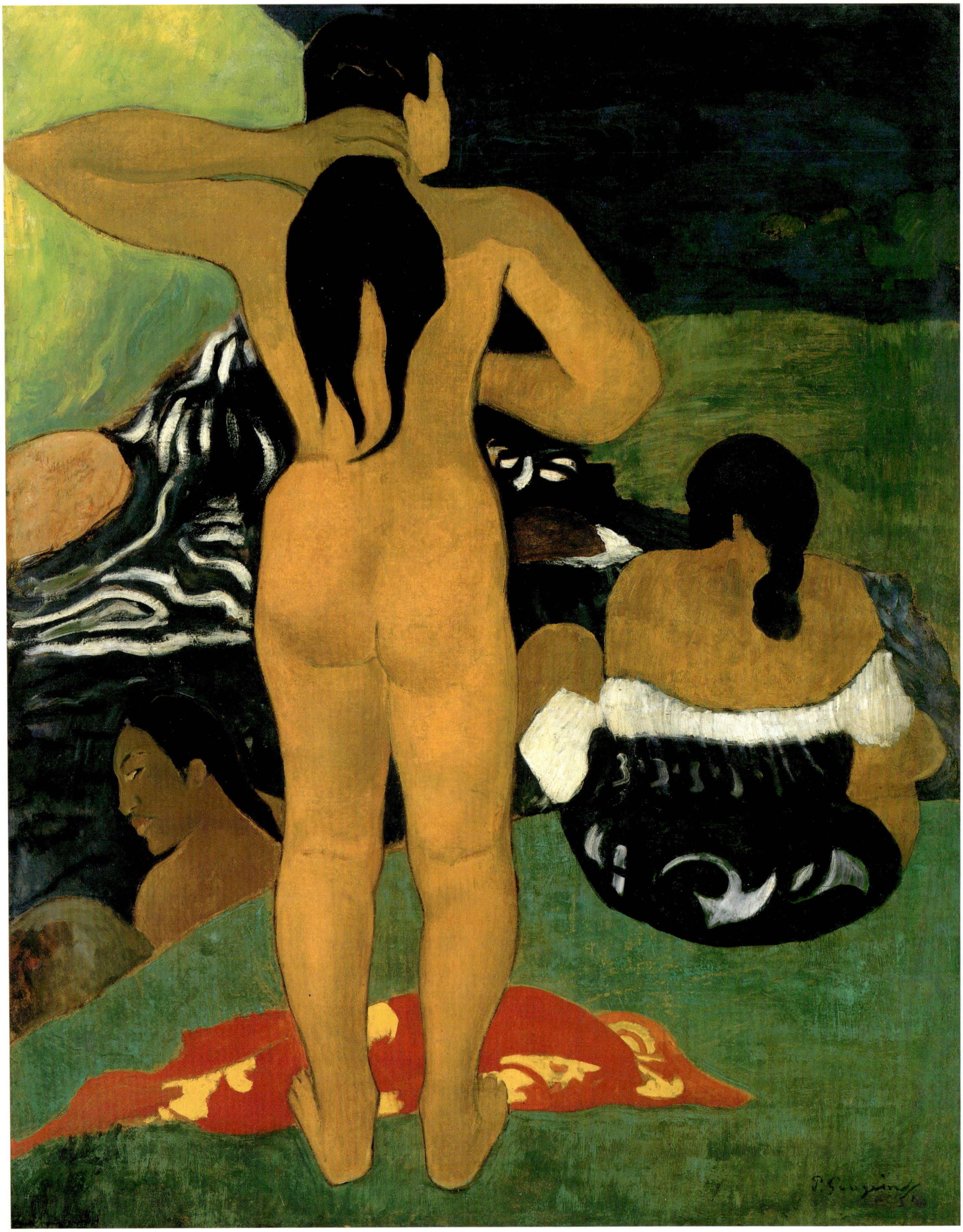

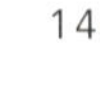

white patterned spume imitative of artists such as Hiroshige. *Tahitian Women at the Beach* is an unusually simplified, even harsh rendition of the bathing motif that Gauguin used in canvases such as his 1892 *Near the Sea (Fatata te Miti*, National Gallery of Art, Washington, D.C.). It is almost unique in Gauguin's oeuvre for several flat, unmodulated passages, particularly in the central figure, and its brushwork.[4]

Gauguin frequently referred to Puvis in his letters, the gist of his comments often being that 'The simplicity [of his works], the nobility, have nothing more to do with the times.'[5] After the older artist's death, he relented, if only in part. In March 1899 he wrote André Fontainas, 'Certainly, Puvis overwhelms me with his talent, and the experience that I don't have: I admire him as much and more than you but for different reasons.... To each his era.'[6]

1. Belinda Thomson, *Gauguin* (New York, 1990), pp. 190-192.
2 Richard S. Field, 'Plagiaire ou créateur,' *Gauguin* (Paris, 1960), 139-169. See generally on this period, Charles F. Stuckey, 'The First Tahitian Years,' in 1988-89, Washington, D.C., National Gallery of Art / Chicago, Art Institute of Chicago / Paris, Grand Palais, *The Art of Paul Gauguin*, pp. 210-216.
3 Related in pose to the figure at right is *Crouching Tahitian Woman Seen From the Back*, a gouache monotype, 533 x 282 mm (Eugene V. Thaw Collection) that has been dated to 1901-02.
4 This may be explained by overpainting, or possibly the painting was begun by Gauguin and finished by another. See Richardson (ref. above) and Field (ref. above).
5 'La simplicité, la noblesse, ne sont plus d'époque.' Jean Loize, 'Un inédit de Gauguin,' *Les Nouvelles Littéraires* (7 May 1953), n. p.
6 'Certes, Puvis m'écrase par son talent, et l'expérience que je n'ai pas: je l'admire autant et plus que vous mais pour des raisons différentes.... Chacun son époque.' in *Lettres de Gauguin à sa femme et à ses amis* (Paris, 1946), p. 289.

149

Maurice Denis (1870-1943)

Nude with Bouquets of Violets / *Nu aux bouquets de violettes* 1894

Signed and dated: MAVD 94
Oil on canvas, 55 x 74.5 cm
Private collection

Provenance Ambroise Vollard, Paris.
Selected Exhibitions December 1894, Paris, Le Barc de Boutteville, no. 51; 1894, Paris, Salon des Indépendants .
Selected References Denis (1890); Denis (1913); Denis (1957) I; Denis (1964); 1975 Toronto, pp. 129-134; 1980, Saint-Germain-en-Laye, Musée départemental du Prieuré, *Symbolistes et Nabis. Maurice Denis et son temps.*

Maurice Denis revered Puvis de Chavannes's work, which was crucial to his own development, both as an artist and as a writer-theoretician. Throughout his life, Denis wrote penetrating analyses of Puvis's work, beginning as a seventeen-year-old when he visited the retrospective of Puvis de Chavannes's work at the Durand-Ruel Gallery. From 1899 he made precise notations on his works as if they were lessons from which he meant to learn.[1] He put Puvis in the front in his 1925 mural tribute to nineteenth-century artists (see fig. 8), and in his writings on French painting Puvis as an innovator was given no less importance. It was in the context of discussing Puvis's *The Poor Fisherman* that Denis launched his famous dictum defining 'Neo-Traditionism' (see p. 50).

Nude with Bouquets of Violets is one of a number of canvases by Maurice Denis that is directly indebted to the imagery of Puvis de Chavannes's work. His nude is based on Puvis's 1872 *Hope* (fig. 4), an image that other artists were also to appropriate. Gauguin incorporated the figure in a ceramic vase, several drawings and paintings (see cat. 146); Renoir copied her in watercolor (Musée du Louvre, Paris);[2] and Amedeo Modigliani drew an *Interpretation of 'Hope'*.[3] Van Gogh also admired Puvis's embodiment of *Hope*.[4] Both critics and other artists took note of the boldly contrived direct self-presentation of the waif-like figure. She was placed to face the viewer with hips and legs pulled forward and to the side on the pictorial plane. Judging from how Denis's strongly defined figure is outlined on the pictorial surface, the way Puvis's *Hope* was configured in two dimensions must have been a particular fascination. *Nude with Bouquets of Violets* also displays the structural containment of Puvis's personification and reflects Denis's later remark that contrasted Puvis's firm colors and silhouettes to Delacroix's 'individuals sacrificed by an artificial shadow.'[5]

Among the many other paintings by Denis that are directly indebted to Puvis de Chavannes's compositions, and in which his decorative aesthetic is clearly articulated, *April* of 1892 (fig. 26) must be singled out for its essential dependency in basic structure and composition on *The Poor Fisherman* (fig. 23), which Denis had so thoroughly analyzed in his writing, and for Denis's radically different iconography. Puvis's flower-picking figure is twice duplicated by Denis. The promontory and background with a winding river and an indication of the city in the background also have antecedents in the topography of *Inter Artes et Naturam* (ill. pp. 214-215). Denis's depiction of the young woman in his *Portrait of Mademoiselle Yvonne Lerolle in Three Poses* (Josefowitz Collection) of 1897 includes the same flower-plucking pose. Moreover, the three poses of the young woman, each in a different direction, re-

14

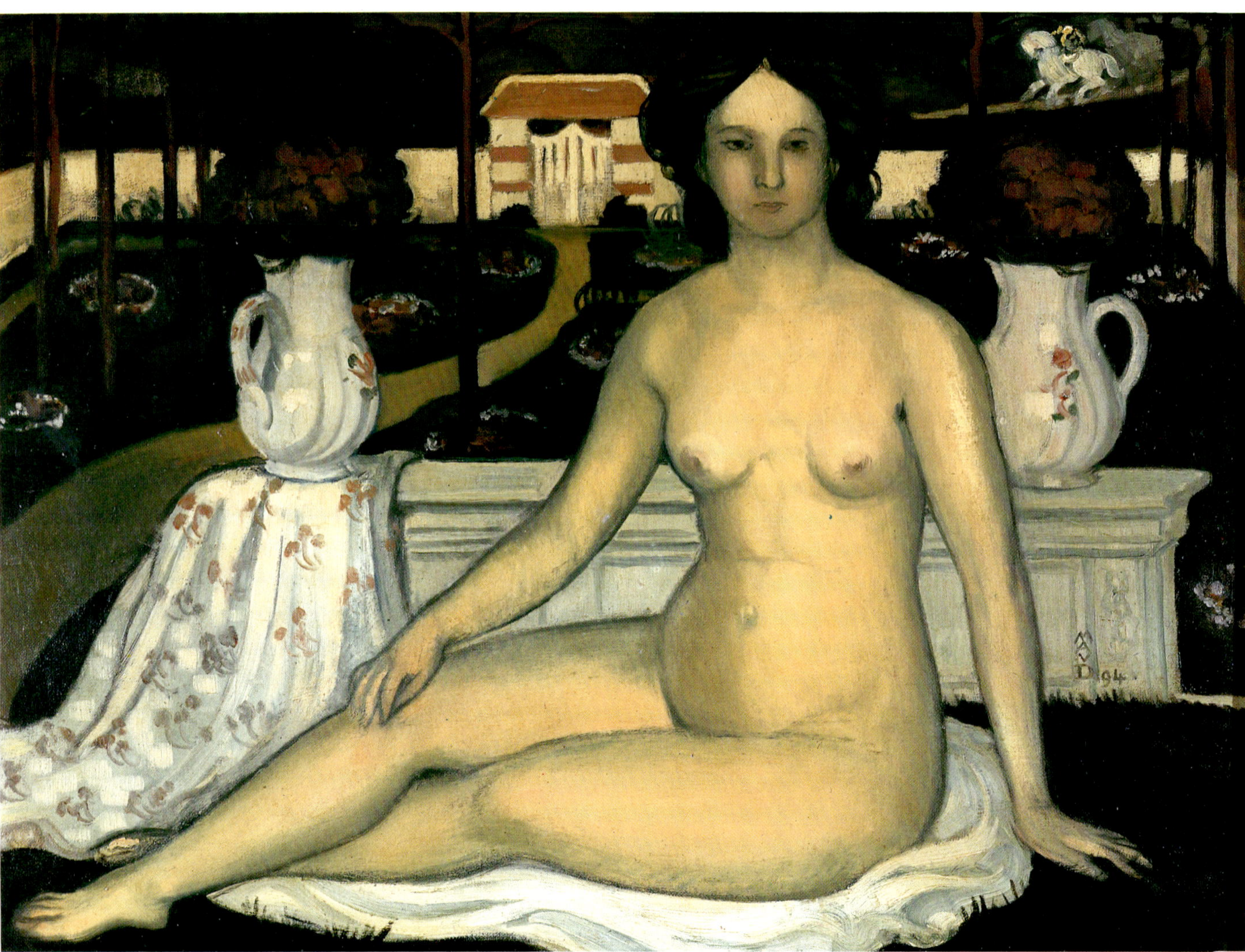

calls the composition of Puvis's *Young Women by the Sea* (fig. 6, cat. 76). Denis's *Childhood* or *Picking Apples* (1896, private collection), a horizontal, frieze-like decoration with painted borders, is also based on *Inter Artes*.[6] Denis's *Sacred Wood* (Musée du Petit Palais, Paris) also bears an interesting relationship to those by Puvis.

More important than any specific instance of Denis's indebtedness to Puvis, however, is the basic and pervasive influence that the work of the older artist had on Denis and his aesthetic idiom and on the group of Post-Impressionists with which Denis was most closely allied, the Nabis. Puvis's work was a model in terms of its decorative aesthetic and flat, circumscribed, opaque forms of equal value. Many critics came to view Denis's work as a continuation of that of Puvis. Like Puvis, Denis also contributed mural decorations to both religious and secular buildings and had a particular affinity for these decorative effects. He articulated much about the special qualities of Puvis's contribution, and what he saw in Puvis's work is underscored in his own: the formal disposition of figures and silhouetted trees, the patterned rhythms of landscape elements – as in *Landscape with Green Trees* of 1893 (private collection) – the pale, flat interlocking forms, and the decorative, overall whitened surfaces that are part of the lightened colors that Puvis was instrumental in establishing, the 'contagion de blanc' ('white epidemic') that one critic accused Puvis of having started.[7]

1 See Denis (1957), I, p. 152, entry of March 1899; p. 197, entry of 15 April 1903; and p. 210, entry of 2 March 1904.

2 Ira Moskowitz and Maurice Serullaz, *Drawings of the Masters: French Impressionists* (New York, 1962), p. 86, repr.; Christopher Riopelle, 'Renoir: The Great Bathers,' *Bulletin. Philadelphia Museum of Arts* (Fall, 1990), p. 16 and repr. fig. 11.

3 *L'Amour de l'art* (May 1931), p. 192, repr.

4 Van Gogh (1958), III, p. 132, no. 574.

5 'personnages sacrifieés par une ombre factice.' Denis (1957), I, pp. 163-164, entry of 1 December 1900.

6 Repr. 1975 Toronto, p. 130, the variant title given there: *Décoration pour la chambre à coucher: L'Amour et la Vie d'une Femme d'après Schumann; L'Enfance ou la Cueillette des pommes*; see also Richard Wattenmaker's analysis p. 134.

7 Gaston Scheffer, *Le Salon de 1897* (Paris, 1897), p. 87.

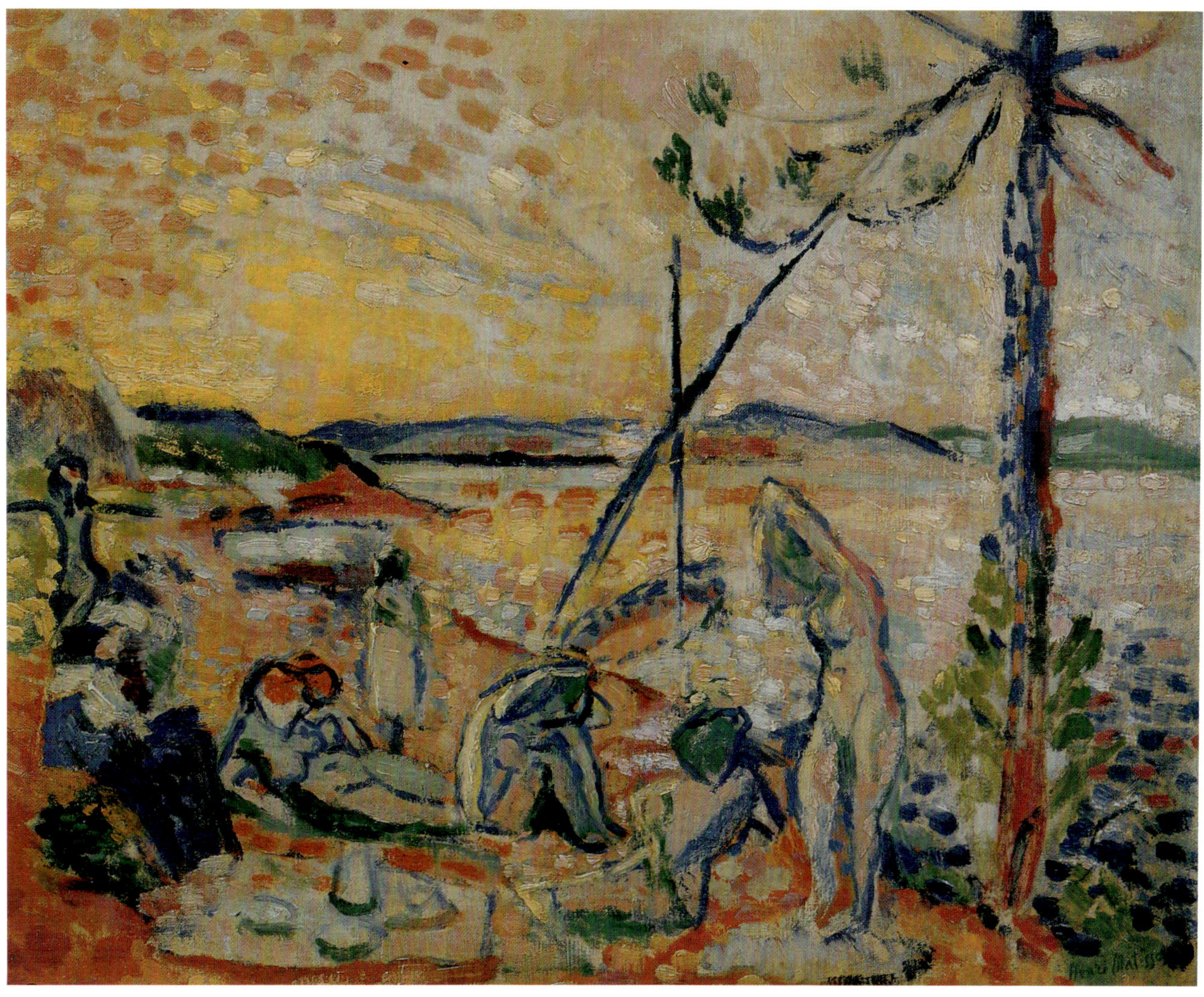

150

Henri Matisse (1869-1954)

Study for 'Luxe, calme et volupté' 1904

Signed l.r.: Henri Matisse
Oil on canvas, 32.2 x 40.5 cm
Mrs. John Hay Whitney

Selected References Alfred H. Barr, Jr., *Matisse. His Art and His Public* (New York, 1951), pp. 34, 53, 59-60; Schneider (1977); Schneider (1984), pp. 99-108, 198-199; Jack Flam, *Matisse. The Man and His Art. 1869-1918* (Cornell, 1986), pp. 19, 107, 292, 118-120.

> 'Là, tout n'est qu'ordre et beauté,
> Luxe, calme et volupté.'

This refrain of Baudelaire's 'L'Invitation au Voyage' provided Matisse with the title for his Arcadian painting. The longing for a fabled Cythera or Golden Age, that Baudelaire expressed in the 'There' of his poem is an unnamed place that is perpetually elsewhere; a place of order and beauty, luxury and serenity from which he felt displaced. It is precisely the ordered place that Puvis de Chavannes posited in his *Pleasant Land* (see cat. 86) and that Matisse's *Luxe, calme et volupté* echoes in its own sensual voluptousness. *Pleasant Land* has been advanced as a key to understanding the pictorial innovations of a Seurat or a Matisse.[1] With his Arcadian motifs, sense of decorative flat shape and will radically to condense his pictorial statements, Puvis's images are a striking antecedent to those of Matisse, especially in the idyllic compositions of about 1904-08. In the case of *Luxe, calme et volupté* the resemblances are remarkable: Matisse here is the continuer of Puvis, not only generally, but most particularly.

Matisse painted two versions of *Luxe, calme et volupté*, working on them in the fall and winter of 1904 after having returned to Paris from Saint-Tropez, where he had spent the summer. There he had executed a study, *The Gulf of Saint-Tropez* (Kunstsammlung Nordrhein-Westfalen, Düsseldorf), that would serve as the basis for their topography. The earlier work shown here, though considered a study for the later canvas, is quite different in its sensibilities and independent of the larger (98.5 x 118 cm) and more deliberate later work (Musée d'Orsay, Paris). The latter consists of more definitely outlined figures, its surface a multicolored confetti of tiny squares (the offshoot of the Neo-Impressionists' points and stitches of color). The former presents a more intimate sensuality, and is no less dazzling for its thoughtfulness. At the time he was working on these canvases, Matisse must have seen the display of Puvis's paintings at the retrospective of his work held at the Salon d'Automne (which opened on 15 October 1904), for he had fourteen paintings and two sculptures of his own on exhibit. Although he could not have seen then and there either version of Puvis's *Pleasant Land*, which is so strikingly close in classicizing feeling and composition to his own canvases, he would doubtless have been familiar with Puvis's work through earlier exhibitions. By the turn of the century, any ambitious and serious artist like Matisse would have known Puvis's work. Moreover, Mécislas Golberg, with whom he was in contact and who reputedly helped him to draft his *Notes d'un peintre* of 1908, was a great advocate of Puvis's painting (see cat. 152) and surely they would have discussed *Pleasant Land*.[2]

In addition, Matisse had been in contact with Puvis in 1896, for he had been nominated by Puvis, then its president, to be an associate member of the Société Nationale des Beaux-Arts. But lest too much be made of this, Puvis was routinely generous to scores of young artists, as thank you letters and cards testify, helping them when he could in his various positions in the art world.

Matisse would have noted the harmonious interdependency in scale between the distinctly outlined lounging figures and the idyllic seaside landscape, with the diagonal of the seashore and hills in the distance. Several of his figures recall Puvis's figures, such as the woman seated on the ground, almost in profile, her back curved and her legs bent. Matisse also may have come to appreciate Puvis through Seurat's modernizing renditions of his work.

What has been noted as the freedoms found so compelling in Matisse's work, the liberation of color from the need to be imitative, for one, a concept that is central to Fauvism, had in fact been achieved by Puvis, in his own muted, but no less audacious way: the burst of yellow in Matisse's canvas is brighter but no more yellow than the yellow gold sky of *Pleasant Land*. More important still, Matisse might have noted the relative size of figures and landscape, their harmonious interdependency, in a number of Puvis's works, but most particularly in *Pleasant Land*.

With all its similarities to *Pleasant Land*, it would seem that the tree to the right of *Luxe, calme et volupté*, along with the boat mast and curved beam, which anchors the composition and balances the ascending diagonal to the left, is derived from the trees that are similarly used to strong compositional effect in Puvis's *Pleasant Land*. But the tree was prominent in Matisse's preliminary landscape study made *sur place* in the South of France that summer. The leaves on the tree at the left of Puvis's idyll show his customary love of flat shapes and would be just the kind of leaf shapes that Matisse would make so much of years hence.

In subtle but important ways Matisse's Arcadianism parallels that of Puvis. Both sought prototypes in the Venus Anadyomenes of Greek art, with women displayed holding up their hair. For both a settled Arcadian calm was integral to their strong sense of two-dimensional decorative embellishment. Both Puvis and Matisse were good Frenchmen with the splendid fictions of classicizing Golden Age pastorals deeply embedded in their psyches. Both had profound feelings for the idea of antiquity. Their sensuality came to them through these ready-made fictions of Hellenic and Greek mythology. Or as Renoir, of whom this was also true, remarked (as if in defeat), 'We want no more of the gods and the gods are necessary to our imagination.'[3]

Again, three years later, the three radically flattened and simplified women, reduced to essential outlines, of Matisse's *Le Luxe I* and *Le Luxe II* (1907, Musée National d'Art Moderne, Paris and Statens Museum for Kunst, Copenhagen) clearly compare to the three figures in Puvis's *Young Women by the Sea* (cat. 76, fig. 6): the central standing figure, the two others separate formally, psychically and physically from her, along a simple seashore. In both these thematic and iconographic ways, but also through its decorative aesthetic, Puvis's work was an important progenitor of that of Matisse.

Recognizing the similarity between Puvis de Chavannes and Matisse, the organizers of the 1913 'Armory Show' in New York hung their works vis-à-vis one another.[4]

1 John Rewald, *Georges Seurat* (Paris, 1948), p. 46; Schapiro (1958), 22-24, 44-45, 52; Herbert (1959).

2 Mécislas Golberg, 'Puvis de Chavannes,' *Cahiers mensuels de Mécislas Golberg* (Paris), (March-April 1901), 33-34; John Richardson, *A Life of Picasso*, with Marilyn McCully, vol. I. *1881-1906* (New York, 1991), p. 424.

3 'On ne veut plus de dieux et les dieux sont nécessaires à notre imagination.' See 'Lettre à M. Henry Mottez,' *L'Occident* (June 1910), 240.

4 Schneider (1984), p. 106.

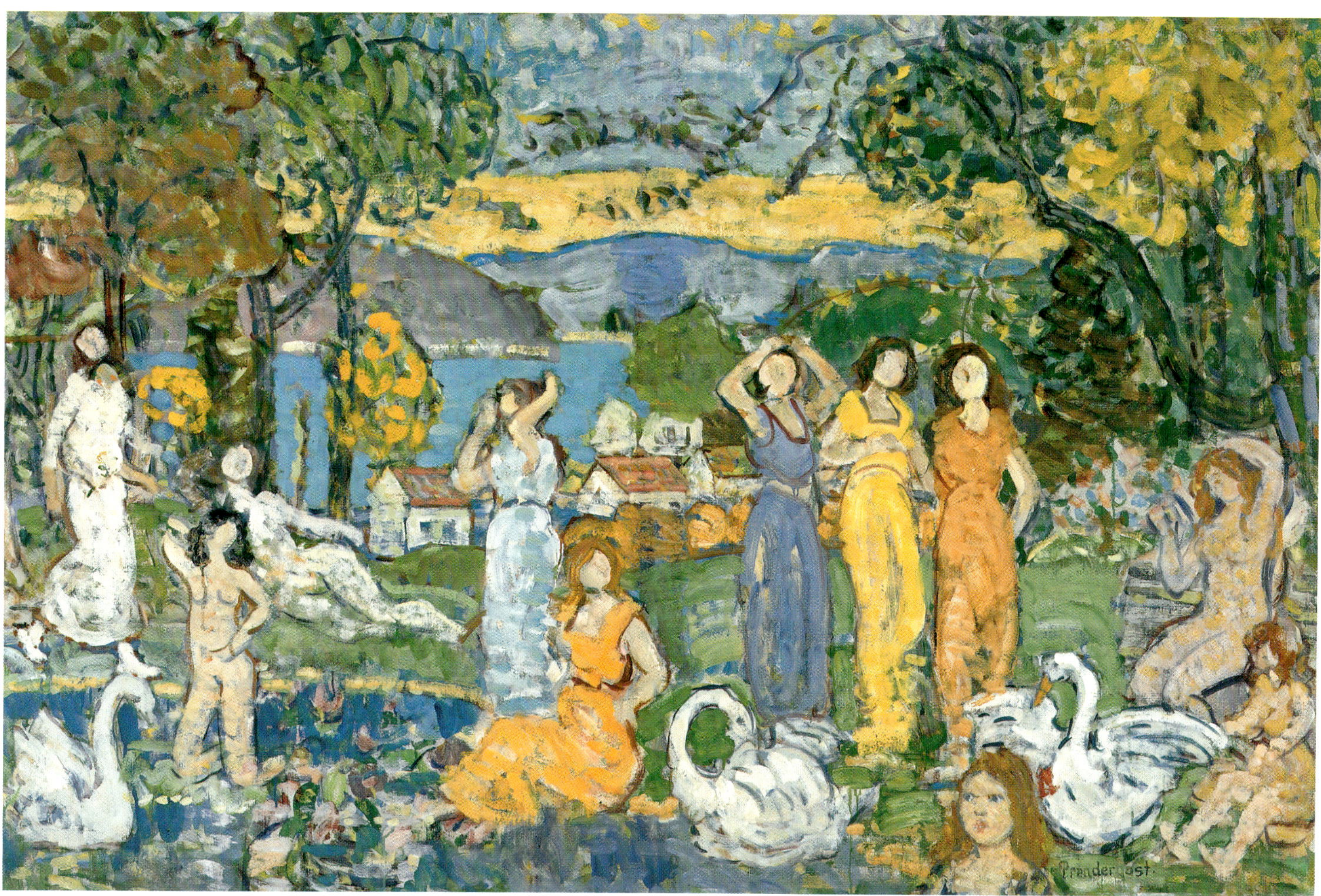

151

Maurice Prendergast (1858-1924)

The Picnic ca. 1914-15

Oil on canvas, 94 x 144.8 cm
National Gallery of Canada, Ottawa (Inv. 4528)

Provenance Artist to John Quinn (1915); Mr. and Mrs. Cornelius Sullivan (1927); Parke-Bernet (1939); Kraushaar Gallery, New York (1939); acquired by the museum (1940).

Selected References Henley Howell Rhys, *Maurice Prendergast: 1859-1924* (Boston and Cambridge, 1960); 1975 Toronto, pp. 188-192; 1990-91, New York, Whitney Museum of American Art / Williamstown, Williams College Museum of Art / Los Angeles County Museum of Art / Washington, D.C., The Phillips Collection, *Maurice Prendergast*; Carol Clark, Nancy Mowll Mathews, Gwendolyn Owens, *Maurice Brazil Prendergast. Charles Prendergast, Catalogue Raisonné* (Munich 1990), no. 388.

The American painter Maurice Prendergast took great interest in a very broad range of artists from the muralists Giotto and Piero della Francesca to such moderns as Cézanne, Matisse, Bonnard, Denis and Vuillard, but the characteristic decorative style of his mature work is particularly beholden to the flat, well-tempered idyllic compositions and decorative aesthetic developed by Puvis de Chavannes.[1] *The Picnic*, a charming frieze -like composition of nude and dressed female figures stationed in horizontal bands in the American Arcadia of a lakeside park, is representative of Prendergast's engaging style of 1913 to 1917 that is so permeated with Puvis's pictorial ideas.[2] Prendergast typically set bathers, picnickers and festive vacationers in such pastoral settings and organized his canvases so that the various elements of his compositions interlock as colored forms on a textured planar surface. In this gaily multi-colored canvas, seated and standing female figures, many with their hands to their hair in the archetypal pose of a Venus or a woman at her toilette, and all twisted to optimum frontality and oriented towards the viewer, are carefully interspersed with swans and trees and landscape elements. Not all American critics were satisfied with the classicizing referents of these compositions, whether nudes or swans (suggesting the story of Leda), and Prendergast was castigated for abandoning the progressive modernism of his earlier work for what was viewed in some circles as the 'sterilities of antiquity.'[3] The colors of Prendergast's paintings are frequently more subdued and whitened than the festive tonalities of *The Picnic*; a variant of this composition, *The Swans* of ca. 1914-15 (Addison Gallery of American Art, Phillips Academy, Andover, Mass.), with its more granular texture, achieves a fresco-like effect. Aware of its special pictorial connotation, from 1908 Prendergast occasionally used the designation 'decoration' to describe certain of his easel paintings, a term which he came to employ often in the period 1910-20. Indeed, the original title for *The Picnic* was *Decoration – Summer*.[4]

Prendergast had worked as a graphic designer in Boston for many years before he first arrived in Paris in 1891, where he stayed until 1894 to study art. Puvis de Chavannes was internationally known by the later 1880s, and well-known artists from other countries who came to Paris would often try to see him, while art students were satisfied with seeing his work. Prendergast must have been aware of Puvis's paintings, but the first sign of any palpable impact on his own work was to come years later. Returning to Boston in 1894, where he then lived until 1914, he could have studied Puvis's great cycle of murals installed with much fanfare in late 1895 and 1896 at the Boston Public Library. Had Prendergast gone to New York in December 1894 he could have seen a major exhibition of Puvis's at the newly opened Durand-Ruel Galleries there. Puvis's work was also exhibited in Boston in 1912 and at the famous 1913 'Armory Show' in New York, the International Exhibition of Modern Art which introduced modern European art to America (see cat. 150) and in which Prendergast exhibited his own work.

From the 1890s Prendergast would have become familiar with new ideas about flat colors and composition, not necessarily through Puvis's works, but through his friend, Arthur Wesley Dow, one of the most important teachers and writers on art in America, whose theories derived from his knowledge of Japanese prints. Moreover, by 1904 Prendergast had befriended the painter Arthur B. Davies (1862-1928) in New York, who was also familiar with Puvis's work and exceedingly influenced by it. Prendergast's compositions of 1902, of parading figures at the seaside or in the country, were already oriented in a frieze-like fashion towards the forward picture plane.

By 1904-05 Prendergast took note of Puvis's paintings. Along with drawings after Giorgione and Poussin in his sketchbooks, the first of two groups of drawings after Puvis's work appeared at this time and included wonderfully sprightly and telling drawings after *Pleasant Land*, presumably copied from a reproduction.[5] Coincidentally, it was just at this moment that Matisse too was remarking on Puvis's Arcadian paintings – specifically *Pleasant Land* – in his own work (see cat. 86). Prendergast's sketchbooks of about 1912 also include drawings after Puvis, and again it was the classicizing idyllic compositions with their flattened figures and topographies that Prendergast drew, *Summer* (see cat. 134) and *Young Women by the Sea* (cat.76, fig. 6).[6]

Prendergast imitated the matte surfaces of Puvis's paintings, first developing his own opaque colors about 1910-11, by mixing transparent watercolors with Chinese white[7] and later sometimes incorporating encaustic in his oil medium to similar effect. Critics describing the surfaces of Prendergast's mature paintings repeatedly called attention to their tapestried effect, just as Puvis's first mural paintings, with their relatively even tonalities, were likened to tapestries in 1861, as were Seurat's painted surfaces a quarter of a century later. Writing of Prendergast's colors in 1925, Dr. Alfred Barnes, the great, independent-minded American collector, singled out their 'lilac-pinks, yellow, pale blue, chalky whites, pale greens and roses.'[8] These were the same colors that were so striking in Puvis's paintings, and the chords which he, in turn, had remarked as admirable in Giotto's frescoes (see p. 16).

Given Puvis's abiding interest in borders and ornamented frames, it is noteworthy that Prendergast, with the instincts of the great decorator that he was, was most attentive to the frames of his paintings. Indeed, the best known of the American painters working abroad, Whistler, also insisted on special frames, a topic of increasing interest among European and American painters in the last decades of the nineteenth century. Maurice's brother Charles, who would become well-known for his carved frames, screens, *cassoni* and decorative carvings, frequently provided frames for Maurice's work, as he did for *The Picnic*.[9]

1 Richard Wattenmaker has ably discussed these links in 1975 Toronto, pp. 188-192.

2 See Clark, Mowll Mathews, Owen (ref. above), generally nos. 353-390; with specific comparisons also to be made, such as that of no. 356, *Red Headed Nude* of 1910-13 (Wadsworth Atheneum, Hartford), to Puvis's *Hope* (fig. 4 of this book).

3 The criticism of Willard Huntington Wright as quoted in Clark, Mowll Mathews, Owen (ref. above), p. 33.

4 1990-91 New York etc. (ref above), p. 32.

5 There are more than 88 sketchbooks; see Clark, Mowll Mathews, Owen (ref. above); these first drawings in Sketchbook no. 13, p. 44, Museum of Fine Arts, Boston.

6 Sketchbook no. 46, ca. 1912, pp. 34, 35, Museum of Fine Arts, Boston; see 1975 Toronto, repr. pp. 189-190.

7 Rhys (ref. above), p. 48.

8 Albert C. Barnes, *The Art In Painting*, 1st ed. (1925), pp. 298-299; quoted in 1975 Toronto, p. 191.

9 See Carol Derby, 'Charles Prendergast's Frames: Reuniting Design and Craftsmanship,' in Clark, Mowll Mathews, Owen (ref. above), pp. 95-105.

152

Pablo Picasso (1881-1973)

Bathers / *Les Baigneuses* 1918

Oil on canvas, 27 x 22 cm
Musée Picasso, Paris (Inv. MP.61)

Selected References Silver (1989), pp. 241-242, 276-281, 289-290 and *passim*.

At several junctures during his prodigious career, Pablo Picasso rearticulated one or another strain of Puvis de Chavannes's imagery in his own powerful manner. Puvis's flat, angular, radically simplified figures, pale blue tonalities and thematics of poverty informed Picasso's Blue Period paintings.[1] The archaizing classicism and pink casts of certain of Puvis's mature classicizing paintings of the 1870s and 1880s[2] were important to the Rose Period. Puvis's work supplied calm, beautiful models to Picasso as he returned in 1918 to whole, integrated forms after a decade in which the kaleidoscopic, fragmented images of his Cubist designs were a preoccupation. And Picasso's radically simplified and monumental classicizing figures of about 1921 to 1924 are indebted to Puvis's Hellenism. Puvis provided important exempla: a mood, a gesture, an unarticulated expanse of landscape, even what through reserve, constraint and asceticism he left undone. Picasso also modeled individual paintings such as *The Bathers* after those by Puvis.

The three bathers in Picasso's small masterpiece – one frolicking with gawky abandon, one languidly dozing, and one seated gathering up her hair – are a charmingly uninhibited reiteration of Puvis de Chavannes's more subdued *Young Women by the Sea* (fig. 6, cat. 76). Picasso's bathers preserve the simple charm, guileless innocence and indolence of Puvis's figures, while emphasis is placed on their endearing awkwardness by intensifying their twisting poses. *The Bathers*, painted in Biarritz in 1918, communicates how much Picasso truly learned from the older artist's work in quoting it and also what particularly charmed him – such inventions as the dreamy, recumbent figure, whom he dressed in an orange bathing suit. Like Puvis's sharply separated, distinctive figures, Picasso's bathers convey a sense of self-absorption and foster a reading not given to narrative. The three figures also resonate against the simple geometry of the tripartite division of shore, sea and sky. The sharply demarcated zones with the single white curved sail recall as well Puvis's *Pleasant Land* (see cat. 86), which Seurat too had modernized in his *A Bathing Place, Asnières*.[3] In Picasso's canvas there is also a dash of Henri Rousseau in the vivid ungainliness of the figural poses and the gaily colored and brightly striped *maillots de bain*.[4] In his 1918 drawings of *Bathers* (Fogg Art Museum, Cambridge, Mass.), Picasso also imitated the lolling, turning poses of several bathers and the nudes half emerging from the water or resting on the shore in Puvis's *Summer* of 1891 (see cat. 134). Indeed two of the poses are identical (though reversed).

Picasso's interest in Puvis may date from even before his first trip to Paris at the turn of the century, when he was in Barcelona, to which city word of Puvis's paintings had spread. The Catalan painter Santiago Rusiñol, who befriended Picasso, had lived in Paris in the 1890s, even attending the famous 1895 banquet honoring Puvis de Chavannes; and Picasso's allusion to Rusiñol and his place in the Paris art world in a small drawing of about 1901 indicates he was well apprised of it.[5] In Barcelona Picasso would have surely also heard of Puvis at the Els Quatre Gats café, which was a major center for exchange on modernist ideas. Moreover, in 1898 there was a session on Puvis at the Club of San Luc.[6] Picasso made three trips to Paris before he finally moved there from Barcelona: in 1900, from June 1901 to January 1902, and from 29 October 1902 until January 1903. In Paris his interest in Puvis would have been further aroused by the Polish anarchist Mécislas Golberg, with whom he came into contact and who was then writing about Puvis.[7] Picasso's keen interest in Puvis's images can first be documented in copybook drawings made between December 1902 and January 1903 after Puvis's first and second campaign murals of Saint Genevieve at the Panthéon. Picasso also based a pastoral drawing on the unusual compositional layout and a figural passage of the first campaign *Saint Genevieve as a Child in Prayer*.[8] Puvis's central motif, Saint Germanus recognizing Genevieve by putting his hand on her upraised profile head, provided the basis for a series of studies of upturned profile heads (Marina Picasso Collection, Fogg Art Museum, Cambridge, Mass.) and for the touching *Old Man and Young Girl* (*The Blind Man*) of 1904 (private collection). Picasso acknowledged Puvis in a drawing based on a passage of the left panel of the second campaign triptych of Saint Genevieve: 'De Pubis en el Panteon/ el cuadro de la hambre/ Mujer joven bien vestida/ hombre de el pueblo/ Mujer vieja;' ('from Pubis [sic] in the Panthéon/ the painting of famine/ well-dressed young woman/ man of the town/ old woman'.[9] The figure Picasso called 'mujer vieja' lies on the ground and has the same essential forward-facing zigzagged angular pose as the figure to the left in Puvis's *Young Women by the Sea*, and is essentially the same figure as the one converted by Picasso into his dozing bather at the center of his 1918 *Bathers*. In addition, there are Picasso's own fantasies based on Puvis's composition of boats with figures and children and disembarkations and drawings similar to *Charity*.[10]

The outcasts of Picasso's Blue Period paintings such as *Woman by the Sea* of 1902 (private collection) and *The Tragedy* of 1903 (fig. 28), with their cramped, stiff, hugged-in gestures and gaunt angularity, indeed the melancholy itself of the paintings, have an important precedent in Puvis's *Poor Fisherman* (see p. 49) and *Charity* (see cat. 140), which Picasso might have seen on any of his early trips to Paris. Picasso was evidently also drawn to the understated austerity of the blue color casts of Puvis's second campaign Saint Genevieve murals of 1896-98 which had a crucial effect on his own paintings from about 1902-05. As part of the decorative aesthetic that he began to formulate in 1859 and 1864, Puvis had painted 'camaïeu' tondi in a variety of tonalities from turquoise to rose (*Return from the Hunt*, reduced variant, Nelson-Atkins Museum of Art, Kansas City; *Contemplation* and *Study* at the Musée de Picardie, Amiens), and continued using prevailing tints through the pinks of his *Antique Vision* (see cat. 105) and the blue grays of his *Charity* (Gifu Museum, Japan).

From distinctive bleached, chalky pink and blue tonalities[11] to general motifs and from specific figures of boys playing pipes to simply stated figures in a landscape, Picasso's Saltimbanques and particularly his Rose Period classicism of 1905-06 follows the stilted classicizing imagery of paintings such as Puvis's *Antique Vision* and *The Shepherd's Song* (1891, Metropolitan Museum of Art, New York). The tender, pale rose colors and fresco-like surfaces of works such as *The Watering Place* (Metropolitan Museum of Art, New York) have an affinity with Puvis's paintings of the late 1870s and 1880s, sometimes by way of Gauguin. There are once again thematic similarities also in paintings such as *The Toilette* (Albright-Knox Art Gallery, Buffalo) and *The Coiffure* (Metropolitan Museum of Art, New York) to the motif of *The Toilette* in Puvis's works of around 1883 (see cat. 96-100).

After the war of 1914-18 as after the 1870-71 Franco-Prussian War (see pp. 16-17), a new ardor for classicizing imagery in France was coupled with the assertion of national identity.[12] Puvis's classicizing images, along with those of Poussin and Ingres, inspired Picasso in this direction. Picasso's great classicizing *Three Women at the Spring* of 1921-22 (Museum of Modern Art, New York), parallels Puvis's painting *At the Fountain* (Boston Museum of Fine Arts, reduced variant of ca. 1885, Musée des Beaux-Arts, Reims),[13] while a series of paintings and drawings of highly simplified monumental classicizing female figures ca. 1921-24, as condensed in impact as they are simple in outline relate to Puvis's images of the 1880s and 1890s: *The Toilette*, *Antique Vision* and to the great *Magdalene* (cat. 145).

1 See Anthony Blunt and Phoebe Pool, *Picasso, The Formative Years, A Study of his Sources* (New York, 1962), pp. 26, 167-170; Juan-Eduardo Cirlot, *Picasso, Birth of a Genius* (New York and Washington, 1972), see figs. 88, 229, 230, 259, 957, 958, 968 for works with special similarity to those by Puvis; Pierre Daix, Georges Boudaille, Joan Rosselet, *Picasso. 1900-1906. Catalogue raisonné de l'oeuvre peint. Les années de formation. La préfauvisme. La Période bleue. La période rose. Le classicisime rose. Le précubisme* (Neuchâtel, 1966), rev. ed. (Neuchâtel, 1988).

2 Meyer Schapiro used the term 'Rosewater Hellenism,' from literary criticism to apply to Puvis; see William Rubin, *Picasso in the Collection of the Museum of Modern Art, New York* (New York, 1972), p. 193, note 5; see also Pool (1965), 122-127.

3 Meyer Schapiro (1958), 22-52.

4 The marrying of the two sources is brilliantly analyzed by Silver (1989), pp. 241-242.

5 1975 Toronto, pp. 162, 168-170; John Richardson, *A Life of Picasso*, with Marilyn McCully, vol. I. *1881-1906* (New York, 1991), pp. 256-257.

6 Blunt and Pool, *op. cit.* (note 1), n.p.

7 Mécislas Golberg, 'Puvis de Chavannes,' *Cahiers mensuels de Mécislas Golberg* (Paris), (March-April 1901), 33-34; Golberg (1901); Brown Price (1972), pp. 204, 212; Richardson, *op. cit.* (note 5), pp. 423-424.

8 Museu Picasso, Barcelona (Inv. MPB 110.546).

9 Museu Picasso, Barcelona (Inv. MPB 110.468).

10 Museu Picasso, Barcelona (Inv. MPB 110.492, MPB 110.493, MPB 110.447 also MPB 110.469). Related to *Charity*, Museu Picasso, Barcelona (Inv. MPB 110.494).

11 Richardson, *op. cit.* (note 5), pp. 424-425.

12 This is a central theme of Silver (1989).

13 Silver (1989), pp. 275-278.

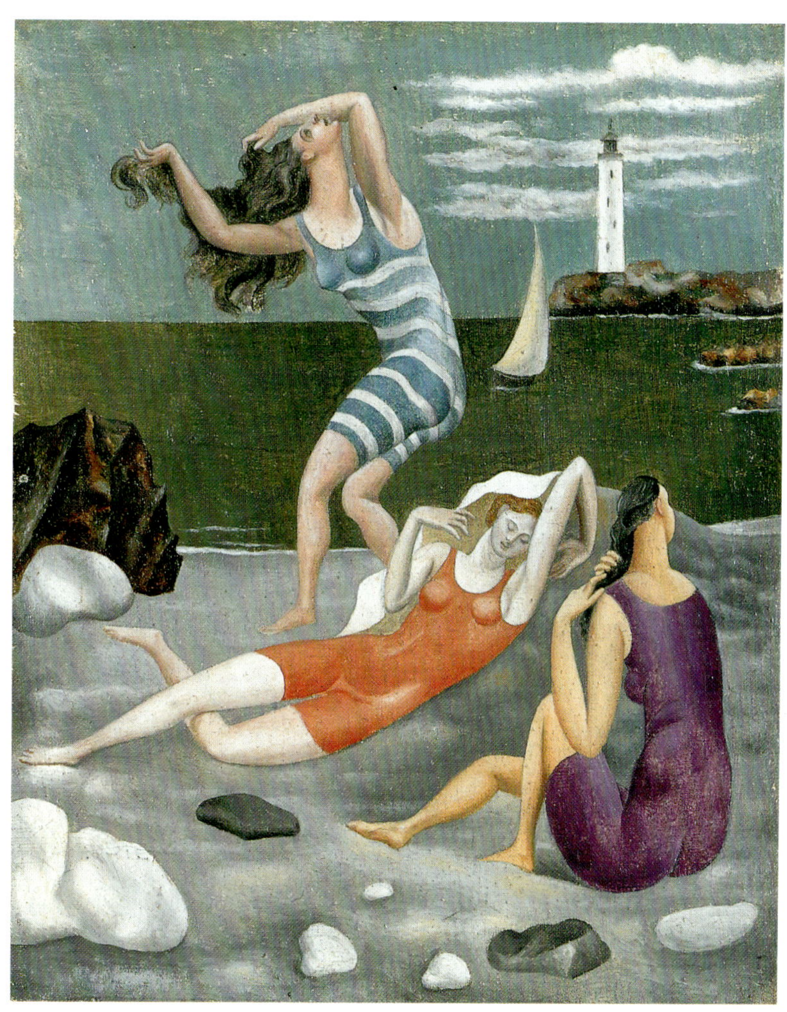

Chronology

With few exceptions, only dated works are listed here. Mural cycles were produced over a span of years; insofar as they were introduced in progressive stages (cartoon, painting, installation), that is so indicated.

Abbreviations: p.c.= private collection; w.u.= whereabouts unknown.

1824

14 December Pierre-Cécile Puvis born in Lyons, France. His father is Marie-Julien-César Joseph Puvis (born 14 March 1785 in Cuiseaux), chief engineer of mines; his mother Marguerite Guyot (born 15 July 1795 at Oullins). Puvis is the youngest of four children.

1830

Attends the Lycée Royal of Lyons, the Collège Saint-Rambert.

1840

27 October Puvis's mother dies.

1841

Puvis is a student at the Lycée Henri IV, Paris.

1842

20 January, 5 March Letters from his father remind Puvis that the Ecole Polytechnique is his goal.

19 November His father hires tutors and promises him drawing lessons, if he will study more.

1843

17 February Puvis's father dies, and he is left of independent means. Illness prevents him from taking the entrance exam to the Ecole Polytechnique and possibly forecloses his attendance at the Faculty of Law, where he is briefly enrolled. He recuperates for two years at Mâcon with his sister Joséphine and her husband, Esprit-Alexandre Jordan; they buy property together in Mervans.

1846

First Italian sojourn probably this year.

Decides to become a painter. He wishes to study with Emile Signol, but Signol does not take students. He approaches Ary Scheffer, who recommends his brother Henri.

1847

Schooled informally by Henri Scheffer for six months, mainly receiving advice and pointers.

1848

Second trip to Italy, with the painter Bauderon de Vermeron. He admires Giotto, the murals of Benozzo Gozzoli at Pisa and of Piero della Francesca at Arezzo. In Florence for almost a year, he works from the model; he visits Naples and the islands of the Adriatic.

Paints: *Three Famous Italians* (Chrysler Museum, Norfolk, Virginia) [inscribed Rome 1848]; probably *Gondolier* (p.c.); *Copy after Veronese's 'Triumph of Venice'* ca. 1848-50 (p.c.).

Introduced by Bauderon, he enters Delacroix's studio, and remains about two weeks before Delacroix, who is ill, closes it. Rents a gymnasium at 50 rue Saint-Lazare, where he works for the next three years.

1848-49

Puvis de Chavannes at Thomas Couture's studio for three months (six months to a year according to some sources); meets Marcellin Desboutin but leaves before Edouard Manet arrives. Later lists himself as a student of Henri Scheffer and Couture in Salon catalogues.

1848-50

Copies at the Musée du Louvre: *Copy after Titian's 'Madonna with a Rabbit'* (p.c.) and a Madonna with Child and Saints after Titian's *Sacra Conversazione* (Eglise de Joude).

1850

Debut at the Salon des Artistes Français (hereafter: Salon) with *Dead Christ* (Mokhtar Museum, Guezira, Cairo); *Negro Boy* (cat. 1); *The Reading Lesson* (p.c.); *Portrait of a Man* (p.c.).

1851

Paints: *Diogenes* (p.c.); *Head of a Woman* (p.c.); *Portrait of Edouard Puvis de Chavannes* (p.c.); *Portrait of Mlle de Vaugelas* (p.c.); *Portrait of Marc Antoine Puvis de Chavannes* (p.c.); *Portrait of a Woman* (p.c.); *Portrait of Marguerite de Vaugelas* (p.c.); *Portrait of Louis de Vaugelas* (p.c.); *Portrait of a Woman* (p.c.); *Portrait of Thomas Alfred Jones* (Musée d'Orsay, Paris); *Portrait of Villiers de l'Isle-Adam* [so-called] (Städelsches Kunstinstitut, Frankfurt); *Jean Cavalier at the Bedside of his Dying Mother* (Musée des Beaux-Arts, Lyons).

1852

24 January Nobiliary titles officially reestablished. The Puvis family, asserting their lineage, would now begin the process of having their name restored.

Submits *Jean Cavalier at the Bedside of his Dying Mother* to the Salon, but it is not accepted. All Puvis's other submissions to the Salon are refused until 1859. During this period he exhibits at the Bazar Bonne-Nouvelle.

15 July Moves to 11 Place Pigalle, where Jean-Jacques Henner, Isidore Pils and Alfred Roll would all have studios. He would remain at the same address until 1897, later also having a large studio in Neuilly.

1852-55

Works with Gustave Ricard, Alexandre Bida, and occasionally the engraver Victor Pollet, drawing from the model in the evenings at their self-styled 'Academy.'

1853

Paints: *Mademoiselle de Sombreuil Drinking a Glass of Blood to Save Her Father's Life* (p.c.).

ca. 1853-54

Collaborates with Alfred Bellet du Poisat on exterior frescoes (his only work in this medium) on an annex at Le Brouchy, the family château.

1854

Paints: *Little Black Turtle Monger, Venice* (p.c.); *Portrait of Forget in Spanish Dress* n.d. (w.u.), may be same as *Calesero, Driver of a Calash in the Surroundings of Madrid* n.d. [before 1855] (w.u.); oil studies for each of the five main murals for the dining room at Le Brouchy (cat. 4; all p.c.).

1854-55

Paints: murals for the dining room at Le Brouchy: *Spring* (*The Miraculous Draught of Fishes*); *Summer* (*Ruth and Boaz in the Fields*); *Autumn* (*The Invention of Wine*); *Winter* (*Esau Returning from the Hunt*); *The Return of the Prodigal Son*; *Overdoor with Helmet*; *Overdoor with Plaster Head*; *Overdoor with Basket*; *Overdoor with Book*.

1855

Exhibits at the Société des Bouches-du-Rhône, Marseilles: *Portrait of M. de St. O[live]* (p.c.); *Calesero, Driver of a Calash in the Surroundings of Madrid*; *Little Black Turtle Monger, Venice*.

1856

Paints: *The Fisherman* (Ohara Museum, Kurashiki, Japan); *Christ Appearing to Saint Paul in Prison* (Church at Bourbon-Lancy, France); *Salome, the Daughter of Herodias, Ordering the Execution of Saint John the Baptist*; *Roosters and Tomatoes* (p.c.).

By 1856 meets Théodore Chassériau and through him the Princess Marie Cantacuzène, who will be his longtime companion.

8 October Chassériau dies.

1857

Paints: *Self-Portrait* (cat. 15); *Julia, the Daughter of Augustus, Returning to the Palace in the Morning, Accompanied by a Servant, is Surprised by Soldiers* ca. 1856-57 (cat. 10); *The Fire* or *The Village Firemen* (Hermitage, Saint Petersburg); *The Martyrdom of Saint Sebastian* (p.c.); *Meditation* (lost/destroyed); *Portrait of a Woman* (ca. 1857; cat. 18); *Study for 'Noli me tangere'* (p.c.); *Noli me tangere* or *Jesus Christ Appearing to the Magdalene* (Musée des Beaux-Arts, Angers).

1857-58

Exhibits at the Exposition de la Société des Amis des Arts de Lyon: *Salome, the Daughter of Herodias, Ordering the Execution of Saint John the Baptist*.

1858

Paints: *Portrait of Alphonse Puvis de Chavannes* (p.c.); *Portrait of Camille Jordan* (p.c.); *Saint Camille at the Bedside of a Dying Man* (p.c.); *Christ Before the Praetorial Court* (church at Champagnat); *Flore* (p.c.).

1858-59

Exhibits at the Exposition de la Société des Amis des Arts de Lyon: *Noli me tangere; The Martyrdom of Saint Sebastian*.

1859

15 April First entry at the Salon since 1850-51; *Return from the Hunt* (Musée des Beaux-Arts, Marseilles); *Young Woman in a Shawl on a Terrace* (w.u.).

20 May The family name, 'Puvis,' legally gains the nobiliary designation 'de Chavanes,' which would be rectified legally to 'de Chavannes' only in 1877.

1861

1 May Puvis exhibits at the Salon: *Concordia* and *Bellum* [listed as 'mural paintings'] (Musée de Picardie, Amiens). Receives second-class medal for History Painting. The former bought by the State, Puvis donates its pendant.

Paints: *Rest* (p.c.); *The Slippers* (p.c.).

July In Karlsruhe, Germany.

1862

Paints: *Labor* (cat. 31) and executes two etchings: *The Martyrdom of Saint Sebastian* and *Return from the Hunt*.

31 August For Théophile Gautier's birthday party in Neuilly, he designs the sets for the theatrical.

December Signs manifesto against photography.

1863

1 May Exhibits at the Salon: *Work* and *Rest* [listed as complementary to the decorative paintings exhibited in 1861]. Both works are acquired by Arthur Diet for the Musée de Picardie (at the time: Musée Napoléon) in Amiens.

1864

February Exhibits at the Société Nationale des Beaux-Arts: *Noli me tangere* (then belonging to Théophile Gautier).

1 May Exhibits at the Salon: *Autumn* (Musée des Beaux-Arts, Lyons), which is awarded a medal.

Paints: *Eight Monumental Figures*: *Abundance*; *Bellona*; *The Harvester*; *The Spinner*; *Desolation*; *The Standard Bearer*; *Contemplation*; *Study* (Musée de Picardie, Amiens).

Concordia, *Bellum*, *Work* and *Rest* are installed at the Musée de Picardie, Amiens.

Commission for *Ave Picardia Nutrix* for the Musée de Picardie, Amiens.

1865

1 May Exhibits at the Salon: *Ave Picardia Nutrix* and *Eight Monumental Figures* [in section 'Public Monuments, paintings'] (installed at the Musée de Picardie, Amiens).

Paints: *The Vintage* or *Autumn* (Wallraf-Richartz Museum, Cologne); *Head of a Young Woman Crowned with Flowers*, *Ceres* or *Spring* (p.c.).

1866

Paints: ensemble for the Hôtel Vignon, Paris: *Vigilance*; *Meditation*; *History* (all three Musée d'Orsay, Paris); *Fantasy* (cat. 43); also *Vigilance* (cat. 45); *Fishing* (w.u.; formerly Ricketts collection).

1 May Exhibits at the Salon (*hors concours*): *Vigilance* (Musée d'Orsay, Paris); *Fantasy*.

1867

Exhibits at the Exposition Universelle: *War*; *Peace*;

Work; *Rest* [reductions of the 1861 and 1863 murals] (cat. 26-29), which are awarded a third prize.

15 April Exhibits at the Salon (*hors concours*): *Sleep* (Musée des Beaux-Arts, Lille).

29 June Named Knight of the Légion d'honneur.

Paints: *Vigilance* or *Truth* (National Gallery of Scotland, Edinburgh); *Contemplation* (p.c.).

25 July Submission for the decoration of the stairway of the new Musée des Beaux-Arts of Marseilles.

1868

1 May Exhibits at the Salon (*hors concours*): *Gaming* [decorative figure for the Cercle de l'Union Artistique] (destroyed).

Exhibits at the Société des Amis des Arts de Bordeaux: *War*; *Peace*; *Work*; *Rest* [reductions].

Meets Berthe Morisot; their correspondence begins.

1869

1 May Exhibits at the Salon: *Massilia, Greek Colony* and *Marseilles, Gateway to the Orient* (installed in the stairway of honor of the Musée des Beaux-Arts, Marseilles).

Paints: *The Beheading of Saint John the Baptist* (cat. 57); *The Magdalene in the Desert* (Städelsches Kunstinstitut Frankfurt); *The Magdalene in the Desert* (cat. 62).

Emma Dobigny begins to pose for Puvis.

1870

1 May Exhibits at the Salon (*hors concours*): *The Beheading of Saint John the Baptist*; *The Magdalene in the Desert* (Städelsches Kunstinstitut Frankfurt).

23 July Commission for the Hôtel de Ville of Poitiers.

Franco-Prussian War: Serves in the National Guard, as do other artists (Manet, Tissot, Bracquemond).

Paints: *The Balloon* or *The Besieged City of Paris Entrusts to the Air Her Call to France* (Musée d'Orsay, Paris).

1871

Paints: *The Carrier Pigeon* or *Having Escaped the Enemy Talon the Awaited Message Exalts the Heart of the Proud City* (cat. 65); *Autumn* or *Children in an Orchard* (Detroit Institute of Arts).

February-May Puvis departs Paris after the capitulation; makes small sketches and watercolors in Versailles.

March-May Commune and civil unrest.

3 June Returns to Paris, finds studio in Neuilly damaged.

Establishment of the Third Republic.

1872

1 May Exhibits at the Salon: *Hope* (Walters Art Gallery, Baltimore). Puvis withdraws from Salon jury. *Death and the Maidens* (Sterling and Francine Clark Art Institute, Williamstown) is refused at the Salon.

1873

15 May Exhibits at the Salon: *Summer* (Musée d'Orsay, Paris).

1874

1 May Exhibits at the Salon: *A.D. 732, Charles Martel Saves Christianity by his Victory over the Saracens near Poitiers* (Hôtel de Ville of Poitiers); *Having Withdrawn to the Convent of the Holy Cross, Radegonde Shelters Poets and Protects Literature from the Barbarism of the Age - 6th Century* [cartoon for a painting destined for the Hôtel de Ville of Poitiers].

7 May Philippe de Chennevières, Directeur des Beaux-Arts, proposes redecoration of the Panthéon.

12 May Commission for *Saint Genevieve* murals in the Panthéon.

1875

1 May Exhibits at the Salon: *Having Withdrawn to the Convent of the Holy Cross, Radegonde Shelters Poets and Protects Literature from the Barbarism of the Age - 6th Century* (installed at the Hôtel de Ville of Poitiers); *The Fisherman's Family* (formerly Staatliche Kunstsammlungen, Dresden, destroyed in World War II).

January Member of provisional committee to form an Académie Nationale des Artistes Français.

1876

1 May Exhibits at the Salon: *Saint Genevieve in Prayer* (Panthéon, then the Church of Saint Genevieve, Paris); *The Childhood of Saint Genevieve* [cartoon].

1877

1 May Exhibits at the Salon: *The Pastoral Life of Saint Genevieve* [in section 'Public Monuments'] (installed at the Panthéon).

Philippe de Chennevières praises Puvis in a speech at the Salon des Artistes Français, and makes him an Officer of the Légion d'honneur.

22 May Inauguration of the Panthéon murals.

1878

25 May Exhibits at the Salon: *Birth of Saint Genevieve*; *Legendary Saints of France* [*Frieze of Saints*] [in section 'Public Monuments'] (installed at the Panthéon).

Frieze installed at the Panthéon.

Begins to work on *Ludus pro Patria* for the Musée de Picardie, Amiens.

1879

12 May Exhibits at the Salon: *The Prodigal Son* (E.G. Bührle Collection, Zurich), *Young Women by the Sea* [listed as 'decorative panel'] (Musée d'Orsay, Paris). Member of jury and award committee.

Paints: *The Poor Fisherman* [painted study] (Pushkin Museum, Moscow).

May Refuses project for three murals for Bordeaux Bourse.

1880

1 May Exhibits at the Salon: *Young Picards Practicing the Javelin* [in section 'Monumental Art'] [project for the Musée d'Amiens, undertaken on speculation, without a commission] (Musées Royaux d'Art et d'Histoire, Brussels). Jury member.

2 May Société des Artistes Français. Takes an active part in organizing an exhibition of Couture's work at the Ecole des Beaux-Arts.

12 July Commission for *Young Picards Practicing the Javelin*.

Suzanne Valadon begins to pose for Puvis.

1881

2 May-30 June Exhibits at the Salon: *The Poor Fisherman* (Musée d'Orsay, Paris).

Committee member setting regulations for the Salon des Artistes Français. Jury member, resigns.

Exhibits at the Exposition de Peinture et Sculpture Moderne de Décoration et d'Ornement in the Musée des Arts Décoratifs, Palais de l'Industrie: *Picardy* [painted sketch; not clear which version]; *Ludus pro Patria* [cartoon]; *Peace, War, Work, Rest* [reductions]; *Figures* [for Amiens]; *Radegonde; Charles Martel* [reductions of cartoons]; *The Life of Saint Genevieve* [sketch for the canvas divided into four parts]; *The Childhood of Saint Genevieve* [painted sketch]; *Young Women by the Sea*; *Sleep*; *The Fishermen*; drawings; photographs.

1882

1 May Exhibits at the Salon: *Young Picards Practicing the Javelin* (*Pro Patria Ludus*) (Musée de Picardie, Amiens); *Pleasant Land* [destined for the hôtel of M.L. Bonnat] (Musée Bonnat, Bayonne).

Committee member Salon des Artistes Français; Jury member. Receives a Medal of Honor. Jules Ferry, Ministre de l'Instruction Publique et des Beaux-Arts, praises Puvis in his awards speech.

Paints: *Portrait of Eugène Benon* (cat. 89).

1883

1 May Exhibits at the Salon: *Portrait of Mme M.C.* [Marie Cantacuzène] (cat. 92); *The Dream* (Musée d'Orsay, Paris). Member of Salon Jury.

Exhibits at the Exposition Nationale des Beaux-Arts ['The Triennale']: *Young Woman at her Toilette* (Musée d'Orsay, Paris); *Young Women by the Sea*; *The Poor Fisherman*; *The Prodigal Son*.

Paints: *Ludus pro Patria* [reduced version] (Walters Art Gallery, Baltimore); *Orpheus* (p.c.).

21 July Mural commission for the stairway of the Musée des Beaux-Arts, Lyons; 11 August: program defined.

1884

1 May Exhibits at the Salon: *The Sacred Wood Dear to the Arts and Muses* (installed at the Musée des Beaux-Arts, Lyons). Jury member.

Exhibits drawings at the Ecole des Beaux-Arts.

Admires Manet's works exhibited at the Ecole des Beaux-Arts.

August Installation of *The Sacred Wood* at the Musée des Beaux-Arts, Lyons.

1885

1 May Exhibits at the Salon: *Autumn* (Museo de Bellas Artes, Caracas). Jury member.

Paints: *Antique Vision* (installed at the Musée des Beaux-Arts, Lyons).

1886

1 May Exhibits at the Salon: *Triptych: (1) Antique Vision; (2) Christian Inspiration; (3) The Rhône and The Saône* (installed at the Musée des Beaux-Arts, Lyons). Jury member.

17 May Commission for the murals for the Great Amphitheater of the Sorbonne.

September/October Installation of murals at the Musée des Beaux-Arts, Lyons.

1887

1 May Exhibits at the Salon (*hors concours*, as 'Sre. Membre de la Société des Artistes Français'): Cartoon of the painting destined for the Great Amphitheater of the Sorbonne. Jury member.

First exhibition in America, at the National Academy of Design, New York (together with Impressionists; through Durand-Ruel). Presents ten works.

19 November The State buys *The Poor Fisherman.*

20 November-20 December Important retrospective at the Galerie Durand-Ruel, Paris, with 84 works.

Paints: *Self-Portrait* (commissioned by the Uffizi Galleries, Florence); *Woman at the Seashore* (Hermitage, Saint Petersburg); *The Fisherman's Family* (Art Institute of Chicago); *executes Pity* [pastel] (cat. 110).

1888

Jury member at the Salon.

The Exposition Internationale d'Art Monumental in Brussels presents seventeen works (eleven of which are photographs).

24 February Commission for the Musée des Beaux-Arts, Rouen.

25 May Awarded a grant to study fresco painting in Italy with his assistant Paul Baudoüin (never realized).

20 December Commission for the Hôtel de Ville of Paris.

Installation of *Ludus pro Patria* at the Musée de Picardie, Amiens.

1889

Exposition Universelle Internationale: *Pro Patria Ludus*; *Antique Vision*; *Christian Inspiration*; *The Rhône and The Saône*; *The Sacred Wood*; *Decoration of the Great Hemicycle of the Sorbonne* [not included; admitted to participate in the awards].

Exhibits at the Exposition Centennale de l'Art Français, Palais du Champ-de-Mars: *Autumn*; *The Beheading of Saint John the Baptist*; *The Prodigal Son*; *Young Women by the Sea*; *The Life of Saint Genevieve*; four watercolor studies for the Hôtel de Ville of Poitiers. Jury member.

June-July Exhibition at the Durand-Ruel Gallery.

Paints: *The Allegory of the Sorbonne* [study] (Metropolitan Museum of Art, New York).

7 August Inauguration of the Sorbonne; made a Commander of the Légion d'honneur by the President of France, Sadi Carnot.

October Member of the jury for the competition for the Paris Hôtel de Ville.

Refuses a commission to represent the French Revolution.

Writes the sculptor Alexandre Falguière that his works are too dispersed to have him be a viable candidate for the Institut.

1890

15 May Foundation of the Société Nationale des Beaux-Arts. Meissonier is president; Puvis is vice-president.

Exhibits at the Salon of the Société Nationale des Beaux-Arts: *Inter Artes et Naturam* (Musée des Beaux-Arts, Rouen).

Exhibits at the Salon of the Société Lyonnaise des Beaux-Arts, Lyons (*hors concours*): *Portrait of Eugène Benon*; *Pottery* and *Ceramics* (Musée des Beaux-Arts, Rouen).

1891

Becomes president of the Société Nationale des Beaux-Arts, after the death of Meissonier.

Exhibits at the Salon of the Société Nationale des Beaux-Arts: *Summer* (Hôtel de Ville, Paris); *Pottery* and *Ceramics*. Rodin exhibits plaster bust of Puvis de Chavannes.

Paints: *Shepherd's Song* (Metropolitan Museum of Art, New York); *Sketch for 'Summer' for the Paris Hôtel de Ville* (Musée du Petit Palais, Paris); *Summer* (cat.134).

16 February Approached by Bordeaux to execute two monumental paintings for the anteroom to their museum (not executed).

30 April Commission for tapestries: *Joan of Arc at Vaucouleurs* and *Joan of Arc at Domrémy* (not executed).

First contact made by the Trustees of the Boston Public Library for a mural commission.

Mural Commission for the ceiling ensemble of the Paris Hôtel de Ville.

Installation of murals at Rouen.

1892

Exhibits at the Salon of the Société Nationale des Beaux-Arts: *Winter* (Hôtel de Ville, Paris).

22 October Presents his project for the ceiling ensemble of the Hôtel de Ville, Paris, to the Administrative Commission.

1893

10 May Exhibits at the Salon of the Société Nationale des Beaux-Arts: *Homage of Victor Hugo to the City of Paris* ['camaïeu'].

Paints: *Child Gathering Apples* or *The Goatherd* (cat. 138); *Normandy* (cat. 137).

20 March Commission for the Panthéon, Paris.

7 July Contract and submission of a mural project for the Boston Public Library.

1894

25 April Exhibits at the Salon of the Société Nationale des Beaux-Arts: 'Decoration Ensemble destined for the Stairway of the Prefecture of the [Paris] Hôtel de Ville. I. Ceiling: *Victor Hugo Offers His Lyre to the City of Paris*. II. Four Vaults: *(1) Patriotism; (2) Charity; (3) Artistic Ardor; (4) Intellectual Home III.* Six tympana: *(1) Intellect; (2) Fantasy; (3) Beauty; (4) Fearlessness; (5) Cult of Remembrance; (6) Urbanity.'*

Exhibits at the Salon of the Libre Esthétique, Brussels.

15 December-31 December Exhibits thirty-two works in New York, at the Durand-Ruel Galleries.

Paints: *Sketch for the Ceiling Ensemble of the Staircase of Honor in the Paris City Hall* (cat. 139); *Charity* (cat. 14).

1895

Exhibits at the Salon of the Société Nationale des Beaux-Arts: *The Inspiring Muses Acclaim the Spirit of Light* (installed at the Boston Public Library).

Paints: *The Inspiring Muses Acclaim the Spirit of Light* [reduced version] (p.c.).

Exhibits at the Biennale, Venice. Committee member.

15 January Large banquet honoring Puvis de Chavannes organized by the magazine *La Plume* and presided over by Auguste Rodin, with some six hundred people present.

October-4 December Victor Koos, Puvis's assistant, in Boston to supervise installation of Puvis de Chavannes's *Inspiring Muses.*

1896

25 April Exhibits at the Salon of the Société Nationale des Beaux-Arts: *Virgil* (*Bucolic Poetry*); *Aeschylus* (*Dramatic Poetry, Aeschylus and the Oceanids*); *Homer Crowned by the Iliad and the Odyssey*; *History* (*History Evokes the Past*); *Astronomy* (*The Chaldean Shepherds Observe the Journey of the Planets*) (all installed at the Boston Public Library); suite of drawings.

Attempts to resign the chair of president of the Société Nationale des Beaux-Arts.

September Exhibits at the Galerie Durand-Ruel, Paris: *Philosophy*, *Chemistry*, *Physics* (Boston Public Library).

Exhibits seven works at the Musée Rath, Geneva (along with works by Rodin and Carrière), including: *Virgil* [reduced versio] (cat. 144); *In the Heather, Nymphs* or *The Toilette of Thetys* (Art Institute of Chicago); *The Young Poet* (National Gallery, Oslo); *Study for 'Winter'* or *Winter* [reduced version] (National Gallery of Victoria, Melbourne).

Sick, he is cared for by the Princess Marie Cantacuzène.

1897

Exhibits at the Salon of the Société Nationale des Beaux-Arts (*hors catalogue*): *Ardent in her Faith and Charity, Genevieve, Not Deterred by the Greatest Perils from Her Task, Revitalizes Paris, Besieged and Menaced with Hunger* [cartoon] (National Gallery of Victoria, Melbourne).

Paints: *The Magdalene* (cat. 145).

March Approached to execute murals for the 'Marriage Chamber' of the Hôtel de Ville of Amiens.

June Moves to the home of the Princess Marie Cantacuzène at 89 avenue de Villiers, Paris.

21 July Marries Marie Cantacuzène.

August In an accident with a vehicle.

1898

January In an accident again.

1 May Exhibits at the Salon of the Société Nationale des Beaux-Arts: *Genevieve in her Pious Solicitude Watches over the Sleeping City* (installed at the Panthéon). (The Panthéon project is left unfinished at the death of the artist.)

29 August Death of the Princess Marie Cantacuzène.

24 October Death of Puvis de Chavannes.

27 October Burial of Puvis de Chavannes at Neuilly.

1899

1 May At the Salon of the Société Nationale des Beaux-Arts *Portrait of Mme Puvis de Chavannes, née Princess Cantacuzène.*

June-July Major retrospective at the Durand-Ruel Gallery, with 103 catalogue entries.

Rodin receives a commission for a commemorative sculpture honoring Puvis.

In accordance with the late artist's wish, his heirs donate a large number of his drawings to several French museums.

Selected Bibliography

Catalogues of exhibitions which included Puvis de Chavannes's works are cited under Selected Exhibitions. Other catalogues are listed here under the name of the city in which the exhibition originated. Titles of works that are pertinent only in very specific instances are not repeated in this bibliography.

Abbreviations used in this bibliography and elsewhere: AN = Archives Nationales, Paris; CMN = Archives de la Commission du Musée Napoléon, Régistres de Correspondance et Procès-verbaux des séances (1852-1964), Bibliothèque de la Société des Antiquaires de Picardie, Musée d'Amiens; n.d. = no date ; n.p. = no place of publication known /no pagination.

Adam, Marcelle *Les Caricatures de Puvis de Chavannes*. Paris, 1906.

Alexandre, Arsène 'Souvenirs sur Puvis de Chavannes.' *La Vie Artistique* (3 November 1898), n.p.

Alexandre, Arsène 'Puvis de Chavannes: sa vie et son oeuvre.' *Le Figaro Illustré*, no. 2 (February 1899), 21-44.

Alexandre, Arsène 'Lettres inédites de Puvis de Chavannes: Epoque de sa jeunesse.' *Le Magasin Pittoresque*, 67e année (15 June 1899), 186-188.

Alexandre, Arsène *Puvis de Chavannes*. London and New York, 1905.

Alexandre, Arsène 'Musée de Picardie, Amiens, Puvis de Chavannes.' *Les Arts*, XV (June 1918), 17-21.

Alexandre, Arsène 'Puvis de Chavannes glorifié; de Rodin à Desbois.' *Renaissance de l'Art* [the full title *Renaissance de l'Art français et des Industries de luxe* is not used here], (January 1925), 1-3.

Alexandre, Arsène 'Les Arts français à l'Age critique: les Salons de 1889 à 1900.' *Gazette des Beaux-Arts*, s6, CXXXIII (1934), 306-320.

Aman-Jean, Edmond-François 'Puvis de Chavannes.' *L'Art dans les Deux Mondes*, I (29 November 1890), 9-11.

Angrand, Pierre 'L'Etat mécène, période autoritaire du Second Empire (1851-1860).' *Gazette des Beaux-Arts*, s6, LXXI (May and June 1968), 303-348.

[Anonymous] 'The Atelier: Puvis de Chavannes.' *The Art Amateur* (December 1890), 5.

[Anonymous] 'Le Banquet Puvis de Chavannes.' *L'Artiste*, IX (January 1895), 45-57.

[Anonymous] 'La Succession de Puvis de Chavannes.' *Le Journal des Artistes* (27 November 1898), 2507-2508.

[Anonymous] 'Puvis de Chavannes.' *Masters in Art*, IV (October 1903), 381-420.

[Anonymous] 'Le Carnet d'un curieux, Puvis de Chavannes à Amiens.' *Renaissance de l'Art*, I (June 1918), 142-143.

[Anonymous] 'Puvis de Chavannes,' *Bulletin de la Société de l'Histoire d'Art Français* (1923), 381.

[Anonymous] 'La Célébration du Centenaire de Puvis de Chavannes.' *Beaux-Arts*, III (1 January 1925), 1-2.

[Anonymous] 'Notices from the Press: The Mural Painters' Exhibition.' *The Brooklyn Museum Quarterly*, XII (April 1925), 83-94.

[Anonymous] 'Vingt Renoirs pour un Puvis de Chavannes.' *Le Bulletin de l'Art* (July 1933), 336-337.

[Anonymous] 'L'Art moderne français dans les collections des musées étrangers: I. Musée d'Art Moderne Occidental à Moscou.' *Cahiers d'Art*, 25e année, II (1950), 335-348.

[Anonymous] 'Peaceful, Exotic, and Decorative; A Current Exhibition of 19th Century Art.' *Illustrated London News*, II (1 December 1951), 904-905.

Aquilino, Marie Jeannine 'Decoration by Design: The Development of the Mural Aesthetic in Nineteenth Century French Painting.' [Unpublished] Doctoral Dissertation, Brown University, 1989 [UMI Facsimile].

Argencourt, Louise d' 'Les peintures murales de Puvis de Chavannes au Musée de Picardie.' [Unpublished] Thèse du doctorat de troisième cycle, Université de Paris, Sorbonne, U.E.R., d'Histoire de l'Art, 1973.

Argencourt, Louise d' 'Puvis de Chavannes, 1824-1898.' *Journal of the National Gallery of Canada* (25 March 1977), 2-8.

Argencourt, Louise d' [see also 1976-77 Paris/Ottawa]

Armand, Edmond 'Puvis de Chavannes.' *Mois Littéraire et Pittoresque* (January-June 1899), 47-63.

Augagneur-Prost, Jean-Yves 'Sur quelques dessin inédits de Puvis de Chavannes.' *Travaux de l'Institut d'histoire de l'art de Lyon*, Cahier no. 14 (1991), 157-170.

Aynard, Edouard *Les Peintures décoratives de Puvis de Chavannes au Palais des Arts*. Lyons, 1884.

Aynard, Edouard 'Les Peintures décoratives de Puvis de Chavannes au Palais des Arts.' *Revue du Lyonnais*, II (September 1886), 241-258.

Azar, L. 'L'Art au Panthéon.' *L'Artiste*, XIII (February 1897), 81-98.

B.B. [Burroughs, Bryson] 'Two Paintings by Puvis de Chavannes,' *The Metropolitan Museum Bulletin*, XI (January 1916), 12-13.

Baignières, Arthur 'La Peinture décorative au XIXe siècle, M. Puvis de Chavannes.' *Gazette des Beaux-Arts*, s2, XXIII (May 1881), 416-426.

Barbier, Pierre 'Exposition de la Société des Amis des Arts; Salon de 1858.' *Revue du Lyonnais* (1858), 338-347.

Baud-Bovy, Daniel 'P. Puvis de Chavannes, E. Carrière, A. Rodin.' *Journal des Artistes*, I (8 March 1896), 1369-1370; II (22 March 1896), 1385-1387; III (5 April 1896), 1401-1402.

Baudelaire, Charles *Oeuvres complètes*. Paris, 1958. Cited as: *OC* (1958).

Baudin, Pierre 'Les Salons de 1904.' *Gazette des*

Beaux-Arts, s3, XXXI (May 1904), 365-371; (June 1904), 468-482.

Baudoüin, Paul 'Souvenirs sur Puvis de Chavannes.' E. Sarradin ed. *Gazette des Beaux-Arts*, s6, XIII (1935), 295-314.

Bénédite, Léonce 'L'Exposition des oeuvres de M. Puvis de Chavannes.' *L'Artiste*, s9, I (1888), 32-37.

Bénédite, Léonce 'Puvis de Chavannes.' *Art et Décoration*, IV (1898), 129-153.

Bénédite, Léonce [signed L. B.] 'Hommage à Puvis de Chavannes.' *Art et Décoration*, IV (November 1898), supplement, 1-2.

Bénédite, Léonce *Les Dessins de Puvis de Chavannes au Musée du Luxembourg, étude et catalogue des dessins exposés au Musée National du Luxembourg*. Paris, 1900.

Bénédite, Léonce 'Les Dessins de Puvis de Chavannes au Musée du Luxembourg.' *Revue de l'Art Ancien et Moderne*, VII (January 1900), 14-28.

Bénédite, Léonce 'A Propos des dessins de Puvis de Chavannes.' *Art et Décoration*, XVI (July 1904), 41-50.

Bénédite, Léonce 'La Légende de Sainte Geneviève.' *Art et Décoration*, XXV (May 1909), 137-152 and supplement (illustration).

Bénédite, Léonce 'Puvis de Chavannes et le Panthéon.' *Paris-Journal* (24 August 1910), 1.

Bénédite, Léonce '"L'Espérance" de Puvis de Chavannes au Musée du Luxembourg.' *Bulletin des Musées de France*, no. 6 (1913), 1-3.

Bénédite, Léonce *Notre art, nos maîtres: Puvis de Chavannes, Gustave Moreau, Burne-Jones, G.F. Watts*. Paris, 1922.

Bénédite, Léonce 'Le Centenaire de Puvis de Chavannes.' *Revue de l'Art Ancien et Moderne*, XLVI, no. 261 (December 1924), 386-388.

Bénédite, Léonce *Théodore Chassériau, sa vie et son oeuvre*. 2 vols. Paris, n.d. [ca. 1931]. Cited as: Bénédite [1931].

Benjamin, Roger 'The Decorative Landscape, Fauvism, and the Arabesque of Observation.' *The Art Bulletin*, LXXV (June 1993), 295-316.

Béraud, Henry 'Puvis de Chavannes.' In *Peintres Lyonnais*, Lyons, 1910, pp. 29-38.

Berger, Klaus 'Ingrism and Pre-Raphaelitism.' *Actes du 19e Congrès International d'Histoire de l'Art* (8-15 September, 1958), pp. 479-486.

Bergerat, Emile 'Un Grotesque de la peinture.' *Le Journal* (1 November 1898), n.p.

Bergerat, Emile *Souvenirs d'un enfant de Paris*. Vol. IV. Paris, 1911.

Bernac, Jean 'The New Style of M. Puvis de Chavannes.' *Art Journal* (1895), 47-48.

Bernard, Emile 'Puvis de Chavannes.' *L'Occident* (December 1903), 273-280.

Beulé, Charles *La Peinture décorative et le grand art*. Paris, 1860.

Biagetta, B. 'Puvis de Chavannes.' *Arte Cristiana*, Anno V (15 May 1917), 130-140.

Bigot, Charles 'Le Salon de 1883,' *Gazette des Beaux-Arts*, s2, XXVII (June 1883), 457-476; s2, XXVIII (July 1883), 5-23.

Blanc, Charles *Grammaire des arts du dessin*. Paris, 1867. 3rd ed. Paris, 1876.

Blanc, Charles *Les artistes de mon temps*. Paris, 1876.

Blanche, Jacques-Emile 'La Peinture murale de la IIIe République: Puvis de Chavannes, Albert Besnard, Alfred Rolle, Duez, Gervex, Martin, Eugène Carrière.' *Art Vivant* (1929), 839-840, 881-882.

Boime, Albert *Thomas Couture and the Eclectic Vision*. New Haven and London, 1980.

Borel, Dominique 'Puvis de Chavannes Dessinateur: La Collection de Lyon.' *Travaux de l'Institut d'Histoire de l'Art de Lyon*, Cahier no. 10 (1986), 93-99.

Boucher, Marie-Christine 'La Décoration de Puvis de Chavannes pour l'Hôtel Vignon.' *La Revue du Louvre et des Musées de France*, XXVIIIe année, no. 2 (1978), 98-106.

Boucher, Marie-Christine *Catalogue des Dessins et Peintures de Puvis de Chavannes*. Palais des Beaux-Arts de la Ville de Paris, Musée du Petit Palais, Paris, 1979.

Bouret, Jean 'Les Dessins de Puvis de Chavannes exposées à la Galerie des Garets.' *Beaux-Arts* (28 May 1948), 3.

Bouret, Jean 'Puvis de Chavannes, Exposition, Galerie des Garets.' *Beaux-Arts* (4 June 1948), 1, 5.

Bourget, J.L. 'Puvis de Chavannes, la peinture claire.' *Vie des Arts* (Spring 1977), 40-42.

Bouyer, Raymond 'Puvis de Chavannes au Musée d'Amiens.' *Renaissance de l'Art*, IV (August 1921), 434-437.

Bouyer, Raymond 'Le Centenaire de Puvis de Chavannes.' *Bulletin de l'Art Ancien et Moderne*, XXVI (December 1924), 275-276.

Bouyer, Raymond 'Le Centenaire de Puvis de Chavannes.' *Le Figaro Artistique*, 2e année (11 December 1924), 129-134.

Bouyer, Raymond 'Hommage à Puvis de Chavannes.' *Bulletin de l'Art Ancien et Moderne*, XXXV (April 1933), 172-173.

Bouyer, Raymond 'Puvis de Chavannes et Hans von Marées.' *Beaux-Arts* (1 October 1937), 1, 2.

Bradley, William Aspen 'Some French Artists During the Siege and Commune.' *The Print Collectors Quarterly*, VI (1916), 190-194.

Bréghot du Lut, F. *Le Peintre Puvis de Chavannes: Son oeuvre et sa famille*. Lyons, 1899.

Bréghot du Lut, F. 'Pierre Puvis de Chavannes.' *Revue du Lyonnais*, XXVII (1899), 266-280, 386-402.

Breton, Jules *Nos peintres du siècle*. Paris, n.d. [1899].

Bricon, Etienne 'Puvis de Chavannes.' *L'Artiste*, s10, I (1898), 289-312.

Briend, Christian 'Un décorateur méconnu, disciple de Puvis de Chavannes.' In *Francis Auburtin, 1866-1930. Le symboliste de la mer*. Paris, n.d. [ca. 1991], pp. 45-63.

Brown Price, Aimée [see Price, Aimée Brown]

Buisson, J. 'Le Salon de 1881.' *Gazette des Beaux-Arts*, s2, XXIII (June 1881), 473-513.

Buisson, J. 'Pierre Puvis de Chavannes - Souvenirs intimes.' *Gazette des Beaux-Arts*, s3, XXII (July 1899), 5-20; (September 1899), 208-225.

Bürger, W. [pseud. of E.J.T. Thoré] *Salons de W. Bürger, 1861 à 1868*. 2 vols. Paris, 1870.

Burkom, Frans van 'Puvis de Chavannes. Ste Geneviève, als kind, in gebed.' *Jong Holland*, no. 4 (1993), 15-19.

Burroughs, Bryson 'Lecture to Art Students.' ['Puvis de Chavannes'] (1915) [unpublished manuscript], Metropolitan Museum of Art Library, New York.

Burroughs, Bryson 'A Loan from the French Government.' *The Metropolitan Museum of Art Bulletin*, XXI (March 1926), 68-72.

Burroughs, Bryson 'The Paintings; The Theodore M. Davis Bequest.' *The Metropolitan Museum of Art Bulletin* (March 1931), 14-16.

Burroughs, Bryson [See also B.B.]

Burty, Philippe 'Exposition de la Société des Amis des Arts de Bordeaux.' *Gazette des Beaux-Arts*, XXIV (1 May 1868), 496-500.

Burty, Philippe 'L'Escalier du Musée de Lyon; Peintures décoratives par P. Puvis de Chavannes.' *L'Express de Lyon* (9 March 1886), n.p.

C., L. 'Studies for the Childhood of St. Geneviève, Puvis de Chavannes.' *Bulletin of the Art Institute of Chicago*, XVIII (January 1924), 117-120.

Cafritz, Robert C., Lawrence Gowing and David Rosand *Places of Delight. The Pastoral Landscape*. Washington, 1988 [published in conjunction with 1988-89, Washington, National Gallery of Art / Phillips Collection, *The Pastoral Landscape: The Legacy of Venice and the Modern Vision*].

Cardon, Emile 'Artistes contemporains, esquisses et portraits, Puvis de Chavannes.' *Moniteur des Arts* (15 September 1895).

Cartwright, Julia 'Puvis de Chavannes.' *Art Journal* (1896), 190-192.

Castagnary, Jules Antoine *Salons, 1857-1879*. 2 vols. Paris, 1892.

Chagny, André 'Puvis de Chavannes: sa jeunesse et ses années de formation.' *L'Echo des Lettres et des Arts* (15 September 1959), n.p.

Chagny, André 'Puvis de Chavannes: Le triomphe: d'Amiens au Panthéon et à Lyon.' *L'Echo des Lettres et des Arts* (22 September 1959), 6.

Chagny, André 'Le Centenaire de Puvis de Chavannes.' *La Vie lyonnaise* [n.d.], 29-34.

Champeaux, A. de *Histoire de la peinture décorative*. Paris, 1890.

Champeaux, A. de *L'Art décoratif dans le vieux Paris*. Paris, 1898.

Chassé, Charles 'Le Mouvement symboliste dans la peinture du XIXe siècle.' *Mercure de France*, CCLXXXVI (15 September 1938), 513-531.

Chassé, Charles *Le Mouvement symboliste dans l'art du XIXe siècle*. Paris, 1947.

Chastel, André 'Au Seuil du XXe siècle: Seurat et Gauguin.' *Art de France*, II (1962), 297-305.

Chaumelin, Marius *L'Art contemporain: la peinture à l'exposition universelle de 1867, Salons de 1868, 1869, 1870*. Paris, 1873.

Chavana, René 'Les Expositions: les Salons de 1924.' *Beaux-Arts* (15 May 1924), 156-158.

Chennevières, Charles Philippe, Marquis de 'Souvenirs d'un Directeur des Beaux-Arts.' *L'Artiste* (March 1883), 159-175; (June 1883), 403-412; (September 1884), 180-204; (October 1884), 257-276; (December 1884), 413-433; last three reprinted in *Les décorations du Panthéon*. Paris, 1885.

Chennevières, Charles Philippe, Marquis de *Souvenirs d'un Directeur des Beaux-Arts*. [reprint of articles in *L'Artiste*, January 1883 - March 1889] Paris, 1979.

Claretie, Jules *Peintres et sculpteurs contemporains*. Paris, 1874.

Claretie, Jules 'Mourning for Puvis de Chavannes.' *Athenaeum* (1898), 614, 644.

Codet, Georges 'Puvis de Chavannes, le fils de l'air.' *Revue des Beaux-Arts et des Lettres* (1 May 1899), 228.

Cogniat, Raymond 'Au Musée Galliera: Puvis de Chavannes.' *Les Arts Plastiques*, s5 (1952), 384-385.

Comte, Jules 'Salon de 1884.' *L'Illustration* (3 May 1884), 283-291, repr. 288.

Comte, Jules 'Salon de 1886: la peinture.' *L'Illustration* (1 May 1886), 282.

Conrad, Michael George 'Puvis de Chavannes und Felicien Rops.' *Gesellschaft* (1899), 34-38.

Cortissoz, Royal *Personalities in Art*. New York and London, 1925.

Cox, Kenyon 'Puvis de Chavannes.' *The Century Magazine*, LX (February 1895), 558-569.

Cox, Kenyon *The Classic Point of View*. New York, 1911.

Crastre, François *Puvis de Chavannes*. Paris, n.d. (English ed. transl. Frederic Taber Cooper. New York, 1912.)

D., Ch. 'Les Doctrines esthétiques de Puvis de Chavannes.' *Le Salut Public* [Lyons] (29 October 1898), 1-2.

Darcel, Alfred 'Le Salon des Arts Décoratifs.' *Gazette des Beaux-Arts*, s2, XXV (June 1882), 583-595.

Dargenty, G. 'Exposition des oeuvres de M. Puvis de Chavannes.' *Courrier de l'Art* (16 December 1887), 393-394.

Davies, Martin and Cecil Gould *National Gallery catalogues. French School. Early Nineteenth Century*. London, 1970.

Dayot, Armand *L'Invasion, Le Siège, La Commune, 1870-1871*. Paris, 1901.

Declairieux, A. *Puvis de Chavannes et ses oeuvres*. Lyons, 1928.

Delaborde, Henri 'La Peinture religieuse en France. M. Hippolyte Flandrin.' *Revue des Deux Mondes* (15 December 1859), 862-892.

Delaney, Caroline White 'Puvis de Chavannes and American Mural Painters.' [Unpublished] M.A. Thesis, New York University, 1939.

Delaroche-Vernet, Marie 'Deux portraits de Puvis de Chavannes.' *Bulletin des Musées de France*, 2e année (July 1930), 143-144.

Delbarre, P. 'Puvis de Chavannes.' *Les Contemporains* [special issue devoted to Puvis de Chavannes], VIII (26 August 1900), n.p.

Delteil, Loys *Manuel de l'amateur d'estampes du XIXe et du XXe siècles*. 2 vols. Paris, 1925.

Denis, Maurice 'Définition du Néo-Traditionnisme.' First published under the pseudonym Pierre Louis in *Art et Critique* (23 and 30 August 1890), 540-542.

Denis, Maurice 'Les Elèves d'Ingres.' *L'Occident*, II (1902), 23-34, 77-112, 142-158.

Denis, Maurice *Théories, 1890-1910*. Paris, 1912; 2nd ed. Paris, 1913; 4th ed. Paris, 1920.

Denis, Maurice 'Puvis de Chavannes.' *Revue Hebdomadaire*, XII (December 1924), 5-12.

Denis, Maurice 'L'Epoque du Symbolisme.' *Gazette des Beaux-Arts*, s6, XI (March 1934), 165-179.

Denis, Maurice 'Ne Vocemini Magistri.' *L'Art Sacré*, I (July 1935), 8-9.

Denis, Maurice *L'Histoire d'art religieux*. Paris, 1939.

Denis, Maurice *Journal*. 3 vols. Paris, 1957-1959.

Denis, Maurice *Théories. Du symbolisme au classicisme*. O. Revault d'Allones, ed. Paris, 1964.

Denoinville, Georges 'Le Banquet de demain.' *Le Journal des Artistes*, 14e année (13 January 1895), 891.

Dessins de Puvis de Chavannes offerts par sa famille à la Ville de Paris. [summary catalogue published on the occasion of the exhibition of the drawings at the Musée Galliera, Paris, 1899].

Desvernay, Félix 'M. Puvis de Chavannes.' *Lyon-Revue*, I (March 1884), 167-169.

Desvernay, Félix 'Les Peintures de la Sorbonne, décoration de l'hémicycle confiée au Lyonnais Puvis de Chavannes.' *Lyon-Revue*, II (July 1886), 62-65.

Dorbec, Prosper 'La Tradition classique dans le paysage au milieu du dix-neuvième siècle.' *Revue de l'Art Ancien et Moderne* XXIV (October 1908), 259-273; (November 1908), 357-368.

Dorbec, Prosper *L'Art du paysage en France: Essay sur son évolution de la fin du XVIIIe siècle à la fin du Second Empire*. Paris, 1925.

Driskel, Michael Paul 'Hippolyte Flandrin and the Mural Painting of the "Renouveau Catholique": The Origin and Meaning of the Hieratic Style of Religious Art in the Nineteenth Century.' [Unpublished] Doctoral Dissertation, University of California, Berkeley, 1980.

Druick, Douglas W. 'Puvis and the Printed Image 1862-1898.' *Nouvelles de l'Estampe*, nos. 34-35 (July-October 1977), 27-35.

Durand-Tahier, H. 'Puvis de Chavannes.' *La Plume* (15-31 January 1895), 27-37.

Duvauchel, Léon 'Ave Picardia Nutrix.' *La Plume* (15-31 January 1895), 38-40.

E. 'Inauguration des peintures de M. Puvis de Chavannes au Musée d'Amiens.' *Chronique des Arts et de la Curiosité* (11 February 1888), 43-44.

Edwards, A. Trystan 'The Mural Decorations of Puvis de Chavannes.' *Architectural Review* [England], XXXVII (May 1915), 85-88; XXXVIII (October 1915), 65-67.

Essarts, Emmanuel des 'De la mélancolie.' *L'Artiste* (1 June 1896), 326-335.

Fabré, Abel 'Puvis de Chavannes.' *Pages d'Art Chrétien*, s4 (1913), 81-90.

Fénéon, Félix *Les Impressionnistes en 1886*. Paris, 1886.

Feydy, Jacques 'Autour du "misérabilisme" de Chateaubriand à Bernard Buffet.' *L'Information Culturelle Artistique*, I, no. 1 (1955-56), 14-21.

Fierens-Gevaert, H. 'L'Hôtel de Ville de Paris.' *Revue de l'art Ancien et Moderne* (October 1899), 281-298; (December 1899), 475-496; (March 1901), 192-210; (April 1901), 193-201, 281-301.

Flagler, Henry Harkness *The Story of a Dream: As It Was Told to the Friends of Mr. Walpole at the Club of Odd Volumes*. Dover, Mass., 1923.

Flament, André *Les Grandes heures de Paris: l'Hôtel de Ville et la Place de la Grève*. Paris, 1966.

Flandreysy, Jeanne de 'La Femme dans l'oeuvre de Puvis de Chavannes.' *Le Figaro*, n.d. [ca. April 1907], n.p.

Flandreysy, Jeanne de 'Les Puvis de Chavannes du Musée de Lyon.' *Le Figaro* (6 April 1907), n.p.

Flat, Paul 'Dessins de Puvis de Chavannes.' *Revue Bleue*, XIII (17 February 1900), 222-223.

Florisoone, Charles 'Puvis de Chavannes.' *Conférence des Rosati Picards*, III (29 October 1898), 5-23.

Fontainas, André and Louis Vauxcelles *Histoire générale de l'art français de la Révolution à nos jours*. Rev. ed. Paris, 1922.

Forges, Marie-Thérèse Lemoyne de 'Un Nouveau tableau de Puvis de Chavannes au Musée du Louvre.' *La Revue du Louvre et des Musées de France*, XXe année, nos. 4-5 (1970), 241-252.

Fosca, François 'Retour à Puvis; à propos de l'Exposition des Quatre-Chemins.' *Beaux-Arts* (24 March 1933), 1, 6.

Foucart, Bruno *Le Renouveau de la peinture religieuse en France (1800-1860)*. Paris, 1987.

Foucart, Jacques 'Puvis de Chavannes.' *Le Petit Journal des Grandes Expositions*, N.S., 41 (November, 1976), 3.

Foucart, Jacques 'Le beau peintre harmonieux des cygnes ... ou le charme de la nostalgie.' In *Francis Auburtin, 1866-1930. Le symboliste de la mer*, Paris, n.d. [ca. 1991], pp. 27-31.

Foucart, Jacques [see also 1976-77 Paris/Ottawa]

Foucart-Borville, Jacques *La Genèse des peintures murales de Puvis de Chavannes au Musée de Picardie*. Amiens, 1976.

Fougerat, Emmanuel de 'Puvis de Chavannes.' *Drogues et Peintures*, no. 9 (1955), n.p.

Fourcaud, Louis de 'Notes sur quelques décorateurs: Pierre Puvis de Chavannes.' *Revue des Arts Décoratifs*, IX (1888-89), 1-10, 74-81.

Fourcaud, Louis de 'Puvis de Chavannes.' *Revue Illustrée*, XVIII (15 May 1894), 365-375.

Fourcaud, Louis de 'Puvis de Chavannes.' *Le Gaulois* (26 October 1898), n.p.

Fourcaud, Louis de 'Au Tombeau de Puvis de Chavannes.' *Le Gaulois* (24 October 1908), 1.

Fry, Roger 'The Sir Hugh Lane Pictures at the National Gallery.' *The Burlington Magazine*, XXX (April 1917), 147-153.

G., H. [Galtier, Hermann] 'Les Dessins de Puvis de Chavannes au Luxembourg.' *Chronique des Arts et de la Curiosité* (20 January 1900), 21-22.

Gaehtgens, Thomas 'Puvis de Chavannes.' *Kunstchronik* (April 1977), 189-196.

Gaillard de Champris, Henry 'Pour le monument de Puvis de Chavannes.' *Le Correspondant*, CCXXXIII, n.s. 197 (10 November 1908), 574-587.

Galtier, Hermann 'Puvis de Chavannes, intime. Documents inédits.' *Revue mondiale*, CLXII (1 December 1924), 262-274.

Galtier, Hermann [see also H. G]

Gautier, Théophile 'La Croix de Berny.' *La Presse* (31 January 1847), 1-2.

Gautier, Théophile 'L'Art en 1848.' *L'Artiste*, s5, I (15 May 1848), 113-115.

Gautier, Théophile 'Palais du Quai d'Orsay. Peintures murales de M. Théodore Chassériau.' *La Presse* (12 December 1848), 1.

Gautier, Théophile *L'Art moderne*. 2 vols. Paris, 1856.

Gautier, Théophile *Les Beaux-Arts en Europe en 1855*. 2 vols. Paris, 1856.

Gautier, Théophile *Histoire de l'art moderne*. Paris, 1856.

Gautier, Théophile *Abécédaire du Salon de 1861*. Paris, 1861.

Gautier, Théophile 'Peintures décoratives de M. Paul Baudry, Salon de M. le Duc de Galiera.' *L'Artiste*, s8, III (1 March 1863), 100-101.

Gautier, Théophile 'Salon de 1863.' *Le Moniteur Universel* (23 May 1863), 801.

Gautier, Théophile *Tableaux de siège, Paris, 1870-1871*. Paris, 1871.

Gautier, Théophile 'Puvis de Chavannes.' *Revue Populaire des Beaux-Arts* (12 February 1898), 270-271.

Geffroy, Gustave *La Vie artistique*. 8 vols. Paris, 1892-1903. [see in particular IV (1895), 127-140].

Geffroy, Gustave 'Puvis de Chavannes.' *La Revue des Beaux-Arts et des Lettres* (1 May 1899), 226-229.

Genet-Delacroix, Marie-Claude 'L'Esthétique officielle et art national sous la Troisième République.' *Le Mouvement sociale*, no. 131 (April-June 1985), 105-120.

Genet-Delacroix, Marie-Claude *Art et état sous la IIIième République. Le système des Beaux-Arts 1870-1940*. Paris, 1992.

Gensel, Walther 'Puvis de Chavannes.' *Deutsche Rundschau* (August 1897), 278-293.

Gensel, Walther 'Wort über Puvis de Chavannes.' *Kunsthalle* [?] (1899), n.p.

Germain, Alphonse 'Théorie des déformateurs.' *La Plume*, IIIe année (1891), 289-290.

Germain, Alphonse 'Le Paysage décoratif.' *L'Ermitage* (November 1891), 641-668.

Germain, Alphonse 'Anecdotes sur Puvis de Chavannes.' *La Plume* (15-31 January 1895), 41-42.

Germain, Alphonse 'Les Artistes lyonnais.' *Gazette des Beaux-Arts*, s3, XXXVIII (November 1907), 424-437.

Germer, Stefan *Historizität und Autonomie. Studien zu Wandbildern im Frankreich des 19. Jahrhunderts: Ingres, Chassériau, Chenavard und Puvis de Chavannes*. Hildesheim, Zürich, New York, 1988.

Gimpel, René *Journal d'un collectionneur marchand de tableaux*. Paris, 1963.

Godet, Pierre 'Puvis de Chavannes et la peinture d'aujourd'hui.' *L'Art Décoratif*, XXVII (20 January 1912), 37-52.

Goffic, Charles le 'Le Hasard chez Puvis de Chavannes.' *Le Mémorial d'Amiens* (27 October 1898), n.p.

Gogh, Vincent van *Verzamelde brieven*. 4 vols. Amsterdam and Antwerpen, 1953-1954.

Gogh, Vincent van *The Complete Letters*. Transl. Mrs. J. van Gogh Bonger and Mr. D. de Dood. 3 vols. Greenwich, 1958.

Golberg, Mécislas *Puvis de Chavannes*. Paris, 1901.

Goldwater, Robert 'Puvis de Chavannes: Some Reasons for a Reputation.' *Art Bulletin*, XXVIII (March 1946), 33-43.

Graul, Richard 'Pierre Puvis de Chavannes.' *Zeitschrift für Bildende Kunst*, X (1899), 86-92.

Greenwood, M. 'Gentle Olympian: Pierre Puvis de Chavannes.' *Artscanada*, XXXIV (October-November 1977), 21-34.

Grimm, Thomas 'Une Vie et une oeuvre.' *Petit Journal* (1 January 1896), 2.

Grinten, E.F. van der 'Puvis de Chavannes, 1824-1898, animateur des murailles.' In *Actes du XXIIe Congrès International d'Histoire de l'Art*, vol. II, Budapest, 1972, pp. 303-308.

Guigou, Paul 'Puvis de Chavannes.' *Revue du Siècle*, VI (January 1892), 1-17.

Guigou, Paul [two articles without title] *La Cocarde* (ca. 16 January 1895), n.p.

Guigou, Paul 'Les Entretiens de Puvis de Chavannes.' In *Interrupta*, Paris, 1898, pp. 261-279.

Guillemot, Maurice 'De l'Ile de la Jatte au Panthéon.' *Commission Municipale Historique et Artistique de Neuilly-sur Seine: Bulletin* (1922), 39-46.

Guillemot, Maurice 'Dessins de maîtres: Puvis de Chavannes.' *La Vie Moderne* [clipping, n.d.], 461.

Guiral, Pierre '"Marseille, Porte de l'Orient" par Puvis de Chavannes.' *Arts et Livres de Provence*, no. 23 (1954), 78-80.

Halluin, D.D. 'Quelques notes d'art à propos de Puvis de Chavannes par un peintre.' *La Revue de Lille* (December 1898-February 1899), 1-25.

Herbert, Robert L. 'Seurat and Puvis de Chavannes.' *Yale University Art Gallery Bulletin*, XXV (October 1959), 22-29.

Hutchins, Will 'Two Composition Sketches by Puvis de Chavannes.' *Art and Understanding*, I (March 1930), 230-239.

Huysmans, Joris-Karl *L'Art moderne*. Paris, 1883.

Huysmans, Joris-Karl *Certains*. Paris, 1889.

Imbert, Daniel 'L'Hôtel de Ville de Paris: genèse républicaine d'un grand décor.' and 'Les décors de L'Hôtel de Ville.' In 1986-87 Paris, pp. 63-71 and 285-288, 279-280 respectively.

Ishikawa, Joseph 'Moderne malgré Lui: The Phenomenon of Puvis de Chavannes.' *Art Journal*, XXVII, no. 4 (Summer 1968), 381-386.

Janneau, Guillaume 'Puvis de Chavannes.' *Bulletin de la Vie Artistique*, V (15 December 1924), 543-545.

Jean, René *Puvis de Chavannes*. Paris, 1914, republished 1925.

Jirat-Wasiutynski, Vojtech 'Puvis de Chavannes at Ottawa.' *Revue d'art canadienne/Canadian Art Review*, IV, no. 2 (1977), 99-101.

Johnson, Una E. *Ambroise Vollard, Editeur: Prints, Books, Bronzes*. New York, 1977.

Johnston, William R. '"L'Espérance" of Puvis de Chavannes.' *Bulletin of the Walters Art Gallery*, XXI (January 1969), 2-4.

Jullian, Camille 'Sainte Geneviève à Nanterre.' *Mélanges offerts à M. Gustave Schlumberger*. Paris, 1924. II, 372-375.

Jullian, P. 'Je parie sur Puvis.' *Connaissance des Arts* (December 1972), 108-117.

Jullian, P. *The Symbolists*. London, 1973.

Jullian, René 'l'Oeuvre de jeunesse de Puvis de Chavannes.' *Gazette des Beaux-Arts*, s6, XX (November 1938), 237-250.

Kahn, Gustave 'Exposition Puvis de Chavannes.' *La Revue Indépendante de littérature et d'art*, VI (January 1888), 142-146.

Karageorgevitch, Prince Bojidar 'Puvis de Chavannes.' *Magazine of Art*, XVII (1894), 73-79.

Karageorgevitch, Prince Bojidar 'Two Great French Artists: A Review; Puvis de Chavannes and Détaille.' *Magazine of Art*, XXII (1898), 659-666.

Keeler, Clinton 'Narrative Without Accent: Willa Cather and Puvis de Chavannes.' *American Quarterly*, XVIII, no. 1 (Spring 1965), 119-126.

Kocks, Dirk 'Puvis de Chavannes oder der humanistische Traum von Arkadien: Grand Palais, Paris, Austellung.' *Pantheon*, XXXV (April 1977), 164-165.

Lacambre, Geneviève and Elisabeth Walter 'Tendances de la Fin du XIXe siècle.' *Etudes de la Revue du Louvre et des Musées de France*, I (1980), 186-189.

La Farge, John 'Puvis de Chavannes.' *Scribner's Magazine*, XXVIII (1900), 672-684.

Lambeau, Lucien *L'Hôtel de Ville de Paris*. Paris, 1908.

Lane, Sir Hugh 'Acquisitions of the National Gallery, London.' *The Connoisseur*, LVII (1920), 180-183.

Larroumet, Gustave *L'Art et l'état en France*. Paris, 1895.

Larroumet, Gustave 'M. Puvis de Chavannes.' In *Etudes de Littérature et d'Art*, Paris, 1895, III, pp. 271-296.

Larroumet, Gustave 'M. Puvis de Chavannes.' *La Vie Contemporaine*, I (15 January 1895), 185-204.

Lechat, Henri 'Puvis de Chavannes au Musée de Lyon: la décoration de l'escalier neuf du Palais des Arts.' *Gazette des Beaux-Arts*, s5, II (October 1920), 234-248; (November 1920), 309-316.

Lecomte, Georges 'Nos chefs-d'oeuvre de peinture décorative.' *Renaissance de l'Art*, I

(September 1918), 254-260.

Levêque, Jean-Jacques 'Au Grand Palais, Puvis de Chavannes L'Imagier des vertus civiques.' *Quotidien de Paris* (27 November 1876), n.p.

Liere, Eldon N. van 'Solutions and Dissolutions: The Bather in 19th C. French Painting.' *Arts Magazine*, LIV (May 1980), 104-114.

Lostalot, Alfred de 'Puvis de Chavannes.' *L'Illustration*, CV, no. 2708 (19 January 1895), 43, repr. 45.

Louis, Pierre [see Denis, Maurice]

Low, Will Hickock 'The Mural Paintings in the Panthéon and the Hôtel de Ville of Paris.' *Scribner's Magazine*, XII (December 1892), 661-677.

Low, Will Hickock 'A Century of Painting, Puvis de Chavannes.' *McClure's Magazine*, VIII (April 1897), 472-482.

M., T.A. 'M. Puvis de Chavannes.' *Courrier de l'Art*, 8e année (24 February 1888), 58-60.

Malitourne, Pierre 'Art monumental. Les Peintures de M. Théodore Chassériau au palais d'Orsay.' *L'Artiste*, s5, II (15 December 1848), 123-125.

Mandach, Conrad de and L. Wehrlé 'Lettres de Puvis de Chavannes.' *La Revue de Paris*, X (15 December 1910), 673-694; XI (1 February 1911), 449-477.

Mantz, Paul 'Salon de 1863.' *Gazette des Beaux-Arts*, XVI (1 June 1863), 481-506.

Mantz, Paul 'Salon de 1865.' *Gazette des Beaux-Arts*, XVIII (1 June 1865), 489-523.

Mantz, Paul 'Salon de 1867.' *Gazette des Beaux-Arts*, XXII (1 June 1867), 513-548.

Mantz, Paul 'Salon de 1869.' *Gazette des Beaux-Arts*, s2, I (1 June 1869), 489-511.

Marks, Montague 'My Note-Book.' *Art Amateur*, XXXVII (August 1897), 24.

Marks, Montague 'The Technic of Puvis de Chavannes.' *Art Amateur*, XXXVII (October 1897), 67-68.

Marlais, Michael 'Seurat et ses amis de l'Ecole des Beaux-Arts.' *Gazette des Beaux-Arts*, s6, CXIV (October 1989), 153-168.

Marthold, Jules 'Sainte Geneviève: Panthéon.' *La Plume* (15-31 January 1895), 37-38.

Martinie, H. 'Puvis de Chavannes.' *Cicerone*, XVII (1 January 1925), 10-16.

Martino, Pierre *Parnasse et symbolisme*. 11th ed. Paris, 1925.

Marty, André 'Puvis de Chavannes.' *Bulletin de la Vie Artistique*, V (15 December 1924), 545-546.

Marx, Roger 'Puvis de Chavannes.' *L'Art et ses Amateurs* (7 November 1898), 1-2.

Marx, Roger 'Puvis de Chavannes.' *La Revue Encyclopédique* (23 December 1899), 1078-1080.

Marx, Roger 'Cartons d'artiste: Puvis de Chavannes.' *L'Image* (July 1917), 241-247.

Marx, Roger 'Le Retour à Puvis.' *Nouvelles Littéraires* (26 February 1938), n.p.

Mathieu, Pierre-Louis 'Puvis de Chavannes ou le peintre et son mur.' *L'Oeil* (November 1976), 20-27.

Mauclair, Camille [pseudonym of Camille Faust] 'La Réforme de l'art décoratif en France.' *La Nouvelle Revue* (February 1896), 724-746.

Mauclair, Camille [pseudonym of Camille Faust] 'Puvis de Chavannes.' *La Nouvelle Revue*, XVIII (15 June 1899), 661-673.

Mauclair, Camille [pseudonym of Camille Faust] 'The Decorators.' In *The Great French Painters and the Evolution of French Painting from 1830 to the Present Day*, London, 1903, pp. 135-154.

Mauclair, Camille [pseudonym of Camille Faust] 'Puvis de Chavannes and Gustave Moreau.' *International Quarterly*, XII (October 1905), 240-254.

Mauclair, Camille [pseudonym of Camille Faust] 'Souvenirs sur Puvis.' *Dépêche de Toulouse* (15 February 1922), n.p. [clipping file, Musée Rodin, Paris].

Mauclair, Camille [pseudonym of Camille Faust] *Puvis de Chavannes*. Paris, 1928.

Mazars, Pierre 'Puvis de Chavannes sort du bois sacré.' *Figaro* (28 December 1976), n.p.

McMullen, Roy *Degas: His Life, Times and Work*. Boston, 1984; London, 1985.

Meissonier, Jean-Louis-Ernest *Funérailles célébrées le 3 février 1891. Discours de M.L. Bourgeois le Cte. Délaborde, Allocution de Puvis de Chavannes*. Paris, n.d. [1891].

Ménard, René 'Les Théoriciens de l'art.' *L'Artiste*, s9, IV (1868), 385-418.

Ménard, René 'L'Enseignement de l'art décoratif à l'Ecole des Beaux-Arts.' *L'Art*, V (1876), 210-214, 230-232.

Mérimée, Prosper 'De la Peinture murale et de son emploi dans l'architecture moderne.' *La Revue générale de l'architecture et des travaux publics*. IX (1851), 258-275, 327-337.

Meyer-Graefe, I. 'From Poussin to Maurice Denis.' *Mir Iscousstva*, IX (1903), 130-136.

Michel, André 'L'Exposition de M. Puvis de Chavannes.' *Gazette des Beaux-Arts*, s2, XXXVII (January 1888), 36-44.

Michel, André 'La Décoration de l'Hôtel de Ville de Paris,' *Gazette des Beaux-Arts*, s2, XXXIX (January 1889), 51-56.

Michel, André 'Puvis de Chavannes.' *Die Graphischen Künste*, XIV (1891), 37-55.

Michel, André 'L'Oeuvre de Puvis de Chavannes.' In *Notes sur l'art moderne (Peinture)*, Paris, 1896, pp. 139-161.

Michel, André and Jean Laran *Puvis de Chavannes*. Paris, 1911; Philadelphia and London, 1912.

Michelet, Emile 'Le Banquet Puvis de Chavannes.' *Le Gaulois* (17 January 1895), 3.

Milner, John *The Studios of Paris, The Capital of Art in the Late Nineteenth Century*. New Haven and London, 1988.

Mirbeau, Octave 'Puvis de Chavannes.' *La France* (8 November 1884), 2-3.

Mitchell, Claudine 'Time and the Idea of Patriarchy in the Pastorals of Puvis de Chavannes.' *Art History*, X (June 1987), 188-202.

Monod, François 'Exposition centennale de l'art français à St. Petersbourg.' *Gazette des Beaux-Arts*, s4, VII (April 1912), 301-326.

Morhardt, Mathias 'Le Banquet de Puvis de Chavannes.' *Mercure de France*, CCLXI (1 August 1935), 499-531.

Morice, Bernard *Paris en son Hôtel de Ville*. Paris, 1974.

Morice, Charles 'A Puvis de Chavannes.' *Mercure de France*, XIII (February 1895), frontispiece, n.p.

Morisot, Berthe *Correspondance*. Documents réunis et présentés par Denis Rouart. Paris, 1950.

Mourey, Gabriel 'Sketches by Puvis de Chavannes.' *The Studio*, XVIII, no. 79 (October 1889), 12-19.

Mourey, Gabriel 'Puvis de Chavannes.' *The Studio* (March 1895), 170-180.

Mourey, Gabriel 'Some French Artists at Home.' *The Studio* (special winter issue, 1896-1897), 25-26.

Mourey, Gabriel 'Pierre Puvis de Chavannes.' *The Studio* (October 1899), 12-18; also in *International Studio* (January 1900), 12-18.

Neff, John H. 'Puvis de Chavannes: Three Easel Paintings.' *Museum Studies*, 4 (1969), 66-86.

Nénot, H.P. *La nouvelle Sorbonne*. Paris, 1895.

Nénot, H.P. *Monographie de la Nouvelle Sorbonne*. Introduction by O. Gréard. Paris, 1903.

Nicolle, Marcel 'Le Musée de Rouen.' *L'Art et les Aristes*, 18e année, no. 47 (May 1924), 293-301.

Nicolson, Benedict 'Reflections on Seurat.' *The Burlington Magazine*, CIV (May 1952), 213-214.

Nicolson, Benedict 'Le Doux Pays.' *The Burlington Magazine*, XCV (December 1953), supplement, n.p.

Pagano, José Léon 'En el centenario de Puvis de Chavannes.' *Formas de vida; filosofia, arte, literatura* (1941), 219-243.

'Le Panthéon,' *Inventaire des richesses d'art de la France, monuments civils*, II (Paris, 1889), 335, 340-341.

Paris, Grand Palais, *La Gloire de Victor Hugo*, 1985-86.

Paris, Grand Palais / Ottawa, National Gallery of Canada / New York, Metropolitan Museum of Art, *Degas*, 1988-89.

Patterson, Annabel *Pastoral and Ideology. Virgil to Valéry*. Berkeley and Los Angeles, 1987.

Pauli, Georg 'Puvis de Chavannes.' *Ord och Bild*, XXVII (1918), 625-639.

Peterson, Ann C. 'A Vision of Antiquity. A Re-evaluatin of Puvis de Chavannes,' [Unpublished] M. A. Thesis, University of Pittsburgh, 1961.

Petrie, Brian 'Puvis de Chavannes and French Symbolist Painting.' *Studio*, CLXXXIII (May 1972), 193-195.

Petrie, Brian 'The art of Influence-hunting.' [review of 1977 Toronto exhibition]. *Times Literary Supplement* (29 April 1977), 525.

Peyre, Henri *Bibliographie critique de l'hellénisme en France de 1843 à 1870*. New Haven, 1932.

Phillips, Sir Claude 'Puvis de Chavannes.' *Magazine of Art*, VIII (1885), 60-68.

Pichon, Alfred 'Puvis de Chavannes, à propos d'un livre récent.' *Revue de Synthèse Historique*, XXVIII (February 1914), 160-167.

Pignatel, Fernand 'Puvis de Chavannes.' *A. B. C., Magazine d'Art* (February 1925), 3-5.

Planche, Gustave 'Peinture monumentale - MM. Eugène Delacroix et Hippolyte Flandrin.' *Revue des Deux Mondes*, s5, XV (1846), 148-161.

Planche, Gustave 'De la Peinture Murale.' In *Etudes sur l'Ecole française (1831-1852)*, Vol. II, Paris, 1855.

La Plume [special issue] (15-31 January 1895).

Poggioli, Renato *The Oaten Flute. Essays on Pastoral Poetry and Pastoral Ideal*. Cambridge, Mass., 1975.

Pool, Phoebe 'The History Paintings of Edgar Degas and their Background.' *Apollo*, ns 80 (October 1964), 306-311.

Pool, Phoebe 'Picasso's Neo-Classicism: First Period, 1905-1906.' *Apollo*, ns 81 (February 1965), pp. 122-127.

Porcellati, Salvatore 'Puvis de Chavannes: A Study of *Le Bois sacré cher aux Arts et aux Muses*.' [Unpublished] M. A. Thesis, Queen's College, City University of New York, 1972.

Price, Aimée Brown 'A Puvis de Chavannes Gouache in the MSU Art Collection.' *Kresge Art Center Bulletin*, II (October 1968), n.p.

Price, Aimée Brown 'Puvis de Chavannes: A Study of the Easel Paintings and a Catalogue of the Painted Work.' [Unpublished] Doctoral Dissertation, Yale University, New Haven, Conn., 1972. [Available through University Microfilms, Ann Arbor, Mich.]

Price, Aimée Brown 'Two Portraits by Vincent van Gogh and Two Portraits by Pierre Puvis de Chavannes.' *The Burlington Magazine* (November 1975), 714-718.

Price, Aimée Brown '"L'Allégorie Réelle" chez Pierre Puvis de Chavannes.' *Gazette des Beaux-Arts* (January 1977), 27-40.

Price, Aimée Brown 'Official Artists and Not-So-Official Art: Covert Caricaturists in Nineteenth-Century France.' *Art Journal* (Winter 1983), 365-370.

Price, Aimée Brown 'Puvis de Chavannes's Caricatures: Manifestoes, Commentary, Expressions.' *The Art Bulletin*, LXXIII (March 1991), 119-140.

Price, Aimée Brown '"Jean Cavalier jouant le choral de Luther devant sa mère mourante" de Puvis de Chavannes.' *Bulletin des Musées et Monuments Lyonnais*, nos. 3-4 (1992), 50-57.

Puvis de Chavannes, Henri 'Pour le centenaire de Puvis de Chavannes.' *Renaissance de l'Art* (October 1924), 548-550.

Puvis de Chavannes, Henri Un Entretien avec M. Edouard Vuillard, contribution à l'histoire de Puvis de Chavannes.' *Renaissance de l'Art*, IX (February 1926), 87-90.

Puvis de Chavannes, Henri 'Puvis de Chavannes et la renaissance de la fresque.' *Beaux-Arts* (1 September 1933), 2.

Puvis de Chavannes, Henri 'Les Muses de Puvis de Chavannes et la Princesse Marie Cantacuzène.' *L'Art et les Artistes* (January 1937), 115-118, 142.

Puvis de Chavannes, Henri 'La Princesse Cantacuzène, muse de Chassériau et de Puvis de Chavannes.' *Le Rempart* (28 May 1938). [Clipping, n.p.]

Puvis de Chavannes, Henri 'Peintures et dessins de Puvis de Chavannes.' *Beaux-Arts* (7 March 1941), 5.

Puvis de Chavannes, Henri 'Puvis de Chavannes et le Bourgogne.' *Bulletin de la Société des Amis du Musée de Dijon* (1949-50), 42-43.

Puvis de Chavannes, Henri 'Puvis de Chavannes, portraitiste.' *Société de l'Histoire de l'Art Français, Bulletin* (1955), 36-41.

Puvis de Chavannes, Pierre 'Personal Recollections.' *The Living Age*, II (28 January 1899), 203-207.

Puvis de Chavannes, Pierre 'Pensées et réflexions, extraites des lettres de Puvis de Chavannes.' *La Revue Encyclopédique* (23 December 1899), 1080-1082.

Puvis de Chavannes, Pierre 'Lettres familières.' *Le Figaro* (31 January 1911), 1-2.

Puvis de Chavannes, Pierre [see also Mandach and Wehrlé]

R., A. 'Exposition de M. Puvis de Chavannes.' *Chronique des Arts et de la Curiosité* (19 November 1887), 267, 284.

Radiot, Paul 'Notre Byzantinisme.' *Revue Blanche*, VI (1894), 110-115.

Raynal, Maurice 'Puvis de Chavannes.' *Montjoie! L'Organe de l'Impérialisme Artistique Français* (14 March 1913), 5-6.

Renan, Ary 'Puvis de Chavannes.' *La Revue de*

Paris, I (15 January 1895), 438-448.

Renan, Ary 'Puvis de Chavannes, à propos d'un livre récent.' *Gazette des Beaux-Arts*, s3, XV (January 1896), 79-85.

La Revue des Beaux-Arts et des Lettres [special issue] (1 May 1899), 225-228.

La Revue Populaire des Beaux-Arts [special issue] (12 February 1898), 258-271.

Rewald, John *Post-Impressionism from Van Gogh to Gauguin*. New York, 1956. Rev. ed. New York, 1962.

Rey, Robert *La Renaissance du sentiment classique dans la peinture française à la fin du XIXe siècle*. Paris, n.d. [ca. 1931].

Rey, Robert '"La Toilette" de Puvis de Chavannes.' *Bulletin des Musées de France*, IVe année (July 1932), 108-110.

Reyszner, G. 'Puvis de Chavannes.' *Die Kunst für Alle*, XIV (1898), 87-92.

Rhys-Jenkins 'Puvis de Chavannes: A Modern Wall-painter.' *Architecture* [England], V-VI (September-October 1928), 146-147.

Ricketts, Charles 'Puvis de Chavannes: A Chapter from "Modern Painters."' *The Burlington Magazine*, XIII (April 1908), 9-18.

Ricketts, Charles *Self-Portrait. Letters and Journals*. Cecil Lewis, ed. London, 1939.

Riotor, Léon 'Le Pauvre pêcheur.' *La Plume* (15-31 January 1895), 40-41.

Riotor, Léon *L'Art et l'idée: Essai sur Puvis de Chavannes*. Paris, 1896; reprint of *L'Artiste*, XI (March 1896), 161-193; (April 1896), 264-277; (May 1896), 357-389.

Riotor, Léon 'Puvis de Chavannes.' *La Revue Populaire des Beaux-Arts* (12 February 1898), 258-270.

Riotor, Léon 'Apothéose de Puvis de Chavannes.' *La Revue des Beaux-Arts et des Lettres* (1 May 1899), 227.

Riotor, Léon 'Puvis de Chavannes,' In *Les Arts et les Lettres*, Paris, 1901, p. 64.

Riotor, Léon *Puvis de Chavannes*. Paris, 1914.

Robertson, Martha Barton 'On the Importance of Puvis de Chavannes.' *The Register of the Museum of Art, University of Kansas*, no. 9 (1957), 10-15.

Robinson, William H. 'Puvis de Chavannes's "Summer" and the Symbolist Avant-Garde.' *The Bulletin of The Cleveland Museum of Art*, LXXVIII, no. 1 (January 1991), 1-27.

Rodenbach, Georges 'Puvis de Chavannes.' In *L'Elite: écrivains, orateurs sacrés peintres-sculpteurs*, Paris, 1899, pp. 219-224.

Roger-Ballu 'Les Peintures de M. Puvis de Chavannes au Panthéon.' *Chronique des Arts et de la Curiosité* (9 June 1877), 212.

Roger-Ballu 'Les Derniers travaux de peinture décorative à Paris.' *Gazette des Beaux-Arts*, s2, XVII (1 February 1878), 142-159.

Roger-Ballu 'M. Puvis de Chavannes.' *Modern Art* (Summer 1895), 74-78.

Roger-Marx, Claude 'La Caricature en France.' *Arts graph* [*iques*?], no. 31 (1932), 57-58.

Roland Holst, R.N 'Puvis de Chavannes.' *Elsevier's geïllustreerd Maandschrift* (July-December 1924), 145-154.

Roland Holst, R.N *Chassériau en Puvis de Chavannes*. Amsterdam, 1928.

Rood, Lily Lewis *Pierre Puvis de Chavannes, a Sketch*. Boston, 1895.

Rood, Lily Lewis 'Puvis de Chavannes as a Painter of the Seasons and Some Allegories.' *Modern Art* (Autumn 1895), 107-108.

Rosenthal, Léon 'La Peinture monumentale.' In *Du Romantisme au réalisme. Essai sur l'évolution de la peinture en France de 1830 à 1848*, Paris, 1914, pp. 298-344.

Roux, Hugues le 'Puvis de Chavannes.' In *Portraits de cire*. 2nd ed. Paris, 1891, pp. 143-156.

Saint-Paul, Albert 'Puvis de Chavannes.' *La Wallonie*, III (January 1888), 72-76.

Sandoz, Marc *Théodore Chassériau: 1819-1856. Catalogue raisonné des peintures et estampes*. Paris, 1974.

Saunier, Charles 'Le Banquet.' *La Plume* (15-31 January 1895), 47-61.

Saunier, Charles 'Le Paysage dans l'oeuvre de Puvis de Chavannes.' *La Plume* (15-31 January 1895), 45-46.

Saunier, Charles 'Petite gazette d'art: Puvis de Chavannes.' *Revue Blanche*, XIX (1899), 384-387.

Schapiro, Meyer 'Joseph C. Sloane's "French Painting Between the Past and the Present."' *Art Bulletin*, XXXVI (June 1954), 163-165.

Schapiro, Meyer 'New Light on Seurat.' *Art News*, LVII (April 1958), 22-24, 44-45, 52.

Schapiro, Meyer 'Seurat: Reflections.' *Art News Annual*, XXIX (1964), 23-38.

Scheid, G. *L'Oeuvre de Puvis de Chavannes à Amiens*. n.p. [Amiens], 1907.

Schmidt, Karl Eugen 'Puvis de Chavannes als Karikaturenzeichner.' *Zeitschrift für bildende Kunst*, XVII (December 1905), 63-65.

Schneider, Pierre 'Puvis de Chavannes: the alternative.' *Art in America*, LXV, no. 3 (May-June 1977), 94-98.

Schneider, Pierre *Matisse*. Transl. Michael Taylor and Bridget Stevens Romer. New York and London, 1984.

Séailles, Gabriel 'Peintres contemporains: Puvis de Chavannes.' *Revue Bleue* (1888), 140-144, 179-185.

Séailles, Gabriel 'Puvis de Chavannes.' *Almanach du Bibliophile*, II (December 1899), 223-264.

Segard, Achille *Peintres d'aujourd'hui. Les Décorateurs*. 2 vols. Paris, 1914.

Segard, Achille 'Fresques inédites de Puvis de Chavannes.' *Les Arts*, XIII (March 1914), 4-16.

Seitz, William 'Some Studies by Puvis de Chavannes.' *Record of the Art Museum, Princeton University*, X, no. 2 (1951), 10-22.

Sharp, William 'Puvis de Chavannes, an Appreciation.' *The Art Journal* [London] (1898), 377-378.

Sherman, Daniel J. 'The Bourgeoisie, Cultural Appropriation and the Art Museum in Nineteenth-Century France.' *Radical History Review*, no. 38 (1987), 38-58.

Sherman, Daniel J. *Worthy Monuments: Art Museums and the Politics of Culture in Nineteenth-Century France*. Cambridge, Mass., 1989.

Signac, Paul *D'Eugène Delacroix au néo-impressionnisme*. Rev. ed. Paris, 1964.

Silver, Kenneth *Esprit de Corps. The Art of the Parisian Avant-Garde and the First World War, 1914-1925*. Princeton, 1989.

Silvestre, Armand 'Puvis de Chavannes.' *La Grande Revue de Paris et St. Petersbourg* (December 1887), 1-3.

Sirieyx de Villers, E. *Les Grands mystiques de la peinture*. Lyons, 1924.

Sizeranne, Robert de la 'Puvis de Chavannes.' *Revue des Deux Mondes*, CL (15 November 1898), 406-420.

Smith, Holmes 'The Technique of Puvis de Chavannes.' *Bulletin of Washington University* (April 1909), 16-24.

Snell, Robert *Théophile Gautier. A Romantic*

Critic of the Visual Arts. Oxford, 1982.

Société Nationale des Beaux-Arts 'Hommages à Puvis de Chavannes.' *Procès-Verbaux des Séances de la Délégation* (24 October 1908), 2e semestre [published at Evreux], n.p.

Souchon, Paul 'Les "Entretiens" de Puvis de Chavannes.' *La Presse* (30 October 1898), n.p.

Sutton, Denys 'An Aristocrat of Idealism.' *Apollo*, XCV (June 1972), 432-439.

'T' [Tabarant, Adolphe?] 'Suzanne Valadon et ses souvenirs de modèle,' *Bulletin de la Vie Artistique*, 7e année (December 1921), 627-628.

Tapley, George Manning, Jr 'The Mural Paintings of Puvis de Chavannes,' [Unpublished] Doctoral Dissertation, University of Minnesota, 1979.

Tardieu, Eugène 'La Peinture et les peintres, M. Puvis de Chavannes.' *L'Echo de Paris* (13 May 1895), 2.

Thévenin, Léon *Puvis de Chavannes*. Paris, 1899.

Thiébault-Sisson, François 'Puvis de Chavannes et son oeuvre.' *La Nouvelle Revue*, XLIX (1 December 1887), 643-648.

Thiébault-Sisson, François *Le Salon de 1895*. Paris, 1895, pp. 5-6.

Thiébault-Sisson, François 'Puvis de Chavannes raconté par lui-même.' *Le Temps* (16 January 1895), 2.

Thiébault-Sisson, François 'The Panels of Puvis de Chavannes: Boston Public Library.' *Harper's Weekly*, XL (23 May 1896), 508-510; (10 October 1896), 1008-1009.

Thiébault-Sisson, François 'Ateliers d'artistes; Chez Puvis de Chavannes.' *Le Figaro Illustré*, s2 (May 1898), 96-99.

Thiébault-Sisson, François 'Puvis de Chavannes d'après des souvenirs personnels.' *Feuilleton du Temps* (11 January 1925), n.p.

Thiébault-Sisson, François 'Puvis de Chavannes nach persönlichen Erinnerungen.' Transl. Gertrud Albahary. *Der Kunstwanderer*, VII (1925-26), 193-195.

Thovez, Enrico 'Artisti Contemporanei: P. Puvis de Chavannes.' *Emporium*, VI (1897), 414-437

Tilanus, Louk 'Rodins portret van Puvis de Chavannes.' *Jong Holland*, no. 4 (1993), 9-14.

Toliver, Harold E. *Pastoral Forms and Attitudes*. Berkeley, Los Angeles, London, 1971.

Topass, Jan 'Puvis de Chavannes, 1824-1898.' Transl. Catherine Beach Ely. *Art in America*, XIII (April 1925), 140-148.

Tougenhold, Jacques [Tougendhold, Jakobà] 'Chtchoukine's Collection of French Paintings.' *Apollon*, nos. 1-2 (1914), 5-46.

Tougendhold, Jakobà *Inootrannbrc Choudojnkn Pjuvis de Chavannes Tekste* [*Puvis de Chavannes*]. Saint Petersburg, n.d.

Vachon, Marius 'Les Peintures de M. Puvis de Chavannes au Panthéon.' *La France* (28 May 1877), n.p.

Vachon, Marius [no title] in *La France* (11 December 1877), n.p. [perhaps the same as:]

Vachon, Marius *Puvis de Chavannes*. N.p. [Amiens], n.d. [ca. 1877, and inscribed 15/7er/1878].

Vachon, Marius 'Puvis de Chavannes.' *La Nouvelle Revue*, XCVII (1895), 483-499.

Vachon, Marius *Puvis de Chavannes*. Paris, 1895; new ed., 1900. Cited as: Vachon (1895).

Vachon, Marius *Un maître de ce temps: Puvis de Chavannes*. Paris, n.d. [1900]. Cited as: Vachon [1900].

Vachon, Marius *L'Hôtel de Ville de Paris, 1535-1905*. Paris, 1905.

Vaisse, Pierre 'Styles et Sujets dans la Peinture Officielle de la IIIe République.' *Bulletin de la Société de l'Histoire de l'Art français* (3 December 1977), 297-299, 302-303, 306-309.

Vaisse, Pierre 'Salons, Expositions et Sociétés d'Artistes en France 1871-1914.' In F. Haskell, *Saloni, Gallerie, Musei e loro Influenza sullo svilippo dell'Arte dei Secoli XIX e XX* in *Atti del XXIV Congresso Internazionale*, n.p., 1979, pp. 141-155.

Vaisse, Pierre 'La Troisième République et les peintres: Recherches sur les rapports des pouvoirs publics et de la peinture en France de 1870 à 1914.' [Unpublished] Thèse de l'Université de Paris, IV, 1980.

Vaisse, Pierre 'La Peinture Monumentale au Panthéon sous la IIIe République,' in 1989, Paris, Hôtel Sully / Montréal, Centre Canadien d'Architecture, *Le Panthéon. Symbole des révolutions*, pp. 252-258.

Vauxcelles, Louis 'Puvis de Chavannes caricaturiste.' *L'Art et les Artistes*, I (1905), 9-13.

Vauxcelles, Louis 'Une Fresque de Puvis, Les Muses inspiratrices....' *Gil Blas* (7 October 1913), 4.

Venturi, Lionello *Les Archives de l'Impressionnisme*. 2 vols. Paris and New York, 1939.

Viéville, Dominique 'Les Peintures murales de Puvis de Chavannes à Amiens.' *Collections Amiens, Musée de Picardie*, no.1 (May 1989), special issue.

Vorst, Marie van 'Puvis de Chavannes.' *The Pall Mall Magazine*, XVII, no. 69 (1899), 312-322.

Waern, Cecilia 'Puvis de Chavannes in Boston.' *The Atlantic Monthly*, LXXIX (February 1897), 251-256.

Wattenmaker, Richard [See 1975 Toronto]

Webster, Sara A 'Puvis de Chavannes: Aspects of his Art before 1883.' [Unpublished] Doctoral Dissertation, University of Cincinnati, 1974.

Werth, Léon 'Puvis de Chavannes.' *Portraits d'Hier*, lère année (1 April 1909), 35-63.

Werth, Léon *Puvis de Chavannes*. Paris, 1926.

Wilhelm, Jacques 'Deux Esquisses inédites de Puvis de Chavannes.' *Bulletin du Musée Carnavalet*, II, no. 1 (1949), 12-13.

Wolfson, Susannah '"L'Hôtel de Ville de Paris," the Hôtel de Ville and the Official Style of the Third Republic.' [Unpublished] graduate student paper, Princeton University, Fall 1986.

Young Ban Lin 'Le Décor peint dans les édifices publics civils à Paris sous la troisième république.' [Unpublished] Thèse de l'Université de Paris, 1964.

Yriarte, Charles 'Six oeuvres de M. Puvis de Chavannes.' *Le Figaro* (10 November 1894), 1.

Zeitler, Rudolf *Klassizismus und Utopia*. Uppsala, 1954.

Selected Exhibitions

The Salons, Expositions Universelles and the principal exhibitions in which Puvis de Chavannes's works were included are listed here, with special attention to exhibitions during his lifetime. With the exception of these and a few other exhibitions, only those exhibitions that included at least three of his works are listed.

An asterisk indicates that the author has not been able to examine the exhibition catalogue to verify specific information.

1850 **Paris** Palais National. *Société des Artistes Français, Exposition publique des ouvrages des artistes vivants. Salon de 1850.* [The Salon began late and ran into 1851.]

1855 **Marseilles** *Exposition de la Société Artistique des Bouches-du-Rhône.**

1858-59 **Lyons** Palais Saint Pierre, Société des Amis des Arts de Lyon. *Salon de 1858.* [The 1976-77 Paris/Ottawa catalogue lists 1857-58, which had no works by Puvis de Chavannes.]

1859 **Paris** Palais des Champs Elysées. *Salon de 1859.*

1861 **Paris** Palais des Champs Elysées. *Salon de 1861.*

1863 **Paris** Palais des Champs Elysées. *Salon de 1863.*

1864 **Paris** Palais des Champs Elysées. *Salon de 1864.*

1864 **Paris** Société Nationale des Beaux-Arts.

1865 **Paris** Palais des Champs Elysées. *Salon de 1865.*

1866 **Paris** Palais des Champs Elysées. *Salon de 1866.*

1867 **Paris** *Exposition Universelle de 1867.*

1867 **Paris** Palais des Champs Elysées. *Salon de 1867.*

1868 **Bordeaux** *Exposition de la Société des Amis des Arts.*

1868 **Paris** Palais des Champs Elysées. *Salon de 1868.*

1869 **Paris** Palais des Champs Elysées. *Salon de 1869.*

1870 **Limoges*** [place and title unavailable]

1870 **Paris** Palais des Champs Elysées. *Salon de 1870.*

1872 **London** *Summer Exhibition of the Society of French Artists.*

1872 **Paris** Palais des Champs Elysées. *Salon de 1872.*

1873 **Paris** Palais des Champs Elysées. *Salon de 1873.*

1874 **Paris** Palais des Champs Elysées. *Salon de 1874.*

1875 **Paris** Palais des Champs Elysées. *Salon de 1875.*

1876 **Paris** Palais des Champs Elysées. *Salon de 1876.*

1877 **Paris** Palais des Champs Elysées. *Salon de 1877.*

1878 **Paris** Palais des Champs Elysées. *Salon de 1878.*

1879 **Paris** Palais des Champs Elysées. *Salon de 1879.*

1880 **Paris** Palais des Champs Elysées. *Salon de 1880.*

1881 **Paris** Musée des Arts Décoratifs, Palais de l'Industrie. *Exposition de peinture et sculpture moderne de décoration et d'ornement.*

1881 **Paris** Palais des Champs Elysées. *Salon de 1881.* [From 1881 through 1889 these Salon exhibitions were held under the auspices of the Société des Artistes Français.]

1882 **Paris** Palais des Champs Elysées. *Salon de 1882.*

1883 **Paris** Palais des Champs Elysées. *Salon de 1883.*

1883 **Paris** Palais de l'Industrie. *Exposition Nationale des Beaux-Arts* ['Le Triennale'].

1884 **Paris** Ecole des Beaux-Arts. *Dessins de l'Ecole Moderne.*

1884 **Paris** Palais des Champs Elysées. *Salon de 1884.*

1885 **Paris** Palais des Champs Elysées. *Salon de 1885.*

1886 **Paris** Palais des Champs Elysées. *Salon de 1886.*

1887 **New York** National Academy of Design. *Celebrated Paintings by French Masters.*

1887 **Paris** Galerie Durand-Ruel. *Exposition de tableaux, pastels, dessins par M. Puvis de Chavannes.*

1887 **Paris** Palais des Champs Elysées. *Salon de 1887.*

1888 **Brussels** *Exposition Internationale d'Art Monumental.*

1889 **Paris** *Exposition Universelle Internationale de 1889.*

1889 **Paris** *Exposition Universelle de 1889. Exposition centennale de l'art français 1789-1889.*

1889 **Paris** *Exposition Universelle de 1889, Exposition de la Société des Pastellistes Français* [special pavillion]

1890 **Lyons** Société Lyonnaise des Beaux-Arts. *Salon de 1890.*

1890 **Paris** Champ-de-Mars, Société Nationale des Beaux-Arts. *Salon de 1890.*

1891 **Paris** Champ-de-Mars, Société Nationale des Beaux-Arts. *Salon de 1891.*

1892 **Paris** Champ-de-Mars, Société Nationale des Beaux-Arts. *Salon de 1892.*

1893 **Paris** Champ-de-Mars, Société Nationale des Beaux-Arts. *Salon de 1893.*

1894 **Brussels** *Salon de la Libre Esthétique.*

1894 **Lyons** *Salon de 1894.*

1894 **New York** Durand-Ruel Galleries. *M. Puvis de Chavannes - Loan Exhibition.*

1894 **Paris** Champ-de-Mars, Société Nationale des Beaux-Arts. *Salon de 1894.*

1894 **Paris** Galerie Durand-Ruel. *Puvis de Chavannes.*

1894 **Vienna** *III. Kunst-Ausstellung im Künstlerhause Wien.**

1895 **Boston** Boston Museum of Fine Arts. *Puvis de Chavannes.*

1895 **Paris** Champ-de-Mars, Société Nationale des Beaux-Arts. *Salon de 1895.*

1895-96 **Paris** Champs Elysées, Pavillon de la Ville [temporary presentation of works belonging to the city of Paris].*

1896 **Geneva** Musée Rath. *L'Exposition d'Oeuvres de Mm. P. Puvis de Chavannes, Auguste Rodin, Eugène Carrière.*

1896 **Lyons** *Salon de 1896.*

1896 **Paris** Champ-de-Mars, Société Nationale des Beaux-Arts. *Salon de 1896.*

1896 **Paris** Galerie Durand-Ruel. *Exposition des trois dernières compositions exécutées par P. Puvis de Chavannes pour l'escalier de la Bibliothèque de Boston.*

1896 **Pittsburgh** Carnegie Institute. *First Annual Exhibition.*

1897 **Copenhagen** Ny Carlsberg Glyptothek. *Internationale Kunstudstillung Kobenhavn.*

1897 **Paris** Société Nationale des Beaux-Arts. *Salon de 1897.*

1897 **Pittsburgh** Carnegie Institute, *Second Annual Exhibition.*

1898 **Paris** Champ-de-Mars, Société Nationale des Beaux Arts. *Salon de 1898.*

1898 **Vienna** *Internationale Kunstausstellung.**

1899 **Paris** Champ-de-Mars, Société Nationale des Beaux-Arts. *Salon de 1899.*

1899 **Paris** Galerie Durand-Ruel. *Tableaux, Esquisses et Dessins de Puvis de Chavannes.*

1899-1900 **Paris** Musée Galliera. *Les dessins de Puvis de Chavannes offerts par sa famille à la Ville de Paris* n.d. [1899-1900].

1900 **Paris** *Exposition Internationale Universelle de 1900*, including *Exposition Centennale de l'Art français, de 1800 à 1889.*

1904 **Lyons** Palais Municipal des Expositions. *Exposition rétrospective des artistes lyonnais; peintres et sculpteurs.*

1904 **Paris** Grand Palais des Champs Elysées. *Société du Salon d'Automne.*

1904 **Saint Louis** Art Palace. *Universal Exposition.**

1905 **Buffalo** Buffalo Fine Arts Academy, Albright Art Gallery. *The Inaugural Loan Collection of Paintings.*

1905 **The Hague** Haagsche Kunstkring. *Puvis de Chavannes.*

1905 **Paris** Galerie A. Bloch. *Puvis de Chavannes* [without catalogue].

1909 **Düsseldorf** *Ausstellung für Christliche Kunst.*

1910 **New York** [?] Alpine Club Gallery. *Twenty-seven drawings and Paintings by Puvis de Chavannes.*

1912 **Frankfurt** Frankfurter Kunstverein. *Die Klassische Malerei Frankreichs im 19. Jahrhundert. Ein Überblick über die Entwicklung der modernen französischen Malerei in ausgewählten Werken der führenden Meister.*

1912 **New York** Durand-Ruel Galleries. *Exhibition of Drawings and Pastels by Chavannes, Degas, Renoir.*

1912 **Paris** Grand Palais. *Salon d'Automne.*

1912 **Saint Petersburg** Institut Français. *Exposition centennale de l'art français à Saint-Petersbourg, 1812-1912.*

1913 **New York** Armory of the 69th Regiment / **Chicago** Art Institute of Chicago / **Boston** Copley Hall, Copley Society of Boston. *International Exhibition of Modern Art* [the `Armory Show'].

1913 **São Paulo** Comité Franco-Amérique. *Exposition d'Art français de Sao-Paulo.* [These may have been photographs, as there is no record of works having been loaned].

1913 **Vienna** Galerie Miethke. *Französische Impressionisten.*

1914 **London** Grosvenor House. *Exhibition of French Painting.** [May be the same as: London, Grosvenor Gallery. *Art Français. Exposition d'Art décoratif contemporain 1800-85.*]

1915 **San Francisco** Palace of Fine Arts. *Panama Pacific International Exhibition.*

1920 **Paris** Grand Palais, Société Nationale des Beaux-Arts. *Salon de 1920.*

1924 **Paris** Grand Palais, Société Nationale des Beaux-Arts. *Salon de 1924* [With *Centenaire P. Puvis de Chavannes*, a retrospective.]

1925 **Brussels** Musées Royaux du Cinquantenaire. *Exposition d'oeuvres de Puvis de Chavannes.*

1925 **Lyons** Chez Marius Audin. *L'Art lyonnais: Exposition organisée au profit de la ligue franco-anglo-américaine et de l'association lyonnaise pour la lutte contre le cancer.*

1926 **Amsterdam** E. J. van Wisselingh & Co. *Teekeningen van Puvis de Chavannes en Lithographien van H. Fantin Latour.*

1926 **Paris** Galerie Hector Brame. *Exposition de dessins par Puvis de Chavannes.*

1927 **Paris** Galerie Max Bine. *Exposition de dessins du XVe siècle au XXe siècle.*

1930 **New York** Durand-Ruel Galleries. *Exhibition of Drawings by Constantin Guys, Puvis de Chavannes, Degas, Cassatt, André and others.*

1930 **New York** Metropolitan Museum of Art. *The H.O. Havemeyer Collection.*

1932 **Buffalo** Buffalo Fine Arts Academy, Albright Art Gallery. *The Nineteenth Century. French Art in Retrospect.*

1932 **London** Royal Academy of Arts. *Exhibition of French Art, 1200-1900.*

1932 **Paris** *L'Exposition du Cinquantenaire de la Société des Artistes français.*

1933 **Chicago** Art Institute of Chicago. *A Century of Progress: Exhibition of Paintings and Sculpture.*

1933 **Hartford** Wadsworth Atheneum and Morgan Memorial. *An Exhibition of Literature and Poetry in Painting since 1850.*

1933 **Paris** Galerie des Quatre Chemins. *Puvis de Chavannes.*

1933 **Paris** Musée des Arts Décoratifs. *Le décor de la vie sous la troisième République.*

1935-36 **New York** Galerie René Gimpel. *Puvis de Chavannes.*

1936 **Lyons** *Exposition diocésaine d'art religieux.*

1936 **Paris** Bibliothèque Nationale. *Cinquantenaire du symbolisme.*

1937 **Lyons** Musée de Lyon. *Puvis de Chavannes et la peinture lyonnaise du XIXe siècle.* Catalogue by Marcelle Lagaisse, with introduction by René Jullian.

1939-40 **San Francisco**, M. H. de Young Memorial Museum / **New York**, Metropolitan Museum of Art / **Chicago**, Art Institute of Chicago / **Los Angeles**, Los Angeles County Museum of Art / **Portland**, Portland Art Museum / **Washington, D.C.**, National Gallery of Art. *French Painting from David to Toulouse-Lautrec.* [same as:] **Buenos Aires** / **Montevideo** / **Santiago de Chile** / **Rio de Janeiro** / **Mexico City**. *Exposiciones de Arte francesa de David a nuestros dias.*

1940-41 San Francisco M. H. de Young Memorial Museum. *The Painting of France Since the French Revolution*. [Perhaps same as above with different catalogue.]

1941 Paris Galerie Jacques Blot. *Quelques dessins et peintures de Puvis de Chavannes, présentés par Maurice Denis*.

1948-49 Paris Orangerie des Tuileries / **Lyons** Musée de Lyon. *La Peinture lyonnaise du XVIe au XIXe siècle*.

1949-50 Paris Orangerie des Tuileries. *Eugène Carrière et le Symbolisme*.

1952 Paris Musée Galliera. *Exposition: `Dessins' et petits tableaux de Pierre Puvis de Chavannes*. Catalogue with introduction by P.L. Rigal and notes by Henri Puvis de Chavannes.

1954 Detroit Detroit Institute of Arts. *The Two Sides of the Medal, French Painting from Gérôme to Gauguin*.

1956 Washington, D.C. Corcoran Gallery of Art. *Visionaries and Dreamers*.

1961 London Roland, Browse and Delbanco. *Paintings by Le Sidaner; Drawings by Puvis de Chavannes and Carrière*.

1962 London Matthiesen Gallery. *Summer Exhibition*.

1962 New York Shepherd Gallery. *The Non-Dissenters*.

1963 Utica Munson-Williams-Proctor Institute / **New York** Armory of the 69th Regiment. *Armory Show, 50th Anniversary Exhibition 1913-1963*.

1964 London Roland, Browse and Delbanco. *French and English Draughtsmen of the 19th and 20th Century*.

1965 Charleroi Palais des Beaux-Arts / **Luxembourg** Musée d'Histoire et d'Art. *Maîtres lyonnais du XIXe siècles*.

1968 New York Shepherd Gallery. *The Non-Dissenters*

1968 Paris Musée National du Louvre. *Maîtres du Blanc et Noir au XIXe siècle*.

1969 Turin Galleria Civica d'Arte Moderna. *Il sacro e il profano nell'arte dei Simbolisti*.

1971-72 Madrid Museo Español de Arte Contemporaneo / **Barcelona** Museo de Arte Moderna. *El Simbolismo en la Pintura Francesa*.

1972 London Hayward Gallery / **Liverpool** Walker Art Gallery. *French Symbolist Painters: Moreau, Puvis de Chavannes, Redon and their Followers*.

1974-75 London Heim Gallery / **Cambridge** Fitzwilliam Museum / **Birmingham** City Museum and Art Gallery / **Glasgow** Glasgow Art Gallery and Museum. *From Poussin to Puvis de Chavannes, A Loan Exhibition of French Drawings from the collections of the Musée des Beaux-Arts at Lille*.

1975 Dijon Musée des Beaux-Arts de Dijon. *Maîtres du blanc et noir au XIXe siècle*.

1975 New York Shepherd Gallery. *Ingres and Delacroix through Degas and Puvis de Chavannes: The Figure in French Art 1800-1870*.

1975 Toronto Art Gallery of Ontario. *Puvis de Chavannes and the Modern Tradition*. Introduction and catalogue by Richard Wattenmaker. Rev. ed. 1976.

1975-76 Rotterdam Museum Boymans-van Beuningen / **Brussels** Koninklijke Musea voor Schone Kunsten van België / **Baden-Baden** Staatliche Kunsthalle / **Paris** Grand Palais. *Symbolism in Europe*.

1976 Paris Galerie Heim / **Lille** Palais des Beaux-Arts / **Strasbourg** Musée des Beaux-Arts. *Cent dessins français du Fitzwilliam Museum Cambridge*.

1976-77 Paris Grand Palais / **Ottawa** National Gallery of Canada. *Puvis de Chavannes, 1824-98*. Catalogue by Louise d'Argencourt and Jacques Foucart with contributions of Marie-Christine Boucher and Douglas Druick and introductory essay by Aimée Brown Price. The second, English language catalogue, revised, 1977.

1978-79 Frankfurt Städtische Galerie / **Hamburg** Kunsthalle. *Courbet und Deutschland*.

1978-79 Philadelphia Philadelphia Museum of Art / **Detroit** Detroit Institute of Arts / **Paris** Grand Palais. *The Second Empire, 1852-70. Art in France Under Napoleon III*.

1980 Montauban Musée Ingres. *Ingres et sa postérité*.

1984-85 Marseilles Musée des Beaux-Arts de Marseille. *Puvis de Chavannes et le Musée des Beaux-Arts de Marseille*.

1984-85 Yamanashi Prefectural Museum of Art / **Kamakura** Museum of Modern Art / **Mié** Prefectural Art Museum. *Gustave Moreau et le Symbolisme*.

1985 Poitiers Crédit Agricole de la Vienne. Musée Sainte-Croix de Poitiers. *Puvis de Chavannes (1824-98), Dessins du Musée Sainte-Croix de Poitiers*.

1986-87 Paris Musée du Petit Palais. *Le Triomphe des Mairies. Grands décors républicains à Paris 1870-1914*.

1990-91 Paris Musée d'Orsay. *De Manet à Matisse. Sept ans d'enrichissements au Musée d'Orsay*.

1991 Paris Grand Palais. Société Nationale des Beaux-Arts Biennale. *Année du Centenaire (1890-1990)*.

Photographs have for the most part been supplied by the owners of the works reproduced. Exceptions and additional credits are listed below.

M. Bellot: cat. 21, 33, 34, 59, 136; Jean Bernard, Aix-en Provence: p. 122; J.L. Boutillier, Amiens: cat. 23, 24, 37, 39; Yves Bresson: cat. 63, 64; Kathleen Culbert-Aguilar, Chicago: fig. 24; J. Diaz, Draguignan: cat. 16; Eschmann, Crêches-sur-Saône: cat. 138; Rene Gerritsen, Amsterdam: cat. 90; André Gontard, Paris: cat. 4, 17, 22, 78, 79, 87, 91, 131; Tom Haartsen, Ouderkerk a/d Amstel: cat. 11 / fig. 26; C. Jean: fig. 30; Walter Klein, Düsseldorf: cat. 102; M.B. Moliterni, Toulouse: cat. 52; Pierrain: cat. 3, 41, 61, 66, 67, 132, 135, 133, 139 / fig. 13, 15, 49, 50; Eric Pollitzer, New York: cat. 150; Georges Poncet, Paris: cat. 93, 94, 95; Etienne Revault, Paris: pp. 192-193; Bernard Ronté, Eybens: cat. 2, 6, 10, 31, 40, 44, 68, 99; Caroline Rose: p. 146, 150; Lynn Rosenthal: cat. 27; A. Szenczi Mária: cat. 145; A. et G. Zimmermann, Genève: cat. 30, 49.
Chicago Historical Society: fig. 10; Bulloz, Paris, © SPADEM: p. 102-103; Caisse Nationale des Monuments Historiques et des Sites, Paris, © SPADEM: pp. 146, 150 / fig. 1; Documentation du Musée d'Orsay, Paris: fig. 18, 19; Giraudon, Paris: pp. 200-201; Haboldt, Paris: p. 10; Lauros-Giraudon, Paris: pp. 214-215; Photothèque des Musées de la Ville de Paris © SPADEM: cat. 3, 15, 41, 61, 66, 67, 132, 133, 135, 139, / fig. 13, 15, 37, 38; Réunion des Musées Nationaux, Paris © SPADEM: cat. 20, 21, 33, 34, 59, 65, 71, 76, 97, 136, 152 / fig. 4, 5, 6, 18, 23, 25, 30, 32, 35; The Art Museum, Princeton University: fig. 36; Atelier Municipal de Photographie, Toulouse: cat. 109; S.T.C., Toulouse: cat. 12, 14, 36, 111.

illustration on page 6
Pierre Puvis de Chavannes
Photograph by Ad. Braun & Cie
Private collection

illustration on page 10
Puvis de Chavannes in his Place Pigalle studio, ca. 1884-87
Photograph by E. Bernard
On the walls the following works can be seen, clockwise starting from the bottom left: the reduced versions of *Rest* and *War* (1867), *The Magdalene in the Desert* (large version, 1869), *Young Women by the Sea* (large version, 1879), an image of the 1884 *Sacred Wood* mural; a drawing for the 1874 *Charles Martel* mural.

illustration on pages 54-55
Puvis de Chavannes's studio at Neuilly, ca. 1894-95
The mural *The Inspiring Muses Acclaim the Spirit of Light* (finished in 1895) can be seen, and, in the back, a small version of the 1892 mural *Winter* and *Jean Cavalier at the Bedside of His Dying Mother* (1851).

illustration on front cover
Young Women by the Sea, cat. 76 (detail)

illustration on back cover
Saint Genevieve as a Child in Prayer, Panthéon, Paris

Colophon

First published in the United States of America in 1994 by
RIZZOLI INTERNATIONAL PUBLICATIONS, INC.
300 Park Avenue South, New York, NY 10010

Published in the Netherlands in 1994 by Waanders Publishers, Zwolle /
Van Gogh Museum, Amsterdam.

ISBN 0-8478-1826-8

LC 94-65750

Concept
Aimée Brown Price

General editor
Martine Stroo

English language editor
John Rudge

Translators
Andrew McCormick (essay by G. Lacambre)
Caroline Meijer (preface)

Research assistants
Lucas Bonekamp, Dorien Wijstma

Design
Pieter Roozen, Amsterdam

Printing
Waanders Printers, Zwolle

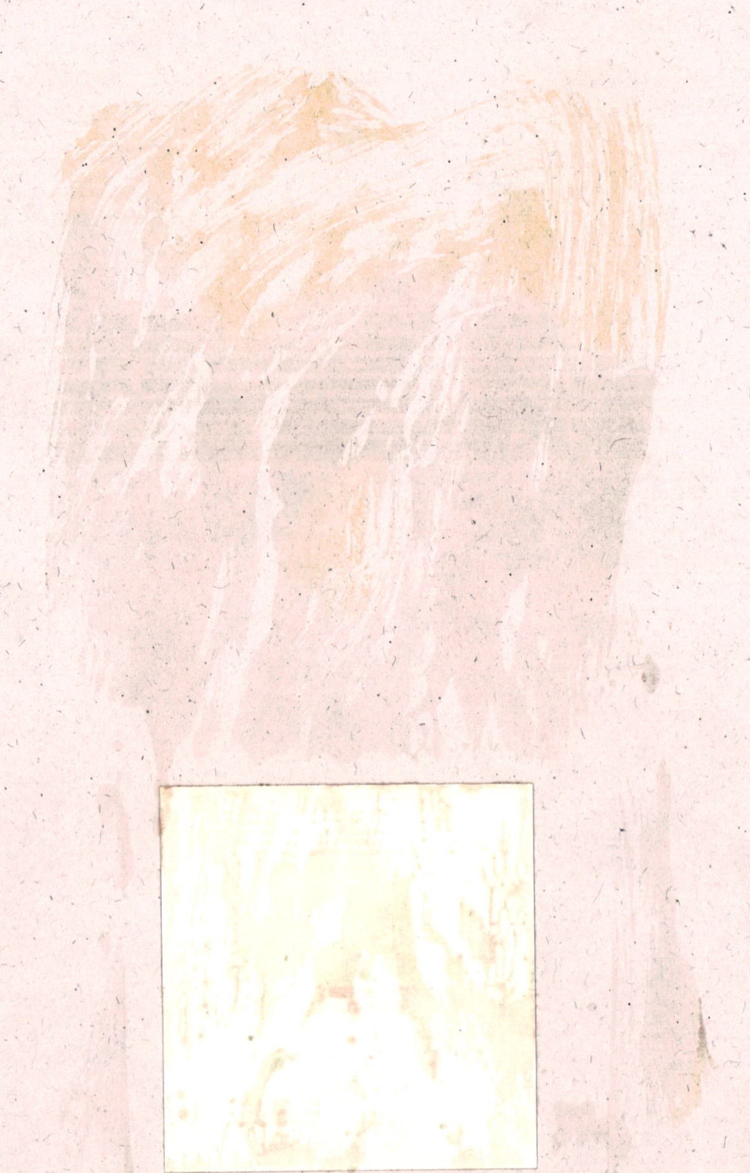